MEN IN SPORTS

ALSO BY BRANDT AYMAR

Cruising Is Fun

The Complete Cruiser

*Guide to Boatmanship, Seamanship,
and Safe Boat Housing*

Cruising Guide

*A Pictorial Treasury of the Marine
Museums of the World*

The Young Male Figure

*A Pictorial History of the World's Great Trials
from Socrates to Jean Harris*
(with Edward Sagarin)

Laws and Trials That Created History
(with Edward Sagarin)

ANTHOLOGIES ALSO COMPILED BY BRANDT AYMAR

Men in the Air

Men at Sea

Treasury of Snake Lore

The Personality of the Cat

The Deck Chair Reader

The Personality of the Bird

The Personality of the Horse

The Personality of the Dog

Men in Sports

Great Sports Stories of All time from the Greek Olympic Games to the American World Series

Edited and with an Introduction by
Brandt Aymar

Crown Trade Paperbacks
New York

To
John Marshall
a good sport always

Originally published in hardcover by Crown Publishers, Inc., in 1994.
Published by Crown Trade Paperbacks, 201 East 50th Street, New York, New York 10022.
CROWN TRADE PAPERBACKS and colophon are trademarks of Crown Publishers, Inc.

Manufactured in the United States of America

Library of Congress Cataloging-in-Publication Data

Men in sports: great sports stories of all time from the Greek Olympic games to the American World Series / edited and with an introduction by Brandt Aymar.
    1. Sports. 2. Sports stories. I. Aymar, Brandt.
GV707.M45 1994
796—dc20   93-19818
CIP

ISBN 0-517-88395-3

10 9 8 7 6 5 4 3 2 1

First Paperback Edition

Contents

Ancient Games

Archery

Auto Racing

Ballooning

Baseball

Basketball

Bicycling

Billiards

Boating

Boxing

Bullfighting

Canoeing

Cricket

Fishing

Football

Golf

Hockey

Horseracing

Hunting

Jai Alai

Jousting

Karate

Mountain Climbing

Polo

Rowing

Scuba Diving

Skiing

Soccer

Surf-Riding

Swimming

Tennis

Track

Wilderness Walking

Wrestling

Yacht Racing

Introduction
by Brandt Aymar

The ashes of the funeral pyre of the recently murdered Greek hero Pa-troklos had scarcely been doused with gleaming wine when Achilles called for the celebratory funeral games to begin. First the fleet chariot racers, whips cracking, sped swiftly over the course plains. Then came boxers, wrestlers, foot racers, spear contestants, weight twirlers, archers, and finally javelin throwers. Thus in his *Iliad* Homer introduces us to these famous ancient Greek sports.

These were the forerunners of the thirty-six different sports that I have included in this anthology: fiction, nonfiction, sports reporting, participating sports, and excerpts from longer works. Since so many individual sports are included, I have arranged them alphabetically, starting with Ancient Games and ending with Yacht Racing. In his book *Sports in America,* James A. Michener lists ninety categories in a Master List of Sports. Although many of these subjects are not suitable for this anthology, I have chosen a number from this list and hope that each fits a criterion of having literary merit or offering informative coverage of the sport in question.

For example, Mary Renault, in another of her brilliant historical reconstructions of ancient Greece, *The Praise Singer,* takes us, along with Simonides, in 520 B.C. to the 64th Olympic Games. How the vast throng cheered when the winner of the four-horse chariot race, Kimon, son of Stesagoras of Athens, won an unheard-of triple crown. How they were stunned to silence and grief shortly after his great victories when he was brutally murdered!

Who has not thrilled to that daring chariot race between the Roman Messala and Ben Hur the Jew in Lew Wallace's vivid tale of the Christian era, *Ben-Hur?* As they raced around the course with Messala always in the lead, the last three pillars were only six hundred feet away at that moment Ben Hur chose to make his dash. As he spurred on his chariot, thousands of spectators in the benches heard a resounding crash—loud enough to send a thrill through the entire Circus.

Although A. Conan Doyle's most famous fictional character was Sherlock Holmes, Mr. Doyle also wrote the novel *The White Company,* containing "A Contest in Archery." In this fourteenth-century medieval tale, the English White Company was encamped close to the French of La Nuit and of the Black Ontingo. Among the elder archers were Samkin Aylward of the English and Brabawt, a cross-bowman of La Nuit. The final contest rested in their hands. As each shot his arrow, the question was, could the longbow outshoot the crossbow?

My Greatest Race, edited by Adrian Ball, contains twenty accounts of the greatest moments in auto racing, written by the men who lived them. None is more exciting and harrowing than Stirling Moss's "The Thousand-Mile Auto Race," in which he became the first Brit to win the 1955 Mille Miglia. Here is his own account of the terrifying maneuvering and cold mechanical expertise of this world-champion driver. Driving a Mercedes with his partner Denis Jenkinson beside him, they roared out of the starting line at Brescia, just outside of Milan, at twenty-two minutes past seven on May 1, 1955. A thousand miles later, after innumerable narrow escapes, they crossed the Brescia finishing line in fine style at 100 mph—impatient to discover whether they had beat Taruffi, their most dangerous competitor. They had their answer when word came through that Taruffi had dropped out of the race with a broken oil pipe.

Jules Verne's stories were mainly about the sea, but in *Five Weeks in a Balloon* his three brilliant sportsmen were caught up in an African equatorial storm that tossed them about unmercifully. Their quandary was whether to descend or try to go up above the water-filled clouds.

While not usually associated with baseball themes, Zane Grey's short story of *The Redheaded Outfield* pits the Rochester Stars against the Providence Grays in the final pennant race. The outcome was decided by the most remarkable outfield ever developed in minor league baseball—three of the nuttiest players imaginable—all redheads.

It is difficult to pick out the best baseball story that Ring Lardner ever wrote, but *Horseshoes* could easily qualify. Connie Mack's unlikely outfielder, Grimes, tells his version of the fracas between himself and Speed Parker that landed McGraw's great third baseman in the hospital. It explains why Parker's calling Grimes "Horseshoes" was at the bottom of it all.

No section on baseball would be complete without a Babe Ruth story, so here is Robert W. Creamer's discussion of *The Magnificent Moment: The Called-Shot Home Run.* At this time the journalists were having a field day arguing whether the Babe did or did not purposefully plan it. You can draw your own conclusion.

Perhaps basketball calls more heavily on the "killer instinct" of its players than any other sport. This is forcefully brought out in this gruesome incident from superstar Bob Cousy's book *Killer Instinct.*

In his highly praised book *Heaven on Earth* Michael D'Antonio tells of a fascinating journey through the beliefs of New Age America. In a chapter called "Mystic Baseball," Bill Lee, a famous Red Sox player, teaches the amateur player D'Antonio how to make the great American pastime a means of spiritual and psychological enrichment.

The first black man ever to become an American sports champion and then a world champion was Marshall W. "Major" Taylor. In his autobiography, *The Fastest Bicycle Rider in the World,* he tells of "My Greatest Race," the one he won in 1898 against Jimmy Michaels, until then the unbeatable Welsh champion. In spite of deep prejudice and efforts to debar him from tracks all over the country, the black contender in this race proved that color could not keep a true champion out of his rightful place in American sports.

Three-cushion billiards was never the same sport without Dan McGoorty, as Robert Byrne laments the passing of its golden age in his book *McGoorty: A Billiard Hustler's Life.* Danny McGoorty wanted desperately to become the ruling champion of the game, but he was ten years too late in conquering his bout with alcohol. Here, in the short story "Three Cushions," Danny tells of a baffling episode in his faded career.

Not all boating trips on a thirty-foot cabin cruiser need to be a two-week vacation to Provincetown and Nantucket. In my book *Cruising Is Fun,* I take three couples out for an evening of fun and games, for a bit of "Moonlight Cruising." After work, we set out from the Harlem Yacht Club at City Island, New York. An hour and a half later, we were anchored in a snug harbor, somewhere off of Long Island Sound. All was peaceful and delightfully serene. No blasting, speeding outboards to mar the occasion. That's where cruising can be fun.

In "A Piece of Steak," one of Jack London's memorable short stories, the master of action fiction has written a classic prize-ring story. Tom King, a typical Australian prizefighter, and his family lived in poverty, with his meager income coming from winning bouts at the Gaiety Club. He badly needed to win his fight that night with Sandel, a Youth incarnate, so his family could eat. In the eleventh round he decked Sandel, who went down for the count, but he was up at "nine." Weak from hunger, this comeback was too much for Tom, and he lost the bout. He lacked enough strength for that one last punch that a piece of steak would have given him.

The Muhammad Ali–George Foreman fight on October 30, 1974 took place in Kinshasa, Zaire. In his autobiography, *The Greatest: My Own Story,* Ali gives a bombastic running account in an explosive chapter called "Bomaye." At the very outset, the angered referee, Zack Clayton, warns Ali he'll stop the fight if Ali's contemptuous talk to his opponent doesn't cease immediately. The fighters return to their corners and come out fighting. Eight rounds later Ali KO's George and regains his World Heavyweight Title.

In *The Presidential Papers* Norman Mailer covers another fight for the Heavyweight Championship—the strange Floyd Patterson–Sonny Liston encounter. Seated next to Jimmy Baldwin, they both were stunned when the fight was over 2:06 of the first round as Liston knocked out Patterson. It must have been the worst fight either boxer had ever had. What happened?

Sidney Franklin reveals in his autobiography how he became *A Bullfighter from Brooklyn.* Not knowing the first thing about bullfighting, he had briefly visited the ranch of Don Abelardo, where he had been introduced to the fundamentals. Imagine his chagrin on arriving in Mexico City to find an enormous sign opposite the ring announcing Sidney Franklin's debut appearance on Sunday, three days hence. The day came and he was herded into the ring by Don Ramos, who pointed out the bull with, "Look, kid, there's the bull. You do anything you want with that bull. But do it! And heaven help us!" Franklin's performance that day was spectacular and the crowd idolized him. "It was at that moment that I knew I would become a bullfighter."

In his first novel, *Deliverance,* James Dickey's four protagonists embark on a three-day canoe trip down a particularly wild section of a river in the heartland of today's South. They are average suburbanites and for them the trip represented a chance for adventure with few risks. Early on the second day, two of the group are suddenly viciously attacked by mountaineers. The canoe trip explodes into a nightmare of horror and murder. In events that follow, the canoes capsize in the treacherous river, as each is called upon to employ every strength and resource to survive and achieve deliverance.

If you're in the mood for a good laugh, then *The Cricket Match* by Robert Stilgoe is your cup of tea, which is exactly what the batsmen interrupted this game for, as their wives served scones of a weight to rival uranium.

From Izaak Walton's unpretentious but classic treatise on angling, *The Compleat Angler,* comes this piscatorial delight on "The Salmon." What amazes Walton is the salmon's ritual of spending their appointed time in fresh water, then going to sea, where they grow big. But then they must return to fresh water to grow fat and spawn. In returning they must force themselves through floodgates, over weirs, hedges, or stops in the water and jump to heights beyond belief, even higher than eight feet above water. And if you want to fish for a salmon, you can share Izaak Walton's secrets of catching them.

Presbyterian ministers are not supposed to go fishing (or play golf, for that matter) on Sunday. However, there are exceptions to every church leader's habits, as Philip Wylie shows in his fishing tale *Once on a Sunday.* The Reverend Doctor Arthur McGill appeared on the Gulf Stream Deck at seven o'clock, ready to spend three days to find out what saltwater fishing was all about. When Sunday came, they still had not had the kind of luck the Reverend had expected. But other fisherman were bringing in scads of fish, he noted. The temptation to fish this last day was too much (although fishing on Sunday was to commit a mortal sin of the first magnitude) so the Reverend took off his collar as he climbed aboard.

In the early seasons of football, the Yale-Princeton game was the most popular. On November 23, 1895 forty thousand people journeyed to Manhattan Field. Richard Harding Davis covers it for *The Journal* in his story "How the Great Football Game Was Played." At the end, just as the Yale men were growing fearful that the game would end in a tie, Captain Thorne of the Yale team made his famous run and settled the question forever.

As an amateur sportsman, a writer, and an anthologist of sport stories, George Plimpton has personally participated as a player in the sports he so superbly writes about. At Pontiac he had been training for three weeks to run against the first-string Detroit defense. In his very successful novel *Paper Lion,* he recounts this harrowing and hilarious experience as "The Five-Play Quarterback." George began calling his signals. He went through five plays with disastrous results on each. He left the field as applause began to sound from the stands. Thinking about it later, he felt that it could only have been in appreciation of the lunacy of his participation.

Peter Gent played football for the Dallas Cowboys. From his brutal, X-rated novel *North Dallas Forty* he covers his participation, play by play, in the New York Giants vs. Dallas Cowboys game. It was an unusually wicked game with tempers on edge and smashed noses, blood pouring from mouths, torn hamstrings. Yet the game went on. With less than two minutes to play, the score read Dallas, 21–New York, 20. On the next play the Dallas ball was intercepted and returned to the Dallas twenty. With fifteen seconds to play, the New York punter kicked his third field goal. New York, 23–Dallas, 21. On the bus to Kennedy, Peter and his quarterback smoked a whole joint in silence.

As with many of his hilarious golf stories, P.G. Wodehouse begins "The Awakening of Rollo Podmarsh" with the Oldest Member snaring a young clubman, reluctant to hear the golf tale he was about to unfold, the story of Rollo Podmarsh, who had yet to break a hundred. Rollo was playing a match teamed with an encouraging Mary, his niece. He started off exceedingly well taking only a forty-six for the first nine holes. With a ninety-six on the last green, he sank his first putt for a ninety-seven. He had achieved his life's ambition of breaking a hundred. Why then did he feel sick?

Ken Dryden was the goalie on the finest Montreal Canadian's championship team. In his book *The Game* he writes entertainingly of what it's really like to be a professional hockey player. In this selection, "The Goalie," he admits that "Playing goal is not fun. Behind a mask, there are no smiling faces. . . . It is a grim, humorless position, largely uncreative, requiring little physical movement. . . . A goalie is simply there." On the other hand, "The great satisfaction of playing goal comes from the challenge it presents. Simply stated, it is to give the team what it needs, when it needs it." And then he proceeds to explain why he enjoys the role he plays and the beauty of the game. And he should know.

Dick Francis has been called "the great thriller writer of the racing world." His story here, "The Day of the Losers," is the only one he has written about the English Grand National. Austin Dartmouth Glenn had £300 to spend on the Races, part of the £15,000 of loot he received for a multimillion bank robbery. Chief Superintendent Crispin had been trying to track down some of these stolen bank notes, hoping some better would try to pass them at this Grand National. Glenn placed £50 on Haunted House to win. They were spotted by a quick-witted teller who reported him to Crispin, who realized that if the robber won he would have to collect at the betting window and could be apprehended. With his usual skill in bringing all the mysterious elements together, Francis keeps the reader guessing as to the enjoyable outcome.

Theodore Roosevelt's account of his hunting days is a sportsman's delight, especially when in the Rockies he went after the giant of all deer, The Moose. In his book *The Wilderness Hunter* he extols the sport: "The chase is among the best of all natural pastimes. . . . No one who has partaken thereof, can understand the keen delight of hunting in lonely lands."

In a short comedy sketch in one of his *Whilomville Stories,* Stephen Crane has Jimmy and his two companions go "Lynx-Hunting." But what he shot sent old Henry Flemming, the owner of the farm, into gales of laughter.

Jai alai is one of the fastest games in the world, as Robert Sylvester shows in an *Esquire* story called "The Monarch's Last Tanto." This was the Monarch's last game, and his first crooked one. In the Havana pelota it was The Monarch and The Flash against Piston and Guillermo. The score changed back and forth but remained even, Blue, 29–White, 29. Until the final tanto.

Jousting was a favorite sport in the medieval ages and Sir Walter Scott a favorite author of these combats. In his novel, *Ivanhoe,* a disinherited knight, at the peril of his life, entered the contest against four champion knights; Brian de Bois-Guillbert was the first. The disinherited knight vanquished him as well as the three that followed. Who was this invincible champion?

In "Legends of Karate," George E. Mattson recounts stories that were told to him while studying karate in Okinawa. Some of the stories had a moral to them; others simply related experiences of the karate masters of the past. Here is The Old Man and the Tiger; The Bluff; The Lesson; Mr. Uochi, Sr. and the Bandits; and Tests of Stability.

A cliff-hanger in every way, Trevanian's suspense novel *The Eiger Sanction* keeps the reader in an edge-of-the-seat excitement until the last absorbing page. This episode, "Descent from the Eiger," is the climax of the hazardous mountain-climbing trip of four men attempting to conquer and scale one of the most treacherous mountain peaks in the Swiss Alps, the Eiger. One of them is engaged in a most hazardous sanction (assassination) assignment. The conclusion of this frightening climb reveals the answer.

In "The Maltese Cat" by Rudyard Kipling, the protagonists in this polo match *should* be experts in this sport. They are the polo ponies themselves.

As they recount the matches for the Upper India Five-for-All Cup, their observations are right from the horses' mouths. At the confused climax, it was the Maltese Cat who saved his owner's life.

Stephen Kiesling served on the U.S. Olympic Team in 1980. As an undergraduate at Yale, he was a member of that crew in the famous annual Yale-Harvard Boat Race at New London, Connecticut. In his book *The Shell Game,* you follow him and his crewmates through the days of preparation, the warm-up before the big race, and every stroke of the four-mile race itself. The close finish was only twenty strokes away—when a blade of the Yale crew caught a little water.

The finest story about scuba diving, I feel, is to be found in James Jones's novel *Go to the Widow-Maker.* Grant had grimly decided he would learn the sport from scratch and hired Al Bonham, an expert teacher who owned a dive shop near the Ganada Bay Yacht Club. In "The Neophyte Diver," after practicing the basics of scuba diving poolside, Bonham decides Grant is ready for his first dive. Their underwater swim was more than Grant had bargained for, especially when they reached the sixty-foot-high cave. Bonham was relentless in the dangerous maneuvers he put Grant through. As they reached their boat and headed back to shore, Grant's elation at his first successful dive knew no bounds.

Maury Allen, one of the country's most competent sports writers, feels that of all the competitive sports, skiing could be the most emotional and most exciting. In his biographical article on Toni Sailer, called "Gold in the Snow," he covers the first ski event of the 1956 Olympics. Toni's first jump was in the giant slalom when he broke an Olympic record. Toni now had two events to go, the special slalom and the downhill race. He took the second in 3:14 to win. The last event was considered a suicide run, 3,622 meters over rolling mountain terrain. As he charged across the finish line in 2:52, he became the first to set a record in all three Alpine events and one of only three skiers in the history of the Olympics to win three gold medals.

Pelé may well be the most famous name in the history of soccer. His autobiography, *Pelé: My Life and the Beautiful Game,* written with Robert L. Fish, opens with the third game between the Soviet Union and Pelé's Brazil in their fight in the Jules Rimet Trophy competition for the soccer championship of the world. Unbelievably, the game ended Brazil, 2–Russia, 0. Time then jumps to a much later game. It is Pelé's 909th, in which he hopes to achieve that magic elusive 1,000th goal. The game was against Vasco da Gama in the Maracana Stadium in Rio. His opponent tripped Pelé and the referee awarded him a penalty kick. While not the way he wanted to make his 1,000th goal, it was successful. The roar of the crowd erupted as hundreds of cheering fans mobbed him. He had reached his 1,000th goal!

Jack London on his cruise to Hawaii aboard his self-built ketch discovered a new sport he immediately decided he must try. It challenged him to wrestle with the sea's breakers and ride to shore upon their backs. He tells of the excitement and dangers inherent in surf-riding in "The Waves at Waikiki," a selection from his book *The Cruise of the Snark.* But he hadn't reckoned with the wonderful sun beating down on a Waikiki beach.

John Cheever's short story "The Swimmer" is a very unusual handling of this sport. On a midsummer Sunday, Neddy Merrill sat by a pool drinking a gin. His own house was in Bullet Park eight miles to the south. It occurred to him that by taking a dogleg to the Southwest he could reach his home by water, by using a string of swimming pools. He would call on his various friends, neighbors, and even a mistress whose pools he would use. As he progressed, the swim became more hazardous; he was caught in a storm, and his dearest friends became hostile strangers. He was perplexed. Was he losing his memory? His answer came when he finally reached his own house.

On August 5, 1976 Diana Nyad was flying British Airways to attempt to become the first woman to complete the double crossing of the English Channel. The swim would be from shore to shore, followed by the permissable ten minutes' rest, and then back again. Her book *Other Shores* contains the inspiring story "Swimming the English Channel," and relates how she fulfilled her psychological and emotional goals by pushing her body to its physical limits.

Bill Tilden was the Golden Age of Tennis, as Richard Schickel tells it in his fast-paced book *The World of Tennis.* In spite of his two prison terms related to his sexual proclivities, just days after his release, an Associated Press poll of sportswriters voted him the greatest athlete in his sport. Schickel follows Tilden as he wins championship after championship matches, not once but time after time: Wimbledon, the Davis Cup, at Forest Hills. In the end, however, he was snubbed unmercifully. For the man who made the world conscious of the game of tennis, there would be no monument.

At the time of the Arthur Ashe vs. Clark Graebner tennis match at Forest Hills, John McPhee decided that both players, being twenty-five, equally matched, and knowing each other half their lives, would be the ideal meeting to cover in his book *Levels of the Game.* He not only offers the game's stunning stroke-by-stroke action but an insight into Arthur Ashe's character as a black championship tennis player against the race prejudices he must accept and overcome.

Billy Sive is a champion long-distance runner, an ideal of American youth, and the best Olympic hope. He is young, proud, and gay. *The Front Runner,* Patricia Nell Warren's best-seller, is a riveting breakthrough novel of homosexual love in the sports world. Billy was the favorite to win the Olympic 5,000 for America. His chief rival was the Finnish star Armas. Fighting it out at the finish of the race, Billy started to pull away. Then tragedy stuck.

The Loneliness of the Long-Distance Runner by Alan Sillitoe is a minor masterpiece, a serious yet wonderfully funny tale of a Borstel boy (a reform school pupil) who seizes a foolproof opportunity during the annual cross-country race to show his defiance of authority. The governor expects his boy to win the Borstel Blue Ribbon Prize Cup for Long Distance Cross Country Running (All England). The gun went off and the race was under-way. The boy gives a running account as he leads the pack almost to the finish. It is there that he reaps his revenge!

Colin Fletcher is a walker. Soon after he moved to Southern California in 1956, he spent the summer walking from Mexico to Oregon, across California's deserts and mountains. In his book *The Secret Worlds of Colin Fletcher,* he has a chapter titled "Beyond the Divide" in which he tells of his walking trip for a week in a valley that "lies west of the Mississippi." Walking, fishing, thinking, "mucking around," the time was well spent. As the ranger said as he returned to his station, "It's done you a whole lot of good."

For a wrestling story I have chosen a selection from Sir Athall Oakeley's book *Blue Blood on my Mat.* In "My American Tour: Casey Berger, the Texas Champ," he tells of his incredible match with a great hulk of an opponent. Although a member of the British International Amateur Wrestling Team, Athall was only a fifteen stoner. As soon as he appeared, the fight crown greeted him with howls of laughter. But they soon changed that to a "Well done, little guy" as David slays Goliath!

"Racing a small yacht across the North Atlantic is not entirely a technical feat, nor even an adventure in the classic sense, but is a great emotional and physical experience for those involved." So wrote Carleton Mitchell in 1952 as a member of the nine-man crew of the yawl *Caribbe,* winner of that year's Transatlantic Race from Bermuda to England. In this selection from his book *Passage East,* he captures this special yachting experience.

In this anthology of both fictional and factual sports literature, I have tried to show the diversity of sports personalities included and the variety of different sports in which they excelled. Any anthology reflects the personal choices of the compiler and I hope you'll enjoy them all. If this should not always be the case, I know you'll be a good sport about it.

OLYMPIC FUNERAL GAMES

By Homer

Thus spáke he, and they hearkened to the fleet-footed son of Peleus. First quenched they with gleaming wine the burning so far as the flame went, and the ash had settled deep: then with lamentation they gathered up the white bones of their gentle comrade into a golden urn and double-folded fat, and placed the urn in the hut and covered it with a linen veil. And they marked the circle of the barrow, and set the foundations thereof around the pyre, and straightway heaped thereon a heap of earth. Then when they had heaped up the barrow they were for going back. But Achilles stayed the folk in that place, and made them sit in wide assembly, and from his ships he brought forth prizes, caldrons and tripods, and horses and mules and strong oxen, and fair-girdled women, and grey iron.

First for fleet chariot-racers he ordained a noble prize, a woman skilled in fair handiwork for the winner to lead home, and an eared tripod that held two-and-twenty measures; these for the first man; and for the second he ordained a six-year-old mare unbroke, with a mule foal in her womb; and for the third he gave a goodly caldron yet untouched by fire, holding four measures, bright as when first made; and for the fourth he ordained two talents of gold; and for the fifth a two-handled urn untouched of fire. Then he stood up and spake a word among the Argies: "Son of Atreus and ye other well-greaved Achaians, for the chariot-racers these prizes lie awaiting them in the lists. If in some other's honour we Achaians were now holding our games, it would be I who should win the first prize and bear it to my hut; for ye know how far my pair of horses are first in excellence, for they are immortal, and Poseidon gave them to my father Peleus, and he again to me. But verily I will abide, I and my whole-hooved horses, so glorious a charioteer have they lost, and one so kind, who on their manes full often poured smooth oil, when he had washed them in clean water. For him they stand and mourn, and their manes are trailing on the ground, and there stand they with sorrow at their hearts. But ye others throughout the host get ye to your places, whosoever of the Achaians hath trust in his horses and firm-jointed car.''

Thus spake the son of Peleus, and the fleet chariot-racers were gathered. First of all arose up Eumelos king of men, Admetos' son, a skilful charioteer; and next to him arose Tydeus' son, valiant Diomedes, and yoked his horses of the breed of Tros, which on a time he seized from Aineias, when Apollo saved their lord. And after him arose Atreus' son, fair-haired heaven-sprung Menelaos, and yoked him a swift pair, Aithe, Agamemnon's mare, and his own horse Podargos. Her unto Agamemnon did Anchises' son Echpolos give in fee, that he might escape from following him to windy Ilios and take his pleasure at home; for great wealth had Zeus given him, and he dwelt in Sikyon of spacious lawns:—so Menelaos yoked her, and she longed exceedingly for the race. And fourth, Antilochos made ready his fair-maned horses, even the noble son of Nestor, high-hearted king, who was the son of Neleus; and fleet horses bred at Pylos drew his car. And his father standing by his side spake counselling him to his profit, though himself was well advised: "Antilochos, verily albeit thou art young, Zeus and Poseidon have loved thee and taught thee all skill with horses; wherefore to teach thee is no great need, for thou well knowest how to wheel round the post; yet are thy horses very slow in the race: therefore methinks there will be sad work for thee. For the horses of the others are fleeter, yet the men know not more cunning than thou hast. So come, dear son, store thy mind with all manner of cunning, that the prize escape thee not. By cunning is a woodman far better than by force; by cunning doth a helmsman on the wine-dark deep steer his swift ship buffeted by winds; by cunning hath charioteer the better of charioteer. For whoso trusting in his horses and car alone wheeleth heedlessly and wide at either end, his horses swerve on the course, and he keepeth them not in hand. But whoso is of crafty mind, though he drive worse horses, he ever keeping his eye upon the post turneth closely by it, neither is unaware how far at first to force his horses by the ox-hide reins, but holdeth them safe in hand and watcheth the leader in the race. Now will I tell thee a certain sign, and it shall not escape thee. A fathom's height above the ground standeth a withered stump, whether of oak or pine: it decayeth not in the rain, and two white stones on either side thereof are fixed at the joining of the track, and all round it is smooth driving ground. Whether it be a monument of some man dead long ago, or have been made their goal in the race by ancient men, this now is the mark fixed by fleet-footed goodly Achilles. Wherefore do thou drive close and bear thy horses and chariot hard thereon, and lean thy body on the well-knit car slightly to their left, and call upon the off-horse with voice and lash, and give him rein from thy hand. But let the near horse hug the post so that the nave of the well-wrought wheel seem to graze it—yet beware of touching the stone, lest thou wound the horses and break the chariot; so would that be triumph to the rest and reproach unto thyself. But, dear son, be wise and on thy guard; for if at the turning-post thou drive past the rest, there is none shall overtake thee from behind or pass thee by, not though he drave the goodly Arion in pursuit, the fleet horse of Adrastos, of divine descent, or the horses of Laomedon, best of all bred in this land.''

Thus spake Neleïan Nestor and sate him down again in his place, when he had told his son the sum of every matter.

And Meriones was the fifth to make ready his sleek-coated steeds. Then went they up into their chariots, and cast in the lots: and Achilles shook them, and forth leapt the lot of Antilochos Nestor's son, and the next lot had lord Eumelos, and next to him the son of Atreus, spear-famed Menelaos, and next to him drew Meriones his place; then lastly Tydeides, far the best of all, drew his lot for his chariot's place. Then they stood side by side, and Achilles showed to them the turning-post, far off in the smooth plain; and beside it he placed an umpire, godlike Phoinix, his father's follower, that he might note the running and tell the truth thereof.

Then all together lifted the lash above their steeds, and smote them with the reins, and called on them eagerly with words: and they forthwith sped swiftly over the plain, leaving the ships behind; and beneath their breasts stood the rising dust like a cloud or whirlwind, and their manes waved on the blowing wind. And the chariots ran sometimes on the bounteous earth, and other whiles would bound into the air. And the drivers stood in the cars, and the heart of every man beat in desire of victory, and they called every man to his horses, that flew amid their dust across the plain.

But when the fleet horses were now running the last part of the course, back toward the grey sea, then was manifest the prowess of each, and the horses strained in the race; and presently to the front rushed the fleet mares of Pheres' grandson, and next to them Diomedes' stallions of the breed of Tros, not far apart, but hard anigh, for they seemed ever as they would mount Eumelos' car, and with their breath his back was warm and his broad shoulders, for they bent their heads upon him as they flew along. Thus would Tydeus' son have either outstripped the other or made it a dead heat, had not Phoebus Apollo been wroth with him and smitten from his hand the shining lash. Then from his eyes ran tears of anger, for that he saw the mares still at speed, even swiftlier than before, while his own horses were thrown out, as running without spur. But Athene was not unaware of Apollo's guile against Tydeides, and presently sped after the shepherd of hosts, and gave him back the lash, and put spirit into his steeds. Then in wrath after the son of Admetos was the goddess gone, and brake his steeds' yoke, and the mares ran sideways off the course, and the pole was twisted to the ground. And Eumelos was hurled out of the car beside the wheel, and his elbows and mouth and nose were flayed, and his forehead bruised above his eyebrows; and his eyes filled with tears and his lusty voice was choked. Then Tydeides held his whole-hooved horses on one side, darting far out before the rest, for Athene put spirit into his steeds and shed glory on himself. Now next after him came golden-haired Menelaos Atreus' son. But Antilochos called to his father's horses: "Go ye too in, strain to your fleetest pace. Truly I nowise bid you strive with those, the horses of wise Tydeides, unto which Athene hath now given speed, and shed glory on their charioteer. But overtake Atreides' horses with all haste, and be not outstripped by them, lest Aithe that is but a mare pour scorn on you. Why are ye outstripped, brave steeds? Thus will I tell you, and verily it shall be brought to pass—ye will find no tendance with Nestor shepherd of hosts, but straightway he will slay you with the edge of the sword if through heedlessness we win but the worse prize. Have after them at your utmost speed, and I for my part will devise a plan to pass them in the strait part of the course, and this shall fail me not.''

Thus spake he, and they fearing the voice of the prince ran swiftlier some little while; and presently did the good warrior Antilochos espy a strait place in a sunk part of the way. There was a rift in the earth, where torrent water gathered and brake part of the track away, and hollowed all the place; there drave Menelaos, shunning the encounter of the wheels. But Antilochos turned his whole-hooved horses out of the track, and followed him a little at one side. And the son of Atreus took alarm and shouted to Antilochos: "Antilochos, thou art driving recklessly—hold in thy horses! The road is straitened, soon thou mayest pass me in a wider place, lest thou foul my chariot and undo us both.''

Thus spake he, but Antilochos drave even fiercelier than before, plying his lash, as though he heard him not. As far as is the range of a disk swung from the shoulder when a young man hurleth it, making trial of his force, even so far ran they on; then the mares of Atreus' son gave back, for he ceased of himself to urge them on, lest the whole-hooved steeds should encounter on the track, and overset the well-knit cars, and the drivers fall in the dust in their zeal for victory. So upbraiding Antilochos spake golden-haired Menelaos: "Antilochos, no mortal man is more malicious than thou. Go thy mad way, since falsely have we Achaians called thee wise. Yet even so thou shalt not bear off the prize unchallenged to an oath.''

Thus saying he called aloud to his horses: "Hold ye not back nor stand still with sorrow at heart. Their feet and knees will grow weary before yours, for they both lack youth.''

Thus spake he, and they fearing the voice of the prince sped faster on, and were quickly close upon the others.

Now the Argives sitting in concourse were gazing at the horses, and they came flying amid their dust over the plain. And the first aware of them was Idomeneus, chief of the Cretans, for he was sitting outside the concourse in the highest place of view, and when he heard the voice of one that shouted, though afar off, he knew it; and he was aware of a horse showing plainly in the front, a chestnut all the rest of him, but in the forehead marked with a white star round like the moon. And he stood upright and spoke among the Argives: "Friends, chiefs, and counsellors of the Argives, is it I alone who see the horses, or do ye also? A new pair seem to me now to be in front, and a new charioteer appeareth; the mares which led in the outward course must have been thrown out there in the plain. For I saw them turning first the hither post, but now can see them nowhere, though my eyes are gazing everywhere along the Trojan plain. Did the reins escape the charioteer so that he could not drive aright round the post and failed in the turn? There, methinks, must he have been cast forth, and have broken his chariot, and the mares must have left the course, in the wildness of their heart. But stand up ye too and look, for myself I discern not certainly, but the first man seemeth to me one of Aitolian race, and he ruleth among Argives, the son of horse-taming Tydeus, stalwart Diomedes.''

Then fleet Aias Oileus' son rebuked him in unseemly sort: ''Idomeneus, why art thou a braggart of old? As yet far off the high-stepping mares are coursing over the wide plain. Neither art thou so far the youngest among the Argives, nor do thy eyes look so far the keenliest from thy head, yet continually braggest thou. It beseemeth thee not to be a braggart, for there are here better men. And the mares leading are they that led before, Eumelos' mares, and he standeth and holdeth the reins within the car.''

Then wrathfully in answer spake the chief of Cretans: ''Aias, master of railing, ill-counselled, in all else art thou behind other Argives, for thy mind is unfriendly. Come then let us wager a tripod or caldron, and make Agamemnon Atreus' son our umpire, which mares are leading, that thou mayest pay and learn.''

Thus said he, and straightay fleet Aias Oileus' son arose angrily to answer with harsh words: and strife between the twain would have gone further, had not Achilles himself stood up and spake a word: ''No longer answer each other with harsh words, Aias and Idomeneus, ill words, for it beseemeth not. Surely ye are displeased with any other who should do thus. Sit ye in the concourse and keep your eyes upon the horses; soon they in zeal for victory will come hither, and then shall ye know each of you the Argives' horses, which follow, and which lead.''

He said, and the son of Tydeus came driving up, and with his lash smote now and again from the shoulder, and his horses were stepping high as they sped swiftly on their way. And sprinklings of dust smote ever the charioteer, and his chariot overlaid with gold and tin ran behind his fleet-footed steeds, and small trace was there of the wheel-tires behind in the fine dust, as they flew speeding on. Then he drew up in the mid concourse, and much sweat poured from the horses' heads and chests to the ground. And Diomedes leapt to earth from the shining car, and leant his lash against the yoke. Then stalwart Sthenelos tarried not, but promptly took the prize, and gave to his proud comrades the woman to lead and the eared tripod to bear away, and he loosed the horses from the yoke.

Then he ordained prizes of the violent boxing match; a sturdy mule he led forth and tethered amid the assembly, a six-year mule unbroken, hardest of all to break; and for the loser set a two-handled cup. Then he stood up and spake a word among the Argives: ''Son of Atreus and ye other well-greaved Achaians, for these rewards we summon two men of the best to lift up their hands to box amain. He to whom Apollo shall grant endurance to the end, and all the Achaians acknowledge it, let him take the sturdy mule and return with her to his hut; and the loser shall take with him the two-handled cup.''

Thus spake he, and forthwith arose a man great and valiant and skilled in boxing, Epeios son of Panopeus, and laid his hand on the sturdy mule and said aloud: "Let one come nigh to bear off the two-handled cup; the mule I say none other of the Achaians shall take for victory with his fists, for I claim to be the best man here. Sufficeth it not that I fall short of you in battle? Not possible is it that in all arts a man be skilled. Thus proclaim I, and it shall be accomplished: I will utterly bruise mine adversary's flesh and break his bones, so let his friends abide together here to bear him forth when vanquished by my hands."

Thus spake he, and they all kept deep silence. And alone arose against him Euryalos, a godlike man, son of king Mekisteus the son of Talaos, Mekisteus, who came on a time to Thebes when Oedipus had fallen, to his burial, and there he overcame all the sons of Kadmos. Thus Tydeides famous with the spear made ready Euryalos for the fight, cheering him with speech, and greatly desired for him victory. And first he cast about him a girdle, and next gave him well-cut thongs of the hide of an ox of the field. And the two boxers being girt went into the midst of the ring, and both lifting up their stalwart hands fell to, and their hands joined battle grievously. Then was there terrible grinding of teeth, and sweat flowed from all their limbs. And noble Epeios came on, and as the other spied for an opening, smote him on the cheek, nor could he much more stand, for his fair limbs failed straightway under him. And as when beneath the North Wind's ripple a fish leapeth on a tangle-covered beach, and then the black wave hideth it, so leapt up Euryalos at that blow. But great-hearted Epeios took him in his hands and set him upright, and his dear comrades stood around him, and led him through the ring with trailing feet, spitting out clotted blood, drooping his head awry, and they set him down in his swoon among them and themselves went forth and fetched the two-handled cup.

Then Peleus' son ordained straightway the prizes for a third contest, offering them to the Danaans, for the grievous wrestling match: for the winner a great tripod for standing on the fire, prized by the Achaians among them at twelve oxen's worth; and for the loser he brought a woman into the midst, skilled in manifold work, and they prized her at four oxen. And he stood up and spake a word among the Argives: "Rise, ye who will essay this match."

Thus said he, and there arose great Aias son of Telamon, and Odysseus of many wiles stood up, the crafty-minded. And the twain being girt went into the midst of the ring, and clasped each the other in his arms with stalwart hands, like gable rafters of a lofty house which some famed crafts-man joineth, that he may baffle the wind's force. And their backs creaked, gripped firmly under the vigorous hands, and sweat ran down in streams, and frequent weals along their ribs and shoulders sprang up, red with blood, while ever they strove amain for victory, to win the wrought tripod. Neither could Odysseus trip Aias and bear him to the ground, nor Aias him, for Odysseus' strength withheld him. But when they began to irk the well-greaved Achaians, then said to Odysseus great Aias, Telamon's son:

"Heaven-sprung son of Laertes, Odysseus of many wiles, or lift thou me, or I will thee, and the issue shall be with Zeus."

Having thus said he lifted him, but Odysseus was not unmindful of his craft. He smote deftly from behind the hollow of Aias' knee, and loosed his limbs, and threw him down backward, and Odysseus fell upon his chest, and the folk gazed and marvelled. Then in his turn much-enduring noble Odysseus tried to lift, and moved him a little from the ground, but lifted him not, so he crooked his knee within the other's, and both fell on the ground nigh to each other, and were soiled with dust. And now starting up again a third time would they have wrestled, had not Achilles himself arisen and held them back: "No longer press each the other, nor wear you out with pain. Victory is with both; take equal prizes and depart, that other Achaians may contend."

Thus spake he, and they were fain to hear and to obey, and wiped the dust from them and put their doublets on.

Then straightway the son of Peleus set forth other prizes for fleetness of foot; a mixing-bowl of silver, chased; six measures it held, and in beauty it was far the best in all the earth, for artificers of Sidon wrought it cunningly, and men of the Phoenicians brought it over the misty sea, and landed it in harbour, and gave it a gift to Thoas; and Euneos son of Jason gave it to the hero Patroklos a ransom for Lykaon Priam's son. Now this cup did Achilles set forth as a prize in honour of his friend, for whoso should be fleetest in speed of foot. For the second he set an ox great and very fat, and for the last prize half a talent of gold. And he stood up and spake a word among the Argives: "Rise, ye who will essay this match."

Thus spake he, and straightway arose fleet Aias Oileus' son, and Odysseus of many wiles, and after them Nestor's son Antilochos, for he was best of all the youth in the footrace. Then they stood side by side, and Achilles showed to them the goal. Right eager was the running from the start, but Oileus' son forthwith shot to the front, and close behind him came noble Odysseus, as close as is a weaving-rod to a fair-girdled woman's breast when she pulleth it deftly with her hands, drawing the spool along the warp, and holdeth the rod nigh her breast—so close ran Odysseus behind Aias and trod in his footsteps or ever the dust had settled there, and on his head fell the breath of noble Odysseus as he ran ever lightly on, and all the Achaians applauded his struggle for the victory and called on him as he laboured hard. But when they were running the last part of the course, forthwith Odysseus prayed in his soul to bright-eyed Athene: "Hearken, goddess, come thou a good helper of my feet."

Thus prayed he, and Pallas Athene hearkened to him, and made his limbs feel light, both feet and hands. But when they were now nigh darting on the prize, then Aias slipped as he ran, for Athene marred his race, where filth was strewn from the slaughter of loud-bellowing oxen that fleet Achilles slew in honour of Patroklos: and Aias' mouth and nostrils were filled with that filth of oxen. So much-enduring noble Odysseus, as he came in first, took up the mixing-bowl, and famous Aias took the ox. And he stood holding in his hand the horn of the ox of the field, sputtering away the filth, and spake among the Argives: "Out on it, it was the goddess who marred my running, she who from of old like a mother standeth by Odysseus' side and helpeth him."

So spake he, but they all laughed pleasantly to behold him. Then Antilochos smiling bore off the last prize, and spake his word among the Argives: "Friends, ye will all bear me witness when I say that even herein also the immortals favour elder men. For Aias is a little older than I, but Odysseus of an earlier generation and earlier race of men. A green old age is his, they say, and hard were it for any Achaian to rival him in speed, save only Achilles."

Thus spake he, and gave honour to the fleet son of Peleus. And Achilles answered him and said: "Antilochos, not unheeded shall thy praise be given; a half-talent of gold I will give thee over and above." He said, and set it in his hands, and Antilochos received it gladly.

[Then Peleus' son brought a long-shadowed spear into the ring and laid it there, and a shield and helmet, the arms of Sarpedon whereof Patroklos spoiled him. And he stood up and spake a word among the Argives: "To win these arms we bid two warriors of the best put on their armour and take flesh-cleaving bronze to make trial of each other before the host whether of the two shall first reach the other's fair flesh and touch the inward parts through armour and dark blood. To him will I give this silver-studded sword, a goodly Thracian sword that I took from Asteropaios; and these arms let both bear away to hold in common, and a fair feast will we set before them in the huts."

Thus spake he, and then arose Telamon's son great Aias, and up rose Tydeus' son, stalwart Diomedes. So when on either side the assembly they had armed them, they met together in the midst eager for battle, with terrible gaze; and wonder fell on all the Achaians. But when they were now nigh in onset on each other, thrice they came on and thrice drew nigh to smite. Then Aias smote on the round shield, but pierced not to the flesh, for the breastplate within kept off the spear. But the son of Tydeus over his great shield kept ever aiming at the neck with the point of his bright spear. Then fearing for Aias the Achaians bade them cease and each take equal prize. But to Tydeus' son the hero gave the great sword, bringing it with its scabbard and well-cut belt.

Then the son of Peleus set an unwrought metal mass which anciently the mighty Eëtion was wont to whirl; but him fleet noble Achilles slew, and brought the mass in his ships with his other possessions. And he stood up and spake a word among the Argives: "Rise, ye who will essay this match. The winner of this, even though his rich fields be very far remote, will have it for use five rolling years, for his shepherd or ploughman will not for want of iron have to go into the town, but this will give it them."

Thus said he, and then arose warlike Polypoites, and the valiant strength of godlike Leonteus, and Aias son of Telamon and noble Epeios. And they stood in order, and noble Epeios took the weight, and whirled and flung it;

and all the Achaians laughed to see it. Then next Leonteus, of the stock of Ares, threw; and thirdly great Aias Telamon's son hurled it from his stalwart hand, and overpassed the marks of all. But when warlike Polypoites took the mass he flung it as far as a herdsman flingeth his staff, when it flieth whirling through herds of kine;—so far cast he beyond all the space, and the people shouted aloud. And the comrades of strong Polypoites arose and bare the king's prize to the hollow ships.

Then for the archers he set a prize of dark iron—ten double-headed axes he set, and ten single; and set up the mast of a dark-prowed ship far off in the sands, and bound a pigeon thereto by the foot with a fine cord, and bade shoot thereat:—"Whosoever shall hit the pigeon let him take all the double axes home with him, and whoso shall miss the bird but hit the cord, he shall take the single, since his shot is worse."

Thus spake he, and then arose the strength of the chief Teukros, and Meriones arose, Idomeneus' brave brother in arms. And they took lots and shook them in a brazen helm, and Teukros drew the first place by lot. Forthwith he shot an arrow with power, but made no vow to offer a famous hecatomb of firstling lambs to the Lord of archery. The bird he missed—Apollo grudged him that—but struck the cord beside its foot, where the bird was tied, and the keen dart cut the cord clean away. Then the bird shot up toward heaven, and the cord hung loose toward earth; and the Achaians shouted. Then Meriones made haste and took from Teukros' hand the bow; —an arrow he had ready, while the other aimed—and vowed withal to far-darting Apollo a famous hecatomb of firstling lambs. High up under the clouds he saw the pigeon; there, as she circled round, he struck her in the midst beneath her wing, and right through her went the dart, and fell back and fixed itself in the ground before Meriones' foot; but the bird lighting on the mast of the dark-prowed ship hung down her neck, and her feathered pinions drooped. And quickly life fled from her limbs, and she fell far down from the mast; and the folk looked on and marvelled. And Meriones took up all the ten double axes, and Teukros bare the single to the hollow ships.]

Then Peleus' son brought and set in the ring a far-shadowing spear and a caldron that knew not the fire, an ox's worth, embossed with flowers; and men that were casters of the javelin arose up. There rose Atreus' son wide-ruling Agamemnon, and Meriones, Idomeneus' brave squire. And swift-footed noble Achilles spake among them: "Son of Atreus, for that we know how far thou excellest all, and how far the first thou art in the might of thy throw, take thou this prize with thee to the hollow ships, and to the hero Meriones let us give the spear, if thou art willing in thy heart: thus I at least advise."

Thus spake he, nor disregarded him Agamemnon king of men. So to Meriones he gave the spear of bronze, but to the herald Talthybios the hero gave the goodliest prize.

ATTENDING THE 64TH OLYMPIC GAMES: 520 B.C.

By Mary Renault

Next year was an Olympic one. The sixty-fourth, it must have been. Why do the Olympics never stale? The last I went to was the seventy-fifth; but it seemed as fresh as ever.

There is the ancient beauty with its changes: the oaks of Kronos may shade one from heat or shelter one from rain; the Alpheus may chuckle low on its pebbles, or rush down in spate; the women across the water may be sunning themselves with straw hats and fans, or huddled in their scented tents; it may be sweet and balmy or grilling hot, the athletes plastered with dust and sweat like clay.

There is always something new; a dedication in the Altis, new craftsmen showing work; the horse-copers' pitches down the road to tempt chariot lords, the bloodstock and handsome mules. I bought a mule that year myself, a sweet grey mare with the smooth pace that feels a part of one. Dear Leuko, she helped me to many a song.

There are new faces, and altered ones: the young wrestler who just held his own last time, now sheathed in bronze muscle in his pride of strength, victor of the pankration; some new poet from Further Greece; a philosopher from Ionia, who'd once have recited his theory in Ephesos or Miletos; a lord who inherited since last time, and is entering a chariot team; boys become youths, youths become men. And the shift of politics between city and city, nowhere to be studied so well as here.

Always I rejoice most in the athletes, dedicating body and spirit to the god: ambitious, emulous, passionate to win; and yet, making their offering. It is nearly always a joy to hymn their victories. There can be bad winners, as there are bad losers, but they are few, after their long training at Olympia itself, when the spirit of the place seeps into them. There are always ways of hymning a man who has won fairly, but whom one does not much like. One goes off into digressions about his ancestors or his city or the family's patron god. They never notice, if the song goes well; and one has earned one's fee without telling lies. Other poets know, but that is our private mystery.

Head and heart of the games is the athlete. You could say of the chariot-race that it is a rich man's toy, a contest whose prize goes to one who did nothing but spend his gold. Yet, like all the rest, I am its captive. After all, in Homer, godlike Achilles put it first, and one can't argue with that.

Though the owners don't mount their chariots, there is no event where you see more endurance, courage or skill. When I was young and poor, and had no one to command a seat for me, I used to spread my blanket over-night on the slope beside the track, stretched out full-length to keep a place for my master, so that he could sleep under cover and come down next day. The last two times, the boy did it for me. I daresay he won't need to again.

That year, though, I got a seat and even an awning. The Archons had brought a large company, with many men of rank. It overflowed the Athenian placings, and but for Hipparchos, we three poets would have had to take our chance on the slopes; it is not every patron will displace minor nobles for bards. Chairs at Olympia are for the great alone; but we had a bench with cushions, were well up the bank, and had a good view of the walk-past.

For the honor of the house, Hippias had entered a chariot. He had barely seen it, leaving everything to Hipparchos; so it was gorgeous, with the Race of Pelops in gilt relief. The horses were good Thessalians, and the driver, who had come with the team, was Thracian. He looked strong, but was rather big; your first-class driver can manage without weight, because he gets the team to think along with him. Such men are rare, however, and we all cheered the chariot on its way.

"Here's Kimon's," said Anakreon, and gave me a nudge.

Kimon son of Stesagoras sat in the row below the Archons; a man getting on in years, high-colored and hawk-nosed. His faded yellow hair was clubbed into a net in the old-fashioned style, and the pins that fixed it were headed with golden grasshoppers, meaning that his Attic ancestry went back forever. He looked a perfect type of the old oligarchs who in their great days had been little lords accountable to no one, ever since the line of High Kings died out. Moreover he was a Philead, and even the Alkmaionids ranked no higher, besides the Phileads having incurred no family curse. At one time they had been at open war with the Pisistratids; most were in exile; and how Kimon, alone of them all, came to be in the seats of honor was already an Olympic legend.

Anakreon, who had kept his eyes on the chariot, suddenly grabbed my arm. "By Zeus, look! It's the same team again!"

For some reason, this was Lasos' first visit to the Olympics. He was short-sighted, which always made him fretful at the races. "The same as what?" he said.

Anakreon and I started together to enlighten him. "Those mares. He won the last two Olympics with that same team." "They must be now— what—ten years old at least, that's if they were two-year-olds the first time." Just then the charioteer raised his arm to salute the owner. "He's the same too," Anakreon said. "That little dark Sicilian." "They look in good shape,'' I said. ''Mares are clever, if they can stay well.'' Then both of us said together, ''What if they win?''

''What if they do?'' said Lasos curiously. ''Will it be a record?''

''No, it's been done by a Spartan once. But don't you know what happened last time; why Kimon is sitting here?''

''Don't tease the poor boy, Simonides. What happened, my dear, was that Kimon proclaimed the victory in Pisistratos' name, instead of his own. He *gave* it to him, an Olympic chariot crown. He might nearly as well have presented him with a city. So the Old Archon shook hands on it, and invited him back from exile. That's why he's here, instead of over there.''

He pointed along the course, to where the Alkmaionids were gathered. It was only at times like this that one ever saw them; and then, if you had sense, it was at a distance.

''Well,'' I said, ''I doubt he could ever have won with two-year-olds; they seldom stay the distance. They may be eleven by now or even twelve.''

''Eleven. They were three-year-olds, he told me so at the time.'' Out of the three of us, only Anakreon had been eminent enough, eight whole years back, to talk with Kimon. ''They'll never do it again,'' I said. ''It's just a fancy the man has taken.''

It was a big entry that year; thirty quadrigas, no less. It seemed to take half the day getting them into the starting-stalls, after the place-lots had been drawn. Each four had a pair of grooms to lead it and help the charioteer; but there were more than the usual run of tangles and bickerings. No owner of sense will run stallions where mares are running, but the horses were excited as always by the crowds, and some charioteers are not above a sly flick of the whip at another team, if the umpire is not looking.

I've never envied those umpires. If the teams were to start from a level line, they'd be in heaps before they were under way; so they have this stepped-back order, one couple of chariots side by side at the apex, the next couple a length behind on each side, and so on outward, like a huge arrowhead. The umpires have to see the gates opened in proper order, the back ones on the outside first, and so on to the foremost that start the last; and I never saw a race yet where some driver did not complain that his gate was slow.

This time it seemed fair enough. The bronze dolphin came clanging down, the bronze eagle was hoisted on its pole over the altar; up went the gates and out went the chariots; the thunder began, and the pale dust rose billowing till it clotted our noses and tongues.

It was a good race that year. I am not one of those who value the event by the number of crashes, and sit near the turn to see them. For me, that is like giving a music prize for loudness. Besides which, I do not like the spectacle; I can picture the death of the blameless hero Hippolytos without seeing it enacted before my eyes. A chariot collision can butcher a good man and a gallant team as bloodily as a god-sent bull from the sea. Most drivers hitch the reins around them for extra grip, and though they wear sharp knives to cut themselves free if they fall, with a broken arm or a kicked head they don't get a chance to use them. Even if the driver escapes alive, it's not often the team gets off without one or all being dragged off the course and slaughtered. It was not for this that Poseidon gave to mankind a creature of such beauty. It is the horse at his godlike best that I love to watch.

It was a dry year; the dust was almost a fog, with people muffling their faces up to the eyes. From our good seats we would see the start and the finish, and all the turns at our end; the further turnpost was invisible in the murk. One saw only a turbulent mass like driftwood in a swirling river, heard the cheers of the crowd, the shouts and neighing that meant a crash or a foul. One chariot at our end had a wheel wrenched off on purpose by another; the charioteer, a fine driver, got his car and horses somehow off the course, and the man who'd fouled him was disqualified. He must have hoped that the dust would hide it. At the far end, we learned later, two teams tangled their yoke-poles and a man was killed. There were one or two other crashes from which men and horses were dragged out with broken bones, the men to race again, the beasts to die.

However, near a turnpost one does not only see disasters; one sees all the skill. All up the straight they have been working and weaving for places inside the turn; but many a driver has taken it too close and wrecked his car on the column. The man who can cut it fine and skim past is a winner, but he needs clever horses, all of whom know him and each other well. All this is as true as when prosy old Nestor instructed his son, who no doubt knew it all already, at Patroklos' funeral games.

The Athenian chariot was running a steady, well-judged race, neither fouling nor being fouled, getting the most from the team, coming fairly close in without collisions. But at each turn one saw, on the outside, a flash of bright yellow swinging round, the outside taken by choice, trusting in speed and in horses who knew their work. The driver in yellow was Kimon's; he showed up well, even after the sixth lap when the pale dust was cloaking horses and men alike. His team knew the track of old; he had no need to whip the outside horse or check the inmost, to get them turning as cleanly as a wheel. You could not have asked better of cavalry chargers with knights on their back to guide them.

At last came the twelfth, last lap. The ancient fever rose; the crowds roaring, the drivers cracking their whips and giving their shrill yells; the horses screaming as they had the last ounce flogged out of them. One team swerved across the course into another still running the lap before, so that they crashed head on; the frightful din of shouts and squeals hardly seemed to increase an uproar that was splitting one's ears already.

Only fifteen chariots finished, about the usual number. The Athenian team came fourth, which was creditable at least. But leading by half a length came Kimon's team with its yellow-robed charioteer and the neat-footed mares, their chestnut sides dappled with foam, their nostrils flaring scarlet, but game to the last, stepping off from the finishing post as prettily as deer.

We turned round to acclaim the owner. He stood up smiling, and lifted an arm to the cheers. In the thrill of the race, I had lost all thought of politics, which are made by men, while beauty and bravery are from the gods. It was not till Anakreon poked me in the ribs that I remembered.

The chief of the judges mounted the platform with the herald. At Olympia, the herald himself is the victor of a heralds' contest held beforehand. This one was a first-class trumpeter with a ringing voice. "In the name of Olympian Zeus, the winner of the four-horse chariot race is Kimon, son of Stesagoras, of Athens."

This time, Kimon of the god-descended Philead clan had claimed his victory for himself.

The chariot drew up before the podium, the mares jingling their harness as they got the air back into their lungs. Above them stood the wiry dark Sicilian, in the stillness this moment demands. He had been through it twice before; from where I sat I could see his eye already stealing down to the foam-flecked mares, with the fondness of a father, longing for all this to be over, waiting to caress them, to give them the little drink they must have before the deep one; to see them rubbed down, and put into their blankets. But he was only the charioteer, and must await the crowning of the victor.

Even at Olympia, I have seldom heard such cheering. People were standing on their seats, tearing the wreaths from their heads to fling flowers and oak-sprays at the podium. In the whole long history of the games, over the centuries, it had only been done once before, three victories running with the same team. It would become a legend.

And when that thought came to me, I saw what else it meant. The legend would be Kimon's, and his alone. Whatever had been proclaimed at the games last time, whoever had worn the crown, it would be forgotten. Men would talk forever of Kimon's triple victory. At that moment, he was bending his head for the olive crown.

In so much commotion, it was quite safe to look round. But if there had been anything to see, we had already missed it. Hippias and Hipparchos were sitting in quiet talk, like any two lords whose rank restrains them from vulgar acclamations.

Anakreon said, "They are taking it very well."

"Of course. They know how to behave in public."

Lasos was still in ecstasy from the race. It took him a moment to follow us. Then he cried in his headlong way, "It was an epic! No one, no man born of woman upon this earth, could be asked to give *that* away!"

"No," I said. "It would have been policy, of course; but policy has its limits."

Anakreon said softly in my ear, "Policy? Well, my dear, that depends upon what he wants."

Neither of us turned to share this thought with Lasos. He was quick-witted, but indiscreet. Before long, he would think for himself what an Olympic chariot crown can mean to a man who aspires to power; power that his forebears held for generations and never surrendered willingly—on sufferance to Solon, to Pisistratos not even that. Let Lasos think for himself, said Anakreon's sidelong eye. When the crowds were breaking up we slipped away from him and strolled off past the Hera temple to the shady slopes of Kronos' oak wood. Of course there were people all about, but one need not be overheard.

Anakreon said, "How much do you think it means?"

"Hard to say. Maybe no more than Lasos sees in it. He took the gift of the god, thinking he'd done enough last time for the Pisistratids, or not thinking about it at all. He could have counted on nothing beforehand. Think of the odds."

"Someone might have murmured to him how acceptable such a thing would be, if the long chance came off."

I said, "His family call him Simple Kimon, because he won't play politics. He lives for his horses and his land; he must have missed them badly in exile. That gift to Pisistratos got him home, which he wanted more than a second victory. On the other hand, he's a Philead, and he may not be so simple after all."

Anakreon picked up a green acorn, and turned it in his hand to admire the gloss. "Isn't his half-brother a petty king somewhere up north?"

"Miltiades? Indeed, and not so petty, sitting there in the Thracian Chersonese on the throat of the Euxine corn-run. You should ask my brother, who's had to pay his tolls. He's been a chariot victor too, it's in the family."

"Then so is money. How did he get among the Thracians?"

"He exiled himself in the Old Archon's time, and was asked by the Dolonkians to command a war for them, because of some oracle they'd had."

"Ah yes, I heard of that in Abydos. They're forever at war. They were grateful and made him King. Could that, too, be in the family?"

"I doubt it's come down to Kimon. He got tarred with the Philead brush, and had to go; you have to take care with a house that goes back to Ajax. But I'd be surprised if he's thinking now of anything much but his crown and his triple victory and his mares. Didn't you see him beaming from ear to ear? Simple Kimon, I thought, and none the worse for that. I should like to make him a praise song, if only for the mares' sake. But I suppose it wouldn't do."

"What I should like would be to be at his party tonight. *That* should be a good one. But I daresay that might not do either . . . *Look,* my dear, at that boy. The curly-haired one. Do you know, he is entered for the *boxing?* How can he do it? He will be ruined in five years."

"He's an Alkmaionid, so if you want to sing about him, leave out his name . . . Anakreon, do you ever wish yourself back in the days when you were an unknown name and a passing face, and could come and go like the breeze?''

"Of course, my dear. As both of us are doing now. But not if I had to pay for it.''

I thought of my shepherd days; of my master dead in his poor Samian room, without help from me; of the girls I had feared to speak to. "No," I said. "Not if I had to pay.''

We agreed together, therefore, that it had better not get about Olympia, however good Kimon's party might be, that it had been graced with the presence of Anakreon and Simonides. Meantime we paid our respects at our own Archons' pavilion. We had delayed long enough already.

It stood up among the lesser tents like a trireme among fishing-boats. Even the Sicilians had brought nothing finer; it must have needed a train of ox-carts to heave it up from the harbor. The canvas was stitched in stripes of yellow and blue. It was far more splendid than in the Old Archon's day; the hand of Hipparchos showed all over it. From a gilded mast heading the tent-pole flew the trident banner of Poseidon, the crest of their god-born ancestor, Neleus of Pylos.

The Archons were in their chairs of state, receiving guests. We joined in compliments on the good run of their chariot. Of course, nobody mentioned Kimon's. It is all very well for the friends of boxers and wrestlers to taunt the losers; but among the chariotry, politer customs rule.

As we went away, I said, "They've got over it, it seems. The odds were too heavy against that victory; it's with things looked forward to that disappointment bites. They were just as usual, Hippias dignified and Hipparchos charming.''

"Oh, indeed . . . But did you notice, with the sun coming through the canvas stripes, that Hippias looked blue and Hipparchos yellow?''

We laughed, and went our separate ways; Anakreon had a host of friends awaiting him, and I had not a few myself. For a while I looked at the stream of Alpheus, and across at the women's side. She would be there, she had told me so; she had even told me the colors of her tent, rose and light blue. But she knew I would not be coming, unless at the end of the games to exchange our gossip. She would be entertaining victors, strong young boxers and wrestlers and hurlers of the disk and javelin, who had said to themselves for months, "If I win, and my city makes me the victory gift, it would buy me a night with Lyra.'' Perhaps Kimon would visit her. Not tonight; he had his feast to see to, and could not ask her across the river to the Altis shore, sacred to men from the beginning.

I was shouldering off through the crowds, when a little dark hand grabbed my arm; and there was Neko, her Egyptian slave-boy, wearing new gold earrings. She spoiled him dreadfully; he was a saucy brat, but at least he was devoted to her. Naturally she had brought him to Olympia, where a girl could run her no errands across the stream.

"Big trouble find you, sir!" he said in his lilting Greek. "My madam she say, nice party tonight, special for friends, you come? Madam say, if you don't come, party no good. I tell her you come, yes?''

"You," I said, noting how gay and cheerful was the scene around me, and wondering why I'd been thinking it a tiresome crowd. "Take this to spend at the fair; and don't forget to tell her.''

For me, this was the first Olympic since I'd known her; for her, it was only the second in her career. Already she knew what was due to her, and began her reign there in style, by holding court.

I think, if there had been room, her rose and blue tent would have held as many men of rank as the Archons'. However, it held fifteen at most, packed in right up to the flaps. She had hand-picked us, and let us know it. Little Neko, who served the wine, could hardly find room to put down his slender feet. It was a splendid party; the night was warm, the tent pegged open, and chosen latecomers were allowed to overflow outside. When it grew late, one or two people came on from Kimon's victory feast, still in the mood for singing. I had something in my head about his gallant mares, and, discreet or not, when the lyre came my way I sang it. The thought of those beautiful creatures, pouring all their virtue into victory, aroused my love of heroes. Surely swift Boreas, from whom all great horses are descended, swept to them in the race and bore them on. As I sang, I saw Lyra look at me under her lashes; but I only threw her a smile. A man must do what he was born to do; and not only when he is hired to do it.

A little later, she said it was unbecoming for a woman to put on contests at Olympia; but Neko should take the omens for her. She bandaged his eyes, not very tightly, and spun him round, and left him to turn again. He came to rest pointing at me, and pulled off the blindfold grinning. I thought it was because of the present I'd given him, till I saw her smile when everyone had gone.

It was the first Olympic night I'd ever spent on the women's side. The Alpheus, low that year, tinkled and gurgled among its pebbles; owls hooted in the sacred oak wood; from the men's side came distant singing, the whinny of a restless horse. A nightjar called. All around us, set to this music, were the voices of Aphrodite, murmurs and laughter and little grunts and squeals. Presently, quite near, came the soft sound of an Egyptian harp. She whispered, "The boy has a great deal of feeling." I don't know if it was he or we who first fell asleep.

The sun was up when we woke; when we had breakfasted, I was already late to get a good place for the pentathlon. Crowds had closed around the Archons' party; I made do near the top of the slope, among a press of Corinthians. None of them knew me, and they talked on among themselves. The Corinthian chariot was one that had not finished the course; it had crashed at the turn in the fifth lap, and they argued about it hotly, Corinthians being great racing men, even if they don't own as much as a donkey. "He should have kept out of the press; that's how Kimon won."

"He won because no one else was trying it. Well, it seems he was too lucky to please some god or other.''

"God?" said a sharp dark young man who had not spoken before. "I hope some god is after the men who did it."

I was all ears now, but did not want to be noticed, and waited for someone else to ask the questions. But I had overslept; they had been asked already.

"In the very precinct!" said an older man. "What times we live in. Cutpurses, sneak-thieves round the tents, cheats in the market, that one expects, with riffraff coming in from everywhere. But to strike down a crowned victor, in the Sacred Truce! I live here in Elis, I've seen the Games since I was six, and in all my years I've known nothing like it."

A Corinthian said, "To give a great feast like that in a foreign city, he'd need to be carrying gold, with something to spare. It's a dark corner, round by the Council Hall; and he'll hardly have been sober, after the party. Well, you can be sure that by now they're far away."

The dark man said, "That's a thing I should like to be sure of."

People looked round, some questioning, some knowingly. The old Elian asked roundly what he meant. He had got as far as, "From what I hear . . ." when the trumpet sounded, and the athletes came marching in.

It was a middling pentathlon that year, the only notable feat a mighty discus-throw by a man from Argos. The first I knew of it was the cheering, and the umpire running out to peg the throw.

I stayed to the end, looking on or thinking, but thinking mostly. When it was over, and shadows began to fall, I threaded the loosening crowd, all talking by now of nothing but the games, and peered about for the red head of Anakreon. He, at least, would not have spent last night over the river.

He was with a crowd when I sighted him. As soon as he saw me, he shed the others with graceful ease, and hurried up to me, saying out of breath, "Wherever have you been? I've been looking all day for you, I thought you'd gone."

"Gone? Where? I was on the women's side."

"Oh, is that all? I wish I'd known."

His face looked quite drawn. I said, "But what did you think? That I'd left Olympia?" He said nothing. "I was all night with Lyra. All I've heard is rumor in the crowd. Are things really so bad? What are they saying? Where can we talk?"

We were by the old Hera temple; there was a quiet corner in its peristyle of black ancient timber. "Anakreon, the Archons cannot have done this thing. Don't tell me you believe it?"

He gave me a long look, and sighed. "My dear, I don't know. I have seen so much evil in my time, there's little I can't believe. You've known them longer. I was hoping that you'd tell *me*."

"Let's walk," I said. We went up into the dusky oak wood. There was an ancient tree split by a thunderbolt, by Zeus in the Titan War as like as not. Half still stood, half was felled, the fire-marks long washed with rain. No one was in earshot, and we sat down.

I said, "My mind's been on it all through the pentathlon. I don't even know who won the foot-race—four years to the next, and by then one may be dead . . . Well, I've thought, and I can't believe it. If it was done, it must have been by Hippias; he's sole ruler in all but name. And he's the most god-fearing man I ever knew; he wakes and sleeps by it. Can you see him violating a sacred precinct *and* a sacred truce, in one stroke? He'd as soon dance naked through the Kerameikos.''

"I think so, too.'' He pulled a piece of pale lichen off the log, shook out the grubs, and peered at it. His short sight hid from him many imperfections; it gave him, I daresay, as much pleasure as it took away. Close to, he could count the veins on a fly's wing. "Exquisite. Like Thessalian goldwork . . . Sometimes I've thought there might be more in Hipparchos than meets the eye. Power does not much concern him. But a slight, I've noticed, concerns him a good deal.''

"Hipparchos!'' I gazed at him amazed. But then, it was true he had seen much evil. "He'd never be a man for a knife in the dark. I suppose like anyone he'd avenge an insult; but he's not had one. Kimon was his father's benefactor, and that's the end of it. He owed nothing to the sons, and he could have promised nothing. It wasn't in his power.''

Anakreon's face lightened. He had been through bad times, and did not want to think they could come again. I could understand it. I went on, "Kimon and Hipparchos can barely know each other. Kimon's a real country squire; the arts mean nothing to him. As for Hipparchos, he likes the graces. He takes nothing very seriously, even love.''

"Fortunate man!'' He sighed and lifted his eyes. "My dear, you have lifted a load from me. If you'd known my need of you, you'd have lain less easy last night.''

I laughed; we brushed the bark from us, and, ready for supper, strolled down among the trees. In the open glade, touched with the yellow light of sunset, people were strolling in twos and threes. "You were saying, my dear, that you missed the winner of the foot-race. Look, there he is. An Athenian, too. The Archons made him a present.''

The young man was dark-haired and dark-eyed, walking lightly, with the springy step of a runner, still wearing the ribbons tied by his friends round his head and arm. "It comes back to me now,'' I said. "He ran a good race and used his head; but I missed his name.''

"I heard it. It will come to me in a moment. Oh, yes. Aristogeiton, son of Theotimos.''

[Kimon's murderers were never found.]

THE CHARIOT RACE

By Lew Wallace

When the dash for position began, Ben-Hur, as we have seen, was on the extreme left of the six. For a moment, like the others, he was half blinded by the light in the arena; yet he managed to catch sight of his antagonists and divine their purpose. At Messala, who was more than an antagonist to him, he gave one searching look. The air of passionless hauteur character-istic of the fine patrician face was there as of old, and so was the Italian beauty, which the helmet rather increased; but more—it may have been a jealous fancy, or the effect of the brassy shadow in which the features were at the moment cast, still the Israelite thought he saw the soul of the man as through a glass, darkly; cruel, cunning, desperate; not so excited as deter-mined—a soul in a tension of watchfulness and fierce resolve.

In a time not longer than was required to turn to his four again, Ben-Hur felt his own resolution harden to a like temper. At whatever cost, at all hazards, he would humble this enemy! Prize, friends, wagers, honor—everything that can be thought of as a possible interest in the race was lost in the one deliberate purpose. Regard for life even should not hold him back. Yet there was no passion, on his part; no blinding rush of heated blood from heart to brain, and back again; no impulse to fling himself upon Fortune: he did not believe in Fortune; far otherwise. He had his plan, and, confiding in himself, he settled to the task never more observant, never more capable. The air about him seemed aglow with a renewed and perfect transparency.

When not half-way across the arena, he saw that Messala's rush would, if there was no collision, and the rope fell, give him the wall; that the rope would fall, he ceased as soon to doubt; and, further, it came to him, a sudden flash-like insight, that Messala knew it was to be let drop at the last moment (prearrangement with the editor could safely reach that point in the contest); and it suggested, what more Roman-like than for the official to lend himself to a countryman who, besides being so popular, had also so much at stake? There could be no other accounting for the confidence with which Messala pushed his four forward the instant his competitors were prudently checking their fours in front of the obstruction—no other except madness.

It is one thing to see a necessity and another to act upon it. Ben-Hur yielded the wall for the time.

The rope fell, and all the fours but his sprang into the course under urgency of voice and lash. He drew head to the right, and, with all the speed of his Arabs, darted across the trails of his opponents, the angle of movement being such as to lose the least time and gain the greatest possible advance. So, while the spectators were shivering at the Athenian's mishap, and the Sidonian, Byzantine, and Corinthian were striving, with such skill as they possessed, to avoid involvement in the ruin, Ben-Hur swept around and took the course neck and neck with Messala, though on the outside. The marvellous skill shown in making the change thus from the extreme left across to the right without appreciable loss did not fail the sharp eyes upon the benches: the Circus seemed to rock and rock again with prolonged applause. Then Esther clasped her hands in glad surprise; then Sanballat, smiling, offered his hundred sestertii a second time without a taker; and then the Romans began to doubt, thinking Messala might have found an equal, if not a master, and that in an Israelite!

And now, racing together side by side, a narrow interval between them, the two neared the second goal.

The pedestal of the three pillars there, viewed from the west, was a stone wall in the form of a half-circle, around which the course and opposite balcony were bent in exact parallelism. Making this turn was considered in all respects the most telling test of a charioteer; it was, in fact, the very feat in which Orestes failed. As an involuntary admission of interest on the part of the spectators, a hush fell over all the Circus, so that for the first time in the race the rattle and clang of the cars plunging after the tugging steeds were distinctly heard. Then, it would seem, Messala observed Ben-Hur, and recognized him; and at once the audacity of the man flamed out in an astonishing manner.

"Down Eros, up Mars!" he shouted, whirling his lash with practised hand—"Down Eros, up Mars!" he repeated, and caught the well-doing Arabs of Ben-Hur a cut the like of which they had never known.

The blow was seen in every quarter, and the amazement was universal. The silence deepened; up on the benches behind the consul the boldest held his breath, waiting for the outcome. Only a moment thus: then, involuntarily, down from the balcony, as thunder falls, burst the indignant cry of the people.

The four sprang forward affrighted. No hand had ever been laid upon them except in love; they had been nurtured ever so tenderly; and as they grew, their confidence in man became a lesson to men beautiful to see. What should such dainty natures do under such indignity but leap as from death?

Forward they sprang as with one impulse, and forward leaped the car. Past question, every experience is serviceable to us. Where got Ben-Hur the large hand and mighty grip which helped him now so well? Where but from the oar with which so long he fought the sea? And what was this spring of the floor under his feet to the dizzy eccentric lurch with which in the old time the trembling ship yielded to the beat of staggering billows, drunk with their power? So he kept his place, and gave the four free rein, and called to them in soothing voice, trying merely to guide them round the dangerous turn; and before the fever of the people began to abate, he had back the mastery. Nor that only: on approaching the first goal, he was again side by side with Messala, bearing with him the sympathy and admiration of every one not a Roman. So clearly was the feeling shown, so vigorous its manifestation, that Messala, with all his boldness, felt it unsafe to trifle further.

As the cars whirled round the goal, Esther caught sight of Ben-Hur's face—a little pale, a little higher raised, otherwise calm, even placid.

Immediately a man climbed on the entablature at the west end of the division wall, and took down one of the conical wooden balls. A dolphin on the east entablature was taken down at the same time.

In like manner, the second ball and second dolphin disappeared.

And then the third ball and third dolphin.

Three rounds concluded: still Messala held the inside position; still Ben-Hur moved with him side by side; still the other competitors followed as before. The contest began to have the appearance of one of the double races which became so popular in Rome during the later Caesarean period —Messala and Ben-Hur in the first, the Corinthian, Sidonian, and Byzantine in the second. Meantime the ushers succeeded in returning the multitude to their seats, though the clamor continued to run the rounds, keeping, as it were, even pace with the rivals in the course below.

In the fifth round the Sidonian succeeded in getting a place outside Ben-Hur, but lost it directly.

The sixth round was entered upon without change of relative position.

Gradually the speed had been quickened—gradually the blood of the competitors warmed with the work. Men and beasts seemed to know alike that the final crisis was near, bringing the time for the winner to assert himself.

The interest which from the beginning had centred chiefly in the struggle between the Roman and the Jew, with an intense and general sympathy for the latter, was fast changing to anxiety on his account. On all the benches the spectators bent forward motionless, except as their faces turned following the contestants. Ilderim quitted combing his beard, and Esther forgot her fears.

"A hundred sestertii on the Jew!" cried Sanballat to the Romans under the consul's awning.

There was no reply.

"A talent—or five talents, or ten; choose ye!"

He shook his tablets at them defiantly.

"I will take thy sestertii," answered a Roman youth, preparing to write.

"Do not so," interposed a friend.

"Why?"

"Messala hath reached his utmost speed. See him lean over his chariot-rim, the reins loose as flying ribbons. Look then at the Jew."

The first one looked.

"By Hercules!" he replied, his countenance falling. "The dog throws all his weight on the bits. I see, I see! If the gods help not our friend, he will be run away with by the Israelite. No, not yet. Look! Jove with us, Jove with us!"

The cry, swelled by every Latin tongue, shook the *velaria* over the consul's head.

If it were true that Messala had attained his utmost speed, the effort was with effect; slowly but certainly he was beginning to forge ahead. His horses were running with their heads low down; from the balcony their bodies appeared actually to skim the earth; their nostrils showed blood-red in expansion; their eyes seemed straining in their sockets. Certainly the good steeds were doing their best! How long could they keep the pace? It was but the commencement of the sixth round. On they dashed. As they neared the second goal, Ben-Hur turned in behind the Roman's car.

The joy of the Messala faction reached its bound: they screamed and howled, and tossed their colors; and Sanballat filled his tablets with wagers of their tendering.

Malluch, in the lower gallery over the Gate of Triumph, found it hard to keep his cheer. He had cherished the vague hint dropped to him by Ben-Hur of something to happen in the turning of the western pillars. It was the fifth round, yet the something had not come; and he had said to himself, the sixth will bring it; but, lo! Ben-Hur was hardly holding a place at the tail of his enemy's car.

Over in the east end, Simonides' party held their peace. The merchant's head was bent low. Ilderim tugged at his beard, and dropped his brows till there was nothing of his eyes but an occasional sparkle of light. Esther scarcely breathed. Iras alone appeared glad.

Along the home-stretch—sixth round—Messala leading, next him Ben-Hur, and so close it was the old story:

> "First flew Eumelus on Pheretian steeds;
> With those of Tros bold Diomed succeeds;
> Close on Eumelus' back they puff the wind,
> And seem just mounting on his car behind;
> Full on his neck he feels the sultry breeze,
> And, hovering o'er, their stretching shadow sees."

Thus to the first goal, and round it. Messala, fearful of losing his place, hugged the stony wall with perilous clasp; a foot to the left, and he had been dashed to pieces; yet, when the turn was finished, no man, looking at the wheel-tracks of the two cars, could have said, here went Messala, there the Jew. They left but one trace behind them.

As they whirled by, Esther saw Ben-Hur's face again, and it was whiter than before.

Simonides, shrewder than Esther, said to Ilderim, the moment the rivals turned into the course: "I am no judge, good sheik, if Ben-Hur be not about to execute some design. His face hath that look."

To which Ilderim answered: "Saw you how clean they were and fresh? By the splendor of God, friend, they have not been running! But now watch!"

One ball and one dolphin remained on the entablatures; and all the people drew a long breath, for the beginning of the end was at hand.

First, the Sidonian gave the scourge to his four, and, smarting with fear and pain, they dashed desperately forward, promising for a brief time to go to the front. The effort ended in promise. Next, the Byzantine and Corinthian each made the trial with like result, after which they were practically out of the race. Thereupon, with a readiness perfectly explicable, all the factions except the Romans joined hope in Ben-Hur, and openly indulged their feeling.

"Ben-Hur! Ben-Hur!" they shouted, and the blent voices of the many rolled overwhelmingly against the consular stand.

From the benches above him as he passed, the favor descended in fierce injunctions.

"Speed thee, Jew!"

"Take the wall now!"

"On! loose the Arabs! Give them rein and scourge!"

"Let him not have the turn on thee again. Now or never!"

Over the balustrade they stooped low, stretching their hands imploringly to him.

Either he did not hear, or could not do better, for halfway round the course and he was still following, at the second goal even still no change!

And now, to make the turn, Messala began to draw in his left-hand steeds, an act which necessarily slackened their speed. His spirit was high; more than one altar was richer of his vows; the Roman genius was still president. On the three pillars only six hundred feet away were fame, increase of fortune, promotions, and a triumph ineffably sweetened by hate, all in store for him! That moment Malluch, in the gallery, saw Ben-Hur lean forward over his Arabs, and give them the reins. Out flew the many-folded lash in his hand; over the backs of the startled steeds it writhed and hissed, and hissed and writhed again and again; and though it fell not, there were both sting and menace in its quick report; and as the man passed thus from quiet to resistless action, his face suffused, his eyes gleaming, along the reins he seemed to flash his will; and instantly not one, but the four as one, answered with a leap that landed them alongside the Roman's car. Messala, on the perilous edge of the goal, heard, but dared not look to see what the awakening portended. From the people he received no sign. Above the noises of the race there was but one voice, and that was Ben-Hur's. In the old Aramaic, as the sheik himself, he called to the Arabs:

"On, Atair! On, Rigel! What, Antares! dost thou linger now? Good horse—oho, Aldebaran! I hear them singing in the tents. I hear the children singing and the women—singing of the stars, of Atair, Antares, Rigel, Aldebaran, victory!—and the song will never end. Well done! Home to-morrow, under the black tent—home! On, Antares! The tribe is waiting for us, and the master is waiting! 'Tis done! 'tis done! Ha, ha! We have overthrown the proud. The hand that smote us is in the dust. Ours the glory! Ha, ha!—steady. The work is done—soho! Rest!''

There had never been anything of the kind more simple; seldom anything so instantaneous.

At the moment chosen for the dash, Messala was moving in a circle round the goal. To pass him, Ben-Hur had to cross the track, and good strategy required the movement to be in a forward direction; that is, on a like circle limited to the least possible increase. The thousands on the benches understood it all: they saw the signal given—the magnificent response; the four close outside Messala's outer wheel, Ben-Hur's inner wheel behind the other's car—all this they saw. Then they heard a crash loud enough to send a thrill through the Circus, and, quicker than thought, out over the course a spray of shining white and yellow flinders flew. Down on its right side toppled the bed of the Roman's chariot. There was a rebound as of the axle hitting the hard earth; another and another; then the car went to pieces; and Messala, entangled in the reins, pitched forward headlong.

To increase the horror of the sight by making death certain, the Sidonian, who had the wall next behind, could not stop or turn out. Into the wreck full speed he drove; then over the Roman, and into the latter's four, all mad with fear. Presently, out of the turmoil, the fighting of horses, the resound of blows, the murky cloud of dust and sand, he crawled, in time to see the Corinthian and Byzantine go on down the course after Ben-Hur, who had not been an instant delayed.

The people arose, and leaped upon the benches, and shouted and screamed. Those who looked that way caught glimpses of Messala, now under the trampling of the fours, now under the abandoned cars. He was still; they thought him dead; but far the greater number followed Ben-Hur in his career. They had not seen the cunning touch of the reins by which, turning a little to the left, he caught Messala's wheel with the iron-shod point of his axle, and crushed it; but they had seen the transformation of the man, and themselves felt the heat and glow of his spirit, the heroic resolution, the maddening energy of action with which, by look, word, and gesture, he so suddenly inspired his Arabs. And such running! It was rather the long leaping of lions in harness; but for the lumbering chariot, it seemed the four were flying. When the Byzantine and Corinthian were halfway down the course, Ben-Hur turned the first goal.

And the race was WON!

The consul arose; the people shouted themselves hoarse; the editor came down from his seat, and crowned the victors.

The fortunate man among the boxers was a low-browed, yellow-haired Saxon, of such brutalized face as to attract a second look from Ben-Hur, who recognized a teacher with whom he himself had been a favorite at Rome. From him the young Jew looked up and beheld Simonides and his party on the balcony. They waved their hands to him. Esther kept her seat; but Iras arose, and gave him a smile and a wave of her fan—favors not the less intoxicating to him because we know, O reader, they would have fallen to Messala had he been the victor.

The procession was then formed, and, midst the shouting of the multitude which had had its will, passed out of the Gate of Triumph.

And the day was over.

A CONTEST IN ARCHERY
By A. Conan Doyle

While the council was sitting in Pampeluna the White Company, having encamped in a neighboring valley, close to the companies of La Nuit and of Black Ortingo, were amusing themselves with sword-play, wrestling, and shooting at the shields, which they had placed upon the hillside to serve them as butts. The younger archers, with their coats of mail thrown aside, their brown or flaxen hair tossing in the wind, and their jerkins turned back to give free play to their brawny chests and arms, stood in lines, each loosing his shaft in turn, while Johnston, Aylward, Black Simon, and half a score of the elders lounged up and down with critical eyes and a word of rough praise or a curt censure for the marksmen. Behind stood knots of Gascon and Brabant cross-bowmen from the companies of Ortingo and La Nuit, leaning upon their unsightly weapons and watching the practice of the Englishmen.

A sunburnt and black-eyed Brabanter had stood near the old archers, leaning upon a large cross-bow and listening to their talk, which had been carried on in that hybrid camp dialect which both nations could understand. He was a squat, bull-necked man, clad in the iron helmet, mail tunic, and woollen gambesson of his class. A jacket with hanging sleeves, slashed with velvet at the neck and wrists, showed that he was a man of some consideration, an under-officer, or file-leader.

"I cannot think," said he, "why you English should be so fond of your six-foot stick. If it amuse you to bend it, well and good; but why should I strain and pull, when my little moulinet will do all for me, and better than I can do it for myself?"

"I have seen good shooting with the prod and with the latch," said Aylward, "but, by my hilt! camarade, with all respect to you and to your bow, I think that it is but a woman's weapon, which a woman can point and loose as easily as a man."

"I know not about that," answered the Brabanter, "but this I know, that though I have served for fourteen years, I have never yet seen an Englishman do aught with the long-bow which I could not do better with my arbalest. By the three kings! I would even go further, and say that I have done things with my arbalest which no Englishman could do with his long-bow!''

"Well said, mon gar!'' cried Aylward. "A good cock has ever a brave call. Now, I have shot little of late, but there is Johnston here who will try a round with you for the honor of the Company.''

"And I will lay a gallon of Jurançon wine upon the long-bow,'' said Black Simon, "though I had rather, for my own drinking, that it were a quart of Twynham ale.''

"I take both your challenge and your wager,'' said the man of Brabant, throwing off his jacket, and glancing keenly about him with his black, twinkling eyes. "I cannot see any fitting mark, for I care not to waste a bolt upon these shields, which a drunken boor could not miss at a village kermesse.''

"This is a perilous man,'' whispered an English man-at-arms, plucking at Aylward's sleeve. "He is the best marksman of all the cross-bow compa-nies, and it was he who brought down the Constable de Bourbon at Brignais. I fear that your man will come by little honor with him.''

"Yet I have seen Johnston shoot this twenty years, and I will not flinch from it. How say you, old war-hound, will you not have a flight-shot or two with this springald?''

"Tut, tut, Aylward!'' said the old bowman. "My day is past, and it is for the younger ones to hold what we have gained. I take it unkindly of thee, Samkin, that thou shouldst call all eyes thus upon a broken bowman who could once shoot a fair shaft. Let me feel that bow, Wilkins! It is a Scotch bow, I see, for the upper nock is without and the lower within. By the black rood! it is a good piece of yew, well nocked, well strung, well waxed, and very joyful to the feel. I think even now that I might hit any large and goodly mark with a bow like this. Turn thy quiver to me, Aylward. I love an ash arrow pierced with cornel-wood for a roving shaft.''

"By my hilt! and so do I,'' cried Aylward. "These three gander-winged shafts are such.''

"So I see, comrade. It has been my wont to choose a saddle-backed feather for a dead shaft, and a swine-backed for a smooth flier. I will take the two of them. Ah! Samkin, lad, the eye grows dim and the hand less firm as the years pass.''

"Come, then, are you not ready?'' said the Brabanter, who had watched with ill-concealed impatience the slow and methodic movements of his antagonist.

"I will venture a rover with you, or try long-butts or hoyles,'' said old Johnston. "To my mind the long-bow is better than the arbalest, but it may be ill for me to prove it.''

"So I think,'' quoth the other with a sneer. He drew his moulinet from his girdle, and, fixing it to the windlass, he drew back the powerful double cord until it had clicked into the catch. Then from his quiver he drew a short thick quarrel, which he placed with the utmost care upon the groove.

Word had spread of what was going forward, and the rivals were already surrounded, not only by the English archers of the Company, but by hundreds of arbalestiers and men-at-arms from the bands of Ortingo and La Nuit, to the latter of which the Brabanter belonged.

"There is a mark yonder on the hill," said he; "mayhap you can discern it."

"I see something," answered Johnston, shading his eyes with his hand; "but it is a very long shoot."

"A fair shoot—a fair shoot! Stand aside, Arnaud, lest you find a bolt through your gizzard. Now, comrade, I take no flight-shot, and I give you the vantage of watching my shaft."

As he spoke he raised his arbalest to his shoulder and was about to pull the trigger, when a large gray stork flapped heavily into view, skimming over the brow of the hill, and then soaring up into the air to pass the valley. Its shrill and piercing cries drew all eyes upon it, and, as it came nearer, a dark spot which circled above it resolved itself into a peregrine falcon, which hovered over its head, poising itself from time to time, and watching its chance of closing with its clumsy quarry. Nearer and nearer came the two birds, all absorbed in their own contest, the stork wheeling upward, the hawk still fluttering above it, until they were not a hundred paces from the camp. The Brabanter raised his weapon to the sky, and there came the short deep twang of his powerful string. His bolt struck the stork just where its wing meets the body, and the bird whirled aloft in a last convulsive flutter before falling wounded and flapping to the earth. A roar of applause burst from the cross-bowmen; but at the instant that the bolt struck its mark old Johnston, who had stood listlessly with arrow on string, bent his bow and sped a shaft through the body of the falcon. Whipping the other from his belt, he sent it skimming some few feet from the earth with so true an aim that it struck and transfixed the stork for the second time ere it could reach the ground. A deep-chested shout of delight burst from the archers at this double feat, and Aylward, dancing with joy, threw his arms round the old marksman and embraced him with such vigor that their mail tunics clanged again.

"Ah, camarade!" he cried, "you shall have a stoup with me! What then, old dog, would not the hawk please thee, but thou must have the stork as well? Oh, to my heart again!"

"It is a pretty piece of yew, and well strung," said Johnston, with a twinkle in his deep-set gray eyes. "Even an old broken bowman might find the clout with a bow like this."

"You have done very well," remarked the Brabanter, in a surly voice. "But it seems to me that you have not yet shown yourself to be a better marksman than I, for I have struck that at which I aimed, and, by the three kings! no man can do more."

"It would ill beseem me to claim to be a better marksman," answered Johnston, "for I have heard great things of your skill. I did but wish to show that the long-bow could do that which an arbalest could not, for you

could not with your moulinet have your string ready to speed another shaft
ere the bird drop to earth.''

"In that you have vantage," said the cross-bowman. "By St. James! it is
now my turn to show you where my weapon has the better of you. I pray
you to draw a flight-shaft with all your strength down the valley, that we
may see the length of your shoot.''

"That is a very strong prod of yours," said Johnston, shaking his grizzled head as he glanced at the thick arch and powerful strings of his rival's
arbalest. "I have little doubt that you can overshoot me, and yet I have seen
bowmen who could send a cloth-yard arrow further than you could speed a
quarrel.''

"So I have heard," remarked the Brabanter; "and yet it is a strange
thing that these wondrous bowmen are never where I chance to be. Pace
out the distances with a wand at every five-score, and do you, Arnaud,
stand at the fifth wand to carry back my bolts to me.''

A line was measured down the valley, and Johnston, drawing an arrow
to the very head, sent it whistling over the row of wands.

"Bravely drawn! A rare shot!" shouted the by-standers. "It is well up to
the fourth mark.''

"By my hilt! it is over it," cried Aylward. "I can see where they have
stooped to gather up the shaft.''

"We shall hear anon," said Johnston quietly, and presently a young
archer came running to say that the arrow had fallen twenty paces beyond
the fourth wand.

"Four hundred paces and a score," cried Black Simon. "I' faith it is a
very long flight. Yet wood and steel may do more than flesh and blood.''

The Brabanter stepped forward with a smile of conscious triumph, and
loosed the cord of his weapon. A shout burst from his comrades as they
watched the swift and lofty flight of the heavy bolt.

"Over the fourth!" groaned Aylward. "By my hilt! I think that it is well
up to the fifth.''

"It is over the fifth!" cried a Gascon loudly, and a comrade came
running with waving arms, to say that the bolt had pitched eight paces
beyond the mark of the five hundred.

"Which weapon hath the vantage now?" cried the Brabanter, strutting
proudly about with shouldered arbalest, amid the applause of his companions.

"You can overshoot me," said Johnston gently.

"Or any other man who ever bent a long-bow," cried his victorious
adversary.

"Nay, not so fast," said a huge archer, whose mighty shoulders and red
head towered high above the throng of his comrades. "I must have a word
with you ere you crow so loudly. Where is my little popper? By sainted
Dick of Hampole! it will be a strange thing if I cannot outshoot that thing
of thine, which to my eyes is more like a rat-trap than a bow. Will you try
another, or do you stand by your last?''

"Five hundred and eight paces will serve my turn," answered the Brabanter, looking askance at this new opponent.

"Tut, John!" whispered Aylward, "you never were a marksman. Why must you thrust your spoon into this dish?"

"Easy and slow, Aylward! There are very many things which I cannot do, but there are also one or two which I have the trick of. It is in my mind that I can beat this shoot, if my bow will but hold together."

"Go on, old babe of the woods! Have at it, Hampshire!" cried the archers, laughing.

"By my soul! you may grin," cried John. "But I learned how to make the long shot from old Hob Miller of Milford."

He took up a great black bow as he spoke, and sitting down upon the ground he placed his two feet on either end of the stave. With an arrow fitted, he then pulled the string toward him with both hands until the head of the shaft was level with the wood. The great bow creaked and groaned and the cord vibrated with the tension.

"Who is this fool's-head who stands in the way of my shot?" said he, craning up his neck from the ground.

"He stands on the further side of my mark," answered the Brabanter, "so he has little fear from you."

"Well, the saints assoil him!" cried John. "Though I think he is over near to be scathed." As he spoke he raised his two feet, with the bow-stave upon their soles, and his cord twanged with a deep, rich hum which might be heard across the valley. The measurer in the distance fell flat upon his face, and then, jumping up again, began to run in the opposite direction.

"Well shot, old lad! It is indeed over his head," cried the bowmen.

"Mon Dieu!" exclaimed the Brabanter, "who ever saw such a shoot?"

"It is but a trick," quoth John. "Many a time have I won a gallon of ale by covering a mile in three flights down Wilverley Chase."

"It fell a hundred and thirty paces beyond the fifth mark," shouted an archer in the distance.

"Six hundred and thirty paces! Mon Dieu! but that is a shoot! And yet it says nothing for your weapon, mon gros camarade, for it was by turning yourself into a cross-bow that you did it."

"By my hilt! there is truth in that," cried Aylward. "And now, friend, I will myself show you a vantage of the long-bow. I pray you to speed a bolt against yonder shield with all your force. It is an inch of elm with bull's hide over it."

"I scarce shot as many shafts at Brignais," growled the man of Brabant; "though I found a better mark there than a cantle of bull's hide. But what is this, Englishman? The shield hangs not one hundred paces from me, and a blind man could strike it." He screwed up his string to the furthest pitch, and shot his quarrel at the shield. Aylward, who had drawn an arrow from his quiver, carefully greased the head of it, and sped it at the same mark.

"Run, Wilkins," quoth he, "and fetch me the shield."

Long were the faces of the Englishmen and broad the laugh of the cross-bowmen as the heavy mantlet was carried toward them, for there in the centre was the thick Brabant bolt driven deeply into the wood, while there was neither sign nor trace of the cloth-yard shaft.

"By the three kings!" cried the Brabanter, "this time at least there is no gainsaying which is the better weapon, or which the truer hand that held it. You have missed the shield, Englishman."

"Tarry a bit! Tarry a bit, mon gar!" quoth Aylward, and turning round the shield he showed a round clear hole in the wood at the back of it. "My shaft has passed through it, camarade, and I trow the one which goes through is more to be feared than that which bides on the way."

The Brabanter stamped his foot with mortification.

THE THOUSAND-MILE AUTO RACE
(MILLE MIGLIA 1955)
By Stirling Moss

Which *was* your greatest race? This is one of the questions which every racing driver finds himself being asked at frequent intervals; and it's one of the most difficult of all to answer truthfully. How do you decide? Is it the race where you won your most convincing victory? Or is it the one where you drove your best, even though you didn't win? Is it the race where luck was on your side, or the one where everything went wrong? Is it your first race, or your last, or one of the hundreds in between?

I don't know how other drivers decide, but for me there is one race out of all the events I entered which gives me the greatest pleasure to look back on. Some of the reasons are obvious enough, if you look in the record books: it was a classic race, with a reputation as one of the most difficult and dangerous events on the calendar. But the reasons which make it stand out in my memory are the more personal and less obvious ones. We accepted it as the challenge it was, sparing no efforts in thinking and planning to get every detail right that we possibly could. I was driving for Mercedes at the time, and in the truest sense of the words, it was a team effort. The racing organisation was an outfit where no task, however long, difficult or expensive, would ever be spared if it might conceivably make the driver's job a little easier. Beside me in the car I had Denis Jenkinson, writer, racing expert and one-time world-champion motor-cycle sidecar racer. And the race I'm talking about? It was the 1955 Mille Miglia.

Just think for a moment what kind of race it was. A fraction short of a thousand miles, over public roads lined with wildly enthusiastic crowds, with every kind of difficulty from tramlines and bumpy pave in city centres to processions of crazy hairpins over mountain passes. An enormous field ranging from bubble cars to the latest and fastest Masaratis and Ferraris, all let loose at minute intervals for hour after hour: the slower cars were just another hazard, mobile instead of stationary, but the local boys in the really fast machinery were what we had to beat. Only Rudolf Caracciola, driving a Mercedes in 1931, had ever beaten the Italian drivers, and most people thought his feat would never be repeated. You can't hope to drive fast enough to win a race unless you know which way the road turns at every bend or over the top of every hill—if you go slowly enough to be able to change your mind, then someone who knows the road will beat you every time. That's why racing drivers have to learn every detail of every circuit— but how could anyone hope to learn a thousand miles of road half as well as drivers like Taruffi, who drove along part of the Mille Miglia route nearly every working day of his life?

There was only one way we could make up for our disadvantages. The rules allowed two people to a car, although most drivers went alone to save weight. What we needed was a two-man team—not driver and co-driver, but driver and navigator. Yet where could we find someone who could sit there at 170 mph plus and stay cool and calm enough to give the driver the right information knowing that the slightest mistake could mean disaster? This was where Denis Jenkinson came in: anyone with his experience of sidecar racing is used to speed, racing speeds, and to relying absolutely on someone else's driving. But how could anyone with even Jenkinson's experience and knowledge of motor-racing hope to memorise every bend, every hill and every junction?

The answer we developed was the one now used by every rally driver: a set of pace notes. We even got a mention in the Guinness Book of Motoring Facts and Feats as the first to use the idea! On an 18-foot roll of paper, Denis Jenkinson wrote down the details of every section of the road— bends were classified as safe, fast, medium, slow, and very slow, and sections with bad bumps or tramlines or level crossings were all marked too. All these details were keyed to landmarks, from kilometre stones to conspicuous houses or road junctions, so we would know exactly where we were all the time. And since you can't hope to hold a conversation in an open sports-racing car going flat out, we worked out a series of hand signals, so that he could tell me exactly what was coming next: a certain wave of his hand would mean right-hand bend, moderately fast, flat out in third gear, then straight afterwards, and so on. In addition to all this, since the crowds lining the kerbs and even spilling out on to the road were such a hazard, he would have to work the linked horn and headlights too.

But the idea was only half the battle—we still had to go out on the route, which apart from the race itself was a set of public roads used by normal traffic, and find out what each and every bend was like so that we could write our notes. And this is where the Mercedes team effort came in: we went round the whole course five times in different cars. We bent one when we arrived on the same bit of road as a flock of sheep, and we crashed another when an Italian army lorry loaded with live shells turned across our path without warning. Alfred Neubauer, Mercedes' team manager, never turned a hair. Mercedes were as committed as we were, and the final result was the only one that counted.

By the time we finished our reconnaissance, we really were working as a team. Denis had enough confidence in me to say that a corner was flat-out when it was, and I had enough confidence in him to take him exactly at his word. We were taking bends at absolutely full speed, something I could never have done on my own on a road I didn't know, and going over blind brows at 170 mph, knowing exactly what lay ahead of us from the notes. But could our communications system stand up under the strain of racing against drivers who carried all this kind of knowledge inside their own heads?

At last we arrived at the starting line at Brescia, just outside Milan, in the early hours of the morning of 1 May 1955. There were four cars in the Mercedes team, the other three being driven by Hermann, Kling, and Fangio. Our car was numbered 722 in the entry list, our starting time being 22 minutes past seven. Thirty seconds before the signal we started up, and when the flag finally dropped, we roared off down the road with a full 300 horsepower at our backs. Now at last we could see whether all the planning and all the practice had been worthwhile.

The first bend we came to was an S-bend, and while approaching it you hadn't a hope of seeing more than a hundred yards round the corner. Denis gave me the signal: flat out in fourth gear. I shifted into fourth and opened the throttle, and through we went. From then on it became almost routine. For each hazard a check of the notes, then the signal, then the action, and then on to the next. Slowly at first, the miles began to tick away, with no sign of the hundreds of other entrants, either ahead or behind. How well were we doing? Then at last, after ten miles of driving, we saw our first car ahead—one of the slower entries who had started before us. We roared past and settled down to watch for the next.

By the time we reached Verona, we were beginning to catch up on gaggles of slower cars. We passed a whole series of Austin-Healeys on the stretch leading to Vicenza, but, although we didn't yet realise it, our own turn was coming. We were making good time after an hour and a quarter's driving, when I saw in the mirror a red car overhauling us. It was no. 723, Eugenio Castellotti, in the big 4.4 litre Ferrari, driving at the absolute limit —having started next behind us, he had gained a whole minute, and was now trying to get past. We shot down the main street of the town, but with Castellotti right on my tail, I found myself approaching the next bend too fast for comfort. I had to stand on the brakes until the very last minute to lose enough speed to get around the corner. We slid across the road and bounced off the bales as I dropped into bottom gear to accelerate away but for a top-class driver that was enough—Castellotti edged past on the inside and was away like a rocket. He was trying everything he knew, showering dust and gravel everywhere as he bounced off the kerbstones. We managed to close up to him once, but we couldn't hold him. In a cloud of dust and burning rubber, he was pulling steadily away.

Through Rovigo we went, and along the banks of the River Po, over the bridge and through the traffic lights into Ferrara—mile after mile blurred past, until we were approaching Ravenna and the first control. We slowed up to less than walking pace, without coming to a dead stop, for cards to be checked and stamped, and collected two bits of very good news. We had broken the record time for this first stage—Castellotti had done even better, but at the price of having to drop out of the race with tyre trouble!

On we went, through Forli and then south-east, straight into the rising sun towards Rimini and the Adriatic coast. Poor Denis was finding the heat, the glare, the strain, and the noise too much for him, and he turned sideways to be sick—the 150-mph slipstream whipped his glasses away as clean as a whistle, which could have been disaster for us. Fortunately, he had another pair in his pocket, and he went on with his notes without missing a signal.

Slowly the sun climbed higher in the sky as our route took us through Pesaro, past several of the smaller, slower cars and one or two crashes by the roadside. We made for a short cut around a level-crossing marked in our notes to find it was blocked by straw bales—too late to change our minds, we had to drive right over them, and fortunately hit nothing more solid on the way through.

Pescara was the second control and the first pit stop. Neubauer had 84 men positioned around the route, working like well-drilled Trojans. They cleaned the dead flies off the screen, poured 18 gallons of fuel into the tank, handed over coffee, chocolate, and peeled bananas and sent us on our way in just 28 seconds!

Pescara saw our second short cut through the straw bales—another car swung in front of us and in avoiding him I locked the wheels, so that we crashed right through the straw barrier—fortunately we were able to carry on along the pavement and pass him before crashing back through the bales on to the road again.

By the next control, at L'Aguila, we were told that Taruffi, called by his Italian fans 'The King of the Mountains', was 18 seconds ahead of us, and the zig-zag drop down to Rome was the part of the course which he knew best. Still, we were determined to make him fight for his lead, and we kept going as hard as we could—we hit one level crossing so hard that we were both flung right up into the slipstream with the shock. We managed to pass Musso's Maserati and Maglioli's Ferrari on this stretch, but on the last lap into Rome it began to seem as if the entire population of Italy was beginning to edge into the middle of the road to get a really close-up view of the race. All we could do was swerve from side to side, horn blaring, and headlamps blazing, as if the car was out of control—it widened the ranks a little bit, but bodies were still too close for comfort as we pulled up at the control after almost 3½ hours driving, at an average of 107 mph.

This was the first time the engine had been stopped since the start of the race. Before we could climb out, Mercedes' devoted pit-team had the car up on jacks, the rear wheels were being changed, and 60 gallons of petrol were pouring into the tanks. Someone came up with an information slip: 'Moss, Taruffi, Kling, Fangio' it read—we had done it, beaten the Mountain King on his home ground by nearly two minutes.

The whole stop took less than a minute, and we were off again. Two bends down the road, and we passed another Mercedes 300SLR, wrecked at the side of the road—it was Karl Kling who had started twenty-one minutes ahead of us. A spectator waved an upraised thumb to show he was all right—we heard later he had escaped with broken ribs.

Now we were trying to fight another tradition. 'He who leads at Rome never leads at Brescia,' said the Mille Miglia veterans—here we were, the leaders at Rome—could we still be leading at the Brescia finishing line? We were on the northward stretch towards Viterbo now, flying over hummocks and hump-backed bridges at top speed. Then we hit one bump which we must have under-estimated—I felt the road shocks through the steering wheel suddenly cease, just as the vibration in an aeroplane stops at the instant of takeoff. Denis and I had time to look at one another—in some surprise—before we touched down again. Fortunately, although we were probably airborne for a good 200 feet, the road was dead straight at this point, and the car touched down in a perfect four-point landing!

In spite of the hundreds of bends and all the signals he had to make, Denis only missed one signal—and this was because, having been showered with petrol from an overfilled tank, he was trying to make sure the fumes were blowing clear of the hot exhaust, otherwise he and the car might have gone up like a torch!

We had another narrow escape when a front wheel locked under heavy braking and we slid into a roadside ditch—happily we were able to crawl out in bottom gear and get back into the race with nothing more than a dented tail. We passed Fangio, stopped temporarily with a broken fuel-injection pipe, and we went through the Siena control so quickly that we found out nothing about our position.

In those circumstances there was only one thing we could do—press on as fast as possible—through the Firenze control and up and over the high passes through the Apennine Mountains—the Futa and the Raticosa. Here the road was so slippery with oil and rubber we had to ease off a little in the interests of staying on the road. Poor Hans Hermann, in the fourth of the works Mercedes, was sitting at the roadside with a split petrol tank— but where was Taruffi?

The run down into Bologna was slower than we hoped, thanks to the slippery roads, so there was no time to stop and make inquiries at the control. Back down on the Emilian plain, the heat really began to build up through the afternoon—here the road was easier, straight and flat, where we could let the car rip to 177 mph in fifth along the stretches into Modena and on to Reggio. At times we were flying so fast that a light aeroplane which was following the route couldn't keep up with us.

This was really one of the most dangerous parts of the race—fatigue and over-confidence could easily make one's judgment relax until you woke up entering a corner 20 mph too fast. We had one anxious moment when the car slid sideways on a patch of melted tar, and we managed to avoid spreading it along a concrete wall by a matter of an inch or two—another came when, with the glare and the dust in our eyes, we hit a gaggle of slower cars doing a mere 110 or so. Fortunately Denis's horn-and-lights symphony got the message through in time.

We finished in fine style—round the last corner to the finishing line with the power full on, crossing the line at well over 100 mph. Yet this is where the deadening sensation of anticlimax really hit us. This was my fourth Mille Miglia, and the only one I had ever finished. But had we won, or not? Slowly we drove around to the team's garages. We had to wait until the news came through that Taruffi had dropped out with a broken oil pipe, and that no one else could possibly beat our record time. We had done it! It was an absolutely unforgettable moment, and even afterwards I found I couldn't unwind from the tension and the reaction of the drive and our victory. In the end I stayed for the celebration dinner with the rest of the team, and then finished the day by driving north through the night, over the Alps to Cologne, because I knew sleep was hopeless. Even now, so many years afterwards, the memory is fresh—of all the races I entered, and finished, and even of those I won, I can't find another to compare with it.

CAUGHT IN A TEMPEST

By Jules Verne

"See," said Joe, "what comes of playing the sons of the moon without her leave! She came near serving us an ugly trick. But say, master, did you damage your credit as a physician?"

"Yes, indeed," chimed in the sportsman. "What kind of a dignitary was this Sultan of Kazeh?"

"An old half-dead sot," replied the doctor, "whose loss will not be very severely felt. But the moral of all this is that honors are fleeting, and we must not take too great a fancy to them."

"So much the worse!" rejoined Joe. "I liked the thing—to be worshipped!—Play the god as you like! Why, what would any one ask more than that? By-the-way, the moon did come up, too, and all red, as if she was in a rage."

While the three friends went on chatting of this and other things, and Joe examined the luminary of night from an entirely novel point of view, the heavens became covered with heavy clouds to the northward, and the lowering masses assumed a most sinister and threatening look. Quite a smart breeze, found about three hundred feet from the earth, drove the balloon toward the north-northeast; and above it the blue vault was clear; but the atmosphere felt close and dull.

The aëronauts found themselves, at about eight in the evening, in thirty-two degrees forty minutes east longitude, and four degrees seventeen minutes latitude. The atmospheric currents, under the influence of a tempest not far off, were driving them at the rate of from thirty to thirty-five miles an hour; the undulating and fertile plains of Mfuto were passing swiftly beneath them. The spectacle was one worthy of admiration—and admire it they did.

"We are now right in the country of the Moon," said Dr. Ferguson; "for it has retained the name that antiquity gave it, undoubtedly, because the moon has been worshipped there in all ages. It is, really, a superb country."

"It would be hard to find more splendid vegetation."

"If we found the like of it around London it would not be natural, but it would be very pleasant," put in Joe. "Why is it that such savage countries get all these fine things?"

"And who knows," said the doctor, "that this country may not, one day, become the centre of civilization? The races of the future may repair hither, when Europe shall have become exhausted in the effort to feed her inhabitants."

"Do you think so, really?" asked Kennedy.

"Undoubtedly, my dear Dick. Just note the progress of events: consider the migrations of races, and you will arrive at the same conclusion assuredly. Asia was the first nurse of the world, was she not? For about four thousand years she travailed, she grew pregnant, she produced, and then, when stones began to cover the soil where the golden harvests sung by Homer had flourished, her children abandoned her exhausted and barren bosom. You next see them precipitating themselves upon young and vigorous Europe, which has nourished them for the last two thousand years. But already her fertility is beginning to die out; her productive powers are diminishing every day. Those new diseases that annually attack the products of the soil, those defective crops, those insufficient resources, are all signs of a vitality that is rapidly wearing out and of an approaching exhaustion. Thus, we already see the millions rushing to the luxuriant bosom of America, as a source of help, not inexhaustible indeed, but not yet exhausted. In its turn, that new continent will grow old; its virgin forests will fall before the axe of industry, and its soil will become weak through having too fully produced what had been demanded of it. Where two harvests bloomed every year, hardly one will be gathered from a soil completely drained of its strength. Then, Africa will be there to offer to new races the treasures that for centuries have been accumulating in her breast. Those climates now so fatal to strangers will be purified by cultivation and by drainage of the soil, and those scattered water supplies will be gathered into one common bed to form an artery of navigation. Then this country over which we are now passing, more fertile, richer, and fuller of vitality than the rest, will become some grand realm where more astonishing discoveries than steam and electricity will be brought to light."

"Ah! sir," said Joe, "I'd like to see all that."

"You got up too early in the morning, my boy!"

"Besides," said Kennedy, "that may prove to be a very dull period when industry will swallow up every thing for its own profit. By dint of inventing machinery, men will end in being eaten up by it! I have always fancied that the end of the earth will be when some enormous boiler, heated to three thousand millions of atmospheric pressure, shall explode and blow up our Globe!"

"And I add that the Americans," said Joe, "will not have been the last to work at the machine!"

"In fact," assented the doctor, "they are great boilermakers! But, without allowing ourselves to be carried away by such speculations, let us rest content with enjoying the beauties of this country of the Moon, since we have been permitted to see it.''

The sun, darting his last rays beneath the masses of heaped-up cloud, adorned with a crest of gold the slightest inequalities of the ground below; gigantic trees, arborescent bushes, mosses on the even surface—all had their share of this luminous effulgence. The soil, slightly undulating, here and there rose into little conical hills; there were no mountains visible on the horizon; immense brambly palisades, impenetrable hedges of thorny jungle, separated the clearings dotted with numerous villages, and immense euphorbiae surrounded them with natural fortifications, interlacing their trunks with the coral-shaped branches of the shrubbery and undergrowth.

Ere long, the Malagazeri, the chief tributary of Lake Taganayika, was seen winding between heavy thickets of verdure, offering an asylum to many water-courses that spring from the torrents formed in the season of freshets, or from ponds hollowed in the clayey soil. To observers looking from a height, it was a chain of waterfalls thrown across the whole western face of the country.

Animals with huge humps were feeding in the luxuriant prairies, and were half hidden, sometimes, in the tall grass; spreading forests in bloom redolent of spicy perfumes presented themselves to the gaze like immense bouquets; but, in these bouquets, lions, leopards, hyenas, and tigers, were then crouching for shelter from the last hot rays of the setting sun. From time to time, an elephant made the tall tops of the undergrowth sway to and fro, and you could hear the crackling of huge branches as his ponderous ivory tusks broke them in his way.

"What a sporting country!" exclaimed Dick, unable longer to restrain his enthusiasm; "why, a single ball fired at random into those forests would bring down game worthy of it. Suppose we just try it once!"

"No, my dear Dick; the night is close at hand—a threatening night with a tempest in the background—and the storms are awful in this country, where the heated soil is like one vast electric battery."

"You are right, sir," said Joe, "the heat has got to be enough to choke one, and the breeze has died away. One can feel that something's coming."

"The atmosphere is saturated with electricity," replied the doctor; "every living creature is sensible that this state of the air portends a struggle of the elements, and I confess that I never before was so full of the fluid myself."

"Well, then," suggested Dick, "would it not be advisable to alight?"

"On the contrary, Dick, I'd rather go up, only that I am afraid of being carried out of my course by these counter-currents contending in the atmosphere."

"Have you any idea, then, of abandoning the route that we have followed since we left the coast?"

"If I can manage to do so," replied the doctor, "I will turn more directly northward, by from seven to eight degrees; I shall then endeavor to ascend toward the presumed latitudes of the sources of the Nile; perhaps we may discover some traces of Captain Speke's expedition or of M. de Heuglin's caravan. Unless I am mistaken, we are at thirty-two degrees forty minutes east longitude, and I should like to ascend directly north of the equator."

"Look there!" exclaimed Kennedy, suddenly, "see those hippopotami sliding out of the pools—those masses of blood-colored flesh—and those crocodiles snuffing the air aloud!"

"They're choking!" ejaculated Joe. "Ah! what a fine way to travel this is; and how one can snap his fingers at all that vermin!—Doctor! Mr. Kennedy! see those packs of wild animals hurrying along close together. There are fully two hundred. Those are wolves."

"No! Joe, not wolves, but wild dogs; a famous breed that does not hesitate to attack the lion himself. They are the worst customers a traveller could meet, for they would instantly tear him to pieces."

"Well, it isn't Joe that'll undertake to muzzle them!" responded that amiable youth. "After all, though, if that's the nature of the beast, me mustn't be too hard on them for it!"

Silence gradually settled down under the influence of the impending storm: the thickened air actually seemed no longer adapted to the transmission of sound; the atmosphere appeared *muffled,* and, like a room hung with tapestry, lost all its sonorous reverberation. The "rover bird" so-called, the coroneted crane, the red and blue jays, the mocking-bird, the flycatcher, disappeared among the foliage of the immense trees, and all nature revealed symptoms of some approaching catastrophe.

At nine o'clock the *Victoria* hung motionless over Mséné, an extensive group of villages scarcely distinguishable in the gloom. Once in a while, the reflection of a wandering ray of light in the dull water disclosed a succession of ditches regularly arranged, and, by one last gleam, the eye could make out the calm and sombre forms of palm-trees, sycamores, and gigantic euphorbiae.

"I am stifling!" said the Scot, inhaling, with all the power of his lungs, as much as possible of the rarefied air. "We are not moving an inch! Let us descend!"

"But the tempest!" said the doctor, with much uneasiness.

"If you are afraid of being carried away by the wind, it seems to me that there is no other course to pursue."

"Perhaps the storm won't burst to-night," said Joe; "the clouds are very high."

"That is just the thing that makes me hesitate about going beyond them; we should have to rise still higher, lose sight of the earth, and not know all night whether we were moving forward or not, or in what direction we were going."

"Make up your mind, dear doctor, for time presses!"

"It's a pity that the wind has fallen," said Joe, again; "it would have carried us clear of the storm."

"It is, indeed, a pity, my friends," rejoined the doctor. "The clouds are dangerous for us; they contain opposing currents which might catch us in their eddies, and lightnings that might set on fire. Again, those perils avoided, the force of the tempest might hurl us to the ground, were we to cast our anchor in the tree-tops."

"Then what shall we do?"

"Well, we must try to get the balloon into a medium zone of the atmosphere, and there keep her suspended between the perils of the heavens and those of the earth. We have enough water for the cylinder, and our two hundred pounds of ballast are untouched. In case of emergency I can use them."

"We will keep watch with you," said the hunter.

"No, my friends, put the provisions under shelter, and lie down; I will rouse you, if it becomes necessary."

"But, master, wouldn't you do well to take some rest yourself, as there's no danger close on us just now?" insisted poor Joe.

"No, thank you, my good fellow, I prefer to keep awake. We are not moving, and should circumstances not change, we'll find ourselves tomorrow in exactly the same place."

"Good-night, then, sir!"

"Good-night, if you can only find it so!"

Kennedy and Joe stretched themselves out under their blankets, and the doctor remained alone in the immensity of space.

However, the huge dome of clouds visibly descended, and the darkness became profound. The black vault closed in upon the earth as if to crush it in its embrace.

All at once a violent, rapid, incisive flash of lightning pierced the gloom, and the rent it made had not closed ere a frightful clap of thunder shook the celestial depths.

"Up! up! turn out!" shouted Ferguson.

The two sleepers, aroused by the terrible concussion, were at the doctor's orders in a moment.

"Shall we descend?" said Kennedy.

"No! the balloon could not stand it. Let us go up before those clouds dissolve in water, and the wind is let loose!" and, so saying, the doctor actively stirred up the flame of the cylinder, and turned it on the spirals of the serpentine siphon.

The tempests of the tropics develop with a rapidity equalled only by their violence. A second flash of lightning rent the darkness, and was followed by a score of others in quick succession. The sky was crossed and dotted, like the zebra's hide, with electric sparks, which danced and flickered beneath the great drops of rain.

"We have delayed too long," exclaimed the doctor; "we must now pass through a zone of fire, with our balloon filled as it is with inflammable gas!"

"But let us descend, then! let us descend!" urged Kennedy.

"The risk of being struck would be just about even, and we should soon be torn to pieces by the branches of the trees!"

"We are going up, doctor!"

"Quicker, quicker still!"

In this part of Africa, during the equatorial storms, it is not rare to count from thirty to thirty-five flashes of lightning per minute. The sky is literally on fire, and the crashes of thunder are continuous.

The wind burst forth with frightful violence in this burning atmosphere; it twisted the blazing clouds; one might have compared it to the breath of some gigantic bellows, fanning all this conflagration.

Dr. Ferguson kept his cylinder at full heat, and the balloon dilated and went up, while Kennedy, on his knees, held together the curtains of the awning. The balloon whirled round wildly enough to make their heads turn, and the aëronauts got some very alarming jolts, indeed, as their machine swung and swayed in all directions. Huge cavities would form in the silk of the balloon as the wind fiercely bent it in, and the stuff fairly cracked like a pistol as it flew back from the pressure. A sort of hail, preceded by a rumbling noise, hissed through the air and rattled on the covering of the *Victoria*. The latter, however, continued to ascend, while the lightning described tangents to the convexity of her circumference; but she bore on, right through the midst of.the fire.

"God protect us!" said Dr. Ferguson, solemnly, "we are in His hands; He alone can save us—but let us be ready for every event, even for fire— our fall could not be very rapid."

The doctor's voice could scarcely be heard by his companions; but they could see his countenance calm as ever even amid the flashing of the lightnings; he was watching the phenomena of phosphorescence produced by the fires of St. Elmo, that were now skipping to and fro along the network of the balloon.

The latter whirled and swung, but steadily ascended, and, ere the hour was over, it had passed the stormy belt. The electric display was going on below it like a vast crown of artificial fireworks suspended from the car.

Then they enjoyed one of the grandest spectacles that Nature can offer to the gaze of man. Below them, the tempest; above them, the starry firmament, tranquil, mute, impassible, with the moon projecting her peaceful rays over these angry clouds.

Dr. Ferguson consulted the barometer; it announced twelve thousand feet of elevation. It was then eleven o'clock at night.

"Thank Heaven, all danger is past; all we have to do now, is, to keep ourselves at this height," said the doctor.

"It was frightful!" remarked Kennedy.

"Oh!" said Joe, "it gives a little variety to the trip, and I'm not sorry to have seen a storm from a trifling distance up in the air. It's a fine sight!"

THE REDHEADED OUTFIELD

By Zane Grey

There was Delaney's red-haired trio—Red Gilbat, left fielder; Reddy Clammer, right fielder, and Reddie Ray, center fielder, composing the most remarkable outfield ever developed in minor league baseball. It was Delaney's pride, as it was also his trouble.

Red Gilbat was nutty—and his batting average was .371. Any student of baseball could weigh these two facts against each other and understand something of Delaney's trouble. It was not possible to camp on Red Gilbat's trail. The man was a jack-o'-lantern, a will-o'-the-wisp, a weird, long-legged, long-armed, red-haired illusive phantom. When the gong rang at the ball grounds there were ten chances to one that Red would not be present. He had been discovered with small boys peeping through knot-holes at the vacant left field he was supposed to inhabit during play.

Of course what Red did off the ball grounds was not so important as what he did on. And there was absolutely no telling what under the sun he might do then except once out of every three times at bat he could be counted on to knock the cover off the ball.

Reddy Clammer was a grand-stand player—the kind all managers hated —and he was hitting .305. He made circus catches, circus stops, circus throws, circus steals—but particularly circus catches. That is to say, he made easy plays appear difficult. He was always strutting, posing, talking, arguing, quarreling—when he was not engaged in making a grand-stand play. Reddy Clammer used every possible incident and artifice to bring himself into the limelight.

Reddie Ray had been the intercollegiate champion in the sprints and a famous college ball player. After a few months of professional ball he was hitting over .400 and leading the league both at bat and on the bases. It was a beautiful and a thrilling sight to see him run. He was so quick to start, so marvelously swift, so keen of judgment, that neither Delaney nor any player could ever tell the hit that he was not going to get. That was why Reddie Ray was a whole game in himself.

Delaney's Rochester Stars and the Providence Grays were tied for first place. Of the present series each team had won a game. Rivalry had always been keen, and as the teams were about to enter the long homestretch for the pennant there was battle in the New England air.

The September day was perfect. The stands were half full and the bleachers packed with a white-sleeved mass. And the field was beautifully level and green. The Grays were practicing and the Stars were on their bench.

"We're up against it," Delaney was saying. "This new umpire, Fuller, hasn't got it in for us. Oh, no, not at all! Believe me, he's a robber. But Scott is pitchin' well. Won his last three games. He'll bother 'em. And the three Reds have broken loose. They're on the rampage. They'll burn up this place today."

Somebody noted the absence of Gilbat.

Delaney gave a sudden start. "Why, Gil was here," he said slowly. "Lord!—he's about due for a nutty stunt."

Whereupon Delaney sent boys and players scurrying about to find Gilbat, and Delaney went himself to ask the Providence manager to hold back the gong for a few minutes.

Presently somebody brought Delaney a telephone message that Red Gilbat was playing ball with some boys in a lot four blocks down the street. When at length a couple of players marched up to the bench with Red in tow Delaney uttered an immense sigh of relief and then, after a close scrutiny of Red's face, he whispered, "Lock the gates!"

Then the gong rang. The Grays trooped in. The Stars ran out, except Gilbat, who ambled like a giraffe. The hum of conversation in the grand stand quickened for a moment with the scraping of chairs, and then grew quiet. The bleachers sent up the rollicking cry of expectancy. The umpire threw out a white ball with his stentorian "Play!" and Blake of the Grays strode to the plate.

Hitting safely, he started the game with a rush. With Dorr up, the Star infield played for a bunt. Like clockwork Dorr dumped the first ball as Blake got his flying start for second base. Morrissey tore in for the ball, got it on the run and snapped it underhand to Healy, beating the runner by an inch. The fast Blake, with a long slide, made third base. The stands stamped. The bleachers howled. White, next man up, batted a high fly to left field. This was a sun field and the hardest to play in the league. Red Gilbat was the only man who ever played it well. He judged the fly, waited under it, took a step back, then forward, and deliberately caught the ball in his gloved hand. A throw-in to catch the runner scoring from third base would have been futile, but it was not like Red Gilbat to fail to try. He tossed the ball to O'Brien. And Blake scored amid applause.

"What do you know about that?" ejaculated Delaney, wiping his moist face. "I never before saw our nutty Redhead pull off a play like that."

Some of the players yelled at Red, "This is a two-handed league, you bat!"

The first five players on the list for the Grays were left-handed batters, and against a right-handed pitcher whose most effective ball for them was a high fast one over the outer corner they would naturally hit toward left field. It was no surprise to see Hanley bat a skyscraper out to left. Red had to run to get under it. He braced himself rather unusually for a fielder. He tried to catch the ball in his bare right hand and muffed it. Hanley got to second on the play while the audience roared. When they got through there was some roaring among the Rochester players. Scott and Captain Healy roared at Red, and Red roared back at them.

"It's all off. Red never did that before," cried Delaney in despair. "He's gone clean bughouse now."

Babcock was the next man up and he likewise hit to left. It was a low, twisting ball—half fly, half liner—and a difficult one to field. Gilbat ran with great bounds, and though he might have got two hands on the ball he did not try, but this time caught it in his right, retiring the side.

The Stars trotted in, Scott and Healy and Kane, all veterans, looking like thunderclouds. Red ambled in the last and he seemed very nonchalant.

"By Gosh, I'd 'a' ketched that one I muffed if I'd had time to change hands," he said with a grin, and he exposed a handful of peanuts. He had refused to drop the peanuts to make the catch with two hands. That explained the mystery. It was funny, yet nobody laughed. There was that run chalked up against the Stars, and this game had to be won.

"Red, I—I want to take the team home in the lead," said Delaney, and it was plain that he suppressed strong feeling. "You didn't play the game, you know."

Red appeared mightily ashamed.

"Del, I'll git that run back," he said.

Then he strode to the plate, swinging his wagon-tongue bat. For all his awkward position in the box he looked what he was—a formidable hitter. He seemed to tower over the pitcher—Red was six feet one—and he scowled and shook his bat at Wehying and called, "Put one over—you wienerwurst!" Wehying was anything but red-headed, and he wasted so many balls on Red that it looked as if he might pass him. He would have passed him, too, if Red had not stepped over on the fourth ball and swung on it. White at second base leaped high for the stinging hit, and failed to reach it. The ball struck and bounded for the fence. When Babcock fielded it in, Red was standing on third base, and the bleachers groaned.

Whereupon Chesty Reddy Clammer proceeded to draw attention to himself, and incidentally delay the game, by assorting the bats as if the audience and the game might gladly wait years to see him make a choice.

"Git in the game!" yelled Delaney.

"Aw, take my bat, Duke of the Abrubsky!" sarcastically said Dump Kane. When the grouchy Kane offered to lend his bat matters were critical in the Star camp.

Other retorts followed, which Reddy Clammer deigned not to notice. At last he got a bat that suited him—and then, importantly, dramatically, with his cap jauntily riding his red locks, he marched to the plate.

Some wag in the bleachers yelled into the silence, "Oh, Maggie, your lover has come!"

Not improbably Clammer was thinking first of his presence before the multitude, secondly of his batting average and thirdly of the run to be scored. In this instance he waited and feinted at balls and fouled strikes at length to work his base. When he got to first base suddenly he bolted for second, and in the surprise of the unlooked-for play he made it by a spread-eagle slide. It was a circus steal.

Delaney snorted. Then the look of profound disgust vanished in a flash of light. His huge face beamed.

Reddie Ray was striding to the plate.

There was something about Reddie Ray that pleased all the senses. His lithe form seemed instinct with life; any sudden movement was suggestive of stored lightning. His position at the plate was on the left side, and he stood perfectly motionless, with just a hint of tense waiting alertness. Dorr, Blake and Babcock, the outfielders for the Grays, trotted round to the right of their usual position. Delaney smiled derisively, as if he knew how futile it was to tell what field Reddie Ray might hit into. Wehying, the old fox, warily eyed the youngster, and threw him a high curve, close in. It grazed Reddie's shirt, but he never moved a hair. Then Wehying, after the manner of many veteran pitchers when trying out a new and menacing batter, drove a straight fast ball at Reddie's head. Reddie ducked, neither too slow nor too quick, just right to show what an eye he had, how hard it was to pitch to. The next was a strike. And on the next he appeared to step and swing in one action. There was a ringing rap, and the ball shot toward right, curving down, a vicious, headed hit. Mallory, at first base, snatched at it and found only the air. Babcock had only time to take a few sharp steps, and then he plunged down, blocked the hit and fought the twisting ball. Reddie turned first base, flitted on toward second, went headlong in the dust, and shot to the base before White got the throw-in from Babcock. Then, as White wheeled and lined the ball home to catch the scoring Clammer, Reddie Ray leaped up, got his sprinter's start and, like a rocket, was off for third. This time he dove behind the base, sliding in a half circle, and as Hanley caught Strickland's perfect throw and whirled with the ball, Reddie's hand slid to the bag.

Reddie got to his feet amid a rather breathless silence. Even the coachers were quiet. There was a moment of relaxation, then Wehying received the ball from Hanley and faced the batter.

This was Dump Kane. There was a sign of some kind, almost imperceptible, between Kane and Reddie. As Wehying half turned in his swing to pitch, Reddie Ray bounded homeward. It was not so much the boldness of his action as the amazing swiftness of it that held the audience spellbound. Like a thunderbolt Reddie came down the line, almost beating Wehying's pitch to the plate. But Kane's bat intercepted the ball, laying it down, and Reddie scored without sliding. Dorr, by sharp work, just managed to throw Kane out.

Three runs so quick it was hard to tell how they had come. Not in the major league could there have been faster work. And the ball had been fielded perfectly and thrown perfectly.

"There you are," said Delaney, hoarsely. "Can you beat it? If you've been wonderin' how the cripped Stars won so many games just put what you've seen in your pipe and smoke it. Red Gilbat gets on—Reddy Clammer gets on—and then Reddie Ray drives them home or chases them home."

The game went on, and though it did not exactly drag it slowed down considerably. Morrissey and Healy were retired on infield plays. And the sides changed. For the Grays, O'Brien made a scratch hit, went to second on Strickland's sacrifice, stole third and scored on Mallory's infield out. Wehying missed three strikes. In the Stars' turn the three end players on the batting list were easily disposed of. In the third inning the clever Blake, aided by a base on balls and a hit following, tied the score, and once more struck fire and brimstone from the impatient bleachers. Providence was a town that had to have its team win.

"Git at 'em, Reds!" said Delaney gruffly.

"Batter up!" called Umpire Fuller, sharply.

"Where's Red? Where's the bug? Where's the nut? Delaney, did you lock the gates? Look under the bench!" These and other remarks, not exactly elegant, attested to the mental processes of some of the Stars. Red Gilbat did not appear to be forthcoming. There was an anxious delay. Capt. Healy searched for the missing player. Delaney did not say any more.

Suddenly a door under the grand stand opened and Red Gilbat appeared. He hurried for his bat and then up to the plate. And he never offered to hit one of the balls Wehying shot over. When Fuller had called the third strike Red hurried back to the door and disappeared.

"Somethin' doin'," whispered Delaney.

Lord Chesterfield Clammer paraded to the batter's box and, after gradually surveying the field, as if picking out the exact place he meant to drive the ball, he stepped to the plate. Then a roar from the bleachers surprised him.

"Well, I'll be dog-goned!" exclaimed Delaney. "Red stole that sure as shootin'."

Red Gilbat was pushing a brand-new baby carriage toward the batter's box. There was a tittering in the grand stand; another roar from the bleachers. Clammer's face turned as red as his hair. Gilbat shoved the baby carriage upon the plate, spread wide his long arms, made a short presentation speech and an elaborate bow, then backed away.

All eyes were centered on Clammer. If he had taken it right the incident might have passed without undue hilarity. But Clammer became absolutely wild with rage. It was well known that he was unmarried. Equally well was it seen that Gilbat had executed one of his famous tricks. Ball players were inclined to be dignified about the presentation of gifts upon the field, and Clammer, the dude, the swell, the lady's man, the favorite of the baseball gods —in his own estimation—so far lost control of himself that he threw his bat at his retreating tormentor. Red jumped high and the bat skipped along the ground toward the bench. The players sidestepped and leaped and, of course, the bat cracked one of Delaney's big shins. His eyes popped with pain, but he could not stop laughing. One by one the players lay down and rolled over and yelled. The superior Clammer was not over-liked by his co-players.

From the grand stand floated the laughter of ladies and gentlemen. And from the bleachers—that throne of the biting, ironic, scornful fans—pealed up a howl of delight. It lasted for a full minute. Then, as quiet ensued, some boy blew a blast of one of those infernal little instruments of pipe and rubber balloon, and over the field wailed out a shrill, high-keyed cry, an excellent imitation of a baby. Whereupon the whole audience roared, and in discomfiture Reddy Clammer went in search of his bat.

To make his chagrin all the worse he ingloriously struck out. And then he strode away under the lea of the grand-stand wall toward right field.

Reddie Ray went to bat and, with the infield playing deep and the outfield swung still farther round to the right, he bunted a little teasing ball down the third-base line. Like a flash of light he had crossed first base before Hanley got his hands on the ball. Then Kane hit into second base, forcing Reddie out.

Again the game assumed less spectacular and more ordinary play. Both Scott and Wehying held the batters safely and allowed no runs. But in the fifth inning, with the Stars at bat and two out, Red Gilbat again electrified the field. He sprang up from somewhere and walked to the plate, his long shape enfolded in a full-length linen duster. The color and style of this garment might not have been especially striking, but upon Red it had a weird and wonderful effect. Evidently Red intended to bat while arrayed in his long coat, for he stepped into the box and faced the pitcher. Capt. Healy yelled for him to take the duster off. Likewise did the Grays yell.

The bleachers shrieked their disapproval. To say the least, Red Gilbat's crazy assurance was dampening to the ardor of the most blindly confident fans. At length Umpire Fuller waved his hand, enjoining silence and call-ing time.

"Take it off or I'll fine you."

From his lofty height Gilbat gazed down upon the little umpire, and it was plain what he thought.

"What do I care for money!" replied Red.

"That costs you twenty-five," said Fuller.

"Cigarette change!" yelled Red.

"Costs you fifty."

"Bah! Go to an eye doctor," roared Red.

"Seventy-five," added Fuller, imperturbably.

"Make it a hundred!"

"It's two hundred."

"Rob-b-ber!" bawled Red.

Fuller showed willingness to overlook Red's back talk as well as costume, and he called, "Play!"

There was a mounting sensation of prophetic certainty. Old fox Wehying appeared nervous. He wasted two balls on Red; then he put one over the plate, and then he wasted another. Three balls and one strike! That was a bad place for a pitcher, and with Red Gilbat up it was worse. Wehying swung longer and harder to get all his left behind the throw and let drive. Red lunged and cracked the ball. It went up and up and kept going up and farther out, and as the murmuring audience was slowly transfixed into late realization the ball soared to its height and dropped beyond the left-field fence. A home run!

Ray Gilbat gathered up the tails of his duster, after the manner of a neat woman crossing a muddy street, and ambled down to first base and on to second, making prodigious jumps upon the bags, and round third, to come down the homestretch wagging his red head. Then he stood on the plate, and, as if to exact revenge from the audience for the fun they made of him, he threw back his shoulders and bellowed: *"Haw! Haw! Haw!"*

Not a handclap greeted him, but some mindless, exceedingly adventurous fan yelled: "Redhead! Redhead! Redhead!"

That was the one thing calculated to rouse Red Gilbat. He seemed to flare, to bristle, and he paced for the bleachers.

Delaney looked as if he might have a stroke. "Grab him! Soak him with a bat! Somebody grab him!"

But none of the Stars was risking so much, and Gilbat, to the howling derision of the gleeful fans, reached the bleachers. He stretched his long arms up to the fence and prepared to vault over. "Where's the guy who called me redhead?" he yelled.

That was heaping fuel on the fire. From all over the bleachers, from everywhere, came the obnoxious word. Red heaved himself over the fence and piled into the fans. Then followed the roar of many voices, the tramping of many feet, the pressing forward of line after line of shirt-sleeved men and boys. That bleacher stand suddenly assumed the maelstrom appearance of a surging mob round an agitated center. In a moment all the players rushed down the field, and confusion reigned.

However, the game had to go on. Delaney, no doubt, felt all was over. Nevertheless there were games occasionally that seemed an unending series of unprecedented events. This one had begun admirably to break a record. And the Providence fans, like all other fans, had cultivated an appetite as the game proceeded. They were wild to put the other redheads out of the field or at least out for the inning, wild to tie the score, wild to win and wilder than all for more excitement. Clammer hit safely. But when Reddie Ray lined to the second baseman, Clammer, having taken a lead, was doubled up in the play.

Of course, the sixth inning opened with the Stars playing only eight men. There was another delay. Probably everybody except Delaney and perhaps Healy had forgotten the Stars were short a man. Fuller called time. The impatient bleachers barked for action.

Capt. White came over to Delaney and courteously offered to lend a player for the remaining innings. Then a pompous individual came out of the door leading from the press boxes—he was a director Delaney disliked.

"Guess you'd better let Fuller call the game," he said brusquely.

"If you want to—as the score stands now in our favor," replied Delaney.

"Not on your life! It'll be ours or else we'll play it out and beat you to death."

He departed in high dudgeon.

"Tell Reddie to swing over a little toward left," was Delaney's order to Healy. Fire gleamed in the manager's eye.

Fuller called play then, with Reddy Clammer and Reddie Ray composing the Star outfield. And the Grays evidently prepared to do great execution through the wide lanes thus opened up. At that stage it would not have been like matured ball players to try to crop hits down into the infield.

White sent a long fly back of Clammer. Reddy had no time to loaf on this hit. It was all he could do to reach it and he made a splendid catch, for which the crowd roundly applauded him. That applause was wine to Reddy Clammer. He began to prance on his toes and sing out to Scott: "Make 'em hit to me, old man! Make 'em hit to me!" Whether Scott desired that or not was scarcely possible to say; at any rate, Hanley pounded a hit through the infield. And Clammer, prancing high in the air like a check-reined horse, ran to intercept the ball. He could have received it in his hands, but that would never have served Reddy Clammer. He timed the hit to a nicety, went down with his old grand-stand play and blocked the ball with his anatomy. Delaney swore. And the bleachers, now warm toward the gallant outfielder, lustily cheered him. Babcock hit down the right-field foul line, giving Clammer a long run. Hanley was scoring and Babcock was sprinting for third base when Reddy got the ball. He had a fine arm and he made a hard and accurate throw, catching his man in a close play.

Perhaps even Delaney could not have found any fault with that play. But the aftermath spoiled the thing. Clammer now rode the air; he soared; he was in the clouds; it was his inning and he had utterly forgotten his team mates, except inasmuch as they were performing mere little automatic movements to direct the great machinery in his direction for his sole achievement and glory.

There is fate in baseball as well as in other walks of life. O'Brien was a strapping fellow and he lifted another ball into Clammer's wide territory. The hit was of the high and far-away variety. Clammer started to run with it, not like a grim outfielder, but like one thinking of himself, his style, his opportunity, his inevitable success. Certain it was that in thinking of himself the outfielder forgot his surroundings. He ran across the foul line, head up, hair flying, unheeding the warning cry from Healy. And, reaching up to make his crowning circus play, he smashed face forward into the bleachers fence. Then, limp as a rag, he dropped. The audience sent forth a long groan of sympathy.

"That wasn't one of his stage falls," said Delaney. "I'll bet he's dead. . . . Poor Reddy! And I want him to bust his face!"

Clammer was carried off the field into the dressing room and a physician was summoned out of the audience.

"Cap., what'd it—do to him?" asked Delaney.

"Aw, spoiled his pretty mug, that's all," replied Healy, scornfully. "Mebee he'll listen to me now."

Delaney's change was characteristic of the man. "Well, if it didn't kill him I'm blamed glad he got it. . . . Cap, we can trim 'em yet. Reddie Ray'll play the whole outfield. Give Reddie a chance to run! Tell the boy to cut loose. And all of you git in the game. Win or lose, I won't forget it. I've a hunch. Once in a while I can tell what's comin' off. Some queer game this! And we're goin' to win. Gilbat lost the game; Clammer throwed it away again, and now Reddie Ray's due to win it. . . . I'm all in, but I wouldn't miss the finish to save my life."

Delaney's deep presaging sense of baseball events was never put to a greater test. And the seven Stars, with the score tied, exhibited the temper and timber of a championship team in the last ditch. It was so splendid that almost instantly it caught the antagonistic bleachers.

Wherever the tired Scott found renewed strength and speed was a mystery. But he struck out the hard-hitting Providence catcher and that made the third out. The Stars could not score in their half of the inning. Likewise the seventh inning passed without a run for either side; only the infield work of the Stars was something superb. When the eighth inning ended, without a tally for either team, the excitement grew tense. There was Reddie Ray playing outfield alone, and the Grays with all their desperate endeavors had not lifted the ball out of the infield.

But in the ninth, Blake, the first man up, lined low toward right center. The hit was safe and looked good for three bases. No one looking, however, had calculated on Reddie Ray's fleetness. He covered ground and dove for the bounding ball and knocked it down. Blake did not get beyond first base. The crowd cheered the play equally with the prospect of a run. Dorr bunted and beat the throw. White hit one of the high balls Scott was serving and sent it close to the left-field foul line. The running Reddie Ray made on that play held White at second base. But two runs had scored with no one out.

Hanley, the fourth left-handed hitter, came up and Scott pitched to him as he had to the others—high fast balls over the inside corner of the plate. Reddy Ray's position was some fifty yards behind deep short, and a little toward center field. He stood sideways, facing two-thirds of that vacant outfield. In spite of Scott's skill, Hanley swung the ball far round into right field, but he hit it high, and almost before he actually hit it the great sprinter was speeding across the green.

The suspense grew almost unbearable as the ball soared in its parabolic flight and the red-haired runner streaked dark across the green. The ball seemed never to be coming down. And when it began to descend and reached a point perhaps fifty feet above the ground there appeared more distance between where it would alight and where Reddie was than anything human could cover. It dropped and dropped, and then dropped into Reddie Ray's outstretched hands. He had made the catch look easy. But the fact that White scored from second base on the play showed what the catch really was.

There was no movement or restlessness of the audience such as usually indicated the beginning of the exodus. Scott struck Babcock out. The game still had fire. The Grays never let up a moment on their coaching. And the hoarse voices of the Stars were grimmer than ever. Reddie Ray was the only one of the seven who kept silent. And he crouched like a tiger.

The teams changed sides with the Grays three runs in the lead. Morrissey, for the Stars, opened with a clean drive to right. Then Healy slashed a ground ball to Hanley and nearly knocked him down. When old Burns, by a hard rap to short, advanced the runners at base and made a desperate, though unsuccessful, effort to reach first the Providence crowd awoke to a strange and inspiring appreciation. They began that most rare feature in baseball audiences—a strong and trenchant call for the visiting team to win.

The play had gone fast and furious. Wehying, sweaty and disheveled, worked violently. All the Grays were on uneasy tiptoes. And the Stars were seven Indians on the warpath. Halloran fouled down the right-field line; then he fouled over the left-field fence. Wehying tried to make him too anxious, but it was in vain. Halloran was implacable. With two strikes and three balls he hit straight down to White, and was out. The ball had been so sharp that neither runner on base had a chance to advance.

Two men out, two on base, Stars wanting three runs to tie, Scott, a weak batter, at the plate! The situation was disheartening. Yet there sat Delaney, shot through and through with some vital compelling force. He saw only victory. And when the very first ball pitched to Scott hit him on the leg, giving him his base, Delaney got to his feet, unsteady and hoarse.

Bases full, Reddie Ray up, three runs to tie!

Delaney looked at Reddie. And Reddie looked at Delaney. The manager's face was pale, intent, with a little smile. The player had eyes of fire, a lean, bulging jaw and the hands he reached for his bat clutched like talons.

"Reddie, I knew it was waitin' for you," said Delaney, his voice ringing. "Break up the game!"

After all this was only a baseball game, and perhaps from the fans' viewpoint a poor game at that. But the moment when that lithe, redhaired athlete toed the plate was a beautiful one. The long crash from the bleachers, the steady cheer from the grand stand, proved that it was not so much the game that mattered.

Wehying had shot his bolt; he was tired. Yet he made ready for a final effort. It seemed that passing Reddie Ray on balls would have been a wise play at that juncture. But no pitcher, probably, would have done it with the bases crowded and chances, of course, against the batter.

Clean and swift, Reddie leaped at the first pitched ball. Ping! For a second no one saw the hit. Then it gleamed, a terrific drive, low along the ground, like a bounding bullet, straight at Babcock in right field. It struck his hands and glanced viciously away to roll toward the fence.

Thunder broke loose from the stands. Reddie Ray was turning first base. Beyond first base he got into his wonderful stride. Some runners run with a consistent speed, the best they can make for a given distance. But this trained sprinter gathered speed as he ran. He was no short-stepping runner. His strides were long. They gave an impression of strength combined with fleetness. He had the speed of a race horse, but the trimness, the raciness, the delicate legs were not characteristic of him. Like the wind he turned second, so powerful that his turn was short. All at once there came a difference in his running. It was no longer beautiful. The grace was gone. It was now fierce, violent. His momentum was running him off his legs. He whirled around third base and came hurtling down the homestretch. His face was convulsed, his eyes were wild. His arms and legs worked in a marvelous muscular velocity. He seemed a demon—a flying streak. He overtook and ran down the laboring Scott, who had almost reached the plate.

The park seemed full of shrill, piercing strife. It swelled, reached a highest pitch, sustained that for a long moment, and then declined.

"My Gawd!" exclaimed Delaney, as he fell back. "Wasn't that a finish? Didn't I tell you to watch them redheads?"

HORSESHOES

By Ring Lardner

The series ended Tuesday, but I had stayed in Philadelphia an extra day on the chance of there being some follow-up stuff worth sending. Nothing had broken loose; so I filed some stuff about what the Athletics and the Giants were going to do with their dough, and then caught the eight o'clock train for Chicago.

Having passed up supper in order to get my story away and grab the train, I went to the buffet car right after I'd planted my grips. I sat down at one of the tables and ordered a sandwich. Four salesmen were playing rum at the other table and all the chairs in the car were occupied; so it didn't surprise me when somebody flopped down in the seat opposite me.

I looked up from my paper and with a little thrill recognized my companion. Now I've been experting round the country with ball players so much that it doesn't usually excite me to meet one face to face, even if he's a star. I can talk with Tyrus without getting all fussed up. But this particular player had jumped from obscurity to fame so suddenly and had played such an important though brief part in the recent argument between the Macks and McGraws that I couldn't help being a little awed by his proximity.

It was none other than Grimes, the utility outfielder Connie had been forced to use in the last game because of the injury to Joyce—Grimes, whose miraculous catch in the eleventh inning had robbed Parker of a home run and the Giants of victory, and whose own homer, a fluky one— had given the Athletics another World's Championship.

I had met Grimes one day during the spring he was with the Cubs, but I knew he wouldn't remember me. A ball player never recalls a reporter's face on less than six introductions or his name on less than twenty. However, I resolved to speak to him, and had just mustered sufficient courage to open a conversation when he saved me the trouble.

"Whose picture have they got there?" he asked, pointing to my paper.

"Speed Parker's," I replied.

"What do they say about him?" asked Grimes.

"I'll read it to you," I said:

" 'Speed Parker, McGraw's great third baseman, is ill in a local hospital with nervous prostration, the result of the strain of the World Series, in which he played such a stellar rôle. Parker is in such a dangerous condition that no one is allowed to see him. Members of the New York team and fans from Gotham called at the hospital to-day, but were unable to gain admittance to his ward. Philadelphians hope he will recover speedily and will suffer no permanent ill effects from his sickness, for he won their admiration by his work in the series, though he was on a rival team. A lucky catch by Grimes, the Athletics' substitute outfielder, was all that prevented Parker from winning the title for New York. According to Manager Mack, of the champions, the series would have been over in four games but for Parker's wonderful exhibition of nerve and——' ' "

"That'll be aplenty," Grimes interrupted. "And that's just what you might expect from one o' them doughheaded reporters. If all the baseball writers was where they belonged they'd have to build an annex to Matteawan."

I kept my temper with very little effort—it takes more than a peevish ball player's remarks to insult one of our fraternity; but I didn't exactly understand his peeve.

"Doesn't Parker deserve the bouquet?" I asked.

"Oh, they can boost him all they want to," said Grimes; "but when they call that catch lucky and don't mention the fact that Parker is the luckiest guy in the world, somethin' must be wrong with 'em. Did you see the serious?"

"No," I lied glibly, hoping to draw from him the cause of his grouch.

"Well," he said, "you sure missed somethin'. They never was a serious like it before and they won't never be one again. It went the full seven games and every game was a bear. They was one big innin' every day and Parker was the big cheese in it. Just as Connie says, the Ath-a-letics would of cleaned 'em in four games but for Parker; but it wasn't because he's a great ball player—it was because he was born with a knife, fork and spoon in his mouth, and a rabbit's foot hung round his neck.

"You may not know it, but I'm Grimes, the guy that made the lucky catch. I'm the guy that won the serious with a hit—a homerun hit; and I'm here to tell you that if I'd had one-tenth o' Parker's luck they'd of heard about me long before yesterday. They say my homer was lucky. Maybe it was; but, believe me, it was time things broke for me. They been breakin' for him all his life."

"Well," I said, "his luck must have gone back on him if he's in a hospital with nervous prostration."

"Nervous prostration nothin'," said Grimes. "He's in a hospital because his face is all out o' shape and he's ashamed to appear on the street. I don't usually do so much talkin' and I'm ravin' a little to-night because I've had a couple o' drinks; but——"

"Have another," said I, ringing for the waiter, "and talk some more."

"I made two hits yesterday," Grimes went on, "but the crowd only seen one. I busted up the game and the serious with the one they seen. The one they didn't see was the one I busted up a guy's map with—and Speed Parker was the guy. That's why he's in a hospital. He may be able to play ball next year; but I'll bet my share o' the dough that McGraw won't reco'nize him when he shows up at Marlin in the spring."

"When did this come off?" I asked. "And why?"

"It come off outside the clubhouse after yesterday's battle," he said; "and I hit him because he called me a name—a name I won't stand for from him."

"What did he call you?" I queried, expecting to hear one of the delicate epithets usually applied by conquered to conqueror on the diamond.

" 'Horseshoes!' " was Grimes' amazing reply.

"But, good Lord!" I remonstrated, "I've heard of ball players calling each other that, and Lucky Stiff, and Fourleaf Clover, ever since I was a foot high, and I never knew them to start fights about it."

"Well," said Grimes, "I might as well give you all the dope; and then if you don't think I was justified I'll pay your fare from here to wherever you're goin'. I don't want you to think I'm kickin' about trifles—or that I'm kickin' at all, for that matter. I just want to prove to you that he didn't have no license to pull that Horseshoes stuff on me and that I only give him what was comin' to him."

"Go ahead and shoot," said I.

"Give us some more o' the same," said Grimes to the passing waiter. And then he told me about it.

Maybe you've heard that me and Speed Parker was raised in the same town —Ishpeming, Michigan. We was kids together, and though he done all the devilment I got all the lickin's. When we was about twelve years old Speed throwed a rotten egg at the teacher and I got expelled. That made me sick o' schools and I wouldn't never go to one again, though my ol' man beat me up and the truant officers threatened to have me hung.

Well, while Speed was learnin' what was the principal products o' New Hampshire and Texas I was workin' round the freighthouse and drivin' a dray.

We'd both been playin' ball all our lives; and when the town organized a semi-pro club we got jobs with it. We was to draw two bucks apiece for each game and they played every Sunday. We played four games before we got our first pay. They was a hole in my pants pocket as big as the home plate, but I forgot about it and put the dough in there. It wasn't there when I got home. Speed didn't have no hole in his pocket—you can bet on that! Afterward the club hired a good outfielder and I was canned. They was huntin' for another third baseman too; but, o' course, they didn't find none and Speed held his job.

The next year they started the Northern Peninsula League. We landed with the home team. The league opened in May and blowed up the third week in June. They paid off all the outsiders first and then had just money enough left to settle with one of us two Ishpeming guys. The night they done the payin' I was out to my uncle's farm, so they settled with Speed and told me I'd have to wait for mine. I'm still waitin'!

Gene Higgins, who was manager o' the Battle Creek Club, lived in Houghton, and that winter we goes over and strikes him for a job. He give it to us and we busted in together two years ago last spring.

I had a good year down there. I hit over .300 and stole all the bases in sight. Speed got along good too, and they was several big-league scouts lookin' us over. The Chicago Cubs bought Speed outright and four clubs put in a draft for me. Three of 'em—Cleveland and the New York Giants and the Boston Nationals—needed outfielders bad, and it would of been a pipe for me to of made good with any of 'em. But who do you think got me? The same Chicago Cubs; and the only outfielders they had at that time was Schulte and Leach and Good and Williams and Stewart, and one or two others.

Well, I didn't figure I was any worse off than Speed. The Cubs had Zimmerman at third base and it didn't look like they was any danger of a busher beatin' him out; but Zimmerman goes and breaks his leg the second day o' the season—that's a year ago last April—and Speed jumps right in as a regular. Do you think anything like that could happen to Schulte or Leach, or any o' them outfielders? No sir! I wore out my uniform slidin' up and down the bench and wonderin' whether they'd ship me to Fort Worth or Siberia.

Now I want to tell you about the miserable luck Speed had right off the reel. He was playin' at St. Louis. They had a one-run lead in the eighth, when their pitcher walked Speed with one out. Saier hits a high fly to centre and Parker starts with the crack o' the bat. Both coachers was yellin' at him to go back, but he thought they was two out and he was clear round to third base when the ball came down. And Oakes muffs it! O' course he scored and the game was tied up.

Parker come in to the bench like he'd did something wonderful.

"Did you think they was two out?" ast Hank.

"No," says Speed, blushin'.

"Then what did you run for?" says Hank.

"I had a hunch he was goin' to drop the ball," says Speed; and Hank pretty near falls off the bench.

The next day he come up with one out and the sacks full, and the score tied in the sixth. He smashes one on the ground straight at Hauser and it looked like a cinch double play; but just as Hauser was goin' to grab it the ball hit a rough spot and hopped a mile over his head. It got between Oakes and Magee and went clear to the fence. Three guys scored and Speed pulled up at third. The papers come out and said the game was won by a three-bagger from the bat o' Parker, the Cubs' sensational kid third base-man. Gosh!

We go home to Chi and are havin' a hot battle with Pittsburgh. This time

Speed's turn come when they was two on and two out, and Pittsburgh a run
to the good—I think it was the eighth innin'. Cooper gives him a fast one
and he hits it straight up in the air. O' course the runners started goin', but
it looked hopeless because they wasn't no wind or high sky to bother
anybody. Mowrey and Gibson both goes after the ball; and just as Mowrey
was set for the catch Gibson bumps into him and they both fall down. Two
runs scored and Speed got to second. Then what does he do but try to steal
third—with two out too! And Gibson's peg pretty near hits the left field
seats on the fly.

When Speed comes to the bench Hank says:

"If I was you I'd quit playin' ball and go to Monte Carlo."

"What for?" says Speed.

"You're so dam' lucky!" says Hank.

"So is Ty Cobb," says Speed. That's how he hated himself!

First trip to Cincy we run into a couple of old Ishpeming boys. They
took us out one night, and about twelve o'clock I said we'd have to go back
to the hotel or we'd get fined. Speed said I had cold feet and he stuck with
the boys. I went back alone and Hank caught me comin' in and put a fifty-
dollar plaster on me. Speed stayed out all night long and Hank never
knowed it. I says to myself: "Wait till he gets out there and tries to play
ball without no sleep!" But the game that day was called off on account o'
rain. Can you beat it?

I remember what he got away with the next afternoon the same as
though it happened yesterday. In the second innin' they walked him with
nobody down, and he took a big lead off first base like he always does.
Benton threw over there three or four times to scare him back, and the
last time he throwed, Hobby hid the ball. The coacher seen it and told
Speed to hold the bag; but he didn't pay no attention. He started leadin'
right off again and Hobby tried to tag him, but the ball slipped out of his
hand and rolled about a yard away. Parker had plenty o' time to get back;
but, instead o' that, he starts for second. Hobby picked up the ball and shot
it down to Groh—and Groh made a square muff.

Parker slides into the bag safe and then gets up and throws out his chest
like he'd made the greatest play ever. When the ball's throwed back to
Benton, Speed leads off about thirty foot and stands there in a trance.
Clarke signs for a pitch-out and pegs down to second to nip him. He was
caught flatfooted—that is, he would of been with a decent throw; but
Clarke's peg went pretty near to Latonia. Speed scored and strutted over to
receive our hearty congratulations. Some o' the boys was laughin' and he
thought they was laughin' with him instead of at him.

It was in the ninth, though, that he got by with one o' the worst I ever
seen. The Reds was a run behind and Marsans was on third base with two
out. Hobby, I think it was, hit one on the ground right at Speed and he
picked it up clean. The crowd all got up and started for the exits. Marsans
run toward the plate in the faint hope that the peg to first would be wild.
All of a sudden the boys on the Cincy bench began yellin' at him to slide,

and he done so. He was way past the plate when Speed's throw got to Archer. The bonehead had shot the ball home instead o' to first base, thinkin' they was only one down. We was all crazy, believin' his nut play had let 'em tie it up; but he comes tearin' in, tellin' Archer to tag Marsans. So Jim walks over and tags the Cuban, who was brushin' off his uniform.

"You're out!" says Klem. "You never touched the plate."

I guess Marsans knowed the umps was right because he didn't make much of a holler. But Speed sure got a pannin' in the clubhouse.

"I suppose you knowed he was goin' to miss the plate!" says Hank sarcastic as he could.

Everybody on the club roasted him, but it didn't do no good.

Well, you know what happened to me. I only got into one game with the Cubs—one afternoon when Leach was sick. We was playin' the Boston bunch and Tyler was workin' against us. I always had trouble with left-handers and this was one of his good days. I couldn't see what he throwed up there. I got one foul durin' the afternoon's entertainment; and the wind was blowin' a hundred-mile gale, so that the best outfielder in the world couldn't judge a fly ball. That Boston bunch must of hit fifty of 'em and they all come to my field.

If I caught any I've forgot about it. Couple o' days after that I got notice o' my release to Indianapolis.

Parker kept right on all season doin' the blamedest things you ever heard of and gettin' by with 'em. One o' the boys told me about it later. If they was playin' a double-header in St. Louis, with the thermometer at 130 degrees, he'd get put out by the umps in the first innin' o' the first game. If he started to steal the catcher'd drop the pitch or somebody'd muff the throw. If he hit a pop fly the sun'd get in somebody's eyes. If he took a swell third strike with the bases full the umps would call it a ball. If he cut first base by twenty feet the umps would be readin' the mornin' paper.

Zimmerman's leg mended, so that he was all right by June; and then Saier got sick and they tried Speed at first base. He'd never saw the bag before; but things kept on breakin' for him and he played it like a house afire. The Cubs copped the pennant and Speed got in on the big dough, besides playin' a whale of a game through the whole serious.

Speed and me both went back to Ishpeming to spend the winter—though the Lord knows it ain't no winter resort. Our homes was there; and besides, in my case, they was a certain girl livin' in the old burg.

Parker, o' course, was the hero and the swell guy when we got home. He'd been in the World Serious and had plenty o' dough in his kick. I come home with nothin' but my suitcase and a hard-luck story, which I kept to myself. I hadn't even went good enough in Indianapolis to be sure of a job there again.

That fall—last fall—an uncle o' Speed's died over in the Soo and left him ten thousand bucks. I had an uncle down in the Lower Peninsula who was worth five times that much—but he had good health!

This girl I spoke about was the prettiest thing I ever see. I'd went with her in the old days, and when I blew back I found she was still strong for me. They wasn't a great deal o' variety in Ishpeming for a girl to pick from. Her and I went to the dance every Saturday night and to church Sunday nights. I called on her Wednesday evenin's, besides takin' her to all the shows that come along—rotten as the most o' them was.

I never knowed Speed was makin' a play for this doll till along last Feb'uary. The minute I see what was up I got busy. I took her out sleigh-ridin' and kept her out in the cold till she'd promised to marry me. We set the date for this fall—I figured I'd know better where I was at by that time.

Well, we didn't make no secret o' bein' engaged; down in the poolroom one night Speed come up and congratulated me. He says:

"You got a swell girl, Dick! I wouldn't mind bein' in your place. You're mighty lucky to cop her out—you old Horseshoes, you!"

"Horseshoes!" I says. "You got a fine license to call anybody Horse-shoes! I suppose you ain't never had no luck?"

"Not like you," he says.

I was feelin' too good about grabbin' the girl to get sore at the time; but when I got to thinkin' about it a few minutes afterward it made me mad clear through. What right did that bird have to talk about me bein' lucky?

Speed was playin' freeze-out at a table near the door, and when I started home some o' the boys with him says:

"Good night, Dick."

I said good night and then Speed looked up.

"Good night, Horseshoes!" he says.

That got my nanny this time.

"Shut up, you lucky stiff!" I says. "If you wasn't so dam' lucky you'd be sweepin' the streets." Then I walks on out.

I was too busy with the girl to see much o' Speed after that. He left home about the middle o' the month to go to Tampa with the Cubs. I got notice from Indianapolis that I was sold to Baltimore. I didn't care much about goin' there and I wasn't anxious to leave home under the circum-stances, so I didn't report till late.

When I read in the papers along in April that Speed had been traded to Boston for a couple o' pitchers I thought: "Gee! He must of lost his rabbit's foot!" Because, even if the Cubs didn't cop again, they'd have a city serious with the White Sox and get a bunch o' dough that way. And they wasn't no chance in the world for the Boston Club to get nothin' but their salaries.

It wasn't another month, though, till Shafer, o' the Giants, quit baseball and McGraw was up against it for a third baseman. Next thing I knowed Speed was traded to New York and was with another winner—for they never was out o' first place all season.

I was gettin' along all right at Baltimore and Dunnie liked me; so I felt like I had somethin' more than just a one-year job—somethin' I could get married on. It was all framed that the weddin' was comin' off as soon as this season was over; so you can believe I was pullin' for October to hurry up and come.

One day in August, two months ago, Dunnie come in the clubhouse and handed me the news.

"Rube Oldring's busted his leg," he says, "and he's out for the rest o' the season. Connie's got a youngster named Joyce that he can stick in there, but he's got to have an extra outfielder. He's made me a good proposition for you and I'm goin' to let you go. It'll be pretty soft for you, because they got the pennant cinched and they'll cut you in on the big money."

"Yes," I says; "and when they're through with me they'll ship me to Hellangone, and I'll be draggin' down about seventy-five bucks a month next year."

"Nothin' like that," says Dunnie. "If he don't want you next season he's got to ask for waivers; and if you get out o' the big league you come right back here. That's all framed."

So that's how I come to get with the Ath-a-letics. Connie give me a nice, comf'table seat in one corner o' the bench and I had the pleasure o' watchin' a real ball club perform once every afternoon and sometimes twice.

Connie told me that as soon as they had the flag cinched he was goin' to lay off some of his regulars and I'd get a chance to play.

Well, they cinched it the fourth day o' September and our next engagement was with Washin'ton on Labor Day. We had two games and I was in both of 'em. And I broke in with my usual lovely luck, because the pitchers I was ast to face was Boehling, a nasty lefthander, and this guy Johnson.

The mornin' game was Boehling's and he wasn't no worse than some o' the rest of his kind. I only whiffed once and would of had a triple if Milan hadn't run from here to New Orleans and stole one off me.

I'm not boastin' about my first experience with Johnson though. They can't never tell me he throws them balls with his arm. He's got a gun concealed about his person and he shoots 'em up there. I was leadin' off in Murphy's place and the game was a little delayed in startin', because I'd watched the big guy warm up and wasn't in no hurry to get to that plate. Before I left the bench Connie says:

"Don't try to take no healthy swing. Just meet 'em and you'll get along better."

So I tried to just meet the first one he throwed; but when I stuck out my bat Henry was throwin' the pill back to Johnson. Then I thought: Maybe if I start swingin' now at the second one I'll hit the third one. So I let the second one come over and the umps guessed it was another strike, though I'll bet a thousand bucks he couldn't see it no more'n I could.

While Johnson was still windin' up to pitch again I started to swing— and the big cuss crosses me with a slow one. I lunged at it twice and missed it both times, and the force o' my wallop throwed me clean back to the bench. The Ath-a-letics was all laughin' at me and I laughed too, because I was glad that much of it was over.

McInnes gets a base hit off him in the second innin' and I ast him how he done it.

"He's a friend o' mine," says Jack, "and he lets up when he pitches to me."

I made up my mind right there that if I was goin' to be in the league next year I'd go out and visit Johnson this winter and get acquainted.

I wished before the day was over that I was hittin' in the catcher's place, because the fellers down near the tail-end of the battin' order only had to face him three times. He fanned me on three pitched balls again in the third, and when I come up in the sixth he scared me to death by pretty near beanin' me with the first one.

"Be careful!" says Henry. "He's gettin' pretty wild and he's liable to knock you away from your uniform."

"Don't he never curve one?" I ast.

"Sure!" says Henry. "Do you want to see his curve?"

"Yes," I says, knowin' the hook couldn't be no worse'n the fast one.

So he give me three hooks in succession and I missed 'em all; but I felt more comf'table than when I was duckin' his fast ball. In the ninth he hit my bat with a curve and the ball went on the ground to McBride. He booted it, but throwed me out easy—because I was so surprised at not havin' whiffed that I forgot to run!

Well, I went along like that for the rest o' the season, runnin' up against the best pitchers in the league and not exactly murderin' 'em. Everything I tried went wrong, and I was smart enough to know that if anything had depended on the games I wouldn't of been in there for two minutes. Joyce and Strunk and Murphy wasn't jealous o' me a bit; but they was glad to take turns restin', and I didn't care much how I went so long as I was sure of a job next year.

I'd wrote to the girl a couple o' times askin' her to set the exact date for our weddin'; but she hadn't paid no attention. She said she was glad I was with the Ath-a-letics, but she thought the Giants was goin' to beat us. I might of suspected from that that somethin' was wrong, because not even a girl would pick the Giants to trim that bunch of ourn. Finally, the day before the serious started, I sent her a kind o' sassy letter sayin' I guessed it was up to me to name the day, and askin' whether October twentieth was all right. I told her to wire me yes or no.

I'd been readin' the dope about Speed all season, and I knowed he'd had a whale of a year and that his luck was right with him; but I never dreamed a man could have the Lord on his side as strong as Speed did in that World's Serious! I might as well tell you all the dope, so long as you wasn't there.

The first game was on our grounds and Connie give us a talkin' to in the clubhouse beforehand.

"The shorter this serious is," he says, "the better for us. If it's a long

serious we're goin' to have trouble, because McGraw's got five pitchers he
can work and we've got about three; so I want you boys to go at 'em from
the jump and play 'em off their feet. Don't take things easy, because it
ain't goin' to be no snap. Just because we've licked 'em before ain't no
sign we'll do it this time."

Then he calls me to one side and ast me what I knowed about Parker.

"You was with the Cubs when he was, wasn't you?" he says.

"Yes," I says; "and he's the luckiest stiff you ever seen! If he got
stewed and fell in the gutter he'd catch a fish."

"I don't like to hear a good ball player called lucky," says Connie. "He
must have a lot of ability or McGraw wouldn't use him regular. And he's
been hittin' about .340 and played a bang-up game at third base. That can't
be all luck."

"Wait till you see him," I says; "and if you don't say he's the luckiest
guy in the world you can sell me to the Boston Bloomer Girls. He's so
lucky," I says, "that if they traded him to the St. Louis Browns they'd
have the pennant cinched by the Fourth o' July."

And I'll bet Connie was willin' to agree with me before it was over.

Well, the Chief worked against the Big Rube in that game. We beat 'em,
but they give us a battle and it was Parker that made it close. We'd gone
along nothin' and nothin' till the seventh, and then Rube walks Collins and
Baker lifts one over that little old wall. You'd think by this time them New
York pitchers would know better than to give that guy anything he can hit.

In their part o' the ninth the Chief still had 'em shut out and two down,
and the crowd was goin' home; but Doyle gets hit in the sleeve with a
pitched ball and it's Speed's turn. He hits a foul pretty near straight up, but
Schang misjudges it. Then he lifts another one and this time McInnes
drops it. He'd ought to of been out twice. The Chief tries to make him hit
at a bad one then, because he'd got him two strikes and nothin'. He hit at it
all right—kissed it for three bases between Strunk and Joyce! And it was a
wild pitch that he hit. Doyle scores, o' course, and the bugs suddenly
decide not to go home just yet. I fully expected to see him steal home and
get away with it, but Murray cut into the first ball and lined out to Barry.

Plank beat Matty two to one the next day in New York, and again Speed
and his rabbit's foot give us an awful argument. Matty wasn't so good as
usual and we really ought to of beat him bad. Two different times Strunk
was on second waitin' for any kind o' wallop, and both times Barry
cracked 'em down the third-base line like a shot. Speed stopped the first
one with his stomach and extricated the pill just in time to nail Barry at
first base and retire the side. The next time he throwed his glove in front of
his face in self-defense and the ball stuck in it.

In the sixth innin' Schang was on third base and Plank on first, and two
down, and Murphy combed an awful one to Speed's left. He didn't have
time to stoop over and he just stuck out his foot. The ball hit it and
caromed in two hops right into Doyle's hands on second base before Plank
got there. Then in the seventh Speed bunts one and Baker trips and falls

goin' after it or he'd of threw him out a mile. They was two gone; so Speed
steals second, and, o' course, Schang has to make a bad peg right at that
time and lets him go to third. Then Collins boots one on Murray and
they've got a run. But it didn't do 'em no good, because Collins and Baker
and McInnes come up in the ninth and walloped 'em where Parker
couldn't reach 'em.

Comin' back to Philly on the train that night, I says to Connie:

"What do you think o' that Parker bird now?"

"He's lucky, all right," says Connie smilin'; "but we won't hold it
against him if he don't beat us with it."

"It ain't too late," I says. "He ain't pulled his real stuff yet."

The whole bunch was talkin' about him and his luck, and sayin' it was
about time for things to break against him. I warned 'em that they wasn't
no chance—that it was permanent with him.

Bush and Tesreau hooked up next day and neither o' them had much
stuff. Everybody was hittin' and it looked like anybody's game right up to
the ninth. Speed had got on every time he come up—the wind blowin' his
fly balls away from the outfielders and the infielders bootin' when he hit
'em on the ground.

When the ninth started the score was seven apiece. Connie and McGraw
both had their whole pitchin' staffs warmin' up. The crowd was wild,
because they'd been all kinds of action. They wasn't no danger of anybody's leavin' their seats before this game was over.

Well, Bescher is walked to start with and Connie's about ready to give
Bush the hook; but Doyle pops out tryin' to bunt. Then Speed gets two
strikes and two balls, and it looked to me like the next one was right over
the heart; but Connolly calls it a ball and gives him another chance. He
whales the groove ball to the fence in left center and gets round to third on
it, while Bescher scores. Right then Bush comes out and the Chief goes in.
He whiffs Murray and has two strikes on Merkle when Speed makes a
break for home—and, o' course, that was the one ball Schang dropped in
the whole serious!

They had a two-run lead on us then and it looked like a cinch for them to
hold it, because the minute Tesreau showed a sign o' weakenin' McGraw
was sure to holler for Matty or the Rube. But you know how quick that
bunch of oarn can make a two-run lead look sick. Before McGraw could
get Jeff out o' there we had two on the bases.

Then Rube comes in and fills 'em up by walkin' Joyce. It was Eddie's
turn to wallop and if he didn't do nothin' we had Baker comin' up next.
This time Collins saved Baker the trouble and whanged one clear to the
woods. Everybody scored but him—and he could of, too, if it'd been
necessary.

In the clubhouse the boys naturally felt pretty good. We'd copped three
in a row and it looked like we'd make it four straight, because we had the
Chief to send back at 'em the followin' day.

"Your friend Parker is lucky," the boys says to me, "but it don't look like he could stop us now."

I felt the same way and was consultin' the time-tables to see whether I could get a train out o' New York for the West next evenin'. But do you think Speed's luck was ready to quit? Not yet! And it's a wonder we didn't all go nuts durin' the next few days. If words could kill, Speed would of died a thousand times. And I wish he had!

They wasn't no record-breakin' crowd out when we got to the Polo Grounds. I guess the New York bugs was pretty well discouraged and the bettin' was eight to five that we'd cop that battle and finish it. The Chief was the only guy that warmed up for us and McGraw didn't have no choice but to use Matty, with the whole thing dependin' on this game.

They went along like the two swell pitchers they was till Speed's innin', which in this battle was the eighth. Nobody scored, and it didn't look like they was ever goin' to till Murphy starts off that round with a perfect bunt and Joyce sacrifices him to second. All Matty had to do then was to get rid o' Collins and Baker—and that's about as easy as sellin' silk socks to an Eskimo.

He didn't give Eddie nothin' he wanted to hit, though; and finally he slaps one on the ground to Doyle. Larry made the play to first base and Murphy moved to third. We all figured Matty'd walk Baker then, and he done it. Connie sends Baker down to second on the first pitch to McInnes, but Meyers don't pay no attention to him—they was playin' for McInnes and wasn't takin' no chances o' throwin' the ball away.

Well, the count goes to three and two on McInnes and Matty comes with a curve—he's got some curve too; but Jack happened to meet it and—Blooie! Down the left foul line where he always hits! I never seen a ball hit so hard in my life. No infielder in the world could of stopped it. But I'll give you a thousand bucks if that ball didn't go kerplunk right into the third bag and stop as dead as George Washington! It was child's play for Speed to pick it up and heave it over to Merkle before Jack got there. If anybody else had been playin' third base the bag would of ducked out o' the way o' that wallop; but even the bases themselves was helpin' him out.

The two runs we ought to of had on Jack's smash would of been just enough to beat 'em, because they got the only run o' the game in their half —or, I should say, the Lord give it to 'em.

Doyle's been throwed out and up come Parker, smilin'. The minute I seen him smile I felt like somethin' was comin' off and I made the remark on the bench.

Well, the Chief pitched one right at him and he tried to duck. The ball hit his bat and went on a line between Jack and Eddie. Speed didn't know he'd hit it till the guys on the bench wised him up. Then he just had time to get to first base. They tried the hit-and-run on the second ball and Murray lifts a high fly that Murphy didn't have to move for. Collins pulled the old bluff about the ball bein' on the ground and Barry yells, "Go on! Go on!" like he was the coacher. Speed fell for it and didn't know where the ball was no more'n a rabbit; he just run his fool head off and we was gettin' all ready to laugh when the ball come down and Murphy dropped it!

If Parker had stuck near first base, like he ought to of done, he couldn't of got no farther'n second; but with the start he got he was pretty near third when Murphy made the muff, and it was a cinch for him to score. The next two guys was easy outs; so they wouldn't of had a run except for Speed's boner. We couldn't do nothin' in the ninth and we was licked.

Well, that was a tough one to lose; but we figured that Matty was through and we'd wind it up the next day, as we had Plank ready to send back at 'em. We wasn't afraid o' the Rube, because he hadn't never bothered Collins and Baker much.

The two lefthanders come together just like everybody's doped it and it was about even up to the eighth. Plank had been goin' great and, though the score was two and two, they'd got their two on boots and we'd hit ourn in. We went after Rube in our part o' the eighth and knocked him out. Demaree stopped us after we'd scored two more.

"It's all over but the shoutin'!" says Davis on the bench.

"Yes," I says, "unless that seventh son of a seventh son gets up there again."

He did, and he come up after they'd filled the bases with a boot, a base hit and a walk with two out. I says to Davis:

"If I was Plank I'd pass him and give 'em one run."

"That wouldn't be no baseball," says Davis—"not with Murray comin' up."

Well, it mayn't of been no baseball, but it couldn't of turned out worse if they'd did it that way. Speed took a healthy at the first ball; but it was a hook and he caught it on the handle, right up near his hands. It started outside the first-base line like a foul and then changed its mind and rolled in. Schang run away from the plate, because it looked like it was up to him to make the play. He picked the ball up and had to make the peg in a hurry.

His throw hit Speed right on top o' the head and bounded off like it had struck a cement sidewalk. It went clear over to the seats and before McInnes could get it three guys had scored and Speed was on third base. He was left there, but that didn't make no difference. We was licked again and for the first time the gang really begun to get scared.

We went over to New York Sunday afternoon and we didn't do no singin' on the way. Some o' the fellers tried to laugh, but it hurt 'em. Connie sent us to bed early, but I don't believe none o' the bunch got much sleep—I know I didn't; I was worryin' too much about the serious and also about the girl, who hadn't sent me no telegram like I'd ast her to. Monday mornin' I wired her askin' what was the matter and tellin' her I was gettin' tired of her foolishness. O' course I didn't make it so strong as that—but the telegram cost me a dollar and forty cents.

Connie had the choice o' two pitchers for the sixth game. He could use Bush, who'd been slammed round pretty hard last time out, or the Chief, who'd only had two days' rest. The rest of 'em—outside o' Plank—had a epidemic o' sore arms. Connie finally picked Bush, so's he could have the Chief in reserve in case we had to play a seventh game. McGraw started Big Jeff and we went at it.

It wasn't like the last time these two guys had hooked up. This time they both had somethin', and for eight innin's runs was as scarce as Chinese policemen. They'd been chances to score on both sides, but the big guy and Bush was both tight in the pinches. The crowd was plumb nuts and yelled like Indians every time a fly ball was caught or a strike called. They'd of got their money's worth if they hadn't been no ninth; but, believe me, that was some round!

They was one out when Barry hit one through the box for a base. Schang walked, and it was Bush's turn. Connie told him to bunt, but he whiffed in the attempt. Then Murphy comes up and walks—and the bases are choked. Young Joyce had been pie for Tesreau all day or else McGraw might of changed pitchers right there. Anyway he left Big Jeff in and he beaned Joyce with a fast one. It sounded like a tire blowin' out. Joyce falls over in a heap and we chase out there, thinkin' he's dead; but he ain't, and pretty soon he gets up and walks down to first base. Tesreau had forced in a run and again we begun to count the winner's end. Matty comes in to prevent further damage and Collins flies the side out.

"Hold 'em now! Work hard!" we says to young Bush, and he walks out there just as cool as though he was goin' to hit fungoes.

McGraw sends up a pinch hitter for Matty and Bush whiffed him. Then Bescher flied out. I was prayin' that Doyle would end it, because Speed's turn come after his'n; so I pretty near fell dead when Larry hit safe.

Speed had his old smile and even more chest than usual when he come up there, swingin' five or six bats. He didn't wait for Doyle to try and steal, or nothin'. He lit into the first ball, though Bush was tryin' to waste it. I seen the ball go high in the air toward left field, and then I picked up my glove and got ready to beat it for the gate. But when I looked out to see if Joyce was set, what do you think I seen? He was lyin' flat on the ground! That blow on the head had got him just as Bush was pitchin' to Speed. He'd flopped over and didn't no more know what was goin' on than if he'd croaked.

Well, everybody else seen it at the same time; but it was too late. Strunk made a run for the ball, but they wasn't no chance for him to get near it. It hit the ground about ten feet back o' where Joyce was lyin' and bounded way over to the end o' the foul line. You don't have to be told that Doyle and Parker both scored and the serious was tied up.

We carried Joyce to the clubhouse and after a while he come to. He cried when he found out what had happened. We cheered him up all we could, but he was a pretty sick guy. The trainer said he'd be all right, though, for the final game.

They tossed up a coin to see where they'd play the seventh battle and our club won the toss; so we went back to Philly that night and cussed Parker clear across New Jersey. I was so sore I kicked the stuffin' out o' my seat.

You probably heard about the excitement in the burg yesterday mornin'. The demand for tickets was somethin' fierce and some of 'em sold for as high as twenty-five bucks apiece. Our club hadn't been lookin' for no seventh game and they was some tall hustlin' done round that old ball park.

I started out to the grounds early and bought some New York papers to read on the car. They was a big story that Speed Parker, the Giants' hero, was goin' to be married a week after the end o' the serious. It didn't give the name o' the girl, sayin' Speed had refused to tell it. I figured she must be some dame he'd met round the circuit somewheres.

They was another story by one o' them smart baseball reporters sayin' that Parker, on his way up to the plate, had saw that Joyce was about ready to faint and had hit the fly ball to left field on purpose. Can you beat it?

I was goin' to show that to the boys in the clubhouse, but the minute I blowed in there I got some news that made me forget about everything else. Joyce was very sick and they'd took him to a hospital. It was up to me to play!

Connie come over and ast me whether I'd ever hit against Matty. I told him I hadn't, but I'd saw enough of him to know he wasn't no worse'n Johnson. He told me he was goin' to let me hit second—in Joyce's place— because he didn't want to bust up the rest of his combination. He also told me to take my orders from Strunk about where to play for the batters.

"Where shall I play for Parker?" I says, tryin' to joke and pretend I wasn't scared to death.

"I wisht I could tell you," says Connie. "I guess the only thing to do when he comes up is to get down on your knees and pray."

The rest o' the bunch slapped me on the back and give me all the encouragement they could. The place was jammed when we went out on the field. They may of been bigger crowds before, but they never was packed together so tight. I doubt whether they was even room enough left for Falkenberg to sit down.

The afternoon papers had printed the stuff about Joyce bein' out of it, so the bugs was wise that I was goin' to play. They watched me pretty close in battin' practice and give me a hand whenever I managed to hit one hard. When I was out catchin' fungoes the guys in the bleachers cheered me and told me they was with me; but I don't mind tellin' you that I was as nervous as a bride.

They wasn't no need for the announcers to tip the crowd off to the pitchers. Everybody in the United States and Cuba knowed that the Chief'd work for us and Matty for them. The Chief didn't have no trouble with 'em in the first innin'. Even from where I stood I could see that he had a lot o' stuff. Bescher and Doyle popped out and Speed whiffed.

Well, I started out makin' good, with reverse English, in our part. Fletcher booted Murphy's ground ball and I was sent up to sacrifice. I done a complete job of it—sacrificin' not only myself but Murphy with a pop fly that Matty didn't have to move for. That spoiled whatever chance we had o' gettin' the jump on 'em; but the boys didn't bawl me for it.

"That's all right, old boy. You're all right!" they said on the bench—if they'd had a gun they'd of shot me.

I didn't drop no fly balls in the first six innin's—because none was hit out my way. The Chief was so good that they wasn't hittin' nothin' out o' the infield. And we wasn't doin' nothin' with Matty, either. I led off in the fourth and fouled the first one. I didn't molest the other two. But if Connie and the gang talked about me they done it internally. I come up again—with Murphy on third base and two gone in the sixth, and done my little whiffin' specialty. And still the only people that panned me was the thirty thousand that had paid for the privilege!

My first fieldin' chance come in the seventh. You'd of thought that I'd of had my nerve back by that time; but I was just as scared as though I'd never saw a crowd before. It was just as well that they was two out when Merkle hit one to me. I staggered under it and finally it hit me on the shoulder. Merkle got to second, but the Chief whiffed the next guy. I was gave some cross looks on the bench and I shouldn't of blamed the fellers if they'd cut loose with some language; but they didn't.

They's no use in me tellin' you about none o' the rest of it—except what happened just before the start o' the eleventh and durin' that innin', which was sure the big one o' yesterday's pastime—both for Speed and yours sincerely.

The scoreboard was still a row o' ciphers and Speed'd had only a fair amount o' luck. He'd made a scratch base hit and robbed our bunch of a couple o' real ones with impossible stops.

When Schang flied out and wound up our tenth I was leanin' against the end of our bench. I heard my name spoke, and I turned round and seen a boy at the door.

"Right here!" I says; and he give me a telegram.

"Better not open it till after the game," says Connie.

"Oh, no; it ain't no bad news," I said, for I figured it was an answer from the girl. So I opened it up and read it on the way to my position. It said:

"Forgive me, Dick—and forgive Speed too. Letter follows."

Well, sir, I ain't no baby, but for a minute I just wanted to sit down and bawl. And then, all of a sudden, I got so mad I couldn't see. I run right into Baker as he was pickin' up his glove. Then I give him a shove and called him some name, and him and Barry both looked at me like I was crazy—and I was. When I got out in left field I stepped on my own foot and spiked it. I just had to hurt somebody.

As I remember it the Chief fanned the first two of 'em. Then Doyle catches one just right and lams it up against the fence back o' Murphy. The ball caromed round some and Doyle got all the way to third base. Next thing I seen was Speed struttin' up to the plate. I run clear in from my position.

"Kill him!" I says to the Chief. "Hit him in the head and kill him, and I'll go to jail for it!"

"Are you off your nut?" says the Chief. "Go out there and play ball—and quit ravin'."

Barry and Baker led me away and give me a shove out toward left. Then I heard the crack o' the bat and I seen the ball comin' a mile a minute. It was headed between Strunk and I and looked like it would go out o' the park. I don't remember runnin' or nothin' about it till I run into the concrete wall head first. They told me afterward and all the papers said that it was the greatest catch ever seen. And I never knowed I'd caught the ball!

Some o' the managers have said my head was pretty hard, but it wasn't as hard as that concrete. I was pretty near out, but they tell me I walked to the bench like I wasn't hurt at all. They also tell me that the crowd was a bunch o' ravin' maniacs and was throwin' money at me. I guess the ground-keeper'll get it.

The boys on the bench was all talkin' at once and slappin' me on the back, but I didn't know what it was about. Somebody told me pretty soon that it was my turn to hit and I picked up the first bat I come to and starts for the plate. McInnes come runnin' after me and ast me whether I didn't want my own bat. I cussed him and told him to mind his own business.

I didn't know it at the time, but I found out afterward that they was two out. The bases was empty. I'll tell you just what I had in my mind: I wasn't thinkin' about the ball game; I was determined that I was goin' to get to third base and give that guy my spikes. If I didn't hit one worth three bases, or if I didn't hit one at all, I was goin' to run till I got round to where Speed was, and then slide into him and cut him to pieces!

Right now I can't tell you whether I hit a fast ball, or a slow ball, or a hook, or a fader—but I hit somethin'. It went over Bescher's head like a shot and then took a crazy bound. It must of struck a rock or a pop bottle, because it hopped clear over the fence and landed in the bleachers.

Mind you, I learned this afterward. At the time I just knowed I'd hit one somewheres and I starts round the bases. I speeded up when I got near third and took a runnin' jump at a guy I thought was Parker. I missed him and sprawled all over the bag. Then, all of a sudden, I come to my senses. All the Ath-a-letics was out there to run home with me and it was one o' them I'd tried to cut. Speed had left the field. The boys picked me up and seen to it that I went on and touched the plate. Then I was carried into the clubhouse by the crazy bugs.

Well, they had a celebration in there and it was a long time before I got a chance to change my clothes. The boys made a big fuss over me. They told me they'd intended to give me five hundred bucks for my divvy, but now I was goin' to get a full share.

"Parker ain't the only lucky guy!" says one of 'em. "But even if that ball hadn't of took that crazy hop you'd of had a triple."

A triple! That's just what I'd wanted; and he called me lucky for not gettin' it!

The Giants was dressin' in the other part o' the clubhouse; and when I finally come out there was Speed, standin' waitin' for some o' the others. He seen me comin' and he smiled. "Hello, Horseshoes!" he says.

He won't smile no more for a while—it'll hurt too much. And if any girl wants him when she sees him now—with his nose over shakin' hands with his ear, and his jaw a couple o' feet foul—she's welcome to him. They won't be no contest!

Grimes leaned over to ring for the waiter.

"Well," he said, "what about it?"

"You won't have to pay my fare," I told him.

"I'll buy a drink anyway," said he. "You've been a good listener—and I had to get it off my chest."

"Maybe they'll have to postpone the wedding," I said.

"No," said Grimes. "The weddin' will take place the day after tomorrow—and I'll bat for Mr. Parker. Did you think I was goin' to let him get away with it?"

"What about next year?" I asked.

"I'm goin' back to the Ath-a-letics," he said. "And I'm goin' to hire somebody to call me 'Horseshoes!' before every game—because I can sure play that old baseball when I'm mad."

THE MAGNIFICENT MOMENT: THE CALLED-SHOT HOME RUN

By Robert W. Creamer

Everything worked for the Yankees in 1932. The infield clicked, the outfield was strong, the catching outstanding (except when Dickey was under a thirty-day suspension for breaking a Washington outfielder's jaw with one punch in a dispute at home plate). The pitching was superb, and the hitting strong and consistent all year long. The team won 107 games and took the pennant by a wide margin.

Ruth pretty much decided when he wanted to play, which was most of the time, but more and more he left the game in the late innings and let young Sammy Byrd or Myril Hoag finish up for him. Ruth's caddies, they were called, or his legs. Babe, now thirty-eight, had a solid enough year, although it was distinctly below his traditional high level of accomplishment. For one thing, he lost the home run championship he had held (except for 1922 and 1925) since 1918. Jimmie Foxx of Philadelphia even threatened Ruth's record of 60, ending with 58. Babe was second, but far behind, with 41. He batted .341, not bad, scored 120 runs and batted in 137, not bad at all. But people like Foxx and Gehrig and Simmons were obviously better hitters than he was now. The only thing the Babe led the league in was bases on balls.

Twice he was out of the lineup for extended periods, the first time in the middle of July after he ruptured the sheath of a muscle in the rear of his leg as he chased a fly ball. He fell in a writhing heap and once again was carried off the field. He was in a hospital for a few days and out of action for the better part of two weeks. Later in the year, in September, he felt shooting pains in his right side during a game in Philadelphia. The Yankees left on a western road trip, pausing first for an exhibition game in Binghamton, New York, and there Ruth felt the pain again. By the time the club reached Detroit he was convinced he had appendicitis. He phoned Barrow in New York, spoke to McCarthy and, with Claire, hurried back to New York for a thorough examination. It may or may not have been his appendix—there was no operation—but he ran a low fever for several days and was kept in bed. Ten days after his return to New York and only ten days before the World Series with the Cubs was due to begin, he got into a uniform and worked out at Yankee Stadium. The team was still on the road and Babe batted against an amateur pitcher, but he was unable to put one ball into the stands. "I'm so weak I don't think I could break a pane of glass," he said, "but I'll be okay in a few days. They had me packed so deep in ice I haven't thawed out yet."

There was considerable doubt that he would be able to play in the Series, but he was in the Yankee lineup for the last five games of the year (he had only three hits in sixteen at bats), and when the Cubs faced the Yankees on Wednesday, September 28, there was Ruth in right field, batting third. This was the World Series that is remembered for Ruth's called home run, the single most famous facet of his legend, yet it was really Gehrig's series. Chicago had a good solid team, representative of the glowing period from 1928 through 1938 when the Cubs won four pennants and never finished lower than third. These Cubs could hit, and indeed they scored almost five runs a game against the excellent Yankee pitching staff, but their own pitchers, a redoubtable collection of first-rate performers (Lon Warneke, Charlie Root, Guy Bush, Burleigh Grimes, Pat Malone), were destroyed by the Yankees, who scored an average of more than nine runs a game. Gehrig had nine hits in the four games, including three home runs and a double, and he scored nine runs and batted in eight as the Yankees won, 12–6, 5–2, 7–5 and 13–6.

Yet Gehrig's exploits were obscured, as they so often were during his career, by a brighter sun, meaning Ruth. Along with being the highest scoring Series ever played, it probably had the most bench jockeying, and the Babe was in the forefront of it. Mark Koenig, who had dropped down to the minors after the Yankees traded him away, had been brought back up by the Cubs late in 1932 to fill a hole at shortstop; he fielded splendidly, batted .353 in 33 games and was a key figure in Chicago's drive to the pennant. But when the Cubs met just before the Series to decide how they would divide their share of the World Series pot, Koenig was voted only a half share. (Rogers Hornsby, who had been fired as manager almost two thirds of the way through the season, received nothing. A young outfielder named Frank Demaree, who was in only 23 games during the season but played center field and batted fifth in two Series games and hit a home run, was given a quarter share.)

The Yankees, led by Ruth, made great capital of Koenig's half share. "Hey, Mark," Babe boomed, "who are those cheapskates you're with?" Variations, richly embellished, followed and never let up. The Cubs struck back, mostly at Ruth, calling him fat and old and washed up, and they dragged out the old "nigger" cry. Guy Bush, a dark-haired, swarthy Mississippian, was Chicago's starting pitcher in the first game, and the Yankees yelled back, "Who are you calling a nigger? Look at your pitcher."

The jockeying continued at this high level as the Yankees won the first two games in New York. Then the Series shifted to Chicago, where thousands of people crammed into La Salle Street Station to see the ball clubs arrive. Ruth, accompanied by Claire, fought his way through the not un-friendly crowd to a freight elevator and then out to a cab. Motorcycle cops had to clear the way for the Yankees, and as Ruth and his wife entered their hotel a woman spat on them.

Such anti-Yankee feeling was isolated on the streets, but it was over-whelmingly evident at Wrigley Field before and during the third game of the Series. Ruth complained a week or so later that the Chicago press had brought the fans down on him with stories about the bench jockeying. "They wrote about me riding the Cubs for being tight and about me calling them cheapskates," he said indignantly.

"Well, didn't you?" he was asked.

"Well, weren't they?" he answered with irrefutable logic. Then he grinned and said, "Jesus, I wish I had known they only voted that kid Demaree a quarter share. Would I have burned them on that one."

Almost 50,000 people were jammed into every part of Wrigley Field, and most of them were yelling at Ruth. Whenever a ball was lofted his way in pregame practice, a lemon or two would come flying out of the bleach-ers. Each time, Babe picked up the lemons and threw them back. He was in a good mood. There was a strong wind blowing toward right field, and during batting practice he and Gehrig put on an awesome show, far more spectacular than the one in Pittsburgh five years earlier. Babe hit nine balls into the stands, Gehrig seven. Ruth yelled at the Cubs, "I'd play for half my salary if I could hit in this dump all the time." Gomez, the non-hitting pitcher, said, "With that wind, I could hit a home run today."

The jockeying between the two teams, or, to be more accurate, between Ruth and the Cubs, became more intense as the game began. Charlie Root was the starting pitcher for Chicago, but Bush and Grimes and Malone were on the top step of the Cub dugout, leading the verbal barrage on Ruth. Andy Lotshaw, the Cubs' trainer, yelled, "If I had you, I'd hitch you to a wagon, you potbelly," Ruth said afterwards, "I didn't mind no ballplayers yelling at me, but the trainer cutting in—that made me sore." As he waited to bat in the first inning, according to Richards Vidmer in the *New York Herald Tribune,* "He paused to jest with the raging Cubs, pointed to the right field bleachers and grinned."

The game started badly for the Cubs. Koenig had hurt his wrist in New York and was out the rest of the Series. His replacement, Billy Jurges, fielded the first ball hit by the Yankees—a grounder by Earle Combs—and threw it all the way into the stands behind first base. Joe Sewell walked, and Ruth came to bat with men on first and second and no one out. Root threw a pitch outside for ball one, another one inside for ball two. Then he threw a fastball on the outside corner and Ruth, swinging at the ball for the first time in a game in Wrigley Field, hit a three-run homer into the right field bleachers to put the Yankees ahead, 3–0, before an out had been made.

Gehrig hit a homer in the third with the bases empty (and Ruth hit a fly to the right center field fence), but the Cubs rallied and in the fourth inning tied the game at 4–4. The tying run was scored by Jurges, who reached second base with a double when Ruth, to the great delight of the crowd, looked foolish missing a try at a shoestring catch.

And so it was 4–4 in a rowdy game as the Yankees came to bat in the fifth. Another lemon bounced toward Ruth as he waited in the on-deck circle while Sewell went out. Boos and hoots rose to a crescendo as he stepped into the batter's box. The Cubs were on the top of the dugout steps, Bush cupping his hands around his mouth as he taunted Ruth. Babe grinned, then stepped in to face Root. The pitcher threw. It was called strike. The crowd cheered, and the Cubs razzed Ruth louder than ever. Still grinning, holding his bat loosely in his left hand, he looked over at the Cubs and raised one finger of his right hand. Root pitched again, in close, for ball one. He pitched again, this time outside, and it was ball two. The crowd stirred in disappointment, and the razzing from the Cubs let up slightly. Again Root pitched, and it was called strike two. The crowd roared, and the Cubs yammered with renewed vigor. Bush was so excited he ran a step or two onto the grass in front of the dugout, yelling at Ruth. Grimes was shouting something. Ruth waved the exultant Cubs back toward their dugout and held up two fingers. Gabby Hartnett, the Chicago catcher, heard him say, "It only takes one to hit it." Root said something from the mound, and Ruth said something back. Gehrig, who was in the on-deck circle, said, "Babe was jawing with Root and what he said was, 'I'm going to knock the next pitch right down your goddamned throat.' "

Root threw again, a changeup curve, low and away. Ruth swung and hit a tremendous line-drive home run deep into the bleachers in center field. Johnny Moore, the center fielder, ran back and stood there looking up as it went far over his head into the stands. It was the longest home run that had ever been hit in Wrigley Field. Ruth ran down the first base line laughing. "You lucky bum," he said to himself. "You lucky, lucky bum." He said something to Charlie Grimm, the Cubs' player-manager first baseman. He said something to second baseman Billy Herman. He shook his clasped hands over his head like a victorious fighter, and as he rounded third base, still laughing, he yelled, "Squeeze the eagle club!" to the now silent Chicago dugout. In a box near home plate Franklin D. Roosevelt, who was running for President against Herbert Hoover, put his head back and laughed, and after the Babe crossed home plate Roosevelt's eyes followed him all the way into the dugout, where he was mauled and pounded by his gleeful Yankee teammates.

Gehrig stepped to the plate, Root threw one pitch and Gehrig hit a home run. Two pitches, two home runs; the Yankees led, 6–4, all their runs coming on homers by Ruth and Gehrig. Root was taken out of the game, and it ended with the Yankees winning, 7–5.

The New York clubhouse roared with noise afterwards. Ruth yelled, "Did Mr. Ruth chase those guys back into the dugout? Mr. Ruth sure did!"

The next day Bush was Chicago's starting pitcher. When Ruth came to

bat in the first inning, Bush hit him on the arm with a blistering fastball.
Babe pretended to flick something off his arm as he trotted down to first
base. "Hey, Lop Ears," he yelled to Bush, "was that your fastball? I
thought it was a gnat." To Gehrig, he called, "Don't look for nothing,
Lou. He ain't got it." And Bush didn't. He faced five men in the inning,
got one out and was lifted from the game. Lazzeri hit two homers, Combs
one, Gehrig batted in three runs, and the Yankees won, 13–6. Ruth had
only one single in five at bats and in the clubhouse afterwards put hot
towels on his arm, which was flaming red and badly swollen where Bush's
gnat had bitten it. Doc Painter, the trainer, said that if the Series had gone
another game, Ruth could not possibly have played in it. But despite the
pain, Ruth was gloriously happy. He even went over to McCarthy and
shook his hand. "What a victory!" he said. "My hat is off to you, Mac."
A few days later, back in New York, he said, "That's the first time I ever
got the players and the fans going at the same time. I never had so much
fun in all my life."

Now. What about the legend? What about the story, often affirmed,
often denied, that Babe pointed to a spot in center field and then hit the ball
precisely to that spot? It is an argument over nothing, and the fact that Ruth
did not point to center field before his home run does not diminish in the
least what he did. He did challenge the Cubs before 50,000 people, did
indicate he was going to hit a home run and did hit a home run. What more
could you ask?

The legend grew, obviously, because people gild lilies and because
sometimes we remember vividly seeing things we did not see. Most of the
contemporary accounts of the game talked about Ruth calling his shot, but
only one that I could find said specifically that he pointed at the fence.
That, written by Joe Williams, sports editor of the Scripps-Howard newspapers, appeared in late editions of afternoon newspapers on Saturday,
October 1, the day of the game. The headline over Williams' story in the
New York World-Telegram said, "RUTH CALLS SHOT AS HE PUTS
HOMER NO. 2 IN SIDE POCKET," and part of his account said, "In the
fifth, with the Cubs riding him unmercifully from the bench, Ruth pointed
to center and punched a screaming liner to a spot where no ball had ever
been hit before." That is the only place in the story where specific reference is made to pointing to center field. Elsewhere in his copy Williams
wrote, "The first strike was called, and the razzing from the Cub bench
increased. Ruth laughed and held up one finger. Two balls were pitched
and Babe jeered the Cub bench, the fans and Root, grinning broadly all the
time. Another strike was called and Bush ran part way out of the dugout to
tell the Babe that he was just a tramp. Ruth hit the next pitch farther than
any other ball ever was hit in this park."

Westbrook Pegler, who wrote a column but not a running account of the
game, said, "Bush pushed back his big ears, funneled his hands at his
mouth and yelled raspingly at the great man to upset him. The Babe
laughed derisively and gestured at him—wait, mugg, I'm going to hit one

out of the yard. Root threw a strike past him and he held up a finger to Bush whose ears flapped excitedly as he renewed his insults. Another strike passed him and Bush crawled almost out of the hole to extend his remarks. The Babe held up two fingers this time. Root wasted two balls and Babe put up two fingers on his other hand. Then with a warning gesture of his hand to Bush he sent the signal for the customers to see. Now, it said, this is the one, look. And that one went riding on the longest home run ever hit in the park. . . . Many a hitter may make two home runs, possibly three, in World Series play in years to come, but not the way Ruth hit these two. Nor will you ever see an artist call his shot before hitting one of the longest drives ever made on the ground in a World Series game, laughing at and mocking the enemy, two strikes gone.''

The story by Williams was the only one I found of those written on the day of the game that interpreted Ruth's gestures as pointing toward center, but two days later Paul Gallico of the *New York Daily News,* a rococo and flamboyant writer, wrote, ''He pointed like a duellist to the spot where he expected to send his rapier home.'' A day after that Bill Corum of the Hearst newspapers wrote that Ruth ''pointed out where he was going to hit the next one, and hit it there,'' but in his game account the day it happened Corum neglected to mention the fact.

Tom Meany, who worked for Williams and sat next to him at the game on Saturday, wrote a story the following Tuesday that said, ''Babe's interviewer then interrupted to point out the hole in which Babe put himself Saturday when he pointed out the spot in which he intended hitting his homer and asked the great man if he realized how ridiculous he would have appeared if he had struck out. 'I never thought of that,' said Babe.'' But it is not clear in Meany's story if the phrase about pointing was in the question put to Ruth or was merely incorporated in the copy as a clarifying description.

Williams was a positive, opinionated observer and a vigorous journalist. Taking an opposite tack some months later, he suggested to Gehrig that Root let Babe hit the ball (''Like hell he did,'' said Gehrig). Meany was a fine reporter, a gifted writer and a superior raconteur of baseball anecdotes. I believe that Williams' strong personality and the wide circulation given his original story in Scripps-Howard newspapers as well as Meany's repeated accounts of that colorful World Series are what got the legend started and kept it going. That the pointing version was often questioned is shown in Meany's biography of Ruth, published in 1947. In it Meany wrote, ''It was then the big fellow made what many believe to be the *beau geste* of his entire career. He pointed in the direction of dead centerfield. Some say it was merely a gesture toward Root, others that he was just letting the Cub bench know that he still had the big one left. Ruth himself has changed his version a couple of times. . . . Whatever the intent of the gesture, the result was, as they say in Hollywood, slightly colossal.''

Ruth told John Carmichael, a highly respected Chicago sportswriter, ''I didn't exactly point to any spot. All I wanted to do was give that thing a ride out of the park, anywhere. I used to pop off a lot about hitting homers, but mostly among the Yankees. Combs and Lazzeri and Fletcher used to yell, 'Come on, Babe, hit one.' So I'd come back, 'Okay, you bums. I'll hit one!' Sometimes I did. Sometimes I didn't. Hell, it was fun.''

His autobiography, published in 1947, not only says he did it but adds the embroidery that he began thinking about it the night before the game, after he and Claire were spat on when they entered their hotel. It says he was angry and hurt because of the taunts of the Chicago players and fans. It says that before the first pitch he pointed to center field and that when Root threw the ball, Babe held up a finger and yelled, "Strike one," before the umpire could call the pitch. And held up two fingers and yelled, "Strike two," after the second pitch. And before the third pitch, he stepped out of the box and pointed to the bleachers again. And then hit the third pitch for the home run. This version is the one that was substantially followed by Hollywood in the movie of Ruth's life that starred William Bendix, and as bad as the movie was it gave the legend the permanence of concrete.

Both autobiography and movie infuriated Charlie Root, who turned the film company down flat when they asked him to portray himself. "Not if you're going to have him pointing," he said. He refused to have anything to do with it, and he went to his grave denying that Ruth had pointed to center field. "If he had I would have knocked him on his ass with the next pitch," he always insisted. Yet Root's memory was hazy on detail. In the mid 1950s, he said, "George Magerkurth, the plate umpire, said in a magazine story that Ruth did point to center field. But to show how far wrong Magerkurth was, he had the count three and two when it was really two strikes and no balls. To me, the count was significant. Why should Ruth point to show where he was going to hit a ball when, with two strikes and no balls, he knew he wasn't apt to get a pitch he could hit at all?" But both Magerkurth and Root were wrong. The count was neither three balls and two strikes nor two strikes and no balls. It was two strikes and two balls. And Magerkurth umpired at first base that day, not behind the plate.

Such fuzziness of detail is evident in several contemporary accounts of the game. Pegler, quoted above, said the count went strike, strike, ball, ball, whereas it was strike, ball, ball, strike. Corum said the count was three and two, and so did the play-by-play account in *The New York Times*. Meany's biography and Ruth's autobiography both say, as Root did, that it was two strikes and no balls. Any lawyer will concede that honest witnesses see the same things differently.

Here are what some witnesses said about it.

Charlie Root: "Ruth did not point at the fence before he swung. If he had made a gesture like that, well, anybody who knows me knows that Ruth would have ended up on his ass. The legend didn't get started until later. I fed him a changeup curve. It wasn't a foot off the ground and it was three or four inches outside, certainly not a good pitch to hit. But that was the one he smacked. He told me the next day that if I'd have thrown him a fastball he would have struck out. 'I was guessing with you,' he said."

Gabby Hartnett, the Chicago catcher: "Babe came up in the fifth and took two called strikes. After each one the Cub bench gave him the business, stuff like he was choking and he was washed up. Babe waved his hand across the plate toward our bench on the third base side. One finger was up. At the same time he said softly, and I think only the umpire and I heard him, 'It only takes one to hit it.' Root came in with a fast one and it went into the center field seats. Babe didn't say a word when he passed me after the home run. If he had pointed out at the bleachers, I'd be the first to say so."

Doc Painter, the Yankee trainer: "Before taking his stance he swept his left arm full length and pointed to the center field fence. When he got back to the bench, Herb Pennock said, 'Suppose you missed? You would have looked like an awful bum.' Ruth was taking a drink from the water cooler, and he lifted his head and laughed. 'I never thought of that,' he said."

Joe McCarthy, the Yankee manager: "I'm not going to say he didn't do it. Maybe I didn't see it. Maybe I was looking the other way. Anyway, I'm not going to say he didn't do it."

Jimmy Isaminger, Philadelphia sportswriter: "He made a satiric gesture to the Cub bench and followed it with a resounding belt that had so much force behind it that it landed in the bleachers in dead center."

The *San Francisco Examiner,* October 2, 1932: "He called his shot theatrically, with derisive gestures towards the Cubs' dugout."

The Reach Guide, covering the 1932 season: "Ruth hit the ball over the center field fence, a tremendous drive, after indicating in pantomime to his hostile admirers what he proposed to do, and did."

Warren Brown, Chicago sportswriter: "The Babe indicated he had one strike, the big one, left. The vituperative Cub bench knew what he meant. Hartnett heard Ruth growl that this was what he meant. Ruth, for a long while, had no other version, nor was any other sought from him."

Ford Frick, who was not at the game, tried to pin Ruth down on the subject when the two were talking about the Series some time later.

"Did you really point to the bleachers?" Frick asked.

Ruth, always honest, shrugged. "It's in the papers, isn't it?" he said.

"Yeah," Frick said. "It's in the papers. But did you really point to the stands?"

"Why don't you read the papers? It's all right there in the papers."

Which, Frick said, means he never said he did and he never said he didn't.

MYSTIC BASEBALL:
A NEW AGE LOOK

By Michael D'Antonio

If there's one thing I learned playing mystic baseball, it's that sometimes you have to go backward before you move forward. Consider a simple throw from shortstop to first base. First you must focus your attention, shutting out all distractions—the crowd, your teammates, the heat of the day. Grasping the ball, you move your hand down and then backward, toward the outfield. Then you swing it up, in an arc that carries the ball past your ear. At the same time your body rocks forward. If you let go of it at the right moment, the ball flies into the first baseman's outstretched mitt. No sore arm. No wild errors. I mention this, not to teach you how to throw a ball, but to begin to explain baseball played the New Age way at the Omega Institute, a spiritual summer camp for adults in upstate New York.

A kind of spa for the mind, body, and soul, Omega is a resort/retreat that offers serious courses on spirituality, alternative medicine, and psychology. But it is also a place where the New Age could be discovered at play: singing, dancing, painting, acting, even gardening. Two of the institute's most popular courses are "Beyond Basketball," taught by Phil Jackson, coach of the Chicago Bulls, and "The Tao of Boxing," led by Floyd Patterson.

"Baseball: The Spirit and Practice of an American Myth" intrigued me. First there was the juxtaposition of the game, an icon of American culture, with the insistently counterculture mentality of the New Age. Second was my own, reflexive response to baseball. My small-town childhood summers had revolved around baseball, almost to the exclusion of everything else. I played countless games, and I was a reverent fan of the Boston Red Sox. On many nights I fell asleep listening to a play-by-play lullaby from the radio hidden under my pillow. One of the teachers Omega had hired had been a Red Sox pitching ace. Outspoken and iconoclastic, Bill Lee was nicknamed "Space Man" because of his eccentric, mystical approach to the game. His teaching partner, Jeffrey McKay, had been a trainer for EST, the controversial and confrontational self-improvement program of the 1970s, and for Actualizations, an EST spinoff. McKay had also played minor-league ball and was a college coach. According to the Omega program, participants in the seminar would "explore baseball as a Way." I signed up. . . .

From my chair in the second row, I scanned the faces of the crowd. Many had come to study meditation, yoga, alternative medicine, and mythology. But I was looking for the baseball players. I wanted to size them up. What I saw did nothing to settle my nerves. Sprinkled among the more typical New Age seekers were several men who wore complete baseball uniforms —jerseys with numbers, stretchy pants, spiked shoes. These were serious ball players. My heart sank.

After orientation the other campers followed their teachers to various classrooms scattered in the woods while the baseball players remained in Main Hall. Lee and McKay came to the front of the room and told us to arrange ourselves in a circle. We did so and then sat, as attentive as kindergartners on the first day of school.

Tall, muscular, with gray hair and blue eyes, forty-four-year-old William Francis "Space Man" Lee wore striped baseball pants and a T-shirt from one of his several mock Presidential campaigns. (Every four years he "declares" for President as a protest against political windbaggery.) The red-white-and-blue shirt was decorated with a picture of a rhinoceros and the words RHINOCEROS PARTY, BILL "SPACE MAN" LEE FOR PRESIDENT. Lee had pulled a Russian Army cap—drab green decorated with a red star—over his bushy hair. He'd gotten the hat in the Soviet Union, where he and McKay had played several exhibition games the week before.

Jeffrey McKay was smaller than Lee. He had the stocky build of a catcher, which had been his position in the minor leagues. He had blond hair, blue eyes, and a youthful, even boyish face. His face reddened a bit as he cleared his throat to speak.

"There's a poem by Walt Whitman, who must have been a baseball fan," McKay began. "In it, he said, 'I am a teacher of athletes. He most honors my style who learns under it to destroy the teacher.' "

After pausing for us to consider this, he went on. "You know, there is a myth in our society that says an athlete is some special person. He's six-foot-four-inches tall and he's very strong and dominating. But it's just a myth. Everyone is an athlete. All you have to do is balance two things, championship and sportsmanship. Championship is playing hard, with all your skill. Sportsmanship is your regard for yourself and the other players. That balance is what we're seeking."

With a John Wayne cadence, Lee added some of his philosophy to McKay's. "I'm on planet Earth to do one thing," he said, "and that's to play baseball my whole life. I'm in search of the perfect game. Every time you play, it could happen. You walk between those white lines and you have the opportunity to create a game that goes on forever. It never ends."

His voice trailed off and he got a faraway look in his eyes. He reminded me of the farmer in *Field of Dreams.* "It's the perfect game. There's no work to go to, nothing to worry about but the game. There's no time limit in baseball. It is the only game unbound by time. It could go on forever.

"Now, my aunt Annabelle Lee is the one who taught me baseball," he continued. (There was apparently no stopping Lee when he started telling baseball stories.) "She pitched for three ball clubs in a professional league during World War Two. She was the only woman to ever pitch a perfect, no-hit game in hardball. She was interviewed about it and the guy said, 'What was it like?' She said, 'Well, twenty-seven came up and twenty-seven made outs.' She was great. She loved the game."

If spirituality is a belief or discipline that gives meaning and purpose to life, then baseball is Lee's spiritual practice. When he talks about baseball, he speaks with the zeal of a true believer and with the energy of an evangelist. McKay, on the other hand, sees baseball in a broader context. He describes a "community of players," a "safe space for play," and the "power of mutual support." He is interested in baseball as a healing practice, a way to soothe wounds and recover strength. I was drawn to this vision of baseball because it freed the game from the fear and anxiety of too much aggressive competition. It promised to free the player—me—to simply play.

Now of course, these two interests, healing and spiritual development, are at the center of the New Age phenomenon and, true to the movement, the ball players who had come to play at Omega were interested in both. . . .

And so it went, with one person after another explaining how baseball had affected his or her emotional or spiritual development. This was mainly a New Age crowd. Several of the women wore crystal earrings. Many of the men had attended other Omega workshops, on shamanism, African drumming, or other topics. And like the other mystically oriented people I had met in my journeys through the New Age, these people were eager for a healing, a transformation. Only this time it wasn't a channel or a psychic that would help them, it was baseball.

"There's a real common thread here," McKay observed before we headed for the practice field. "What I hear is that everybody's ten years old again. People want to heal some of the wounds from back there so they can move on."

"Hey, baseball has its assholes, we all know it," cracked Lee. "I was kicked out of Little League, kicked out of Pony League, kicked off the Red Sox because I stuck up for Bernie Carbo, and kicked off Toronto because I stood up for Rodney Scott."

The Space Man had been an extremely controversial ball player. In Boston he had annoyed management by standing on his head in center field and speaking his mind to the press about everything from the team's managers to racism in Boston. Lee's book, *The Wrong Stuff,* is the only ball player's autobiography that touches on holistic medicine, the concept of karma, and the teachings of Buckminster Fuller. He writes as much about mystics and psychics and Carlos Casteneda as he does about the mechanics of pitching. On the cover he is pictured winding up to pitch, dressed in an astronaut's suit and a Red Sox cap with a tiny propeller whirling on its peak. My favorite line from the book: "You are the baseball, the baseball is you."

Lee picked up that theme as he continued to expound on his unique approach to the game. "The key is to put everything but the baseball out of your mind when you are on the field. Look at Jody Reed," he continued. Reed, the Red Sox first baseman, is as consistent as the turning of the seasons. "Jody is in a nice Zen trance when he's in the game, at bat or on the field. He's relaxed, centered, his eyes are focused. That's the way you've gotta be."

"There will be a lot of joy here this weekend, but also some tears," added McKay. "Whatever we do, let's support each other. Now, let's play ball."

We split into two groups. One followed McKay to the tennis courts, where they would hit little spongy balls against a fence. The rest of us went into the meadow beside Main Hall to practice throwing and catching. The field was big, about two hundred yards by one hundred yards, and the grass was long, like hay, and so wet with dew that our feet were quickly soaked. It was like the schoolyard where I had played as a boy. In the summer the grass grew so long that a ground ball could disappear in the infield.

Although we were eager to start throwing and catching, first we had to learn to stand. We set our feet shoulder's width apart and put our weight forward, on the balls of our feet. Our knees were to be slightly bent, and our shoulders were to be rounded. "It's called striking the horse," Lee said. "It is the best position to do anything in life." We all "struck the horse," looking like so many bow-legged cowboys with baseball mitts. But standing there, knees bent, my weight slightly forward, I did feel well-balanced and ready to spring into action.

From there Lee showed us the proper way to grip a baseball in order to throw fastballs, sliders, and curves, and he demonstrated the smooth, backward-then-forward method of throwing. Along with the baseball mechanics, there was always philosophy. "The key is to be fluid. I didn't learn to be fluid until I read *Autobiography of a Yogi*. That guy taught me a lot about baseball. You've also got to be willing to fail. Failure is the beginning of success. Besides, if you do it right all the time, you'll be like José Canseco, and then you'll be an asshole."

We paired off to practice throwing. As I threw the ball back and forth with a curly-haired man in blue jeans named Chris, I tried to be willing to fail. I experimented with grips, used the backward-then-forward method, and gave up the stiff-armed, forced way of throwing I had always used. After heaving a few over Chris's head and into the woods, I slowly improved. Soon I was throwing the ball with speed, accuracy, and little effort.

My arm was working as a lever, swinging down and back and then forward. And I shut out every distraction. I quieted my doubts and used my
mind like a laser targeting device, guiding the ball to Chris's mitt.

Standing there in the field, playing catch with Chris, I felt as competent
as I had ever felt with a baseball in my hands. I felt the flow. He seemed to
feel it, too.

"Hey, Mike. I'm going to try a curve!" he called.

The ball came in on an arc, curving right into my glove.

"You did it! It really curved!" I shouted.

Then I tried it. It was amazing. For the first time in my life, I could throw
a curve ball, or a fastball, or a slider, at will.

After the throwing clinic we went to the tennis courts to learn hitting.
McKay began by having us select bats. Then he told us to throw them on
the ground before us. With hollow clunks, eighteen bats hit the dirt.

"Now pick it up, feel it," he said. "Run your hand along its finish. Feel
the weight of the bat. Feel how it's balanced. Get to know this bat until it
feels like it's an extension of you. It's not just a dumb piece of wood. It's
like an extension of your consciousness. It's something that can work with
you. Respect it."

All around me, people caressed and shook their bats. Some talked to
their bats. Others swung them through the air. I did the same, trying to feel
its weight, to feel how it responded as an extension of my arm and my
mind.

"The swing involves the power of Earth, fire, wind, and water," McKay
continued. It begins with the batter "grounding" himself in the Earth of
the batter's box. As batters dig in, they establish a relationship with the
Earth. They also begin a ritual that puts them in a state of heightened
consciousness, ready to hit the ball. Using a round bat to hit a baseball
that's going eighty miles per hour obviously requires extraordinary concentration. The trance heightens concentration in a way that makes hitting
possible.

The element of fire is tapped when the hitter "hits from his belly,"
McKay continued, pointing to a spot below his navel. "You use the fire in
your whole body, not just the arms." The element of the air would be
expressed in loud exhaling as we hit the ball. Jimmy Connors does this
every time he hits the tennis ball. "The Chinese call it *kee-ah,*" he said.
"And water symbolizes fluidity. It is all one, fluid movement."

For the next hour we practiced the ritual of batting, paying attention to
Earth, fire, wind, and water. (One of the pagan chants I had learned from
Ayisha—"Earth my body, water my blood, air my breath, and fire my
spirit"—invaded my mind from time to time as I did this.) Working in
teams of two, we hit little foam baseballs—powder puffs with stitches—
against the fences at Omega's tennis courts. With all the grunting and
exhaling that went on, we sounded like eighteen Jimmy Connors hitting
groundstrokes in a championship match. We also became smoother, more
powerful, and more focused hitters.

After these morning drills we answered the call of the conch shell, eating a quick lunch of tofu, sprouts, salad, and broccoli at the Omega cafeteria. I used the time to chat briefly with one of Omega's founders, a woman named Elizabeth Lesser. Lesser began by informing me that she was concerned about my intentions. A *New York Times* reporter had recently visited and wrote an article depicting Omega as a 1960s holdover catering to a rather small segment of the population: self-indulgent liberals with spiritual yearnings. Lesser told me that the *New York Times* reporter "had been a pretty charming guy, too," but that she felt betrayed. "So," she asked bluntly, "where are you coming from on this?"

"I'm not here to trash Omega," I said. "I am here to do something lighthearted. To have fun." But as long as she was speaking bluntly, I added, "The only thing I can see about this place that makes me uncomfortable is it's a pretty elite crowd—all white, all highly educated, all middle or upper class." Indeed, I was starting to think that everyone in the New Age belonged to the same demographic group.

"We do serve a very moneyed group," Lesser allowed. "They are not rich compared with Club Med, but it is a certain upper-middle-class group." Many of them are also professional helpers—social workers, doctors, activists—who are anything but elitists, she added. "They are interested in social change, in making the world a better place. But often those are the same people who need to be healed themselves. They can't be very helpful to others if they are rageful or angry inside. Here they work on it in an environment that is a real community of people who form trusting relationships."

Omega is a place where people explore some of the more painful aspects of life. The institute offers seminars on illness, AIDS, divorce, and the study of death and dying. "These are middle-class people, and you might be cynical about all this, but middle-class pain is real, just as real as any other," said Lesser.

Where did all this pain come from? Lesser believed it came, in part, from the disillusionment that followed the 1950s and '60s. "The baby-boomers were the most well-cared-for generation of children in history. We were so rich. Life was so good. We were supposed to have conquered pain. There was supposed to be no suffering. We didn't see people get born or die. We took the old people out of our communities, and we became very good at emphasizing our individuality. Too good. We destroyed our communities and created very sterile environments."

When the inevitable pain of real life finally visited the baby-boom generation, they became overwhelmed, she suggested. They were not supposed to experience losses or defeats, and when they did, they had no idea how to cope with them. "At the same time, churches and other institutions have declined," said Lesser. "Our lives have contracted into these very limited spheres. Our contacts with each other are very minimal. That's one reason a lot of people come here. They come to find that community that has been lost."

In my case, this would be done through baseball. Mystic baseball promised to be a method—a Zen "Way"—to achieve both inner harmony and outer grace. I imagine this could be done with most any activity—painting, music, writing, work—but baseball had a certain power over me, and many of the others. It stirred both sweet and painful memories that might be used to teach us something about life as play and practice.

I had to hurry from my lunch with Lesser to get a ride in the caravan that would take us all to Rhinebeck High School's playing fields. We were to try the ideas and techniques we had learned that morning in real, nine-inning games.

At the high school we quickly divided ourselves into four teams. It was a sticky, windless, ninety-degree afternoon, and as I waited for the teams to be organized, I felt as though the sun was pushing me down, into the ground. In the harsh glare my confidence began to wane.

Fielding practice only made me feel worse. Taking my position at second base, I promptly called for a pop-up that was coming down about twenty feet behind me. I might as well act like I know what I'm doing, I thought.

I back-pedaled confidently, watching the ball as I moved. Then I made my big mistake. I put my glove up. It blocked the ball from view.

Panic. A hard, heavy object was hurtling toward me like a satellite crashing out of orbit. But all I could see was the sun. I moved my glove down.

There it was, about ten feet above my head. I raised my gloved hand again, to defend myself. I felt the ball slam into the pocket and, for a moment, I hoped that I had caught it.

But there was no reassuring weight in my glove. The ball had disappeared. I whirled to look for it, but I was half-blinded by the sun. By the time my eyes adjusted, the right fielder was picking it up.

I waited for the groans, the complaints, the recriminations. After all, I had called for the ball. It was probably the right fielder's play. Who did I think I was?

"Nice hustle back there, Mike!" shouted McKay, who was over at the bench.

"Hey, good try," said the right fielder. "But I can help you with those. They get lost in the sun."

There would be no criticisms. At first I thought this was a pose, that I was being patronized. But it wasn't so. These New Age ball players reassured every infielder who lost a ground ball and every batter who struck out. They also whooped their approval for the occasional spectacular play. They were sincere.

When the game finally started, I knew that everyone—both my teammates and our opponents—was hoping I would play well. And I did, sort of. Sure, a few ground balls got by me, and my throws were shaky. But in one inning, three batters hit the ball to second base and I made all three plays. It felt wonderful. I had done something as well as I could do it. It's a feeling we don't often get in real life. I remembered it from my sandlot days. I was ten years old again.

I wasn't the only one. Between innings Will, the gray-haired church leaguer from Memphis, told me he was feeling like a kid again, and it didn't feel good.

"God, I'm in first grade again and everyone knows what they're doing but me," he said. He mopped his face with a towel and swallowed three cups of water. "I've been very interested in the warrior archetype," he said. "It's something we all need, especially men."

(Mythological archetypes—warrior, wise man, crone, maiden, king, and queen—are at the core of widely popular books by Joseph Campbell and the poet Robert Bly. Author of a series of books on myth, Campbell became a household name in the late 1980s via TV interviews with writer/broadcaster Bill Moyers. Building on the theories of psychiatrist C. G. Jung, Campbell argued that mythological archetypes lie within all of us, supplying subconscious inspiration, motivation, and blueprints for behavior. Robert Bly turned Campbell and Jung into poetry and prose about the modern male. He also led so-called "Gatherings of Men," weekend-long meetings at which men explored the archetypes through dance, songs, storytelling, and conversation. These gatherings are part of a growing "men's movement" that is reevaluating the male role in the family and larger society. Bly argues that the Industrial Revolution took men out of the home and destroyed their relationships with daughters and sons. He advocates a stronger male presence in family life and encourages men to be mentors and better friends to one another. Moyers's programs with Campbell and later with Bly kindled such widespread interest in mythology, especially among New Agers, that Will would assume that our conversation about "the warrior within" required no preliminary explanations.)

"What I'm really stuck on," Will continued, "is the fact that the warrior is so skilled. You don't just feel the warrior in you and have it. No, you have to have the warrior's skills, and right now I don't."

In a baseball sense, Will was right. So far, he was no-hit and no-field. But when it came to confronting the pain of his past, he was a very skilled warrior indeed. Middle-aged and out of shape, he nevertheless took to the field doggedly, exposing himself to potential embarrassment, ridicule, and disappointment. Each time that it failed to materialize, the burden of his past grew lighter.

Will seemed like a warrior to me. He was just so mired in self-criticism, he didn't know it yet.

As we chatted, a remarkable display of both talent and errors unfolded on the field. Slow grounders trickled between infielders feet, and outfielders misjudged fluttering pop-ups. But some of the batters hit Lee's pitches solidly, and a center fielder made a series of three running catches. Top-notch players shared the diamond with raw beginners, and no one seemed to care. Somehow, the game proceeded smoothly.

It was not a gentle, passionless game. We played hard. We played to win. In the third inning Chris—my catch-mate from the morning—barreled into me at second to break up a double play. The impact catapulted me into right field.

In between the third and fourth innings, I overcame my pride and asked Jeff for some pointers on throwing the ball. This was more difficult than it might seem. There I was, a thirty-five-year-old man, asking another man to teach me something little boys are supposed to learn by the time they are six years old. But McKay answered me as a teacher, not a competitive male rival. He again reviewed for me the backward-then-forward motion, and he patiently tossed the ball back and forth with me while I worked the kinks out of my motion. When I went back onto the field, I was able to scoop up a grounder and throw the ball to first base with new confidence. But more important, I had asked another man for help and he had responded with kindness and respect. This is the kind of man-to-man exchange Robert Bly and other leaders of the men's movement mean when they talk about new, positive ways for men to relate to one another.

My team lost by one or two runs. I didn't pay close attention to the score. No one else seemed to, either. But I had noticed the "flow." I had narrowed my focus, shutting out all distractions until all I could see was the ball as it left the pitcher's hand, met the bat, and skidded across the grass to my position. Time had seemed to stand still, and my reactions were quicker, surer.

I think others had the same sorts of experiences that day. I know that as a group, we had created an atmosphere that was free of criticism and recrimination. For a few moments, most of us had felt the bliss of being fully immersed in the game, concerned only with what was going on between the foul lines. It was mystic baseball.

WINNING AND LOSING

By Bob Cousy with John Devaney

It was April 1963. I had just arrived in Los Angeles with the Boston Celtics for the final game of the National Basketball Association championship playoffs. After thirteen years with the Celtics this would be my last game.

I walked into my hotel room and locked the door. For the next thirty-six hours I stayed inside that locked room alone. I ordered all my meals sent up. I talked to no one. I didn't answer the telephone. I thought so long and so intensely about Frank Selvy, the Laker guard I would be playing against, that if he had walked into that room I might have leaped at his throat and tried to strangle him. If anyone had touched me or even talked to me, I might have tried to kill him. Or, more likely, I would have broken down and wept.

The next day I ran onto the court to play for that championship with my insides as taut as violin strings, my throat too tight for speaking. Yet outwardly I appeared to be calm, almost daydreamy. My body was under rein, ready to function.

This state—controlled on the outside, emotions erupting inside me—was my most important asset as a competitor. I could be like that, I believed, because I inherited two contrasting personalities. My father was as low-keyed and complacent as you can get. My mother is an emotional, very high-strung person. My father gave me self-control in time of stress; my mother, the overdrive to succeed whatever the cost.

I think you will find this dual personality in many successful people in any competitive profession. The obvious prerequisite for success in competition is an abundance of talent. But as you rise to higher levels you compete against other people who are equally talented. Then you need intensity, a killer instinct that impels you to keep going the extra mile to reach a goal when others slow down or stop.

On a basketball court I had that instinct. I would climb over anyone or anything to succeed, whatever the cost to me or anyone else. Some years ago I was playing in an ordinary three-on-three half-court game at my basketball camp for boys in New hampshire. One of the players was a boy from Colgate named Duffy, who worked for me as a counselor at the camp. Everyone liked him—he was a decent, nice young man.

Well, we were banging around under the hoop and he made contact with me. I went wild. I flung an elbow into his face. He fell to the ground but he still had a grip on the ball. As if I hadn't done enough, I went right after him and stole the ball. And while I was jerking the ball away, I kicked him in the face—not intentionally, but not accidentally, either. Blood poured from a cut above his eye.

I didn't even stop playing. Someone else took the kid's place while I went on doing my thing out there, playing better now because of the anger he had aroused.

As soon as the game ended, what I hope is my basic nature came to the fore. I felt terrible. I went to the infirmary and spent about an hour with Duffy, telling him how badly I felt.

Yet I knew I would do the same thing again in the heat of competition. In fact, even during meaningless regular-season games I hoped that someone would knock me down, because I played better when I was angry. I believe that if I had never had this killer instinct, this inner drive to keep going when others slowed down, I would have been just another of those six-foot guards who wander briefly into the NBA and then disappear without a trace.

We won that game against the Lakers for the National Basketball Association championship, the fifth in a row for the Boston Celtics. After that game I retired. I was thirty-five and I could have played for another year or two. But I had always wanted to retire when the Celtics and I were on top.

I was well prepared to leave basketball. I had signed contracts with three companies to do public relations and sales work. I was the partner in an insurance company in Worcester, Massachusetts, where I lived with my wife, Missie, and our two daughters. I had come to Worcester eighteen years earlier, as a freshman at Holy Cross, and had lived there ever since.

But I didn't want to leave basketball. For one thing, it's only natural to love something you do well. And I had learned from working at my camp that I enjoyed teaching the game to young players. There was more to it than that, though. Looking back, I realize that I was reluctant to give up competition. I had honed my life to a competitive edge, and now, if I couldn't compete myself, I could at least compete through the team I coached.

So when Boston College offered me the position of basketball coach, I thought: *Exactly what I want to do.* The job would keep my hand in the game yet would last only from September to March, leaving me time for my other commitments. And I would be close to home. BC's campus at Chestnut Hill is only an hour's drive from Worcester.

Like many men dedicated to a career, I had been able to give little time to being a family man. From the day I came out of college, I had been wrapped up in my career: traveling with the Celtics during the season, keeping myself prepared physically and mentally, doing all the things that seem to be required of sports celebrities. I had not had the hours to devote to my wife and daughters, who were by this time almost teenagers. Now I thought I could be home with them more often without leaving basketball altogether.

As a coach I had high hopes that the Cousy name would attract the kind of player I wanted—poor and as hungry to succeed as I had been. I grew up in a poor neighborhood on New York's East Side and moved to Queens when I was twelve. There I played schoolyard basketball on the twin principles that you gave it back "in spades" to anybody who gave it to you and that every loose ball was mine.

In my years at BC we tried to develop that kind of player. These young men received a basketball education and a good college education, as well. And in the process I got an education, too.

I experienced the many pressures that most college coaches (and others in competitive businesses) must cope with. The biggest pressure of all was to win games. Though some of the pressure came from others, much of it I put on myself. But there were other conflicting demands—demands that you be honest with your players, that you live within the rules governing college basketball and that you hold on to your own sense of right and wrong. I learned that there were some situations where my killer instinct conflicted with my need to stay honest. And I came to see for the first time that winning might not always mean success and happiness. I had always assumed that winning *was* success.

MY GREATEST RACE

By Marshall W. "Major" Taylor

I have been asked thousands of questions relative to my career on the bicycle track that range from how I happened to start riding a bicycle to what I considered my hardest race. What was my fastest time for a mile, and how I got the name Major, how I managed to get out of pockets. Since every heat leading up to every final that I figured in during my almost 17 years of racing was desperately fought every inch of the way, because of that color business, it is no easy matter for me to answer that last question. However, my special match race against Jimmie Michaels at the Manhattan Beach track in the summer of 1898 was perhaps my greatest achievement. Incidentally, I believe it was also my most spectacular victory.

As I delved into my records and scrap-books to get data on which to base my answer to that greatest question, I came across a number of entries including the following:—"Major Taylor easily won the championship" and "Major Taylor easily breaks world's records." I might say at this time that the impression that I won my races easily was perhaps due in a great measure to my own peculiar position on my wheel. It was distinct from that of any other rider on the track—in fact, it was my own invention which was made necessary when I adopted extension handle bars for my sprint races. I was a pioneer among the sprint riders to adopt the extension handle bars. Today the extension handle bars and the position I perfected for myself on my racing wheel, are accepted as the standard by bicycle sprinters the world over.

My racing position was made conspicuous because of the absence of any unnecessary motion of the head or body, awkward or otherwise, which was so noticeable in some riders. I reasoned that any unnecessary motions only tended to impede the rider's efforts, whereas, if the same amount of exertion were employed in the only motion necessary, from the hips down, with a light, quick motion of the ankle, it would not only produce a maximum of efficiency, but by constant practice it would produce an easy, graceful celerity of motion that is pleasing to the eye. It would also conserve the rider's energy for the final lap where it is most needed. So carefully had I worked out my racing style that newspaper men in general always conceded that I was the most graceful rider on the track.

But to get back to what I consider was undoubtedly my hardest race. Jimmie Michaels, the famous little Welshman, and myself were in excellent physical trim for this race of races on the historic Manhattan Beach track on a mid-summer afternoon 28 years ago.

We found the three-lap cement track at Manhattan Beach lightning fast on that torrid afternoon, because of the absence of the usual gale which swept the track. In the grandstand and strewn out along the rail that bordered the track was one of the greatest throngs that ever witnessed a sporting event in this country. Newspapers had devoted considerable space to the event because of the spectacular way in which this special match race was brought about. Mr. William A. Brady, of New York, who was manager of James J. Corbett when he was the heavyweight champion boxer of the world, was looking after my interest at the time. His challenges on my behalf fell on deaf ears as regarded the other crack sprinters of the day. The great Eddie (Cannon) Bald refusing to be matched against me on grounds that it would effect him socially. In desperation he assembled the sporting editors of the New York daily papers and requested them to broadcast his willingness to wager $1,000 on a winner-take-all basis, and that I could defeat any one of them in a one-mile paced sprint race. Jimmie Michaels was the only one of the bunch that accepted the defy. It was agreed between Michaels and myself that the prize would go to the rider winning two out of three races from a standing start with pace.

I daresay no bicycle race that was ever conducted in this country received the amount of space in the daily sporting pages that this one did. The outstanding reason for this keen interest was the fact that Michaels was at the moment the King of the paced riders of the world while the experts generally conceded that I held the same position among the sprinters. As a matter of prestige, however, the victory meant far more to me than to my worthy opponent, as the event in which we were to participate was classed as a sprint race even though it was to be paced. Michaels stepped out of his class when he consented to ride a short distance while I did likewise by undertaking to ride behind pace. Michaels through his long experience riding behind pace entered this match race with a decided advantage over me, inasmuch as following pace was an innovation for me at that time.

The inside story of Mr. Brady's anxiety to arrange a match race between myself and the cream of the sprinters of the country, including Eddie Bald, Tom Cooper, Earl Kiser and Arthur Gardiner, widely known as the "big-four," centered about the rough treatment accorded me on the Brooklyn track one week before my race with Jimmie Michaels. I quote the following paragraph from one of the New York papers to explain Mr. Brady's attitude on the race referred to and his determination to match me against those who would have prevented my winning any of the prize money at the Brooklyn event:

"On Saturday last the bicycle racers seemed determined to prevent Major Taylor, the colored youth, from winning any prize money in the Brooklyn track meet. However, Major Taylor was equal to the occasion, wiggled in and out of pockets set for him and won the one-mile handicap event in addition to finishing second in the one-mile national championship event.

"Mr. Brady was indignant at the show of race prejudice against the colored cyclist in the Brooklyn events. He claims that under his handling Major Taylor will develop into a world-beater. He has been riding very fast this season and is now up in fourth place in the percentage table, and only a few points behind the leader. Brady claims that if the rest of the racers give Taylor a fair shake he will win every sprint race in which he starts. 'Unhampered, Major Taylor is the fastest man on the track today. Just think of the great odds he has to ride under and then give a thought to the great number of races he wins year in and year out against the cream of the world. Of course it is humiliating to have a colored boy win over them, but Taylor turns the trick honestly and carefully and in racing parlance there is not a whiter man on the track, he is game to the core, and you never hear him complain or protest about his ill treatment,' said Mr. Brady."

It was due to the observations Mr. Brady made at those races in Brooklyn that he challenged the sprinters to meet me in a match race for $1,000. He told the newspaper men that he had implicit confidence in my ability and that if he had not he would never put up $1,000 on me.

Now to get back to this all important race between Jimmie Michaels and myself on the Manhattan Beach track. The press conceded that the rider who got away in front in our race would have a slight edge on his opponent in the dash for the tape. Again I quote further from the same clipping referred to above:—"But this does not mean to say that he will necessarily win the race which will be the best second and third heat struggle with quintet pacing. It will be a wild rush on the part of the two contestants to locate themselves behind their big pacing machines at the getaway and the same sort of a wild scramble will ensue in the concluding few yards when they leave the protection of their multicycles to sprint for the tape."

"The colored rider gets away very fast and the Welsh boy is not negligent in this respect. The battle between the two will be the first of its kind ever staged in this country, and should prove to be a heartbreaker."

The following article appeared in the New York *Journal* the morning after our race:—Major Taylor a winner. Phenomenal performances in Special Match Race. Major Taylor runs away from Jimmie Michaels and establishes a new World's Record of 1:41 which will, no doubt, stand for years."

"The Welsh Rider was hissed while the Colored Rider was cheered."

Major Taylor, the colored cyclist, met and defeated Jimmie Michaels in the special match race yesterday afternoon at Manhattan Beach. Michaels winning the first heat easily. Major Taylor's pacing quintet going wrong in the final lap. Major Taylor's riding was wonderful both from a racing and a time standpoint, having established a new world's record, which was absolutely phenomenal. For the first time in his racing career Michaels was hissed by the spectators as he passed in front of the grandstand deserted and dejected by Major Taylor's overwhelming victory.

"Immediately after the third heat was finished, and before the time was announced, William A. Brady, who championed the colored boy during the entire season, quickly issued a sweeping challenge to match Taylor against Michaels for any distance up to 100 miles, for from $5,000.00 to $10,000.00 a side. The challenge was received with tumultuous shouts, yelling and continued applause from the large assembly, and the colored rider was lionized when his time was announced.

"Edward Taylore, the French rider, had held the world's competition record of 1.45 for that distance in a contest paced from a standing start. The world's record against time was made by Platt Betts, of England, which was 1.43–3. Michaels broke Edward Taylore's record by four-fifths of a second. Major Taylor wiped out this new mark and tied Betts' record against time. In the second heat Taylor rode on the outside for nearly two and one half laps, it can be easily seen that he rode more than a mile in the time, and shrewd judges who watched the race said that Major Taylor would do even better in his third attempt.

"That he justified this belief goes without saying. After taking up his position on the pole, Taylor jumped away at a hair-raising clip and opened up a gap of 10 lengths. In the first lap of the last heat Michaels never had a 'look-in' after his adversary entered the second lap, as Taylor skimmed along as swiftly as the flight of a swallow, and on the back stretch of the last lap Michaels sat upright and pedalled leisurely to the tape, for he saw it was useless to attempt to catch his speedy rival. The Welsh rider was as pale as a corpse as he jumped from his wheel, he had no excuse to offer for his defeat, for at no time could he keep up with the terrible pace set by Taylor.

"Major Taylor's wonderful performance undoubtedly stamped him as the premier sprinter of the world and judging from the staying qualities that he exhibited in the six-day race, the middle distance championship may yet be his also before the season is over."

After having lost the first heat because of a mishap to my pacing machine, I went to the tape for the second heat fairly bubbling over with confidence that I could take my opponent's measure this time, providing my pacing machine gave me no further trouble. I felt this way even after Michaels had again won the toss for the pole position which gave him the advantage.

After two or three false attempts to get away, due to the snapping of chains on our pacing machines, which was caused by over anxiety on the part of our pacemakers, we finally got off to a perfect start.

I will now relate the most amazing part of this widely advertised match race which the press did not get, and which is told here for the first time.

I was always credited with being the fastest man in the world, off the mark, among the sprinters, while my opponent enjoyed the same distinction among the paced riders. Michaels, having won the favored position on the pole in this heat, the second, experienced little difficulty in getting away first, well in the lead, but my pacers dashed after them with a vengeance. As we turned into the back stretch they were confident that I could hang on to them regardless of their speed and with this thought in their minds they tore down the back stretch and around the turn at a rate of speed that must have given the crowd a rare thrill.

After the most furious efforts ever seen in pace-racing, we succeeded in closing the big gap gained by Michaels at the getaway. We were on even terms crossing tape at the end of the first torrid lap, when fresh teams picked us up with desperate though marvelous accuracy, because in changing pace from one machine to another the slightest possible miscue means certain defeat. Michaels and I were both struggling for dear life to hold on to our big machines as the pace was waxing hotter and hotter with every turn of the pedals. Being obliged to fight around on the outside of the track for the entire distance, the heart-breaking speed was now beginning to have its effect on me.

Immediately after I had changed over to my fastest pacing team steered by Austin Crooks with Allie Newhouse coaching on the rear seat, this team having been held in reserve to cover that last feverish lap, I felt my strength ebbing very fast. It was just as I was turning into the last lap and despite my utmost effort the rear wheel of my big quintet was getting away from me, inch by inch. My pacemakers were straining every muscle and fiber in their well-trained legs and were pedalling with perfect rhythm, apparently satisfied that I could take all the speed that they could give me. At this tense moment when we were in the back stretch of the last lap, Michaels was slightly ahead, although our elbows were almost touching, and we were racing neck and neck.

Our coachers on the rear seats of the big pacing machines were shrieking frantically, "C'mon, C'mon." It now seemed only a question of which of us would be shaken off first, and it really seemed that it would be me, for at this point in the race I was more than a yard off the rear wheel of my quintet after having failed in my last super-effort to regain it. In another fraction of a second I would have been defeated and badly crushed, but at this point the unexpected happened.

Michaels, who was now leading by more than two yards, could withstand the great strain no longer. He yelled frantically to his coach, "Steady, Steady" which was synonymous for "Slow, Slow." When I heard Michaels' cry "Steady, Steady" to his pacemakers I could scarcely believe my ears. That proved to be the psychological turning point of that race, the one I now consider my greatest achievement.

Michaels' urgent plea of "Steady, Steady" sounded his death knell and simultaneously inspired me to my supreme efforts which were shortly culminated by a remarkable victory. Up to the moment that I heard Michaels direct his pacemakers to slacken their speed I felt certain he would defeat me. I was absolutely burned out.

Just how I ever managed to kick up to the rear wheel of my pacing machine will always remain a mystery to me, but in a flash I got it and was yelling like mad, "Go, Go," and go they did, with every ounce of energy they had left in them. They were delighted to hear me call for a faster pace and on they dashed as we rounded into the home stretch. It was a glorious sensation to see victory now within my grasp, when only a few seconds before inevitable defeat stared me in the face. As we made for the finishing line I was even bold enough to jump from the rear of my pacing machine and beat it across the tape, breaking the record established by Michaels in the preceding heat, and leading him over the line by 200 feet.

Both my pacing-team and that of Michaels were pedalling desperately in that heat for supremacy of speed and low score. For that reason Michaels' pacers disregarded his distressful cry of "Steady, Steady"—their one thought being to lead my boys over the finishing line. This they did but only because my pacers had to fight hard all the way around on the outside of the track. However, it gave my pacing quintet no little satisfaction to know that they had finished the race with me hanging onto them while the rival quintet had left their star away back on the track.

I never heard such applause as that which greeted me when I dismounted and started for my dressing room. I was pretty well "baked," and nearly dropped twice, but the cheers of the crowd did much to revive and stimulate me and by the time I reached my cot I was in pretty good condition. At this point I resorted to some strategy which I always regarded as one of my best cards. It was in effect to have the third and final heat of the race run off as quickly as possible. I always felt that since I was in such perfect physical condition throughout the racing year that I could recuperate more quickly after a gruelling race than any of my competitors. Therefore, my anxiety was to get Michaels out for the final heat at the earliest possible moment. Mr. Brady, my manager, saw to it that we were called out again in short order. Excitement was at a high pitch as Michaels and I took up our positions to start the final heat. Interest in this final sprint for the $1,000 prize, was at fever heat since each of us had won a heat with a record attached to each whirl around the track. I have seen enthusiastic gatherings at bicycle race tracks all over the country but I never saw one more on edge than the assembly that witnessed the final heat in this great race with Michaels. Incidentally thousands of dollars were waged on the outcome with the odds being two to one on me.

I noticed that as Michaels came to the tape for the final test his face was colorless. His countenance plainly showed that he had been through a trying ordeal in the last heat. When I won the toss for the pole position Michaels seemed to grow even paler. That position gave me a slight advantage such as he had over me in the other two heats. As he stood over on the track it was apparent that Michaels realized that all the breaks were in my favor, and he seemed especially conscious of the bad defeat he had received in the last heat. The mental suffering and physical strain under which Michaels was laboring at the moment seemed to bewilder him. I felt I had him beaten even before the race started.

I jumped to the front at the crack of the gun, taking the lead by 10 or 12 wheel lengths, which I steadily increased as the race continued. The pace in this heat was terrific and I could tell from the outset that we were travelling in record time. Still it did not seem to have the same strenuous effect on me that I had experienced in the second heat and several times I called for more pace.

After the start I did not see my opponent again until the race was concluded. Michaels quit somewhere on the last lap, and for the first time in his life he was roundly hissed as he rode past the grand stand. I felt sorry for him, because Michaels was the best man in the world at middle-distance racing. But he had made the mistake of his life by going out of his class just as I did sometime later when he defeated me in the 20-mile paced race which was his favorite distance. As I made my way to the dressing room it dawned upon me, as never before, that the public is always with the winner, regardless of color.

It was a well-known fact among trainers, managers, riders and newspaper men that Jimmie Michaels was practically unbeatable as long as he could maintain the lead. However, it was agreed among them that if for any reason he lost the front position he was at that moment a beaten man. In a word he could not fight an up-hill battle to win a race. I knew this before we started that epoch-making race referred to above.

As a result of this extraordinary match race with Jimmie Michaels I gained a distinction that never befell the lot of any other racing cyclist in the world, and created a precedent in bicycle racing that has never been equalled, let alone excelled in the history of any athletic sport as far as I have been able to learn.

In all three heats the world's record for the one-mile competition, standing start, 1.45, which was established by Edward Taylore, the famous French rider, was broken. In the first heat Michaels turned the trick in 1:44–1; in the second heat I set the new mark at 1:43–3, and in the final heat I lowered that mark to 1:41–2, a world's record which has not been bettered in the 29 intervening years. Incidentally in the second heat I set up a mark of 1:43–3 equalling the world's record established by Platt Betts in a mile race with a flying start behind human pace several years before. In the final heat I not only lowered the world's record for the standing start competition to its present figure, 1:41–2, but I also shaved 2:1–5 from Betts' world's record. Therefore, I had the honor of having tied the world's record and beating it in successive heats.

So highly elated was Mr. Brady, my manager, that he made me a present of $1,000 for defeating Michaels. Of course, I was delighted with such a material token of his appreciation for my efforts, or as he so generously put it, "Just a little present from one good sport to another."

Deeply mindful of the important part played by my pacemakers leading up to my victory over Michaels, I decided to split Mr. Brady's thousand dollars with them. At first they were reluctant to do this claiming that they were amply repaid for their efforts by the sincere thanks that I had bestowed upon them as soon as we had entered our dressing room. They also took no little pride in the fact that in that furious second heat they were able to furnish me speed and more speed when I really needed it in my mad dash for the tape and victory. Nevertheless, I insisted and Mr. Brady's generous gift was split among them.

Incidentally, no man was ever more grateful to a group of coworkers than I was to those pacemakers who served me so loyally and well in my defeat of the great Jimmie Michaels. Had any one of them so desired he could have brought about my defeat absolutely without one of his team mates even suspecting a plot. I will always be grateful to my pacemakers on that occasion as they played no small part in what is considered the greatest paced race in the history of the sport in this country.

All of my pacemakers in my race against Michaels were white while I was black, but color evidently was neither a burden, handicap or drawback in this instance. Those fine sportsmen, who paced me in that epoch-making race against Michaels, admired me as an athlete, respected me as a man, and gave their utmost in as trying a race as has ever been ridden, that I might achieve victory over the remarkable Jimmie Michaels.

The following paragraph is quoted from a New York newspaper:

"Major Taylor's victory over Jimmie Michaels, coming as it did just after the unsuccessful efforts of certain race meet managers to debar him from their tracks on account of his color, and for no other reason, has established fortune for him. Now the colored boy's services will have to be sought after by the race track promoters as he is among the very best, if not the very best drawing card among the racing men of the country.

"In view of his newly acquired standing, Major Taylor will doubtless know how to deal with those who have sought to retard his progress and injure his prospects as a National Circuit rider. As for those circuit riders who have heretofore given Taylor the cold shoulder, and sought by unfair and unsportsmanlike methods to compass his defeat in past races, they will now do well if they entertain the slightest hope of defeating or making a creditable showing against this new star, to get a match with him without delay. Their mere suggestions in arranging a match with the colored boy will bring most of them greater prestige than they have ever enjoyed in their careers, while to defeat Major Taylor would make them famous."

THREE CUSHIONS
By Robert Byrne

Bums play pool, gentlemen play billiards. It was as true fifty years ago as it is today. Walk in any room that has both pool and billiard tables and look at the difference between the players. All of the jerks, drifters, bums, hoodlums, loudmouths, and pimps will be playing pool. The guys playing billiards will be a different sort entirely, doctors and dentists, businessmen, professional people, serious-minded types. Sure, you can find college professors playing pool and cornholers playing billiards, but I am talking about the average. Why is this? The way I figure it, billiards is a tougher game . . . you have to be a good pool player to even think about playing billiards, so only those with some staying power get from one game to the other. And there is something about the games themselves that sorts people out. Pool is so obvious. Just knock the fucking ball in the hole—any idiot can see it. But in three-cushion billiards, where there are no holes, where you have to map out inside your skull the path the balls have to take around the table . . . well, there you have something that takes some brains. You can study three-cushion for a lifetime and learn tricks and variations right up to the end. I've been studying it for fifty years, and I've learned probably fifty new shots in the last five years alone.

Bums play pool, gentlemen play billiards. I noticed it the minute I lit in Chicago. The pool tables were either in the back of the room, or in the basement, so that the pool players wouldn't bother the billiard players. If you walked in a joint needing a shave, they would escort you right to the back, where the rest of the bums were. There was always a sign over the pool tables: "No loud talking. No swearing. No gambling. No massé shots." When one of the players missed a massé shot for some money, he might holler, "Goddam sonofabitching motherfucker!" and the house man would shout, "Shuddup, you stupid cocksucker! Can't you read?"

They didn't need signs like that for the billiard players, because they weren't the type of people who hollered and cussed; they were allowed to shoot massé shots because they knew what they were doing.

I was a no-good, useless, drunken bum, but I wanted to be a gentleman.

The only way open to me was to take up billiards. I didn't think of it that way at the time . . . Christ, I didn't think much about anything. I was just trying to get through each day as best I could. All I knew was that there was something *important* about billiards, something high class. All the billiard players seemed to have made something of themselves. Playing billiards was like belonging to a private club. Willie Hoppe, Welker Cochran, Jake Schaefer, they were players famous all over the world and they played billiards, not pool. When they saw a pool table they got sick to their stomachs.

When I arrived on the scene, straight billiards—where all you have to do to score a point is make the cueball hit the two other balls—was already in limbo. Jake Schaefer's father had killed it as a spectator sport. That old codger would get the balls trapped against the rail or in a corner and run thousands of points. The only way to stop him from scoring was hit him on the head with a club. When the game was over the ushers would have to slap the spectators in the faces to wake them up.

Something had to be done to make the game tougher. One of the ideas was to make the player hit a rail before hitting the second object ball, or hit the red ball first. Another idea was balkline, where they divided the table up with chalk lines. You couldn't make more than one or two points of straight billiards in any area without driving at least one of the balls into a different area. Things settled down finally to 18.2 balkline, where the lines are drawn eighteen inches from the rails, and you are allowed two points before you have to drive a ball out.

The record book shows that the first big balkline tournament was held in 1903 in Paris. Maurice Vigneaux, a frog, was the winner. I never saw the guy, but I know they called him The Lion because he had a big head of hair. He was the one Hoppe beat in 1906 to win the world title at the age of eighteen. It was a sensation at the time—front-page news, not sports-page news—and from then on you always had to pay money to see Hoppe play.

The first balkline tournament I saw was held in 1921 in the Grand Ballroom of the Congress Hotel in Chicago and was considered a very important event for the whole town. The *Chicago Daily News,* the *Herald Examiner,* the *Tribune,* those papers wrote it up as if the Prince of Wales was playing polo on Michigan Boulevard. The spectators had to be very well dressed to get in, and the players wore tuxedos. No kids allowed. No screaming meemies in mothers' arms. The room was plush, with big chandeliers, private boxes all around at the balcony level, a brass rail between the audience and the arena, gold drapes. Just one table. That shit about having more than one table at a time got started much later. I can remember looking up at the ladies in the boxes, watching the game through opera glasses, and wondering if they knew what the hell was going on. Everything was so lavish . . . God, they did things up big then. They packed the people in . . . for an attraction that wouldn't draw flies today. Of course, billiards was a very big sport. In the Loop, at that time, there were at least five hundred billiard tables, and in the middle of the afternoon every one was busy.

The same thing killed balkline that killed straight rail: the players got so good they were boring to watch for the general public. They kept the balls in a little cluster and made cozy shots about an inch long that you couldn't see unless you were kneeling on the table. When a ball had to be driven to the other end of the table, it always came to the cluster as if it was tied to a long rubber band. If Hoppe or Cochran or Schaefer got the balls straddling a chalk line they kept making points until somebody turned out the lights or sprayed them with a hose. Cochran made one run of 684. To wake the audience up after that they had to shoot off a cannon.

Three-cushion—where the cueball has to hit at least three rails and one ball, in any order, before it hits the second ball—is a better spectator sport so it has stayed alive. In three-cushion the shots are big—even the spectators in the cheap seats can see them. Sometimes in order to score you have to drive the cueball forty feet, or twice around the table. The game is so tough it is impossible to really master it. If you make a run of fifteen points in a row you get a standing ovation.

At Bensinger's in Chicago, the billiard tables were on one floor and the pool tables on another. The elevator was an open wrought-iron cage, and I could see the billiard games as I rode up to join the hoodlums on the next floor. After getting hoisted through that billiard atmosphere a thousand times, I decided to get off and see what it was all about. I have never been the same since.

When I stepped off the elevator a broad was right there to take my coat. Thank God I was well dressed that day. She led me to a table covered with beautiful new green cloth . . . Number One Simonis from Belgium, naturally. The best. She spilled out the three balls—clear heart ivory from Zanzibar. Lately we have been running out of elephants, so most billiards today is played with plastic balls, which is not too bad, but nothing like good ivory. The sound ivory balls make when they click together, the way they hesitate before the English takes, the way they hold the spin off the third rail—you just can't beat it. The girl asked me what weight cue I wanted, and when I told her twenty ounces with a twelve-millimeter tip she brought me one that was a dream—two-piece bird's-eye maple, brass joint, inlaid butt, ivory ferrule. I wanted somebody to play with, so she put up a little sign next to the table that said "Three-cushion player wanted." In other words, she treated me as if I *was* somebody, somebody special, when, as I said, I was nothing but a no-good, useless, drunken fucking bum.

It was quiet as a library in that billiard room. All you could hear was the clicking of the ivory and the bump of the balls against the rubber. If you shouted or swore they were liable to bar you for life. Even if you coughed a little they might ask you to step outside till you got control of yourself. Nothing was allowed that might be the least bit distracting. It almost makes me cry to remember the respect they used to have for billiard players.

A fellow showed up to play me. He was probably a corporation lawyer or a Superior Court judge, for all I know. At least a bail bondsman. He tried to get me to play for a little something, but I ducked that. He beat me without any trouble, but I enjoyed it, enjoyed the atmosphere. When you get beat at something and enjoy it, you've got to like it.

What makes three-cushion a great game is that every move you make is half offense and half defense. Like chess. I don't play chess myself, but that is what chess players tell me. When you study a three-cushion shot you have to estimate the odds of making it, the odds of leaving your opponent a tough shot if you miss, or yourself an easy one if you score. There are damned few really easy shots, but some are easier than others. If you can score one point an inning, on the average—one point each time you get a turn at the table—you are in the world-championship class. In rack pool the top players average about fifteen points an inning, in balkline about thirty-five.

The shots in three-cushion are so tough it is a pleasure when you make one. And it is a pleasure to watch the cueball do what you want it to do—slow down, speed up, curve. When you know what you are doing you can make that cueball act as if it had a mind of its own.

After that afternoon in Bensinger's, I was hooked, and I played three-cushion almost every day from then on. I was hungry for knowledge, and I drove some of the older players nuts with questions. It wasn't long before I was making people sit up and take notice. In 1924 something happened that sealed my fate as billiard bum for life: I won the Chicago Junior Amateur Tournament. There were twenty-four players in it, some of them very good, but all of them fairly young and green. We played twenty-five points of three-cushion in a different place every night—Rogers Park, Evanston, Arlington, all over. My record was 23–1, and for a while there I was the toast of the town. Well, housewives weren't hoisting glasses to me, but I was big in the Loop poolrooms. Up-and-coming young player, and all that.

I was introduced to Willie Hoppe and I almost pissed my pants. You can't believe what an honor it was to shake his hand—it was like meeting Babe Ruth. The fans wanted to see how I would do against various people, so some matches were arranged. I played Alfredo De Oro, who already was pretty old, maybe sixty, and got beat, but I dumped Leon Magnus, who was so old he shook like a leaf. Magnus had won the first three-cushion tournament ever held—in 1878. I'll bet I'm the only guy that has played him, the first champ, and Ceulemans, the current one. In fact, I've played almost all the champs in between, too.

Augie Kieckhefer set up a match for me against Johnny Layton, who was the reigning three-cushion king at the time. He went right through me, but he was a hell of a nice guy and I didn't mind too much. Not on the outside, anyway. Underneath, I promised myself I would learn how he made it look so easy, and why it was when I stepped to the table I never seemed to have anything to shoot at.

A fellow by the name of Dick Adams took me under his wing and was a big help to me. He ran a billiard room on 63rd between University and Woodlawn. According to him I had a perfect billiard stroke and could go all the way to the top if I would quit drinking and learn to control my speed and how to lock up my short-angle shots. What I had to do, he said, was play balkline, and play it, play it, play it. So we played, he and I did, at his place every morning for a year. Every morning it was 200 points of 18.2, and I hated it. It was too small a game for me; I wanted to let my stroke out and see those balls *move*. Adams taught me the massé, the dead-ball draw, how to kill the speed of the cueball with reverse English off the rail, how to spread the balls so the next shot brought them back together, a hundred things like that. There is no question that learning balkline helped me. There's nothing like it for short shots, speed, and position. Every three-cushion player should practice balkline once in a while. I tell all my students to do it, but few of them do. I can tell by the way they look at me what they are thinking. They are thinking: "What the fuck does that old fart know about it?"

Next time the Junior Amateur came around, in 1925, I was barred. I *gambled,* the other players said. I hung around with people like Bad Eye and Scarface Foreaker and The Eagle, they said. I was not the clean-cut type of youngster the amateur billiard program was designed to promote, or some such shit, they said. The other players just wanted me out, that's all. I was plenty clean-cut enough when they thought they could beat me. So I learned another important lesson: The better you get the bigger prick you become. You don't really change, but you do in the eyes of your competitors. Everybody loves you as long as they can beat your brains out.

Sure, I hung around with Bad Eye and Scarface. I had to win a match with Scarface, in fact, to get that game with Layton. I've heard people whisper about Scarface, but he is a perfectly fine guy in my book. Last time I saw him was in Sacramento, California. He was running down a sidewalk, going so fast his raincoat was standing straight out behind him. I didn't find out what he had done because I couldn't catch him. All I know is that he was getting *lost.*

The best three-cushion players in the world were concentrated in Chicago during the 1920's, and I watched them whenever I could. It was in 1923 that the Interstate League started, which really put three-cushion on the map and killed balkline. The Interstate League started out with about a dozen players, each one sponsored by a room in a different town. Every guy had to play every other guy two matches, one at home and one away . . . a double round robin for the championship of the world. They charged $1.10 for front-row seats at the matches, and the rooms were always packed to the rafters. My God, the players . . . the players were the best in the world: Johnny Layton out of Sedalia, Missouri, Tiff Denton playing for Kling and Allen in Kansas City, Augie Kieckhefer representing himself, Bob Cannafax out of Detroit, Gus Copulus playing for the Euclid Arcade in Cleveland, Otto Reiselt for Allinger's in Philadelphia—that gives you an idea of the caliber of play. Hoppe, Cochran, and Schaefer weren't in it. They were opposed to three-cushion. They had balkline locked up—nobody could come close to them—so they fought against three-cushion and didn't take it up until balkline died completely in the 1930's.

There were always at least two of the league players in Chicago, and they kept an open game going in the back room of Kieckhefer's most of the day. Seven points for two dollars. Anybody could play, but you got no spot. There were no spectators allowed . . . this was strictly a players' game. I got in and played with them every chance I could, and it was like going through a meat grinder. If there were, say, six players in the game, you never got more than two or three shots. Somebody would run seven and out, or a four and a three. For a year and a half I played, and one day I broke even. Broke even! I went right out and got drunk, I was so happy.

But it was the best training I could have got. If I became some kind of half-ass billiard player, I owe it to playing in those pot games. It cost me at least ten bucks a day, but it was priceless experience. Cheaper than taking lessons. They didn't mind me, so long as I brought my money and didn't ask for a spot. If I had asked for a spot, they would have said, "Don't let the door hit you in the ass." When they had picked me clean I would race out to Dick Adams's joint and set up shots I had seen played, particularly by Reiselt, who was terrific, and I would talk them over with Dick. "Why did he play it off the white instead of the red? Why did he elevate his cue a little? Why did he bank for this one instead of going cross table? Why did he slow the ball down?" Between the two of us we would figure out the answers. To beat a kiss. To drop the red into the opposite corner. To leave a tough shot. To drive a ball five rails for position.

I didn't quit playing pool entirely, because I had to hustle pool here and there to make a living between jobs, but three-cushion was what I enjoyed doing most. Besides, it is a big help to a hustler to know all games. After beating a guy in rotation it is nice to have him propose a little game of billiards for higher stakes.

I used to make swings through Indiana and Ohio, hustling both pool and billiards, whichever presented itself. One night I was lining up a shot, looking down my cue toward the front door, when I saw a police car pull up in front of the joint. The house man said to me, "Look, kid, I'm going to do you a favor. I called the cops on you. How am I going to make any money off my customers if you get it all? Now beat it out the back way."

He had a point, and I thanked him as I disappeared.

It is much nicer to hustle three-cushion instead of pool, because you rob a more refined type of person. In three-cushion, the worst that can happen is to have the guy ask you if you will take a check. But you beat a guy out of a few bucks in a pool game and he might pick up the cueball and knock your teeth out.

I have never taken a ball in the teeth, but I have taken checks. I was working for Cliquot Club as a salesman. One morning after the daily sales meeting, the pep talk—"Get out there and *sell* . . ." and so on—I ducked into 18 East Randolph Street. It was winter, the air was full of those white flies, the streets were a mess of dirty slush. I wanted to play billiards, I didn't want to get out there and sell. I got a set of balls and was knocking them here and there when a very solid citizen type asked me if I wanted to indulge in a little game.

"Why not?" I said. "I have to wait here until my secretary calls, anyway."

The guy had a big stickpin in his tie with a headlight on it, and another flasher on his ring. "Care to make it interesting?" he said while he chalked his cue.

"Anything you say, pal." I had plenty of money. I was doing well enough hustling so that my commissions from Cliquot Club were going right in the bank.

We decided on ten points for two dollars. After the first few shots I saw that the guy couldn't even *spell* billiards. We played six games and he never got more than five points.

When we quit he went up to the desk and paid the time with a bill he peeled off a roll he could hardly get his fingers around. Then to me he said, "I trust you will accept a check?"

"Holy shit," I said, "you got a roll you couldn't flush down a toilet and you want to give me a check?"

"I assure you the check is good. Furthermore, I enjoyed playing with you and I would like to meet you here next Friday at the same time for another session, and the Friday after that."

Talk about the soft con! But there was something solid about him. I took a chance.

The check was on the LaSalle Trust and Savings at LaSalle and Monroe, where I happened to know a teller by the name of Shorty Hackman. I busted over there through the slush.

"Say, Shorty, how good is this check?"

"Just a minute and I'll tell you if it is any good at all." He looked something up. "The check is good."

"Shorty, how good is it?"

"Danny, my friend, you could sign a long string of zeros on the end of it."

At 9:30 next Friday morning I came out of the sales meeting at Cliquot Club. It was a beautiful day—no slush, no white flies. A good day to call on my accounts and try to work up some new business. But it was the appointed hour, so I ducked into Kieckhefer's. There were fifty-five tables on one floor . . . forty billiards in front and fifteen pockets in the back. At that time of day there was nothing doing but one snooker game way in the corner. I hung around the top of the stairs, and sure enough, here came my opponent through the door. I raced to the back of the room and slumped into a chair and pretended to be watching the snooker game. He looked around, spotted me, walked back to where I was sitting, and tapped me on the shoulder.

"Well, hello!" I said.

"Shall we play?" he said.

We played every Friday for six weeks. He never won a game and his checks never bounced. I could count on twelve bucks a week like clockwork. Plenty of my so-called friends tried to get him away from me, but he wasn't interested. He had taken a liking to me, or some damned thing. I was supposed to be a killer, but I got to feeling a little sorry for this particular guy. One day I showed up half drunk after being out all night. As we were lagging for the break I turned to him and said, "Listen, why don't you smarten up? You won't beat me in a thousand years."

What he said to me made me feel about an inch tall. He said, "I know that, Dan, but don't you think I'm improving?"

A couple of Fridays later he didn't show up. I figured he was sick, and I half expected him to phone in or send a note. When he didn't show the next week either, or the week after, I went over to see Shorty at the bank.

"Hey, what happened to my meal ticket?"

Shorty looked in a few filing cabinets. "Danny, he's moved his account to Boston. He's gone."

"Who the hell was he, anyway?"

"You didn't know? He's the vice president of the Metropolitan Life Insurance Company."

"The vice *president?*"

"That's right. One of the richest legitimate guys in the country. He probably paid you by check so he could deduct you from his income tax or put you on his expense account."

I've often wondered how he handled that, how he accounted for all those "Pay to the order of Danny McGoorty . . . $12.00." Maybe he put me down as a consulting engineer. Or a ballet teacher.

MOONLIGHT CRUISING

By Brandt Aymar

Not all the fun in cruising comes from those long trips to Nantucket, Block Island, Marblehead, or wherever you may head. No, indeed. Not by a long shot. There are weekend cruises to nearby resorts where you sail in upon friends who own castles by the sea, or get-togethers of the U. S. Power Squadron, where beer flows freely and the musical yarns of the sea go round and round. But best of all, by the light of the silvery moon, you streak through the rippleless water with the greatest of ease and a happy group of moonlight sailors in your charge.

This can happen any night in the week, but Friday seems the ideal time, because few, if any, of your guests will go to work on the morrow—most offices being closed Saturdays during the summer. This does away with rushing back to your home port so you and your guests can catch two winks of sleep before the dawn hits as squarely as did the daiquiris of the night before.

On a boat around forty feet long I should call six people an ample complement of moonlight cruisers. Three of each will make it all the more cozy, and at least three semi-private nooks can be found on and around a forty footer—we must take full advantage of a full moon. This, of course, presupposes everybody to be young enough for that sort of thing. But who isn't?

Having invited the five people I want with me for the evening, I ask that they be at the dock between six o'clock and six-thirty, at the latest. At four o'clock I go out and buy the supplies. First comes the question of drinks. Shall it be cocktails? If so, what kind? After running the gantlet of the various kinds of mixed drinks, visualizing how thrilled they'll all be to get frozen daiquiris, I then decide, since I'll have to do all the work of making them, that we'll have plain Manhattans. A dash of vermouth—one part, to be exact, and three parts of rye (I prefer Golden Wedding, a smooth blend of all straight whiskies), and a lot of cracked ice. There you have it without the slightest trouble! In fact, you don't even have to have a cocktail shaker to mix it in—any bowl or cooking pot will do, although it isn't quite as appetizing in appearance. For after dinner, it's a snap to mix rye highballs with water, soda or ginger ale. So first I visit the liquor store and buy one bottle of vermouth and two or three of rye. To hell with the bitters!

Next, off to the grocery store which carries frozen foods and boasts a meat counter as well. For my guests' protein diet, six large, juicy, tender lamb chops will do very well. While the meat cleaver is fixing them up real fancy, I step over to the other side of the store, across the invisible dividing line, and order three cans of consomme madrilene or chicken gumbo, as suits my fancy. A dozen rolls, hard or soft, a half-pound of butter, and perhaps a bottle of Sauce Diable to add an indescribable something to the chops. Then two or three boxes of frozen-food peas or six ears of frozen-food corn on the cob, again as the spirit of Epicurus moves me. A little salad goes well if it isn't too much trouble, so one head of lettuce and three tomatoes, plus a bottle of Monk Dressing, go down on the slip. For after-dinner coffee, a dozen powdered coffee packages join the rest of the para-phernalia (I wouldn't "perc" coffee for any six people in the world, aboard ship). While the butcher is fixing the chops, while the grocer is rounding up the rest, I run over to the baker's and pick up a chocolate devil's food cake. Back again, I find everything ready, pay for it, discover I have forgotten the soda and ginger ale, get them, and presto, I am ready to go ahead for my boat. All this takes just about twenty minutes at the outside. Where, oh where are these housewives who loudly complain that they have to spend their entire lives in the market place?

After it has taken you a good half-hour to reach your yacht club or place of mooring, you row out to your boat just as the village bell tolls five. For half an hour you open your boat, airing it out, tuning up the motor, stowing the essentials in the icebox (especially the cold soup, which requires sev-eral hours to jell), arranging chairs for the guests to sit in, mopping up the effects of the sea gulls who have assumed squatter rights on your boat during the week without having duly charted it, and generally putting your "pride and joy" into immaculate, ship-shape order. At a quarter of six, spotless as an arctic glacier, you bring your boat into the dock. At six your guests arrive to change the whole picture. Well anyway, it once looked like a boat!

Six-thirty sees the last couple running, racing, tripping down the dock and puffing out the usual excuse about just having missed the 5:15 train and having had to wait half an hour for the next. By their breath you can tell they have made very good use of that half-hour and several other half-hours before. But off in a blaze of glorious sunset you go, proud to be at the helm of your ship, with the responsibility of the lives and good time of the five other people planted squarely on your shoulders. You head your boat for a nice, quiet, sheltered harbor, where the forest in all its primeval glory comes down to the water's edge and only nature is within miles of you. The run will consume an hour, possibly an hour and a half. Of course the first thing one of your female guests wants to do is to steer the boat. You acquiesce, giving her a full minute's course on the subject of piloting, which, by the blank expression on the young lady's face, you can tell isn't penetrating even a sixteenth of an inch. Then, noting that no matter which way she runs the boat, there's nothing she can hit, you give up and go below to mix cocktails. Immediately the young lady, as long as she isn't being told how to do it, handles the wheel like a veteran. You can always count on beginner's luck like that. Well, from then on, you are not permitted to touch the wheel once, but everybody else must take his turn. In fact, once having relinquished the wheel, you cease to be anything more than a galley slave and chief steward on your own boat. Even so, you do a bit of 5th-Column snooping every few seconds to make sure nothing is approaching your course and all's safe on the Sound. Once cocktails are made and you're on deck serving them up, you feel a little closer to the vital workings of your ship.

An hour or so later on, approaching the entrance of the harbor in which you plan to anchor, you again take over command of your ship. Your guests are only too glad at this point to relinquish control, since they have seen a buoy or two with land looming up close, and they do not know exactly what to do. Before taking over, you have loosened the anchor from its holdings and cleared the anchor rope. Then picking out the ablest-bodied seaman of your group, you instruct him in the simple art of dropping the anchor overboard when you give the signal. Returning to the wheel you take over just about the time the first channel buoy comes abeam. In a few minutes you are inside and enjoying the excited ohs and ahs of your friends at the beauty of so lovely a place. A dozen times you must explain how you managed to discover such a seaside Shangri-La. In the midst of all this you bring your boat up near the shore at just the spot you want, knowing that there will always be at least four feet of water underneath, but near enough to the shore to swim or even wade in. You call to your anchor man to "heave the anchor over," which he actually does, in spite of all your admonitions to the contrary. (Well, you shouldn't have used a nautical phrase to begin with.) And there you are, safe and sound on the first leg of your moonlight sail. (The moon will be coming up any minute now.)

Once securely at anchor, there's a rush for the cabin, to change into bathing suits and see who can be the first over the side. If there are two fairly private sections to your boat, everyone can don his or her bathing suit at the same time. If not, the winner of a race to reach the cabin, boy or girl, holds the fort for his or her sex. Of course, if chivalry has not died, that's another story. But I'm afraid it has. Anyway it doesn't make a great deal of difference, for a split second is about all the time needed to get out of one's clothes. Soon the whole crowd is sporting around in the water, ducking the ladies, diving under and catching hold of their legs, to the general accompaniment of wild screams of terror and delight. Naturally everyone swims to shore the first thing, just to prove it can be done. A bright idea strikes you. Out comes the pneumatic mattress, it is blown up and heaved into the water. A mad scramble ensues and the bully of the crowd succeeds in making himself master of the castle, until a conspiracy gangs up on him and overthrows the dictatorship of the pneumatic mattress. If the shadows are lengthening in the West and darkness beginning to creep in, get out your lantern with a floodlight attachment, or turn your searchlight on the swimmers. Yours is still the responsibility for their safety. If it is really dark, warn everyone to stay within the range of the floodlight, and see to it that your warning is heeded. I found that even the smartest Alec, who on land would ordinarily thumb his nose at any such advice, will obey your command implicitly, if your voice carries the right tone of indisputable authority, which any good skipper must use on such occasions.

After fifteen to twenty minutes of this romping about, the idea suddenly dawns en masse that a drink is in order. Having foreseen this bit of inevitability, and having cut your swim short by five minutes, you have already prepared another round of Manhattans and set them up in an enticing way on your table. Now is the time to toss your guests towels and let them dry themselves on deck or in the stern before they turn the cabin into a regular Niagara. Like a hungry baby nippling at his first bottle (only this is a different kind of bottle and the babies slightly older), everyone becomes very contented and somewhat quieter and relaxed. With a little introspection they suddenly realize how wonderful it all is to be sipping cocktails on a gently rocking boat in the very heart of all this wild splendor. And to top it all off . . . the moon has come up! Yes, a gorgeous, silvery full moon, shining so clear that the broad grin on the man in the moon's face is as plain as the nose on your own. Wonder what he's grinning about? Is it so hard to guess?

Such silent contentment is but a fleeting fancy when the hour approaches nine and appetites are whetted (and how) to the quick. "Whatta we got for dinner?" a voice ravenous with hunger calls out. And from the galley where you've been working this past number of minutes you call out, "Menu coming right up, Sir!" Once again you are merely a scullion of the galley and at your guests' service. Up you pop and recite the table d'hote for the evening.

Jellied Consomme Madrilene
Spring Lamb Chops au Diable
Fresh Peas au Beurre
Lettuce and Tomato Salad à la Monk
Pan Rolls and Butter
Devil's Food Layer Cake Shrapnel Icing
After-Dinner Coffee

Then back you pop to prepare this pretentious bill of fare. And for all its splendiferous sounding, it's the easiest thing in the world to do. First off, you use only paper plates and cups to avoid the necessity of washing. At your side is a huge brown paper bag in which to dispose of garbage. On the two-burner alcohol stove sits a large frying pan with a high cover that turns it into a broiler. All six chops fit easily into it. Use a small square of butter

if you want to grease the pan, or let the natural fat of the chops do this for
you. On the other burner you are boiling water in which to drop the frozen-
food peas. Don't forget to put in salt when preparing vegetables. While
your two hot dishes are cooking merrily away, minding their own business,
you tend to the business of opening the cold consomme cans. There are
two big portions to each can. You open all three and divide the contents
into six paper cups. Use your own silverware (or a reasonable facsimile
thereof) rather than paper spoons and forks. At this point, if you own some
sort of tray to hold glasses or paper cups, it comes in mighty handy. Slip
the six cups of consomme into the tray, a spoon in each cup, and hand
them to your eager friends. Since the hot dishes require time to cook,
maybe fifteen minutes or so, you can take this opportunity to join the
others and enjoy your cup of soup with them.

Don't be worried when the Madrilenc vanishes as if a hundred hungry
hounds were devouring chopped meat. Tell your guests to take it easy,
because they've got to wait a while for the rest, anyway. Tell them that. It
won't do any good. Soup over, you throw the empty cups directly into the
big brown paper bag. The spoons you collect in the sink half-full of water.
To prepare the Plate du Jour, bring out those three-compartment paper
plates with which your boat ought to be well stocked, and in one of the
compartments make the individual salad. Much the wisest procedure is to
serve everything on individual plates, to avoid the confusion of everyone
getting up and crowding around a central table trying to help himself. A
few leaves of lettuce, three slices of tomato, and a generous dash of Monk
Dressing, and the salad is ready. In the larger partition of each plate put a
lamb chop. Because you've broiled them, these chops will not be brown,
but they'll taste just as good. Browning thick meats by frying is somewhat
difficult on your ship's stove, especially if you've got to cook quite a batch
in a hurry. Just make sure the chops are sufficiently but not too well done.
Inside they should be nice and pink, not broiled to death. After you've put
a chop on each plate, spread with Sauce Diable. Fill the remaining portion
of the plate with peas, and, on top of these, set a good-sized square of
butter. Somewhere on each plate add a buttered roll. This complete operation, the work of but a very few minutes, turns out a really royal spread to
set before the crew. Don't think they won't appreciate it, even marvel at
the apparent ease with which you have so quickly fostered up a feast.
(They can't even cook toast without burning it.)

Since everything has been served at once, you can again enjoy the
luxury of eating your own dinner with your guests. Conversation definitcly
goes overboard at this time, as all with one accord go to it hand and tooth.
If they ask, you'll have to disappoint them on seconds. But just remind
them that when they order a dish at the Ritz, they don't get seconds there
either.

For dessert serve the coffee and cake together. Use small paper dessert
plates and paper coffee cups, the kind which really will hold hot drinks
without the bottom falling out when you're half way through. In case

Shrapnel Icing has you baffled, that's just what's known as Shot or little sprinkles of chocolate on top of the regular chocolate icing. Lots of cakes come this way. Those spoons that have been soaking in water since the first course, dry them off and use them for the coffee. If you know most of your crew prefer sugar and cream in their coffee, use the condensed milk you always keep on board or remember to add fresh cream to your shopping list. Then, as they all finish and lie back contentedly, you collect the dirty plates and throw them all with one fell swoop into the brown bag. Remove the silverware first, of course. As you survey the whole task of cleaning up after the banquet is over, you find you have exactly 6 spoons, 6 forks, 6 knives, one kitchen knife, one frying pan and top, and one pot to be cleaned. All of which adds up to exactly nothing to speak of! Where are those housewives who spend three days in preparation for entertaining six for dinner?

Having noted that I, as skipper of the boat, have done what adds up to approximately 100% of the work, you are justified in lifting your eyebrows at the apparent laxness of my crew. Let me say that every guest I ever had on board was willing and more than willing to do his share. But the crowded confines of the galley, coupled with the time consumed in instructing the newcomer in the whys and whereabouts of utensils, food, pots, pans—not to mention his inability, albeit willingness, to cook the precise dinner you want to serve—make it decidedly impractical to take advantage of his offers to help. You've played the slave so often that the whole routine is more or less mechanical on your part. Of course, if some of your guests happen to be old friends who come out with you often, that's a totally different question. They can relieve you of much of the work. Or if you are married and your wife is as efficient in running the galley as she is in telling you how to run it, you're saved! Let her do all the work, while you bask in your own ego as Captain. Wake up, Skipper. Quit dreaming!

As an antidote to the very undignified gorging to which everyone has abandoned himself for the past hour, there's nothing quite like a cooling highball. Now you can bring out your highball glasses, for no tall drink tastes any good in paper cups. Anyway, each one will be using the same glass for the rest of the evening, and the work of cleaning them later is inconsequential. And now, with everybody's one hand happily around his or her own glass, and the other hand equally happy around what-have-you, the time has come to douse the lights. (Bad for the batteries, you know, to keep up that constant drain of current.)

Bathed in the silvery beams of the moon, the still, silent night has become the nearest thing to a lover's paradise. Only the sounds of softly rippling waters on the sands of the shore, a lone bird calling for his mate, or a light breeze sporting in and out around the tall, bushy trees. How can such wonders fail to bring out the poet in every man? And not only the poet! Pretty soon one couple decides they must explore the bow. (They've been looking at it all evening, what's there to explore?) Another wonders if the top of the cabin is really strong enough to support two. This leaves for the Captain and Mate, whether he wants it or not, the aft cockpit. "Ain't Nature grand!"

Occasionally a male will return to the cabin and replenish two empty highball glasses.

Funny how, on the water, most people show so little the effects of liquor. It's not at all the same as on land.

Funny too how time flies in that quiet haven, halfway to heaven. But there's still an hour's run ahead, and already it's well past midnight. You cautiously hint that maybe it's getting late. If you get any answer you're lucky. Half an hour later you inform the gang that not only is the dawn approaching, but so is a fog, and, if they want to get home at all, they and you had better get under way. To which they answer in no uncertain terms that they don't give a hoot if they *never* get back. And neither do you! That's what makes the situation all the more difficult. At about one-thirty you take a decided stand by turning on all the lights, including shining the searchlight on the bow. THAT brings results! Everyone finally assembles aft. Where's the fog, asks one. There isn't any, say you. That was just a ruse. Didn't work, did it, says he smugly.

On the run home you keep the wheel all the way. Nor do any of your guests feel much like relieving you, for they have all snuggled down in their chairs and are already in the arms of Morpheus. Chances are, too, no one else knows how to pilot well enough to keep on a compass course. Needless to say, before beginning the return trip, you have plotted your course on the chart, converted it to Compass and allowed for any current effects. Also, you have noted just what lights you're going to pass and their individual characteristics. Any ranges which may be of assistance have been duly noted, especially the range which will bring you safely into your own harbor. All these facts you have written on your chart, which you keep in front of you and refer to constantly all the way home. Just between you and your binnacle, night navigating is about the most fun of any phase of cruising. When you pull gracefully up to the old dock at home and land her without a jolt, you've got something. You've not only had the time of your life—and so have all the others—but you've earned the undying respect of your crew for the expert and seamanlike manner in which you have handled your boat. And, just to celebrate, you all drink a last round before everyone, tired but walking on air, wends his way home. If you're wise, this night you'll stay on board. So you cast off and put out for your mooring as the others wave a "thanks for everything" goodbye, and the moon shines down with that same mirthful smile he's had all evening. Perhaps one other stays with you that night, and together you enjoy the solitude of the wee, early hours of the morning. Perhaps even watch the morning sunrise.

A PIECE OF STEAK

By Jack London

With the last morsel of bread Tom King wiped his plate clean of the last particle of flour gravy and chewed the resulting mouthful in a slow and meditative way. When he arose from the table he was oppressed by the feeling that he was distinctly hungry. Yet he alone had eaten. The two children in the other room had been sent early to bed in order that in sleep they might forget they had gone supperless. His wife had touched nothing, and had sat silently and watched him with solicitous eyes. She was a thin, worn woman of the working class, though signs of an earlier prettiness were not wanting in her face. The flour for the gravy she had borrowed from the neighbor across the hall. The last two ha'pennies had gone to buy the bread.

He sat down by the window on a rickety chair that protested under his weight, and quite mechanically he put his pipe in his mouth and dipped into the side pocket of his coat. The absence of any tobacco made him aware of his action and, with a scowl for his forgetfulness, he put the pipe away. His movements were slow, almost hulking, as though he were burdened by the heavy weight of his muscles. He was a solid-bodied, stolid-looking man, and his appearance did not suffer from being overprepossessing. His rough clothes were old and slouchy. The uppers of his shoes were too weak to carry the heavy resoling that was itself of no recent date. And his cotton shirt, a cheap, two-shilling affair, showed a frayed collar and ineradicable paint stains.

But it was Tom King's face that advertised him unmistakably for what he was. It was the face of a typical prizefighter; of one who had put in long years of service in the squared ring and, by that means, developed and emphasized all the marks of the fighting beast. It was distinctly a lowering countenance, and, that no feature of it might escape notice, it was clean-shaven. The lips were shapeless and constituted a mouth harsh to excess, that was like a gash in his face. The jaw was aggressive, brutal, heavy. The eyes, slow of movement and heavy-lidded, were almost expressionless under the shaggy, indrawn brows. Sheer animal that he was, the eyes were the most animal-like feature about him. They were sleepy, lion-like—the eyes of a fighting animal. The forehead slanted quickly back to the hair, which, clipped close, showed every bump of the villainous-looking head. A nose, twice broken and moulded variously by countless blows, and a cauliflower ear, permanently swollen and distorted to twice its size, completed his adornment, while the beard, fresh-shaven as it was, sprouted in the skin and gave the face a blue-black stain.

Altogether, it was the face of a man to be afraid of in a dark alley or lonely place. And yet Tom King was not a criminal, nor had he ever done anything criminal. Outside of brawls, common to his walk of life, he had harmed no one. Nor had he ever been known to pick a quarrel. He was a professional, and all the fighting brutishness of him was reserved for his professional appearances. Outside the ring he was slow-going, easy-natured, and, in his younger days when money was flush, too open-handed for his own good. He bore no grudges and had few enemies. Fighting was a business with him. In the ring he struck to hurt, struck to maim, struck to destroy; but there was no animus in it. It was a plain business proposition. Audiences assembled and paid for the spectacle of men knocking each other out. The winner took the big end of the purse. When Tom King faced the Woolloomoolloo Gouger, twenty years before, he knew that the Gouger's jaw was only four months healed after having been broken in a Newcastle bout. And he had played for that jaw and broken it again in the ninth round, not because he bore the Gouger any ill will, but because that was the surest way to put the Gouger out and win the big end of the purse. Nor had the Gouger borne him any ill will for it. It was the game, and both knew the game and played it.

Tom King had never been a talker, and he sat by the window, morosely silent, staring at his hands. The veins stood out on the backs of the hands, large and swollen; and the knuckles, smashed and battered and malformed, testified to the use to which they had been put. He had never heard that a man's life was the life of his arteries, but well he knew the meaning of those big, upstanding veins. His heart had pumped too much blood through them at top pressure. They no longer did the work. He had stretched the elasticity out of them, and with their distention had passed his endurance. He tired easily now. No longer could he do a fast twenty rounds, hammer and tongs, fight, fight, fight, from gong to gong, with fierce rally on top of fierce rally, beaten to the ropes and in turn beating his opponent to the ropes, and rallying fiercest and fastest of all in the last, twentieth round, with the house on its feet and yelling, himself rushing, striking, ducking, raining showers of blows upon showers of blows and receiving showers of blows in return, and all the time the heart faithfully pumping the surging blood through the adequate veins. The veins, swollen at the time, had always shrunk down again, though not quite—each time, imperceptibly at first, remaining just a trifle larger than before. He stared at them and at his battered knuckles, and, for the moment, caught a vision of the youthful excellence of those hands before the first knuckle had been smashed on the head of Benny Jones, otherwise known as the Welsh Terror.

The impression of his hunger came back on him.

"Blimey, but couldn't I go for a piece of steak!" he muttered aloud, clenching his huge fists and spitting out a smothered oath.

"I tried both Burke's an' Sawley's," his wife said half apologetically.

"An' they wouldn't?" he demanded.

"Not a ha'penny. Burke said——" She faltered.

"G'wan! Wot'd he say?"

"As how 'e was thinkin' Sandel ud do ye tonight, an' as how yer score was comfortable big as it was."

Tom King grunted, but did not reply. He was busy thinking of the bull terrier he had kept in his younger days to which he had fed steaks without end. Burke would have given him credit for a thousand steaks—then. But times had changed. Tom King was getting old; and old men, fighting before second-rate clubs, couldn't expect to run bills of any size with the tradesmen.

He had got up in the morning with a longing for a piece of steak, and the longing had not abated. He had not had a fair training for this fight. It was a drought year in Australia, times were hard and even the most irregular work was difficult to find. He had had no sparring partner and his food had not been of the best nor always sufficient. He had done a few days' navvy work when he could get it, and he had run around the Domain in the early mornings to get his legs in shape. But it was hard training without a partner and with a wife and two kiddies that must be fed. Credit with the tradesmen had undergone very slight expansion when he was matched with Sandel. The secretary of the Gayety Club had advanced him three pounds —the loser's end of the purse—and beyond that had refused to go. Now and again he managed to borrow a few shillings from old pals, who would have lent more only that it was a drought year and they were hard put themselves. No—and there was no use in disguising the fact—his training had not been satisfactory. He should have had better food and no worries. Besides, when a man is forty it is harder to get into condition than when he is twenty.

"What time is it, Lizzie?" he asked.

His wife went across the hall to inquire and came back.

"Quarter before eight."

"They'll be startin, the first bout in a few minutes," he said. "Only a try-out. Then there's a four-round spar 'tween Dealer Wells an' Gridley, an' a ten-round go 'tween Starlight an' some sailor bloke. I don't come on for over an hour."

At the end of another silent ten minutes he rose to his feet.

"Truth is, Lizzie, I ain't had proper trainin'."

He reached for his hat and started for the door. He did not offer to kiss her—he never did on going out—but on this night she dared to kiss him, throwing her arms around him and compelling him to bend down to her face. She looked quite small against the massive bulk of the man.

"Good luck, Tom," she said. "You gotter do 'im."

"Ay, I gotter do 'im," he repeated. "That's all there is to it. I jus' gotter do 'im."

He laughed with an attempt at heartiness, while she pressed more closely against him. Across her shoulders he looked around the bare room. It was all he had in the world, with the rent overdue, and her and the kiddies. And he was leaving it to go out into the night to get meat for his mate and cubs—not like a modern workingman going to his machine grind, but in the old, primitive, royal, animal way, by fighting for it.

"I gotter do 'im," he repeated, this time a hint of desperation in his voice. "If it's a win, it's thirty quid—an' I can pay all that's owin', with a lump o' money left over. If it's a lose I get naught—not even a penny for me to ride home on the tram. The secretary's give all that's comin' from a loser's end. Good-by, old woman. I'll come straight home if it's a win."

"An' I'll be waitin' up," she called to him along the hall.

It was a full two miles to the Gayety, and as he walked along he remembered how in his palmy days—he had once been the heavyweight champion of New South Wales—he would have ridden in a cab to the fight, and how, most likely, some heavy backer would have paid for the cab and ridden with him. There were Tommy Burns and that Yankee nigger, Jack Johnson—they rode about in motor cars. And he walked! And, as any man knew, a hard two miles was not the best preliminary to a fight. He was an old un, and the world did not wag well with old uns. He was good for nothing now except navvy work, and his broken nose and swollen ear were against him even in that. He found himself wishing that he had learned a trade. It would have been better in the long run. But no one had told him, and he knew, deep down in his heart, that he would not have listened if they had. It had been so easy. Big money—sharp, glorious fights—periods of rest and loafing in between—a following of eager flatterers, the slaps on the back, the shakes of the hand, the toffs glad to buy him a drink for the privilege of five minutes' talk—and the glory of it, the yelling houses, the whirlwind finish, the referee's "King wins!" and his name in the sporting columns next day.

Those had been times! But he realized now, in his slow, ruminating way, that it was the old uns he had been putting away. He was Youth, rising; and they were Age, sinking. No wonder it had been easy—they with their swollen veins and battered knuckles and weary in the bones of them from the long battles they had already fought. He remembered the time he put out old Stowsher Bill, at Rush-Cutters Bay, in the eighteenth round, and how old Bill had cried afterward in the dressing-room like a baby. Perhaps old Bill's rent had been overdue. Perhaps he'd had at home a missus an' a couple of kiddies. And perhaps Bill, that very day of the fight, had had a hungering for a piece of steak. Bill had fought game and taken incredible punishment. He could see now, after he had gone through the mill himself, that Stowsher Bill had fought for a bigger stake, that night twenty years ago, than had young Tom King, who had fought for glory and easy money. No wonder Stowsher Bill had cried afterward in the dressing-room.

Well, a man had only so many fights in him, to begin with. It was the iron law of the game. One man might have a hundred hard fights in him, another man only twenty; each, according to the make of him and the quality of his fiber, had a definite number, and when he had fought them he was done. Yes, he had had more fights in him than most of them, and he had had far more than his share of the hard, grueling fights—the kind that worked the heart and lungs to bursting, that took the elastic out of the arteries and made hard knots of muscle out of youth's sleek suppleness, that wore out nerve and stamina and made brain and bones weary from excess of effort and endurance overwrought. Yes, he had done better than all of them. There was none of his old fighting partners left. He was the last of the old guard. He had seen them all finished, and he had had a hand in finishing some of them.

They had tried him out against the old uns, and one after another he had put them away—laughing when, like old Stowsher Bill, they cried in the dressing-room. And now he was an old un, and they tried out the youngsters on him. There was that bloke, Sandel. He had come over from New Zealand with a record behind him. But nobody in Australia knew anything about him, so they put him up against old Tom King. If Sandel made a showing he would be given better men to fight, with bigger purses to win; so it was to be depended upon that he would put up a fierce battle. He had everything to win by it—money and glory and career; and Tom King was the grizzled old chopping-block that guarded the highway to fame and fortune. And he had nothing to win except thirty quid, to pay to the landlord and the tradesmen. And, as Tom King thus ruminated, there came to his stolid vision the form of Youth, glorious Youth, rising exultant and invincible, supple of muscle and silken of skin, with heart and lungs that had never been tired and torn and that laughed at limitation of effort. Yes, Youth was the Nemesis. It destroyed the old uns and recked not that, in so doing, it destroyed itself. It enlarged its arteries and smashed its knuckles, and was in turn destroyed by Youth. For Youth was ever youthful. It was only Age that grew older.

At Castlereagh Street he turned to the left, and three blocks along came to the Gayety. A crowd of young larrikins hanging outside the door made respectful way for him, and he heard one say to another: "That's 'im! That's Tom King!"

Inside, on the way to his dressing-room, he encountered the secretary, a keen-eyed, shrewd-faced young man who shook his hand.

"How are you feelin', Tom?" he asked.

"Fit as a fiddle," King answered, though he knew that he lied, and that if he had a quid he would give it right there for a good piece of steak.

When he emerged from the dressing-room, his seconds behind him, and came down the aisle to the squared ring in the center of the hall, a burst of greeting and applause went up from the waiting crowd. He acknowledged salutations right and left, though few of the faces did he know. Most of them were the faces of kiddies unborn when he was winning his first laurels in the squared ring. He leaped lightly to the raised platform and ducked through the ropes to his corner, where he sat down on a folding stool. Jack Ball, the referee, came over and shook his hand. Ball was a broken-down pugilist who for over ten years had not entered the ring as a principal. King was glad that he had him for referee. They were both old uns. If he should rough it with Sandel a bit beyond the rules he knew Ball could be depended upon to pass it by.

Aspiring young heavyweights, one after another, were climbing into the ring and being presented to the audience by the referee. Also, he issued their challenges for them.

"Young Pronto," Ball announced, "from North Sydney, challenges the winner for fifty pounds side bet."

The audience applauded, and applauded again as Sandel himself sprang through the ropes and sat down in his corner. Tom King looked across the ring at him curiously, for in a few minutes they would be locked together in merciless combat, each trying with all the force of him to knock the other into unconsciousness. But little could he see, for Sandel, like himself, had trousers and sweater on over his ring costume. His face was strongly handsome, crowned with a curly mop of yellow hair, while his thick, muscular neck hinted at bodily magnificence.

Young Pronto went to one corner and then the other, shaking hands with the principals and dropping down out of the ring. The challenges went on. Ever Youth climbed through the ropes—Youth unknown, but insatiable— crying out to mankind that with strength and skill it would match issues with the winner. A few years before, in his own heyday of invincibleness, Tom King would have been amused and bored by these preliminaries. But now he sat fascinated, unable to shake the vision of Youth from his eyes. Always were these youngsters rising up in the boxing game, springing through the ropes and shouting their defiance; and always were the old uns going down before them. They climbed to success over the bodies of the old uns. And ever they came, more and more youngsters—Youth unquenchable and irresistible—and ever they put the old uns away, themselves becoming old uns and traveling the same downward path, while behind them, ever pressing on them, was Youth eternal—the new babies, grown lusty and dragging their elders down, with behind them more babies to the end of time—Youth that must have its will and that will never die.

King glanced over to the press box and nodded to Morgan, of the Sportsman, and Corbett, of the Referee. Then he held out his hands, while Sid Sullivan and Charley Bates, his seconds, slipped on his gloves and laced them tight, closely watched by one of Sandel's seconds, who first examined critically the tapes on King's knuckles. A second of his own was in Sandel's corner, performing a like office. Sandel's trousers were pulled off and, as he stood up, his sweater was skinned off over his head. And Tom

King, looking, saw Youth incarnate, deep-chested, heavy-thewed, with muscles that slipped and slid like live things under the white satin skin. The whole body was acrawl with life, and Tom King knew that it was a life that had never oozed its freshness out through the aching pores during the long fights wherein Youth paid its toll and departed not quite so young as when it entered.

The two men advanced to meet each other and, as the gong sounded and the seconds clattered out of the ring with the folding stools, they shook hands with each other and instantly took their fighting attitudes. And instantly, like a mechanism of steel and springs balanced on a hair trigger, Sandel was in and out and in again, landing a left to the eyes, a right to the ribs, ducking a counter, dancing lightly away and dancing menacingly back again. He was swift and clever. It was a dazzling exhibition. The house yelled its approbation. But King was not dazzled. He had fought too many fights and too many youngsters. He knew the blows for what they were— too quick and too deft to be dangerous. Evidently Sandel was going to rush things from the start. It was to be expected. It was the way of Youth, expending its splendor and excellence in wild insurgence and furious onslaught, overwhelming opposition with its own unlimited glory of strength and desire.

Sandel was in and out, here, there and everywhere, light-footed and eager-hearted, a living wonder of white flesh and stinging muscle that wove itself into a dazzling fabric of attack, slipping and leaping like a flying shuttle from action to action through a thousand actions, all of them centered upon the destruction of Tom King, who stood between him and fortune. And Tom King patiently endured. He knew his business, and he knew Youth now that Youth was no longer his. There was nothing to do till the other lost some of his steam, was his thought, and he grinned to himself as he deliberately ducked so as to receive a heavy blow on the top of his head. It was a wicked thing to do, yet eminently fair according to the rules of the boxing game. A man was supposed to take care of his own knuckles, and if he insisted on hitting an opponent on the top of the head he did so at his own peril. King could have ducked lower and let the blow whiz harmlessly past, but he remembered his own early fights and how he smashed his first knuckle on the head of the Welsh Terror. He was but playing the game. That duck had accounted for one of Sandel's knuckles. Not that Sandel would mind it now. He would go on, superbly regardless, hitting as hard as ever throughout the fight. But later on, when the long ring battles had begun to tell, he would regret that knuckle and look back and remember how he smashed it on Tom King's head.

The first round was all Sandel's, and he had the house yelling with the rapidity of his whirlwind rushes. He overwhelmed King with avalanches of punches, and King did nothing. He never struck once, contenting himself with covering up, blocking and ducking and clinching to avoid punishment. He occasionally feinted, shook his head when the weight of a punch landed, and moved stolidly about, never leaping or springing or wasting an ounce of strength. Sandel must foam the froth of Youth away before discreet Age could dare to retaliate. All King's movements were slow and methodical, and his heavy-lidded, slow-moving eyes gave him the appearance of being half asleep or dazed. Yet they were eyes that saw everything, that had been trained to see everything through all his twenty years and odd in the ring. They were eyes that did not blink or waver before an impending blow, but that coolly saw and measured distance.

Seated in his corner for the minute's rest at the end of the round, he lay back with outstretched legs, his arms resting on the right angle of the ropes, his chest and abdomen heaving frankly and deeply as he gulped down the air driven by the towels of his seconds. He listened with closed eyes to the voices of the house. "Why don't yeh fight, Tom?" many were crying. "Yeh ain't afraid of 'im, are yeh?"

"Muscle-bound," he heard a man on a front seat comment. "He can't move quicker. Two to one on Sandel, in quids."

The gong struck and the two men advanced from their corners. Sandel came forward fully three-quarters of the distance, eager to begin again; but King was content to advance the shorter distance. It was in line with his policy of economy. He had not been well trained and he had not had enough to eat, and every step counted. Besides, he had already walked two miles to the ringside. It was a repetition of the first round, with Sandel attacking like a whirlwind and with the audience indignantly demanding why King did not fight. Beyond feinting and several slowly-delivered and ineffectual blows he did nothing save block and stall and clinch. Sandel wanted to make the pace fast, while King, out of his wisdom, refused to accommodate him. He grinned with a certain wistful pathos in his ring-battered countenance, and went on cherishing his strength with the jealousy of which only Age is capable. Sandel was Youth, and he threw his strength away with the munificent abandon of Youth. To King belonged the ring generalship, the wisdom bred of long, aching fights. He watched with cool eyes and head, moving slowly and waiting for Sandel's froth to foam away. To the majority of the onlookers it seemed as though King was hopelessly outclassed, and they voiced their opinion in offers of three to one on Sandel. But there were wise ones, a few, who knew King of old time and who covered what they considered easy money.

The third round began as usual, one-sided, with Sandel doing all the leading and delivering all the punishment. A half-minute had passed when Sandel, overconfident, left an opening. King's eyes and right arm flashed in the same instant. It was his first real blow—a hook, with the twisted arch of the arm to make it rigid, and with all the weight of the half-pivoted body behind it. It was like a sleepy-seeming lion suddenly thrusting out a lightning paw. Sandel, caught on the side of the jaw, was felled like a bullock. The audience gasped and murmured awestricken applause. The man was not muscle-bound, after all, and he could drive a blow like a triphammer.

Sandel was shaken. He rolled over and attempted to rise, but the sharp yells from his seconds to take the count restrained him. He knelt on one knee, ready to rise, and waited, while the referee stood over him, counting the seconds loudly in his ear. At the ninth he rose in fighting attitude, and Tom King, facing him, knew regret that the blow had not been an inch nearer the point of the jaw. That would have been a knockout, and he could have carried the thirty quid home to the missus and the kiddies.

The round continued to the end of its three minutes, Sandel for the first time respectful of his opponent and King slow of movement and sleepy-eyed as ever. As the round neared its close King, warned of the fact by sight of the seconds crouching outside ready for the spring in through the ropes, worked the fight around to his own corner. And when the gong struck he sat down immediately on the waiting stool, while Sandel had to walk all the way across the diagonal of the square to his own corner. It was a little thing, but it was the sum of little things that counted. Sandel was compelled to walk that many more steps, to give up that much energy and to lose a part of the precious minute of rest. At the beginning of every round King loafed slowly out from his corner, forcing his opponent to advance the greater distance. The end of every round found the fight manoeuvered by King into his own corner so that he could immediately sit down.

Two more rounds went by, in which King was parsimonious of effort and Sandel prodigal. The latter's attempt to force a fast pace made King uncomfortable, for a fair percentage of the multitudinous blows showered upon him went home. Yet King persisted in his dogged slowness, despite the crying of the young hotheads for him to go in and fight. Again, in the sixth round, Sandel was careless, again Tom King's fearful right flashed out to the jaw, and again Sandel took the nine seconds' count.

By the seventh round Sandel's pink of condition was gone and he settled down to what he knew was to be the hardest fight in his experience. Tom King was an old un, but a better old un than he had ever encountered—an old un who never lost his head, who was remarkably able at defense, whose blows had the impact of a knotted club and who had a knockout in either hand. Nevertheless, Tom King dared not hit often. He never forgot his battered knuckles, and knew that every hit must count if the knuckles were to last out the fight. As he sat in his corner, glancing across at his opponent, the thought came to him that the sum of his wisdom and Sandel's youth would constitute a world's champion heavyweight. But that was the trouble. Sandel would never become a world champion. He lacked the wisdom, and the only way for him to get it was to buy it with Youth; and when wisdom was his, Youth would have been spent in buying it.

King took every advantage he knew. He never missed an opportunity to clinch, and in effecting most of the clinches his shoulder drove stiffly into the other's ribs. In the philosophy of the ring a shoulder was as good as a punch so far as damage was concerned, and a great deal better so far as concerned expenditure of effort. Also, in the clinches King rested his weight on his opponent and was loth to let go. This compelled the interference of the referee, who tore them apart, always assisted by Sandel, who had not yet learned to rest. He could not refrain from using those glorious flying arms and writhing muscles of his, and when the other rushed into a clinch, striking shoulder against ribs and with head resting under Sandel's left arm, Sandel almost invariably swung his right behind his own back and into the projecting face. It was a clever stroke, much admired by the audience, but it was not dangerous, and was, therefore, just that much wasted strength. But Sandel was tireless and unaware of limitations, and King grinned and doggedly endured.

Sandel developed a fierce right to the body, which made it appear that King was taking an enormous amount of punishment, and it was only the old ringsters who appreciated the deft touch of King's left glove to the other's biceps just before the impact of the blow. It was true, the blow landed each time; but each time it was robbed of its power by that touch on the biceps. In the ninth round, three times inside a minute, King's right hooked its twisted arch to the jaw; and three times Sandel's body, heavy as it was, was level to the mat. Each time he took the nine seconds allowed him and rose to his feet, shaken and jarred, but still strong. He had lost much of his speed and he wasted less effort. He was fighting grimly; but he continued to draw upon his chief asset, which was Youth. King's chief asset was experience. As his vitality had dimmed and his vigor abated he had replaced them with cunning, with wisdom born of the long fights and with a careful shepherding of strength. Not alone had he learned never to make a superfluous movement, but he had learned how to seduce an opponent into throwing his strength away. Again and again, by feint of foot and hand and body he continued to inveigle Sandel into leaping back, ducking or countering. King rested, but he never permitted Sandel to rest. It was the strategy of Age.

Early in the tenth round King began stopping the other's rushes with straight lefts to the face, and Sandel, grown wary, responded by drawing the left, then by ducking it and delivering his right in a swinging hook to the side of the head. It was too high up to be vitally effective; but when first it landed King knew the old, familiar descent of the black veil of unconsciousness across his mind. For the instant, or for the slightest fraction of an instant rather, he ceased. In the one moment he saw his opponent ducking out of his field of vision and the background of white, watching faces; in the next moment he again saw his opponent and the background of faces. It was as if he had slept for a time and just opened his eyes again, and yet the interval of unconsciousness was so microscopically short that there had been no time for him to fall. The audience saw him totter and his knees give, and then saw him recover and tuck his chin deeper into the shelter of his left shoulder.

Several times Sandel repeated the blow, keeping King partially dazed, and then the latter worked out his defense, which was also a counter. Feinting with his left he took a half-step backward, at the same time uppercutting with the whole strength of his right. So accurately was it timed that it landed squarely on Sandel's face in the full, downward sweep of the duck, and Sandel lifted in the air and curled backward, striking the mat on his head and shoulders. Twice King achieved this, then turned loose and hammered his opponent to the ropes. He gave Sandel no chance to rest or to set himself, but smashed blow in upon blow till the house rose to its feet and the air was filled with an unbroken roar of applause. But Sandel's strength and endurance were superb, and he continued to stay on his feet. A knockout seemed certain, and a captain of police, appalled at the dreadful punishment, arose by the ringside to stop the fight. The gong struck for the end of the round and Sandel staggered to his corner, protesting to the captain that he was sound and strong. To prove it he threw two back air springs, and the police captain gave in.

Tom King, leaning back in his corner and breathing hard, was disappointed. If the fight had been stopped the referee, perforce, would have rendered him the decision and the purse would have been his. Unlike Sandel, he was not fighting for glory or career, but for thirty quid. And now Sandel would recuperate in the minute of rest.

Youth will be served—this saying flashed into King's mind, and he remembered the first time he had heard it, the night when he had put away Stowsher Bill. The toff who bought him a drink after the fight and patted him on the shoulder had used those words. Youth will be served! The toff was right. And on that night in the long ago he had been Youth. Tonight Youth sat in the opposite corner. As for himself, he had been fighting for half an hour now, and he was an old man. Had he fought like Sandel he would not have lasted fifteen minutes. But the point was that he did not recuperate. Those upstanding arteries and that sorely-tried heart would not enable him to gather strength in the intervals between the rounds. And he had not had sufficient strength in him to begin with. His legs were heavy under him and beginning to cramp. He should not have walked those two miles to the fight. And there was the steak which he had got up longing for that morning. A great and terrible hatred rose up in him for the butchers who had refused him credit. It was hard for an old man to go into a fight without enough to eat. And a piece of steak was such a little thing, a few pennies at best; yet it meant thirty quid to him.

With the gong that opened the eleventh round Sandel rushed, making a show of freshness which he did not really possess. King knew it for what it was—a bluff as old as the game itself. He clinched to save himself, then, going free, allowed Sandel to get set. This was what King desired. He feinted with his left, drew the answering duck and swinging upward hook, then made the halfstep backward, delivered the uppercut full to the face and crumpled Sandel over to the mat. After that he never let him rest, receiving punishment himself, but inflicting far more, smashing Sandel to the ropes, hooking and driving all manner of blows into him, tearing away from his clinches or punching him out of attempted clinches, and ever, when Sandel would have fallen, catching him with one uplifting hand and with the other immediately smashing him into the ropes where he could not fall.

The house by this time had gone mad, and it was his house, nearly every voice yelling: "Go it, Tom!" "Get 'im! Get 'im!" "You've got 'im, Tom! You've got 'im!" It was to be a whirlwind finish, and that was what a ringside audience paid to see.

And Tom King, who for half an hour had conserved his strength, now expended it prodigally in the one great effort he knew he had in him. It was his one chance—now or not at all. His strength was waning fast, and his hope was that before the last of it ebbed out of him he would have beaten his opponent down for the count. And as he continued to strike and force, coolly estimating the weight of his blows and the quality of the damage wrought, he realized how hard a man Sandel was to knock out. Stamina and endurance were his to an extreme degree, and they were the virgin stamina and endurance of Youth. Sandel was certainly a coming man. He had it in him. Only out of such rugged fiber were successful fighters fashioned.

Sandel was reeling and staggering, but Tom King's legs were cramping and his knuckles going back on him. Yet he steeled himself to strike the fierce blows, every one of which brought anguish to his tortured hands. Though now he was receiving practically no punishment he was weakening as rapidly as the other. His blows went home, but there was no longer the weight behind them, and each blow was the result of a severe effort of will. His legs were like lead, and they dragged visibly under him; while Sandel's backers, cheered by this symptom, began calling encouragement to their man.

King was spurred to a burst of effort. He delivered two blows in succession—a left, a trifle too high, to the solar plexus, and a right cross to the jaw. They were not heavy blows, yet so weak and dazed was Sandel that he went down and lay quivering. The referee stood over him, shouting the count of the fatal seconds in his ear. If before the tenth second was called he did not rise the fight was lost. The house stood in hushed silence. King rested on trembling legs. A mortal dizziness was upon him, and before his eyes the sea of faces sagged and swayed, while to his ears, as from a remote distance, came the count of the referee. Yet he looked upon the fight as his. It was impossible that a man so punished could rise.

Only Youth could rise, and Sandel rose. At the fourth second he rolled over on his face and groped blindly for the ropes. By the seventh second he had dragged himself to his knee, where he rested, his head rolling groggily on his shoulders. As the referee cried "Nine!" Sandel stood upright, in proper stalling position, his left arm wrapped about his face, his right wrapped about his stomach. Thus were his vital points guarded, while he lurched forward toward King in the hope of effecting a clinch and gaining more time.

At the instant Sandel arose King was at him, but the two blows he delivered were muffled on the stalled arms. The next moment Sandel was in the clinch and holding on desperately while the referee strove to drag the two men apart. King helped to force himself free. He knew the rapidity with which Youth recovered and he knew that Sandel was his if he could prevent that recovery. One stiff punch would do it. Sandel was his, indubitably his. He had outgeneraled him, outfought him, outpointed him. Sandel reeled out of the clinch, balanced on the hairline between defeat or survival. One good blow would topple him over and down and out. And Tom King, in a flash of bitterness, remembered the piece of steak and wished that he had it then behind that necessary punch he must deliver. He nerved himself for the blow, but it was not heavy enough nor swift enough. Sandel swayed but did not fall, staggering back to the ropes and holding on. King staggered after him and, with a pang like that of dissolution, delivered another blow. But his body had deserted him. All that was left of him was a fighting intelligence that was dimmed and clouded from exhaustion. The blow that was aimed for the jaw struck no higher than the shoulder. He had willed the blow higher, but the tired muscles had not been able to obey. And from the impact of the blow Tom King himself reeled back and nearly fell. Once again he strove. This time his punch missed altogether, and, from absolute weakness, he fell against Sandel and clinched, holding on to him to save himself from sinking to the floor.

King did not attempt to free himself. He had shot his bolt. He was gone. And Youth had been served. Even in the clinch he could feel Sandel growing stronger against him. When the referee thrust them apart, there, before his eyes, he saw Youth recuperate. From instant to instant Sandel grew stronger. His punches, weak and futile at first, became stiff and accurate. Tom King's bleared eyes saw the gloved fist driving at his jaw and he willed to guard it by interposing his arm. He saw the danger, willed the act; but the arm was too heavy. It seemed burdened with a hundredweight of lead. It would not lift itself, and he strove to lift it with his soul. Then the gloved fist landed home. He experienced a sharp snap that was like an electric spark and, simultaneously, the veil of blackness enveloped him.

When he opened his eyes again he was in his corner, and he heard the yelling of the audience like the roar of the surf at Bondi Beach. A wet sponge was being pressed against the base of his brain and Sid Sullivan was blowing cold water in a refreshing spray over his face and chest. His gloves had already been removed and Sandel, bending over him, was shaking his hand. He bore no ill will toward the man who had put him out, and he returned the grip with a heartiness that made his battered knuckles protest. Then Sandel stepped to the center of the ring and the audience hushed its pandemonium to hear him accept young Pronto's challenge and offer to increase the side bet to one hundred pounds. King looked on apathetically while his seconds mopped the streaming water from him, dried his face and prepared him to leave the ring. He felt hungry. It was not the ordinary, gnawing kind, but a great faintness, a palpitation at the pit of the stomach that communicated itself to all his body. He remembered back into the fight to the moment when he had Sandel swaying and tottering on the hairline balance of defeat. Ah, that piece of steak would have done it!

He had lacked just that for the decisive blow, and he had lost. It was all because of the piece of steak.

His seconds were half-supporting him as they helped him through the ropes. He tore free from them, ducked through the ropes unaided and leaped heavily to the floor, following on their heels as they forced a passage for him down the crowded center aisle. Leaving the dressing-room for the street, in the entrance to the hall, some young fellow spoke to him.

"W'y didn't yuh go in an' get 'im when yuh 'ad 'im?" the young fellow asked.

"Aw, go to hell!" said Tom King, and passed down the steps to the sidewalk.

The doors of the public house at the corner were swinging wide, and he saw the lights and the smiling barmaids, heard the many voices discussing the fight and the prosperous chink of money on the bar. Somebody called to him to have a drink. He hesitated perceptibly, then refused and went on his way.

He had not a copper in his pocket and the two-mile walk home seemed very long. He was certainly getting old. Crossing the Domain he sat down suddenly on a bench, unnerved by the thought of the missus sitting up for him, waiting to learn the outcome of the fight. That was harder than any knockout, and it seemed almost impossible to face.

He felt weak and sore, and the pain of his smashed knuckles warned him that, even if he could find a job at navvy work, it would be a week before he could grip a pick handle or a shovel. The hunger palpitation at the pit of the stomach was sickening. His wretchedness overwhelmed him, and into his eyes came an unwonted moisture. He covered his face with his hands and, as he cried, he remembered Stowsher Bill and how he had served him that night in the long ago. Poor old Stowsher Bill! He could understand now why Bill had cried in the dressing room.

BOMAYE

By Muhammad Ali
with Richard Durham

I wondered if it would feel strange to strip down for a fight at 4 A.M. in Zaire, Africa, but it feels the same as stripping down for a fight at 9 P.M. in Madison Square Garden, the corresponding time in New York, the usual fight time.

In the four months since the fight was announced, Zairian craftsmen have converted an old, dilapidated arena, built in 1917 by the Belgians, into a fresh modern stadium. My dressing room is the cleanest and best I ever had for a fight.

Herbert and I step into the shower room, hold our last conference, give thanks to Allah, and briefly review what is at stake. We embrace warmly as only two old, close friends can, who have for eight years shared success and setbacks together, trials and triumphs, and are now at the crossroads.

In the dressing room I dance lightly, looking in the mirror. I feel the nervous tingle that comes when I know whatever is about to happen will change my life.

"How much time, Blood?"

His hands are trembling as he seals my water bottles with adhesive so they look like little Egyptian mummies. Once they're sealed, only Blood and Bundini will be allowed to touch them.

Angelo's watch has stopped. Bundini says, "The clock on the wall is slow."

No one knows for sure until Blood sends out Lieutenant Bomba Nsakala, assigned to me since I flew here fifty-five days ago. Nsakala pushes through the crowd jammed around the dressing room door, goes directly to the timekeeper and synchronizes his watch, comes back out of breath and speaks low, as though there's some tactical advantage in only me knowing. "Fifteen minutes. The whole world's out there."

"Is President Mobutu out there?"

"Our President will view the fight from his home."

"Is George out there?"

"George wants you out first. He says he's The Champion."

"I'm The Champion before daybreak."

The lieutenant smiles.

An African reporter from Zambia, one of a handful of writers in the room, asks, "What goes through your mind before such a fight?"

I tell him, "I think over what's at stake. I go over every preparation I've made. My roadwork was right. My diet was right. The way I trained was right. My sleep was right. My timing was right. For thirty days I timed my roadwork to take place at 4 A.M., so when I step into the stadium at 4 A.M. it's like going for an exercise in the gym."

Then I speak to all my handlers. "This is just like an exercise in the gym, just another day."

But the mood in the dressing room doesn't change. Usually I'm the one who finds the dressing-room atmosphere before a fight too free, and usually I'm the one who brings the trainers and Angelo around to take these moments seriously. I feel uneasy and in danger when trainers and handlers take a fight lightly, but this morning they came into the dressing room as though they were walking behind a coffin. My coffin. Even Bundini is grim.

"It's just another exercise in the gym," I say. "From now on, time will fly."

I throw a flurry of punches at the mirror, and I see Dr. Pacheco. A close friend of Angelo's, he has been with me since the night I stopped Sonny Liston at Miami Beach, and with me for most of my fights. They call him "the boxing doctor," because he attends the fighters in Angelo's Fifth Street Gym. He's a sophisticated man, a painter, a musician and an artist. His eyes meet mine, and when the handful of writers are out of hearing range I take him to my inner dressing room.

It's about my hands.

Each fight I have to think of the shape my hands are in. Pain has tortured me through so many of my fights since I came back from exile. I hold up my hands to the light, flex them, wishing I could see what's inside them that might cripple me tonight. I'm fighting the youngest, most powerful opponent I've ever faced, and one with the highest knockout percentage in history. The odds are four to one against me in America, three to one in Europe—even three to one in Tokyo, where I'm popular. So pessimistic is the mood in Tokyo over my chances that actor-producer Shintaru Katsu, the "Marlon Brando" of Japan, has dropped his company's option to include the fight in Zaire in his documentary on my life. In England, where I was a favorite even when I was in exile, and even when I was fighting against their own champions, the odds this morning are two to one against me. And Angelo has handed me this week's Chicago *Tribune*, which says, ALI NEEDS A MIRACLE TO SURVIVE.

On the other hand, throughout all of Africa, cards, telegrams and greetings are pouring into my camp, hailing my victory even before I get in the ring and thanking my manager for his support of Black Africa's fight against South African racism. Herbert has refused to honor any contract which calls for me to fight inside South Africa until that country gives freedom to its black majority.

All this is flashing through my mind as I make a fist and bang my knuckles together harder and harder to arouse the pain. A trickle of sweat is coming from under my arms.

A fighter's only weapons are his hands. If they go, he goes. I've been using these hands in rings and gyms almost constantly for twenty-two years to strike against the hardest thing on a man's body, his head.

Sometimes something happens to the bones inside—microscopic chips, calcium deposits, so many things. It has changed my fighting style many times. Sometimes I've had to hold up on follow-through punches, because I can stand my opponent's blows easier than I can stand the pain when I deliver one to him.

I once heard Howard Cosell commenting on my fight with Dutch Heavyweight Champion Rudi Lubbers: "Ali hasn't used his right hand six times throughout the entire fight. Is something wrong with it? What is he saving it for? His fight with Joe Frazier?"

Yes. I was saving it for my second fight with Frazier, coming up next. But while training for Frazier the pain was almost unbearable. Even to be hit on the hands by sparring partners when blocking blows was torture. At first it was only the right hand, but then both hands.

Herbert had asked me to fly into Boston to see the famous hand specialist Dr. Richard Smith, at Massachusetts General Hospital. I knew my days as a fighter were numbered, but the treatment they prescribed seemed too costly, complex and long.

Besides, when I got back to camp, the pain had eased. I began tearing into sparring partners and the heavy bag to make up for lost time. Then suddenly it was back again and worse.

"Sparring partners now hit you with blows a baby could get away from," Bundini lamented. "Champ, if there's something wrong, let's leave boxing. We can make it somewhere else."

"Frazier is like a tank," Blood said. "You need anti-tank guns, Champ. You ain't got no anti-tank guns now. They broke."

It was less than three weeks before I was scheduled to go in the ring against Frazier. I wanted the return match with Joe Frazier not only to wipe out the first decision against me, but because Frazier was probably the most ruthless, aggressive and competitive heavyweight in modern times. I had to whip Frazier to establish any claim to a title fight. Then, too, a deep personal feud had grown up between us. Our fights were not just for money, but for our lives. Whatever would happen to me in the future, my body was now at its peak. I had everything it took to master Frazier or any other fighter.

Herbert was on the phone. "If the hands are no better in two weeks, we're calling the Garden to cancel the fight. It's better we bow out of boxing now than risk any injury. Nothing in boxing is worth that.''

"I think they're getting better," I said. "They'll be all right."

"I hear what you say. I know why you say it," Herbert answered. "But just the same . . ."

Herbert had assigned C.B. to report on my hands early in training, not only during the Frazier training but during my training for Norton and Quarry. Now they had Blood and Bundini watching me for signs that might indicate danger.

I remember it was in mid-January of 1974 that I had a feeling close to desperation. I had just passed my thirty-second birthday, and I knew if I lost the chance to fight Frazier this time, I might never have another. I had wiped out a decision Norton held over me. I wanted to do the same with Frazier.

Joe stood like a stone wall against giving me a return match after our first "Fight of the Century," even when all those around him, including his manager and beloved "ring father" Yank Durham, were pleading with him to fight me again—if for no other reason than that it meant millions for both of us.

"I'll never fight that bastard for even money again," Frazier told Yank, and he meant it. "I'd rather die and go to hell first."

But it was Yank who died and went somewhere first, only a month after he and Herbert had met secretly to maneuver a return match between Joe and me. Joe flew into a rage about that meeting and accused Yank of doublecrossing him.

Boxing officials had warned Joe that the year was almost up, that he must make a defense of his title against me or Foreman, the top-ranking contenders, or forfeit the title. He had a clear-cut choice between signing for four million dollars to fight me or eight hundred thousand to fight Foreman.

He overruled everybody, flew down to Jamaica, underprepared and overconfident, and George wiped him out, took the title.

But in January of 1974 I had not wiped out my defeat by Frazier and I was afraid that if Frazier fought a return match with Foreman and won, he would never get in the ring with me in this world or the next unless on terms too humiliating for me to accept. C.B. said Herbert wanted me to go back to Massachusetts General Hospital and have the treatment. But I refused; their verdict could end my career.

Rocky Aioka, a Japanese wrestling champion who was with me in the Rome Olympics, now owner of the Benihana restaurant empire, came up to the mountains around that time and saw me pawing away at sparring partners. He was so alarmed that he wired back to Tokyo for the leading Japanese orthopedic specialist. I refused to let him come.

But I knew I had to have help, so when Lou Beltrami, a friend since I moved up to the mountains, asked me to go to a nearby town to see his personal physician, Dr. Peter Greco, I agreed. "By the condition of your hands now," the doctor said, "I would say you should cancel the fight."

I felt hostile. "That's a judgment for me to make," I said. "All I want to know is if there's anything that can be done to help them before I fight Frazier."

He said he'd try. And almost every day he came to camp to give me cortisone and hot wax treatments. I bought a hot wax applicator, and all through the day and evening I doused my hands. Slowly, they seemed to improve.

But by the day of the weigh-in the New York Boxing Commission had heard reports of my trip to a doctor. Reporters who saw sparring partners push me around the ring wrote that something was wrong. For the first time in my career I was asked to have my hands x-rayed.

It was the quickest, most casual x-ray I'd ever taken. They found nothing.

Hal Conrad, Top Rank veteran boxing consultant, saw my puzzled look when I left the room. "They had to satisfy the reporters," he said. "The Garden's sold out. You can't beg, borrow or steal tickets. Nobody's gonna find anything wrong with the fighters at this late date. Two legs missing and one eye in the middle of your forehead might help. Otherwise, good luck."

In the quiet of my dressing room, twenty minutes before the fight, I held up my hands and flexed them. They felt better, but I decided to be careful.

This may have saved Frazier from a knockout in the second round of that last fight. I had him groggy and weaving, but did not follow up, not only because the timekeeper rang the bell too soon, but because I was saving my hands. I wasn't sure I had hit him that hard.

Nsakala appears in the doorway. "We go on in twelve minutes."

This may be the final fight of my life. I don't care how bad my hands hurt. I'll hit him until the pain tears them off at the wrists. I'll gamble on the weapons I got. Everything I want in life is on the line tonight.

"Countdown! Countdown is on!" Blood says in his intense, hushed way.

But my own countdown has already begun. I check over everything. One thing the countdown always brings is the urge to pee. I have the urge now, although I emptied myself before I left my villa. The urge is so overpowering that I get up from the training table and go to the toilet. I stand there over the bowl and try. I squeeze, but nothing comes out. Still the urge is there. I don't want to be in the ring during the seventh or eighth round in a hot exchange of blows with George and feel this urge. How could I say, "George, my black brother, hold that uppercut while I go over to my corner and pee in my bucket. I'd do the same for you." George would say, "Oh no you don't," hit me in the kidneys, and out it would come. I can see the late Jimmy Cannon rising from his grave and writing his most triumphant column: CHRISTIAN BEATS THE PEE OUT OF BLACK MUSLIM. Dick Young, New York *Daily News* sportswriter, banging out the beginning of his column: FOREMAN MAKES ALI WET HIS PANTS IN SEVENTH ROUND. Red Smith saying: ALI POURED OUT MORE PEE THAN PUNCHES TONIGHT.

It would be the same way when I finished fighting that morning, when they carried me through the screaming crowd back into the dressing room. There were two doctors I'd never seen before, one European and one Zairian, asking for urine specimens.

"Before you do anything else," the Zairian doctor said even before I undressed, "we need a urine specimen."

The European explained casually, "Since you took so many body blows, there is fear that your kidneys might be injured."

They gave me a flask. We went into the toilet and I tried. Not a drop came out. They looked disappointed.

"Maybe if you follow me home," I suggested, "maybe I can do better. Do you mind riding in my car?"

I took them in my caravan along the road to Nsele. The storm that had held off for four weeks broke out a half-hour after the fight. Of all the unexplained miracles in my life, the long overdue torrential rain poured down in sheets so heavy that the very ring we fought in was wrecked and the stadium flooded. All of Hank Schwartz's Video Technique signal-bearing equipment went out of order. I sat back during the drive, wondering at the miracle; if it had come two hours earlier, I wouldn't be riding out of the stadium as World Heavyweight Champion. The fight would have been postponed for the final time. George would have gone back to his initial plan—to avoid me until I'm "a little older and slower." I'd be flying home as the old fighter who the oddsmakers said couldn't have beaten young George anyway.

But none of those tons of water got into me. When we reached the villa and I went to the bathroom to try again, nothing.

"You sweated it all out," one doctor said. "There is very little excess liquid left in your body."

I apologized and suggested that they come back in the morning when I woke up. "Tomorrow morning maybe I can do you justice."

But they gave up on it. They never came back.

I was told later they were doctors from the WBA. They were looking to examine my urine to see if I had taken any drugs that had enabled me to be so energetic while George seemed to wear down. And if they had found any, I was to be immediately disqualified and the title reverted back to George.

Dr. Williams, my own physician, said later, "They kept me in a room, quizzing me for two hours after the fight. Trying to get me to tell them if I had given you any medicine for any reason seventy-two hours before the fight. They were surprised that you seemed so strong and Foreman so weak. They wouldn't give up until they were certain they didn't have a leg to stand on to strip you of the title once more.''

I sit on the training table and Angelo tapes my hands with rows of thin gauze. Doc Nick Broadus comes over from George's camp to watch the wrapping, an ancient precaution designed to let each side see that no horseshoes or brass knuckles are taped on a fighter. We send Dr. Pacheco to George's room, but George has him kicked out. Broadus has to take him back to verify his credentials.

It's nice to know George is so suspicious and uneasy. Maybe it's because only last night a rumor circulated that George's aides tried to force an additional five hundred thousand from John Daly, the young London executive of Hemdale Leisure Corporation who advanced the original million and a half used by Don King and Hank Schwartz to start the mechanics of the title fight. According to the rumor, the aide told him that unless the five hundred thousand was delivered before the fight, George would not step into the ring. The Zaire venture, now up to a fifty-million-dollar outlay, would collapse.

George didn't know what I'd learned in my association with Daly, the son of a Welsh prizefighter. In spite of his rosy schoolboy look, Daly is as shrewd and tough in his business as George is in his—maybe more so.

"It was a delicate thing," Daly told me after the fight. "I felt the fight was in the balance. I had to give his man an empty suitcase and allow him to fly to London for the money."

Right now George's man is supposedly sitting in a London hotel, waiting to have the suitcase filled with five hundred thousand dollars in U.S. currency. Later we heard that Scotland Yard cooperated with Daly in having his outgoing phone calls cut off.

But another rumor in Kinshasa is that Daly was so certain I would be annihilated and George the dominant figure in boxing for years to come that he offered George the half-million if he would sign for Daly to handle his future title defenses. And crafty George insisted on having the money before the fight.

Somehow, I have no fear about George being foolish enough not to show up. Both The Champion and I have met President Mobutu Sese Seko, face to face, and if George is as feeble a judge of character as his aide, I would hate to be his wife, waiting for the day he gets out of Africa.

Nsakala whispers, "Seven minutes."

The countdown goes on.

I warm up before the mirror, throwing my punches, and two minutes later I go to the inside room with Herbert. We say a prayer of thanks to Allah. I come out and shadowbox again, lightly, keeping my body at a certain temperature.

"Five minutes."

Blood begins to stick his mummies in the water bucket. The only thing new in one of the bottles is a solution of honey, orange juice and water, a formula from Dr. Charles Williams of Chicago, who had analyzed the fatigue I felt while training in Philadelphia. I will do like Sugar Ray Robinson did when he fought, take a nip of sweets in between rounds.

Bundini throws the towels across his shoulders. The room is moving toward the door. A hand-picked squad of paratroopers is receiving last-second instructions from Lieutenant Nsakala. The line forms around me.

A young Zaire reporter with a scratch pad slips through to whisper to me, "What does a fighter think about these last minutes?" As though I'm a condemned man going for execution.

It's too late to answer. But I go over in my mind how I will pull every ounce of strength and endurance out of my body to defeat George.

I remember the signs President Mobutu has strung along the highway between the airport and the city, slogans to welcome visitors to Zaire. One describes this fight as a "Sport Between Two Brothers." But there's no one I feel more unbrotherly toward at this moment than George. I tighten my fist. I may not be able to stop the pain, but no pain will stop me from throwing blows at George.

We're at the door. Bundini has circled the editorial of a magazine, and reads it in my ear like a prayer: "So it boils down to this: 'Foreman-Ali, $5 million each in a battle in Zaire, Africa. Forget everything else, every fight that has been won or lost before and all of those that will be contested in years to come. Forget every battle of man against man, of mind against mind, of soul against soul. This is the one. This is the greatest.' "

I nod to him. The line is moving.

"This is it." Bundini's voice is husky. Then he cries out loud:

> *"THE LAMB'S COME BACK TO CLAIM HIS OWN!*
> *GET THE PRETENDER OFF THE THRONE!"*

"What does the fighter think these last minutes?" the reporter keeps trying to ask.

I think of who I am and who my opponent is. Who is he? He is White America, Christianity, the Flag, the White Man, Porkchops. But George is The Champion, and the world listens to The Champion. There are things I want to say, things I want the world to hear. I want to be in a position to fight for my people. Whatever I have to do tonight, George will not leave Africa The Champion.

"It's time!" Nsakala snaps, and the whole line moves faster.

I feel chilly, nervous. I want to pee. They push and pull us through the door, we're out into the hall now, and the people jammed in the corridor see me. The chants start:

"ALI! ALI! BOMAYE! ALI! ALI! BOMAYE!"

The sound booms through the corridor, stays with us until we make the turn up the ramp to the opening into the stadium. We move almost on the double, and burst into the grounds. Lights flood the stadium like poured-down sunshine. Zairians in bright clothes of all colors fill the arena and make it alive with chants, songs, cheers.

It's a quarter to four. The moon is still out, but the stadium is lit up like high noon. Spotlights crisscross, searching for my crew, and when the light finds them the stadium explodes from all sides:

"ALI! ALI! BOMAYE! ALI! ALI! BOMAYE!"

I'm behind Lieutenant Nsakala; Angelo is behind me, Bundini on my side, Blood and his bucket coming up. We swing down the aisle that leads to my corner.

I reach the four steps to the ring, climb up to my corner and see the full sweep of the stadium; people are on the walls, on the tracks, every space is filled. They cheer and I raise my hand and salute them back.

They respond as though we've been rehearsing together all our lives. I look up at the roof that stretches above us, forty feet across the field, so that if the overdue rains come, the fight will still go on. The people will be drenched, but the fighters will have no excuse. We fight for the Title to the World.

I raise my hand again and dance from one end of the ring to the other. I dance by George's empty corner. The crowd roars—they understand. I'm moving easy. Sweat comes down my chest and I feel good. I know George has already lost a heavy point by not coming into the ring at the same time.

"Maybe he's holding out for something," Blood says.

But I know he'll be here. There is no force on earth that can resist the power of these people and they want us both here.

"ALI! ALI! BOMAYE! ALI! ALI! BOMAYE!"

Bundini is frowning. "Champ," he whispers, "I forgot to do it."

"What?"

"I forgot the flags."

I smile. Bundini had planned that I would enter the ring with flags, in memory of George during the Olympics in Mexico when he waved an American flag to counteract the Black Power salutes of the black champions who were protesting race discrimination in America. I would enter the ring waving a Zairian flag, a flag representing the Organization of African Unity, and the UN flag. But Bundini had no time to get it together.

"George is playing prima donna," Angelo says. "He wants to make you wait."

I understand George's play. He thinks this will make me nervous, worn and edgy by the time the fight begins. But he has given me an edge I know how to take advantage of, a chance to study the crowd, to get to know their ego, their personality. Crowds exert pressure on you. Every crowd feels strange at first, no matter who they cheer for. But when I warm up, I feel their good vibrations, the pulsebeats. George has given me time to test the ropes and to get the feel of the distance between the center and the corner. I circle the ring. I look at the crowd from different angles, from the corner, the center, all sides. I get used to the heat from the lights.

Newsmen who've described my circling the ring before the fight as all showmanship do not understand there's more to it than that. Instead of starting out cold, I will know more about the atmosphere than my opponent.

My feet get the feel of the canvas. I feel the soft spots, the firm spots. Ordinarily, there's no time to do this. Usually I try to enter a stadium the night before, as I did the ring in Madison Square Garden before I fought Frazier—move about and make myself known to the square I do my life's work in.

Angelo looks at his watch. "He's gonna be more than ten minutes late."

I look around at ringside, nod to people I know. I see Jim Brown, Miriam Makeba, Lloyd Price, Bill Withers. I nod to the press: Red Smith, Jack Griffin, Dave Anderson, Switzerland's Mario Widmar.

"The Champ's getting ready to cook!" Bundini is shouting. "Cook tonight, Champ! Cook!"

The longer The Champion lingers, the more I like it. By the time George comes out, he will be a total stranger in a house I know all about. I've looked into all the closets, the exits, the basement, the bedrooms. I'm at home. George will be my unwelcome guest, one I must not allow to stay too long.

"FOREMAN! FOREMAN! FOREMAN!"

I see Angelo's neck jerk. The audience on the west side starts a chant. It's for The Champion!

"THERE HE IS!"

The Champion is coming down the aisle, his entourage around him. His hands are up in the Olympic salute. I watch him climb up the steps behind his crew, Dick Sadler, Archie Moore, Sandy Saddler. He goes immediately to his stool. He doesn't move about the ring to get the feel of it. He doesn't test the ropes or get the feel of the crowd. He slumps on his stool and will stay there until the referee comes to the center of the ring.

I dance lightly and steadily. I glance across the ring and see Sadler whispering in George's ear. Now Zack Clayton, the referee, comes to the center. George is poised to get up.

The referee motions to us.

The greatest roar I've ever heard fills the air. We stand up face to face.

"ALI! ALI! BOMAYE! ALI! ALI! BOMAYE!"

"FOREMAN! FOREMAN! THE CHAMPION! THE CHAMPION!"

"ALI! ALI! BOMAYE! ALI! ALI! BOMAYE!"

Our eyes are locked like gunfighters' in a Wild West movie. Angelo and Bundini rub my shoulders. Sandy and Archie stand with George. In his eyes, I see Sonny Liston glaring at me ten years ago at Miami Beach, a fresh, young, powerful, taller, stronger Liston. Now I think this will answer the question critics have been asking since I first won the title from an "aging Liston": Could I have defeated a young Sonny Liston?

Clayton begins his instructions. "Now, both of you know the rules. When I step back, you break clean. No hitting on the breaks . . ."

But I draw my guns first. I lean close to George's ear, and since I obviously have his undivided attention, I think we should get a few things straight that the referee might overlook. "Chump," I say with all the contempt I can muster. "You're gonna get yourself beat tonight in front of all these Africans."

The referee's head jerks up. "Ali, no talking! Listen to the instructions." He goes on. "No hitting below the belt. No kidney punches . . ."

"Never mind that stuff, sucker." I speak low. "I'm gonna hit you everywhere but under the bottom of your big funky feet, Chump! You got to go, sucker!"

"Ali, I warned you," the referee snaps. "Be quiet!"

George bites his lips and his eyes glare.

"Ref," I say. "This sucker is in trouble. He ain't nobody's Champ!"

George's eyes go from me to the referee. He wants Clayton to chastise me, but I pull his eyes back to mine. The referee talks on mechanically while I say to George, "You heard about me for years, sucker! All your life you been hearing about Muhammad Ali. Now, Chump, you gotta face me!"

"Ali, I'm warning you for the last time!"

George's eyes are tight. His head is close to mine.

"You been hearing about how bad I am since you were a little kid with mess in your pants! Tonight"—I say it loud—"I'm gonna whip you till you cry like a baby."

"If you don't stop talking, I'll disqualify you." Clayton is furious, his hands shake. "I want a good, clean, sportsman fight, or I will absolutely call a halt to it."

"That's the only way you gonna save this sucker," I say. "He's doomed!"

Sweat is coming down George's forehead. Archie Moore is rubbing his shoulders.

"If you talk while fighting," the referee says, "I'm going to stop this fight, you hear? I'll stop it!"

I've been told this before, but where does it say in the rules that fighters can't have an orderly discussion while they work as long as they perform properly? Where does it say that they cannot discuss some personal problems or world problems?

The only other time objections were raised to my talking was when I fought Oscar Bonavena in Madison Square Garden, and the New York Boxing Commissioner, Dooley, put in a special rule aimed at me which declared that if either fighter talked during the fight a fine of five thousand dollars would be levied, which I thought was a compliment, since Bonavena understands no English and I speak no Spanish.

I keep talking. Too much is at stake to stop this fight. Too much has gone into making it; a billion people around the world are watching it. I'm not worried about the referee. After all, he knows I will not neglect my work while I lecture George. I will enlighten his mind while I whip him.

The public will not be cheated. In fact, I will perform even better than if I go out slugging like a deadpan Frankenstein robot.

"Sucker," I explain, "I'm too fast for a big, slow mummy. Your title is gone. You never should have come to Africa."

"All right, all right!" Clayton gives up. "Go to your corners and come out fighting when you hear the bell, and may the best man . . ."

I flip around and dance to my corner. The thunderous roars come in waves, chants, yells, shouts.

"ALI! ALI! BOMAYE!"

"FOREMAN! THE CHAMPION!"

I've never fought in a stadium like this. I feel at home. So much so, I look across at George and take his measurements as though I'm his undertaker's tailor, outfitting him for the suit he's to wear in his casket. How soon shall I go all out? How soon shall I gamble on getting him in the half-dream?

I've called it the half-dream room since I was a boy, boxing in Louisville, and was knocked down and almost out in the gym for the first time. I went home and thought about it all night. I had seen champions, contenders, professional boxers on TV get knocked down and out. Now I knew how it felt.

It's like in the Golden Gloves tournaments. I'm hit, knocked groggy. The feeling is like being half awake and half dreaming. And your awake half knows what you're dreaming about. In fact, it follows the whole scene. A heavy blow takes you to the door of this room. It opens, and you see neon, orange and green lights blinking. You see bats blowing trumpets, alligators play trombones, and snakes are screaming. Weird masks and actor's clothes hang on the wall.

The first time the blow sends you there, you panic and run, but when you wake up you say, "Well, since it was only a dream, why didn't I play it cool, put on the actor's clothes, the mask, and see what it's like? Only you have to fix it in your mind and plan to do it long before the half-dream comes. For when it comes, time stretches out slow. You have to put the plan in your mind long before you need it. The blow makes your mind vibrate like a tuning fork. You can't let your opponent follow up. You've got to stop the fork from vibrating.

I know how to do it now, like when Frazier knocked me down in the fifteenth round. I get up groggy. I go on the defensive. I act until my head clears, as I did when Norton broke my jaw in the second round and opened the door of the half-dream room. I acted it out until the fight was over.

I know George has never been hurt or dazed. He has never been behind in a single round. Shall I gamble in the first round? When should I go all out to take him to the dream room? Will he know what to do? Has The Champion thought it out as I have?

*   *   *

CLANG! ROUND ONE.

I move out and dance straight into George and throw a fast left. He's bearing down on me, and I dance away and flick out more jabs. I say nothing for the first full minute, but if he thinks this is going to be all work and no education, he's mistaken. Then:

"Come on, Chump! Now's your chance! Show me what you got!"

"You been hitting kindergarten kids!"

A quick jab in the face and his eyes blink.

"Here comes another one, Chump! Another one!"

"Didn't I tell you I was the fastest heavyweight that ever lived?"

"Didn't they tell you, sucker?"

"The round's half over, and you ain't landed a good shot yet."

But in the second half of the round George is executing what he's practiced for months. He's cutting the ring off and forcing me to move six steps to his two, and he's doing it better than anyone I've been up against. I've had fighters chase me—most fighters chase me—but I make them match me step for step. George is the first fighter to consistently cut me off.

He corners me for a few seconds, and I find myself lying against the ropes. The Champion moves in, throwing long rights and lefts, haymaker hooks. He's at the peak of his strength, and he hurls one left, his "anywhere" punch that strikes and makes me feel exactly as Bossman Jones described it.

"DANCE, CHAMP! DANCE!" I hear Bundini crying out.

"MOVE, ALI! MOVE!" Angelo is calling.

All during training I had planned to stay off the ropes. Now I move off and circle the ring, but before the end of the round I know I've got to change my plans. Sadler and Archie have drilled George too well. He does his job like a robot, but he does it well.

I'm famous for being hard to hit in the first rounds, but no fighter can last fifteen if he has to take six steps to his opponent's three. When the first round is over, when I'm back in my corner, Angelo's voice is urgent: "Keep moving. You've got to stay off those ropes!"

The only thing my cornermen see out there is that I need to move, but I see something else. In the first three minutes I felt George's power, and I understand how Frazier and Norton were destroyed. I see what his Board of Strategy has planned.

I'm looking directly across into his corner when Blood alerts me that George's man, Doc Broadus, has come over and is standing at the foot of the stairs, directly under my corner, to hear what I'm saying. Blood wants to throw him out. I shake my head. "Leave him alone. I'm the only one George is listening to out there."

"Move and sting him!" Angelo is whispering. "Sting him!"

*   *   *

CLANG! ROUND TWO.

I move to the center, jab and dance and jab. But I know now that my danger is not in the corners or on the ropes, but in dancing six steps to George's three. His Board of Strategy knows at that pace he's forcing me to move. It won't be George who will be exhausted by round nine. It'll be me.

"ALI! DANCE! DANCE, CHAMP! DANCE!"

I dance, and in a clinch, glance down at those on ringside. My eyes fall for a split second on Eddie Futch, manager of Joe Frazier, once manager of Ken Norton, yelling up encouragement to George. New York newspapers are hailing Futch as the only trainer who has had fighters to defeat Ali, and Futch predicts: "George will corner Muhammad and destroy him. Nothing in the world can keep George from driving him into a corner, and when he does . . . George has the power of Joe Louis and Rocky Marciano combined. I pray for Ali's life."

I feel a shot of adrenalin. I have avenged my defeat by Futch's fighters. Now I will defeat Futch.

"DANCE, CHAMP! FLOAT LIKE A BUTTERFLY, STING LIKE A BEE!"

"ALI! ALI! BOMAYE!"

But I've moved into a corner, and my back is against the ropes. George eagerly comes in after me. For the first time in all my fights, I decide not to wait until I'm tired to play the ropes, but to take to the corners while I'm fresh and still strong, to gamble on the ropes all the way.

"Come on, sucker. Show me something, Chump!" . . . "They say you hit hard?" . . . "Is that the best you can do, sissy?"

My cornermen are screaming. I hear friends at ringside, pleading. Some get out of their chairs, come up to the lap of the ring.

"ALI! MOVE OUT OF THE ROPES!"

I taunt George. I goad him.

"You ain't got no punch, you phony!" . . . "Show me something, sucker!"

George roars in like a mob. He's throwing punches with tonnage I never thought a fist could carry. A crowbar in George's right hand crashes through my guard into my head, knocks me into the room of half-dream. My head vibrates like a tuning fork. Neon lights flash on and off.

I've been here before.

I say to myself: I've been hit. I've been hit.

I fight to open the door and go in the room.

"ALI, MOVE!" my cornermen are screaming. In all my life I've never heard the sound of fear from my corner before. "DANCE, CHAMP, DANCE!"

I hear them from far away, for I have crossed into another world and I will never come back to dance in this fight.

I tell myself: I must not get hit again. The tuning fork must stop vibrating. I must open the door of the room—the room I planned to take George into, the half-dream room. He has brought me here first. Only, I've been here before. I know about it. When I see the masks and the actor's clothes hanging on the walls, the lizards playing saxophones and the bats blowing trumpets, I don't panic and run out. I put on actor's clothes. I go on the defensive.

I know the best defense is an offense, that when you give up offense your opponent is free to take his best shots. George's blows explode into my kidneys, my ribs, my head. I lean back. I slip and slide. I catch some on my arms, off my elbows, but I stay on the ropes.

"GET OFF THE ROPES, CHAMP! MOVE!"

But they don't know what I know. I stay on the ropes. Then near the end of the round I rise up and shoot quick, straight jabs and right crosses directly into George's head. POW! POW! POW!

And I must carry on my educational program. I must not let him think his blows can stop me from talking. If I stop talking now, he knows I'm hurt.

"Sucker, is that all you got? Is that the hardest you can hit?"

When the bell rings, I go back to my corner. I see concern, confusion and fear in the eyes of my cornermen. They have strong advice about what I should do, but my head is on the line, not theirs. I've felt the hot breath of The Monster, and they do not know what I know. Even Angelo doesn't remember that for years I've practiced blocking heavy punches at close range from heavyweights in the gym. For years my trainers and advisers have screamed and begged and pleaded in the gyms while I worked laying against the ropes to test the endurance of heavyweights.

I have a theory about speed and endurance in my own weight. I like to test a heavyweight when he's throwing his best shots wide open, to find out how long he can keep it up. I need to know, because I'll have to wear down an opponent stronger than me, and in the gym, practicing year after year, I've discovered something—that heavyweights usually burn down when the wide-open opportunity to punch and punch is in front of him. But this is a gamble now, because George is the strongest heavyweight in the world. Yet I know, too, that George is gambling on knocking me out, at least in the third round.

I've studied George too closely not to know that at times he's a fine, skillful boxer, who can execute the amazing moves and maneuvers he picked up from Saddler and Moore. I've seen him do it. But George has twenty-three knockout victims behind him. It's got to be hard for him to believe that the same methods he used on the others will not make me the twenty-fourth.

Can I make George the victim of his own fantastic success? It's not easy for him to change a habit that works so well.

In a few seconds the bell for round three will ring. George has not had to go beyond round three in five years. He will come at me now with all he's got. Everything in his ego and his psyche is at stake now.

"THE FLEA IN THREE!"

Suddenly the sound of a voice through a megaphone cuts across the arena. It takes my eyes off George and over to the left side of the ring. Elmo Henderson, The Champion's chief clown, is barking through a white megaphone. I expected it, but I still feel a chill. The secret inside Foreman's camp is that I will and must be destroyed by round three.

"OH, YEA! OH, YEA!

"THE FLEA IN THREE!"

Henderson, a tall, lanky retired heavyweight, a natural tout man, devotes his life to "giving the spirit to The Champion." All night he has walked through Kinshasa hotel lobbies and streets, screaming into his megaphone:

"OH, YEA! OH, YEA!

"TODAY IS THE DAY!

"THE FLEA IN THREE!

"GEORGE THE EAGLE WILL FLY!

"ALI THE BUTTERFLY WILL DIE!

"TODAY IS THE DAY!

"OH, YEA! OH, YEA!"

Bundini clashed with Henderson in the hotel lobbies and tried to outshout him: "You can't beat God's son! Put your money where your mouth is!" But Henderson's voice is even louder than Bundini's. He would stand before a crowd and shout until Bundini would fade away saying, "I can't deal with a nut."

Angelo is pleading in my ear, "Keep off the ropes. Keep in the center of the ring. Make him box!"

And Elmo rings out his prophecy:

"THE FLEA IN THREE!"

CLANG! ROUND THREE.

I move quick and shoot jabs with sting. POW! POW! POW! George blinks, but moves forward like a big tank. He controls the center of the ring, as though he expects me to challenge him, but I go back to the ropes and to the corner. And I call to him: "All right, sucker! This is where you want me. Come on, man!"

I'm talking louder and louder, and the referee is hissing at me, "Be quiet, Ali. Be quiet. I warned you the last time! Stop talking!"

His voice makes me look at his face. It's tight, tense. Zack has refereed a thousand fights. He was the third man in the ring when I knocked out Sonny Liston in Maine. He anticipates the action in a fight better than any referee in the ring, and he knows this is George's "murder" round. But if he expects me to be quiet on the day I'm supposed to die, he's mistaken.

I'm snapping jabs in George's face and talking through my mouthpiece: "Where's your punch, sucker? Show me! You ain't got nothin'! Show me somethin'!" . . . "Here I am! Come and get me!"

My corner is screaming, "ALI, GET OFF THE ROPES! STICK HIM! JAB! MOVE OFF THE ROPES!"

George is throwing bombs at my head. I lean back, but he stays on top of me. I'm amazed at how he can pack power into every punch. Every punch is a haymaker. I block them from my head, and suddenly he switches, comes up from the floor with an uppercut that seems to blow my jaw off. I'm hurt. I try to hold on.

"GET OFF THE ROPES! DANCE, CHAMP, DANCE!"

I try to move off, but he pushes me back like a rag doll. The tuning fork in my head is humming. I've got to hold on. I've got to keep him from following up. George senses that I'm hurt, and he's coming in for the kill. I block, move back and weave. It's the longest round I've ever fought in my life, but near the end my head begins to clear.

George keeps roaring in with his head straight up, confident all I will do is take cover. Suddenly I come out from under with straight lefts and rights directly into his face. WHAM! WHAM! WHAM!

The crowd roars. They come to life as if they're seeing me rise from the dead.

WHAM! WHAM! WHAM! They're not powerful punches, but they shake him up.

"MOVE, CHAMP! DANCE! MOVE, CHAMP!"

George looks startled. He throws his heaviest bomb, it curls around my head and we clinch so tight I feel his heart pounding. I bite his ear. "Is that the best you can do, sucker? Is that all you got, Chump? You ain't got no punch! You in big trouble, boy!"

I feel his breath coming in gasps, and I know I'm taking something out of him. I know this round will go down on the judges' scorecards as belonging to George, but there's something in it that belongs to me.

When the round ends, my head is humming. But the round of my execution is over, and all I will do now is plot the time when my turn comes. I take a deep swig from my water bottle and wash the blood out of my mouth.

Bundini is crying, "Champ, you got to move! You got to stick and move!"

"He wants you on the ropes. Don't let him!" Angelo is desperate.

I rarely ask for advice from my corner, and seldom accept what they say. And now, more than any time, I know they do not understand what's happening out there.

The stadium crowd is all I'm listening to:

"ALI! ALI! BOMAYE! ALI! ALI! BOMAYE!"

They chant in Lingala, but I know that "Bomaye" means:

"KNOCK HIM DOWN! KILL HIM DEAD!"

They've seen me take the worst shelling I've had in my life, and they still believe I can take the fight. It's like a charge of electricity.

"ALI! ALI! BOMAYE! ALI! ALI! BOMAYE!"

I remember looking down at ringside. My eyes meet Jim Brown's.

Brown has publicly predicted George would knock me out. I lean out of the ring. "Jim Brown! You bet on the wrong horse! This sucker don't have a chance! You lost your money! He can't fight no better than you can act!"

"George is going to lynch you!" a disbeliever next to Brown jumps up and screams.

I can see all of George's corner looking over at me, shocked that instead of resting I'm taking the entire time educating the disbelievers around the ring. Before the bell rings, I stand up and wave my gloves to direct my choir.

"ALI! ALI! BOMAYE!"

CLANG! ROUND FOUR.
CLANG! ROUND FIVE.
CLANG! ROUND SIX.
CLANG! ROUND SEVEN.

I lay on the ropes through them all, and I come to life near the end of each round just when George thinks my life is over.

WHAM! WHAM! WHAM! WHAM! into The Champion's face and head. In the clinches, I measure his heavy breathing. The slowdown in his punches, the weakening of his recoil. And I talk to him like an old friend, louder and louder: "You gone six rounds, sucker, and you ain't hit me yet! Who said you could hit? Come on! I'll give you a chance. Swing, sucker! Swing!"

Then, WHAM! WHAM! WHAM! I pop him straight in the eye. "Look at your eye, sucker! I ain't even touched the cut eye yet. I'm hittin' the good eye!"

But George keeps driving on like a one-way tank, every ounce of his 220 pounds behind his blows. I'm draining him, but it's coming near time when I've got to go all out before he gets his second wind. Tired as he is, it will take the heaviest blows I've ever thrown to bring him down.

When the seventh round nears the end, I clinch him tightly and give my best advice: "You got eight more rounds to go, sucker! Eight more rounds, and look how tired you are. I ain't even got started, and you out of breath! Look at you! Out of gas, and I'm whippin' you."

He throws a long, almost slow-motion swing, and I block it and come in with two quick jabs to his face. POP! POP! "Look at your eye, chump! Ain't you 'shamed? Those pretty African girls sittin' out there lookin' at your eye all messed up?"

Sadler is yelling at him from the corner. Archie Moore is trying to say something to him. But I know he's listening to me. "Don't listen to those fools in your corner. Don't listen to Archie and Sadler. They're foolin' you. They didn't tell you how bad I was, did they? They didn't tell you I was the baddest in the world. They lied to you. You got eight—EIGHT— long rounds to go, sucker! And you can hardly make it past this one."

The bell rings, and I feel pain all over me. Even my cornermen now sense something is being turned around.

I sit down, but I feel uneasy. The pace is killing George, but it's also taking a heavy toll on me. I've got to go for the kill before he gets his second wind. I know The Champion is more exhausted than I am, but how long can I stand up under this barrage? I look at George's corner. He's had to go into the eighth round only three times in his life. Every minute now will be strange, unsure.

I remember catching the eye of a tall African girl walking by, flashing the number of the upcoming round. She winks at me. I wink back and feel better.

CLANG! ROUND EIGHT.

George storms out, still only one thing on his mind: knockout. But now his blows come slower, take longer to reach me. I know fire and pain are inside his stomach and lungs, and every breath is torture, just as it is for me. I see him draw back for a mighty swing with all his power, and I slip aside and he tangles himself in the ropes. "Sucker!" I say. "You missed by a mile! You look bad, chump!"

I keep my eyes pinned on his eyes. I never even blink. I don't want to miss anything his face might say, and his eyes tell me everything. As I watch him pull himself back into the ring, I suddenly think of Joe Frazier. Have I been treating George as though he's another Frazier? If you knock Frazier down, he'll get up almost before he hits the canvas and come back at you. His heart is a lion. When Frazier comes at you, his blood and marrow and muscles all scream at you: "If you can't kill me, get out of my way, or I'll kill you!" He'll fight way beyond exhaustion and still come on. Even when his lungs are tired and burning, when every ounce of blood is drained out of him, he still keeps coming. Whatever the price, he'll pay it. You can knock him down a dozen times, and he'll still bounce back up and come again.

George *looks* like King Kong when he comes at you, but does he have the heart—of a Joe Louis, Rocky Marciano, Henry Armstrong? A Joe Frazier?

Only a man who knows what it is to be defeated can reach down to the bottom of his soul and come up with the extra ounce of power it takes to win when the match is even. I know George wants to keep The Champion's crown. He wants the crown, but is he willing to pay the price? Would he lay out his life?

It's time to go all out. Toe to toe. George pours out a long left, and I cross my right over it. Now I've got to lay it all down on the line. If the price of winning is to be a broken jaw, a smashed nose, a cracked skull, a disfigured face, you pay it if you want to be King of the Heavyweights. If you want to wear the crown, you can play it careful only until you meet a man who will die before he lets you win. Then you have to lay it all on the line or back down and be damned forever.

The crowd eggs me on: "ALI! ALI! BOMAYE!"

I hear Kid Gavilan, the old Cuban Champion of a thousand fights, telling me, "Ali, the crowd'll push you on like they own a piece of you, like there's something in their life that depends on whether you live or die. And you'll get into something too deep to back down. You've been calling out, 'I'm the prettiest. I'm the greatest. See how pretty I am. Not a scratch!' They laugh, but one day the people will test you out. They will send you into a den to take meat out of the lion's mouth and see who comes out the prettiest. If you die trying, they'll be sorry for you, but if you back down, they'll remember you as a phony forever. When you fight for the title, you lay it all on the line."

I know it's time for the test. I see George trying to lumber back, to regain his poise. I shoot a straight right to his jaw with all the snap and power that's in me. I strike him almost flush on the chin, and he stands still.

Archie Moore will say the blow would have knocked out anybody, but I know, had I thrown it in the earlier rounds, George would have been strong enough to shake it off.

I'm ready to follow through with combinations, but I see he's slowly falling, a dazed look in his eyes. I know he's entering the room of the half-dream for the first time in his life. George is down, his eyes glazed. He's listening to the tuning forks humming in his head, bats blowing saxophones, alligators whistling, neon signs blinking.

The referee begins the count. George will later protest that he was the victim of a short count, and I can understand why. In the half-dream room time seems to stretch out slow, like rubber, and unless you've been there before, you'll never know how fast it goes by.

I watch every lift of the referee's arm. I remember thinking again of Frazier. He would never lose the crown lying on the floor. No referee could count over his body as long as he had blood in it.

"Six . . . seven . . . eight . . ."

George is turning over slowly.

"Nine . . . ten!"

George is on his feet, but it's over. The referee raises my hand in victory.

And the stadium explodes. People break past the paratroopers and climb over the press tables, climb into the ring.

Archie has wrapped his arms around George, and I holler, "Archie, am I too old?"

Archie jerks his head my way. There's a gleam in his eye. He raises his fists and shouts, "Your time is coming! Your day will come!"

And this I know. But the referee is raising *my* hand, and the whole world is screaming, "ALI! ALI! ALI! ALI!"

A reporter claws his way through the crowd and yells at me, "How did you do it, World Heavyweight Champion? What you think of George now?''

I shake my head. I want to go to my dressing room. I don't want to tell him what George has taught me. That too many victories weaken you. That the defeated can rise up stronger than the victor.

But I take nothing away from George. He can still beat any man in the world.

Except me.

THE PATTERSON-LISTON FIGHT

By Norman Mailer

On the afternoon of the night Emile Griffith and Benny Paret were to fight a third time for the welterweight championship, there was murder in both camps. "I hate that kind of guy," Paret had said earlier to Pete Hamill about Griffith. "A fighter's got to look and talk and act like a man." One of the Broadway gossip columnists had run an item about Griffith a few days before. His girl friend saw it and said to Griffith, "Emile, I didn't know about you being that way." So Griffith hit her. So he said. Now at the weigh-in that morning, Paret had insulted Griffith irrevocably, touching him on the buttocks, while making a few more remarks about his manhood. They almost had their fight on the scales.

The accusation of homosexuality arouses a major passion in many men; they spend their lives resisting it with a biological force. There is a kind of man who spends every night of his life getting drunk in a bar, he rants, he brawls, he ends in a small rumble on the street; women say, "For God's sakes, he's homosexual. Why doesn't he just turn queer and get his suffering over with." Yet men protect him. It is because he is choosing not to become homosexual. It was put best by Sartre who said that a homosexual is a man who practices homosexuality. A man who does not, is not homosexual—he is entitled to the dignity of his choice. He is entitled to the fact that he chose not to become homosexual, and is paying presumably his price.

The rage in Emile Griffith was extreme. I was at the fight that night, I had never seen a fight like it. It was scheduled for fifteen rounds, but they fought without stopping from the bell which began the round to the bell which ended it, and then they fought after the bell, sometimes for as much as fifteen seconds before the referee could force them apart.

Paret was a Cuban, a proud club fighter who had become welterweight champion because of his unusual ability to take a punch. His style of fighting was to take three punches to the head in order to give back two. At the end of ten rounds, he would still be bouncing, his opponent would have a headache. But in the last two years, over the fifteen-round fights, he had started to take some bad maulings.

This fight had its turns. Griffith won most of the early rounds, but Paret knocked Griffith down in the sixth. Griffith had trouble getting up, but made it, came alive and was dominating Paret again before the round was over. Then Paret began to wilt. In the middle of the eighth round, after a clubbing punch had turned his back to Griffith, Paret walked three disgusted steps away, showing his hindquarters. For a champion, he took much too long to turn back around. It was the first hint of weakness Paret had ever shown, and it must have inspired a particular shame, because he fought the rest of the fight as if he were seeking to demonstrate that he could take more punishment than any man alive. In the twelfth, Griffith caught him. Paret got trapped in a corner. Trying to duck away, his left arm and his head became tangled on the wrong side of the top rope. Griffith was in like a cat ready to rip the life out of a huge boxed rat. He hit him eighteen right hands in a row, an act which took perhaps three or four seconds, Griffith making a pent-up whimpering sound all the while he attacked, the right hand whipping like a piston rod which has broken through the crankcase, or like a baseball bat demolishing a pumpkin. I was sitting in the second row of that corner—they were not ten feet away from me, and like everybody else, I was hypnotized. I had never seen one man hit another so hard and so many times. Over the referee's face came a look of woe as if some spasm had passed its way through him, and then he leaped on Griffith to pull him away. It was the act of a brave man. Griffith was uncontrollable. His trainer leaped into the ring, his manager, his cut man, there were four people holding Griffith, but he was off on an orgy, he had left the Garden, he was back on a hoodlum's street. If he had been able to break loose from his handlers and the referee, he would have jumped Paret to the floor and whaled on him there.

And Paret? Paret died on his feet. As he took those eighteen punches something happened to everyone who was in psychic range of the event. Some part of his death reached out to us. One felt it hover in the air. He was still standing in the ropes, trapped as he had been before, he gave some little half-smile of regret, as if he were saying, "I didn't know I was going to die just yet," and then, his head leaning back but still erect, his death came to breathe about him. He began to pass away. As he passed, so his limbs descended beneath him, and he sank slowly to the floor. He went down more slowly than any fighter had ever gone down, he went down like a large ship which turns on end and slides second by second into its grave. As he went down, the sound of Griffith's punches echoed in the mind like a heavy ax in the distance chopping into a wet log.

Paret lay on the ground, quivering gently, a small froth on his mouth. The house doctor jumped into the ring. He knelt. He pried Paret's eyelid open. He looked at the eyeball staring out. He let the lid snap shut. He reached into his satchel, took out a needle, jabbed Paret with a stimulant. Paret's back rose in a high arch. He writhed in real agony. They were calling him back from death. One wanted to cry out, "Leave the man alone. Let him die." But they saved Paret long enough to take him to a hospital where he lingered for days. He was in coma. He never came out of it. If he lived, he would have been a vegetable. His brain was smashed. But they held him in life for a week, they fed him chemicals, and made exploratory operations into his skull, and fed details of his condition to The Goat. And The Goat kicked clods of mud all over the place, and spoke harshly of prohibiting boxing. There was shock in the land. Children had seen the fight on television. There were editorials, gloomy forecasts that the Game was dead. The managers and the prizefighters got together. Gently, in thick, depressed hypocrisies, they tried to defend their sport. They did not find it easy to explain that they shared an unstated view of life which was religious.

It was of course not that religion which is called Judeo-Christian. It was an older religion, a more primitive one—a religion of blood, a murderous and sensitive religion which mocks the effort of the understanding to approach it, and scores the lungs of men like D. H. Lawrence, and burns the brains of men like Ernest Hemingway when they explore out into the mystery, searching to discover some part of the secret. It is the view of life which looks upon death as a condition which is more alive than life or unspeakably more deadening. As such it is not a very attractive notion to the Establishment. But then the Establishment has nothing very much of even the Judeo-Christian tradition. It has a respect for legal and administrative aspects of justice, and it is devoted to the idea of compassion for the poor. But the Establishment has no idea of death, no tolerance for Heaven or Hell, no comprehension of bloodshed. It sees no logic in pain. To the Establishment these notions are a detritus from the past.

Like a patient submerged beneath the plastic cover of an oxygen tent, boxing lives on beneath the cool, bored eyes of the doctors in the Establishment. It would not take too much to finish boxing off. Shut down the oxygen, which is to say, turn that switch in the mass media which still gives sanction to organized pugilism, and the fight game would be dead.

But the patient is permitted to linger for fear the private detectives of the Establishment, the psychiatrists and psychoanalysts, might not be able to neutralize the problem of gang violence. Not so well as the Game. Of course, the moment some piece of diseased turnip capable of being synthesized cheaply might prove to have the property of tranquilizing a violent young man for a year, the Establishment would wipe out boxing. Every time a punk was arrested, the police would prescribe a pill, and violence would walk the street sheathed and numb. Of course the Mob would lose revenue, but then the Mob is also part of the Establishment, it, and the labor unions and the colleges and the newspapers and the corporations are all part of the Establishment. The Establishment is never simple. It needs the Mob to grease the chassis on its chariot. Therefore, the Mob would be placated. In a society with strong central government, it is not so difficult to turn up a new source of revenue. What is more difficult is to enter the plea that violence may be an indispensable element of life. This is not the place to have the argument: it is enough to say that if the liberal Establishment is right in its unstated credo that death is a void, and man leads out his life suspended momentarily above that void, why then there is no argument at all. Whatever shortens life is monstrous. We have not the right to shorten life, since life is the only possession of the psyche, and in death we have only nothingness. What then can there be said in defense of sports-car racing, war, or six-ounce gloves?

But if we go from life into a death which is larger than our life has been, or into a death which is small, if death comes to nothing for one man because he swallowed his death in his life, and if for another death is alive with dimension, then the certitudes of the Establishment lose power. A drug which offers peace to a pain may dull the nerve which could have taught the mind how to carry that pain into the death which comes on the next day or on the decades that follow. A tranquilizer gives coma to an anxiety which may later smell of the dungeon, beneath the ground. If we are born into life as some living line of intent from an eternity which may have tortured us or nurtured us in death, then we may be obliged to go back to death with more courage and art than we left it. Or face the dim end of going back with less.

That is the existential venture, the unstated religious view of boxers trying to beat each other into unconsciousness or, ultimately, into death. It is the culture of the killer who sickens the air about him if he does not find some half-human way to kill a little in order not to deaden all. It is a defense against the plague, against that plague which comes from violence converted into the nausea of all that nonviolence which is void of peace. Paret's death was with horror, but not all the horror was in the beating, much was in the way his death was cheated. Which is to say that his death was twice a nightmare. I knew that something in boxing was spoiled forever for me, that there would be a fear in watching a fight now which was like the fear one felt for any *novillero* when he was having an unhappy day, the bull was dangerous, and the crowd was ugly. You knew he would get hurt. There is fascination in seeing that the first time, but it is not as enjoyable as one expects. It is like watching a novelist who has written a decent book get run over by a car.

Something in boxing was spoiled. But not the principle, not the right for one man to try to knock another out in the ring. That was perhaps not a civilized activity, but it belonged to the tradition of the humanist, it was a human activity, it showed a part of what man was like, it belonged to his ability to create art and artful movement on the edge of death or pain or danger or attack, and it had much to say about the subtleties of human style. For there are boxers whose bodies move like a fine brain, and there are others who pound the opposition down with the force of a trade-union leader, there are fools and wits and patient craftsmen among boxers, wild men full of a sense of outrage, and steady oppressive peasants, clever spoilers, dogged infantrymen who walk forward all night, hypnotists (like

Liston), dancers, lovers, mothers giving a scolding, horsemen high on their legs. There is knowledge to be found about our nature, and the nature of animals, of big cats, lions, tigers, gorillas, bears, walruses (Archie Moore), birds, elephants, jackals, bulls. No, I was not down on boxing, but I loved it with freedom no longer. It was more like somebody in your family was fighting now. And the feeling one had for a big fight was no longer clear of terror in its excitement. There was awe in the suspense.

But then there is nothing else very much like being at a Heavyweight Championship fight. It is to some degree the way a Hollywood premiere once ought to have been; it's a big party with high action—there is the same rich flush of jewelry, bourbon, bare shoulders, cha-cha, silk, the promise that a life or two will be changed by tonight; it is even a bit like a political convention; it is much more like an event none of us will ever see —conceive of sitting in a classic arena waiting for a limited war with real bullets to begin between a platoon of Marines and two mounted squads of Russian Cossacks—you'd have the sensation of what a Heavyweight Championship can promise. A great heavyweight fight could take place in the center of a circus.

Ideally, it should take place in New York. Because Broadway turns out and Hollywood flies in with Las Vegas on the hip, and many of the wings and dovecotes and banlieues of what even a couple of years ago was called Café Society is there, and International Set (always seeing their first fight), and Big Business, and every good-looking call girl in New York, and some not so good-looking, and all the figures from the history pages of prizefighting in America, as well as ghosts there are some to claim—the ghost of Benny Leonard, the ghost of Harry Greb. Plus all the models, loose celebrities, socialites of high and lower rank, hierarchies from the racetrack, politicians, judges, and—one might offer a prayer if one really cared—one sociologist of wit and distinction ought to be there to capture for America the true status of its conflicting aristocracies: does Igor Cassini rate with Mickey Rooney or does Roger Blough get a row in front of Elizabeth Taylor? Is Frank Sinatra honored before Mrs. Woodward? Does Zsa Zsa Gabor come in ahead of Mayor Wagner? The First Sociologists of America are those professionals who sell the hot seats for a big fight in New York.

In Chicago, there was little of this. If there are nine circles to Hell, there were nine clouds over this fight. D'Amato was not licensed to manage in New York. Small matter. Patterson once again would fight in New York without him. But Liston was not cleared to fight by the State Boxing Commission—the shadow of the Establishment lay against him. So the fight was transferred to Chicago which promptly took fire. If Patterson-Liston was not clean enough for New York, it was not cool enough for Chicago. The local newspapers gave the kind of publicity one tastes in cold canned food. The stories on training were buried. Interest was greater outside the city than within. Yet little of Broadway arrived and less of Hollywood. You cannot get producers and movie stars to travel a distance to watch two Negroes fight. A bitch lives to see a white man fight a black man. She's not prejudiced—depending on the merits, she'll root for either, but a Negro against a Negro wets no juice.

And then there was poor weather. The day before the fight was misty, chilly. It rained on and off, and cleared inconclusively on Tuesday, which was cold. Fight night was cold enough to wear a topcoat. Comiskey Park was far from filled. It could hold fifty thousand for a big fight; it ended with less than twenty in paid admissions. Twenty-six thousand people showed. Proportions were poor. Because of theatre television, Patterson would make more money on this fight than any fighter had ever made, and there was much local interest in cities all over America. Parties were got up to go to the theatre, see it on television. The press coverage was larger than average, larger let us say than any of the three Johansson fights or the Marciano-Walcott fights. It was the biggest fight in ten years, it was conceivably the biggest fight since Louis fought Schmeling the second time, and yet nobody in the city where it was fought seemed to care. Radio, with its roaring inside hysteria, had lost to television, that grey eminence which now instructed Americans in the long calm of Ecclesiastes: vanity of vanities, all events are vanity.

So for a celebrity hunter, ringside was nothing formidable at this fight. The good people of Chicago turned out modestly. The very good people—which is to say, the very rich—turned out for ringside, and had a chance to cross the outfield grass, luminous green in the half-light of the baseball towers, and walk to their seats under the great folded wings of the grandstand. Ever since the Romans built the Colosseum, arenas take on a prehistoric breath at night—one could be a black ant walking inside the circle a pterodactyl must have made with its wing as it slept. Or is it hills like dark elephants of which we speak?

I had a seat in the working press five rows from the ring. An empty seat away was Jimmy Baldwin. There had been a chill between us in the last year. Not a feud, but bad feeling. We had been glad, however, to see each other in Chicago. Tacitly, settling no differences, not talking about it, we had thought to be friendly. But the unsettled differences were still there. Two nights ago, at a party, we had had a small fight. We each insulted the other's good intentions and turned away. Now we sat with a hundred-pound cake of ice on the empty seat between us. After ten minutes, I got up and went for a walk around the ring.

The Press section occupied the first six rows. Back of us was an aisle which made a larger square around the square of the ring. On the other side of this aisle was the first row of ringside seats. This was as close as you could come to the fight if you had entered by buying a ticket. So I took a sampling of the house as I walked around the square. If this had been New York, you would expect to find twelve movie stars in the front row. But this was Chicago. Behind us were a muster of local Irish politicians, big men physically in the mold of Jimmy Braddock, not unhappy tonight with their good seats.

The front row to my right and the front row across the ring from me was given over in part to the Mob. They were the most intricate faces one would find this side of Carpaccio or Bellini, chins with hooks and chisels, nostrils which seemed to screw the air up into the head, thin-lipped mouths like thin-nosed pliers, eyes which behind their dark glasses scrutinized your interior until they could find the tool in you which would work for them, and then would flip away like the turning of a card. Yes, those two rows of seats made up a right angle of *don capos* and a few very special Catholic priests, thin, ascetic, medieval in appearance, as well as a number of field officers dressed in black like subalterns, but older, leaner, with more guilds at their command. They were well-seated. They filled close to every seat around the corner.

It proved to be Patterson's corner.

That was art. They did not have to do much more. Sitting there, they could devote their study to Patterson. He would see them when he came back to his corner, his seconds would be obliged to look at them each time a new round began and they climbed down the steps from the corner. The back of the cornermen's necks would be open to detailed inspection, the calves of Patterson's leg, as he sat resting on the stool, would be a ready target for mental arrows. Like Lilliputians they could shoot thousands of pins into Gulliver.

I completed the tour. The last row, Liston's corner, was routine: musclemen, mobsters, business-sporting, a random sample. Turning the angle I came back to my seat, and sat watching a preliminary, shivering a little in the cold. It was much too cold for a fight. The sensitivity to magic I had felt earlier in the evening would not come back. There was just a dull sense of apprehension. Everything was wrong.

The preliminaries ended. Visiting fighters were called up from the crowd to take a bow. Archie Moore drew a large hand: he was wearing a black-silk cape with a white lining and he twirled the cape with éclat. It said: ''Go away, all solemn sorcerers, the magic man is here.''

Patterson and Liston arrived within a minute of each other. The visiting fighters who were gathered in the ring said hello to each man, shook their gloves, and went back to their seats.

The Star-Spangled Banner was played. Liston stood in his corner with his handlers, the referee stood in the middle of the ring, and Cus D'Amato stood alone, eight feet away from Patterson and his seconds. Since D'Amato was across from me, I could see his face clearly. It was as pale as his white sweater. His face was lifted to the sky, his eyes were closed. While the anthem played, D'Amato held his hand to his heart as if he were in anguish. I had the impression he was praying with fear.

The anthem ended, the fighters took their instructions from the referee, and stripped their robes. Their bodies made a contrast. Liston, only an inch taller than Patterson, weighed 214 pounds to Patterson's 189. But the difference was not just in weight. Liston had a sleek body, fully muscled, but round. It was the body of a strong man, but the muscles looked to have been shaped by pleasure as much as by work. He was obviously a man who had had some very good times.

Whereas Patterson still had poverty in his muscles. He was certainly not weak, there was whipcord in the way he was put together, but it was still the dry, dedicated body of an athlete, a track man, a disciplinarian: it spoke little of leisure and much of the gym. There was a lack eating at it, some misery.

The bell rang.

Liston looked scared.

Patterson looked grim.

They came together with no vast impact, trying for small gains. Each was moving with large respect for the other. Liston had the unhappy sweaty look in his eye of the loudest-talking champion on a city block— he has finally gotten into a fight with one of the Juniors, and he knows this Junior can fight. If he loses he's got much to lose. So Liston was trying to make Junior keep distance.

Patterson was not doing much. He threw a fast left hook which missed, then he circled a bit, fighting from a crouch. He lunged in once very low, trying to get under Liston's long jab and work to the stomach, but his timing was not acute and he drew back quickly. There had been no inspiration, no life, and a hint of clumsiness. But it had been intellectually sound. It caused no harm. Then he tried again, feinting a left hook, and slipping Liston's left jab, but as he came in close, Liston grabbed him with both arms, and they bulled back and forth until the referee separated them. Now, they each had an unhappy look on their faces as if they were big men who had gotten into an altercation in a bar, and didn't like the physical activity of fighting. Each of them looked like it would take three or four rounds to warm up.

All this had used a minute. Liston seemed to have gained the confidence that he was stronger, and he began crowding Patterson to the rope, throwing a good many punches, not left hooks, not left jabs, not uppercuts or straight rights, just thick, slow, clubbing punches. None of them landed on Patterson's body or head, they all banged on his arms, and occasionally Patterson would bang Liston back on the arm. It is a way of fighting. A strong slow fighter will sometimes keep hitting the other man on the shoulder or the biceps until his arms go dead. If the opponent is in condition, it is a long procedure. I was surprised at how slow Liston's punches were. From ringside, they looked easy to block. He had a way of setting himself and going "ahem" before he threw the punch. It is, of course, one thing to block punches from your seat at ringside, and another to block them in a ring, but when a fighter is punching with real speed and snap, you can't block the punches from where you sit. Even from thirty feet away, you are fooled.

All that was fooling me now was Patterson. He seemed sluggish. He was not getting hit with Liston's punches, but he was not hitting back, he seemed to miss one small opportunity after another. He was fighting like a college heavyweight who has gone in to work with a professional and is getting disheartened at the physical load of such sparring. He had the expression on his face of somebody pushing a Cadillac which has run out of gas.

Then occurred what may have been the most extraordinary moment ever seen in a championship fight. It was very spooky. Patterson, abruptly, without having been hurt in any visible way, stood up suddenly out of his crouch, his back a foot from the ropes, and seemed to look half up into the sky as if he had seen something there or had been struck by something from there, by some transcendent bolt, and then he staggered like a man caught in machine-gun fire, and his legs went, and he fell back into the ropes. His left glove became tangled in the top rope, almost as Paret's arm had been tangled, and that murmur of death, that visitation which had passed into Madison Square Garden on the moment Paret began to die, seemed a breath from appearing now, Patterson looked at Liston with one lost look, as if somehow he had been expecting this to happen ever since the night it happened to Paret; it was the look of a man saying, "Don't kill me," and then Liston hit him two or three ill-timed punches, banging a sloppy stake into the ground, and Patterson went down. And he was out. He was not faking. He had started to pass out at the moment he stood straight on his feet and was struck by that psychic bolt which had come from wherever it had come.

Patterson rolled over, he started to make an attempt to get to his feet, and Baldwin and I were each shouting, "Get up, get up!" But one's voice had no force in it, one's will had no life.

Patterson got up somewhere between a quarter and a half second too late. You could see the critical instant pass in the referee's body, and Patterson was still getting his glove off the ground. The fight was over: 2:06 of the First. It must have been the worst fight either fighter had ever had.

Liston looked like he couldn't believe what had happened. He was blank for two or three long seconds, and then he gave a whoop. It was an artificial, tentative whoop, but it seemed to encourage him because he gave another which sounded somewhat better, and then he began to whoop and whoop and laugh and shout because his handlers had come into the ring and were hugging him and telling him he was the greatest fighter that ever lived. And Patterson, covered quickly with his bathrobe, still stunned, turned and buried his head in Cus D'Amato's shoulder.

From the stands behind us came one vast wave of silence. Here and there sounded cheers or applause, but you could hear each individual voice or pair of hands clapping into the silence.

"What happened?" said Baldwin.

*   *   *

What did happen? Everybody was to ask that question later. But in private.

The descriptions of the fight fed next morning to The Goat showed no uncertainty. They spoke of critical upper-cuts and powerful left hooks and pulverizing rights. Liston talked of dominating Patterson with left hands, Patterson's people said it was a big right which did the job, some reporters called the punches crunching, others said they were menacing, brutal, demolishing. One did not read a description of the fight which was not authoritative. The only contradiction, a most minor contradiction, is that with one exception, a wire-service photograph used everywhere of a right hand by Liston which has apparently just left Patterson's chin, there were no pictures—and a point was made of looking at a good many—which show Liston putting a winning glove into Patterson's stomach, solar plexus, temple, nose, or jaw. In fact there is not a single picture of Liston's glove striking Patterson at all. It is not highly probable the photographers missed every decent punch. Fight photographers are capable of splitting the strictest part of a second in order to get the instant of impact. The fine possibility is that there was no impact. There was instead an imprecise beating, that is a beating which was not convincing if the men were anywhere near to equal in strength. Something had happened to Patterson, however. He fought as if he were down with jaundice. It was not that he did not do his best; he always did his determined best; he did just that against Liston. It is just that his best this night was off the spectrum of his normal condition. Something had struck at him. From inside himself or from without, in that instant he straightened from his crouch and stared at the sky, he had the surprise of a man struck by treachery.

Now I am forced to give a most improper testimony, because I felt as if I were a small part of that treachery and one despairs of trying to explain how that could be so.

A man turns to boxing because he discovers it is the best experience of his life. If he is a good fighter, his life in the center of the ring is more intense than it can be anywhere else, his mind is more exceptional than at any other time, his body has become a live part of his brain. Some men are geniuses when they are drunk; a good fighter feels a bit of genius when he is having a good fight. This illumination comes not only from the discipline he has put on his body or the concentration of his mind to getting ready for his half hour in the open, but no, it comes as well from his choice to occupy the stage on an adventure whose end is unknown. For the length of his fight, he ceases to be a man and becomes a Being, which is to say he is no longer finite in the usual sense, he is no longer a creature of a given size and dress with a name and some habits which are predictable. Liston-in-the-ring was not just Sonny Liston; much more he was the nucleus of that force at Comiskey Park (and indeed from everywhere in the world from which such desire could reach) which wished him to win or hated

him with an impotence that created force, to wit, hated him less than it
feared him, and so betrayed its hate since the telepathic logic of the unconscious makes us give our strength to those we think to hate but favor
despite ourselves. Just so, Patterson-in-the-ring was not Floyd Patterson
sparring in his gym, but was instead a vehicle of all the will and all the
particular love which truly wished him to win, as well as a target of all the
hatred which was not impotent but determined to strike him down.

When these universes collided, the impact if not clear was total. The
world quivered in some rarefied accounting of subtle psychic seismo-
graphs, and the stocks of certain ideal archetypes shifted their status in our
country's brain. Sex had proved superior to Love still one more time, the
Hustler had taken another pool game from the Infantryman, the Syndicate
rolled out the Liberal, the Magician hyped the Artist, and, since there were
more than a few who insisted on seeing them simply as God and the Devil
(whichever much or little of either they might be), then the Devil had
shown that the Lord was dramatically weak.

The Goat would demand that this fight be reported in a veritable
factology of detail. America could not listen to questions. The professional
witnesses to the collision, the pipers of cancer gulch, were obliged to
testify to a barrage of detailed punches, and the fighters reexamining their
own history in such a mirror of prose would be forced to remake the event
in their mind. Yet so long as one kept one's memory, the event was unclear. The result had been turned by betrayal. And it was by one's own
person that the guilt was felt. I had been there with half a body from half a
night of sleep for too many nights, and half a brain from too many bouts of
drinking drinks I did not want that much, and dim in concentration because
I was brooding about the loss of a friendship which it was a cruel and
stupid waste to lose. And Baldwin too had been brooding. We had sat there
like beasts of burden, empty of psychic force to offer our fighter.

Now, too late, in the bout's sudden wake, like angels whose wings are
wet, we buried our quarrel; this time it might stay buried for a while. "My
Lord," said Jimmy, "I lost seven hundred and fifty dollars tonight."

Well, we laughed. I had lost no more than a paltry twenty-eight.

Later, I went back to the dressing room. But Patterson's door was
locked. Over a hundred reporters were jammed into Liston's room, so
many that one could not see the new champion, one could only hear his
voice. He was resounding very much like Clark Gable now, late Gable
with the pit of his mannerism—that somewhat complacent jam of much
too much love for the self. Liston had the movie star's way of making the
remark which cuts, then balming it with salve. "Did you take your ugly
pills?" says the actor to the leading lady, and gives his smile at her flush.
"Why honey, dear child, I'm only kidding." So Liston said. "The one
time he hurt me was when he got up to a knee at nine. I was afraid he
would come all the way up." Which was class. It whipped. A minute later,
some banana oil was uncorked. "Yessir," said Liston at large, "Floyd is a
heck of a man."

I left that dressing room and tried to get into Patterson's, but the door was still locked. Ingemar Johansson was standing nearby. They were interviewing him over a pay telephone for a radio program. Johansson had a bewildered combative look as if someone had struck him on the back of the head with a loaded jack. He had knocked Patterson down for seven times in one round, there had been wild lightning and "toonder," but he had not been able to keep Patterson down. Now Liston had taken Floyd out with a punch or two or three no witness would agree upon.

"Do you think you can beat Liston," was the interviewer's question.

"I don't know," said Johansson.

"Do you think you have a chance?"

Johansson looked sad and Swedish. "One always has a chance," he said. "I would make my fight and fight it, that's all."

One never did get into Patterson's dressing room. After a while I left and walked around the empty ringside seats. It was cold now. Some of the events of the last few days were coming back to mc in the cold air of Comiskcy Park. They were not agreeable to contemplate. I had done a few unattractive things. I did not want to count them.

A BULLFIGHTER FROM BROOKLYN

By Sidney Franklin

With very little sleep and a corking hangover I barely made the train. On the trip back to Mexico City I took stock and tried to figure out what had happened. I began to feel uneasy. There was much more to bullfighting than I had ever dreamed. I began to understand in part why everyone had seemed so skeptical at what I thought were simple statements. Thank goodness things had turned out as well as they had.

But all that had happened before was nothing to compare with the shock I got when we arrived in the city. Across from the station on a rooftop was an enormous sign which announced my debut for Sunday, September 30! And this was Friday the twenty-eighth! No, I thought, they couldn't mean me! Who would have dared to do that without first consulting me? I was so upset that I didn't stop to read the details. I hailed a cab and went directly to the offices of the promoters.

Don Ramon was waiting for me. "Let me be the first to congratulate you," he said.

"Look out!" I yelled. "Don't touch me. I'm all banged up! What's the big idea, anyway? Why didn't you wait to speak to me first before going ahead with it? Besides, I need a lot more practice before I'll be ready. I'm all bruised and I can hardly move! How do you expect me to do anything decent on such short notice?"

"Wait a minute. Take it easy. You remember when I sent you to Xochitl I said if you showed any promise I'd put you on as soon as possible? Well, this Sunday is the last fight of the season. So unless you want to wait for another year, this is your only chance! Another thing. If you take it easy now, by the middle of the week you really will be stiff and it will take you at least a month to get over it. You've got to get right into action so you'll force the circulation, and by Monday you'll never know anything ever happened."

"Let's not kid ourselves, Don Ramon," I said. "I found out I don't know the first thing about bullfighting and I want to be sure I know enough before I go into the ring in public."

"Look, kid," he said. "You get in there Sunday and do half of what you did on the ranch and you'll knock them all cold! You should have heard them over the phone from San Juan del Rio each night when they gave us the reports of what you were doing. I sure wish I had been there to see it! I knew you could do it!"

"But what's the use, Don Ramon," I said, really worried. "I only had a chance to practice with the cape and this is more than I bargained for. Besides, I haven't a uniform or anything, and I don't have the slightest idea of where to go in the ring or what to do. There's an awful lot to this that I don't know anything about!"

He ignored me. Turning to the office force, he asked them to tell me the effects of the reports of what I had done on the ranch. "And tell him how the sale of tickets for his debut is going!" he said.

When he saw that I was getting angry, he said bluntly, "We can't pull back now. If we had to refund any money on the tickets already sold, the whole country would know you had backed out. And there would be only one reason they could think of. Besides, what about all the money we've spent on publicity?"

I didn't know what to say. The office force of about twenty were pretending to work; but every once in a while they would glance up and wink. Then Don Ramon told me to sit down and take it easy. "All you have to do," he said, "is to march across the arena in the parade. Then you get behind the fence and we'll tell you what to do, when, and where. Then do a few of the things you did on the ranch. It will be easier here, because there will be more order in this ring. That's simple enough, isn't it?"

"It sounds simple all right. But what'll I do about a uniform?" I said.

"I have the best uniform in the city for you. I remember your saying that you like pearl gray and gold because that was Belmonte's favorite. Well," he continued, "this one belonged to Chato Valencia and should fit you as though painted on you."

We still argued over a few details. Then, when he realized that he had finally convinced me, he handed me a block of tickets. "Here are some tickets for your friends. What time do you want us to have the car call for you on Sunday morning?"

"Why Sunday morning?" I said. "What will I do with the car until the afternoon?"

"Don't you know you're fighting at eleven in the morning?" he said. "How silly can you be?"

Then I realized that I wasn't even to appear in the big ring. The whole thing seemed to fall apart. At this point I could easily have walked out of Don Ramon's office. There was no power on earth that could have made me go through with his plans if I didn't want to. But still it seemed to me that I had no alternative. All I could manage to say was that I wanted the uniform to try on to be sure it fit properly. Besides, I wanted to take some posed studio photographs. At least I'd have that to remember. So he gave me the uniform, and that was that.

Saturday I spent most of the afternoon in the photographer's studio. Once I got into that uniform, I couldn't get away from the mirror. The only thing that made me realize how vain I was getting was the photographer's constant reminder that he wasn't going to be there all night, and that I'd better get it over with. Then I went to see my girl friend Elvira.

I was all mixed up. One minute I'd be tickled and the next I'd feel like backing out. I couldn't make up my mind. I purposely avoided the places where I'd be likely to meet friends. I didn't want to have to explain anything. Elvira would understand.

Elvira was a lovely girl. She was two years older than I. She and two older orphaned sisters were living with an American who had married her aunt. She was noncommittal when I first told her I was going to take up bullfighting to try for the charity festivals. But when I entered the house that night, she flew at me almost in tears. "What's the big idea?" she wailed. "Have you gone out of your mind? Don't you know that if you appear in professional uniform, even in a *novillada* or semi-pro fight, as you are advertised, my family won't let me have anything to do with you? We're in Mexico, you know! There are certain things we can do here and others we can't. This isn't the States, where anything goes!"

"Wait a minute," I said. "Just catch your breath! I'm going with you and not your family. If you think more of your family than you do of me, then that's okay with me! There's no use telling you what happened. You wouldn't understand anyway. But I have to go through with this and work it out in my own way. And I want you and the family to be there to see it, that's all. Here are the tickets. Take the family and give the rest to whomever you want."

"How ridiculous," she said. "If you go ahead with this we're through! It's all over between us!"

"It's a good thing this came up now and not later," I said. "If you really care for me, you'll be there. If you're not there tomorrow—*and I want you to sit right in the center of your whole group*—then I'll know it's all over. That's all there is to it!" I stalked out of the house and slammed the door.

I didn't sleep that night. Every few minutes I'd jump up startled. I spent the whole night in a semi-somnambulous state that left me as limp as a rag by morning. I got up at seven and, knowing I wasn't supposed to eat before the fight, started to dress. I called Don Ramon and asked him to have his chauffeur bring the car around at eight. By eight-thirty I was in the car, fully uniformed. I ordered the chauffeur to drive slowly through the center of town. The morning was beautiful. Although I was jittery I couldn't imagine such a beautiful day being anything other than a good omen. We finally got to the Chapultepec bull ring fifteen minutes before the fight began.

The place was jammed. People were milling everywhere. All the boys on the card were there and took me to the little private chapel under the stands reserved for bullfighters only. Then after introductions all around, we took our positions near the *puerta de cuadrillas,* or main parade gate. Someone showed me how to wrap the embroidered dress cape around me and when the bugle blew we marched across the arena. I bowed as I had been told to do and went to look for Elvira. The only empty seat was obviously hers. Her sister said she couldn't come. All the rest of the family were there. That struck me as being odd. But things were about to begin, so I threw my cape to them and they spread it on the rail in front of them. Then I went behind the fence and prepared to enjoy the show.

From the remarks shouted at me from all sides I knew the crowd thought I didn't know anything and expected to have a grand time at my expense. But I was being smug. I'd give them the surprise of their lives, I thought, when the proper time came. As long as they expected nothing, then anything I might do should prove satisfactory.

A bull had entered the ring. He was quite a bit larger than the ones I had practiced with at Xochitl. But he wasn't mine, so I relaxed.

The *banderillerós,* or assistants, did the preliminary cape work and Juan Espinosa, a dark Indian boy who was using the name of "Armilla," stepped out and went to work. I recall that I applauded him openly when I thought he had done something worth while and razzed him at other times when I didn't approve. I acted as though I were a spectator in the stands. Several assistants tried to explain that one professional doesn't do such things to another. But I wasn't a professional and didn't pay attention to what they were saying. As a beginner I could flout bull-ring etiquette.

When Armilla had killed the bull and it had been dragged from the arena, my assistants told me to get ready. I looked to see if Don Ramon were anywhere around. I didn't see him, so I acted as though this had nothing to do with me. But when cushions and bottles began to fall from the stands, I hastily sent for Don Ramon.

He was sweating copiously by the time he got to me. He had been checking the gate receipts. The thought that I might have backed out brought him on the double. "What's going on here?" he demanded. All this time the crowd was getting nastier. They were at near-riot pitch.

"You told me you would tell me when to go in and what to do," I said as casually as I could manage.

"Is that all that's bothering you?" he shouted. "Oh, why did I ever get mixed up with you anyway?" he said, looking to the stands for sympathy. Then turning to me he asked, "What bull is this?"

"It's the second. Armilla just finished the other one," I said.

"Then this one is yours. Now stop acting so silly and get out there."

"Where?" I said, badgering for time.

"Look, kid," he said, suddenly going white. "There's the bull! Right? And there's the ring! Right? Well, you get in that ring anywhere you want and do whatever you want with that bull. But do it! And heaven help us!" He made the sign of the cross and leaned on the wall of the stands.

The crowd seemed fascinated momentarily by the altercation going on in the runway behind the fence between Don Ramon and me. The assistants were giving them a running account in sign language while it went on. Then, when I saw there was nothing more to do, I took a grip on my cape and stalked through the shelter and into the arena. The crowd quieted down although they stood in their seats in gleeful anticipation.

The bull was on the far side of the ring and when he saw me coming, alone, he started toward me at a full gallop. He stopped suddenly about fifteen feet away. For the first time I saw how big he was. He was twice the size of the biggest animal I had worked out with on the ranch. And what horns! But I couldn't do anything about it, so I shook my cape and waited. The bull just glared and snorted and shook his head as though wondering what this apparition in front of him was. When I thought I had waited long enough, I backed to the fence and came out to face him at a slight trot, jolting to a sudden stop when I had reached the desired spot at half the previous distance. He took one startled look, as though in disbelief, and charged.

The crowd let out a horrified shriek which turned to a triumphant shout as they saw the bull pass me. I'm sure they were incredulous and refused to believe their eyes. Meanwhile, the bull had circled back and charged at me from the other side. I just stood my ground like a post, moving only my arms, and blithely passed him right by me. The thunderous shout and applause that went up from the stands rang in my ears. From that moment until quite some time later I couldn't hear a thing except when an assistant came close and spoke slowly.

And now that I saw I had made those two passes so well, with terrible form, of course, I thought it proper to give the crowd a real surprise. So in the next verónica I passed the cape over my shoulder and brought it down in back of me in preparation for a "Gaonera" pass. As I raised my arms over my head in this maneuver, momentarily my ears came unplugged and I heard a terrific roar that seemed louder than the most thunderous surf I had ever heard. Then I seemed to go deaf again.

I had successfully completed two Gaoneras and when at the beginning of the third I must have overstepped my bounds, everything went blank and then exploded! I didn't know it but I had been tossed fifteen feet in the air and landed about twenty feet away. And I landed right on my head!

A moment later some assistants were standing over me and helping me up. I shook myself and pushed them away. Yelling for my cape, which I couldn't seem to find, I ran toward the bull. That was when the crowd really went wild. The fact that I hadn't stopped to see if I was hurt was the best gesture I could have made.

On the way to the bull, one of the boys gave me my cape. I went right back to what I had been doing when tossed.

I did about ten Gaoneras with the bull actually rubbing ribs with me. Then Augustín, one of my assistants, yelled to me to finish off the series in a *serpentina,* or swirl pass. When he caught on to the fact that I didn't know how, he tried to get the bull away from me. He shouldn't have done that, because the bull caught me and tossed me in the air.

As I was coming down, I saw in a flash I would land on his back. Automatically I grabbed for him as I had done with the smaller animals on the ranch. I caught a hold far back around his neck and hung on for dear life. But my middle came down between his horns with my legs dangling loosely in front of his head. He ran around that ring tossing his head and trying to shake me off. But I wouldn't let go.

The first few times he tossed his head, I felt the breath jolted out of me each time my middle bumped down on his forehead. Then I managed to clamp my legs around his snoot and practically shut off his vision. When he slowed down a little, Augustín grabbed his tail and shouted for me to let go. As soon as I realized what he was shouting, I dropped to the ground. There was a mad scramble of all the boys to get the bull away from me. I got up, shaken a bit, with my uniform in tatters but otherwise unharmed.

As I walked to the fence, I became aware of the madhouse in the stands. Battles were going full tilt between spectators in all sections. Everyone was sure I had been torn limb from limb. There wasn't a soul present who remained unaffected by what he had seen. They were gasping for air. Red Cross nurses were administering first aid to those who had fainted. Half of the spectators didn't dare to look at me for fear of seeing me suddenly fall apart before their eyes. It was incredible that nothing had happened to me.

I got in back of the fence where the sword handler tried to mend my uniform as best he could. He used strings, pieces of cloth, and handkerchiefs, as well as a needle and thread. I washed my face in a stream of water from a jug and heaved a sigh of relief. My job was done. Lucky for me it was over! Everyone who could catch his breath tried to speak to me at the same time. And before I knew it the banderillas had been placed in the bull's shoulders and Augustín told me to get ready to work with the muleta and sword and kill the bull.

"Not for me, brother!" I said. "That's not for me! I don't know the first thing about it. I don't even know which end to hold the sword by!"

Then I learned how fickle the public can be. Whereas a moment before they would have died for me, now that they thought they were being cheated and I was refusing to go on with the fight they began to get nastier than before. They wanted to kill me if I didn't kill that bull. And when word reached Don Ramon, he appeared from nowhere. The specter of refunding all that money must have had its effect on him.

"What's eating you now?" he demanded.

"Nothing," I said. "I already did all I'm going to do for the day! I told you I didn't practice with anything but the cape. And I can't use the sword because I don't even know how to hold it!"

In all the time I had known Don Ramon he never gave me the slightest indication that he knew or understood a word of English. I always had to make myself understood to him in Spanish, no matter how badly. But at this moment I guess he couldn't contain himself any longer. "Look, you fool!" he hissed in perfect English. "This has gone far enough! You insisted on being billed as a matador. Well, the word matador comes from the verb *matar*, which means to kill. Now either you get out there and kill that bull or I won't be responsible for what this crowd will do to you! You've been tossed a couple of times by this bull, so you know what he can do. But you don't know, as I do, what that crowd can do when it gets real nasty! And they paid to see you kill that bull," he said as he walked away.

Well, this time the world fell in on me. I had asked for it. I had no business to start this whole thing anyway. But there was nothing I could do about it now except go ahead. When the mob saw me go through the shelter and out into the ring, they quieted down again, but grudgingly.

I went to the sword handler and took the sword and the muleta from him. He told me to bow in front of the mayor's box, dedicate the bull to someone I knew, and then go ahead. After bowing to the mayor, I went over and dedicated the bull to Don Ramon. Elvira wasn't there, and no one else meant anything to me. "Here's hoping everything comes out all right," I said, and left my *montéra,* or hat, with him as is the ritual.

I stopped by the fence to ask Augustín if he'd show me how to manipulate the muleta and hold the sword. I truly didn't know the first thing about them. He came into the ring and took the muleta and sword from me. The bull was alone on the opposite side as we started to walk across. Every couple of steps Augustín stopped to show me how to make another pass and how to integrate them. After he would show me how, he would give me the muleta and have me do it. Then we would continue.

All this while the crowd were looking on fascinated. Some of them realized I didn't know a thing about what I was doing. But most of them insisted it was an act that I was putting on purposely. Well, when we reached the bull, Augustín told me to start with the *pase de la muerte,* or death pass. This is done as the man stands rigidly and makes absolutely no movement other than raising the cloth in a straight line upward. I just stood there, holding muleta and sword in my right hand. The bull couldn't seem to make up his mind as to what to do. Then my arm began to go dead on me. It felt paralyzed. Muleta and sword seemed to weigh a ton.

I brought my arm down slowly and put the muleta in my left hand to give my right arm a rest. As I was opening out the folds of the muleta with the point of the sword, the bull suddenly charged. I heard his snort and grunt as he started. It was so sudden that I froze. I couldn't move a muscle. I must have jerked the cloth because the bull went by me in a whoosh. But I had frozen so completely that I couldn't turn my head to see where he went.

I heard the clop-clop of his hoofs as he came at me from the other side but I was so scared I didn't see a thing. And he went past me a second time. I do remember that as he went past I instinctively pulled in my middle. And each successive time he went past, I pulled in some more. By the time he passed the fourth time, I must have been so bent over that it appeared I was sitting on the ground. How I retained my balance and didn't actually sit down I'll never know. But as he came toward me for the fifth consecutive charge, I saw from the corner of my eye that he was headed toward the back of me. What made him change his course I will never know. Maybe the wind caught the end of the cloth. Maybe I jerked it inadvertently. I don't know. But as he reached me, he stretched his neck and passed in front of me so closely that he hit me with the pallette, or foreshoulder. In doing so, I came to life. When the bull had circled, he stopped momentarily. Augustín rushed up and shouted for me to kill the bull. "You've got the crowd nuts again," he shouted. "You've got them in the palm of your hand. Kill that bull before you spoil everything!"

"I don't know how!" I moaned.

He came up behind me. After making me take the proper position, he took my left arm from in back and furled the muleta on its stick. "Bring your sword up like this," he said as he helped me to do it. "Now sight along the blade and put it in that little spot where the neck and shoulder blade meet."

"But how do I get past the horns?" I said. I had barely finished with the question with my head turned toward him when Augustín gave me a push. He did it so unexpectedly that I closed my eyes and expected the worst. But, strange as it seems, nothing happened. The bull had gone past me and I was left standing there with just the muleta in my left hand. But where was the sword? I looked around quickly but couldn't find it. So I ran to the fence and demanded another from the sword handler.

He stood there gawking at me, and said, as though I were asking the impossible, "What do you want with another sword?"

"Cut the comedy," I said, annoyed. "Give me another one, quick, before the time passes and they take him out alive. I don't want that to happen in my very first fight. Are you against me too?"

He motioned me to come closer. "For the sake of all that's holy, get over to that bull before even I begin to think you're batty!"

I stole a quick glance and saw that the sword was in the bull in the proper place, right up to the hilt! Imagine that! The whole thing struck me as being so ludicrous that I began to feel the waves of laughter. But rather than have that crowd think I was pulling their leg or laughing in their faces, I quickly pulled out my handkerchief and covered my face while I ran toward the bull. I got there just in time to take one of the classical poses in front of the vanquished enemy. I held that pose, grinning from ear to ear, while photographers clicked their cameras furiously.

Then, as I came back across the arena, the mob poured into the ring and paraded me around on their shoulders. They carried me out and all the way to my home, ten miles away. As we went through town, more and more people swelled the crowd of frantic well-wishers. By the time we reached home, there were about two thousand sweating fans pouring into the house and gardens.

I ordered the maids to open all the bottles on hand and spread all the food we had. The mauling I got from that crowd was almost as bad as the one I'd received from the bulls at Xochitl. Most of my uniform was gone. Pieces had been torn or cut off by the souvenir hunters.

After I had changed into a business suit and sat with a horde of friends and new admirers, there began a period of questioning I'll never forget. Why did I do this and why did I do that? And before I could recall the incident they were discussing, someone would chime in with what seemed the most plausible answer. They never gave me a chance to answer a single question. Well, that set me to thinking. Mind you, I still didn't believe a man could be hurt. The horses? Yes, because they were made to stand still. But the man could move out of harm's way if he knew what he was about.

The thought struck me that if all I had to do was take an occasional beating and have everyone solve all my problems for me, and be paid handsomely for it while I was enjoying myself—well, what was I waiting for? Then, too, bullfighters traveled to many lands in great style. And I loved to travel. Here was an opportunity to travel while being paid for it. Also, bullfighters were idolized in a manner I never had seen before. It was probably at that moment that I knew I would become a bullfighter.

CAPSIZING IN THE RAPIDS
By James Dickey

We started back. I couldn't tell anything about our back trail, but Lewis kept stopping and looking at a wrist compass, and it seemed to me that we were going more or less in the right direction; it was the direction I would have followed if I had been by myself.

We came out upstream of where the canoe was. The water was running toward the river, and we went with it, down the secret pebbles of the creek-bed, stooping under the leaves of low branches, mumbling to ourselves. I felt separated from the others, and especially from Lewis. There was no feeling any longer of helping each other; I believed that if I had stepped into a hole and disappeared the others would not have noticed, but would have gone on faster and faster. Each of us wanted to get out of the woods in the quickest way he could. I know I did, and it would have taken a great physical effort for me to turn back and take one step upstream, no matter what trouble one of the others was in.

When we got to the canoe we all got in. Drew an Lewis paddled, and I felt the long surges of Lewis' strokes move us as I wanted us to move. Drew fended off the low branches, and we went back to the river faster than I thought possible.

The other canoe was where we had left it, softly shaking against the bank.

"Let's get the hell out of here," Bobby said.

"Let me figure a minute," Lewis said. "This is no time for vanity or hurt feelings. How much work can you do, Bobby?"

"I don't know, Lewis," Bobby said. "I'll try."

"It's not your fault," Lewis said. "But trying is not going to be enough. We've got to get the best combinations we can get. I expect I'd better take Bobby with me, Ed, how much have you got left?"

"I don't know. Some."

"All right. You and Drew take my boat. Bobby and I will take everything we can in the other one. We'll try to keep up with you, but it'll be better if you lead off, so that we can see you if you get into trouble. I hate to tell you, but from what little I know, we haven't hit the rough part of this river yet.''

"The part that was going to be fun," Bobby said.

"The part that's going to knock your stupid brains out if you don't do exactly what I tell you to do," Lewis said, without raising his voice. "Come on; let's get whatever else we can carry out of my canoe. You want out of this, don't you?''

We took about ten minutes shifting equipment around.

"Take everything, if you can take it, Lewis," I said. "If Drew and I have to go through these damned rapids first, I want a boat I can at least halfway handle. And I don't want things wrapping around me in the water.''

"I don't blame you," Lewis said. "We'll take all we can."

"All I want is a weapon," I said. "I'll take my bow."

"I'd think twice about that," Lewis said. "If you think tents can be bad, you wait'll those bare broadheads gore you a few times when you're in the water with them.''

"I'll take it anyway," I said. "And I sure wish we still had that guy's gun. Why the hell did we leave it with *him?*''

"The gun is better right where it is," Lewis said.

"We could have got rid of it later."

"No, too risky. Every mile we carried that shotgun with us would increase the danger of our being caught with it. That could be the thing, buddy. That could be the thing.''

We were ready. Drew crawled into the front of the aluminum canoe. I was glad he was there; I could work with him. He sat with the paddle just out of the river, shaking his head. Neither of us said anything until I told him to push off.

It was about four o'clock, and the thought of spending another night in the woods paralyzed me. The problems and the physical work of the burial had taken my mind off our situation, but now the thought of it and of what might happen to us surrounded me; I felt driven into it by a hammer. But something came to an edge in me, also. The leaves glittered, all mysterious points, and the river and the light on it were nothing but pure energy. I had never lived sheerly on nerves before, and a gigantic steadiness took me over, a constant trembling of awareness in a hundred places that added up to a kind of equilibrium, that made my arms move in long steady motions and showed me where the rocks were by the differences in the swirling of the water.

We moved well for the better part of an hour. Lewis was keeping up, too, driving the almost-buried canoe forward with an effort I could not even guess at. He liked to take things on himself and, because he could, do more than anyone else. And I was glad to see that in an emergency his self-system didn't fold up on him, but carried on the same, or even stronger.

But I was also very glad that Drew and I were light and maneuverable. There were no rapids, but the river seemed to be moving faster. There was an odd but definite sensation of going downhill in a long curving slant like a ramp. I noticed this more and more, and finally it occurred to me that the feeling was caused by what the land on both sides was doing. At first it had lifted into higher banks, the left higher than the right, and now it was going up raggedly and steadily, higher and higher, changing the sound of the river to include a kind of keep beating noise, the tone coming out more and more as the walls climbed, shedding their trees and all but a few bushes and turning to stone. Most of the time the sides were not vertical, but were very steep, and I knew we would be in real trouble if we spilled. I prayed that there would be no rapids while we were in the gorge, or that they would be easy ones.

We pulled and pulled at the river. Drew was hunched forward in a studious position like a man at a desk, and at every stroke the old GI shirt he wore took a new hold across his shoulders, one which was the old hold as well.

I looked back. We had opened up a little distance on the other canoe; it was about thirty yards behind us. I thought I heard Lewis holler to us, probably to slow down, but the voice, thinly floating through the boom of wall-sound, had no authority and very little being at all.

The walls were at least 150 feet high on both sides of us now. The cross-reverberation seemed to hold us on course as much as the current did; it was part of the same thing—the way we had to move to get through the gorge.

I looked around again, and Lewis and Bobby had gained a little. They were too close to us for running rapids, but there was nothing I could do about it; as far as I was concerned they were going to have to take their chances.

As we cleared each turn, before Drew swung across in front of me I kept looking for white water, and when I'd checked for that I looked along both banks as far downriver as I could see, to try to tell if either of them was lowering. There was no white water, and the walls stayed like they were, gray and scrubby, limestonish, pitted and scabby.

But the sound was changing, getting deeper and more massively frantic and authoritative. It was the old sound, but it was also new, it was a fuller one than the reverberations off the walls, with their overtones and under-tones; it was like a ground-bass that was made of all the sounds of the river we'd heard since we'd been on it. God, God, I thought, I know what it is. If it's a falls we're gone.

The sun fell behind the right side of the gorge, and the shadow of the bank crossed the water so fast that it was like a quick step from one side to the other. The beginning of darkness was thrown over us like a sheet, and in it the water ran even faster, frothing and near-foaming under the canoe.

My teeth were chattering; I felt them shaking my skull, as though I had already been in the river and now had to suffer in the stone shade of the bank. We seemed to leap, and then leap from that leap to another down the immense ditch, like flying down an underground stream with the ceiling ripped off.

We couldn't make it to Aintry by dark; I knew that now. And we couldn't survive on the river, even as it was here, without being able to see. The last place I wanted to be was on the river in the gorge in the dark. It might be better to pull over while there was still light and find a flat rock or a sandbar to camp on, or get ready to sleep in the canoes.

We came around one more bend, and at the far end of it the river-bed began to step down. There was a succession of small, rough rapids; I couldn't tell how far they went on. About the only thing I had learned about canoeing was to head into the part of the rapids that seemed to be moving the fastest, where the most white water was. There was not much light left, and I had already made up my mind to get through this stretch of water and pull over to the bank, no matter what Lewis and Bobby decided to do.

The water was throwing us mercilessly. We came out in a short stretch between rapids, but we were going too fast to get out of the middle of the river before the next rocks. I didn't want to risk getting the canoe broadside to the river and then be sucked into the rocks. That would not only spill us, but would probably wedge the canoe on the rocks, and the force of water against it would keep it there. And we couldn't make it downriver with four of us in one canoe, as low in the water and hard to turn as it would be. I tried to hold Drew centered on the white water, to line him up and shoot him through the rocks; if I could get him through, I'd be with him.

"Give me some speed, baby," I hollered.

Drew lifted his paddle and started to dig in long and hard.

Something happened to him. It looked at first—I can see it in my mind in three dimensions and slow motion and stop action—as if something, a puff of wind, but much more definite and concentrated, snatched at some of the hair at the back of his head. For a second I thought he had just shaken his head, or had been jarred by the canoe in some way I hadn't felt, but at the same instant I saw this happen I felt all control of the canoe go out of it. The river whirled the paddle from Drew's hand as though it had never been there. His right arm shot straight out, and he followed it, turning the whole canoe with him. There was nothing I could do; I rolled with the rest.

In a reflex, just before my head smashed face-first into the white water with the whole river turning around in midair and beginning to swing upside down, I let go the paddle and grabbed for the bow at my feet, for even in panic I knew I would rather have a weapon than the paddle, as dangerous as it would be to have the naked broadheads near me in such water.

The river took me in, and I had the bow. My life jacket brought me up, and Lewis' canoe was on top of me like a whale, rising up on the current. It hit me in the shoulder, driving me down where the rocks swirled like marbles, and something, probably a paddle, thrust into the side of my head as Lewis or Bobby fended me off like a rock. I kicked at the rushing stones and rose up. Downstream, the green canoe drove over the broadside other one, reared nearly straight up, and Bobby and Lewis pitched out on opposite sides. A rock hit me and I felt some necessary thing—a muscle or bone—go in my leg. I kicked back with both feet and caught something solid. I must have been upside down, for there was no air. I opened my eyes but there was nothing to see. I threw my head, hoping I would be throwing it clear of the water, but it did not clear. I was not breathing and was being beaten from all sides, being hit and hit at and brushed by in the most unlikely and unexpected places in my body, rushing forward to be kicked and stomped by everything in the river.

I turned over and over. I rolled, I tried to crawl along the flying bottom. Nothing worked. I was dead. I felt myself fading out into the unbelievable violence and brutality of the river, joining it. This is not such a bad way to go, I thought; maybe I'm already there.

My head came out of the water, and I actually thought of putting it under again. But I got a glimpse of the two canoes, and that interested me enough to keep me alive. They were together, the green one buckled, rolling over and over each other, like logs. Something was nailing one of my hands, the left one, to the water. The wooden canoe burst open on a rock and disappeared, and the aluminum one leapt free and went on.

Get your feet forward of you, boy, I said, with my mouth dragging through the current. Get on your back.

I tried, but every time I came up with my feet I hit a rock either with my shins or thighs. I went under again, and faintly I heard what must have been the aluminum canoe banging on the stones, a ringing, distant, beautiful sound.

I got on my back and poured with the river, sliding over the stones like a creature I had always contained but never released. With my life preserver the upper part of my body drew almost no water. If I could get my feet—my heels—over the stones I slid over like a moccasin, feeling the moss flutter lightly against the back of my neck before I cascaded down into the next rapids.

Body-surfing and skidding along, I realized that we could never have got through this stretch in canoes. There were too many rocks, they were too haphazardly jumbled, and the water was too fast; faster and faster. We couldn't have portaged, either, because of the banks, and we couldn't have got out and walked the canoes through. We would have spilled one way or the other, and strangely I was just as glad. Everything told me that the way I was doing it was the only way, and I was doing it.

It was terrifyingly enjoyable, except that I hurt in so many places. The river would shoot me along; I'd see a big boulder looming up, raise my feet and slick over, crash down on my ass in a foaming pool, pick up speed and go on. I got banged on the back of the head a couple of times until I learned to bend forward as I was coming down off the rock, but after that nothing new hurt me.

I was already hurt, I knew. But I was not sure where. My left hand hurt pretty bad, and I was more worried about it than anywhere else, for I couldn't remember having hit it with anything. I held it up and saw that I had hold of the bow by the broadheads and was getting cut in the palm every time I flinched and grabbed. The bow was also clamped under my left arm, and now I took it out and swung the heads away from me, just before I went over another rock. As I slid down I saw calm water below, through another stretch of rapids: broad calm, then more white water farther down, far off into evening. I relaxed again, not even touching the stones of the passage this time, but riding easily along through the flurrying cold ripples into the calm water, cradling the bow.

I was floating, not flowing anymore. Turning idly in the immense dark bed, I looked up at the gorge side rising and rising. My legs were killing me, but I could kick them both, and as far as I could tell neither was broken. I lifted my hand from the water; it was nicked and chopped a little in places, but not as badly as it might have been; there was a diagonal cut across the palm, but not a deep one—a long slice.

I floated on, trying to recover enough to think what to do. Finally I started to struggle weakly around to look upstream for the others. My body was heavy and hard to move without the tremendous authority of the rapids to help it and tell it what to do.

Either upstream or down, there was nobody in the river but me. I kept watching the last of the falls, for I had an idea that I might have passed the others, somewhere along. There had probably been several places where the water split and came down through the rocks in different ways; all three of them might be back there somewhere, dead or alive.

As I thought that, Bobby tumbled out of the rapids, rolling over and over on the slick rocks, and then flopped belly-down into the calm. I pointed to the bank and he began to work toward it. So did I.

"Where is Lewis?" I yelled.

He shook his head, and I stopped pulling on the water and turned to wait in midstream.

After a minute or two Lewis came, doubled-up and broken-looking, one hand still holding his paddle and the other on his face, clasping something intolerable. I breast-stroked to him and lay beside him in the cold coiling water under the falls. He was writhing and twisting uselessly, caught by something that didn't have hold of me, something that seemed not present.

"Lewis," I said.

"My leg's broke," he gasped. "It feels like it broke off."

The water where we were did not change. "Hold on to me," I said.

He moved his free hand through the river and fixed the fingers into the collar of my slick nylon outfit, and I moved gradually crossways on the water toward the big boulders under the cliff. The dark came on us faster and faster as I hauled on the crossgrain of the current with Lewis' choking weight dragging at my throat.

From where we were the cliff looked something like a gigantic drive-in movie screen waiting for an epic film to begin. I listened for interim music, glancing now and again up the pale curved stone for Victor Mature's stupendous image, wondering where it would appear, or if the whole thing were not now already playing, and I hadn't yet managed to put it together.

As we neared the wall, I saw that there were a few random rocks and a tiny sand beach where we were going to come out; where Bobby was, another rock. I motioned to him, and he unfolded and came to the edge of the water, his hands embarrassing.

He gave me one of them, and I dragged us out. Lewis hopped up onto a huge placid stone, working hard, and then failed and crumpled again. The rock, still warm with the last of the sun that had crossed the river on its way down, held him easily, and I turned him on his back with his hand still over his face.

"Drew was shot," Lewis said with no lips. "I saw it. He's dead."

"I'm not sure," I said, but I was afraid that's what it was. "Something happened to him. But I don't know. I don't know."

"Let's take his pants down," I said to Bobby.

He looked at me.

"God*damn* phraseology," I said. "We're in another bag, now, baby. Get his pants off him and see if you can tell how bad he's hurt. I've got to try to get that goddamned canoe, or we'll stay here."

I turned back to the river. I waded in, feeling the possibility of a rifle shot die with the very last light, moving back into the current like an out-of-shape animal, taking on the familiar weight and lack-of-weight of water. Very clearheaded, I sank down.

The depth came into me, increasing—no one can tell me different—with the darkness. The aluminum canoe floated palely, bulging half out of the total dark, making slowly for the next rapids, but idly, and unnaturally slowed and stogged with calm water. Nearly there, I ran into a thing of wood that turned out to be a broken paddle. I took it on.

I swam slow-motion around the canoe, listening for the rifle shot I would never hear if it killed me; that I had not heard when it killed Drew, if it did. Nothing from that high up could see me, and I knew it, though it might see the canoe. Even that was doubtful, though, and the conviction enlarged on me that I could circle the canoe all night, if I chose, in the open.

The calm was deep; there was no place to stand to dump the water out. I hung to the upside-down gunwale, tipping it this way and that, trying to slip the river out of the factory metal. Finally it rolled luckily, and the stream that had been in it began to flow again; the hull lightened and climbed out of the water, and was mostly on top of it. I pushed on the sharp stern, keeping it going with excruciating frog legs. The current went around me, heading into the darkness downstream. I could see a little white foaming, but it was peacefully beyond, another problem for another time. I turned to the cliff and called softly out to Bobby, and he answered.

I looked up and could barely make out his face. The canoe went in to him, guided by the same kind of shove I gave Dean when he was first learning to walk. He waded and drew it up onto the sand by the bow rope, and we beached it under the overhang.

I moved onto land, not saying anything.

"For God's sake," Bobby said, "don't be so damned quiet. I'm flipping already."

Though my mouth was open, I closed it against the blackness and moved to Lewis, who was now down off the rock and lying in the sand. His bare legs were luminous, and the right leg of his drawers was lifted up to the groin. I could tell by its outline that his thigh was broken; I reached down and felt it very softly. Against the back of my hand his penis stirred with pain. His hair gritted in sand, turning from one side to the other.

It was not a compound fracture; I couldn't feel any of the bone splinters I had been taught to look for in innumerable compulsory first-aid courses, but there was a great profound human swelling under my hand. It felt like a thing that was trying to open, to split, to let something out.

"Hold on, Lew," I said. "We're all right now."

It was all-dark. The river-sound enveloped us as it never could have in light. I sat down beside Lewis and motioned to Bobby. He crouched down as well.

"Where is Drew?" Bobby asked.

"Lewis says he's dead," I said. "Probably he is. He may have been shot. But I can't really say. I was looking right at him, but I can't say."

Lewis' hand was pulling at me from underneath. I bent down near his face. He tried to say something, but couldn't. Then he said, "It's you. It's got to be you."

"Sure it's me," I said. "I'm right here. Nothing can touch us."

"No. That's not . . ." The river had the rest of what he said, but Bobby picked it up.

"What are we going to do?" he made the dark say; night had taken his red face.

"I think," I said, "that we'll never get out of this gorge alive."

Did I say that? I thought. Yes, a dream-man said, you did. You did say it, and you believe it.

"I think he means to pick the rest of us off tomorrow," I said out loud, still stranger than anything I had ever imagined. When do the movies start, Lord?

"What . . . ?"

"That's what I'd do. Wouldn't you?"

"I don't . . ."

"If Lewis is right, and I think he is, that toothless bastard drew down on us while we were lining up to go through the rapids, and before we were going too fast. He killed the first man in the first boat. Next would have been me. Then you.''

"In other words, it's lucky we spilled.''

"Right. Lucky. Very lucky.''

THE CRICKET MATCH
By Richard Stilgoe

Ever since a life assurance company began to sponsor Test matches, the City of London has taken a renewed interest in cricket. Of course, the City has had for years the oddity of its own cricket field. It lies between the City Road and Bunhill Row, and since 1538 the Honourable Artillery Company have played cricket on it, despite the fact that if they stopped playing cricket on it and sold it to a developer, they could probably buy another twenty million pounds worth of artillery.

You might thing it surprising that a group of part-time soldiers enjoy such expansive and expensive sporting facilities, in view of the fact that the City's other major cricket club has no home ground at all. But the City's other club is of recent formation. The H.A.C. annexed its oval before property prices passed through the false ceiling, the insulation and the roof in the 'sixties. The P.C.C.C.C. had no chance to show such foresight, as this is their first season. They are the Post-Cardiac City Cricket Club. To join, you have to be a City businessman who has survived both a major heart-attack and the ministrations of a particular heart specialist whose sworn opinion it is that heart sufferers should thenceforward play cricket, since it gives gentle exercise and cannot possibly excite. This, anyway, is his theory. At first, all went well. The P.C.C.C.C. turned up gently and punctually at eleven villages on eleven Saturdays, and each time managed to engineer the result most dear to the true cricket-lover's heart—a draw interrupted by rain.

In truth, the itinerant nature of the team is their own choice, spurred on by their doctor. He feels that these trips to havens of rural peace are as therapeutic as the game, serving to remove his ex-patients from the City with its associations of competition and stress. Had he decided otherwise —that the team must grasp the nettle and play always within the City, to exorcise their ghost by meeting it first bounce and despatching it over long-on—then the H.A.C.'s ground might have been under threat. For the P.C.C.C.C.'s dozen or so founder-members were among the richest men in the City, in England, in Europe, probably in the World, and raising twenty

million pounds between them would have been the work of the few moments it takes to oversubscribe a new share issue. But their specialist had
doomed them to wander the village greens of England and so they did as
they were bid, for they believed it made them able to carry on juggling
seven different burning currencies with two hands from Monday to Friday
in the City, not half a mile from the H.A.C. ground.

The twelfth Saturday of their existence found the P.C.C.C. at TOILCHARD
REGIS in Wiltshire, not far from Marlborough and not far from Hungerford,
but not very near to either. Too far from London to commute, but too near
to escape its influence. Much of Toilchard Regis is thatched unnaturally
well, as second-home buyers have moved in and improved the houses to
the point where no native of Toilchard Regis can afford them any more.
Luckily, a large group of speculative post-war houses was built to attract
people to the village. These now house the locals, who got them quite
cheaply, the newcomers having eyes only for the thatch, the beams, the
bread oven and the inglenook. Toilchard Regis's cricket team divided
roughly half and half—well, exactly, not roughly, since most Saturdays
either ten or twelve turn up and insist on playing—between seven-
day-a-week residents and two-day-a-week residents. Of a Saturday they
meet before lunch at the Bull and Bear on the village green, where they
have a clear view of the cricket pitch and usually the opposition—for
visiting cricket teams also tend to sniff out the nearest pub to soothe the
effects of the journey, to try and catch a glimpse of the home side, to ask
the landlord what they might expect in the way of fast bowling, reliable
batting or (worst of all) a proper wicket-keeper, and generally to analyse
the atmosphere of the alien planet on whose surface they find themselves.

    Thus it was that Joe Painter, Alan Tremoyne, Ned Deering, Tom Deer-
ing, Jim Trance and the others sat and watched while the Bull and Bear's
car park filled with two Daimler Double-Sixes, two Range Rovers, a
Maserati Bora, a Porsche Turbo, a black Renault 5 with a telephone in it
and four Silver Shadows (three of them with race-horse mascots replacing
the flying lady). These, instead of the more normal motor-coach, represented the team transport of the eleven heart patients who now stood in the
saloon bar, holding eleven neat tonic waters in eleven slightly shaking
hands.

    The rules of village cricket decree that, at about 1.30, the two teams
shall set off from the pub to the pavilion, and on the way shall pretend to
have seen each other for the first time. So it was that at 1.32, halfway
across the village green, Alan Tremoyne of Toilchard Regis turned to a
man who had walked with him for the last hundred yards or so and said,
'You'll be the chaps from London, I suppose. My name's Tremoyne. I'm
the village captain, for my sins.' He smiled, and stuck out a hand.

    His walking companion took it in a larger, redder hand, and shook it briefly. 'Hogdirt,' he said, 'Alec Hogdirt. Well, SIR ALEC HOGDIRT, if you insist. Not ashamed of it. It was these hands got it for me.'

'Are you the captain, er, Sir Alec?' asked Tremoyne.

'I am not, son, though there are those as says I should be. Oh yes. Alec, they say, you should be captain. Well, *Sir* Alec, in fact, they say, but I don't stand on ceremony. But I'm not captain, and that's that, so I pull my weight and bide my time, Sir Alec or no. You want the General, Sir Eric.' And he indicated a small, brown husk of a man with a grey toothbrush tethered to his upper lip.

'Are you all Sir Something?' Tremoyne asked.

'Nay lad,' said Sir Alec. 'Just three of us. Eric over there, Tag, of course, and me. Sir Alec. I got mine eight years ago. Tag's is only two years old. Eric got his for being in the army. It didn't cost him a penny, so it doesn't really count. But they still made him captain. There are those who say that this country's decline is due to that kind of thinking, and I'm not saying I'm not one of them. But that's how it is, General!' he shouted, and the long, pale linen jacket ahead stiffened, and turned slowly. 'This is the home team's captain. He thought I was the captain. Easy mistake to make. I told him you were captain. For the moment.' Sir Alec looked belliger-ently at the general, who stared past him at Tremoyne, and offered a desiccated hand.

'SIR ERIC GOLDHAT is my name,' he said, pleasantly enough. Alan Tremoyne took the hand. 'Tremoyne,' he said. 'Alan Tremoyne.'

The General looked interested. 'Tremoyne, eh? Any relation to D.R.T. Tremoyne? Green Jackets?'

'Not that I know of,' said Alan. 'Sorry.'

'B.J.M.?' said the General.

'I beg your pardon?'

'B.J.M.,' repeated the General. 'B.J.M. Tremoyne. Younger brother of D.R.T. Got a D.S.O. in Burma.'

'I don't think any of my family was in the army, sir,' Alan explained.

The General looked at him suspiciously. 'You're not Welsh, are you?' he asked after a pause.

Alan pretended not to hear and changed the subject. 'Don't you think we ought to toss, sir?' he said. The two teams were now moving into the pavilion in dribs and drabs, and it was getting late.

The General agreed, and asked his players if any of them had any money. They all denied possession of the smallest sou, as they did regu-larly to all inquiries. No really rich man ever admits to having any money. 'Liquidity problem,' said Sir Eric. 'What would you do if you won the toss?'

Alan hesitated. 'Put you into bat, sir,' he said.

'Set yourself a target, eh!' barked Sir Eric. 'Good ploy. I always bat first meself. Not saying you're not right. No need to toss, though. We bat first. Good decision, young Tremoyne. Tell me, were your father's initials S.E.J.?'

'No sir, T.K.A.' replied Alan.

'T.K.A., eh?' mused the General.

'No, just one "A",' said Alan.

The General looked at him, and again wondered if he was Welsh.

It was only five minutes past two when, to the surprise of the Toilchard Regis faithful, the umpires came out. By the standards of village cricket, this is punctuality almost to the point of pedantry. But the P.C.C.C.C., for all their lack of a coin to toss up with, were not men who had earned their millions by turning up late. Each one, invalid or no, was in his office every morning before his secretary, to sort through the mail and see which letters were for her to pass to him, and which for her to pass on to the ground-lings. So the P.C.C.C.C. batting order was already on a typed slip of paper. The presence of a scorer and two umpires had been checked by phone and confirmed by letter (by one of the secretaries who arrived at the office after the team members). Indeed, the delay of five minutes was only due to the absence of a wicket-keeper's glove, which had been borrowed by the wife of the wicket-keeper to remove the vol-au-vents from the oven, so they would have plenty of time to go cold before the tea interval. The glove having been returned, Alan Tremoyne (an efficient, if rather harassed, person and a trainee estate manager) led his ten men on to the field, full of hope that the eleventh would arrive when he saw the rigours of fielding waning, and the chance of a bowl and a bat waxing.

The opening pair of millionaires were Sir Alec Hogdirt (whom we have met, who had progressed from Pigs to Bacon to Pork Pies to Wholesale and Retail until he controlled all food that grunted from squealing piglet to smoky-bacon-flavoured crisps and pork scratchings) and GILES T. HAIRCORD, whose capacity for seeing carpet in terms of acres rather than yards had made him at thirty-four very rich and very worried. His carpets had made him a pile, his friends said. He had piles, his enemies said. Either way, his incipient angina had greatly strengthened the team's bat-ting, as had the fact that, though ambitious and greedy, he was hardly mad at all. As the Toilchard Regis clock struck eight, he looked at his digital watch. It was 2.06.00 (and 10.06.00 in Perth, Western Australia. It was that sort of watch). Sir Alec took middle and leg from the local magistrate, looked round the field and began to pat Wiltshire with his bat.

In village cricket, each bowler's first ball is special. The batsman has no idea whether the new bowler is fast, medium slow, an absolute rabbit, keen but mediocre, a man with a grudge against batsmen, or worst of all, a halfway competent cricketer. The batsman finds out all these things during the first few seconds. This makes that first ball harder than anything Test cricket has to offer. In Test cricket the bowler is Lever, left-arm fast-medium, tending to swing the ball in. In village cricket the bowler is the grocer, and the umpire thinks he's right-handed from the way he works the bacon slicer.

So with trepidation Sir Alec Hogdirt faced the first ball from the Toilchard Regis grocer, Joe Painter. It turned out to be a fast in-swinger, but only the square-peg umpire could see whether or not it swung before it whistled past him. The magistrate signalled four wides. Two German tourists in deck chairs consulted each other on what this might mean. Giles T. Haircord walked over to the point where the ball had bounced—a point about fifteen yards away from the pitch—and prodded it. He was wondering whether to open more branches of Ambience, a chain of shops he had successfully started which sold uncomfortable knotty-pine beds and corduroy curtains, or merely to take over Environ, his principal rival. He was still wondering when the grocer bowled his second ball, a mirror image of the first, which hit cover point in the kidneys on its way to the boundary. 'Next one should be bang on middle stump,' said the umpire cheerfully, lowering his arms once the scorer had acknowledged four more wides. It was, and it duly bowled Sir Alec Hogdirt, who stood his ground firmly until the umpire raised his finger, then glared at him and walked sullenly towards the pavilion, crossing as he did so the incoming batsman, who was the frozen-food magnate, Harold Icegrist.

A small, dogged man with a healthy doormat of grey hair, Harold Icegrist came from Barnsley and therefore believed himself invincible at all forms of sport. This belief generally stood him in good stead, since self-confidence daunts an opponent more than almost anything else. He and Giles T. Haircord took the score to 31 before Giles T. Haircord was run out. Well, hardly run out, because he made no effort to run at all, standing instead deep in concentration. (It had just occurred to him that to bring the South Korean occasional tables in through Ireland might avoid the tariff controls—if not even attracting a subsidy.) He smiled sheepishly, collected his pocket calculator from the umpire and departed. The two German tourists clapped politely, and checked their rule book.

Harold Icegrist lasted not much longer, giving his wicket away in order to be back in the pavilion for a three o'clock transatlantic phone call. By the time he hung up the P.C.C.C.C. had scored 65 for 4 with Lord A.G. Christie not out 11 and Sir Eric Goldhat not out 9, the innings of Aristide Glorch, the shipping magnate, having lasted only two balls. It should be said that the first of these went for six over square-leg. The second went to the same place, but this time square-leg did not get out of the way in time and was forced to catch the ball to save himself serious injury.

It is a fine thing to watch two old English patricians at the wicket. Arthur Gervaise Christie, six foot three of him from his grey socks to his bald head, like a Georgian folly topped by a dome, and Sir Eric Goldhat, nearly as tall but with an Old Wellingtonian tie holding up his trousers in contrast to Lord A. G. Christie's Etonian one. As they cantered their sweetly stroked runs, they looked like a pair of threadbare greyhounds with striped girths. Lord Christie's fifty was followed by Sir Eric's and their success so demoralized the Toilchard Regis team that the batsmen who followed them were also able to score freely—apart, that is, from the merchant banker HEROD GILTRAISE, whose company, GIRO CASHIER LTD, had doubled its value in the previous weeks thanks to judicious investment in the Middle East. Thinking of the Middle East, Herod Giltraise remembered that he should not be playing cricket on a Saturday and his concentration suffered. When the post-cardiac team's innings ended at 4.28, the score sheet read like this:

Sir Alec Hogdirt b. Painter	0
Giles T. Haircord run out	14
Harold Icegrist c. Trance b. Tremoyne	16
Lord A.G. Christie not out	77
Aristide Glorch c. Deering N. b. Deering T	6
Sir Eric Goldhat lbw b. Painter	51
Horst I. Claridge c. Trance b. Deering T	22
Sir Tag Chloride hit wkt b. Jordan	24
Giles R. Richtoad c. Tremoyne b. Deering T	18
Herod Giltraise b. Jordan	0
Lord Cigar-Heist ret hurt	1
Extras (w. 8, nb. 1, leg byes 2)	11
Total	240

So it was in cheerful mood that the team sat down to tea (well, LORD CIGAR-HEIST didn't sit down, the wild stumping attempt from Jim Trance having hit him firmly on the coccyx), for 240 is a formidable score in village cricket. They might even win! The Post-Cardiac City Cricket Club had never yet won a match. Normally they batted for a gentle couple of hours, scored ninety or so, had a frugal tea, misfielded for an hour while the home team approached their score, got rained on, shook hands with everyone and drove home. But today—well, it was obviously the arrival in the team of Lord Christie (promoted on the death of SIR GODRIC LEATH, the Governor of the Bank of England, who had been run over while trying to pick up a penny that had rolled into the middle of the North Circular Road) which had strengthened the side. None of them knew him well. He was not a City man generally, but he came up from the country occasionally to try and attract sponsorship for the ballet festival he ran at his house, Glen Underboy, and several of them had been approached in this capacity. Well, none of them was averse to sponsoring art if the return was reasonable, and if he went on playing his late cut as sweetly, Lord Christie could look forward to an easier passage in the future. 'Perhaps he might be able to bowl as well,' they said to one another. And with this pleasing thought in mind, they sat down to tea.

The wives of the Toilchard Regis team had excelled themselves. They had not only cooled the vol-au-vents, but had curled the sandwiches and dried the tops with a hair-dryer. The biscuits had been dampened, the fair cakes' chocolate icing had been melted, then allowed to set again. Scones of a weight to rival uranium—and roughly as beneficial to the human body —had been buttered with butter whose sell-by date had long passed. There were flapjacks of a consistency to challenge the whole falseteeth fixative industry and sticky things made of Weetabix and cocoa, while the sandwich fillings—the work of Mrs Deering (N)—were a tour de force: white of egg with cress and earth, cheese and mould, hundreds and thousands with lemon curd, and ham fat; each one a noble complement for the furry aluminium pot of already sugared tea. With 240 on the board, The P.C.C.C.C. tucked in—so much that when the four strongest ladies carried in the fruit cake, the magnates could manage scarcely two slices each. The remainder had to be sold to the two German tourists, who gave every sign of approval at being charged only 94p a slice, for they too had been to London.

When the teams returned to the field, it turned out that Lord Christie could indeed bowl. Sir Eric Goldhat invited him to take the second over instead of Sir Alec Hogdirt, who had expended so much energy in telling everyone how he had been unfairly dismissed that he was now too tired to bowl. The first over had been bowled by SIR TAG CHLORIDE, founder and managing director of DIGITAL SCHROER, a multinational whose purpose was clear to very few people below presidential rank. Sir Tag had conceded four wides and two runs, from a lucky snick by Ichabod Jordan over the head of the P.C.C.C.C.'s other Giles, GILES R. RICHTOAD, who was to assets what Nitromors is to paint. His concentration at what the rest of the team called 'first strip' was impaired by his listening throughout the game to a long memo from a New York colleague on his miniature earphone.

Lord A. G. Christie's first over was bowled at a speed which would not have disgraced Larwood himself (on whose style it was based). The effect was the more terrifying for the loud grunt that accompanied the delivery of the ball, and for the fact that Lord Christie did not stop when the ball left his hand, but carried on running down the wicket as if helpless without a braking parachute. This so surprised the opening batsman that he watched the progress of the galloping peer rather than the ball, which whistled unheeded past him and dislodged his off stump. His successor was less distracted, and played carefully forward—only to find himself caught by the bowler who had got within five feet of overhauling the ball. At the end of two overs the Toilchard Regis team were 6 for 2 and even some of the wives had come out of the pavilion to watch. They stood, ranged directly behind the bowler's arm, drying plates with flapping white tea-cloths.

The city cricketers clapped Lord Christie warmly on the back, and took their places for Sir Tag Chloride's next over. A new spirit was abroad. Better, a new spirit was in Wiltshire, which isn't abroad at all. Sir Tag's over conceded but one run, and that should have been a boundary but for Aristide Glorch throwing himself—nay, hurling himself—into the path of the ball, and returning it to the wicket-keeper with a smile his face had not seen since the invention of flags of convenience.

That same wicket-keeper's moment of glory was yet to come. After six overs, with the score at 29 for 6, Sir Eric Goldhat felt emboldened to change the bowling and allow his off-breaks their weekly outing. As he ran up he saw to his surprise that the wicket-keeper was standing right behind the stumps, not twenty yards back as he usually did. HORST I. CLARIDGE, hotelier and restaurateur, was remembering the happy days at G. CARRIDI'S HOTEL, when he was reception clerk. And now, again, he had moved from the office at the back to the front door. Let no cricket ball try to pass *him* without a tie! Sir Eric duly bowled, the demoralized batsman duly played and missed and Horst I. Claridge, sweating a little, gathered the ball and removed the bails as if spinning a visitor's book round to face a guest. 'Porter!' he cried, forgetting himself for a moment. And the umpire, who was very deaf, raised his finger. Sir Eric Goldhat ran to congratulate the keeper, his Adam's apple bobbing furiously.

From then on, as each wicket fell, the Post-Cardiac Cricket Club ran excitedly to whoever was responsible and patted him, talking volubly, congratulating each other and giving little jumps. They were going to win. They liked winning. They were used to winning from Mondays to Fridays, but not used to winning at cricket. They were going to win, and it wasn't even going to rain.

When Alan Tremoyne came out to bat, his side had 43 runs on the board for the loss of nine wickets. The faces of the fielders were almost derisive as he took guard and looked around him. Four slips, a gully, silly mid-off, silly mid-on, leg-slip and a square-leg, all crouching with eyes unnaturally bright. The capillaries popped in their cheeks, the veins throbbed in their temples. Lord Christie, whose figures stood at 6 for 17 after ten high-speed overs, ignored the silver flecks that danced before his eyes as he walked back to bowl.

Alan Tremoyne had decided to have a tonk. He might as well. He wasn't really a batsman. Nobody expected him to score the 198 necessary for victory. So, at what he judged the appropriate moment, he shut his eyes and carved the air massively with his bat. The ball shot straight up in the air, followed by the gleaming eyes of the fielders. This was it. It would be caught. They had won. It was falling towards Sir Alec Hogdirt at square leg. 'Yours, Alec!' cried one of the fielders. '*Sir* Alec!' shouted Sir Alec, but didn't take his eyes from the red ball descending towards him. It was getting bigger. It was very red indeed, and huge. The whole sky was red and flaming. Why was somebody pulling a piano wire tight around his chest? Why were they hitting the backs of his legs with hammers? As Sir Alec pitched forward the ball hit him in the small of the back and bounced away. One by one the entire City eleven rolled his eyes, clutched at his throat and fell. The Toilchard Regis team ran on to the field, and with commendable unself-consciousness began giving their prone opponents the kiss of life. The Toilchard Regis wives ran on to the field as well, with the remains of the tea and a plate of headless gingerbread men.

The two German tourists, who had thought they were just getting the hang of it, looked at the eleven flannelled couples kissing on the ground and reflected that cricket was indeed a game hard to understand. But they took a photograph of it anyway.

THE SALMON
By Izaak Walton

The Salmon is accounted the King of freshwater fish; and is ever bred in rivers relating to the sea, yet so high, or far from it, as admits of no tincture of salt, or brackishness. He is said to breed or cast his spawn, in most rivers, in the mouth of August: some say, that then they dig a hole or grave in a safe place in the gravel, and there place their eggs or spawn, after the melter has done his natural office, and then hide it most cunningly, and cover it over with gravel and stones; and then leave it to their Creator's protection, who, by a gentle heat which he infuses into that cold element, makes it brood, and beget life in the spawn, and to become Samlets early in the spring next following.

The Salmons having spent their appointed time, and done this natural duty in the fresh waters, they then haste to the sea before winter, both the melter and spawner; but if they be stopt by flood-gates or weirs, or lost in the fresh waters, then those so left behind by degrees grow sick and lean, and unseasonable, and kipper, that is to say, have bony gristles grow out of their lower chaps, not unlike a hawk's beak, which hinders their feeding; and, in time, such fish so left behind pine away and die. 'Tis observed, that he may live thus one year from the sea; but he then grows insipid and tasteless, and loses both his blood and strength, and pines and dies the second year. And 'tis noted, that those little Salmons called Skeggers, which abound in many rivers relating to the sea, are bred by such sick Salmons that might not go to the sea, and that though they abound, yet they never thrive to any considerable bigness.

But if the old Salmon gets to the sea, then that gristle which shews him to be kipper, wears away, or is cast off, as the eagle is said to cast his bill, and he recovers his strength, and comes next summer to the same river, if it be possible, to enjoy the former pleasures that there possest him; for, as one has wittily observed, he has, like some persons of honour and riches which have both their winter and summer houses, the fresh rivers for summer, and the salt water for winter, to spend his life in; which is not, as Sir Francis Bacon hath observed in his *History of Life and Death,* above ten years. And it is to be observed, that though the Salmon does grow big in the sea, yet he grows not fat but in fresh rivers; and it is observed, that the farther they get from the sea, they be both the fatter and better.

Next, I shall tell you, that though they make very hard shift to get out of the fresh rivers into the sea, yet they will make harder shift to get out of the salt into the fresh rivers, to spawn, or possess the pleasures that they have formerly found in them: to which end, they will force themselves through floodgates, or over weirs, or hedges, or stops in the water, even to a height beyond common belief. Gesner speaks of such places as are known to be above eight feet high above water. And our Camden mentions, in his *Britannia,* the like wonder to be in Pembrokeshire, where the river Tivy falls into the sea; and that the fall is so downright, and so high, that the people stand and wonder at the strength and sleight by which they see the Salmon use to get out of the sea into the said river; and the manner and height of the place is so notable, that it is known, far, by the name of the Salmon-leap. Concerning which, take this also out of Michael Drayton, my honest old friend; as he tells it you, in his *Polyolbion:*

> And when the Salmon seeks a fresher stream to find;
> (Which hither from the sea comes, yearly, by his kind,)
> As he towards season grows; and stems the watry tract
> Where *Tivy,* falling down, makes an high cataract,
> Forc'd by the rising rocks that there her course oppose,
> As tho' within her bounds they meant her to inclose;
> Here when the labouring fish does at the foot arrive,
> And finds that by his strength he does but vainly strive;
> His tail takes in his mouth, and, bending like a bow
> That's to full compass drawn, aloft himself doth throw,
> Then springing at his height, as doth a little wand
> That bended end to end, and started from man's hand,
> Far off itself doth cast; so does that Salmon vault:
> And if, at first, he fail, his second summersault
> He instantly essays, and, from his nimble ring
> Still yerking, never leaves until himself he fling
> Above the opposing stream.

This Michael Drayton tells you, of this leap or summersault of the Salmon.

And, next, I shall tell you, that it is observed by Gesner and others, that there is no better Salmon than in England; and that though some of our northern counties have as fat, and as large, as the river Thames, yet none are of so excellent a taste.

And as I have told you that Sir Francis Bacon observes, the age of a Salmon exceeds not ten years; so let me next tell you, that his growth is very sudden: it is said, that after he is got into the sea, he becomes, from a Samlet not so big as a Gudgeon, to be a Salmon, in as short a time as a gosling becomes to be a goose. Much of this has been observed, by tying a riband, or some known tape or thread, in the tail of some young Salmons which have been taken in weirs as they have swimmed towards the salt water; and then by taking a part of them again, with the known mark, at the same place, at their return from the sea, which is usually about six months after; and the like experiment hath been tried upon young swallows, who have, after six months' absence, been observed to return to the same chimney, there to make their nests and habitations for the summer following; which has inclined many to think, that every Salmon usually returns to the same river in which it was bred, as young pigeons taken out of the same dovecote have also been observed to do.

And you are yet to observe further, that the Hesalmon is usually bigger than the Spawner; and that he is more kipper, and less able to endure a winter in the fresh water than the She is: yet she is, at that time of looking less kipper and better as watry, and as bad meat.

And yet you are to observe, that as there is no general rule without an exception, so there are some few rivers in this nation that have Trouts and Salmon in season in winter, as 'tis certain there be in the river Wye in Monmouthshire, where they be in season, as Camden observes, from September till April. But, my scholar, the observation of this and many other things I must in manners omit, because they will prove too large for our narrow compass of time, and, therefore, I shall next fall upon my directions how to fish for this Salmon.

And, for that: First you shall observe, that usually he stays not long in a place, as Trouts will, but, as I said, covets still to go nearer the spring-head: and that he does not, as the Trout and many other fish, lie near the waterside or bank, or roots of trees, but swims in the deep and broad parts of the water, and usually in the middle, and near the ground, and that there you are to fish for him, and that he is to be caught, as the Trout is, with a worm, a minnow which some call a penk, or with a fly.

And you are to observe, that he is very seldom observed to bite at a minnow, yet sometimes he will, and not usually at a fly, but more usually at a worm, and then most usually at a lob or garden-worm, which should be well scoured, that is to say, kept seven or eight days in moss before you fish with them: and if you double your time of eight into sixteen, twenty, or more days, it is still the better; for the worms will still be clearer, tougher, and more lively, and continue so longer upon your hook. And they may be kept longer by keeping them cool, and in fresh moss; and some advise to put camphire into it.

Note also, that many used to fish for a Salmon with a ring of wire on the top of their rod, through which the line may run to as great a length as is needful, when he is hooked. And to that end, some use a wheel about the middle of their rod, or near their hand, which is to be observed better by seeing one of them than by a large demonstration of words.

And now I shall tell you that which may be called a secret. I have been a-fishing with old Oliver Henly, now with God, a noted fisher both for Trout and Salmon; and have observed, that he would usually take three or four worms out of his bag, and put them into a little box in his pocket, where he would usually let them continue half an hour or more, before he would bait his hook with them. I have asked him his reason, and he has replied, ''He did but pick the best out to be in readiness against he baited his hook the next time'': but he has been observed, both by others and myself, to catch more fish than I, or any other body that has ever gone a-fishing with him, could do, and especially Salmons. And I have been told lately, by one of his most intimate and secret friends, that the box in which he put those worms was anointed with a drop, or two or three, of the oil of ivy-berries, made by expression or infusion; and told, that by the worms remaining in that box an hour, or a like time, they had incorporated a kind of smell that was irresistibly attractive, enough to force any fish within the smell of them to bite. This I heard not long since from a friend, but have not tried it; yet I grant it probable, and refer my reader to Sir Francis Bacon's *Natural History,* where he proves fishes may hear, and, doubt-less, can more probably smell: and I am certain Gesner says, the Otter can smell in the water; and I know not but that fish may do so too. 'Tis left for a lover of angling, or any that desires to improve that art, to try this conclusion.

I shall also impart two other experiments, but not tried by myself, which I will deliver in the same words that they were given me by an excellent angler and a very friend, in writing: he told me the latter was too good to be told, but in a learned language, lest it should be made common.

''Take the stinking oil drawn out of polypody of the oak by a retort, mixed with turpentine and hive-honey, and anoint your bait therewith, and it will doubtless draw the fish to it.'' The other is this: ''Vulnera hederae grandissimae inflicta sudant balsamum oleo gelato, albicantique persimile, odoris verò longè suavissimi''. '' 'Tis supremely sweet to any fish, and yet assa foetida may do the like.''

But in these I have no great faith; yet grant it probable; and have had from some chymical men, namely, from Sir George Hastings and others, an affirmation of them to be very advantageous. But no more of these; especially not in this place.

I might here, before I take my leave of the Salmon, tell you, that there is more than one sort of them, as namely, a Tecon, and another called in some places a Samlet, or by some a Skegger; but these, and others which I forbear to name, may be fish of another kind, and differ as we know a Herring and a Pilchard do, which, I think, are as different as the rivers in which they breed, and must, by me, be left to the disquisitions of men of more leisure, and of greater abilities than I profess myself to have.

And lastly, I am to borrow so much of your promised patience, as to tell you, that the trout, or Salmon, being in season, have, at their first taking out of the water, which continues during life, their bodies adorned, the one with such red spots, and the other with such black or blackish spots, as give them such an addition of natural beauty as, I think, was never given to any woman by the artificial paint or patches in which they so much pride themselves in this age. And so I shall leave them both; and proceed to some observations of the Pike.

ONCE ON A SUNDAY
By Philip Wylie

Somewhere up the river a noon whistle blew; quiet came over the boatyard. The band saw stopped screaming first; mallets and hammers fell
silent; old man Kane's handsaw was last. Crunch Adams, acting yard
superintendent that day, picked up the box of lunch his wife, Sari, had
prepared for him and walked over to the lean, gnarled shipwright. Crunch
inspected the intricately worked chunk of madeira—looked his thoughts—
and the old fellow nodded with satisfaction.

Crunch sat in the shade of a cabbage palm, out of the heat. Kane moved
beside him and opened a pasteboard shoebox. The two men began to eat.
Multiple riffles moved along the turgid river at their feet.

"Mullet," Crunch said.

"Mullet," the old man agreed.

The backdrop of Miami glittered in the sunlight and murmured with an
abnormal springtime industry occasioned by the presence of thousands of
soldiers and sailors. By and by Crunch's eyes traveled purposefully to the
blue-grey sides of the hauled crash boat on which they were working.
"Navy'd like to have her back in the water tomorrow night."

"No doubt," said the skillful old man. "But it's Sunday."

The *Poseidon*'s skipper nodded. "Yeah." He let time pass. They
watched a brace of pelicans float up the river on stiff wings. "Enemy
works on Sunday, though. Usually attacks then, if possible."

Mr. Kane spat. "Swine."

"Short-handed," Crunch went on. "We are. Everybody is. If we could
get that piece fitted tomorrow morning, they could paint it later—"

"I'm a strict Presbyterian," the old man replied firmly. "At eleven
tomorrow, I'll be in church, that's where I'll be."

"I know how it is." Crunch's expression was innocent. "I fished a
Presbyterian minister once—on a Sunday."

"You don't *say!*"

*   *   *

Desperate, the *Poseidon*'s mate, was swabbing down. The sun was a red disc—a stagy decoration; it emitted no glare but it dyed the line of boats at the Gulf Stream Dock a faint orange. Soon it would be gone. Crunch and Sari were up on the pier, laughing with the last customer. A tall stranger made his way past them, stared at the boats' names, and walked lithely to the stern of the *Poseidon*.

"Are you Crunch Adams?" he asked. His "r's" burred with a trace of Scotland and the voice that pronounced them had a slow sonority.

"I'm Des, the mate. Crunch is yonder."

The eyes of the stranger were cavernous. His nose was large and beak-like; above the six-foot level of his craggy head was a shock of iron-grey hair. Des wondered what sort of man he was and had a partial answer when the man saw young Bill Adams. Bill was three, then—proudly toting a suitcase for his father. The evening breeze stirred his blond curls. He tugged and grunted—a scale model of Hercules, in a blue sunsuit. A twinkle came in the man's recessed eyes and his broad mouth broke into a smile. "Likely lad!"

"Crunch's. The skipper's."

"I've been told he's the best. It shows—in the offspring."

Des began to like the guy. "Hey, Crunch!" he called.

"My problem," said the man, as he and the two charter-boatmen put their heads together, "is as difficult as it is simple. I'm a minister o' the gospel—a Presbyterian—though I wouldn't like it to be held against me."

Crunch and Des chuckled.

"When I went to school in Edinburgh—which was a considerable long while ago—I used to slip out as often as the opportunity afforded and cast a fly for trout and sometimes for salmon. I haven't wet a line since." He rubbed his chin. "My daughter spends her winters here with her husband, who's a man of means. I've joined them for a few days' vacation and my son-in-law insists I put in a few on the sea. He's footing the bill—and a man ought to keep in good with his son-in-law, don't you think?" He beamed.

"Very sound," Crunch said.

"But there's more to it than that," the man went on. "Do you mind if I light a pipe? It's safe on these gasoline boats?"

Crunch struck the match.

The prospective customer sat down with a sigh of composure. He sniffed the air. "Salty. I like it. Smells as good as the recollection of a frith. Unfortunately, for the past twenty-five years, I've hardly smelled it at all. I've been preaching the gospel inland. Not that it isn't as desperately needed there as n the coasts. I am simply explaining the rest of my predica-ment—an altogether happy one, as it chances. This vacation I'm on comes between my old church and a new one I'm to take directly after Christmas. What's that yonder?'' He pointed with the stem of his pipe.

Crunch looked in time to see the triangular top of a dark fin ease into the blue water. "Porpoise.''

"You don't say! They come here in this Bay?''

"Some of 'em live in here.''

"Well!'' He watched the big mammal rise and blow. "Fine creature! But to get to the point. Where I'm taking the new pastorate, fishing is partly a business and largely a recreation, besides. It's in New Jersey, at a place called Antasquan—a big town or small city, whichever you will. Some of my new congregation are commercial fishermen, and some of the wealthier ones are boat-owners, like yourselves. They go out for big tunny, I understand. Then, there's something called 'blues' they're partial to—''

"We know a little about it,'' Crunch said appreciatively. "We've fished a few summers from the Manasquan nearby.''

The minister smiled. "Which, no doubt, is one of the reasons my son-in-law stipulated you two! What can a man expect in a corporation lawyer, though, except guile? At any rate, I've got a congregation of fishermen—and golf players, to boot. Being a Scot, I can handle the golf, on week days, though it somewhat drains my congregations on the Sabbath, I hear. As fishing does, to an even greater degree, in the summer. But I like to know something of the pursuits of the men I preach to. So I'm doubly glad to be able to take advantage of this vacation to find out what I can of salt-water fishing. Have I made myself clear?''

"You sure have, Mr.—?''

"McGill. The Reverend Doctor Arthur McGill. And if, in the heat of excitement in the three days I've got to fish, it should become necessary to use a shorter term, you'll find I respond to 'Mac.' ''

He shook hands with them to seal the bargain.

When he was gone, Des grinned at the descending twilight. "The trouble is, there aren't enough ministers like that. If there were, I'd go to church oftener, myself.''

"Just what I was thinking,'' his skipper agreed.

The Reverend Doctor Arthur McGill appeared on the Gulf Stream Dock at seven o'clock the following morning—a green-visored hat flopping above his grey mane and a huge hamper carried lightly over his bony arm. He took the gap between dock and stern in an easy stride and deposited the basket.

It was a cool, breezy day—it would be choppy outside—but, if he knew it, he did not seem concerned. "Bracing weather,'' he said. "I hadn't expected it of the tropics. I rose before the servants and picked my own grapefruit from a tree in the yard. There was something burning out toward the Everglades and it recalled my autumn fire anywhere in the world. But the grapefruit was a distinctly pagan note; it made me understand a little why it is that north country men always have a sense of guilt in the south. It ought to be snowing and blowing—and here you are picking fruit!''

Des was already hanging the bow lines on the dolphins. The *Poseidon* pushed into the ship channel and started east. At the jetty-mouth, the outgoing tide, bulled by the easterly wind, threw up an unpredictable maelstrom of lumpy current; the *Poseidon* tossed, smashed hard and found her sea gait for the day. Three warm December weeks had changed, overnight, into the Floridian equivalent of a winter day—a day with a twelve-mile breeze and a temperature in the shade of sixty—a "cold" day, in the opinion of the natives.

Crunch cut baits. The minister wrapped an elbow around one of the canopy supports and watched, his eyes bright under his tangled brows. Once or twice, the skipper glanced at him covertly; he wasn't going to be seasick. He took in each detail, as the strip was sliced wafer-thin, tapered, pointed, beveled, and pierced for the hook. "It's an art, I can see that."

"The idea is to make it flutter in the water—like a fish with a busy tail." Crunch dropped over a bait on a leader and tested it to make sure it would not spin and wind up—or unwind—the line. He handed the rod to Reverend McGill and, under the same intense scrutiny, he arranged two balao on the outrigger lines. Then, because his passenger looked quizzical, he explained the operation of outriggers.

"You see," said the minister, "I'm a dub and a tyro and I have plenty of need to learn all this. A congregation of fishing enthusiasts will listen with a polite and patronizing interest if their dominie discusses the fine points of netting fishes in the Sea of Galilee two thousand years ago. But if you can bring the matter up to date—put it in terms of outriggers, so to speak—and use it in an illustration, you may even wake up the habitual sleepers."

Crunch laughed. "I get the idea, parson. Now. About 'blues.' Being a part-time Jersey fisherman myself, I understand the Jersey attitude. It's cold today—and we may run along like this for hours without a strike—so I'll explain what they do off the 'Squan Inlet—and why. Their fishing is done this way—and other ways."

"I'd appreciate it." The minister snuggled into the fighting chair and pulled his muffler tighter.

Crunch was deep in a lucid description of the art of chumming for tuna —remembering to cite the fact that Jersey old-timers still call them "horse mackerel"—when there was a splash behind the center bait. Reverend McGill went taut as his reel warbled.

"Bonita!" Crunch said. "Just hang on till he gets that run out of his system."

Reverend McGill hung on—and hung on properly—with his rod high enough so that no sudden bend could snap it over the stern and low enough so that he had room to lift it and take in slack in the event the fish turned suddenly. It did. The rod went higher and the minister began to reel. He brought the bonita to within a few yards of the boat and it sounded a good seventy-five feet. His rod tip shivered with the rapid tail action. He pumped the fish up, under Crunch's instruction. It sounded again—ran again—and came to gaff.

Crunch brought it aboard and the exhilarated minister looked. "Magnificent creature! Herringbone back—and the underside as white and sleek as alabaster! Funny thing! It's almost as big as any fish I ever caught in my life—and yet it pulled so hard I expected a fish my own size!"

"Bonitas are strong," Crunch said. He resumed his discussion of chumming. His back was turned to the water when Reverend McGill has his second strike. The minister handled the fish with considerable skill. " 'Cuda," Crunch said, after a moment.

It proved to be a barracuda. Crunch flipped it over the gunwale, showed the ferocious teeth by clamping the fish's head under the lid of the box in the stern, and removed the hook with pliers in a gingerly fashion. The *Poseidon* ran steadily for some two hours after that. Then there was a bluish flash under one of the outrigger baits and its line drifted gently down to the water only to spring tight like the wire of a snare. Crunch eyed the line as it cut the surface—pointing, in a curve, to a fish that was barely under the water. "Dolphin," he explained. "Get ready for him to jump. And when he does jump—watch him."

When the fish jumped, it was quite a sight. This particular dolphin at the particular instant was green and silver. Sometimes they are luminous cobalt and silver or gold—with pale blue spots. Sometimes they are almost pure gold or silver. Their rainbow patterns cannot be predicted—they change in seconds—and they range through all the natural colors save red and those with red in them, as well as through the spectra of precious metals.

"I know," the minister said quietly and between breaths, when Crunch gaffed the dolphin, "why people write poetry about them." He watched Crunch bait up again and went back to his vigil. "It's amazing," he continued, "what eyes you have. Now, in all three strikes, all I saw was a flicker and a lot of spray. But—each time—you saw the fish and named it correctly."

Crunch laughed. "I didn't see the fish, itself, any time. Except, as you say, an impression of a fish. I could tell what they were by the way your rod tip behaved—by the angle at which the fish fought—by a lot of little things."

"They must be fine points, for fair! I don't suppose you reveal them to the novitiate—the lucky novitiate, I might add?"

"Why not?" Crunch grinned benignly. "Take—the bonita. He was first. He hits hard and fast, usually at a sharp angle to the course of the bait. When he feels the hook he puts on every ounce of power he's got. He goes away, maybe for thirty yards or so, and then, still feeling the hook, he goes down. He'll bore straight down or go down in a spiral, like an auger. Now there's a fish out here that's related to the tuna, called an albacore. He does the same thing. But when the albacore swims, it's like a glide, all power and no wiggle. With a bonita there's the wiggle. A flutter. You see it in the rod tip. You feel it in your arms."

"You do that," the minister agreed.

" 'Cuda's can sound—or run—or jump. In fact, they usually give a jump or two like a pike or a muskie. On the same tackle, they're even stronger, I believe. But they do one thing that's characteristic—the jerk. If you get one near the boat you can see him do it under water. He'll yank his head back and forth trying to get rid of the hook or to break the line, just the way a bulldog yanks.''

"And the dolphin?''

"He always skims along at a terrific rate right below the surface. You can tell that because your line, instead of boring down into the sea, will be stretching out over it for a long way. Then the dolphin will circle, first one way and then the other, in big arcs. That is, he will unless he's foul-hooked. Hooked from the outside, in the back, say. Or hooked through the eye. In that case, he's very apt to sound—and if you haven't seen him when he hit, you'll be hard put to guess what you're fighting. Of course, you occasionally do see dolphin before they hit, because they sometimes make several bounds into the air to get the bait, as if they were impatient with the resistance of the water.''

"I see." The minister mused, "Funny, that. If you're fishing for salmon —you take salmon. You know what you've got when you have your rise. Trout, too, unless you happen to encounter a chub or dace. Here, though, the possibilities are vast.''

"There are hundreds.''

The minister thought that over. "And what would a sailfish be like? That is, if we were to have the fantastic good fortune—?''

So Crunch told him about the ways of sailfish. And in the end, he was, as usual, completely at a loss: "What I've said goes for the average sail-fish. But you're continually running into the exception. The fellow who just gulps the bait and runs. The one who strikes like a bonita—with only a flash under the bait. And then, when you know it was a sail because you saw its high fin and its bill—and you hook it—it'll possibly turn out to be a white marlin.''

"I presume, in the three days I have, there's no chance of that?''

"I dunno," Crunch answered. "There's always some chance. They're tailing today, though. I've seen a couple. They don't strike, as a rule, when they're running south from a cold snap.''

The minister nodded. Crunch knew by his attitude during the discussion of sailfish that the Reverend Doctor McGill had a very definite dream about his three days of deep-sea angling and the dream was centered around that particular breed of fish. In his mind's eye, the minister wanted not only what knowledge of marine angling he could glean from the pe-riod, but a particular object, a mounted sail, to hang, probably, in his study, where the visiting members of his new congregation could observe it and admire. Reverend McGill did not say so. He was too humble a man. But Crunch knew.

While the skipper was contemplating that matter, the novice in the *Poseidon*'s stern had another strike. The reel sang. The fish ran. Then it went deep. The rod tip fluttered. "A bonita!" the preacher cried with certainty.

"Well—it's not quite like a bonita. A little, just a shade, less powerful. Not quite so vicious. It might be a small bonita, at that. But I think it's a kingfish."

It was a kingfish. The minister chuckled. "You're not giving away all your trade secrets in one day!"

"Well, that one wasn't easy. I couldn't be sure myself. If we call three quarters of them correctly we're doing fine."

"I won't be so rash and conceited on the next," the minister promised. But there wasn't any "next." They ate the excellent lunch in the big hamper. They trolled the length of the island that is Miami Beach. Then they turned south and went as far as the old lighthouse. But there were no more strikes upon which the minister could test his fresh knowledge.

That evening the *Poseidon* came in as late as the winter sun would allow. "I've had a wonderful day," the minister said. "I've thought of at least six new sermons. I've settled in my head a minute point of ethics brought to me by one of my former flock which stuck me for a long time. I've caught four prime fish—whoppers, all—and two of 'em, you say, are superb eating. There's a good fifteen pounds of meat for the larders of myself and the friends of my son-in-law. And I'll never be able to thank you enough. The best part of it all is," his eyes crinkled, "we'll be at it again in the morning—and the day after, also. That's what they mean when they call this place a paradise on earth!"

Crunch stopped the recital and carefully poured a cup of coffee from his thermos. He raised his eyebrows enquiringly at old man Kane. The shipwright nodded and held out a cup from which he had been drinking milk. "Thanks, Crunch. So—what happened? Did he get a sail?"

"No," Crunch said. He peered reminiscently at the murky river and tossed a coral pebble to break the immaculate surface. "No. Doctor McGill never caught a sail, so far as I am aware."

"I'm disappointed."

"Maybe he wasn't! Des and I got fond of that gent. Whatever a good man is, he's it. And by that I mean he was both a man, and good. We fished Friday, from seven till dark, and got skunked. It was raw and windy with low clouds. Not a strike. But the old boy saw a whale, a finback, that came up close to the *Poseidon* and cruised along, blowing—and he insisted it made the day worth while.

"Then—Saturday came. His last day. He was going home Monday and he was planning to take in a couple of Miami preachers Sunday and Sunday night. So we started at six, in the dark, and we dragged a bait till night. He caught one grouper over the reef, and a rock hind, and he had one sailfish rise. I swear the old boy's hair stood on end. The sail came like an upside-down yacht with her keel out, and it followed the bait for a mile, but it never hit. Old Mac McGill stood up the whole time, muttering. First I thought he was praying and then I had a kind of shock because I thought he was swearing, but he wasn't doing either—he was just coaching the fish—like a quarterback on the bench when his team's in a spot. The fish never did hit, just eyed that bait, wallowed behind it, and finally swam away. And then it got dark and we came in and the dominie's vacation was over. He said he'd be back some day when his pocketbook could stand it and he said he'd had more fun than ever before in his life. His eyes shot sparks and he meant every word of it. He was disappointed, I am certain, but not as much disappointed as pleased. Des and I, of course, tried to make up for the thin fishing by telling him as many stories as we could—and by giving him as much dope as we knew how.''

"A good sport," Kane nodded.

"The real thing. Well, he shook our hands and thanked us and went away. Mr. Williams, the dock manager, had us down Sunday for a party—we didn't know the people—and we sat around Saturday evening feeling pretty low about the preacher. Sunday, we got down about seven and our party hadn't shown up. So we just sat around some more. Lots of people get a special kick out of deep-sea fishing for the main and simple reason that you don't have to get out at the crack of dawn. I mean, they'll hit at noon just as often as they'll hit at daybreak, which isn't like freshwater stuff. Anyway——"

During the night the wind had hauled. The norther had blown itself out and the Trade Wind, dawdling back from the southeast, had taken its place, pushing the cold air aside, dissipating the lowering clouds, and substituting the regimented wool-balls of Caribbean cumulus. The thermometer, between midnight and sunrise, had gone up fifteen degrees and a balminess characteristic of Florida had supplanted the sharp chill. Even the first level bars of sunshine were warm and it was certain that by noon the temperature in the shade would be eighty. On such days, after a cold-weather famine, the sailfish are likely to be ravenous. Crunch knew it, and Des, and they wondered in their separate silences what Reverend McGill would think about it. Because he knew, too. They'd told him how, as a rule, the sailfish would come up fighting on these days when the weather broke.

By nine o'clock, they were getting restless. Their party hadn't appeared. All the other boats were out, with the exception of one, engine parts of which were strewn over its stern cockpit for repair. Des was commenting on the laggardliness of some people when Crunch said, "Look. There's Reverend McGill."

The minister stepped from a car. He was wearing a neat serge suit and a high, starched collar. He walked down the dock with a sheepish expression and said, "That was my son-in-law. Off to play golf—like too many in my own congregations! I went along with him this far—I can walk the balance of the way to the kirk.'' Then he realized that the boats had gone. ''How does it happen you're still hanging to the pilings?''

''We were chartered,'' Des said bitterly, ''by some slug-a-bed named Ellsworth Coates.''

The minister turned pale. He swallowed. ''That,'' he finally murmured, ''is the name of my son-in-law—the heathen tempter!''

Crunch merely glanced up at the tall man on the dock. Then he squinted across the Bay. He neither smiled nor frowned—just squinted. I guess he must have seen the weather prediction—and realized what it would probably be like out there today.''

Reverend McGill sat down shakily. ''It's like him! The lawyer's guile! Dropping me here to walk to church! And with you two boys waiting, steam up and bait in the box! What does he take me for—a weakling? Is some crafty second-rate, amoral attorney to be the first to make me break the Sabbath? Not that, in the proper cause, I mightn't! I'm none of your hardshell preachers! I've been known far and wide as a liberal man, these long years! But a precedent is a precedent and I've kept the Lord's day, in my own fashion, as an example. Fie to Ellsworth—the wretch!''

''This might turn out to be a good cause,'' Des said. ''After all, it's a day in a hundred, and you wanted your future parish to feel you were one of them.''

''It could be a day in a million!'' the minister said scornfully.

Time passed—a good deal of time. Crunch began to repair a light rod which had lost a guide in an encounter with a wahoo. Up where the Gulf Stream Dock joined the Florida shore a school of big jack got under a walloping school of small mullet. The result was aquatic chaos: fish showered into the air as if they were being tossed up in barrelfuls by Davy Jones himself. The minister watched, goggle-eyed, and said something that Crunch thought was, ''It's more than flesh can withstand!'' But Crunch wasn't certain.

And then the *Clarissa B.* came in. She came in because one of her four passengers, a novice, had been taken ill—although the sea was smooth: only a vague ground swell kept it from being as calm as pavement. The *Clarissa,* as she approached, throwing two smart wings of water from her bows, was flying four sailfish flags.

''Four of them!'' Reverend McGill whispered disconsolately. ''I could have stood two—or possibly three—!''

The boat turned, backed in smartly, and deposited her shaky passenger with little ceremony: the other anglers were manifestly annoyed at the interruption and anxious to get back on the Gulf Stream. She pulled away from her slip again—showing four forked tails above her gunwales.

''Good fishing, eh?'' Crunch called to the skipper.

''They'll jump in the boat!'' he yelled back. ''It's red-hot! We've already had a triple and two doubleheaders and a single!'' He turned his wheel and purred into the blue distance.

Reverend McGill sighed and stood up. He shook out his full length of supple anatomy. He brushed back his iron-grey hair. "In any event," he said, grinning, "I'll not rationalize. I had it on the tip of my tongue to say that the Reverend Doctor Stone, whom I had intended to hear this morning, isn't so much of a preacher-man. We'll agree that he's the finest preacher in the south—and that by going fishing, I'm committing a mortal sin of the first magnitude. But—boys—let's get a lunch on board and make all the haste we can to violate the canon that has to do with this precious and altogether magnificent day!" He took off his collar as he came aboard.

By four o'clock in the afternoon, the lone passenger was stunned. In the interim, no less than seven sailfish had come up from the purple depths and done their best to be caught by the cleric. But in each instance that gentleman, through bad luck and inexperience, had failed to bring his fish to boat. In testament of his effort there was a broken rod. There were blisters on his fingers. There was a burn on his left arm where the running line had cut him. There was an empty reel from which the line had been stripped. And there was on the deck, a leader to which was still attached the upper half of a broken hook. But no sailfish flag flew from the *Poseidon*'s outrigger.

The loquacious Reverend McGill was dour, and his accent had become more Scottish. "I will nae say it's injustice," he proclaimed morosely, "an' a' would not ha' missed this day for the worrld—but it's a sterrn way to remind a mon of his evil intent!"

Crunch and Des exchanged glances. "There'll be more of 'em, parson," Des said encouragingly. "Just—take it easy."

And, even while he spoke, the outrigger line on the port side fell again and a big boil of water showed briefly where the bait had been. The line came tight and the minister struck to set the hook. The fish ran off rapidly for about forty yards and sounded. "It's no sailfish this time," he cried. "A bonita, I think. At least, perhaps we'll ha' one small fishie to show for our sins!"

Crunch looked critically at the bend in the rod. "If it's a bonita, it's the father of all bonitas," he said quietly.

"Very unlikely," Reverend McGill replied as he jockeyed to get in a few feet of slack. "Nothing sensational. The last two hours, I've realized I was predestined to have misfortune to the end of the day. But at least my face will be saved. I'll never have to exhibit a sailfish I caught on Sunday and acknowledge my guilt. The deed will be a secret between the two of us —and my son-in-law—who will use it, no doubt, for some blackmailing tomfoolery, one day. Now—he's coming toward us nicely!"

The fish swam toward the *Poseidon* for several yards. Then it turned, still deep under the water, and ran three hundred yards with the speed of an express train. The reel screamed. Crunch yelled. Des brought the *Poseidon* around in a fast arc. They chased the fish at full throttle for five hundred yards more before the minister stopped losing line from a spool that was by then no thicker than his thumb.

"It must be a sailfish, after all," Reverend McGill murmured.

"It's no sailfish," Crunch replied. His mouth was tight and he shot an enquiring glance at Des.

"What then?"

"I dunno. I dunno, Reverend. Maybe a marlin—"

"A marlin! It isn't possible—!"

"I think," Des called, "it's an Allison tuna. Better take it easy, Mac. You've got a long fight on your hands if it is."

"I'll gentle it like a baby," the angler promised. "I'm getting a bit of line, now." He tried tentatively and then with fury. "He's running to us— *to* us—faster than I can reel!"

Crunch waved—and waved again. The *Poseidon* leaped away from the fish but even at full gun she barely made enough speed so that the man on the rod could keep his line taut. Presently Crunch signalled again and the boat stood still. "Mac," as Des had called him in the stress of excitement, began to horse his fish toward the boat, lifting slowly until his bowed rod came high, dropping the tip swiftly, and winding in the slack thus gained. Two feet at a time, he brought the fish toward the place where the two guides leaned in tense concentration and where he labored sweatily. When the reel-spool was well filled with line, the fish turned and raced away again—a hundred yards, two, three. The process was repeated. The fish ran.

On the fifth struggle to the boat Reverend McGill gasped, "It's a new tribulation! I've hung a whale! Every joint in me is protesting—!"

"Stay with it," Crunch breathed fervently.

"Mon—I'm a *Scot.*"

He stayed with it. Stayed with it until it tired and until, an hour and three quarters after he had hooked it, a head and jaws rolled out of water not forty feet from the *Poseidon.* Crunch felt himself grow weak. He just stood there. Des said in a small voice, "You see it?"

"Yeah."

"What is it?"

"I dunno." Crunch repeated the words as if they angered him. "I dunno. It was red—wasn't it?"

"Yeah. It was red."

"But it wasn't a snapper," Crunch continued. "Not a snapper—not a monster mangrove snapper. I never saw it before. Mac—take it mighty easy, now. It's something new you've got there."

"I couldn't put any strength on it if I had to," the minister said grittily. Then he did put on strength. The fish made a last flurry—a rush, a mighty splash—and Crunch got the leader in his gloved hand. Swiftly, skillfully, he rammed home the gaff. The tail hammered on the boat's hull like a piston. Des jumped clear down from the canopy without hanging and made a noose around the leader. He dropped the rope into the sea. The two men pulled, and the fish came aboard tail first.

It was red, scarlet, from mouth to caudal. Its underside was greenish-white. It had big fins and a square tail. It was toothed. Its eyes were green. It gasped like a grouper and flopped heavily. They guessed it weighed about a hundred and eighty.

The minister flexed his raging arms slowly, caught some of his wind, stirred his back a little as if he were afraid any further motion would shatter it, and he looked and looked at the fish. "You mean—this is one you boys can't give a name to?"

Crunch said slowly, "No, Mac. And I don't think anybody—any taxidermist, any ichthyologist—can give it a name, either. I think it's a new one. Somebody comes in with a brand-new one every year or so, around these parts. Tonight you're gonna, Mac."

"Whatever the name is," Des said with the voice of a man who had seen a miracle, "part of it will probably be McGill—forever."

Crunch walked stiffly to the radio telephone. He put in a call for Hal—and for Bob Breastedt—the two foremost piscatorial authorities on the coast. "It's built like an amberjack—something," he said into the transmitter. "Fought like one—more or less. But it has scales like a tarpon, almost, and fins like a bass, and the darned thing's red all over!"

The experts came to the dock to meet the *Poseidon*—and so did the reporters.

It was a new one. Part of its long scientific name eventually became McGillia.

Many weeks later, Crunch had a letter from the minister. It was postmarked "Antasquan, N.J." It said, in part:

". . . and the celebrated catch we made that memorable day has become a not unmixed blessing. It served the purpose of giving my new flock an advance notice that I'm a fisherman of distinction. Indeed, the reputation carried ahead of me by the national publicity was so great that I'm alarmed whenever I remember that next summer I'll have to go out and show my lack of proficiency on the blues and the school tuna—not to mention the great horse mackerel. However, I'll take my chances on that.

"The point is, the fact that I caught the fish on the Sabbath was one which the press associations did not glaze over. On the contrary, they prominently noted it, and my congregation here was quick to make the discovery. Some of them chided me. And all of those who fish, and those who play golf, are smugly planning to be absent from their pews as soon as the spring weather breaks. After all, their dominie fishes on Sunday! This, however, has set me thinking—this—and the lesson in wiliness I learned from my son-in-law.

"Even now, war work is engaging the daytime hours of some of my people on Sunday—so I have stressed the evening service. It is already a feature in this city and the kirk is full every Sunday night though it was formerly sparsely attended at that hour. Come spring, my friends, and I expect to have most of the golfers and anglers in the evening habit and it'll be another bit of triumph I can credit to you and your fine ship! In short, I'm punished by the richly deserved lampoons of a fine group of people—

and rewarded with an evening attendance that beats the old morning service average!

"The fish itself arrived in due course—splendidly mounted and a thing of wonder. In that, I lost out, also—because I still have no symbol of my dubious skill to hang on my study wall. One of my parishioners is on the board of the American Museum of Natural History—and there the creature hangs. Still—I think the day was well spent—for myself and my fellow men—don't you?"

Crunch rose and stretched. He looked at his watch. One o'clock. Presently, the sound of the band saw rent the air. The boatyard resumed work for the U.S. Navy. Crunch had been reading the letter—having taken it from his hip pocket at the proper moment. He handed it, now, to the old shipwright, who stared blankly.

"You mean—you brought this thing here this morning?"

"Sure," Crunch said.

"You knew I was going to tell you I wouldn't work tomorrow?"

Crunch nodded. "Yep. But we need you—if we're going to get that job back in the water on time for Uncle Sam."

Kane glanced down at the name of the church on the letterhead. He sucked his teeth. "Well," he said slowly, "if that preacher can go fishing —and have it turn out all right—I guess I can work."

"It was for a cause. So's this."

"I still don't get it! You planned to tell me this story—and brought the letter to prove it was the truth—"

"I'm like the preacher's son-in-law," Crunch said as he walked away. "Guileful."

HOW THE GREAT FOOTBALL GAME WAS PLAYED

By Richard Harding Davis

Some football players can make football scores—a very few players can make football history. Yesterday afternoon when the Princeton and Yale elevens met at Manhattan Field Captain Thorne of Yale showed that he belongs to the class of players who make history.

"Tilly" Lamar ten years ago ran through the entire Yale eleven, and that run was of so sensational a character that it has been quoted ever since as the greatest run made on a football field in America. Yesterday Captain Thorne effaced the memory of Lamar's run and made a new record. It will probably be another ten years before anyone will eclipse the memory of Captain Thorne. His run took place late in the game, when he was tired and his energy nearly spent, and, as there were many things happened before that climax to the day's excitement, it is best to merely say here that such a run was made, and then go back and lead up to it properly. But, as it was the event that made yesterday's game memorable, it had to be recorded first.

The reason the annual football match between Yale and Princeton has a greater interest for the public than any of the games between the other colleges is because it is played on a football field where everyone can see it, and not in committee rooms and through the mails.

According to college tradition and their places on the map, Yale and Harvard should grow up hating one another with a fierce rivalry. They should be natural enemies and opponents, and Princeton and Pennsylvania football players should, according to their past history, jump at the chance to meet and roll each other around in the mud. But they are contented nowadays to stand haughtily aloof, each in his own yard, and write letters. Yale and Princeton, on the contrary, go out once a year to a whitewashed gridiron and play ball. They have been doing this ever since football was imported into this country, and that is what tends to make their match the popular one with the masses and the classes, and the public is grateful.

About 40,000 people showed how grateful they were yesterday by journeying out to Manhattan Field and paying from $3 to $10 for a seat, or by standing for hours on the side of a hill and watching these two great teams struggle in the arena.

It seems a bold thing to say; but there was a time within the memory of men now living when the sport of letter writing was as absolutely unknown in this country as the game of golf, and there are some who claim to remember when men who were rich enough to own yachts used to put them in the water and race them over a prescribed course whether the water was obstructed by fish or not; and when prizefighters voluntarily and of their own free will and without being pushed by anyone would step into a ring and find out which was the better man. In those old-fashioned days college boys, after training six months to play football, made it a point to roam around seeking whom they might beat at that game in order that so much good energy might not be wasted. Today they train just as hard or harder, but they allow the Alumni Advisory Committees and the Faculty to fight the game for them with typewritten letters. This has been a great year for the epistolary sportsman, from Jim Corbett down to the Earl of Dunraven, but the public likes the old way best, as it showed yesterday when Yale defeated Princeton by a score of 20 to 10. To report the game properly it was necessary to send many young men to Manhattan Field, and the one who has this part to write is uncertain whether he should tell of it from the point of view of the man in the crowd who had seen every Yale-Princeton game since '84, or from the point of view of the young woman who saw a football match yesterday for the first time. For these two spectators saw very different things. The latter saw only what was put before her; the former saw the game as one of a series of games, the crowd as a crowd made up of old friends and familiar faces; he appreciated that months of abstinence, of obedience, of hard work and physical discomfort, had fitted those twenty-two dirty and desperate young men before him for that restless two hours of fierce and soul-racking combat, and in many instances he knew what was coming even before it took place, as soon as the captain glanced over the bent shoulders of his men and signalled "Twelve, sixty, twenty-three."

But if Somebody's Sister in one of the grandstands did not get quite as near to the inwardness of what was going forward as did the explayers and coaches along the line, she at least witnessed a spectacle that was worth crossing a continent to see. The majority of the spectators yesterday belonged to the class of the unseeing ones. They came because it was the thing to do, just as they went to the Horse Show to see the people on exhibition there, and to the opera to look at the boxes and not to listen to the music, and their interest in Yale and Princeton was of the slightest, and their knowledge of the game even less. But that did not interfere with their enjoyment of the day or prevent them from rising in their places and shouting as they had never shouted before.

Five minutes after the game began they were as excited over it as though they had graduated from one of the two opposing universities and their sons and brothers were at that moment in the thick of the fight before them. That is what happens when 40,000 people get together and grow excited. Excitement spreads like smallpox germs, and before very long the enthusiasm of the man who is only interested in Yale because he has purchased a paper muslin flag with a blue Y on it is as great as that of the Yale freshman who has bet his entire allowance that the Tigers won't score. What the unseeing ones saw when they arrived at Manhattan Field was something like this: They saw a level turf marked out with lines of whitewash like a gridiron, and surrounded by walls of living people that started from the substitutes lying on the ground itself, and rose from those to the people in the lower boxes to those on the coaches to those in the five great stands, and higher yet to those on the Washington Bridge, and still higher to those on Googan's Bluff, which last were so far away that you could only distinguish that they were human beings by the aid of a field-glass.

It was like a great crater of living people, and those who were on a level with the players saw the blue sky above them as a man sees it from the bottom of a well. A circle a half of a mile in circumference, and composed of people rising one above another as high as a three-story house, is a very remarkable sight, and when half of these people leap suddenly to their feet and wave blue flags and yell, and then sink back as the man they have been cheering is tackled and thrown, and the other half jump up in their turn and wave orange and black flags, the effect is something which cannot be duplicated in this country or in any other. There are layers and tissues of people in this valley of human beings, each with a somewhat different interest, and each with a different point of view. On the lowest level next to the line are the substitutes, wrapped in blankets, and watching the game with the same intimate knowledge of what is being attempted and what has failed that the physician possesses when he holds the pulse of a patient. They are like a small army of understudies standing in the wings, each hoping some of the chief actors in the cast will grow ill, and that he can take his place. They have also been compared to vultures hovering over a battlefield, trusting that someone will soon be carried out on a blanket. Back of them are the people in the ground boxes, pretty girls with bunches of violets or chrysanthemums, which flowers seem to have been specially adopted for Yale-Princeton games, and excited parents who have sons at one of the colleges, and back of them are the sons and heirs themselves, on breaks and coaches and omnibuses, which are draped with colored bunting and which rock like small boats in a choppy sea when the men on top leap up and down in unison as they give their college cheer. On the other side of the field are the reporters and artists and photographers and telegraph operators, who have to tell the people around the bulletin boards down town exactly who made a run and who stopped him from making a longer one, while another run is being made, and the whole scene is changing like figures in a kinetoscope. Back of the reporters are their natural enemies, the ungrateful "general admissions", who stand ten deep behind a wooden fence, and yell "Down in front!" from the moment the game begins until the whistle blows for the last time. And their joy is greater when they can force a policeman to his knees than when one of the players scores a touchdown.

Behind the "general admissions" are the covered stands, in which the people sit, one above the other in solid ranks, separated by alleys of steps. As the game changes, they rise and fall like Mussulmans in a mosque, now straining forward and sinking back, now turning their faces to the right about as the ball flies through the air, and then looking back to the left as it is returned by the half-back who received it. The top layer of all are the people on Washington Bridge and Googan's Bluff, and the housetops and along the railroad buildings. Even with glasses they can understand but little of the game, but they remain at their posts all the afternoon, from luncheon time on till sunset, when the sky against which they are outlined turns a sullen red, and they stand out against it as clearly and as motionless as figures cut in black marble.

The score gives no idea of the game yesterday. The teams were much more evenly matched than 20 to 10 would seem to signify, and up to the last of the first half it was anybody's game. Why Princeton waited until the second half before deigning to show the stuff that was in her is one of the problems only known to the members of the team. And, except that post-mortem discussions are of interest only as guides for the future, it is of no consequence now. As a matter of record, however, the game began evenly, and continued unenlivened by any scoring until a fumble gave Bass the ball. It was one of those things that are generally considered as "against history". It seldom happens that the ball rolls off by itself, leaving twenty-two men struggling with each other and utterly unconscious that the object of their struggle is taking a little journey on its own account. But that is what happened yesterday. The ball rolled out from beneath a mass of men with an air of saying, "You don't need me, I am going to rest a while." And then Bass saw it, and stooping, scooped it up in his arms, and then they all saw it—when it was too late. Bass had forty-five yards to run to reach the goal line and absolutely no one in front of him. There were eleven Princeton men behind him, but there were also ten Yale men whose business it was to see that they did not have a clear course and get too near to Bass. There was no one in front of him whom he had to dodge, and there was no danger of the referee's whistle bringing him back, for the ball was fairly in play. His mind, in fact, was free from all anxiety, and all he had to do was to run. And he ran. It is very much easier to run away from something than to run after something. So Bass reached the goal line first and then the real excitement of the afternoon broke forth and the air shook with the roars of the Yale enthusiasts. Men stood up and threw their heads back and yelled and danced and tossed their hats above their heads and pounded each other in the sides, and the substitutes seized each other around the waist and waltzed over the turf or ran screaming down the lines, shaking their colored blankets in the air and turning handsprings. They had been training four months to make that touchdown, against Harvard if possible, and failing Harvard, against Princeton, and now that it was an accomplished fact they were letting out four months of bottled-up enthusiasm and anxiety and expressing their infinite relief. It seemed after that touchdown had been made as though everyone was aroused to greater interest, and the excitement grew and fed on itself and waxed stronger every minute up to the moment when the curtain fell.

The touchdown that followed was made within a minute of the end of the first half, and the score of 12 to 0 left the Yale men cheering grandly with blissful satisfaction, and threw the Princeton sympathizers into a state of silent, depressed and exasperated impatience.

But it did not last long.

The second half introduced a team that made the audience rub their eyes and sit up with excited wonder. They were apparently the same men, but they were rejuvenated, refreshed and desperate. They worked the ball down the field a few yards at a time, but with a rush and impetus that carried it thirty yards before they lost it. That was the best exhibition of team play that was seen during the day. The ground was not gained by one man or through a fumble on the part of their opponents. It was won by hard, scientific football, where every man did his share and helped his neighbor like the several parts of an engine. Not a cog slipped or a piston clutch or a driving rod failed in its duty. It was a beautiful exhibition.

And when the line was crossed at last, once Princeton had scored, the air turned so yellow that the place looked as if every seat in it was occupied by Princeton men, and everybody was of their way of thinking. Five minutes later Princeton scored again, and after that there was an antiphonal chorus of yells and cheers and calls that never slackened.

A clever stage manager, with a view to keeping up the interest, could not have arranged the game better. First Yale had scored so heavily that her students were already laying out in their minds the money they had won, and Princeton people were trying to remember who it was who had told them Yale would not last out the first half, and hoping that that man had backed his opinion himself. When just as all seemed lost, the Princeton team jumped to the front, and scored twice in two minutes, bringing the score up from 0 to 16 to 10 to 16.

It was obviously easy after that to argue that if the Tigers had scored twice in ten minutes they could at least score once more in the fifteen minutes still remaining to them, or even snatch a victory out of defeat. And at the thought of this the yells redoubled, and the air shook, and every play, good, bad or indifferent, was greeted with shouts of encouragement that fell like the blows of a whip on one side, and that tasted like wine to the other. People forgot for a few precious minutes to think about themselves, they enjoyed the rare sensation of being carried completely away by something outside of themselves, and the love of a fight, or a struggle, or combat, or whatever you choose to call it, rose in every one's breast and choked him until he had either to yell and get rid of it or suffocate. Men acted like maniacs, and the air was filled with the cheers of the opposing factions, until they swept against the walls of people and echoed back again, rent and broken.

The clamor ceased once absolutely, and the silence was even more impressive than the tumult that had preceded it. It came toward the end of the second half, when the light had begun to fail and the mist was rising from the ground. The Yale men had forced the ball to within two yards of Princeton's goal, and they had still one more chance left them to rush it across the line. While they were lining up for that effort the cheering died away, the yells, both measured and inarticulate, stopped, and the place was so still that for the first time during the day you could hear the telegraph instruments chirping like crickets from the side line. Forty thousand people in a state of breathless silence is more impressive than forty thousand people making all the noise they possibly can. But Princeton blocked the ball, and the goal was saved.

And then, just as the Yale men were growing fearful that the game would end in a tie, and while the Princeton men were shrieking their lungs out that it might, Captain Thorne made his run, and settled the question forever.

It is not possible to describe that run. It would be as easy to explain how a snake disappears through the grass, or an eel slips from your fingers, or to say how a flash of linked lightning wriggles across the sky.

Thorne was standing about forty yards from the Princeton goal, far over on the left of the field. When he got the ball in his hands there were two courses open to him. At least, one of them was open; the other was blocked with Princeton men. If he ran straight ahead, he had to pass through a mass of them; if he ran to the right, he had an open course, but as he would have to run diagonally across the field he would have just that much more ground to cover.

He took the shorter course, either by instinct or luck or by good judgment. If it was by good judgment, he has the gift of deciding quickly under disturbing circumstances so highly developed that he makes the difficulties of a captain in the conning tower of a ship of war during a naval battle seem contemptible. But, however he came to lay out his course, he followed it to the end. It was all over in five seconds, during which time he had dodged the Princeton team, slipping through their hands, jumping over their bodies, sweeping them out of his way and mowing them down before him. When he crossed the line one Princeton man was left hanging to his ankles, and the impetus of the run sent them into a policeman and knocked him flat so quickly that his head struck the ground before he knew his feet had left it.

The speed, the driving power and the agility of Thorne on this great march across the field was a most amazing thing. It was the sort of thing that one would have to see before it could be believed. At more than one spot along the field his advance seemed to be blocked beyond any chance of picking up more ground, but his flying feet still kept their way yard after yard. Whitney, a former Harvard star, and one of the best in the country, was sitting on the grass at my right and John Sears, the captain of the Harvard eleven in '89, was on the left. They looked as though they had seen a ghost. "That," said Whitney solemnly, "is the greatest run I have ever seen, or that we will ever see."

The game went on after that, but it was an anti-climax. The one run was worth the whole of it, and the people who saw that run need not distress themselves when they are told of the sensational efforts of Lamar and Laurie Bliss, of McClung, of Dean and of "Jim" Lea. They can boast that they saw Thorne; that should satisfy them.

THE FIVE-PLAY QUARTERBACK

By George Plimpton

Jack Benny used to say that when he stood on the stage in white tie and tails for his violin concerts and raised his bow to begin his routine—scraping through "Love in Bloom"—that he *felt* like a great violinist. He reasoned that, if he wasn't a great violinist, what was he doing dressed in tails, and about to play before a large audience?

At Pontiac I *felt* myself a football quarterback, not an interloper. My game plan was organized, and I knew what I was supposed to do. My nerves seemed steady, much steadier than they had been as I waited on the bench. I trotted along easily. I was keenly aware of what was going on around me.

I could hear Bud Erickson's voice over the loudspeaker system, a dim murmur, telling the crowd what was going on. He was telling them that number zero, coming out across the sidelines was not actually a rookie, but an amateur, a writer, who had been training with the team for three weeks and had learned five plays, which he was now going to run against the first-string Detroit defense. It was like a nightmare come true, he told them, as if one of *them,* rocking a beer around in a paper cup, with a pretty girl leaning past him to ask the hot-dog vendor in the aisle for mustard, were suddenly carried down underneath the stands by a sinister clutch of ushers. He would protest, but he would be encased in the accoutrements, the silver helmet, with the two protruding bars of the cage, jammed down over his ears, and sent out to take over the team—that was the substance of Erickson's words, drifting across the field, swayed and shredded by the steady breeze coming up across the open end of Wisner Stadium from the vanished sunset. The crowd was interested, and I was conscious, just vaguely, of a steady roar of encouragement.

The team was waiting for me, grouped in the huddle watching me come. I went in among them. Their heads came down for the signal. I called out, "Twenty-six!" forcefully, to inspire them, and a voice from one of the helmets said, "Down, down, the whole stadium can hear you."

"Twenty-six," I hissed at them. "Twenty-six near oh pinch; on three.

Break!'' Their hands cracked as one, and I wheeled and started for the line behind them.

My confidence was extreme. I ambled slowly behind Whitlow, poised down over the ball, and I had sufficient presence to pause, resting a hand at the base of his spine, as if on a windowsill—a nonchalant gesture I had admired in certain quarterbacks—and I looked out over the length of his back to fix in my mind what I saw.

Everything fine about being a quarterback—the embodiment of his power—was encompassed in those dozen seconds or so: giving the instructions to ten attentive men, breaking out of the huddle, walking for the line, and then pausing behind the center, dawdling amidst men poised and waiting under the trigger of his voice, cataleptic, until the deliverance of himself and them to the future. The pleasure of sport was so often the chance to indulge the cessation of time itself—the pitcher dawdling on the mound, the skier poised at the top of a mountain trail, the basketball player with the rough skin of the ball against his palm preparing for a foul shot, the tennis player at set point over his opponent—all of them savoring a moment before committing themselves to action.

I had the sense of a portcullis down. On the other side of the imaginary bars the linemen were poised, the lights glistening off their helmets, and close in behind them were the linebackers, with Joe Schmidt just opposite me, the big number 56 shining on his white jersey, jumpjacking back and forth with quick choppy steps, his hands poised in front of him, and he was calling out defensive code words in a stream. I could sense the rage in his voice, and the tension in those rows of bodies waiting, as if coils had been wound overtight, which my voice, calling a signal, like a lever would trip to spring them all loose. "Blue! Blue! Blue!" I heard Schmidt shout.

Within my helmet, the schoolmaster's voice murmured at me: "Son, nothing to it, nothing at all . . ."

I bent over the center. Quickly, I went over what was supposed to happen—I would receive the snap and take two steps straight back, and hand the ball to the number two back coming laterally across from right to left, who would then cut into the number six hole. That was what was designated by 26—the two back into the six hole. The mysterious code words "near oh pinch" referred to blocking assignments in the line, and I was never sure exactly what was meant by them. The important thing was to hang on to the ball, turn, and get the ball into the grasp of the back coming across laterally.

I cleared my throat. "Set!" I called out—my voice loud and astonishing to hear, as if it belonged to someone shouting into the earholes of my helmet. "Sixteen, sixty-five, forty-four, *hut* one, *hut* two, *hut* three," and at three the ball slapped back into my palm, and Whitlow's rump bucked up hard as he went for the defensemen opposite.

The lines cracked together with a yawp and smack of pads and gear. I had the sense of quick, heavy movement, and as I turned for the backfield, not a second having passed, I was hit hard from the side, and as I gasped the ball was jarred loose. It sailed away, and bounced once, and I stumbled after it, hauling it under me five yards back, hearing the rush of feet, and the heavy jarring and wheezing of the blockers fending off the defense, a great roar up from the crowd, and above it, a relief to hear, the shrilling of the referee's whistle. My first thought was that at the snap of the ball the right side of the line had collapsed just at the second of the handoff, and one of the tacklers, Brown or Floyd Peters, had cracked through to make me fumble. Someone, I assumed, had messed up on the assignments designated by the mysterious code words "near oh pinch." In fact, as I discovered later, my *own man* bowled me over—John Gordy, whose assignment as offensive guard was to pull from his position and join the interference on the far side of the center. He was required to pull back and travel at a great clip parallel to the line of scrimmage to get out in front of the runner, his route theoretically passing between me and the center. But the extra second it took me to control the ball, and the creaking execution of my turn, put me in his path, a rare sight for Gordy to see, his own quarterback blocking the way, like coming around a corner in a high-speed car to find a moose ambling across the center line, and he caromed off me, jarring the ball loose.

It was not new for me to be hit down by my own people. At Cranbrook I was knocked down all the time by players on the offense—the play patterns run with such speed along routes so carefully defined that if everything wasn't done right and at the proper speed, the play would break down in its making. I was often reminded of film clips in which the process of a porcelain pitcher, say, being dropped by a butler and smashed, is shown in reverse, so that the pieces pick up off the floor and soar up to the butler's hand, each piece on a predestined route, sudden perfection out of chaos. Often, it did not take more than an inch or so off line to throw a play out of kilter. On one occasion at the training camp, practicing handoff plays to the fullback, I had my chin hanging out just a bit too far, something wrong with my posture, and Pietrosante's shoulder pad caught it like a punch as he went by, and I spun slowly to the ground, grabbing at my jaw. Brettschneider had said that afternoon: "The defense is going to rack you up one of these days, if your own team'd let you *stand* long enough for us defense guys to get *at* you. It's aggravating to bust through and find that you've already been laid flat by your own offense guys."

My confidence had not gone. I stood up. The referee took the ball from me. He had to tug to get it away, a faint look of surprise on his face. My inner voice was assuring me that the fault in the tumble had not been mine. "They let you down," it was saying. "The blocking failed." But the main reason for my confidence was the next play on my list—the 93 pass, a play which I had worked successfully in the Cranbrook scrimmages. I walked into the huddle and I said with considerable enthusiasm, "All right! All right! Here we *go!*"

"Keep the voice down," said a voice. "You'll be tipping them the play."

I leaned in on them and said: "Green right" ("Green" designated a pass play, "right" put the flanker to the right side), "three right" (which put the three back to the right), "ninety-three" (indicating the two primary receivers; nine, the right end, and three, the three back) "on *three* . . . *Break!*"—the clap of the hands again in unison, the team streamed past me up to the line, and I walked briskly up behind Whitlow.

Again, I knew exactly how the play was going to develop—back those seven yards into the defensive pocket for the three to four seconds it was supposed to hold, and Pietrosante, the three back, would go down in his pattern, ten yards straight, then cut over the middle, and I would hit him.

"Set! . . . sixteen! . . . eighty-eight . . . fifty-five . . . *hut* one . . . *hut* two . . . *hut* three . . ."

The ball slapped into my palm at "three." I turned and started back. I could feel my balance going, and two yards behind the line of scrimmage I *fell down*—absolutely flat, as if my feet had been pinned under a trip wire stretched across the field, not a hand laid on me. I heard a great roar go up from the crowd. Suffused as I had been with confidence, I could scarcely believe what had happened. Mud cleats catching in the grass? Slipped in the dew? I felt my jaw go ajar in my helmet. "Wha'? Wha'?''—the mortification beginning to come fast. I rose hurriedly to my knees at the referee's whistle, and I could see my teammates' big silver helmets with the blue Lion decals turn toward me, some of the players rising from blocks they'd thrown to protect me, their faces masked, automaton, prognathous with the helmet bars protruding toward me, characterless, yet the dismay was in the set of their bodies as they loped back for the huddle. The schoolmaster's voice flailed at me inside my helmet. "Ox!" it cried. "Clumsy oaf."

I joined the huddle. "Sorry, sorry," I said.

"Call the play, man," came a voice from one of the helmets.

"I don't know what happened," I said.

"Call it, man."

The third play on my list was the 42, another running play, one of the simplest in football, in which the quarterback receives the snap, makes a full spin, and shoves the ball into the four back's stomach—the fullback's. He has come straight forward from his position as if off starting blocks, his knees high, and he disappears with the ball into the number two hole just to the left of the center—a straight power play, and one which seen from the stands seems to offer no difficulty.

I got into an awful jam with it. Once again, the jack-rabbit speed of the professional backfield was too much for me. The fullback—Danny Lewis —was past me and into the line before I could complete my spin and set the ball in his belly. And so I did what was required: I tucked the ball into my own belly and followed Lewis into the line, hoping that he might have budged open a small hole.

I tried, grimacing, my eyes squinted almost shut, and waiting for the impact, which came before I'd taken two steps—I was grabbed up by Roger Brown.

He tackled me high, and straightened me with his power, so that I churned against his three-hundred-pound girth like a comic bicyclist. He began to shake me. I remained upright to my surprise, flailed back and forth, and I realized that he was struggling for the ball. His arms were around it, trying to tug it free. The bars of our helmets were nearly locked, and I could look through and see him inside—the first helmeted face I recognized that evening—the small, brown eyes surprisingly peaceful, but he was grunting hard, the sweat shining, and I had time to think, "It's Brown, it's *Brown!*" before I lost the ball to him, and flung to one knee on the ground I watched him lumber ten yards into the end zone behind us for a touchdown.

The referee wouldn't allow it. He said he'd blown the ball dead while we were struggling for it. Brown was furious. "You taking that away from *me,*" he said, his voice high and squeaky. "Man, I took that ball in there good."

The referee turned and put the ball on the ten yard line. I had lost twenty yards in three attempts, and I had yet, in fact, to run off a complete play.

The veterans walked back very slowly to the next huddle.

I stood off to one side, listening to Brown rail at the referee. "I never scored like that befo'. You takin' that away from me?" His voice was peeved. He looked off toward the stands, into the heavy tumult of sound, spreading the big palms of his hands in grief.

I watched him, detached, not even moved by his insistence that I suffer the humiliation of having the ball stolen for a touchdown. If the referee had allowed him his score, I would not have protested. The shock of having the three plays go as badly as they had left me dispirited and numb, the purpose of the exercise forgotten. Even the schoolmaster's voice seemed to have gone—a bleak despair having set in so that as I stood shifting uneasily watching Brown jawing at the referee, I was perfectly willing to trot in to the bench at that point and be done with it.

Then, by chance, I happened to see Brettschneider standing at his corner linebacker position, watching me, and beyond the bars of his cage I could see a grin working. That set my energies ticking over once again—the notion that some small measure of recompense would be mine if I could complete a pass in the Badger's territory and embarrass him. I had such a play in my series—a slant pass to the strong-side end, Jim Gibbons.

I walked back to the huddle. It was slow in forming. I said, "The Badger's asleep. He's fat and he's asleep."

No one said anything. Everyone stared down. In the silence I became suddenly aware of the feet. There are twenty-two of them in the huddle, after all, most of them very large, in a small area, and while the quarterback ruminates and the others await his instruction, there's nothing else to catch the attention. The sight pricked at my mind, the oval of twenty-two football shoes, and it may have been responsible for my error in announcing the play. I forgot to give the signal on which the ball was to be snapped back by the center. I said: "Green right nine slant *break!*" One or two of the players clapped their hands, and as the huddle broke, some of them automatically heading for the line of scrimmage, someone hissed: "Well, the *signal,* what's the signal, for Chrissake."

I had forgotten to say "on two."

I should have kept my head and formed the huddle again. Instead, I called out "Two!" in a loud stage whisper, directing my call first to one side, then the other, *"two! two!"* as we walked up to the line. For those that might have been beyond earshot, who might have missed the signal, I held out two fingers spread like a V, which I showed around furtively, trying to hide it from the defense, and hoping that my people would see.

The pass was incomplete. I took two steps back (the play was a quick pass, thrown without a protective pocket) and I saw Gibbons break from his position, then stop, buttonhooking, his hand, which I used as a target, came up, but I threw the ball over him. A yell came up from the crowd seeing the ball in the air (it was the first play of the evening which hadn't been "blown"—to use the player's expression for a missed play), but then a groan went up when the ball was overshot and bounced across the sidelines.

"Last play," George Wilson was calling. He had walked over with a clipboard in his hand and was standing by the referee. "The ball's on the ten. Let's see you take it all the way," he called out cheerfully.

One of the players asked: "Which end zone is he talking about?"

The last play of the series was a pitchout—called a flip on some teams— a long lateral to the number four back running parallel to the line and cutting for the eight hole at left end. The lateral, though long, was easy for me to do. What I had to remember was to keep on running out after the flight of the ball. The hole behind me as I lateraled was left unguarded by an offensive lineman pulling out from his position and the defensive tackle could bull through and take me from behind in his rush, not knowing I'd got rid of the ball, if I didn't clear out of the area.

I was able to get the lateral off and avoid the tackler behind me, but unfortunately the defense was keyed for the play. They knew my repertoire, which was only five plays or so, and they doubted I'd call the same play twice. One of my linemen told me later that the defensive man opposite him in the line, Floyd Peters, had said, "Well, here comes the forty-eight pitchout," and it *had* come, and they were able to throw the number four back, Pietrosante, who had received that lateral, back on the one yard line—just a yard away from the mortification of having moved a team backward from the thirty yard line into one's own end zone for a safety.

As soon as I saw Pietrosante go down, I left for the bench on the sidelines at midfield, a long run from where I'd brought my team, and I felt utterly weary, shuffling along through the grass.

Applause began to sound from the stands, and I looked up, startled, and saw people standing, and the hands going. It made no sense at the time. It was not derisive; it seemed solid and respectful. "Wha'? Wha'?" I thought, and I wondered if the applause wasn't meant for someone else—if the mayor had come into the stadium behind me and was waving from an opentopped car. But as I came up to the bench I could see the people in the stands looking at me, and the hands going.

I thought about the applause afterward. Some of it was, perhaps, in appreciation of the lunacy of my participation, and for the fortitude it took to do it; but most of it, even if subconscious, I decided was in *relief* that I had done as badly as I had: it verified the assumption that the average fan would have about an amateur blundering into the brutal world of professional football. He would get slaughtered. If by some chance I had uncorked a touchdown pass, there would have been wild acknowledgment— because I heard the groans go up at each successive disaster—but afterward the spectators would have felt uncomfortable. Their concept of things would have been upset. The outsider did not belong, and there was comfort in that being proved.

Some of the applause, as it turned out, came from people who had enjoyed the comic aspects of my stint. More than a few thought that they were being entertained by a professional comic in the tradition of baseball's Al Schacht, or the Charlie Chaplins, the clowns, of the bullfights. Bud Erickson told me that a friend of his had come up to him later: "Bud, that's one of the funniest goddamn . . . I mean that guy's *got* it," this man said, barely able to control himself.

I did not take my helmet off when I reached the bench. It was tiring to do and there was security in having it on. I was conscious of the big zero on my back facing the crowd when I sat down. Some players came by and tapped me on the top of the helmet. Brettschneider leaned down and said, "Well, you stuck it . . . that's the big thing."

The scrimmage began. I watched it for a while, but my mind returned to my own performance. The pawky inner voice was at hand again. "You didn't stick it," it said testily. "You funked it."

At half time Wilson took the players down to the band shell at one end of the stadium. I stayed on the bench. He had his clipboards with him, and I could see him pointing and explaining, a big semicircle of players around him, sitting on the band chairs. Fireworks soared up into the sky from the other end of the field, the shells puffing out clusters of light that lit the upturned faces on the crowd in silver, then red, and then the reports would go off, reverberating sharply, and in the stands across the field I could see the children's hands flap up over their ears. Through the noise I heard someone yelling my name. I turned and saw a girl leaning over the rail of the grandstand behind me. I recognized her from the Gay Haven in Dearborn. She was wearing a mohair Italian sweater, the color of spun pink sugar, and tight pants, and she was holding a thick folding wallet in one hand along with a pair of dark glasses, and in the other a Lion banner, which she waved, her face alive with excitement, very pretty in a perishable, childlike way, and she was calling, "Beautiful; it was beautiful."

The fireworks lit her, and she looked up, her face chalk white in the swift aluminum glare.

I looked at her out of my helmet. Then I lifted a hand, just tentatively.

THE PRO-FOOTBALL GAME

By Peter Gent

The crowd bellowed as our kicker bore down on the ball, the roar increasing as the ball sailed through the air. It sounded as if they were surprised he hit it. They apparently knew about our kicker. The sounds of the crowd, although having a definite pattern, don't seem to coincide with their wishes. The clamor rose again as the New York receiver caught the ball and moved upfield. The noise reached its peak as our coverage team knocked the shit out of him.

As the eleven men on the New York offense huddled in the middle of the field, I watched the other twenty-nine men walk to the bench to find their numbers and sit down. I pointed this out to Maxwell. He didn't seem interested.

On first down, New York ran an unsuccessful trap for a loss of two yards. Maxwell quit playing catch, picked up his helmet, and walked to the sideline. I moved close to B.A. by the phone table and watched O.W. Meadows bat away a second down pass. On third, New York lost two on a draw when the back fumbled the handoff in the backfield. The crowd booed their offense to the bench.

New York lined up to punt. Alan Claridge and Delma Huddle were back to receive as Bobby Joe Putnam lofted the ball from his twenty-five. Alan caught it and started back upfield. He was turning the corner, trying to get behind his blocking wall, when a New York tackler hit him head on. The ball popped straight up, hanging in the air an eternity, and then dropping straight into the arms of another New York player. He looked around startled and then ran the thirty yards to our end zone unmolested. B.A. threw his hat down and glared Claridge to the bench.

After the official time-out to sell beer and shaving lotion, the crowd settled down. B.A. put his hat back on, and New York kicked off. The kick was short and Huddle raced forward to grab it. Misjudging his stride and the condition of the field, he overran the ball, tried to stop, and slipped down. The ball bounced off his shoulder. New York recovered on our nineteen. B.A. hit himself in the forehead with the palm of his hand and walked to the phone table. He picked up a headset and screamed at one of the assistants in the press box.

New York quickly lined up at scrimmage, snapped the ball, and ran a reverse, handing off to the split end. Nineteen yards later the split end slammed the ball onto the end zone grass. He was so excited, he raced to the bench and leaped on Tarkenton's back. They both fell in a heap on the sidelines. New York 14-Dallas 0.

Maxwell stood at the far end of our bench. He stared at the scoreboard. The kickoff went out of the end zone and Maxwell walked slowly toward the forming huddle.

"Elliott." B.A. called me to his side as the huddle broke. He put his arm around my shoulder and leaned close to my ear, ready to send me in with instructions.

Stepping quickly under the center, Maxwell went on a quick count, not bothering to set the line. He caught the defense in the middle of a shift. Both backs faked into the line, while Maxwell kept and rolled to the weak side, laying the ball out in front of Delma Huddle five yards behind the New York secondary. Delma stepped out of bounds on the five.

Seeing the completion, B.A. pushed me away and strode down the sideline yelling encouragement.

A dive play didn't fool anybody. On second and goal, a picture pass over the middle hit Billy Gill in the face and fell harmlessly to the ground. Maxwell had barely gotten the ball off ahead of a blitz and sat on the ground watching Gill walk back to the huddle.

I could tell by the third down formation it would be another pass to Gill. It was like Maxwell to come right back to a receiver who had just dropped a pass. He did it for me often enough. I tried not to hope Gill would drop the difficult outside throw, but I did, and he did.

The field goal team passed Gill and Maxwell as they left the field. Gill extended his arms to show Seth how far he thought the ball was off target.

The field goal was blocked and New York recovered on their own fourteen.

Tarkenton was unsuccessful in moving the Giants the first two downs, and on third and nine his deep post was intercepted by safetyman John Wilson and returned to the New York twenty.

Maxwell took the offense back on the field, turning back to yell at B.A. and point at me. The first play was a strongside pitch to Andy Crawford trying to sweep the end. Morris, New York's strong safety, came up fast behind his linebacker and quickly forced the play, dodging the tackle's block and stopping Crawford at the line of scrimmage.

"Elliott. Elliott." B.A. was motioning for me. "Get in there and tell Seth to watch for a sara blitz."

Gill saw me coming, dropped his head, and trotted off the field. Neither of us said a word as we passed.

I stepped into the circle of heavily breathing men. Maxwell was down on one knee looking up at me expectantly.

"All he said was to watch for that strongside blitz." I shrugged.

"Okay," he said. "Fire ninety T pull pass. Wing zig out."

It was a good call, faking the fullback into the line while Crawford flared wide from the halfback spot with the tackle pulling and leading, faking a run. If Morris, the strong safety, forced the run fake, I would be man to man against Ely, the cornerback. Ely's tendency to look constantly into the backfield should set him up perfectly for Maxwell's pump fake on the inside move of the zig out.

Schmidt, the center, snapped the ball. The tackle, the two backs, and Maxwell executed their fakes, forcing the strong-side linebacker and safety to play the run and leaving me one on one against Ely.

I drove down hard slightly to the cornerback's inside, making him adjust his outside position. He was inching in, afraid of the quick-breaking post route. The play fake had robbed him of any inside help. At six yards I made my inside break. Ely went with me driving strong toward me trying to close the distance between us. He was covering the quick post well. I swiveled my head looking into our backfield. Maxwell brought the ball up high and made a strong pump fake at me. I planted my left foot and drove back outside, passing under Ely, still covering the inside move.

"Goddammit," Ely said as I slid beneath him and headed at a forty-five degree angle for the sideline.

As he released the ball, Maxwell was hit from the blind side and the pass took off. I turned quickly back to my left, diving for the ball as it wobbled toward the ground. I caught it with my right hand and bounced into the end zone on my head and left shoulder. Sitting up, I checked for flags. Seeing the official with his hands up, I slowly got to my feet and started toward the bench, where Maxwell stood smiling with his hands on his hips.

B.A. would leave me in until I made a mistake. I would try not to make any.

The defense held New York again on the next series, and, after a fair catch by Delma Huddle, we took over on our thirty-five.

There was an official television time-out as we were forming our huddle on the twenty-five. Maxwell stood back on the twenty alone looking toward the other end zone. The rest of us milled around giving each other encouragement. The whistle blew and Schmidt, the center, raised his hands and called the huddle on him. We were all waiting expectantly when Maxwell stepped back into the circle. He was singing.

"It wasn't God that made honky-tonk angels . . . I shoulda knowed that you'd never make a wiiiife . . ." He stopped, looked around the huddle smiling, and called a play.

During that series of downs Maxwell was superb, mixing his passes and runs, and in ten plays completed the drive with an audible pass to Delma Huddle. The split end stole the ball from the hands of Davey Waite, New York's right cornerback, for fifteen yards and the score. I had two catches during the drive, for eight and fifteen yards. The fifteen yarder was a good catch, going over the top of two defenders. Both catches were third downs. I was having a good day.

We went to the locker room tied 14-14.

The tops of the equipment trunks were covered with cans of Coca-Cola and Dr. Pepper. The Cokes were disappearing quickly. As far as I knew, Maxwell, Jo Bob, and O.W. Meadows were the only Dr. Pepper drinkers.

I sat in front of my locker wiping the sweat from my eyes and trying to catch my breath. Ever since I had been benched, I had trouble getting my second wind. Sometimes I thought it was conditioning, other times panic.

Several players were sprawled around the floor smoking cigarettes and coughing. Maxwell sat down next to me with a lighted cigarette and a Dr. Pepper.

"All I need now is a moon pie," he said, grinning and dropping his voice to a rasp, "and halftime would be hog heaven." He was confident and it was contagious. I felt my spirits rise.

On the blackboard was a list of the first half Giant defenses. B.A. and Jim Johnson were standing beside the board studying them and listing the offensive formations we would use the second half to penetrate those defenses.

Our defense was huddled in the back of the dressing room considering the most systematic way to stop Tarkenton's scrambling. Except for that and the one end around, the New York offense had been powerless.

Over by the wooden tables, the trainers were patching a hole in the bridge of Jo Bob's nose. His helmet had smashed down and gouged out a quarter-sized hunk of flesh from between his eyes. Red rivulets had been running down both sides of his nose since the start of the second quarter. It looked as if he was crying blood. The doctor was bent over John Wilson, shooting his hip full of Novocain again. Three or four others were waiting their turn for treatment, blood pouring from torn flesh and joints swelling as body fluids pumped out of mutilated vessels.

The cigarette smoke began to get thick and I moved back to the showers to get some air. I took two more codeine.

Halftime was just long enough for muscles and ligaments to stiffen, while America sat and watched Dick Butkus shave without water. Many teams lost their momentum at the half, slowed by too many cigarettes and too much advice.

I watched O.W. Meadows down two fifteen-milligram Dexamyl Spansules. The pills wouldn't start working until the fourth quarter and maybe not until after the game. Dexamyl Spansules were one reason why Meadows never shut up all the way home after a road game. Spurred on by a goodly amount of bootlegged liquor, he would babble incredible shit at the top of his lungs about his personal philosophy of life, which fell somewhere between Spartacus and the Marquis de Sade.

I walked nervously into the bathroom and met John Wilson as he came out wiping his hands on the front of his silver pants.

"Pissed all over 'em," he said, holding the hands out for my inspection.

Most of the team was up and milling around. The coaches were still next to the blackboard talking over last-minute strategy that would be forgotten as soon as we hit the field.

Alan Claridge lay face down on a table while the doctor probed and prodded his right hamstring. Finding the knot, the doctor held his thumb on it and reached for a syringe. He drove the needle deep into Claridge's leg, moved it around, and emptied the syringe into the muscle. Repeating the procedure twice more, he deadened a large portion of the hamstring. If Claridge reinjured the leg in the second half, he wouldn't know until it was too late, but with luck he would finish the game with little problem.

The referee stuck his head in the door and signaled five minutes remaining in the halftime. As he opened the door, I could hear the distant strains of "Raindrops Keep Fallin' on My Head." I hoped everything was going off like clockwork for the boys with the sousaphones.

"Okay, listen up," B.A. said, walking to the middle of the room. "We've had some bad breaks out there, but we've come back and it's a brand-new game. We receive this half, so let's take it to 'em. The same team that started the game starts the second half."

Since Gill was the only starter on the bench, it would have been easier just to tell him and me. But B.A. didn't believe in dealing in personalities.

The crowd was back from the hot dog stand and America had returned safely, if somewhat confused, from CBS Control, when we took the field for the second half. The shadow of the stadium had moved almost halfway across the playing field, adding a dimension of time to the vacuum of fear. It was beginning to get cold and the sky was a fast-darkening gray.

The third quarter went quickly, with me alternating my attention from the field to the clock, hoping New York would get out ahead and I would get back into the game. The shadow steadily moved across the yardlines.

The Giants didn't move in the third quarter and Gill played a steady game, catching a nice turn in and a difficult sideline. I waited vainly for a signal from B.A. to carry in a play. Feeling powerless as my fate was being decided by twenty-two other men, I sat silently hating football, B.A., Conrad Hunter, Maxwell, my teammates, and the color guard from New Jersey. I could do nothing but wait and wish bad luck on my own team.

Near the end of the third quarter, Crawford fumbled a pitchout and my spirits rose. The Giants recovered on our thirty-five. Three plays later our defense had pushed them back to the forty. I could feel B.A.'s eyes searching me out as the ball hit the crossbar and bounced over. New York 17–Dallas 14.

"Elliott."

That familiar cry, cloud of dust, and a hearty hi-ho.

I turned my smile into a grimace and walked quickly to his side, trying my best to look as dedicated as I felt.

"Go in for Gill on the next series," he said, never taking his eyes off the field.

"Yes, sir," I said, immediately changing my allegiances and looking for

Maxwell to discuss how we could salvage a victory. He was at the phones talking to a coach in the press box. His face was ashen and he was talking rapidly.

"Goddammit," he shouted into the phone, "I haven't had time to throw a deep zig out all day, maybe that's why they ain't coverin' it. Fuck you, don't tell me, you cocksucker, tell your fuckin' lineman."

Slamming down the earphones, Maxwell took a cup of water from one of the trainers. Looking over the rim of the cup, he watched me approach. The cup came away from his face.

"You in?" he asked, his breath coming in gasps. I nodded.

"Good. I wanna try and run wide and I want you cracking back on Whitman."

That news took the edge off the thrill of playing. It wasn't the fear of hitting the 235-pound linebacker, although that was substantial. It was the fear of missing him. If I missed and Maxwell didn't run me off the field, B.A. certainly would. The only way I could be sure of making the block was to spear him with my head; for me, it was the surest of open field blocks. I would dive headfirst at his knees, making it next to impossible to miss. The drawback was that I wouldn't have any control over where I took the blow—head, face, neck, back. It all depended on whether Whitman saw me sneaking back down the line at him and what kind of evasive technique he used if he did.

I watched Claridge bring the kickoff out from three yards deep in the end zone. Reaching the twenty-yard line, he suddenly straightened up and grabbed the back of his leg. He went rigid and as he fell forward Bobby Joe Putnam hit him full speed flush in the face with his headgear.

Seeing the ball torn loose elated me for an instant. Then guilt washed over me as I realized I was back in the game and had changed sides. I felt as if I had wished the fumble. I felt no better when Tarkenton scrambled to the five on the first play from scrimmage and the quarter ended.

The fourth quarter started. We were trailing 17–14 and New York had the ball, first and goal, on our five. Tarkenton tried to roll out, was trapped, and reversed his field back to the twenty-five, dancing around our exhausted defensive linemen for a full thirty seconds, finally making it back to the ten. New York was penalized for holding the next two plays in a row, and on second and goal from the forty Meadows trapped Tarkenton back at the New York forty-five. The next play we were called for pass interference and New York took the five-yard penalty and automatic first down.

They stayed on the ground the remainder of the drive, pushing out three first downs, getting the final yards on fourth down each time. They stalled on our eighteen and settled for a field goal. New York 20–Dallas 14.

I moved around the sidelines to loosen up, waiting for the network to return the slightly altered television audience so New York could kick off. Several people were standing over Claridge, who was stretched out face down on the bench. The doctor was digging his fingers in the hamstring he had anesthetized at halftime.

"See," the doctor said, "feel this. The hole? I can put my four fingers in it. It's torn pretty bad."

Claridge had his face turned away, into the back of the bench. He appeared to be in great pain, mumbling and crying apologies for the fumble. I knelt down next to him and put my hand on his shoulder. I shook him gently. I was going to explain that New York only got a field goal and we would get that back this series. I was again amazed at how quickly the team spirit possessed me when I was in the game.

Claridge turned to me; he was covered with blood. His double bar mask was shattered and his face was swollen and discolored a purplish-black. It seemed lopsided, twisted into a grotesque scowl, the running blood continually changing the expression. His nose was smashed flat and split open as if someone had sliced the length of it with a razor. The white cartilage shone brightly from the red-black maw that had been his nose. His eyes were wide and bright but seemed sightless. He tried to say something, raising his hand, but it was lost in a gurgle as black blood poured from his mouth.

"Goddam," I screamed. "Goddam, somebody get over here and fix his face!"

Claridge had apparently gotten off the field under his own power and collapsed on the bench. Face down was the only way he could keep from strangling on the blood. I held his head up slightly, gripping his headgear through the earholes.

My cries brought several people and directed the doctor's attention from one end of Claridge to the other.

"Did he bite his tongue?" The doctor shoved a finger into Claridge's mouth and searched for his tongue, making sure he hadn't bitten it off or swallowed it. "We'd better get him to a hospital."

"What happened?" B.A. was peering over the huddle around Claridge.

"Smashed up his nose pretty bad," the doctor said. "Better take him to the hospital."

"Oh." B.A. nodded, and turned back to the field.

The crowd noises indicated America had returned to her living room and New York was about to kick off. Backing away from the mutilated man, I heard the kick but couldn't take my eyes off the black blood running through the slats in the bench and into the damp sand below.

The ball sailed out of the end zone and I walked slowly alongside Maxwell to the huddle at the ten-yard line.

"Jesus," I said, recalling the face that didn't resemble Claridge and the pitiful mindless eyes, "did you see Claridge's face?"

"I ain't got time to worry about that shit," he said, his mouth drawn and his eyes tired. "If you can't take it . . . ." He broke into a trot and hurried to the huddle before he finished.

I followed a few steps behind.

The men in the huddle were tired and openly hostile to each other, the day's frustrations pushing several to the breaking point. The spirit and attitude had degenerated markedly from the first half.

"Goddammit, Andy. Hold onto the fuckin' ball this time."

"Fuck you, Schmidt. You just snap the ball, I'll take care of myself."

"All right, quiet down," Maxwell instructed angrily, kneeling into the huddle. "I'm the only one that talks in this huddle. All you guys shut up unless I ask you somethin'."

I looked around the huddle at the battered, bruised, and exhausted men, some already worrying about mistakes they would have to explain next Tuesday. Scared to death and angry, it would be a miracle if they could even get off on the same count, let alone outthink, outmaneuver, and outmuscle the men of similar talent across the line.

The shadows of the stadium had covered the field, adding further gloom to an already dismal afternoon.

"All right," Maxwell ordered. "Red right dive forty-one G pull. On two."

It was a simple trap up the middle. Jo Bob Williams jumped offsides. We walked back five yards.

"Goddammit, Jo Bob, pay attention to the count."

"Shove it up your ass, Schmidt. Who died and left you in charge?"

"Okay, I'm telling you guys," Maxwell shouted. "You better shut the fuck up in my huddle."

The huddle was silent as the quarterback scanned the grimy, sweaty faces. The gouge in Jo Bob's nose had opened up again and the blood was running into his mouth, turning his lips shiny red. He licked them nervously.

"Okay, Brown right dive forty-nine G take. On three."

It was a pitchout with a guard lead, coming off a fullback slant fake over the tackle. We ran it from a set backfield and the key block was our tight end against their defensive end Deyer. Deyer made the tackle for a two-yard loss.

"Jesus Christ," Crawford yelled, straightening his helmet as he regained his feet. "What the fuck is goin' on?" He wobbled back to the huddle, spitting out grass and mud.

"Sorry, Andy."

"Fuckin' sorry ain't gonna get it."

"Come on. Knock it off—"

"All right," Maxwell screamed. "This is the last time I'm gonna say it. Shut the fuck up in my huddle."

"If the dumb cocksuckers would do their jobs." Bill Schmidt, the center, was talking. Because he was a member of the original expansion family and worked for Conrad Hunter personally in the off season, Schmidt considered himself a player-coach and the leader of the offensive line.

"Shut your mouth, Schmidt," Maxwell ordered, "or you're off the field."

"Bullshit, I am," Schmidt shot back, glaring at the quarterback.

Maxwell looked up, shocked, and returned Schmidt's gaze thoughtfully for a few seconds, then shook his head and stepped from the huddle. He walked in measured steps to the referee and then on to the sidelines.

The official signaled a Dallas time-out. The huddle dissolved into a group of pointless men, pulling off their helmets and kneeling down, or standing and looking around aimlessly, waiting for Maxwell to return. Nobody said a word. I looked over at Delma Huddle and he flashed a big smile and gave me the thumbs up sign. I smiled back. Looking up into the stands at the mass of gray dots that were faces, perched atop flashes of colors that expressed their egos, I suddenly realized how peculiar we must look. I thought of Al Capp shmoos paying six dollars a head to watch and scream while trained mice scurried around in panic.

Eddie Rand, his whites smudged and bloodied at the end of a long day, started out on the field with towels and water. Maxwell stopped him and sent him back to the sidelines.

B.A. walked a few steps onto the field to meet with Maxwell. Neither man looked at each other, Maxwell had turned almost away from his coach and seemed to be staring out at the milling, disorganized rabble that was his command. B.A. was looking down to one end zone and the scoreboard. The stadium band broke into a halting "Tea for Two Cha Cha." Maxwell suddenly whirled around and pointed his finger directly into B.A.'s face. The coach dropped his head momentarily, then nodded and turned back to the bench. Maxwell returned to the huddle.

"Schmidt," he said, matter-of-factly, "you're out."

Marion Konklin, a backup guard who doubled at center only in practice, lumbered onto the field.

Schmidt stared at Maxwell with pure animal hatred. Maxwell turned his back and stepped into the huddle already forming around Konklin. The veteran center turned and walked rapidly to the sidelines, throwing his helmet into a crowd of his teammates. The row of players lining the sidelines opened up slightly to dodge the helmet and let Schmidt pass, then closed as the furious man disappeared.

"All right, goddammit," Maxwell ordered. "This time we go. I wanted you out here, Konklin. Don't lemme down. You know what to do on a draw delay trap?"

It was third and fifteen.

"I'm not sure."

Several players coughed and moved uneasily.

"Just set for pass. Then fire out and get the middle linebacker. It's no sweat," Maxwell reassured the frightened substitute.

The whistle blew, signaling time back in.

"All right. Red right draw delay trap on two. Got it Marion? On two."

Maxwell stepped up behind Konklin and patted him reassuringly on the hip. The terrified center nearly leaped into New York's secondary. Maxwell shouted out the defensive alignment, set the line, and stood scanning the linebackers and deep backs. The middle linebacker moved up into the line showing blitz. I watched Maxwell as he considered an audible against the blitz. Konklin's legs started shaking slightly. Maxwell decided against the audible. Konklin would certainly miss it. Maxwell was gambling the linebacker was faking.

By the time Maxwell called the second hut, Konklin's legs were shaking noticeably. He slammed the ball up into Maxwell's hands and shot into the middle linebacker. He forgot about waiting to show pass set. It couldn't have worked better if it had been executed correctly. The straight power block caught the linebacker guessing. He had been expecting a pass or at least a pass set. The block caught him totally unprepared and he went right over backward with Konklin on top of him. Crawford carried for fourteen and the first down.

"That's a start. That's a start," Maxwell chattered confidently, clapping his hands and smiling broadly. He slipped into a heavy Texas drawl. "We're gonna run an' tho' this ball rat down their throats."

The huddle formed around Konklin, who was smiling broadly as everyone congratulated him. The energy was returning.

"All right. All right." Maxwell knelt back into the huddle. "Fire draw forty-one Y zig out on two. Now come on, you guys. I didn't leave them sand hills jest to come to the big city an' git beat." The huddle broke with a low grunt.

Maxwell hit Delma going out of bounds on the New York thirty-five. They had two men on him when he caught the ball.

The sound waves from fifty thousand diaphragms blew through our bodies. It was innervating. My stomach started to churn violently. I needed to evacuate; the pressure was intense. I farted and felt better.

"Who the hell did that?"

"Goddam."

The huddle started to break up as players fanned at the air in front of their faces and scowled with disgust.

"All right, you guys. Get back in here," Maxwell ordered. "Jesus, who did that?" He looked around the huddle. I looked accusingly at Crawford next to me. "Okay," Maxwell began again. "Red right freeze protection. Wing out at six yards. You linemen on the strongside cut block to get their hands down."

I took long strides heading for Ely's outside shoulder forcing him back. On my fourth step I made a rounded cut with no fake and drove hard for the sideline. The ball was in the air when I looked back. I grabbed it and put it away quickly. I planted my right foot, dropped my shoulder, and turned upfield. Ely drilled me in the chest with his headgear and knocked me flat on my back at the twenty-five. The back of my head slammed into the ground, making my nose burn and my eyes water. The roof of my mouth hurt.

"All right. All right. Green right pitch twenty-nine wing T pull. On two."

My heart jumped and my mouth went dry at the call. I would have to crack back on Whitman, the outside linebacker on the right-hand side. Crawford would try to get outside of my block with the help of the strong-side tackle.

Whitman moved toward the sideline in a low crouch, stringing the play out and watching Andy and the leading tackle. At the last second he felt me coming back down the line at him. I dove headlong as he turned. He tried to jump the block and his knees caught me in the forehead and the side of the neck. We went down in a jumble of arms and legs, my shoulder went numb, and a hot burn shot up my neck and into the back of my head. The play gained eight yards.

"All right. All right. Here we go." Maxwell looked up at me. I was shrugging my shoulders and rolling my neck, trying to ease the sting. "You okay?" he asked.

"Yeah, I'm fine."

"All right. All right. Here we go. Red right freeze. Wing out and go. You guys cut block just like the out but tie 'em up an' gimme some more time."

Just before the snap Ely moved up close to the line and played me tight, bumping me as I sprinted off the line. He covered the out move I had beaten him on earlier. I took three hard strides to the sideline, looking back for the ball, then planted hard and turned upfield past him.

"Son of a bitch!" he yelled when he realized Maxwell's pump was a fake and his interception had dissolved.

I caught the ball on the five and ran it into the end zone. Dallas 21–New York 20.

Our defense kept New York bottled up inside their own twenty and after a long punt by Bobby Joe Putnam we took over on our own thirty-five. There were less than two minutes to play.

An I formation tackle slant was good for three yards and we were huddling up for the second and seven situation when Billy Gill raced in from the sidelines. He slapped me on the shoulder and delivered a play to Seth.

B.A. waved me to his side when I reached the bench. He put his arm around me, keeping his eyes on the field as our huddle broke and the team lined up to run the play. It was a draw delay trap. The fullback made it to the line of scrimmage.

It was third and ten.

"Tell him to roll weakside and hit Delma on a sideline. Or run with it himself."

I turned and raced to the already forming huddle.

I repeated the order, leaning into the huddle.

"Okay," Maxwell nodded. "Green left. Roll right Y sideline at twelve. Okay, Delma?"

"You get it there, Bubba, and I'll catch it."

The Giants rolled up into a zone against Delma. He dodged the cornerman's cut block and curled out to the sideline in front of the deep covering safety. Maxwell dropped the ball right in the hole to him. Delma dodged the fast-closing deep man and was cutting across the grain heading down the middle for the end zone. The middle linebacker made a desperate dive and hooked his arm. The ball popped free. Lewis, the Giant free safety, scooped up the crazily bouncing ball and returned it to our twenty. Gogolak kicked his third field goal of the day with fifteen seconds to play.

New York 23–Dallas 21

The locker room was almost deserted. The equipment man was finishing packing the soiled and bloody uniforms into the blue trunks and was making a last-minute check of the lockers. He found Jo Bob's headgear. "Goddam Williams," he grumbled. "He'd ferget his ass if he wasn't always on it."

An aged black stadium custodian swept the used tape and gauze, the disposable syringes and needles, and the discarded paper cups and drink cans into a pile in the center of the room.

The last sportswriter had just left after listening to B.A. "reluctantly" place the blame on several players, most notably Delma Huddle and Alan Claridge.

The last bus to the airport was outside the stadium, its exhaust blowing white in the cold New York twilight. The first bus was well on its way to Kennedy.

The trainer had just given me a muscle-relaxant shot, had rubbed down and rewrapped my legs, and had strapped my arm to my chest. The taping gave protective support to the shoulder that had collided with Whitman.

I heard the sound of running water in the shower room. I pulled my coat on over my shoulders and walked back to investigate. Seth Maxwell was sitting in a steel folding chair, his head on his chest and a steady stream of water pounding on the back of his neck. His ankles were still taped. Every now and then he rotated his right arm at the shoulder and flexed his fingers. I watched him silently for several minutes. Finally I broke in.

"Hey, man, the last bus goes in about twenty minutes."

"Okay, okay," he responded instantly. "Throw me some tape cutters."

I borrowed cutters from the trainers and tossed them to Maxwell. He quickly sliced off the tape and slammed the water-soaked bandages against the shower floor.

"Cocksucker. Cocksucker," he shouted, punctuating the epithets by whacking the tape on the wet tile. "Cocksucker!"

"Shit," I said, smiling and trying to adjust my taped shoulder comfortably. "The way it went today, I'm surprised you hit the floor."

I ducked aside and the tape cutters clanged on the wall behind my head.

"That's more like it," I said, wincing slightly. Dodging the cutters had made my shoulder throb. I pushed up on my tightly bound forearm. "Come on, get dressed and let's find someplace to get high."

The trainers were taking their showers when we left the locker room. In the tunnel, the equipment man was loading the trunks into the back of an air-freight van for transport to Kennedy, where an orange Braniff 727 with a galley full of dry chicken sandwiches and eighty warm beers sat waiting.

"I sure could use me a Cutty and water," Maxwell rasped, his hands thrust deep in the pockets of his brown cashmere coat. His hair was slicked back and still slightly wet from his shower. Little beads of perspiration dotted his forehead.

"I mentioned it to Mary Jane on the way up. I'm sure she'll have us something."

The leather trench coat started slipping off my taped shoulder. I tried to pull it back on with my free hand but the twisting motion sent hot pains into my head. Maxwell noticed my struggle, grabbed the coat and reseated it on my shoulder.

As we reached the exit to the parking lot Maxwell went past and started up the ramp to the stadium seats. I followed, after making sure the bus was still waiting.

"We don't have much time," I called, as Maxwell disappeared into the stadium.

The covered seats were in such deep shadows that I had to stop for a moment to let my eyes adjust before I located Maxwell. He was sitting on the aisle four rows in front of me.

"You got a joint?" he asked.

There was a determination, a destructiveness, in his voice. He kept his eyes fixed on the field, almost totally lost in darkness. It looked cold and barren in the gray city dusk.

"Yeah, I think so. But we'll have to hurry." My caution drew a look of distaste.

"Sometimes I wonder about your manhood," he said.

The insult puzzled me, but I avoided his eyes and dug in my pocket for a joint. As long as I played well I was seldom upset by a loss. I looked at winning or losing as someone else's benefit, distantly removed from my daily struggles for existence. Maxwell took losses to heart, regardless of his personal performance.

I lit the joint and inhaled deeply; it made my shoulder hurt. I leaned over and passed to Maxwell, at the same time looking around the stadium for the police I knew were hiding behind every pillar. Maxwell pushed his cowboy hat down over his eyes, propped his feet on the seat in front, took a long, loud drag, and passed back to me. We smoked the whole joint in silence. Finally Maxwell stood up and flicked the glowing roach away.

"Well," he said, starting back down the ramp to the waiting bus, "she whipped me again."

THE AWAKENING
OF ROLLO PODMARSH

By P.G. Wodehouse

Down on the new bowling-green behind the club-house some sort of competition was in progress. The seats about the smooth strip of turf were crowded, and the weak-minded yapping of the patients made itself plainly audible to the Oldest Member as he sat in his favourite chair in the smoking-room. He shifted restlessly, and a frown marred the placidity of his venerable brow. To the Oldest Member a golf-club was a golf-club, and he resented the introduction of any alien element. He had opposed the institution of tennis courts; and the suggestion of a bowling-green had stirred him to his depths.

A young man in spectacles came into the smoking-room. His high forehead was aglow, and he lapped up a ginger-ale with the air of one who considers that he has earned it.

"Capital exercise!" he said, beaming upon the Oldest Member.

The Oldest Member laid down his *Vardon On Casual Water,* and peered suspiciously at his companion.

"What did you go round in?" he asked.

"Oh, I wasn't playing golf," said the young man. "Bowls."

"A nauseous pursuit!" said the Oldest Member, coldly, and resumed his reading.

The young man seemed nettled.

"I don't know why you should say that," he retorted. "It's a splendid game."

"I rank it," said the Oldest Member, "with the juvenile pastime of marbles."

The young man pondered for some moments.

"Well, anyway," he said at length, "it was good enough for Drake."

"As I have not the pleasure of the acquaintance of your friend Drake, I am unable to estimate the value of his endorsement."

"*The* Drake. The Spanish Armada Drake. He was playing bowls on Plymouth Hoe when they told him that the Armada was in sight. 'There is time to finish the game,' he replied. That's what Drake thought of bowls."

"If he had been a golfer he would have ignored the Armada altogether."

"It's easy enough to say that," said the young man, with spirit, "but can the history of golf show a parallel case?"

"A million, I should imagine."

"But you've forgotten them, eh?" said the young man, satirically.

"On the contrary," said the Oldest Member. "As a typical instance, neither more nor less remarkable than a hundred others, I will select the story of Rollo Podmarsh." He settled himself comfortably in his chair, and placed the tips of his fingers together. "This Rollo Podmarsh—"

"No, I say!" protested the young man, looking at his watch.

"This Rollo Podmarsh—"

"Yes, but—"

This Rollo Podmarsh (said the Oldest Member) was the only son of his mother, and she was a widow; and like other young men in that position he had rather allowed a mother's tender care to take the edge off what you might call his rugged manliness. Not to put too fine a point on it, he had permitted his parent to coddle him ever since he had been in the nursery; and now, in his twenty-eighth year, he invariably wore flannel next his skin, changed his shoes the moment they got wet, and—from September to May, inclusive—never went to bed without partaking of a bowl of hot arrowroot. Not, you would say, the stuff of which heroes are made. But you would be wrong. Rollo Podmarsh was a golfer, and consequently pure gold at heart; and in his hour of crisis all the good in him came to the surface.

In giving you this character-sketch of Rollo, I have been at pains to make it crisp, for I observe that you are wriggling in a restless manner and you persist in pulling out that watch of yours and gazing at it. Let me tell you that, if a mere skeleton outline of the man has this effect upon you, I am glad for your sake that you never met his mother. Mrs. Podmarsh could talk with enjoyment for hours on end about her son's character and habits. And, on the September evening on which I introduce her to you, though she had, as a fact, been speaking only for some ten minutes, it had seemed like hours to the girl, Mary Kent, who was the party of the second part to the conversation.

Mary Kent was the daughter of an old school-friend of Mrs. Podmarsh, and she had come to spend the autumn and winter with her while her parents were abroad. The scheme had never looked particularly good to Mary, and after ten minutes of her hostess on the subject of Rollo she was beginning to weave dreams of knotted sheets and a swift getaway through the bedroom window in the dark of the night.

"He is a strict teetotaller," said Mrs. Podmarsh.

"Really?"

"And has never smoked in his life."

"Fancy that!"

"But here is the dear boy now," said Mrs. Podmarsh, fondly.

Down the road towards them was coming a tall, well-knit figure in a Norfolk coat and grey flannel trousers. Over his broad shoulders was suspended a bag of golf-clubs.

"Is *that* Mr. Podmarsh?" exclaimed Mary.

She was surprised. After all she had been listening to about the arrow-root and the flannel next the skin and the rest of it, she had pictured the son of the house as a far weedier specimen. She had been expecting to meet a small, slender young man with an eyebrow moustache, and pince-nez; and this person approaching might have stepped straight out of Jack Dempsey's training-camp.

"Does he play golf?" asked Mary, herself an enthusiast.

"Oh, yes," said Mrs. Podmarsh. "He makes a point of going out on the links once a day. He says the fresh air gives him such an appetite."

Mary, who had taken a violent dislike to Rollo on the evidence of his mother's description of his habits, had softened towards him on discovering that he was a golfer. She now reverted to her previous opinion. A man who could play the noble game from such ignoble motives was beyond the pale.

"Rollo is exceedingly good at golf," proceeded Mrs. Podmarsh. "He scores more than a hundred and twenty every time, while Mr. Burns, who is supposed to be one of the best players in the club, seldom manages to reach eighty. But Rollo is very modest—modesty is one of his best qualities—and you would never guess he was so skilful unless you were told."

"Well, Rollo darling, did you have a nice game? You didn't get your feet wet, I hope? This is Mary Kent, dear."

Rollo Podmarsh shook hands with Mary. And at her touch the strange dizzy feeling which had come over him at the sight of her suddenly became increased a thousand-fold. As I see that you are consulting your watch once more, I will not describe his emotions as exhaustively as I might. I will merely say that he had never felt anything resembling this sensation of dozed ecstasy since the occasion when a twenty-foot putt of his, which had been going well off the line, as his putts generally did, had hit a worm-cast sou'-sou'-east of the hole and popped in, giving him a snappy six. Rollo Podmarsh, as you will have divined, was in love at first sight. Which makes it all the sadder to think Mary at the moment was regarding him as an outcast and a blister.

Mrs. Podmarsh, having enfolded her son in a vehement embrace, drew back with a startled exclamation, sniffing.

"Rollo!" she cried. "You smell of tobacco smoke."

Rollo looked embarrassed.

"Well, the fact is, mother—"

A hard protuberance in his coat-pocket attracted Mrs. Podmarsh's notice. She swooped and drew out a big-bowled pipe.

"Rollo!" she exclaimed, aghast.

"Well, the fact is mother—"

"Don't you know," cried Mrs. Podmarsh, "that smoking is poisonous, and injurious to the health?"

"Yes. But the fact is, mother—"

"It causes nervous dyspepsia, sleeplessness, gnawing of the stomach, headache, weak eyes, red spots on the skin, throat irritation, asthma, bronchitis, heart failure, lung trouble, catarrh, melancholy, neurasthenia, loss of memory, impaired will-power, rheumatism, lumbago, sciatica, neuritis, heartburn, torpid liver, loss of appetite, enervation, lassitude, lack of ambition, and falling out of hair."

"Yes, I know, mother. But the fact is, Ted Ray smokes all the time he's playing, and I thought it might improve my game."

And it was at these splendid words that Mary Kent felt for the first time that something might be made of Rollo Podmarsh. That she experienced one-millionth of the fervour which was gnawing at his vitals I will not say. A woman does not fall in love in a flash like a man. But at least she no longer regarded him with loathing. On the contrary, she found herself liking him. There was, she considered, the right stuff in Rollo. And if, as seemed probable from his mother's conversation, it would take a bit of digging to bring it up, well—she liked rescue-work and had plenty of time.

Mr. Arnold Bennett, in a recent essay, advises young bachelors to proceed with a certain caution in matters of the heart. They should, he asserts, first decide whether or not they are ready for love; then, whether it is better to marry earlier or later; thirdly, whether their ambitions are such that a wife will prove a hindrance to their career. These romantic preliminaries concluded, they may grab a girl and go to it. Rollo Podmarsh would have made a tough audience for these precepts. Since the days of Antony and Cleopatra probably no one had ever got more swiftly off the mark. One may say that he was in love before he had come within two yards of the girl. And each day that passed found him more nearly up to his eyebrows in the tender emotion.

He thought of Mary when he was changing his wet shoes; he dreamed of her while putting flannel next his skin; he yearned for her over the evening arrowroot. Why, the man was such a slave to his devotion that he actually went to the length of purloining small articles belonging to her. Two days after Mary's arrival Rollo Podmarsh was driving off the first tee with one of her handkerchiefs, a powder-puff, and a dozen hairpins secreted in his left breast-pocket. When dressing for dinner he used to take them out and look at them, and at night he slept with them under his pillow. Heavens, how he loved that girl!

One evening when they had gone out into the garden together to look at the new moon—Rollo, by his mother's advice, wearing a woollen scarf to protect his throat—he endeavoured to bring the conversation round to the important subject. Mary's last remark had been about earwigs. Considered as a cue, it lacked a subtle something; but Rollo was not the man to be discouraged by that.

"Talking of earwigs, Miss Kent," he said, in a low musical voice, "have you ever been in love?"

Mary was silent for a moment before replying.

"Yes, once. When I was eleven. With a conjurer who came to perform at my birthday-party. He took a rabbit and two eggs out of my hair, and life seemed one grand sweet song."

"Never since then?"

"Never."

"Suppose—just for the sake of argument—suppose you ever did love any one—er—what sort of a man would it be?"

"A hero," said Mary, promptly.

"A hero?" said Rollo, somewhat taken aback. "What sort of hero?"

"Any sort. I could only love a really brave man—a man who had done some wonderful heroic action."

"Shall we go in?" said Rollo, hoarsely. "The air is a little chilly."

We have now, therefore, arrived at a period in Rollo Podmarsh's career which might have inspired those lines of Henley's about "the night that covers me, black as the pit from pole to pole." What with one thing and another, he was in an almost Job-like condition of despondency. I say "one thing and another," for it was not only hopeless love that weighed him down. In addition to being hopelessly in love, he was greatly depressed about his golf.

On Rollo in his capacity of golfer I have so far not dwelt. You have probably allowed yourself, in spite of the significant episode of the pipe, to dismiss him as one of those placid, contented—shall I say dilettante?—golfers who are so frequent in these degenerate days. Such was not the case. Outwardly placid, Rollo was consumed inwardly by an everburning fever of ambition. His aims were not extravagant. He did not want to become amateur champion, nor even to win a monthly medal; but he did, with his whole soul, desire one of these days to go round the course in under a hundred. This feat accomplished, it was his intention to set the seal on his golfing career by playing a real money-match; and already he had selected his opponent, a certain Colonel Bodger, a tottery performer of advanced years who for the last decade had been a martyr to lumbago.

But it began to look as if even the modest goal he had marked out for himself were beyond his powers. Day after day he would step on to the first tee, glowing with zeal and hope, only to crawl home in the quiet evenfall with another hundred and twenty on his card. Little wonder, then, that he began to lose his appetite and would moan feebly at the sight of a poached egg.

With Mrs. Podmarsh sedulously watching over her son's health, you might have supposed that this inability on his part to teach the foodstuffs to take a joke would have caused consternation in the home. But it so happened that Rollo's mother had recently been reading a medical treatise in which an eminent physician stated that we all eat too much nowadays, and that the secret of a happy life is to lay off the carbohydrates to some extent. She was, therefore, delighted to observe the young man's moderation in the matter of food, and frequently held him up as an example to be noted and followed by little Lettice Willoughby, her grand-daughter, who was a good and consistent trencherwoman, particularly rough on the puddings. Little Lettice, I should mention, was the daughter of Rollo's sister Enid, who lived in the neighbourhood. Mrs. Willoughby had been compelled to go away on a visit a few days before and had left her child with Mrs. Podmarsh during her absence.

You can fool some of the people all the time, but Lettice Willoughby was not of the type that is easily deceived. A nice, old-fashioned child would no doubt have accepted without questioning her grandmother's dictum that roly-poly pudding could not fail to hand a devastating wallop to the blood pressure, and that to take two helpings of it was practically equivalent to walking right into the family vault. A child with less decided opinions of her own would have been impressed by the spectacle of her uncle refusing sustenance, and would have received without demur the statement that he did it because he felt that abstinence was good for his health. Lettice was a modern child and knew better. She had had experience of this loss of appetite and its significance. The first symptom which had preceded the demise of poor old Ponto, who had recently handed in his portfolio after holding office for ten years as the Willoughby family dog, had been this same disinclination to absorb nourishment. Besides, she was an observant child, and had not failed to note the haggard misery in her uncle's eyes. She tackled him squarely on the subject one morning after breakfast. Rollo had retired into the more distant parts of the garden, and was leaning forward, when she found him, with his head buried in his hands.

"Hallo, uncle," said Lettice.

Rollo looked up wanly.

"Ah, child!" he said. He was fond of his niece.

"Aren't you feeling well, uncle?"

"Far, far from well."

"It's old age, I expect," said Lettice.

"I feel old," admitted Rollo. "Old and battered. Ah, Lettice, laugh and be gay while you can."

"All right, uncle."

"Make the most of your happy, careless, smiling, halcyon childhood."

"Right-o, uncle."

"When you get to my age, dear, you will realise that it is a sad, hopeless world. A world where, if you keep your head down, you forget to let the club-head lead: where even if you do happen by a miracle to keep 'em straight with your brassie, you blow up on the green and foozle a six-inch putt."

Lettice could not quite understand what Uncle Rollo was talking about, but she gathered broadly that she had been correct in supposing him to be in a bad state, and her warm, childish heart was filled with pity for him. She walked thoughtfully away, and Rollo resumed his reverie.

Into each life, as the poet says, some rain must fall. So much had recently been falling into Rollo's that, when Fortune at last sent along a belated sunbeam, it exercised a cheering effect out of all proportion to its size. By this I mean that when, some four days after his conversation with Lettice, Mary Kent asked him to play golf with her, he read into the invitation a significance which only a lover could have seen in it. I will not go so far as to say that Rollo Podmarsh looked on Mary Kent's suggestion that they should have a round together as actually tantamount to a revelation of undying love; but he certainly regarded it as a most encouraging sign. It seemed to him that things were beginning to move, that Rollo Preferred were on a rising market. Gone was the gloom of the past days. He forgot those sad, solitary wanderings of his in the bushes at the bottom of the garden; he forgot that his mother had bought him a new set of winter woollies which felt like horsehair; he forgot that for the last few evenings his arrowroot had tasted rummy. His whole mind was occupied with the astounding fact that she had voluntarily offered to play golf with him, and he walked out on to the first tee filled with a yeasty exhilaration which nearly caused him to burst into song.

"How shall we play?" asked Mary. "I am a twelve. What is your handicap?"

Rollo was under the disadvantage of not actually possessing a handicap. He had a sort of private system of bookkeeping of his own by which he took strokes over if they did not seem to him to be up to sample, and allowed himself five-foot putts at discretion. So he had never actually handed in the three cards necessary for handicapping purposes.

"I don't exactly know," he said. "It's my ambition to get round in under a hundred, but I've never managed it yet."

"Never?"

"Never! It's strange, but something always seems to go wrong."

"Perhaps you'll manage it to-day," said Mary, encouragingly, so encouragingly that it was all that Rollo could do to refrain from flinging himself at her feet and barking like a dog. "Well, I'll start you two holes up, and we'll see how we get on. Shall I take the honour?"

She drove off one of those fair-to-medium balls which go with a twelve handicap. Not a great length, but nice and straight.

"Splendid!" cried Rollo, devoutly.

"Oh, I don't know," said Mary. "I wouldn't call it anything special."

Titanic emotions were surging in Rollo's bosom as he addressed his ball. He had never felt like this before, especially on the first tee—where as a rule he found himself overcome with a nervous humility.

"Oh, Mary! Mary!" he breathed to himself as he swung.

You who squander your golden youth fooling about on a bowling-green will not understand the magic of those three words. But if you were a golfer, you would realise that in selecting just that invocation to breathe to himself Rollo Podmarsh had hit, by sheer accident, on the ideal method of achieving a fine drive. Let me explain. The first two words, tensely breathed, are just sufficient to take a man with the proper slowness to the top of his swing; the first syllable of the second "Mary" exactly coincides with the striking of the ball; and that final "ry!" takes care of the follow-through. The consequence was that Rollo's ball, instead of hopping down the hill like an embarrassed duck, as was its usual practice, sang off the tee with a scream like a shell, nodded in passing Mary's ball, where it lay some hundred and fifty yards down the course, and, carrying on from there, came to rest within easy distance of the green. For the first time in his golfing life Rollo Podmarsh had hit a nifty.

Mary followed the ball's flight with astonished eyes.

"But this will never do!" she exclaimed. "I can't possibly start you two up if you're going to do this sort of thing."

Rollo blushed.

"I shouldn't think it would happen again," he said. "I've never done a drive like that before."

"But it must happen again," said Mary, firmly. "This is evidently your day. If you don't get round in under a hundred to-day, I shall never forgive you."

Rollo shut his eyes, and his lips moved feverishly. He was registering a vow that, come what might, he would not fail her. A minute later he was holing out in three, one under bogey.

The second hole is the short lake-hole. Bogey is three, and Rollo generally did it in four; for it was his custom not to count any balls he might sink in the water, but to start afresh with one which happened to get over, and then take three putts. But to-day something seemed to tell him that he would not require the aid of this ingenious system. As he took his mashie from the bag, he *knew* that his first shot would soar successfully on to the green.

"Ah, Mary!" he breathed as he swung.

These subtleties are wasted on a worm, if you will pardon the expression, like yourself, who, possibly owing to a defective education, is content to spend life's springtime rolling wooden balls across a lawn; but I will explain that in altering and shortening his soliloquy at this juncture Rollo had done the very thing any good pro. would have recommended. If he had murmured, "Oh, Mary! Mary!" as before he would have over-swung. "Ah, Mary!" was exactly right for a half-swing with the mashie. His ball shot up in a beautiful arc, and trickled to within six inches of the hole.

Mary was delighted. There was something about this big, diffident man which had appealed from the first to everything in her that was motherly.

"Marvellous!" she said. "You'll get a two. Five for the first two holes! Why, you simply must get round under a hundred now." She swung, but too lightly; and her ball fell in the water. "I'll give you this," she said, without the slightest chagrin, for this girl had a beautiful nature. "Let's get on to the third. Four up! Why, you're wonderful!"

And not to weary you with too much detail, I will simply remark that, stimulated by her gentle encouragement, Rollo Podmarsh actually came off the ninth green with a medal score of forty-six for the half-round. A ten on the seventh had spoiled his card to some extent, and a nine on the eighth had not helped, but nevertheless here he was in forty-six, with the easier half of the course before him. He tingled all over—partly because he was wearing the new winter woollies to which I have alluded previously, but principally owing to triumph, elation, and love. He gazed at Mary as Dante might have gazed at Beatrice on one of his particularly sentimental mornings.

Mary uttered an exclamation.

"Oh, I've just remembered," she exclaimed. "I promised to write last night to Jane Simpson and give her that new formula for knitting jumpers. I think I'll phone her now from the club-house and then it'll be off my mind. You go on to the tenth, and I'll join you there."

Rollo proceeded over the brow of the hill to the tenth tee, and was filling in the time with practice-swings when he heard his name spoken.

"Good gracious, Rollo! I couldn't believe it was you at first."

He turned to see his sister, Mrs. Willoughby, the mother of the child Lettice.

"Hallo!" he said. "When did you get back?"

"Late last night. Why, it's extraordinary!"

"Hope you had a good time. What's extraordinary? Listen, Enid. Do you know what I've done? Forty-six for the first nine! Forty-six! And holing out every putt."

"Oh, then that accounts for it."

"Accounts for what?"

"Why, your looking so pleased with life. I got an idea from Letty, when she wrote to me, that you were at death's door. Your gloom seems to have made a deep impression on the child. Her letter was full of it."

Rollo was moved.

"Dear little Letty! She is wonderfully sympathetic."

"Well, I must be off now," said Enid Willoughby. "I'm late. Oh, talking of Letty. Don't children say the funniest things! She wrote in her letter that you were very old and wretched and that she was going to put you out of your misery."

"Ha ha ha!" laughed Rollo.

"We had to poison poor old Ponto the other day, you know, and poor little Letty was inconsolable till we explained to her that it was really the kindest thing to do, because he was so old and ill. But just imagine her thinking of wanting to end *your* sufferings!"

"Ha ha!" laughed Rollo. "Ha ha h—"

His voice trailed off into a broken gurgle. Quite suddenly a sinister thought had come to him.

The arrowroot had tasted rummy!

"Why, what on earth is the matter?" asked Mrs. Willoughby, regarding his ashen face.

Rollo could find no words. He yammered speechlessly. Yes, for several nights the arrowroot had tasted very rummy. Rummy! There was no other adjective. Even as he plied the spoon he had said to himself: "This arrowroot tastes rummy!" And—he uttered a sharp yelp as he remembered—it had been little Lettice who had brought it to him. He recollected being touched at the time by the kindly act.

"What *is* the matter, Rollo?" demanded Mrs. Willoughby, sharply. "Don't stand there looking like a dying duck."

"I am a dying duck," responded Rollo, hoarsely. "A dying man, I mean. Enid, that infernal child has poisoned me!"

"Don't be ridiculous! And kindly don't speak of her like that!"

"I'm sorry. I shouldn't blame her, I suppose. No doubt her motives were good. But the fact remains."

"Rollo, you're too absurd."

"But the arrowroot tasted rummy."

"I never knew you could be such an idiot," said his exasperated sister with sisterly outspokenness. "I thought you would think it quaint. I thought you would roar with laughter."

"I did—till I remembered about the rumminess of the arrowroot."

Mrs. Willoughby uttered an impatient exclamation and walked away.

Rollo Podmarsh stood on the tenth tee, a volcano of mixed emotions. Mechanically he pulled out his pipe and lit it. But he found that he could not smoke. In this supreme crisis of his life tobacco seemed to have lost its magic. He put the pipe back in his pocket and gave himself up to his thoughts. Now terror gripped him; anon a sort of gentle melancholy. It was so hard that he should be compelled to leave the world just as he had begun to hit 'em right.

And then in the welter of his thoughts there came one of practical value. To wit, that by hurrying to the doctor's without delay he might yet be saved. There might be antidotes.

He turned to go and there was Mary Kent standing beside him with her bright, encouraging smile.

"I'm sorry I kept you so long," she said. "It's your honour. Fire away, and remember that you've got to do this nine in fifty-three at the outside."

Rollo's thoughts flitted wistfully to the snug surgery where Dr. Brown was probably sitting at this moment surrounded by the finest antidotes.

"Do you know, I think I ought to—"

"Of course you ought to," said Mary. "If you did the first nine in forty-six, you can't possibly take fifty-three coming in."

For one long moment Rollo continued to hesitate—a moment during which the instinct of self-preservation seemed as if it must win the day. All his life he had been brought up to be nervous about his health, and panic gripped him. But there is a deeper, nobler instinct than that of self-preservation—the instinctive desire of a golfer who is at the top of his form to go on and beat his medal-score record. And little by little this grand impulse began to dominate Rollo. If, he felt, he went off now to take antidotes, the doctor might possibly save his life; but reason told him that never again would he be likely to do the first nine in forty-six. He would have to start all over afresh.

Rollo Podmarsh hesitated no longer. With a pale, set face he teed up his ball and drove.

If I were telling this story to a golfer instead of to an excrescence—I use the word in the kindliest spirit—who spends his time messing about on a bowling-green, nothing would please me better than to describe shot by shot Rollo's progress over the remaining nine holes. Epics have been written with less material. But these details would, I am aware, be wasted on you. Let it suffice that by the time his last approach trickled on to the eighteenth green he had taken exactly fifty shots.

"Three for it!" said Mary Kent. "Steady now! Take it quite easy and be sure to lay your second dead."

It was prudent counsel, but Rollo was now thoroughly above himself. He had got his feet wet in a puddle on the sixteenth, but he did not care. His winter woollies seemed to be lined with ants, but he ignored them. All he knew was that he was on the last green in ninety-six, and he meant to finish in style. No tame three putts for him! His ball was five yards away, but he aimed for the back of the hole and brought his putter down with a whack. Straight and true the ball sped, hit the tin, jumped high in the air, and fell into the hole with a rattle.

"Oo!" cried Mary.

Rollo Podmarsh wiped his forehead and leaned dizzily on his putter. For a moment, so intense is the fervour induced by the game of games, all he could think of was that he had gone round in ninety-seven. Then, as one waking from a trance, he began to appreciate his position. The fever passed, and a clammy dismay took possession of him. He had achieved his life's ambition; but what now? Already he was conscious of a curious discomfort within him. He felt as he supposed Italians of the Middle Ages must have felt after dropping in to take pot-luck with the Borgias. It was hard. He had gone round in ninety-seven, but he could never take the next step in the career which he had mapped out in his dreams—the money-match with the lumbago-stricken Colonel Bodger.

Mary Kent was fluttering round him, bubbling congratulations, but Rollo sighed.

"Thanks," he said. "Thanks very much. But the trouble is, I'm afraid I'm going to die almost immediately. I've been poisoned!"

"Poisoned!"

"Yes. Nobody is to blame. Everything was done with the best intentions. But there it is."

"But I don't understand."

Rollo explained. Mary listened pallidly.

"Are you sure?" she gasped.

"Quite sure," said Rollo, gravely. "The arrowroot tasted rummy."

"But arrowroot always does."

Rollo shook his head.

"No," he said. "It tastes like warm blotting-paper, but not rummy."

Mary was sniffing.

"Don't cry," urged Rollo, tenderly. "Don't cry."

"But I must. And I've come out without a handkerchief."

"Permit me," said Rollo, producing one of her best from his left breast-pocket.

"I wish I had a powder-puff," said Mary.

"Allow me," said Rollo. "And your hair has become a little disordered. If I may—" And from the same reservoir he drew a handful of hairpins.

Mary gazed at these exhibits with astonishment.

"But these are mine," she said.

"Yes. I sneaked them from time to time."

"But why?"

"Because I loved you," said Rollo. And in a few moving sentences which I will not trouble you with he went on to elaborate this theme.

Mary listened with her heart full of surging emotions, which I cannot possibly go into if you persist in looking at that damned watch of yours. The scales had fallen from her eyes. She had thought slightingly of this man because he had been a little over-careful of his health, and all the time he had had within him the potentiality of heroism. Something seemed to snap inside her.

"Rollo!" she cried, and flung herself into his arms.

"Mary!" muttered Rollo, gathering her up.

"I told you it was all nonsense," said Mrs. Willoughby, coming up at this tense moment and going on with the conversation where she had left off. "I've just seen Letty, and she said she meant to put you out of your misery but the chemist wouldn't sell her any poison, so she let it go."

Rollo disentangled himself from Mary.

"What?" he cried.

Mrs. Willoughby repeated her remarks.

"You're sure?" he said.

"Of course I'm sure."

"Then why did the arrowroot taste rummy?"

"I made inquiries about that. It seems that mother was worried about your taking to smoking, and she found an advertisement in one of the magazines about the Tobacco Habit Cured in Three Days by a secret method without the victim's knowledge. It was a gentle, safe, agreeable method of eliminating the nicotine poison from the system, strengthening the weakened membranes, and overcoming the craving; so she put some in your arrowroot every night."

There was a long silence. To Rollo Podmarsh it seemed as though the sun had suddenly begun to shine, the birds to sing, and the grasshoppers to toot. All Nature was one vast substantial smile. Down in the valley by the second hole he caught sight of Wallace Chesney's plus-fours gleaming as their owner stooped to play his shot, and it seemed to him that he had never in his life seen anything so lovely.

"Mary," he said, in a low, vibrant voice, "will you wait here for me? I want to go into the club-house for a moment."

"To change your wet shoes?"

"No!" thundered Rollo. "I'm never going to change my wet shoes again in my life." He felt in his pocket, and hurled a box of patent pills far into the undergrowth. "But I *am* going to change my winter woollies. And when I've put those dashed barbed-wire entanglements into the club-house furnace, I'm going to 'phone to old Colonel Bodger. I hear his lumbago's worse than ever. I'm going to fix up a match with him for a shilling a hole. And if I don't lick the boots off him you can break the engagement!"

"My hero!" murmured Mary.

Rollo kissed her, and with long, resolute steps strode to the club-house.

THE GOALIE

By Ken Dryden

I have always been a goalie. I became one long enough ago, before others'
memories and reasons intruded on my own, that I can no longer remember
why I did, but if I had to guess, it was because of Dave. Almost six years
older, he started playing goal before I was old enough to play any position,
so by the time I was six and ready to play, there was a set of used and
discarded equipment that awaited me—that and an older brother I always
tried to emulate.

I have mostly vague recollections of being a goalie at that time. I remember the spectacular feeling of splitting and sprawling on pavement or
ice, and feeling that there was something somehow noble and sympathetic
about having bruises and occasional cuts, especially if they came, as they
did, from only a tennis ball. But if I have one clear image that remains, it is
that of a goalie, his right knee on the ice, his left leg extended in a half
splits, his left arm stretching for the top corner, and, resting indifferently in
his catching glove, a round black puck.

It was the posed position of NHL goalies for promotional photos and
hockey cards at the time and it was a position we tried to re-enact as often
as we could in backyard games. There was something that looked and felt
distinctly major league about a shot "raised" that high, and about a clean,
precise movement into space to intercept it. Coming as it did without
rebound, it allowed us to freeze the position as if in a photo, extending the
moment, letting our feelings catch up to the play, giving us time to step
outside ourselves and see what we had done. In school, or at home, with
pencil and paper, sometimes thinking of what I was doing, more often just
mindlessly doodling, I would draw pictures of goalies, not much more than
stick figures really, but fleshed out with parallel lines, and always in that
same catching position. Each year when my father arranged for a photographer to take pictures for our family's Christmas card, as Dave and I readied
ourselves in our nets, the shooter was told to shoot high to the glove side,
that we had rehearsed the rest.

To catch a puck or a ball—it was the great joy of being a goalie. Like a young ballplayer, too young to hit for much enjoyment but old enough to catch and throw, it was something I could do before I was big enough to do the rest. But mostly it was the feeling it gave me. Even now, watching TV or reading a newspaper, I like to have a ball in my hands, fingering its laces, its seams, its nubby surface, until my fingertips are so alive and alert that the ball and I seem drawn to each other. I like to spin it, bounce it, flip it from hand to hand, throw it against a wall or a ceiling, and catch it over and over again. There is something quite magical about a hand that can follow a ball and find it so crisply and tidily every time, something solid and wonderfully reassuring about its muscular certainty and control. So, if it was because of Dave that I became a goalie, it was the feeling of catching a puck or a ball that kept me one. The irony, of course, would be that later, when I finally became a real goalie instead of a kid with a good glove hand, when I learned to use the other parts of a goaltender's equipment—skates, pads, blocker, stick—it could only be at the expense of what had been until then my greatest joy as a goalie.

I was nineteen at the time. It surely had been happening before then, just as it must before any watershed moment, but the time I remember was the warm-up for the 1967 NCAA final against Boston University. For the first few minutes, I remember only feeling good: a shot, a save, a shot, a save; loose, easy, the burn of nerves turning slowly to a burn of exhilaration. For a shot to my right, my right arm went up and I stopped it with my blocker; another, low to the corner, I kicked away with my pad; along the ice to the other side, my skate; high to the left, my catching glove. Again and again: a pad, a catching glove, a skate, a stick, a blocker, whatever was closest moved, and the puck stopped. For someone who had scooped up ice-skimming shots like a shortstop, who had twisted his body to make back-handed catches on shots for the top right corner, it was a moment of great personal triumph. I had come of age. As the warm-up was ending, I could feel myself becoming a goalie.

Goaltending is often described as the most dangerous position in sports. It is not. Race drivers die from racing cars, jockeys die, so do football players. Goalies do not die from being goalies. Nor do they suffer the frequent facial cuts, the knee and shoulder injuries, that forwards and defensemen often suffer. They stand as obstacles to a hard rubber disc, frequently shot at a lethal speed, sometimes unseen, sometimes deflected; the danger to them is obvious, but it is exaggerated—even the unthinkable: a goalie diving anxiously out of the way of a 100 m.p.h. slap shot, the shooter panicking at his own recklessness, the fans "ah"-ing at the near miss. Except for that one, feared time, the time it doesn't happen that way, when the puck moves too fast and the goalie too slow, and, hit in the head, he falls frighteningly to the ice. Moments later, up again, he shakes his head, smiling as others slowly do the same, again reminded that he wears a mask which at other times he sees through and forgets. The danger of playing goal is a *potential* danger, but equipment technology, like a net below a trapeze act, has made serious injury extremely unlikely.

From the time I was six years old, until as a freshman at Cornell I was required to wear a mask, I received fifteen stitches. Since then I have had only four—from a Dennis Hull slap shot that rebounded off my chest, hitting under my chin, in my first playoff year. I have pulled groins and hamstrings, stretched, twisted, and bruised uncounted times various other things, sent my back into spasm twice, broken a toe, and torn the cartilege in one knee. In almost eight years, after more than 400 games and 1000 practices, that's not much.

Yet, I am often afraid. For while I am well protected, and know I'm unlikely to suffer more than a bruise from any shot that is taken, the puck hurts, constantly and cumulatively: through the pillow-thick leg pads I wear, where straps pulled tight around their shins squeeze much of the padding away; through armor-shelled skate boots; through a catching glove compromised too far for its flexibility; with a dull, aching nausea from stomach to throat when my jock slams back against my testes; and most often, on my arms, on wrists and forearms especially, where padding is light and often out of place, where a shot hits and spreads its ache, up an arm and through a body, until both go limp and feel lifeless. Through a season, a puck hurts like a long, slow battering from a skillful boxer, almost unnoticed in the beginning, but gradually wearing me down, until two or three times a year, I wake up in the morning sore, aching, laughing/moaning with each move I make, and feel a hundred years old. It is on those days and others that when practice comes, I shy away.

The puck on his stick, a player skates for the net. Deep in my crouch, intent, ready, to anyone watching I look the same as I always do. But, like a batter who has been knocked down too many times before, when I see a player draw back his stick to shoot, at the critical moment when concentration must turn to commitment, my body stiffens, my eyes widen and go sightless, my head lifts in the air, turning imperceptibly to the right, as if away from the puck—I bail out, leaving only an empty body behind to cover the net. I yell at myself as others might ("you chicken"). I tell myself reasonably, rationally, that lifting my head, blanking my eyes, can only put me in greater danger; but I don't listen. In a game, each shot controlled by a harassing defense, with something else to think about I can usually put away fear and just play. But in practice, without the distraction of a game, seeing Tremblay or Lambert, Risebrough, Chartraw, or Lupien, dangerous, uncontrolled shooters as likely to hit my arms as a corner of the net, I cannot. In time the fear gradually shrinks back, manageable again, but it never quite goes away.

I have thought more about fear, I have been afraid more often, the last few years. For the first time this year, I have realized that I've only rarely been hurt in my career. I have noticed that unlike many, so far as I know, I carry with me no permanent injury. And now that I know I will retire at the end of the season, more and more I find myself thinking—*I've lasted this long: please let me get out in one piece.* For while I know I am well protected, while I know it's unlikely I will suffer any serious injury, like every other goalie I carry with me the fear of the *one big hurt* that never comes. Recently, I read of the retirement of a race-car driver. Explaining his decision to quit, he said that after his many years of racing, after the deaths of close friends and colleagues, after his own near misses, he simply "knew too much." I feel a little differently. I feel I have known all along what I know now. It's just that I can't forget it as easily as I once did.

Playing goal is not fun. Behind a mask, there are no smiling faces, no timely sweaty grins of satisfaction. It is a grim, humorless position, largely uncreative, requiring little physical movement, giving little physical pleasure in return. A goalie is simply there, tied to a net and to a game; the game acts, a goalie reacts. How he reacts, how often, a hundred shots or no shots, is not up to him. Unable to initiate a game's action, unable to focus its direction, he can only do what he's given to do, what the game demands of him, and that he must do. It is his job, a job that cannot be done one minute in every three, one that will not await rare moments of genius, one that ends when the game ends, and only then. For while a goal goes up in lights, a permanent record for the goal-scorer and the game, a save is ephemeral, important at the time, occasionally when a game is over, but able to be wiped away, undone, with the next sho . It is only when a game ends and the mask comes off, when the immense challenge of the job turns abruptly to immense satisfaction or despair, that the unsmiling grimness lifts and goes away.

If you were to spend some time with a team, without ever watching them on the ice, it wouldn't take long before you discovered who its goalies were. Goalies are different. Whether it's because the position attracts certain personality types, or only permits certain ones to succeed; whether the experience is so intense and fundamental that it transforms its practitioners to type—I don't know the answer. E ut whatever it is, the differences between "players" and "goalies" are manifest and real, transcending as they do even culture and sport.

A few years ago, at a reception at the Canadian Embassy in Prague, the wife of Jiri Holecek, former star goalie for Czechoslovakia, was introduced to Lynda, and immediately exclaimed, "The players think my Jiri's crazy. Do they [my teammates] think your husband's crazy too?" (No more of the conversation was related to me.) For his book on soccer goalies, English journalist Brian Glanville chose as his title *Goalkeepers Are Different*. It is all part of the mythology of the position, anticipated, expected, accepted, and believed; and in many ways real.

Predictably, a goalie is more introverted than his teammates, more serious (for team pictures, when a photographer tells me to smile, unsmilingly I tell him, "Goalies don't smile"), more sensitive and moody ("ghoulies"), more insecure (often unusually "careful" with money; you might remember Johnny Bower and I *shared* a cab). While a goalie might sometimes be gregarious and outgoing, it usually manifests itself in binges—when a game is over, or on the day of a game when he isn't playing—when he feels himself released from a game. Earlier this season, minutes before a game with the Rangers in the Forum, Robinson looked across the dressing room at me and asked, "Who's playing?" Before I could answer, Shutt yelled back, "I'll give ya a hint, Bird," he said. "Bunny's in the shitter puking; Kenny hasn't shut up since he got here." While teams insist on togetherness, and on qualities in their teammates that encourage it both on and off the ice, a goalie is the one player a team allows to be different. Indeed, as perplexed as anyone at his willingness to dress in cumbrous, oversized equipment to get hit by a puck, a team allows a goalie to sit by himself on planes or buses, to disappear on road trips, to reappear and say nothing for long periods of time, to have a single room when everyone else has roommates. After all, *shrug,* he's a goalie. What can you expect? Flaky, crazy, everything he does accepted and explained away, it offers a goalie wonderful licence. It was what allowed Gilles Gratton to "streak" a practice, and Gary Smith to take showers between periods. In many ways, it is also why my teammates accepted my going to law school.

Good goalies come in many shapes, sizes, and styles. So do bad goalies. A goalie is often plump (Savard, a defenceman, always insists "I like my goalies fat"), sometimes unathletic, and with reflex reactions surprisingly similar to those of the average person (recently at a science museum, with a flashing light and a buzzer I tested my eye-hand reactions against Lynda's; she was slightly faster). While most might agree on what the ideal physical and technical goalie-specimen might look like, it almost certainly would be a composite—the physical size of Tretiak, the elegance of Parent, the agility of Giacomin or Cheevers, the bouncy charisma of Vachon or Resch—with no guarantee that *supergoalie* would be any good. For while there are certain minimum standards of size, style, and agility that any goalie must have, goaltending is a remarkably aphysical activity.

If you were to ask a coach or a player what he would most like to see in a goalie, he would, after some rambling out-loud thoughts, probably settle on something like: consistency, dependability, and the ability to make the big save. Only in the latter, and then only in part, is the physical element present. Instead, what these qualities suggest is a certain character of mind, a mind that need not be nimble or dextrous, for the demands of the job are not complex, but a mind emotionally disciplined, one able to be focused and directed, a mind under control. Because the demands on a goalie are mostly mental, it means that for a goalie the biggest enemy is himself. Not a puck, not an opponent, not a quirk of size or style. Him. The stress and anxiety he feels when he plays, the fear of failing, the fear of being embarrassed, the fear of being physically hurt, all are symptoms of his position, in constant ebb and flow, but never disappearing. The successful goalie understands these neuroses, accepts them, and puts them under control. The unsuccessful goalie is distracted by them, his mind in knots, his body quickly following.

It is why Vachon was superb in Los Angeles and as a high-priced free-agent messiah, poor in Detroit. It is why Dan Bouchard, Tretiak-sized, athletic, technically flawless, lurches annoyingly in and out of mediocrity.

It is why there are good "good team" goalies and good "bad team" goalies—Gary Smith, Doug Favell, Denis Herron. The latter are spectacular, capable of making near-impossible saves that few others can make. They are essential for bad teams, winning them games they shouldn't win, but they are goalies who need a second chance, who need the cushion of an occasional bad goal, knowing that they can seem to earn it back later with several inspired saves. On a good team, a goalie has few near-impossible saves to make, but the rest he must make, and playing in close and critical games as he does, he gets no second chance.

A good "bad team" goalie, numbed by the volume of goals he cannot prevent, can focus on brilliant saves and brilliant games, the only things that make a difference to a poor team. A good "good team" goalie cannot. Allowing few enough goals that he feels every one, he is driven instead by something else—the penetrating hatred of letting in a goal.

The great satisfaction of playing goal comes from the challenge it presents. Simply stated, it is to give the team what it needs, when it needs it, not when I feel well-rested, injury-free, warmed-up, psyched-up, healthy, happy, and able to give it, but when *the team* needs it. On a team as good as the Canadiens, often it will need nothing; other times, one good save, perhaps two or three; maybe five good minutes, a period, sometimes, though not often, a whole game. Against better teams, you can almost predict what and when it might be; against the rest, you cannot. You simply have to be ready.

During my first two years with the team, for reasons none of us could figure out, we would start games slowly, outplayed for most of the first period, occasionally for a little longer. It happened so regularly that it became a pattern we anticipated and prepared for, each of us with a special role to play. Mine was to keep the score sufficiently close in the first period, usually to within one goal, so as not to discourage any comeback—their role—that otherwise we would almost certainly make. We were a good combination. I could feel heroically beleaguered the first period, all the time knowing that it would end, that we would soon get our stride, and when we did that I would become a virtual spectator to the game.

That has changed. It began to change the next season, and for the last four years, the change has been complete. A much better team than earlier in the decade, it needs less from me now, just pockets of moments that for me and others sometimes seem lost in a game. But more than that, what it needs now is not to be distracted—by bad goals, by looseness or uncertainty in my play. It needs only to feel secure, confident that the defensive zone is taken care of; the rest it can do itself.

It makes my job different from that of every other goalie in the NHL. I get fewer shots, and fewer *hard* shots; I must allow fewer goals, the teams I play on must win Stanley Cups. Most envy me my job, some are not so sure. Once Vachon, my predecessor in Montreal, in the midst of one of his excellent seasons in Los Angeles, told me that he wasn't sure he would ever want to play for the Canadiens again, even if he had the chance. He said he had come to enjoy a feeling he knew he would rarely have in Montreal—the feeling of winning a game for his team—and he wasn't sure how well he could play without it. In a speech a few years ago, my brother talked about the heroic self-image each goalie needs and has, and is allowed to have because of the nature and perception of his position. "A solitary figure," "a thankless job," "facing an onslaught," "a barrage," "like Horatio at the bridge"—it's the stuff of backyard dreams. It is how others often see him; it is how he sometimes sees himself. I know the feeling Vachon described because I felt it early in my career, when the team wasn't as good as it is now. It is a feeling I have learned to live without.

But something else has changed, something that is more difficult to live without. Each year, I find it harder and harder to make a connection between a Canadiens win and me—nothing so much as my winning a game for the team, just a timely save, or a series of saves that made a difference, that arguably made a difference, that *might* have made a difference, that, as with a baseball pitcher, can make a win feel mine and ours. But as the team's superiority has become entrenched, and as the gap between our opponents and us, mostly unchanged, has come to seem wider and more permanent, every save I make seems without urgency, as if it is done completely at my own discretion, a minor bonus if made, a minor inconvenience, quickly overcome, if not.

A few months ago, we played the Colorado Rockies at the Forum. Early in the game, I missed an easy shot from the blueline, and a little unnerved, for the next fifty minutes I juggled long shots, and allowed big rebounds and three additional goals. After each Rockies goal, the team would put on a brief spurt and score quickly, and so with only minutes remaining, the game was tied. Then the Rockies scored again, this time a long, sharp-angled shot that squirted through my legs. The game had seemed finally lost. But in the last three minutes, Lapointe scored, then Lafleur, and we won 6–5. Alone in the dressing room afterwards, I tried to feel angry at my own performance, to feel relieved at being let off the uncomfortable hook I had put myself on, to laugh at what a winner could now find funny; but I couldn't. Instead, feeling weak and empty, I just sat there, unable to understand why I felt the way I did. Only slowly did it come to me: I had been irrelevant; I couldn't even lose the game.

I catch few shots now, perhaps only two or three a game. I should catch more, but years of concussion have left the bones in my hand and wrist often tender and sore, and learning to substitute a leg or a stick to save my hand, my catching glove, reprogrammed and out of practice, often remains at my side. Moreover, the game has changed. Bigger players now clutter the front of the net, obstructing and deflecting shots, or, threatening to do both, they distract a goalie, causing rebounds, making clean, precise movements into space—commitments to a single option unmindful of possible deflection or rebound—an indulgence for which a price is too often paid. What I enjoy most about goaltending now is the game itself: feeling myself slowly immerse in it, finding its rhythm, anticipating it, getting there before it does, challenging it, controlling a play that should control me, making it go where I want it to go, moving easily, crushingly within myself, delivering a clear, confident message to the game. And at the same time, to feel my body slowly act out that feeling, pushing up taller and straighter, thrusting itself forward, clenched, flexed, at game's end released like an untied balloon, its feeling spewing in all directions until the next game.

I enjoy the role I play—now rarely to win a game, but not to lose it; a game fully in my hands, fully in the hands of my teammates, and between us an unstated trust, a quiet confidence, and the results we want. Our roles have changed, but we remain a good combination, and I find that immensely satisfying.

THE DAY OF THE LOSERS
By Dick Francis

He set off to the Grand National with £300 in his pocket and a mixture of guilt and bravado in his mind.

Austin Dartmouth Glenn knew he had vowed not to put banknotes into premature circulation.

Not for five years, he had been sternly warned. Five years would see the heat off and the multi-million pound robbery would be ancient history.

The police would be chasing more recent villains and the hot serial numbers would have faded into fly-blown obscurity on out-of-date lists.

In five years it would be safe to spend the £15,000 he had been paid for his part in springing the bank-robbery boss out of unwelcome jail.

That was all very well, Austin told himself aggrievedly, looking out of the train window. What about inflation? In five years' time £15,000 might not be worth the paper it was printed on.

Or the colour and size of fivers might be changed. He'd heard of a frantic safe-blower who'd done 12 years and gone home to a cache full of the old thin white stuff.

All that time served for a load of out-of-date, uncashable, rubbish. Austin Glenn's mouth twisted in sympathy at the thought. It wasn't going to happen to him, not ruddy well likely.

Austin had paid for his train ticket with ordinary currency, and ditto for the cans of beer, packages of cellophaned sandwiches, and copy of the *Sporting Life.*

The hot £300 was stowed safely in an inner pocket, not to be risked before he reached the bustling anonymity of the huge crowd converging on the Aintree race course.

He was no fool, of course, he thought complacently. A neat pack of 60 fivers, crisp, new, and consecutive, might catch the most incurious eyes.

But no one would look twice now that he had shuffled them and crinkled them with hands dirtied for the purpose.

He wiped beer off his mouth with the back of his hand; a scrawny fortyish man with neat, thin grey-black hair, restless eyes, and an overall air of self-importance.

A life spent on the fringes of crime had given him hundreds of dubious acquaintances, an intricate memory bank of information and a sound knowledge of how to solicit bribes without actually cupping the palm.

No one liked him very much but Austin was not sensitive enough to notice.

Nearer the front of the same train Jerry Springwood sat and sweated on three counts. For one thing, he was an outdoor man, and found the heat excessive, and for another, owing to alcohol and sex, he had no time to spare and would very likely lose his job if he arrived late; but above all, he sweated from fear.

Jerry Springwood, at 32, had lost his nerve and was trying to carry on the trade of steeplechase jockey without anyone finding out. The old days, when he used to ride with a cool brain and discount intermittent bangs as merely a nuisance, were long gone.

For months now he had travelled with dread to the meetings, imagining sharp ends of bone protruding from his skin, imagining a smashed face or a severed spine . . . imagining pain.

For months he had been unable to take risks he would once not have seen as risks at all.

For months he had been unable to urge his mounts forward into gaps, when only such urging would win; and unable to stop himself steadying his mounts to jump, when only kicking them on would do.

The skill which had taken him to the top was now used to cover the cracks, and the soundness of his long-time reputation bolstered the explanations for defeat which he gave to owners and trainers.

Only the most discerning saw the disguised signs of disintegration, and fewer still had put private doubts into private words.

The great British public, searching the list of Grand National runners for inspiration, held good old Jerry Springwood to be a plus factor in favour of the third favourite, Haunted House.

A year ago, he reflected drearily, as he stared out at the passing fields, he would have known better than to go to a party in London on the night before the big race.

A year ago he had stayed near the course, drunk maybe a couple of beers, gone to bed early, slept alone. He wouldn't have dreamed of making a four-hour dash south after Friday's racing, or getting drunk, or going to bed at two with a girl he'd known three hours.

He hadn't needed to blot out the thought of Saturday afternoon's marathon, but had looked forward to it with zest, excitement, and unquenchable hope.

Oh God, he thought despairingly, what has happened to me?

He was small and strong, with wiry mid-brown hair, deep set eyes, and a nose flattened by too much fast contact with the ground. A farmer's son, natural with animals, and with social manners sophisticated by success.

People usually liked Jerry Springwood, but he was too unassuming to notice.

The crowds poured cheerfully into Aintree race course, primed with hope, faith, and cash. Austin peeled off the first of the hot fivers at the turnstiles, and contentedly watched it being sucked into the anonymity of the gate receipts.

He safely got change for another in a crowded bar, and for a third from a stall selling form sheets.

Money for old rope, he thought sardonically. It didn't make sense, holding on to the stuff for five years.

The Tote, as usual, had opened its windows an hour before the first race to take bets on the Grand National, because there was not time after the second to sell tickets to all who wanted to buy for the big third.

There were long queues already when Austin went along to back his fancy, for like him they knew from experience that it was best to bet early if one wanted a good vantage point in the stands.

He waited in the shorter queue for the £5 window, writing his proposal on his race card.

When his turn came, he said, 'Fifty to win, number twelve,' and counted off the shuffled fivers without a qualm.

The busy woman behind the window gave him his tickets with barely a glance. 'Next?' she said, looking over his shoulder to the man behind.

Dead easy, thought Austin smugly, stuffing his tickets into his jacket pocket. Fifty on number twelve, to win. No point in messing about with place money, he always said. Mind you, he was a pretty good judge of form: He always prided himself on that.

Nothing in the race had a better chance than the third favourite, Haunted House, and you couldn't want a better jockey than Springwood, now could you? He strolled with satisfaction back to the bar and bought another beer.

In the changing room Jerry Springwood had no difficulty in disguising either his hangover or his fear. The other jockeys were gripped with the usual pre-National tension, finding their mouths a little dry, their thoughts a little abstracted, their flow of ribald jokes silenced to a trickle.

Twice over Becher's, Jerry thought hopelessly: the Canal Turn, the Chair, how in God's name am I going to face it?

The Senior Steward of the Jockey Club was lunching a party of eminent overseas visitors in a private dining room when Chief Superintendent Crispin interrupted the roast saddle of lamb.

'I want to speak to you urgently, sir,' the policeman said, bending down to the Turf's top ear.

Sir William Westerland rested his bland gaze briefly on the amount of brass on the navy blue uniform. 'You're in charge here?'

'Yes, sir. Can we talk privately?'

'I suppose so, if it's important.' Sir William rose, glanced regretfully at his half-eaten lunch, and led the policeman to the outdoor section of his private box high in the grandstand. The two men stood hunched in the chilly air, and spoke against the background noise of the swelling crowd and the shouts of the bookmakers offering odds on the approaching first race.

Crispin said, 'It's about the Birmingham bank robbery, sir.'

'But that happened more than a year ago,' Westerland protested.

'Some of the stolen notes have turned up here, today, on the race course.'

Westerland frowned, not needing to be told details. The blasting open of the supposedly impregnable vault, the theft of more than £3½ million, the violent getaway of the thieves, all had been given wider coverage than the death of Nelson.

Four men and a small boy had been killed by the explosion outwards of the bank wall, and two housewives and two young policemen had been gunned down later.

The thieves had arrived in a fire engine before the crashing echoes died, had dived into the ruins to carry out the vault's contents for 'safekeeping', and driven clear away with the loot.

They were suspected only at the very last moment by a puzzled constable, whose order to halt had been answered by a spray of machine-gun bullets.

Only one of the gang had been recognised, caught, tried, and sentenced to 30 years; and of that he had served precisely 30 days before making a spectacular escape. Recapturing him, and catching his confederates, was a No 1 police priority.

'It's the first lead we've had for months,' Crispin said earnestly. 'If we can catch whoever came here with the hot money . . .'

Westerland looked down at the scurrying thousands. 'Pretty hopeless, I'd have thought,' he said.

'No, sir,' Crispin shook his neat greying head. 'A sharp-eyed checker in the Tote spotted one of the notes, and now they've found nine more. One of the sellers in the £5 windows remembers selling £50 worth of tickets early on to a man who paid in fivers which *felt* new, although they had been roughly creased and wrinkled.'

'But even so . . .'

'She remembers he backed only one horse to win, which is unusual on Grand National Day.'

'Which horse?'

'Haunted House, sir. And so, sir, if Haunted House wins, our fellow will bring his batch of £50 worth of winning tickets to the pay-out, and we will have him.'

'But,' Westerland objected, 'What if Haunted House DOESN'T win?'

Crispin gazed at him steadily. 'We want you to arrange that Haunted House DOES win. We want you to fix the Grand National!'

Down in Tattersall's enclosure Austin Dartmouth Glenn passed two hot fivers to a bookmaker who stuffed them busily into his satchel without looking. A tenner to win on Spotted Tulip, at eight to one.

In the noise, haste, and flurry of the last five minutes before the first race Austin elbowed his way up the stands to find the best view of his money on the hoof, smirking with satisfaction.

In the changing room Jerry Springwood reluctantly climbed into his thin white breeches and fumbled with the buttons of his shiny red and white striped colours.

His mind was filling like a well with panic, the terrible desire to cut and run growing deeper and deadlier with every passing minute. He had difficulty in concentrating and virtually did not hear when anyone spoke to him.

His hands trembled. He felt cold. There was another hour to live through before he would have to force himself out to the parade ring, onto the horse, down to the start, and right round those demanding four and a half miles and over 30 huge fences.

I can't do it, he thought numbly. I can't face it. Where can I hide?

The four Stewards in charge of the meeting sat gloomily round their large table, reacting with varying degrees of incredulity and uneasiness to the urgings of Chief Superintendent Crispin.

'There's no precedent,' said one. 'It's out of the question. There isn't time,' said another.

A third said: 'You'd never get the trainers to agree.' 'And what about the owners?' asked the fourth.

Crispin held racing in as little esteem as crooked politicians and considered that catching the Birmingham mob was of far greater social importance than any particular horse finishing first.

His inner outrage at the obstructive reaction of the Stewards seeped unmistakably into his voice.

'The Birmingham robbers murdered nine people,' he said forcefully. 'Everyone has a public duty to help the police catch them.' 'Surely not to the extent of ruining the Grand National,' insisted the Stewards.

'I understand,' Crispin said, 'that in steeple-chasing in general few stud values are involved, and in this year's National the horses are all geldings. It is not as if we were asking you to spoil the Stud Book by fixing the Derby.'

'All the same, it would be unfair on the betting public,'' said the Stewards.

'The people who died were part of the betting public. The next people to die, in the next violent bank raid, will also be the betting public.'

Sir William Westerland listened to the arguments with his bland expression unimpaired. He had gone far in life by not declaring his views before everyone else had bared their breasts, their opinions, and their weaknesses.

His mild subsequent observations had a way of being received as revealed truth, when they were basically only unemotional common sense.

He watched Crispin and his fellow Stewards heat up into emphasis and hubbub, and begin to slide towards prejudice and hostility. He sighed internally, looked at his watch, and noisily cleared his throat.

'Gentlemen,' he said calmly and distinctly. 'Before we reach a decision, I think we should consider the following points. First, possibility. Second, secrecy. Third, consequences.'

Stewards and policemen looked at him with united relief.

'Jump jockeys,' Westerland said, 'are individualists. Who do you think is going to persuade them to fix the race?'

No answer.

'Who can say that Haunted House will not fall?'

No answer.

'How long do you suppose it would be before someone told the Press? Do we want the uproar which would follow?'

No answer, but a great shaking of stewardly heads.

'But if we refuse Chief Superintendent Crispin's request, how would we feel if another bank was blown apart and more innocent people killed, knowing we took no action to prevent it?'

The meeting looked at him in silence, awaiting his lead.

Jerry Springwood's head felt like a balloon floating somewhere above his unco-ordinated body. The call of 'Jockeys out, please', had found him still unable to think of a way of escape. Too many people knew him.

How can I run? he thought; how can I scramble to the gate and find a taxi when everyone knows I should be walking out to ride Haunted House?

Can I faint? he thought. Can I say I'm ill?

He found himself going out with the others, his leaden legs trudging automatically while his spirit wilted.

He stood in the parade ring with his mouth dry and his eyes feeling like gritty holes in his skull, not hearing the nervously hearty pre-race chit-chat of owner and trainer.

I can't, he thought. I can't.

The senior steward of the Jockey Club, Sir William Westerland, walked up to him as he stood rigidly in his hopeless hell.

'A word in your ear, Jerry,' he said.

Jerry Springwood looked at him blankly, with eyes like smooth grey pebbles. Westerland, who had seen that look on other faces and knew what it foreboded, suffered severe feelings of misgiving.

In spite of Chief Superintendent Crispin's opposition, he secured the stewards' whole-hearted agreement. The National could not be fixed— even to catch murderers.

He came to the conclusion that both practically and morally, it was impossible. The police would just have to keep a sharper check on future meetings, and one day soon, perhaps, they would catch their fish as he swam again to the Tote.

All the same, Westerland had seen no harm in wishing Jerry Spring- wood success; but he perceived now that Crispin had no chance of catching his men today. No jockey in this state of frozen fear could win the Na- tional.

The backers of Haunted House would be fortunate if their fancy lasted half a mile before he pulled up, or ran out, or refused to jump because of the stranglehold on his reins.

'Good luck,' said Westerland lamely, with regret.

Jerry made no answer, even ordinary politeness being beyond him.

Up on his vantage point in the stands, Austin Glenn watched the long line of runners walk down the course. Ten minutes to race time, with half the bookies suffering from sore throats and the massed crowds buzzing with rising excitement.

Austin, who had lost his tenner on Spotted Tulip in the first, and fifteen more to bookmakers on the second, was biting his knuckles over Haunted House.

Jerry Springwood sat like a sack in the saddle, shoulders hunched. The horse, receptive to his rider's mood, plodded along in confusion, not able to sort out whether or not he should respond to the crowd instead.

To Austin and many others, horse and rider looked like a grade one losing combination.

William Westerland shook his head ruefully, and Crispin wondered irri- tably why that one horse, out of all of them, looked half asleep.

Jerry Springwood got himself lined up for the start by blotting out every thought. The well of panic was full and trying to flood over.

Jerry, white and clammily sweating, knew that in a few more minutes he would have to dismount and run.

Have to.

When the starter let them go, Haunted House was standing flat-footed. Getting no signal from the saddle, he started hesitantly after the departing field.

The horse knew his job—he was there to run and jump and get his head in front of the next.

But he was feeling rudderless, without the help and direction he was used to.

His jockey stayed on board by instinct, the long years of skill coming to his aid, the schooled muscles acting in a pattern that needed no conscious thought.

Haunted House jumped last over the first fence, and was still last five fences later, approaching Becher's.

Jerry Springwood saw the horse directly in front of him fall, and knew remotely that if he went straight on he would land on top of him.

Almost without thinking he twitched his right hand on the rein, and Haunted House, taking fire from this tiniest sign of life, swerved a yard, bunched his quarters, and put his great equine soul into clearing the danger.

Haunted House knew the course: had won there, with Jerry Springwood up, in shorter races. His sudden surge over Becher's melted his jockey's defensive blankness and thrust him into freshly vivid fear.

Oh God, Jerry thought, as Haunted House took him inexorably towards the Canal Turn, how can I? How can I?

He sat there, fighting his panic, while Haunted House carried him surefootedly round the Turn, and over Valentine's and all the way to The Chair.

Jerry thought forever after that he'd shut his eyes as his mount took the last few strides towards the most testing steeplechase fence in the world, but Haunted House met it perfectly and cleared the huge spread without the slightest stumble.

Over the water jump in front of the stands, and out again towards Becher's, with the whole course to jump again. Jerry thought, if I pull up now, I'll have done enough.

Horses beside him tired and stopped or slid and fell but Haunted House galloped at a steady 30 miles an hour with scant regard for his fate.

Austin Glenn on the stands, and William Westerland in his private box, and Chief Superintendent Crispin tense in front of a television set, all watched with faster pulses as Haunted House made progress through the field.

By the time he reached Becher's on the second circuit he lay 10th, and seventh at the Canal Turn, and fifth after the third last fence, a mile from home.

Jerry Springwood saw a gap on the rails and didn't take it. He checked his mount before the second-last fence so they jumped it safely but lost two lengths.

On the stands William Westerland groaned aloud, but on Haunted House Jerry Springwood just shrivelled inside at his own fearful cowardice. It's useless, he thought. I'd be better off dead.

The leader of the field had sprinted a long way ahead, and Jerry saw him ride over the last fence while Haunted House was a good 40 lengths in the rear. One more, Jerry thought. Only one more fence. I'll never ride another race. Never.

He locked his jaw as Haunted House gathered his muscles and launched his half ton weight at the green-faced birch. If he rolls on me, Jerry thought . . . if I fall and he crashes on top of me . . . Oh God, he thought, take me safely over this fence.

The horse in front, well-backed and high in the handicap, took the last flat half-mile at a spanking gallop. Jerry Springwood and Haunted House, still on their feet, had left it too late to make a serious bid to catch them, but with a surge of what Jerry knew to be release from purgatory they raced past everything else in a flat-out dash to the post.

Austin Glenn watched Haunted House finish second by 20 lengths. Cursing himself a little for not bothering about place money, he took out his tickets, tore them philosophically across, and let the pieces flutter away to the four winds.

William Westerland rubbed his chin and wondered whether Jerry Springwood could have won if he'd tried sooner. Chief Superintendent bitterly cursed the 20 lengths by which his quarry would escape.

Sir William took his eminent foreign visitors down to watch the scenes of jubilation round the winner in the unsaddling enclosure, and was met by flurried officials with horrified faces.

'The winner can't pass the scales,' they said.

'What do you mean?' Westerland demanded.

'The winner didn't carry the right weight! The trainer left the weight-cloth hanging in the saddling box when he put the saddle on his horse. The winner ran all the way with 10lb less than he should have done . . . and we'll have to disqualify him.'

Forgetting the weight-cloth was done often enough; but in the National! William Westerland took a deep breath and told the aghast officials to relay the facts to the public over the tannoy system.

Jerry Springwood heard the news while he was sitting on the scales and watching the pointer swing round to the right mark. He felt, not joyful, but overwhelmingly ashamed, as if he'd won the prize by cheating.

Crispin stationed his men strategically, and alerted all the Tote pay-out windows.

Up on the stands, Austin Glenn searched for the pieces in a fury, picking up every torn and trampled scrap and peering at it anxiously.

What if someone else picked up his tickets, and claimed his winnings? The idea enraged him: and what was more, he couldn't stay on the course indefinitely because he had to catch his return train. He couldn't afford to be late; he had to work that night.

Crispin's men shifted from foot to foot as time went by, and were left there growing more and more conspicuous while the crowd thinned and trouped out through the gates.

When the Tote closed for the day the Chief Superintendent called them off in frustrated rage, and conceded that they would have to wait for another day after all.

In the weighing room Jerry Springwood bore the congratulations as best he could, and announced to surprised television millions that he would be hanging up his boots in a few weeks, at the end of the season.

Austin Dartmouth Glenn travelled home empty-handed and in a vile mood. He cursed his wife and kicked the cat, and after a hasty supper he put on his neat navy blue uniform.

Then he went off scowling to work his usual night shift as a warder in the nearby high security jail.

THE MOOSE

By Theodore Roosevelt

The moose is the giant of all deer, and many hunters esteem it the noblest of American game. Beyond question there are few trophies more prized than the huge shovel horns of this strange dweller in the cold north-land forests.

I shot my first moose after making several fruitless hunting trips with this special game in view. The season I finally succeeded it was only after having hunted two or three weeks in vain, among the Bitter Root Mountains, and the ranges lying southeast of them.

I began about the first of September by making a trial with my old hunting friend Willis. We speedily found a country where there were moose, but of the animals themselves we never caught a glimpse. We tried to kill them by hunting in the same manner that we hunted elk; that is, by choosing a place where there was sign, and going carefully through it against or across the wind. However, this plan failed; though at that very time we succeeded in killing elk in this way, devoting one or two days to their pursuit. There were both elk and moose in the country, but they were usually found in different kinds of ground, though often close alongside one another. The former went in herds, the cows, calves, and yearlings by themselves, and they roamed through the higher and more open forests, well up towards timber line. The moose, on the contrary, were found singly or in small parties composed at the outside of a bull, a cow, and her young of two years; for the moose is practically monogamous, in strong contrast to the highly polygamous wapiti and caribou.

The moose did not seem to care much whether they lived among the summits of the mountains or not, so long as they got the right kind of country; for they were much more local in their distribution, and at this season less given to wandering than their kin with round horns. What they wished was a cool, swampy region of very dense growth; in the main chains of the northern Rockies even the valleys are high enough to be cold. Of course many of the moose lived on the wooded summits of the lower ranges; and most of them came down lower in winter than in summer, following about a fortnight after the elk; but if in a large tract of woods the cover was dense and the ground marshy, though it was in a valley no higher than the herds of the ranchmen grazed, or perchance even in the immediate neighborhood of a small frontier hamlet, then it might be chosen by some old bull who wished to lie in seclusion till his horns were grown, or by some cow with a calf to raise. Before settlers came to this high mountain region of Western Montana, a moose would often thus live in an isolated marshy tract surrounded by open country. They grazed throughout the summer on marsh plants, notably lily stems, and nibbled at the tops of the very tall natural hay of the meadows. The legs of the beast are too long and the neck too short to allow it to graze habitually on short grass; yet in the early spring when greedy for the tender blades of young, green marsh grass, the moose will often shuffle down on its knees to get at them, and it will occasionally perform the same feat to get a mouthful or two of snow in winter.

The moose which lived in isolated, exposed localities were speedily killed or driven away after the incoming of settlers; and at the time that we hunted we found no sign of them until we reached the region of continuous forest. Here, in a fortnight's hunting, we found as much sign as we wished, and plenty of it fresh; but the animals themselves we not only never saw but we never so much as heard. Often after hours of careful still-hunting or cautious tracking, we found the footprints deep in the soft earth, showing where our quarry had winded or heard us, and had noiselessly slipped away from the danger. It is astonishing how quietly a moose can steal through the woods if it wishes: and it has what is to the hunter a very provoking habit of making a half or three quarters circle before lying down, and then crouching with its head so turned that it can surely perceive any pursuer who may follow its trail. We tried every method to outwit the beasts. We attempted to track them; we beat through likely spots; sometimes we merely "sat on a log" and awaited events, by a drinking hole, meadow, mud wallow or other such place (a course of procedure which often works well in still-hunting); but all in vain.

Our main difficulty lay in the character of the woods which the moose haunted. They were choked and tangled to the last degree, consisting of a mass of thick-growing conifers, with dead timber strewn in every direction, and young growth filling the spaces between the trunks. We could not see twenty yards ahead of us, and it was almost impossible to walk without making a noise. Elk were occasionally found in these same places; but usually they frequented more open timber, where the hunting was beyond comparison easier. Perhaps more experienced hunters would have killed their game; though in such cover the best tracker and still-hunter alive cannot always reckon on success with really wary animals. But, be this as it may, we, at any rate, were completely baffled, and I began to think that this moose-hunt, like all my former ones, was doomed to end in failure.

However, a few days later I met a crabbed old trapper named Hank Griffin, who was going after beaver in the mountains, and who told me that if I would come with him he would show me moose. I jumped at the chance, and he proved as good as his word; though for the first two trials my ill luck did not change.

At the time that it finally did change we had at last reached a place where the moose were on favorable ground. A high, marshy valley stretched for several miles between two rows of stony mountains, clad with a forest of rather small fir-trees. This valley was covered with reeds, alders, and rank grass, and studded with little willow-bordered ponds and island-like clumps of spruce and graceful tamaracks.

Having surveyed the ground and found moose sign the preceding afternoon, we were up betimes in the cool morning to begin our hunt. Before sunrise we were posted on a rocky spur of the foot-hills, behind a mask of evergreens; ourselves unseen we overlooked all the valley, and we knew we could see any animal which might be either feeding away from cover or on its journey homeward from its feeding ground to its day-bed.

As it grew lighter we scanned the valley with increasing care and eagerness. The sun rose behind us; and almost as soon as it was up we made out some large beast moving among the dwarf willows beside a little lake half a mile in our front. In a few minutes the thing walked out where the bushes were thinner, and we saw that it was a young bull moose browsing on the willow tops. He had evidently nearly finished his breakfast, and he stood idly for some moments, now and then lazily cropping a mouthful of twig tips. Then he walked off with great strides in a straight line across the marsh, splashing among the wet water-plants, and ploughing through boggy spaces with the indifference begotten of vast strength and legs longer than those of any other animal on this continent. At times he entered beds of reeds which hid him from view, though their surging and bending showed the wake of his passage; at other times he walked through meadows of tall grass, the withered yellow stalks rising to his flanks, while his body loomed above them, glistening black and wet in the level sunbeams. Once he stopped for a few moments on a rise of dry ground, seemingly to enjoy the heat of the young sun; he stood motionless, save that his ears were continually pricked, and his head sometimes slightly turned, showing that even in this remote land he was on the alert. Once, with a somewhat awkward motion, he reached his hind leg forward to scratch his neck. Then he walked forward again into the marsh; where the water was quite deep he broke into the long, stretching, springy trot, which forms the characteristic gait of his kind, churning the marsh water into foam. He held his head straight forwards, the antlers resting on his shoulders.

After awhile he reached a spruce island, through which he walked to and fro; but evidently could find therein no resting-place quite to his mind, for he soon left and went on to another. Here after a little wandering he chose a point where there was some thick young growth, which hid him from view when he lay down, though not when he stood. After some turning he settled himself in his bed just as a steer would.

He could not have chosen a spot better suited for us. He was nearly at the edge of the morass, the open space between the spruce clump where he was lying and the rocky foothills being comparatively dry and not much over a couple of hundred yards broad; while some sixty yards from it, and between it and the hills, was a little hummock, tufted with firs, so as to afford us just the cover we needed. Keeping back from the edge of the morass we were able to walk upright through the forest, until we got the point where he was lying in a line with this little hummock. We then dropped on our hands and knees, and crept over the soft, wet sward, where there was nothing to make a noise. Wherever the ground rose at all we crawled flat on our bellies. The air was still, for it was a very calm morning.

At last we reached the hummock, and I got into position for a shot, taking a final look at my faithful 45-90 Winchester to see that all was in order. Peering cautiously through the shielding evergreens, I at first could not make out where the moose was lying, until my eye was caught by the motion of his big ears, as he occasionally flapped them lazily forward. Even then I could not see his outline; but I knew where he was, and having pushed my rifle forward on the moss, I snapped a dry twig to make him rise. My veins were thrilling and my heart beating with that eager, fierce excitement, known only to the hunter of big game, and forming one of the keenest and strongest of the many pleasures which with him go to make up "the wild joy of living."

As the sound of the snapping twig smote his ears the moose rose nimbly to his feet, with a lightness on which one would not have reckoned in a beast so heavy of body. He stood broadside to me for a moment, his ungainly head slightly turned, while his ears twitched and his nostrils snuffed the air. Drawing a fine bead against his black hide, behind his shoulder and two thirds of his body's depth below his shaggy withers, I pressed the trigger. He neither flinched nor reeled, but started with his regular ground-covering trot through the spruces; yet I knew he was mine, for the light blood sprang from both of his nostrils, and he fell dying on his side before he had gone thirty rods.

Later in the fall I was again hunting among the lofty ranges which continue towards the southeast the chain of the Bitter Root, between Idaho and Montana. There were but two of us, and we were travelling very light, each having but one pack-pony and the saddle animal he bestrode. We were high among the mountains, and followed no regular trail. Hence our course was often one of extreme difficulty. Occasionally, we took our animals through the forest near timber line, where the slopes were not too steep; again we threaded our way through a line of glades, or skirted the foot-hills, in an open, park country; and now and then we had to cross stretches of tangled mountain forest, making but a few miles a day, at the cost of incredible toil, and accomplishing even this solely by virtue of the wonderful docility and sure-footedness of the ponies, and of my companion's skill with the axe and thorough knowledge of woodcraft.

Late one cold afternoon we came out in a high alpine valley in which there was no sign of any man's having ever been before us. Down its middle ran a clear brook. On each side was a belt of thick spruce forest, covering the lower flanks of the mountains. The trees came down in points and isolated clumps to the brook, the banks of which were thus bordered with open glades, rendering the travelling easy and rapid.

Soon after starting up this valley we entered a beaver meadow of considerable size. It was covered with lush, rank grass, and the stream wound through it rather sluggishly in long curves, which were fringed by a thick growth of dwarfed willows. In one or two places it broadened into small ponds, bearing a few lily-pads. This meadow had been all tramped up by moose. Trails led hither and thither through the grass, the willow twigs were cropped off, and the muddy banks of the little black ponds were indented by hoofmarks. Evidently most of the lilies had been plucked. The footprints were unmistakable; a moose's foot is longer and slimmer than a caribou's, while on the other hand it is much larger than an elk's, and a longer oval in shape.

Most of the sign was old, this high alpine meadow, surrounded by snow mountains, having clearly been a favorite resort for moose in the summer; but some enormous, fresh tracks told that one or more old bulls were still frequenting the place.

The light was already fading, and, of course, we did not wish to camp where we were, because we would then certainly scare the moose. Accordingly we pushed up the valley for another mile, through an open forest, the ground being quite free from underbrush and dead timber, and covered with a carpet of thick moss, in which the feet sank noiselessly. Then we came to another beaver meadow, which offered fine feed for the ponies. On its edge we hastily pitched camp, just at dusk. We tossed down the packs in a dry grove, close to the brook, and turned the tired ponies loose in the meadow, hobbling the little mare that carried the bell. The ground was smooth. We threw a cross-pole from one to the other of two young spruces, which happened to stand handily, and from it stretched and pegged out a piece of canvas, which we were using as a shelter tent. Beneath this we spread our bedding, laying under it the canvas sheets in which it had been wrapped. There was still bread left over from yesterday's baking, and in a few moments the kettle was boiling and the frying-pan sizzling, while one of us skinned and cut into suitable pieces two grouse we had knocked over on our march. For fear of frightening the moose we built but a small fire, and went to bed soon after supper, being both tired and cold. Fortunately, what little breeze there was blew up the valley.

At dawn I was awake, and crawled out of my buffalo bag, shivering and yawning. My companion still slumbered heavily. White frost covered whatever had been left outside. The cold was sharp, and I hurriedly slipped a pair of stout moccasins on my feet, drew on my gloves and cap, and started through the ghostly woods for the meadow where we had seen the moose sign. The tufts of grass were stiff with frost; black ice skimmed the edges and quiet places of the little brook.

I walked slowly, it being difficult not to make a noise by cracking sticks or brushing against trees, in the gloom; but the forest was so open that it favored me. When I reached the edge of the beaver-meadow it was light enough to shoot, though the front sight still glimmered indistinctly. Streaks of cold red showed that the sun would soon rise.

Before leaving the shelter of the last spruces I halted to listen; and almost immediately heard a curious splashing sound from the middle of the meadow, where the brook broadened into small willow-bordered pools. I knew at once that a moose was in one of these pools, wading about and pulling up the water-lilies by seizing their slippery stems in his lips, plunging his head deep under water to do so. The moose love to feed in this way in the hot months, when they spend all the time they can in the water, feeding or lying down; nor do they altogether abandon the habit even when the weather is so cold that icicles form in their shaggy coats.

Crouching, I stole noiselessly along the edge of the willow-thicket. The stream twisted through it from side to side in zigzags, so that every few rods I got a glimpse down a lane of black water. In a minute I heard a slight splashing near me; and on passing the next point of bushes, I saw the shadowy outline of the moose's hindquarters, standing in a bend of the water. In a moment he walked onwards, disappearing. I ran forward a couple of rods, and then turned in among the willows, to reach the brook where it again bent back towards me. The splashing in the water, and the rustling of the moose's body against the frozen twigs, drowned the little noise made by my moccasined feet.

I strode out on the bank at the lower end of a long narrow pool of water, dark and half frozen. In this pool, half way down and facing me, but a score of yards off, stood the mighty marsh beast, strange and uncouth in look as some monster surviving over from the Pliocene. His vast bulk loomed black and vague in the dim gray dawn; his huge antlers stood out sharply; columns of steam rose from his nostrils. For several seconds he fronted me motionless; then he began to turn, slowly, and as if he had a stiff neck. When quarter way round I fired into his shoulder; whereat he reared and bounded on the bank with great leap, vanishing in the willows. Through these I heard him crash like a whirlwind for a dozen rods; then down he fell, and when I reached the spot he had ceased to struggle. The ball had gone through his heart.

LYNX-HUNTING

By Stephen Crane

Jimmie lounged about the dining room and watched his mother with large, serious eyes. Suddenly he said, "Ma—now—can I borrow pa's gun?"

She was overcome with the feminine horror which is able to mistake preliminary words for the full accomplishment of the dread thing. "Why, Jimmie!" she cried. "Of al-l wonders! Your father's gun! No indeed you can't!"

He was fairly well crushed, but he managed to mutter, sullenly, "Well, Willie Dalzel, he's got a gun." In reality his heart had previously been beating with such tumult—he had himself been so impressed with the daring and sin of his request—that he was glad that all was over now, and his mother could do very little further harm to his sensibilities. He had been influenced into the venture by the larger boys.

"Huh!" the Dalzel urchin had said; "your father's got a gun, hasn't he? Well, why don't you bring that?"

Puffing himself, Jimmie had replied, "Well, I can, if I want to." It was a black lie, but really the Dalzel boy was too outrageous with his eternal bill-posting about the gun which a beaming uncle had entrusted to him. Its possession made him superior in manfulness to most boys in the neighbor-hood—or at least they enviously conceded him such position—but he was so overbearing, and stuffed the fact of his treasure so relentlessly down their throats, that on this occasion the miserable Jimmie had lied as natu-rally as most animals swim.

Willie Dalzel had not been checkmated, for he had instantly retorted, "Why don't you get it, then?"

"Well, I can, if I want to."

"Well, get it, then!"

"Well, I can, if I want to."

Thereupon Jimmie had paced away with great airs of surety as far as the door of his home, where his manner changed to one of tremulous misgiv-ing as it came upon him to address his mother in the dining room. There had happened that which had happened.

When Jimmie returned to his two distinguished companions he was blown out with a singular pomposity. He spoke these noble words: "Oh, well, I guess I don't want to take the gun out today."

They had been watching him with gleaming ferret eyes, and they detected his falsity at once. They challenged him with shouted gibes, but it was not in the rules for the conduct of boys that one should admit anything whatsoever, and so Jimmie, backed into an ethical corner, lied as stupidly, as desperately, as hopelessly as ever lone savage fights when surrounded at last in his jungle.

Such accusations were never known to come to any point, for the reason that the number and kind of denials always equaled or exceeded the number of accusations, and no boy was ever brought really to book for these misdeeds.

In the end they went off together, Willie Dalzel with his gun being a trifle in advance and discoursing upon his various works. They passed along a maple-lined avenue, a highway common to boys bound for that free land of hills and woods in which they lived in some part their romance of the moment, whether it was of Indians, miners, smugglers, soldiers, or outlaws. The paths were their paths, and much was known to them of the secrets of the dark green hemlock thickets, the wastes of sweet fern and huckleberry, the cliffs of gaunt bluestone with the sumach burning red at their feet. Each boy had, I am sure, a conviction that some day the wilderness was to give forth to him a marvelous secret. They felt that the hills and the forest knew much, and they heard a voice of it in the silence. It was vague, thrilling, fearful, and altogether fabulous. The grown folk seemed to regard these wastes merely as so much distance between one place and another place, or as a rabbit-cover, or as a district to be judged according to the value of the timber; but to the boys it spoke some great inspiring word, which they knew even as those who pace the shore know the enigmatic speech of the surf. In the meantime they lived there, in season, lives of ringing adventure—by dint of imagination.

The boys left the avenue, skirted hastily through some private grounds, climbed a fence, and entered the thickets. It happened that at school the previous day Willie Dalzel had been forced to read and acquire in some part a solemn description of a lynx. The meager information thrust upon him had caused him grimaces of suffering, but now he said, suddenly, "I'm goin' to shoot a lynx."

The other boys admired this statement, but they were silent for a time. Finally Jimmie said, meekly, "What's a lynx?" He had endured his ignorance as long as he was able.

The Dalzel boy mocked him. "Why, don't you know what a lynx is? A lynx? Why, a lynx is a animal somethin' like a cat, an' it's got great big green eyes, and it sits on the limb of a tree an' jus' glares at you. It's a pretty bad animal, I tell you. Why, when I—"

"Huh!" said the third boy. "Where'd you ever see a lynx?"

"Oh, I've seen 'em—plenty of 'em. I bet you'd be scared if you seen one once."

Jimmie and the other boy each demanded, "How do you know I would?"

They penetrated deeper into the wood. They climbed a rocky zigzag path which led them at times where with their hands they could almost touch the tops of giant pines. The gray cliffs sprang sheer toward the sky. Willie Dalzel babbled about his impossible lynx, and they stalked the mountain-side like chamois-hunters, although no noise of bird or beast broke the stillness of the hills. Below them Whilomville was spread out somewhat like the cheap green-and-black lithograph of the time— "A Bird's-eye View of Whilomville, N.Y."

In the end the boys reached the top of the mountain and scouted off among wild and desolate ridges. They were burning with the desire to slay large animals. They thought continually of elephants, lions, tigers, crocodiles. They discoursed upon their immaculate conduct in case such monsters confronted them, and they all lied carefully about their courage.

The breeze was heavy with the smell of sweet fern. The pines and hemlocks sighed as they waved their branches. In the hollows the leaves of the laurels were lacquered where the sunlight found them. No matter the weather, it would be impossible to long continue an expedition of this kind without a fire, and presently they built one, snapping down for fuel the brittle under branches of the pines. About this fire they were willed to conduct a sort of play, the Dalzel boy taking the part of a bandit chief, and the other boys being his trusty lieutenants. They stalked to and fro, long-strided, stern yet devil-may-care, three terrible little figures.

Jimmie had an uncle who made game of him whenever he caught him in this kind of play, and often this uncle quoted derisively the following classic: "Once aboard the lugger, Bill, and the girl is mine. Now to burn the château and destroy all evidence of our crime. But, hark 'e, Bill, no violence." Wheeling abruptly, he addressed these dramatic words to his comrades. They were impressed; they decided at once to be smugglers, and in the most ribald fashion they talked about carrying off young women.

At last they continued their march through the woods. The smuggling *motif* was now grafted fantastically upon the original lynx idea, which Willie Dalzel refused to abandon at any price.

Once they came upon an innocent bird which happened to be looking another way at the time. After a great deal of maneuvering and big words, Willie Dalzel reared his fowling piece and blew this poor thing into a mere rag of wet feathers, of which he was proud.

Afterward the other big boy had a turn at another bird. Then it was plainly Jimmie's chance. The two others had, of course, some thought of cheating him out of this chance, but of a truth he was timid to explode such a thunderous weapon, and as soon as they detected this fear they simply overbore him, and made it clearly understood that if he refused to shoot he would lose his caste, his scalp-lock, his girdle, his honor.

They had reached the old death-colored snake-fence which marked the limits of the upper pasture of the Fleming farm. Under some hickory trees the path ran parallel to the fence. Behold! a small priestly chipmunk came to a rail and, folding his hands on his abdomen, addressed them in his own tongue. It was Jimmie's shot. Adjured by the others, he took the gun. His face was stiff with apprehension. The Dalzel boy was giving forth fine words. "Go ahead. Aw, don't be afraid. It's nothin' to do. Why, I've done it a million times. Don't shut both your eyes, now. Jus' keep one open and shut the other one. He'll get away if you don't watch out. Now you're all right. Why don't you let 'er go? Go ahead."

Jimmie, with his legs braced apart, was in the center of the path. His back was greatly bent, owing to the mechanics of supporting the heavy gun. His companions were screeching in the rear. There was a wait.

Then he pulled trigger. To him there was a frightful roar, his cheek and his shoulder took a stunning blow, his face felt a hot flush of fire, and, opening his two eyes, he found that he was still alive. He was not too dazed to instantly adopt a becoming egotism. It had been the first shot of his life.

But directly after the well-mannered celebration of this victory a certain cow, which had been grazing in the line of fire, was seen to break wildly across the pasture, bellowing and bucking. The three smugglers and lynx-hunters looked at each other out of blanched faces. Jimmie had hit the cow. The first evidence of his comprehension of this fact was in the celerity with which he returned the discharged gun to Willie Dalzel.

They turned to flee. The land was black, as if it had been overshadowed suddenly with thick storm-clouds, and even as they fled in their horror a gigantic Swedish farm hand came from the heavens and fell upon them, shrieking in eerie triumph. In a twinkle they were clouted prostrate. The Swede was elate and ferocious in a foreign and fulsome way. He continued to beat them and yell.

From the ground they raised their dismal appeal. "Oh, please, mister, we didn't do it! He did it! I didn't do it! We didn't do it! We didn't mean to do it! Oh, please, mister!"

In these moments of childish terror little lads go half blind, and it is possible that few moments of their after life made them suffer as they did when the Swede flung them over the fence and marched them toward the farmhouse. They begged like cowards on the scaffold, and each one was for himself. "Oh, please let me go, mister! I didn't do it, mister! He did it! Oh, p-l-ease let me go, mister!"

The boyish view belongs to boys alone, and if this tall and knotted laborer was needlessly without charity, none of the three lads questioned it. Usually when they were punished they decided that they deserved it, and the more they were punished the more they were convinced that they were criminals of a most subterranean type. As to the hitting of the cow being a pure accident, and therefore not of necessity a criminal matter, such reading never entered their heads. When things happened and they were caught, they commonly paid dire consequences, and they were accustomed to measure the probabilities of woe utterly by the damage done, and not in any way by the culpability. The shooting of the cow was plainly heinous, and undoubtedly their dungeons would be knee-deep in water.

"He did it, mister!" This was a general outcry. Jimmie used it as often as did the others. As for them, it is certain that they had no direct thought of betraying their comrade for their own salvation. They thought themselves guilty because they were caught; when boys were not caught they might possibly be innocent. But captured boys were guilty. When they cried out that Jimmie was the culprit, it was principally a simple expression of terror.

Old Henry Fleming, the owner of the farm, strode across the pasture toward them. He had in his hand a most cruel whip. This whip he flourished. At his approach the boys suffered the agonies of the fire regions. And yet anybody with half an eye could see that the whip in his hand was a mere accident, and that he was a kind old man—when he cared.

When he had come near he spoke crisply. "What you boys ben doin' to my cow?" The tone had deep threat in it. They all answered by saying that none of them had shot the cow. Their denials were tearful and clamorous, and they crawled knee by knee. The vision of it was like three martyrs being dragged toward the stake. Old Fleming stood there, grim, tight-lipped. After a time he said, "Which boy done it?"

There was some confusion, and then Jimmie spake. "I done it, mister."

Fleming looked at him. Then he asked, "Well, what did you shoot 'er fer?"

Jimmie thought, hesitated, decided, faltered, and then formulated this: "I thought she was a lynx."

Old Fleming and his Swede at once lay down in the grass and laughed themselves helpless.

THE MONARCH'S LAST TANTO

By Robert Sylvester

The Monarch started forward as soon as the hard, white ball struck the frontwall. He picked up speed, turned into the granite sidewall and took three quick steps up its perpendicular height, like a man running up a short flight of stairs. The ball was coming back at him along the sidewall, high and hugging the surface the way extra spin will make them do, but he trapped it in the curved basket and shoved himself clear of the wall with his feet. He wanted to make his return throw while he was still plummeting back to the court, but he felt the ball bounce crazily around in his basket and then fly out onto the court.

These new pelotas were too light, he told himself in disgust. They weren't anything like the sound, true Basque balls which could be depended upon not to try any fancy Cuban tricks. These Havana pelotas acted just like Cubans. You never knew which way they were going. The Monarch blew in disgust and signaled for time out. He walked over to the low bench off the rear of the court, savagely ripping at the long binding cord which laced the curved cesta—a reed basket woven to a supple frame—to his thick right hand.

He made a brief show of examining his cesta for flaws. Actually, the cesta meant little to him, flaws or no flaws. The giant Negro who made cestas for all the Havana players, weaving them out of flat reed and cutting the leather gloves to tailored measurement, made his cestas by the dozen. He had none of the personal feeling for one that a ballplayer, for example, feels toward an old glove or bat. The Monarch used cestas as extravagantly as he used bath towels in the shower room. Once he had smashed nine cestas during a single thirty-point game—some by accident and some out of sheer temper.

But he made a pretense of examining it closely while, actually, he was studying to see how his legs were behaving. He stood very still, for a minute, and assured himself that his legs hadn't started any telltale trembling. He looked carefully at the back of his right hand, ridged by the tight binding of the glove cord, and noted that the hand hadn't started to swell. It

was important that he know about these things, tonight. Tonight of all
nights. He mustn't overestimate anything tonight.

He leaned back on the bench, sweating healthily, and looked up the
court. It stretched before him to the frontwall 250 feet away, its green walls
rising to the high-netted skylight of the huge auditorium. Up forward his
nimble frontwall partner, the blue-shirted Armando Martínez, walked jerkily back and forth. Down at midcourt his white-shirted opponents, Piston
and Guillermo, stood and talked things over, bobbing their heads up and
down and talking in Basque.

At his right, where the concrete of the concha floor ended in the red foul
line and met the wooden floor of the auditorium, the vertical wire screen
protected the tiers of customers. Down close to the floor level the customers stood in knots around the bookmakers, arguing and betting, and the
tiers ran sharply up to the high boxes under the eaves, where Havana
socialites and visiting Americanos del Norte sat in their boxes and drank
what the messengers brought them.

The Monarch sensed that everything was in its place, but he didn't
bother to make sure. There really wasn't anything about this jai-alai concha—or any jai-alai concha anywhere in the world—that he didn't know
all about. On this one he could about tell by the sound of the ball striking
the frontwall just about how it was going to act on the rebound. And he
could close his eyes on any part of the court and know just how many steps
he could run before he'd crash into the vertical screen. He had been at it
for twenty-five years, a quarter of a century. A long time.

Too long, he thought, just to make himself feel better about what he had
agreed to do. Had anybody else been an established professional pelotari,
or player, at the age of eleven? Had anybody else been undisputed champion for fifteen consecutive years? And wasn't he still a famous, if fading,
star at the advanced age of thirty-six? Well, then, nobody could say he
hadn't been in it long enough or given it all he had, either.

But somehow this reasoning didn't make him feel any better. The habits
of twenty-five years aren't much more easily broken than the granite of the
concha, and no matter how he argued with himself it still didn't make him
feel any easier about the fact that tonight, in what would be his last game,
he was playing crooked. His first crooked game, and his last one. Tonight
The Monarch was abdicating, stepping down after long and honorable
service. And even though nobody else in the world would ever know that
he abdicated dishonestly, that still wouldn't alter the fact that he knew it.

"I will think about all this later," he told himself. He strapped on his
cesta and walked back on the court. Guillermo—The Ox—was playing
backwall against him, and he came down the court with his short, decep-
tive steps. The Monarch watched him closely to see just how far he came.
At The Monarch's age it was wise and worthwhile to make a study of the
opponents' positions. Piston, The Ox's frontwall partner, edged over to his
own right and scowled darkly, testing the pelota which had just been
thrown into the game. Piston didn't want a pelota that was too fast. The

Monarch was thirty-six years old, but he still threw a ball like a bullet and nobody wanted to give him a fast one. Better use a slower ball and let the old devil chase it around on his tired legs.

The Monarch watched Piston trying to find a dead ball for a minute and then looked up the court for his partner, Señor Armando Martínez, belovedly hailed in the Havana press as The Cuban Flash. The Flash was sprawled out in the center of the court, arms and legs extended, in the attitude of a martyr who rests from superhuman effort. The Monarch sneered in irritation.

"Señorito," he told himself. A fancy little man. He strapped on his cesta and looked up at the scoreboard. It read: Blue 26—White 26.

"Must you wrap your life in the cover of a pelota," Miguelito Quintero had sneered at him as they sat drinking the pale Cuban beer. They had chosen a table apart from the others and Miguelito had leaned forward, talking with speed and animation while Chinita, saying nothing, studied him enigmatically with her lovely, mysterious eyes. The Monarch had listened a long while, looking from one to the other and then out across the Malecón toward the darkened ships in the harbor and the darker bulk of the Morro Castle against the ocean sky. For a moment his thoughts had wandered to the amount of treachery which had been plotted within and without those tragic old walls, and he had started a mirthless smile. Chinita had reached out and grasped his hand, pressing it a little as if to emphasize Miguelito's words.

"Don't be a Gallego all your life," Miguel had yapped. "What has the game ever done for you? Maybe you think this Cuban management will give you a nice, fat pension, now that your usefulness had ended. Or maybe you think that nobody can see that you are almost through. Maybe that's it. Or are you depending upon the Montepío to take care of you in your old age?"

It was the mention of the Montepío, which The Monarch had helped to found, that had brought him to at least partial surrender. There had been 275,000 dollars in the Montepío treasury in Barcelona at the outbreak of the Spanish Civil War. It was an accumulation of dues and fines and payments sent home by Basque jai-alai players in Mexico and Cuba and Peru and Shanghai and Manila and Florida and, also, from all over Spain. It was money which assured every old or crippled pelotari of a decent pension. Money from an organization which took care of its members and kept them honest, too. Protected them from just such treachery as was being plotted with Miguelito, and disgraced them when it couldn't protect them.

The Monarch had laughed briefly, and silently, when he had thought of that part of the Montepío treasury which was rightfully his. Where was it now, he had wondered? In some lobster's pocket. Or buying more bullets to kill more Basques. Or maybe spent for the shells which destroyed Guernica, that fine old Basque city which had sent so many fine young Basques out onto the conchas of the world.

Thinking his troubled thoughts of the Montepío, he had turned and looked at Chinita. She had lifted her head and looked fully into his face, her black and faintly slanted eyes warming him as they always did.

"There are other places in the world, my heart," she had said softly. "We could go to Mexico and watch the bullfights. Miguelito is intelligent. We must think about us, you and I."

He had hesitated only a moment or two longer, but that had been enough to win him at least a partial compromise with his conscience. Miguelito had sighed in disgust.

"Well, then," he had snapped, lighting a cigarette, "if you can't get any sense in your hard head, then listen to our second offer. Play to win, but play it our way. At least you will keep your honor"—here he had sneered faintly—"if you win, even if you win crookedly. We will have to do some other fixing and we can't make so much money this way. But we can make enough. You want to listen?"

"Estanislao," the Chinita had said softly, pleadingly.

"Tell me this other plan," The Monarch demanded. His hand had trembled a little when he poured the cold bottled beer into the glass. He wasn't sure, then or later, whether he had trembled at the realization of how badly he would soon need money or because, for the first time in his life, he was joining hands with the thieves.

Piston bounced the new pelota once or twice, ran at the serving line and rocketed a curving service against the frontwall. The ball came back on an angle and glanced off the sidewall before striking the floor. It came at The Monarch knee high and he was on it like a cat. He was going to win this point. He had to. This was one night when he had to win and lose points according to somebody else's schedule. It wasn't easy, but it had to be done.

He stopped the pelota backhanded and let the momentum of his run carry him forward. He swept his cesta shoulder high and whipped it forward sidearm, like a left-handed batter swinging at a high pitch. He hoped he had put enough spin on it to make the ball come back and strike too far forward for Guillermo to take in the air and the bounce too high from The Ox to recover.

Guillermo was playing too far forward, as usual, but he covered more ground than a cathedral. He took The Monarch's shot just as it struck the concrete and slammed it back high and hard. It carried all the way to the backwall and The Monarch, pedaling back furiously on his old legs, just managed to take it on the rebote, and send it along the sidewall past Piston's ears.

This was to be a real good point. Piston speedily took the pelota in the air, stole a crafty glance over his shoulder, and lofted midway between The Cuban Flash and The Monarch. The Cuban Flash came running back, but The Monarch shouted him off.

"Yo, yo," he yelled. He smashed a forehand shot that skidded teasingly along the wall, never bouncing off or quite curving out.

Three thousand spectators stood, their heads swiveling from right to left with the white ball. The Monarch guessed that the point lasted over two minutes before Guillermo, lunging off balance for a faulty rebote from the backwall, fouled out. This time it was Guillermo who called time. The Monarch sat on the bench and stole a look into the stands.

He could distinguish the shrill screams of the bookmakers, and he frowned, puzzled at the odds they offered. With the score 27 to 26 in favor of The Monarch and The Flash, it was strange that the odds held at even money. They ought to be more like 10 to 7. The Monarch searched the rows of seats until he saw Chinita, the soft fur coat he had bought her thrown back off the slim shoulders, and Miguelito.

Miguelito was yelling at a white-coated bookmaker who had pushed his red beret off his sweating forehead, screamed some reply and held up nine fingers. The bookmaker tucked a slip of paper in a hollow rubber ball and tossed it up into the stands. Miguelito caught it deftly, removed the slip, wadded some money inside and tossed it back.

Well, The Monarch considered, he had just seen another payment made on the farm or whatever it was which would occupy him the rest of his days. He and Chinita could live easily . . .

It was funny, though, why the odds were staying the way they were. He couldn't understand.

"Never mind who we have to fix," Miguelito had said that night at the café. "Just don't get more than one point ahead after the 26 tanto. Keep it exactly even, losing and winning, losing and winning, until the last point. Then just play anyway you like. You won't lose the last point and your precious conscience will be clear. If you won't make a lot of money by losing, at least make some money doing what we tell you."

Riding home in the big car which wasn't yet paid for, Chinita had sighed happily and rubbed her sleek head against the hard muscles of his shoulder. Driving through the soft night he had thought of the thirty-four pelotaris in Manila, Basques all, and wondered if they were in prison or hiding in the hills or dead.

"It is no use," he had told himself. "Pelota is dead along with the Basque homeland, its songs and language and its freedom. What matters if I drive one more nail into a dead man's coffin? What matters a little evil when there is so much evil?"

*   *   *

He sighed, a tired man's sigh, and returned to the court. His partner prepared to serve. The Monarch tested the ball briefly. This was one of the points he didn't want to play, one of the crooked ones. His legs began to tremble. The white ball was in play with a sound like a shot.

The Monarch made two easy returns, watched The Flash make a nice play on one of Piston's murderous angle shots and then, purposely misjudging a rebote from the backwall, threw a "cripple" to Guillermo. The Ox took it like a delighted kid. He smashed an angled return which hit the backwall just where it joined the floor and skipped out safely clear of The Monarch's basket.

It was: Blue 27–White 27.

He took his position again and accepted Piston's service. Guillermo took The Monarch's next smash in the air and threw a low ball which came straight back at Martínez.

"Dale candela, chaval," he shouted. "Give it a hit, kid." The kid gave it his best, sending an angle shot skipping at Piston's ankles. Piston somehow made a recovery.

A real good boy, Piston. But then all Basques were real good boys. He lowered his head and started for the backwall to take a floating rebote. He got his basket on the ball, pivoted hard, like a hammer thrower, and sent a high shot forward with all the spin he could put on it.

Guillermo had backed up to take a straight smash and saw his mistake just a half step too late.

The scoreboard changed to White 28–Blue 27.

Again The Monarch felt his legs tremble as the ball went into play. This was to be another crooked point. Fortunately he didn't have to worry about it. The Cuban Flash, trying to outslug the catlike Piston in a duel of angle shots, was badly outsmarted. So the point was lost honestly, after all. The score was 28 to 28.

One more equalization, The Monarch told himself. One more igualana and then the final tanto; he wished he could stop now. He would like to leave things just as they were. He didn't want to have to think about crookedly losing another point. He called time and sat down.

Chinita, he thought fondly. He remembered when he had first seen her sitting alone in the stands and had sent a boy with a message. When the boy returned with the news that she had ripped the note to shreds without even opening it, he was delighted. It had reassured him, he who had reason to be cynical about lone women in tropical countries. He had inquired about to find somebody who knew her and, surprisingly, Guillermo knew her.

Her name was Maraquita Valdez. Guillermo understood there was a trace of Chinese in her ancestry. What did she do? Guillermo had been evasive.

A lifetime of strict physical discipline had brought The Monarch no sophistication or subtlety. But his life was lonely, and lately the loneliness seemed more important than in earlier, happier days. It wasn't long before he decided this woman with the exciting, exotic eyes was the one thing in the world he wanted and was determined to have.

There had been times when Guillermo and Piston and other old Basque friends had haltingly tried to discourage the romance. The Monarch had laughed. Let the Basques have their old-fashioned moral codes. That was about all a Basque had left. He had the girl with the pointed eyes, the sleek beauty, the subtle fire which struck right into his tired and battered body.

He pulled himself out of his reverie. Guillermo was standing in front of him, talking.

"I say it again," Guillermo repeated, spitting contemptuously, "that Piston and I do not talk with our mouths no matter what we think with our heads. So tell us how you are going to do it and we will make some money on the point-by-point betting, too."

The Monarch felt his back go rigid and the hot sweat on the back of his neck suddenly turned cold. He stood up quickly, his green eyes narrowing quickly under the heavy black brows and his square head thrust forward. He reached out, apparently carelessly, and grasped The Ox's left arm in a vise of thick fingers.

Suddenly, like the crooked pieces of a puzzle falling into place by themselves, he knew what it was that had been making him uneasy. If he was playing this game crookedly to win, then somebody else was playing it crookedly to lose. He realized that it was Piston and Guillermo.

"No Dios ni Hostia," he said aloud, in wonder. He was a fool; neither God nor the Holy Ghost could induce those two Basques to lose a game crookedly.

"Guillermo," he said quickly, "for the sake of our years together, tell me what you know."

Guillermo's eyes widened.

"What I know?" he sneered. "Listen to the odds. You, the great Estanislao Amuchastegui, have the partido at 28 to 28 and the apostadores, the bookmakers, make Piston and me 10 to 7 favorite? What else is there to know, when your woman and a common gambler sit in the stands and bet your money against you?"

"Bet how?" The Monarch snarled his question.

"Bet against you, you foolish old goat," Guillermo said, contempt in his voice. "Do you pretend that you do not know this?"

"Give me a minute," The Monarch said, sitting down slowly on the bench. It couldn't be, he thought, but it was. He could hear the cries of the bookmakers. The odds had changed to 10 to 6 in favor of Guillermo and Piston . . . 10 to 6 against The Monarch.

Footsteps came padding at him and as he looked up, his partner, the señor Armando Martínez, came back and made a pretense of washing out his mouth. Guillermo moved away. Martínez spoke softly, insinuatingly, hardly moving his lips.

"Monarca," he said in his soft Cuban blur, "when comes the final tanto, let me play the first return. I have the instructions." He spit water off the court and walked jerkily away.

The Monarch thought he walked crookedly. Yes! The last crooked piece in the crooked puzzle.

They had him in the middle, all right. It would be the Cuban Flash who lost the final tanto, the last point. But the talk, when it started, would not be of the final tanto. The talk would be about the money bet by The Monarch's girl and by the professional gambler. Money bet by people close to The Monarch and bet against him, bet against him from the start.

He had been smartly swindled by a woman and a gambling thief, like poor Argarate that time in Mexico. He, The Monarch.

"Manolo," he called sharply. The young mulatto came running with a paper water cup which looked like any other paper cup full of water. The Monarch drained the draught of Spanish brandy. Passing behind Guillermo, he spoke rapidly in Basque.

"As a favor, chaval," he said. "Throw me just one rebote."

Guillermo's face was impassive and the ball went into play. Piston and the Cuban kept it up around the front wall for four returns and Guillermo took it and arched a high, floating shot to the backwall. The Monarch turned and waited for the rebound.

It came off the backwall and he took the ball backhand in his cesta and pivoted hard. Midway through his pivot he let his right leg, the one which had been injured, collapse under him. Before he fell, twisting, to the floor, he sent the rockhard pelota flying up the court as hard as he could.

It carried straight, not more than a foot above the floor, and struck Armando Martínez just below the knee. The Monarch, lying sprawled on the court, could hear the bone break. Then he arose and joined Piston and Guillermo over the injured Flash.

"An accident," he said in concern. "My old knee again."

It was: White 29–Blue 28.

The referee, came lumbering down, staring at The Monarch.

"You know the rules. You can stop and this is the final score. Or you can play it out alone."

"We play it out," he said.

"You old goat," Piston cried, "you haven't seen a day in ten years you could beat us alone."

"We play it out," he repeated.

"Well, then, hurry it up." Estévez told him. Lumbering over to the wire screen, he told an attendant to make the announcement. The stands roared and the odds rose to 10 to 3.

"Come on," The Monarch said furiously to Piston. "Throw the ball. Let's see how good you are."

Piston bounced the pelota twice, ran at the serving line, twisted, and made his service.

It came back truly and The Monarch ran forward. Piston had given him a fair serve, instead of sending it up the court where his partner should be, and Guillermo made a return as hard as he could. No fancy tricks. They weren't going to give him anything crookedly easy, but they weren't going to make it crookedly hard for him either.

They were good, honest boys. He arched his broad back and smashed away.

Maybe he was washed up; maybe it was time he quit. But he would quit the way he had always done everything, putting everything he had into it. Maybe he could even salvage this game at the final tanto. He only had to win this one and then win one more. He made a nice pickup and told himself that winning was what he was used to. Winning was easy for him. He laughed aloud when he thought of what Miguelito and the slant-eyed woman were thinking and saying or doing. Whatever they were doing, they weren't going to have time enough to do all the necessary undoing. He slammed a backhand shot as hard as he had ever slammed one in his life.

The score: Blue 29–White 29.

He took the ball to serve and laughed again. The final tanto. The last point. He didn't bother to look to see just where his opponents were playing. He'd play this final tanto the way he had always played it. He was The Monarch, wasn't he? The Champion. The greatest since . . .

He grunted and sent the service up against the frontwall.

He felt wonderful . . .

THE TOURNAMENT
By Sir Walter Scott

In the midst of Prince John's cavalcade, he suddenly stopt, and appealing to the Prior of Jorvaulx, declared the principal business of the day had been forgotten.

"By my halidom," said he, "we have forgotten, Sir Prior, to name the fair Sovereign of Love and of Beauty, by whose white hand the palm is to be distributed. For my part, I am liberal in my ideas, and I care not if I give my vote for the black-eyed Rebecca."

"Holy Virgin," answered the Prior, turning up his eyes in horror, "a Jewess!—We should deserve to be stoned out of the lists; and I am not yet old enough to be a martyr. Besides, I swear by my patron saint, that she is far inferior to the lovely Saxon, Rowena."

"Saxon or Jew," answered the Prince, "Saxon or Jew, dog or hog, what matters it? I say, name Rebecca, were it only to mortify the Saxon churls."

A murmur arose even among his own immediate attendants.

"This passes a jest, my lord," said De Bracy; "no knight here will lay lance in rest if such an insult is attempted."

"It is the mere wantonness of insult," said one of the oldest and most important of Prince John's followers, Waldemar Fitzurse, "and if your Grace attempts it, cannot but prove ruinous to your projects."

"I entertained you, sir," said John, reining up his palfrey haughtily, "for my follower, but not for my counsellor."

"Those who follow your Grace in the paths which you tread," said Waldemar, but speaking in a low voice, "acquire the right of counsellors; for your interest and safety are not more deeply engaged than their own."

From the tone in which this was spoken, John saw the necessity of acquiescence. "I did but jest," he said; "and you turn upon me like so many adders! Name whom you will, in the fiend's name, and please yourselves."

"Nay, nay," said De Bracy, "let the fair sovereign's throne remain unoccupied, until the conqueror shall be named, and then let him choose the lady by whom it shall be filled. It will add another grace to his triumph,

and teach fair ladies to prize the love of valiant knights, who can exalt
them to such distinction.''

"If Brian de Bois-Guilbert gain the prize," said the Prior, "I will gage
my rosary that I name the Sovereign of Love and Beauty."

"Bois-Guilbert," answered De Bracy, "is a good lance; but there are
others around these lists, Sir Prior, who will not fear to encounter him."

"Silence, sirs," said Waldemar, "and let the Prince assume his seat.
The knights and spectators are alike impatient, the time advances, and
highly fit it is that the sports should commence."

Prince John, though not yet a monarch, had in Waldemar Fitzurse all the
inconveniences of a favourite minister, who, in serving his sovereign, must
always do so in his own way. The Prince acquiesced, however, although his
disposition was precisely of that kind which is apt to be obstinate upon
trifles, and, assuming his throne, and being surrounded by his followers,
gave signal to the heralds to proclaim the laws of the tournament, which
were briefly as follows:—

First, the five challengers were to undertake all comers.

Secondly, any knight proposing to combat, might, if he pleased, select a
special antagonist from among the challengers, by touching his shield. If
he did so with the reverse of his lance, the trial of skill was made with what
were called the arms of courtesy, that is, with lances at whose extremity a
piece of round flat board was fixed, so that no danger was encountered,
save from the shock of the horses and riders. But if the shield was touched
with the sharp end of the lance, the combat was understood to be at
outrance; that is, the knights were to fight with sharp weapons, as in actual
battle.

Thirdly, when the knights present had accomplished their vow, by each
of them breaking five lances, the Prince was to declare the victor in the first
day's tourney, who should receive as prize a warhorse of exquisite beauty
and matchless strength; and in addition to this reward of valour, it was now
declared, he should have the peculiar honour of naming the Queen of Love
and Beauty, by whom the prize should be given on the ensuing day.

Fourthly, it was announced, that, on the second day, there should be a
general tournament, in which all the knights present, who were desirous to
win praise, might take part; and being divided into two bands of equal
numbers, might fight it out manfully, until the signal was given by Prince
John to cease the combat. The elected Queen of Love and Beauty was then
to crown the knight whom the Prince should adjudge to have borne himself
best in the second day, with a coronet composed of thin gold plate, cut into
the shape of a laurel crown. On this second day the knightly games ceased.
But on that which was to follow, feats of archery, of bull-baiting, and other
popular amusements, were to be practiced, for the more immediate amuse-
ment of the populace. In this manner did Prince John endeavour to lay the
foundation of a popularity, which he was perpetually throwing down by
some inconsiderate act of wanton aggression upon the feelings and prejudices of the people.

The lists now presented a most splendid spectacle. The sloping galleries were crowded with all that was noble, great, wealthy, and beautiful in the northern and midland parts of England; and the contrast of the various dresses of these dignified spectators, rendered the view as gay as it was rich, while the interior and lower space, filled with the substantial burgesses and yeomen of merry England, formed, in their more plain attire, a dark fringe, or border, around this circle of brilliant embroidery, relieving, and, at the same time, setting off its splendour.

The heralds finished their proclamation with their usual cry of "Largesse, largesse, gallant knights!" and gold and silver pieces were showered on them from the galleries, it being a high point of chivalry to exhibit liberality towards those whom the age accounted at once the secretaries and the historians of honour. The bounty of the spectators was acknowledged by the customary shouts of "Love of Ladies—Death of Champions—Honour to the Generous—Glory to the Brave!"—to which the more humble spectators added their acclamations, and a numerous band of trumpeters the flourish of their martial instruments. When these sounds had ceased, the heralds withdrew from the lists in gay and glittering procession, and none remained within them save the marshals of the field, who, armed cap-a-pie, sat on horseback, motionless as statues, at the opposite ends of the lists. Meantime, the enclosed space at the northern extremity of the lists, large as it was, was now completely crowded with knights desirous to prove their skill against the challengers, and, when viewed from the galleries, presented the appearance of a sea of waving plumage, intermixed with glistening helmets, and tall lances, to the extremities of which were, in many cases, attached small pennons of about a span's breadth, which, fluttering in the air as the breeze caught them, joined with the restless motion of the feathers to add liveliness to the scene.

At length the barriers were opened, and five knights, chosen by lot, advanced slowly into the area; a single champion riding in front, and the other four following in pairs. All were splendidly armed, and my Saxon authority (in the Wardour Manuscript) records at great length their devices, their colours, and the embroidery of their horse trappings. It is unnecessary to be particular on these subjects. To borrow lines from a contemporary poet, who has written but too little—

> The knights are dust,
> And their good swords are rust,
> Their souls are with the saints, we trust.[1]

---

[1] These lines are part of an unpublished poem by Coleridge, whose Muse so often tantalizes with fragments which indicate her powers, while the manner in which she flings them from her betrays her caprice, yet whose unfinished sketches display more talent than the laboured masterpieces of others.

Their escutcheons have long mouldered from the walls of their castles. Their castles themselves are but green mounds and shattered ruins—the place that once knew them, knows them no more—nay, many a race since theirs has died out and been forgotten in the very land which they occupied, with all the authority of feudal proprietors and feudal lords. What, then, would it avail the reader to know their names, or the evanescent symbols of their martial rank!

Now, however, no whit anticipating the oblivion which awaited their names and feats, the champions advanced through the lists, restraining their fiery steeds, and compelling them to move slowly, while, at the same time, they exhibited their paces, together with the grace and dexterity of the riders. As the procession entered the lists, the sound of a wild Barbaric music was heard from behind the tents of the challengers, where the performers were concealed. It was of Eastern origin, having been brought from the Holy Land; and the mixture of the cymbals and bells seemed to bid welcome at once, and defiance, to the knights as they advanced. With the eyes of an immense concourse of spectators fixed upon them, the five knights advanced up the platform upon which the tents of the challengers stood, and there separating themselves, each touched slightly, and with the reverse of his lance, the shield of the antagonist to whom he wished to oppose himself. The lower orders of spectators in general—nay, many of the higher class, and it is even said several of the ladies, were rather disappointed at the champions choosing the arms of courtesy. For the same sort of persons, who, in the present day, applaud most highly the deepest tragedies, were then interested in a tournament exactly in proportion to the danger incurred by the champions engaged.

Having intimated their more pacific purpose, the champions retreated to the extremity of the lists, where they remained drawn up in a line; while the challengers, sallying each from his pavilion, mounted their horses, and, headed by Brian de Bois-Guilbert, descended from the platform, and opposed themselves individually to the knights who had touched their respective shields.

At the flourish of clarions and trumpets, they started out against each other at full gallop; and such was the superior dexterity or good fortune of the challengers, that those opposed to Bois-Guilbert, Malvoisin, and Front-de-Boeuf, rolled on the ground. The antagonist of Grantmesnil, instead of bearing his lance-point fair against the crest or the shield of his enemy, swerved so much from the direct line as to break the weapon athwart the person of his opponent—a circumstance which was accounted more disgraceful than that of being actually unhorsed; because the latter might happen from accident, whereas the former evinced awkwardness and want of management of the weapon and of the horse. The fifth knight alone maintained the honour of his party, and parted fairly with the Knight of St. John, both splintering their lances without advantage on either side.

The shouts of the multitude, together with the acclamations of the heralds, and the clangour of the trumpets, announced the triumph of the victors and the defeat of the vanquished. The former retreated to their pavilions, and the latter, gathering themselves up as they could, withdrew from the lists in disgrace and dejection, to agree with their victors concerning the redemption of their arms and their horses, which, according to the laws of the tournament, they had forfeited. The fifth of their number alone tarried in the lists long enough to be greeted by the applauses of the spectators, amongst whom he retreated, to the aggravation, doubtless, of his companions' mortification.

A second and a third party of knights took the field; and although they had various success, yet, upon the whole, the advantage decidedly remained with the challengers, not one of whom lost his seat or swerved from his charge—misfortunes which befell one or two of their antagonists in each encounter. The spirits, therefore, of those opposed to them, seemed to be considerably damped by their continued success. Three knights only appeared on the fourth entry, who, avoiding the shields of Bois-Guilbert and Front-de-Boeuf, contented themselves with touching those of the three other knights, who had not altogether manifested the same strength and dexterity. This politic section did not alter the fortune of the field, the challengers were still successful; one of their antagonists was overthrown, and both the others failed in the *attaint*,[2] that is, in striking the helmet and shield of their antagonist firmly and strongly, with the lance held in a direct line, so that the weapon might break unless the champion was overthrown.

After this fourth encounter, there was a considerable pause; nor did it appear that any one was very desirous of renewing the contest. The spectators murmured among themselves; for, among the challengers, Malvoisin and Front-de-Boeuf were unpopular from their characters, and the others, except Grantmesnil, were disliked as strangers and foreigners.

But none shared the general feeling of dissatisfaction so keenly as Cedric the Saxon, who saw, in each advantage gained by the Norman challengers, a repeated triumph over the honour of England. His own education had taught him no skill in the games of chivalry, although, with the arms of his Saxon ancestors, he had manifested himself, on many occasions, a brave and determined soldier. He looked anxiously to Athelstane, who had learned the accomplishments of the age, as if desiring that he should make some personal effort to recover the victory which was passing into the hands of the Templar and his associates. But, though both stout of heart, and strong of person, Athelstane had a disposition too inert and unambitious to make the exertions which Cedric seemed to expect from him.

"The day is against England, my lord," said Cedric, in a marked tone; "are you not tempted to take the lance?"

"I shall tilt to-morrow," answered Athelstane, "in the *mêlée;* it is not worth while for me to arm myself to-day."

[2] This term of chivalry, transferred to the law, gives the phrase of being attainted by treason.

Two things displeased Cedric in this speech. It contained the Norman word *mêlée,* (to express the general conflict,) and it evinced some indifference to the honour of the country; but it was spoken by Athelstane, whom he held in such profound respect, that he would not trust himself to canvass his motives or his foibles. Moreover, he had no time to make any remark, for Wamba thrust in his word, observing, "It was better, though scarce easier, to be the best man among a hundred, than the best man of two."

Athelstane took the observation as a serious compliment; but Cedric, who better understood the Jester's meaning, darted at him a severe and menacing look; and lucky it was for Wamba, perhaps, that the time and place prevented his receiving, not withstanding his place and service, more sensible marks of his master's resentment.

The pause in the tournament was still uninterrupted, excepting by the voices of the heralds exclaiming—"Love of ladies, splintering of lances! stand forth, gallant knights, fair eyes look upon your deeds!"

The music also of the challengers breathed from time to time wild bursts expressive of triumph or defiance, while the clowns grudged a holiday which seemed to pass away in inactivity; and old knights and nobles lamented in whispers the decay of martial spirit, spoke of the triumphs of their younger days, but agreed that the land did not now supply dames of such transcendent beauty as had animated the jousts of former times. Prince John began to talk to his attendants about making ready the banquet, and the necessity of adjudging the prize to Brian de Bois-Guilbert, who had, with a single spear, overthrown two knights, and foiled a third.

At length, as the Saracenic music of the challengers concluded one of those long and high flourishes with which they had broken the silence of the lists, it was answered by a solitary trumpet, which breathed a note of defiance from the northern extremity. All eyes were turned to see the new champion which these sounds announced, and no sooner were the barriers opened than he paced into the lists. As far as could be judged of a man sheathed in armour, the new adventurer did not greatly exceed the middle size, and seemed to be rather slender than strongly made. His suit of armour was formed of steel, richly inlaid with gold, and the device on his shield was a young oak-tree pulled up by the roots, with the Spanish word *Desdichado,* signifying Disinherited. He was mounted on a gallant black horse, and as he passed through the lists he gracefully saluted the Prince and the ladies by lowering his lance. The dexterity with which he managed his steed, and something of youthful grace which he displayed in his manner, won him the favour of the multitude, which some of the lower classes expressed by calling out "Touch Ralph de Vipont's shield—touch the Hospitaller's shield; he has the least sure seat, he is your cheapest bargain."

The champion, moving onward amid these well-meant hints, ascended the platform by the sloping alley which led to it from the lists, and, to the astonishment of all present, riding straight up to the central pavilion, struck with the sharp end of his spear the shield of Brian de Bois-Guilbert until it rung again. All stood astonished at his presumption, but none more than the redoubted Knight whom he had thus defied to mortal combat, and who, little expecting so rude a challenge, was standing carelessly at the door of the pavilion.

"Have you confessed yourself, brother," said the Templar, "and have you heard mass this morning, that you peril your life so frankly?"

"I am fitter to meet death than thou art," answered the Disinherited Knight; for by this name the stranger had recorded himself in the books of the tourney.

"Then take your place in the lists," said Bois-Guilbert, "and look your last upon the sun; for this night thou shalt sleep in paradise."

"Gramercy for thy courtesy," replied the Disinherited Knight; "and to requite it, I advise thee to take a fresh horse and a new lance, for by my honour you will need both."

Having expressed himself thus confidently, he reined his horse backward down the slope which he had ascended, and compelled him in the same manner to move backward through the lists, till he reached the northern extremity, where he remained stationary, in expectation of his antagonist. This feat of horsemanship again attracted the applause of the multitude.

However incensed at his adversary for the precautions which he recommended, Brian de Bois-Guilbert did not neglect his advice; for his honour was too nearly concerned, to permit his neglecting any means which might ensure victory over his presumptuous opponent. He changed his horse for a proved and fresh one of great strength and spirit. He chose a new and a tough spear, lest the wood of the former might have been strained in the previous encounters he had sustained. Lastly, he laid aside his shield, which had received some little damage, and received another from his squires. His first had only borne the general device of his rider, representing two knights riding upon one horse, an emblem expressive of the original humility and poverty of the Templars, qualities which they had since exchanged for the arrogance and wealth that finally occasioned their suppression. Bois-Guilbert's new shield bore a raven in full flight, holding in its claws a skull, and bearing the motto, *Gare le Corbeau.*

When the two champions stood opposed to each other at the two extremities of the lists, the public expectation was strained to the highest pitch. Few argued the possibility that the encounter could terminate well for the Disinherited Knight, yet his courage and gallantry secured the general good wishes of the spectators.

The trumpets had no sooner given the signal, than the champions vanished from their posts with the speed of lightning, and closed in the centre of the lists with the shock of a thunderbolt. The lances burst into shivers up to the very grasp, and it seemed at the moment that both knights had fallen, for the shock had made each horse recoil backwards upon its haunches. The address of the riders recovered their steeds by use of the bridle and spur; and having glared on each other for an instant with eyes which seemed to flash fire through the bars of their visors, each made a demi-volte, and, retiring to the extremity of the lists, received a fresh lance from the attendants.

A loud shout from the spectators, waving of scarfs and handkerchiefs, and general acclamations, attested the interest taken by the spectators in this encounter; the most equal, as well as the best performed, which had graced the day. But no sooner had the knights resumed their station, than the clamour of applause was hushed into a silence, so deep and so dead, that it seemed the multitude were afraid even to breathe.

A few minutes' pause having been allowed, that the combatants and their horses might recover breath, Prince John with his truncheon signed to the trumpets to sound the onset. The champions a second time sprung from their stations, and closed in the centre of the lists, with the same speed, the same dexterity, the same violence, but not the same equal fortune as before.

In this second encounter, the Templar aimed at the centre of his antago-nist's shield, and struck it so fair and forcibly, that his spear went to shivers, and the Disinherited Knight reeled in his saddle. On the other hand, that champion had, in the beginning of his career, directed the point of his lance towards Bois-Guilbert's shield, but, changing his aim almost in the moment of encounter, he addressed it to the helmet, a mark more difficult to hit, but which, if attained, rendered the shock more irresistible. Fair and true he hit the Norman on the visor, where his lance's point kept hold of the bars. Yet, even at this disadvantage, the Templar sustained his high reputation; and had not the girths of his saddle burst, he might not have been unhorsed. As it chanced, however, saddle, horse, and man, rolled on the ground under a cloud of dust.

To extricate himself from the stirrups and fallen steed, was to the Tem-plar scarce the work of a moment; and, stung with madness, both at his disgrace and at the acclamations with which it was hailed by the specta-tors, he drew his sword and waved it in defiance of his conqueror. The Disinherited Knight sprung from his steed, and also unsheathed his sword. The marshals of the field, however, spurred their horses between them, and reminded them, that the laws of the tournament did not, on the present occasion, permit this species of encounter.

"We shall meet again, I trust," said the Templar, casting a resentful glance at his antagonist; "and where there are none to separate us."

"If we do not," said the Disinherited Knight, "the fault shall not be mine. On foot or horseback, with spear, with axe, or with sword, I am alike ready to encounter thee."

More and angrier words would have been exchanged, but the marshals, crossing their lances betwixt them, compelled them to separate. The Disin-herited Knight returned to his first station, and Bois-Guilbert to his tent, where he remained for the rest of the day in an agony of despair.

Without alighting from his horse, the conqueror called for a bowl of wine, and opening the beaver, or lower part of his helmet, announced that he quaffed it, "To all true English hearts, and to the confusion of foreign tyrants." He then commanded his trumpet to sound a defiance to the challengers, and desired a herald to announce to them, that he should make no election, but was willing to encounter them in the order in which they pleased to advance against him.

The gigantic Front-de-Boeuf, armed in sable armour, was the first who took the field. He bore on a white shield a black bull's head, half defaced by the numerous encounters which he had undergone, and bearing the arrogant motto, *Cave, adsum.* Over this champion the Disinherited Knight obtained a slight but decisive advantage. Both Knights broke their lances fairly, but Front-de-Boeuf, who lost a stirrup in the encounter, was adjudged to have the disadvantage.

In the stranger's third encounter with Sir Philip Malvoisin, he was equally successful; striking that baron so forcibly on the casque, that the laces of the helmet broke, and Malvoisin, only saved from falling by being unhelmeted, was declared vanquished like his companions.

In his fourth combat with De Grantmesnil, the Disinherited Knight shewed as much courtesy as he had hitherto evinced courage and dexterity. De Grantmesnil's horse, which was young and violent, reared and plunged in the course of the career so as to disturb the rider's aim, and the stranger, declining to take the advantage which this accident afforded him, raised his lance, and passing his antagonist without touching him, wheeled his horse and rode back again to his own end of the lists, offering his antagonist, by a herald, the chance of a second encounter. This De Grantmesnil declined, avowing himself vanquished as much by the courtesy as by the address of his opponent.

Ralph de Vipont summed up the list of the stranger's triumphs, being hurled to the ground with such force, that the blood gushed from his nose and his mouth, and he was borne senseless from the lists.

The acclamations of thousands applauded the unanimous award of the Prince and marshals, announcing that day's honours to the Disinherited Knight.

LEGENDS OF KARATE

By George E. Mattson

Until the present time there has been very little written about karate. All of the history was passed down from master to student by word of mouth. Much of the history was in the form of stories. Some of these stories had a moral behind them while others simply related experiences of the masters in China. Many times the masters would tell a story to clear up a certain point or to stress an important point. Following are some of the stories that were told to me while I was studying karate in Okinawa.

The Old Man and the Tiger

When Mr. Uechi, Sr., was studying karate in China sixty years ago, the Chinese people had few ways of protecting themselves other than with their bare hands. Because the people were relatively helpless in an emergency, they depended upon the karate masters for protection. The village karate master was called upon in any situation that would require someone with authority.

Mr. Uechi and his teacher were training one evening at home when a group of farmers from the outskirts of the village hurried to tell the teacher of their latest trouble. A huge man-eating tiger had come down from the mountains and was killing the livestock. The farmers pleaded with the teacher to help them kill the tiger. Mr. Uechi believed that the teacher was too old to attempt such a feat, so he volunteered himself for the job.

When Mr. Uechi said that he would go alone to slay the tiger, the teacher said that the task would require two men and he too would go. That night they set out to deal with the tiger.

At daybreak they arrived at the spot where the tiger had last struck. Mr. Uechi tied a small lamb to a post, and then the two men stood back to back about three feet from the lamb to begin their wait for the tiger. The teacher appeared calm and ready, but Mr. Uechi was a bit upset at the thought of the huge man-eating tiger lurking somewhere in the woods. The plan was to remain until the tiger attacked the lamb. The two men would then attempt to kill the tiger by striking it in the heart with a knuckle strike. Being back to back, the two men would not fall victim to a surprise attack. The day passed slowly, and both men grew quite weary. Mr. Uechi was now afraid that he would be too tired to fight the tiger if it attacked.

Suddenly they heard a movement in the woods. As it came closer, Mr. Uechi immediately became ready. He assumed a sanchin stance and prepared himself for the attack. Instead of a tiger, an old man with a flowing white beard walked into the clearing. He asked the two men why they were standing as they were. The teacher told the old man about the tiger and advised him to find a place of protection until it was killed.

The old man smiled and said that he had killed the tiger a short time before. He pointed back toward the woods in the direction from which he had come. Mr. Uechi and the teacher thought the old man was crazy, for how could an old man possibly kill a tiger that was three times as large as he?

Mr. Uechi asked the old man his name, and the old man started to walk away, detecting the sarcasm and disbelief in the tone of Mr. Uechi's voice. Mr. Uechi again asked the old man his name. This time the old man turned and said: "Never mind what my name is." Saying this, he walked into the woods.

The two men walked into the woods in the direction that the old man had indicated. About a quarter of a mile along the path they came to a clearing. Both men stared in amazement, for on the ground lay the dead tiger, just as the old man had said. The men examined the animal for weapon marks but could find none. Mr. Uechi turned the tiger over and saw that the animal's back had left an impression in the ground an inch deep.

The two men only guessed at what had happened, but it seemed sure that the tiger's back had been broken. Apparently the tiger had jumped the old man from the rear, and he had grabbed the animal's fore-feet and thrown it over his shoulder, snapping its back as he did. The deep imprint in the ground indicated that the old man must have possessed great strength and speed.

Mr. Uechi believed that the old man was a monk and a great karate master from another province. Neither Mr. Uechi nor his teacher ever saw him or heard of him again.

The Bluff

When karate was at its height in China about two hundred years ago, there was much rivalry among the masters. Usually the teachers would remain in their own districts and would not attempt to set up schools where another karate master was already teaching, but this was not always the case.

A young karate student who was exceptionally good at karate believed that he was better than any master and was set to prove it. He decided to take a trip to a nearby province where an old master was teaching. The young man knew that the only way he could prove to himself that he was tougher than the master was to fight him. The young man also knew it was next to impossible to provoke a master into a fight, so he devised a plan which he believed would make the master angry enough to fight.

The master lived at the top of a hill in a small home with his wife and three children. The season was fall, and the master and his family had just completed working in his garden, picking beans. The master was drying the beans on a blanket of grass on both sides of a path at the side of his house. The arrogant student believed that he could provoke the master into a fight by the following plan. He would carry a pole long enough to extend over both sides of the path alongside the master's house and would carry buckets filled with manure at both ends of the pole. When he reached the master's house, he would jostle the pole enough to spill the manure over the master's beans. "This," thought the student, "will surely get the master fighting mad, and then I will show him who is stronger."

When the student reached the master's house, he began to shake the manure over the master's beans and succeeded in making the master come running from his house. "What are you doing?" exclaimed the master. "Do you not realize that my family and I must eat these beans that you are so thoughtlessly ruining?"

"Yes, I realize that," said the student, "but I will continue to do what I am doing because you are not man enough to stop me."

The master smiled to himself, knowing now that this overconfident young man was a karate student who had not been trained properly and was now trying to prove his ability by fighting with him.

When the master smiled at the student, the student became enraged. "Why are you afraid to fight me?" he asked. "Are you afraid that you will lose respect in your village, or is it that you are just afraid?"

The master still said nothing but again smiled at the student.

The young man, now in a frenzy, dropped the buckets from the pole and held the pole in front of the master, saying that he was stronger than any man in China. He twisted the pole with all his might until it broke. He then threw the broken pole at the master's feet, saying: "You had better leave this area immediately, because I am going to start teaching karate here. You are an old man and should feel lucky that I do not beat you up before making you leave."

The master did not say a word but turned around and walked into the house. The student was elated that he had won this battle with a karate master who had the reputation of being one of the greatest masters in China. He felt that he surely proved that he was the strongest man in China.

The student was surprised when he saw the master come back carrying a large bamboo pole twice the size of the one he had just broken. The old man smiled as he offered the pole to the student, saying: "You are a strong young man. You have impressed me so much with your strength that I feel you will be able to break this pole also.''

The student took the pole and began to twist it. He twisted with all his might, but to no avail. For fifteen minutes he tugged, twisted, and pulled. He finally gave up, exhausted. He dropped the pole to the ground, saying that it was an impossible task. No human being could break this pole.

No sooner had the words been said than the old man picked up the pole and, with a tremendous twist, broke it in two. He smiled as he gave the two pieces to the young man and said: "Go back to your master and tell him to train your mind as well as he has trained your body. Then come back to visit me as a friend when you are able to duplicate this senseless feat of strength, so that we may smile together over your youthful and unwise act." The master then turned and walked back to his home and family.

The student went back to his master and began to study karate as the old man had advised.

The Lesson

Many of the stories of karate relate incidents concerning young men who had the wrong idea of karate. In these stories the young men usually learn a lesson in conduct and in respect.

A young man who had been studying karate for three years began using his knowledge to terrorize the people of a nearby village. Every week he would go into this village and bully people by pushing them around or beating them up if they resisted him in any way.

One afternoon while he was making his rounds of the taverns and market places of the village, he happened to bump into an old man who was stooped with age. The old man nearly fell over. Instead of helping him to his feet, the boy turned to the old man and said: "Why don't you watch where you are going? Do you not know better than to bump into me?"

The old man told him that he should be more respectful of his elders and should not be such a bully. At this the young man began to shout abuses and threats at the old man. He told him that he was crazy and stupid.

The old man was standing now, and he was again in the young man's path. The boy yelled at him again, telling him to get out of his way. The old man, however, told him that he should help him to his destination rather than ask him to move aside. At this the boy nearly exploded. He grabbed the old man, saying that he would teach him to respect the strong and that when he had finished with him the old man would know better than to ever talk back to him again.

There followed a one-sided battle in which the young man believed that he was nearly killing the old man. Punches and kicks flew to all parts of the old man's body until finally he was lying still on the ground. The boy was jubilant, for the old man had been able to strike him only once near the heart with a weak blow. So light was the blow that he could hardly feel it.

The boy left the spot where the old man was lying and returned to his village.

A group of people who had witnessed the incident rushed to the old man and offered to help him, but he got up without any help, stood up straight, and walked briskly to his home.

About two weeks after the incident, the boy began to feel strange. He felt nauseated after all his meals, and he could not sleep well. After five weeks, he could not hold anything in his stomach. By the end of six weeks he had lost twenty pounds and was nearly dead. He then knew that the old man had done this to him. He now realized that what he had done was wrong, and he wished that he could be forgiven by the old man. Feeling certain that he was going to die, the boy sent his brother to search for the old man.

The old man had left word in the town of his whereabouts, as if he knew that the boy would try to contact him. The boy's brother found him the next day. Together they went to the boy's home.

When the boy saw the old man, he begged forgiveness for all the things he had done. The old man, seeing that the boy was truly sorry, told him that he would help his condition. He gave the boy some liquid to drink, and soon after that the boy was asleep. In a week he was on his feet again and feeling much better.

The old man then told the boy that the village people had sent for him from another district to cope with the young man. He also told the boy that he was a karate teacher. The boy immediately begged the old man to take him as student. The old man accepted him, and the boy became his best student.

Mr. Uechi, Sr. and the Bandits

Shortly before Mr. Uechi, Sr., came back to Okinawa, he went to visit all of his friends. On one such visit, which took him deep into a wooded area infested with bandits, he found occasion to use his karate.

When it came time for Mr. Uechi to return home, the hour was late. His friend urged him to stay the night because of the dangerous bandits that lurked along the path. Mr. Uechi had to be in his village the following morning, so he had to decline the invitation.

Walking along the wooded path, he was confronted by five bandits who demanded all his money. "I have no money, kind sirs, so please let me pass," said Mr. Uechi.

The leader of the bandits, a burly, rough-looking fellow, said: "If you have no money, we will take your clothes." Mr. Uechi replied that he would need his clothes to protect him from the insects on his way home.

Hearing this, the leader was furious. "I am a karate expert and am very strong," he said. "You had better take your clothes off and do it quickly, or I will punish you severely." Again Mr. Uechi refused, and the bandit, enraged, rushed at him.

Mr. Uechi calmly deflected the powerful thrust and counterattacked with a blow that instantly killed the bandit. Looking at the other bandits, he said: "Come and pick up your leader and dispose of him. I think this is great sport. Are there any more of you who wish to take my clothes?"

There was no response, so Mr. Uechi continued: "I will travel this district every night from now on in hopes of amusing myself. The next time, do not tell me of your whereabouts. Jump me silently from behind so that you do not make defending myself so easy." Mr. Uechi then walked home.

Every night for a week he walked the road to his friend's home, but he met with no further trouble. In fact, the area had no trouble with bandits for many years after.

Mr. Uechi, Sr., studied karate as hard as any other person in China while he was there. He loved the exercises and movements, but most of all he enjoyed doing sanchin. His Chinese instructor told him that through sanchin training he would be able to perform feats of strength with his body that would appear to be impossible. He studied sanchin diligently from the time that he began his training in 1900 until he died in 1947 at the age of seventy-nine. He returned to Okinawa and demonstrated some of these amazing feats which new students of karate find hard to believe possible.

Tests of Stability

Mr. Uechi performed these feats not to show how strong he was but to prove to his students that the human body has not so many limitations as most people believe it to have. He wanted to stress the importance of sanchin by doing feats which he said required no other training except sanchin.

The first feat he demonstrated was the stability test. He asked two of his largest and strongest students to pick up a large bamboo pole hanging over the door to his school and place it against his stomach. He then positioned himself in a sanchin stance and requested the two students to push as hard as they could. They did so for a minute or two, but they were unable to budge Mr. Uechi an inch.

There were no tricks involved in this feat. Mr. Uechi loved karate too much to have degraded it with trickery of any sort. He told his students that they could all duplicate the feat if they perfected sanchin to a high degree. Mr. Uechi, Jr., believes that the feat was performed by controlling the stomach muscles to such an extent that all the power of the men pushing the pole was absorbed by his body. No one knows for sure. The pole still hangs over the door, waiting for someone else to duplicate the feat.

After another workout, Mr. Uechi instructed his wife to bring him six fragile china teacups. He arranged these six cups about twelve inches apart in a straight line. He then instructed his smallest student, who weighed about ninety pounds, to walk from one cup to another until he had walked on all six cups.

The student placed his foot on the first cup, slowly putting his weight on it. Immediately the cup shattered. Mr. Uechi told him to try another cup—any cup along the line. The student broke the third cup in the row after trying to place his weight on it.

Mr. Uechi instructed his wife to bring out two more cups to replace the broken ones. He then placed his right foot on the first cup, putting all his weight on it. The cup did not break. Then he walked in a sanchin position from cup to cup, not breaking a single cup. He told his students that they also could learn to do this if they studied sanchin enough.

DESCENT FROM THE EIGER

By Trevanian

The four figures were as motionless as the mountain they huddled against. Their clothing was stiff with a brittle crust of ice, just as the rock was glazed over with a shell of frozen rain and melt water. It was not yet dawn, but the saturation of night was diluting in the east. Jonathan could dimly make out the ice-scabbed folds of his waterproof trousers. He had been crouched over for hours, staring sightlessly into his lap, ever since the force of the storm had abated sufficiently to allow him to open his eyes. Despite the penetrating cold that followed the storm, he had not moved a muscle. His cringing posture was exactly what it had been when the *foehn* struck, tucked up in as tight a ball as his stance permitted, offering the elements the smallest possible target.

It had broken upon them without warning, and it was not possible to reckon the time it had lasted—one interminable moment of terror and chaos compounded of driving rain and stinging hail, of tearing wind that lashed around them and wedged itself between man and rock, trying to drive them apart. There were blinding flashes and blind darkness, pain from clinging and numbness from the cold. But most of all there had been sound: the deafening crack of thunder close at hand, the persistent scream of the wind, the roar and clatter of the avalanche spilling to the right and left and bouncing in eccentric patterns over the outcropping of rock that protected them.

It was quiet now. The storm was gone.

The torrent of sensation had washed Jonathan's mind clean, and thought returned slowly and in rudimentary forms. He told himself in simple words that he was looking at his pants. Then he reasoned that they were covered with a crust of ice. Eventually, he interpreted the pain as cold. And only then, with doubt and wonder, but no excitement, he knew that he was alive. He must be.

The storm was over, but the dark and the cold only slowly retreated from his consciousness, and the transition from pain and storm to calm and cold was an imperceptible blend. His body and nerves remembered the fury, and his senses told him it had passed, but he could recall neither the end of the storm nor the beginning of the calm.

He moved his arm, and there was a noise, a tinkling clatter as his movement broke the crust of ice on his sleeve. He clenched and unclenched his fists and pressed his toes against the soles of his boots, forcing his thickened blood out to his extremities. The numbness phased into electric tingle, then into throbbing pain, but these were not unpleasant sensations because they were proofs of life. The dark had retreated enough for him to make out Karl's bowed and unmoving back a few feet from him, but he wasted no thought on Karl's condition; all his attention was focused on the returning sense of life within himself.

There was a sound just beneath him.

"Anderl?" Jonathan's voice was clogged and dry.

Anderl stirred tentatively, like a man checking to see if things were still working. His coating of ice shattered with his movement and tinkled down the face. "There was a storm last night." His voice was gruffly gay. "I imagine you noticed."

With the advance of dawn came a wind, persistent, dry, and very cold. Anderl squinted at his wrist altimeter. "It reads forty meters low," he announced matter-of-factly. Jonathan nodded. Forty meters low. That meant the barometric pressure was two points higher than normal. They were in a strong, cold high that might last any amount of time.

He saw Anderl move cautiously along his ledge to attend to Jean-Paul, who had not yet stirred. A little later Anderl set to the task of brewing tea on the spirit stove, which he placed for balance against Jean-Paul's leg.

Jonathan looked around. The warmth of the foehn had melted the surface snow, and it had frozen again with the arrival of the cold front. An inch of ice crusted the snow, slippery and sharp, but not strong enough to bear a man's weight. The rocks were glazed with a coat of frozen melt water, impossible to cling to, but the crust was too thin to take an ice piton. In the growing light, he assessed the surface conditions. They were the most treacherous possible.

Karl moved. He had not slept, but like Anderl and Jonathan he had been deep in a protective cocoon of semiconsciousness. Pulling himself out of it, he went smoothly and professionally through the task of checking the pitons that supported him and Jonathan, then he exercised isometrically to return circulation to his hands and feet, after which he began the simple but laborious job of getting food from his kit—frozen chocolate and dried meat. All through this, he did not speak. He was humbled and visibly shaken by the experiences of the night. He was no longer a leader.

Anderl twisted against the rope holding him into his nook and stretched up to offer Jonathan a cup of tepid tea. "Jean-Paul . . ."

Jonathan drank it down in one avaricious draught. "What about him?" He passed the metal cup back down and licked the place where his lip had adhered to it and torn.

"He is dead." Anderl refilled the cup and offered it up to Karl. "Must have gone during the storm," he added quietly.

Karl received the tea and held it between his palms as he stared down at the rumpled and ice-caked form that had been Jean-Paul.

"Drink it," Jonathan ordered, but Karl did not move. He breathed orally in short, shallow breaths over the top of the cup, and the puffs of vapor mixed with the steam rising off the tea.

"How do you know he is dead?" Karl asked in an unnaturally loud, monotonic voice.

"I looked at him," Anderl said as he refilled the small pot with ice chips.

"You saw he was dead! And you set about making a cup of tea!"

Anderl shrugged. He did not bother to look up from his work.

"Drink the tea," Jonathan repeated. "Or pass it over here and let me have it before it gets cold."

Karl gave him a look saturated with disgust, but he drank the tea.

"He had a concussion," Anderl said. "The storm was too much. The man inside could not keep the man outside from dying."

For the next hour, they swallowed what food they could, exercised isometrically to fight the cold, and placated their endless thirsts with cup after cup of tea and bouillon. It was impossible to drink enough to satisfy themselves, but there came a time when they must move on, so Anderl drank off the last of the melted ice and replaced the pot and collapsible stove in his pack.

When Jonathan outlined his proposal for action, Karl did not resist the change in leadership. He had lost the desire to make decisions. Again and again his attention strayed and his eyes fixed on the dead man beneath him. His mountain experience had not included death.

Jonathan surveyed their situation in a few words. Both the rock and the snow were coated over with a crust of ice that made climbing up out of the question. A frigid high, such as the one then punishing them with cold could last for days, even weeks. They could not hole up where they were. They must retreat.

To return down Karl's chute was out of the question. It would be iced over. Jonathan proposed that they try to get down to a point just above the Eigerwand Station Window. It was just possible that they might be able to rope down from there, despite the beetling overhang. Ben, waiting and watching them from the ground, would realize their intention, and he would be waiting with help at the Window.

As he spoke, Jonathan read in Anderl's face that he had no great faith in their chances of roping down from above the Station Window, but he did not object, realizing that for reasons of morale, if nothing else, they had to move out. They must not stay there and face the risk of freezing to death in bivouac as, years before, Sedlmayer and Mehringer had done not a hundred meters above them.

Jonathan organized the rope. He would lead, slowly cutting big, tublike steps in the crusted snow. Karl would be next on the rope. A second, independent line would suspend Jean-Paul's body between them. In this way Karl could belay and protect Jonathan without the additional drag of Jean-Paul, then, when they were both in established stances, they could maneuver the load down, Jonathan guiding it away from snags, Karl holding back against gravity. As the strongest in the party, Anderl would be last on the rope, always seeking a protected stance in case a slip suddenly gave him the weight of all three.

Although the dangers of the descent were multiplied by bringing Jean-Paul with them, no one thought of leaving him behind. It was mountain tradition to bring your dead with you. And no one wanted to please the Eiger Birds by leaving a grisly memento on the face that would tingle and delight them at their telescopes for weeks or months until a rescue team could retrieve it.

As they packed up and tied Jean-Paul into the sleeping bag that would act as a canvas sled, Karl grumbled half-heartedly against the bad luck that had kept them from bagging the mountain. Anderl did not mind retreating. With surface conditions like these, it was equally difficult to move in either direction, and for him the challenge of climbing was the point of it all.

Watching the two men at their preparations, Jonathan knew he had nothing to fear from his sanction target, whoever it was. If they were to get down alive, they would have to cooperate with every fiber of their combined skill and strength. The matter would be settled in the valley, if they reached the flat land intact. In fact, the whole matter of his SS assignment had the unreal qualities of a fantastic operetta, viewed in terms of the grim presence of the mountain.

The descent was torturously slow. The frozen crust of the snow was such that at one step the surface was so hard the crampons would take no bite, but at the next the leg would break through to the softer snow below and balance would be lost. The snowfield clung to the face at an angle of 50°, and Jonathan had to lean out and down from the edge of each big step to chop out the next with his ice axe. He could not be content with those stylish toe steps that can be formed with two skillful swings of the axe; he had to hack out vast tubs, big enough to hold him as he leaned out for the next, and big enough to allow Anderl to take a belaying stance at each step.

The routine was complicated and expensive of energy. Jonathan moved down alone for one rope length, belayed from above by Karl who, in turn, was held by Anderl. Then he cut out an especially broad stance from the protection of which he carefully guided Jean-Paul's body down to him as Karl let the burden slip bit by bit, always fighting its tendency to tear itself from his grip and fly down the face carrying all of them with it. When the canvas bundle reached Jonathan, he secured it as best he could, driving Jean-Paul's ice axe into the crust and using it as a tie-off. Then Karl came down to join him, moving much more quickly down the big steps. The third phase of the pattern was the most dangerous. Anderl had to move down half the distance to them, where he could jam himself into one of the better steps and set his body to protect them through the next repetition of the cycle. Anderl moved essentially without protection, save for the "psychological rope" that regularly slackened between him and Karl. Any slip might knock his fellow climbers out of their step or, even should his line of fall miss them, they would have very little chance of withstanding the shock of a fall twice the length of the rope. Anderl knew his responsibility and moved with great care, although he continually called down to them cheerfully, grousing about the pace or the weather or any other trivial matter that came to mind.

Slow though their progress was, for Jonathan, who had to cut each of the steps and who could rest only while the others closed up from above, it was desperately tiring.

Three hours; two hundred and fifty meters.

He panted with exertion; the cold air seared his lungs; his arm was leaden with swinging the axe. And when he stopped to receive Jean-Paul and let the others close up, one torture was exchanged for another. At each rest, the frigid wind attacked him, freezing the perspiration to his body and racking him with convulsions of shivering. He wept with the pain of fatigue and cold, and the tears froze on his stubbled cheeks.

The goal of the cliffs above the Eigerwand Station was too demoralizingly distant to consider. He concentrated on objectives within human scope: one more swing of the axe, one more step to hack out. Then move on.

Five hours; three hundred twenty-five meters.

Progress diminishing. Must rest.

Jonathan conned his body, lured it into action. One more step then you can rest. It's all right. It's all right. Now, just one more step.

The jagged edges of the ice crust around each deep step cut through his waterproof pants as he leaned out. It cut through his ski pants. It cut into his flesh, but the cold dulled the hurt.

One more step, then you can rest.

Since the first light of dawn Ben had been in the meadow, scanning the face with his telescope. The young climbers who had volunteered for the rescue grouped themselves around him, their faces tight with concern. No one could recall weather this cold so late in the season, and they estimated in low voices what it must be like up on the face.

Ben had prepared himself psychologically to find nothing on the face. In his mind he had rehearsed the calm way he would stroll back to the hotel and send off telegrams to the Alpine Clubs sponsoring the climbers. Then he would wait in his room, perhaps for days, until the weather softened and he could organize a team to recover the bodies. He promised himself one petcock for his emotions. He was going to hit somebody: a reporter, or better yet an Eiger Bird.

He swept the telescope back and forth over the dark crease beside the Flatiron where, just before nightfall, he had seen them making bivouac. Nothing. Their clothing iced over, the climbers blended invisibly into the glazed rock.

On the hotel terrace Eiger Birds were already queued up at the telescopes, stamping about to warm themselves, and receiving great bowls of steaming coffee from scuttling waiters. The first rumors that there was nothing to be seen on the face had galvanized the tourists. Hungry for sensation and eager to display depths of human sympathy, Eiger Hens told one another how terrible it all was, and how they had had premonitions during the night. One of the twits Anderl had used burst suddenly into tears and ran back into the hotel, refusing to be consoled by her friends. When they took her at her word and left her alone in the empty lobby for twenty full minutes, she found the inner resources to return to the terrace, red-eyed but brave.

The Eiger Cocks nodded to one another significantly and said that they had known it all along. If anyone had had the sense to ask their advice, they would have told them that the weather looked ugly and changeable.

Muffled up securely against the cold, and convoyed by a solicitous entourage, the Greek merchant and his American wife walked through the crowd which grew silent and pressed back to make way for them. Nodding to the left and right, they assumed their roles as major mourners, and everyone said how especially hard this must be on them. Their tent had been kept warm through the night by two portable gas stoves, but still they had to endure the rigors of chill wind as they took turns rising from breakfast to scan the mountain with the telescope that had been reserved for their private use.

Ben stood in the meadow, sipping absently at the tin cup of coffee one of the young climbers had pressed anonymously into his hand. A murmur, then a squealing cheer came from the terrace. Someone had spied a trace of movement.

He dropped the cup on the rimed grass and was at the eyepiece in an instant. There were three of them moving slowly downward. Three—and something else. A bundle. Once they were well out onto the snow, Ben could make out the colors of their windbreakers. Blue (Jonathan) was in the lead. He was moving down very slowly, evidently cutting out wide steps of the kind that cost time and energy. He inched down almost a rope's length before the second man—red (Karl)—began to lower a gray-green something—lump—down to him. Then Karl descended relatively quickly to join Jonathan. The last—yellow (Anderl)—climbed carefully down, stopping halfway and setting a deep belay. There was no one behind Anderl.

The bundle must be Jean-Paul. Injured . . . or dead.

Ben could imagine what that surface must be like after the melting foehn and the hard freeze. A treacherous scab of ice that might pull away from the under snow at any time.

For twenty minutes Ben remained at the telescope, his tightly reined body aching to do something helpful, but uncertain of the intentions of the climbers. Finally, he forced himself to straighten up and stop the torment of guessing and hoping. At their terribly slow pace, it would be hours before he could be certain of how they would try to execute their retreat. He preferred to wait in his room where no one could observe his vicarious fear. They might attempt the long traverse over the classic route. Or they might retrace their line of ascent, forgetting that Karl's chute was iced over now. There was a third possibility, one Ben prayed Jonathan would have vision enough to elect. They might try for the cliffs above the Eigerwand Station Window. It was remotely possible that a man might rope down to the safety of that lateral gallery. No one had ever attempted it, but it seemed the best of a bad lot of alternatives.

"Morning! Are you going to be using your telescope?"

Ben turned to see the confident, boyish smile of the actor beaming at him. The stiffly made-up actress wife stood beside her husband, her sagging throat bound up in a bright silk neckerchief, shivering in the stylish ski clothes that had been specifically designed to make her appear taller and less dumpy.

The actor modulated richly, "The lady would hate to go home without having seen anything, but we really can't have her standing around in line with those other people. I know you understand that."

"You want to use *my* telescope?" Ben asked, unbelieving.

"Tell him we'll pay for it, love," the wife inserted, then she blessed the young climbers with her handsome eyes.

The actor smiled and used his most chocolate voice. "Of course we'll pay for it." He reached out for the instrument, smiling all the while his effective, disarming grin.

Contrary to subsequent news reports, Ben never really hit him.

The actor reacted to the flash of Ben's hand and winced away with surprising celerity. The movement cost him his balance, and he fell on his back on the frozen ground. Instantly, the wife screamed and threw herself over her fallen mate to protect him from further brutality. Ben snatched her up by the hair and bent over them, speaking in rapid, hushed tones. "I'm going up to my room, and I'm leaving this telescope right where it is. If either of you fucking ghouls touches it, your doctor's going to have one hell of a time getting it out."

He walked away to the sound of laughter from the young climbers and a spate of scatological vitriol from the actress that revealed her familiarity with most of the sexual variants.

Ben bore across the terrace with his energetic, hopping stride, not swerving an inch from his course through the milling crowd, and taking a retributive pleasure in each jolting impact that left one of the Eiger Birds dazed and startled in his wake. In the deserted bar he ordered three bottles of beer and a sandwich. While he waited, Anna approached, pressing through the terrace throng to join him. He did not want to talk to her, but the barman was slow.

"Is Jean-Paul all right?" She asked as she neared him.

"No!" He took up the clinking bottles between the fingers of one hand and the sandwich in the other, and he left the bar for his room.

He ate and drank sitting morosely on the edge of his bed. Then he lay down, his fingers locked behind his head, staring at the ceiling. Then he got up and walked around the room, pausing at the window at each circuit. Then he lay down again. And got up again. Two hours dragged on in this way before he gave up the attempt to rest.

At the telescope in the meadow again, Ben was nearly certain that the climbers were making for the cliffs above the station window. They were near the edge of a rock pitch that separates the ice field from the small shelf of snow above the window. The distance between them and safety could be covered by a thumb at arm's length, but Ben knew there were hours of labor and risk in that stretch. And the sun was slipping down. He had made arrangements for a special train to carry the rescue team up the cogwheel railroad that bore through the heart of the mountain. They would depart when the time was right and be at the window to receive the climbers.

He hunched over his telescope, pouring sympathetic energy up the line of visual contact.

His whole body jolted convulsively when he saw Anderl slip.

There was a grating sound, and Anderl realized the surface was moving beneath him. A vast scab of crusted snow had loosened from the face and was slipping down, slowly at first, and he was in the middle of the doomed island. It was no use digging in; that would be like clinging to a falling boulder. Reacting automatically, he scrambled upward, seeking firm snow. Then he was tumbling sideward. He spread his limbs to stop the deadly roll and plunged his axe into the surface, covering it with his body. And still he slipped down and sideward, a deep furrow above him from the dig of his axe.

Jonathan had been huddled with Karl and Jean-Paul in the deep step he had just cut out. His eyes were fixed on the snow before him, his mind empty, and he shivered convulsively as he had at each *étape*. At Karl's shout, a sudden squirt of adrenalin stopped the shivering instantly and, his eyes glazed with fatigue, he watched with a stupid calm the snowslide come at him.

Karl pushed Jonathan down upon the encased corpse and covered both with his body, locking his fingers around the ice axe that was their belay point. The avalanche roared over them, deafening and suffocating, clutching at them, piling up under them and trying to tug them away from their step.

And with a sudden ringing silence, it was over.

Jonathan clawed his way up past Karl's limp body and scooped the fresh snow out of the step. Then Karl scrambled up, panting, his hands bleeding, skin still stuck to the cold axe. Jean-Paul was half covered with snow, but he was still there.

"I can't move!" The voice was not far from them.

Anderl was spread-eagled on the surface of the snow, his feet not three meters from the edge of the rock cliff. The snow-slide had carried him down, then had capriciously veered aside, over the others, and left him face down, his body still covering the axe that had broken his slide. He was unhurt, but each attempt to move caused him to slip downward a few inches. He tried twice, then had the good judgment to remain still.

He was just out of reach, and the freshly uncovered snow was too unstable to be crossed. The rope from Karl to Anderl lay in a hairpin loop up toward his earlier stance and back sharply, but only the two ends of it emerged from the snow that had buried it.

Anderl slipped down several inches, this time without attempting to move.

Jonathan and Karl tugged and whipped the rope, trying desperately to unbury it. They dared not pull with all their strength lest it suddenly come free and precipitate them off the face.

"I feel foolish," Anderl called. And he slipped farther down.

"Shut up!" Jonathan croaked. There was nothing for an ice piton to hold onto, so he hurriedly slapped his axe and Karl's deep into the soft snow, then he laced the slack they had tugged in from Anderl's line back and forth between the two axe handles. "Lie down on that," he ordered, and Karl mutely obeyed.

Jonathan unroped himself and started up Anderl's buried line, alternately clinging to it and ripping it out of the snow. Each time he gained a little slack he lay still on the steeply inclined surface as Karl whipped the loose rope around the axes. It was all-important that there be as little slack as possible when the line came free. Once he reached the point at which the rope began to curve down toward Anderl, he had to move quickly, knowing that he must be very close to Anderl when the line came free. Movement now was most awkward, and the adrenalin that had fed Jonathan's body was burning off, leaving heavy-limbed nausea in its stead. He wrapped his legs around the rope and tugged it loose with one hand, expecting at any moment to come sliding down on top of Anderl as they both snapped to the end of their slack.

It happened when they were only ten feet apart, and fate was in a humorous mood. The line slipped slowly out of the snow and they skidded gently sideward, Jonathan atop Anderl, until they were directly below Karl and the protection of the big step, their feet overhanging the lip of the rock cliff. They scrambled up with little difficulty.

The instant he fell into the almost vertical snow cave, Jonathan collapsed from within. He crouched near Jean-Paul's body, shivering uncontrollably, limp with fatigue.

Anderl was cheerful and talkative, and Karl was obedient. Between them they widened the step, and Anderl set about making tea. The first cup he gave to Jonathan with two small red pills, heart stimulants.

"I certainly felt ridiculous out there. I wanted to laugh, but I knew that the motion would make me slip, so I bit my lip. It was wonderful the way you came out to get me, Jonathan. But in the future I wish you would not use me to ride around on like a sled. I know what you were doing. Showing off for the people down on the terrace. Right?" He babbled on, brewing tea and passing it around like a solicitous Austrian aunt.

The heart stimulant and the tea began to make inroads on Jonathan's fatigue. He practiced controlling his shivering as he stared at the maroon ooze of blood around the rips in his pants. He knew he would not be able to stand another night in open bivouac. They had to move on. His exhalations were whimpers: for him, the last stages of fatigue. He was not certain how long he could continue to wield the ice axe. The muscles of his forearms were knotted and stiff, and his grip was a thing of rusted metal. He could clamp his fist shut or release it totally, but he had no control over the middle pressures.

He knew perfectly well that, in this condition, he should not be leading. But he did not dare turn the rope over to either of the younger men. Karl had retreated into automaton depression, and Anderl's brassy chatter had a disturbing note of hysteria about it.

They collected themselves to move out. As he took the metal cup back, Anderl examined Jonathan's gray-green eyes as though seeing him for the first time. "You're very good, you know, Jonathan. I've enjoyed climbing with you."

Jonathan forced a smile. "We'll make it."

Anderl grinned and shook his head. "No, I don't think so. But we shall continue with style."

They took the cliff quickly, rappelling on a doubled rope. That which looked most daring to Eiger Birds below was in reality much less demanding than slogging down through the snowfields. Evening was setting in, so they did not waste time retrieving Anderl's rope.

Months later it could still be seen dangling there, half rotten.

One more snowfield to cross and they would be perched above the station windows. The brutal cycle began again. It was colder now with the sun going. Jonathan set his jaw and turned off his mind. He cut step after step, the shocks against the axe head traveling up his throbbing arm directly to the nape of his neck. Chop. Step down. Lean out. Chop. And shiver convulsively as the others close up. The minutes were painfully long, the hours beyond the compass of human time.

*   *   *

Time had been viscous for Ben too; there would have been consolation in action, but he controlled his impulse to move until he was sure of their line of descent. When he had seen the last man rappel from the cliff and move out onto the final, relatively narrow snowfield, he stood up from the telescope. "All right," he said quietly, "let's go."

The rescue team trudged to the train depot, making a wide arc around the hotel to avoid arousing the interest of reporters and rubbernecks. However, several newsmen had received reports from the PR-minded railroad authorities and were waiting at the platform. Ben was sick of dealing with them, so he did not argue about taking them along, but he made it most clear what would happen to the first man who got in the way.

Despite the arrangements made earlier, time was wasted convincing the Swiss officials that the costs of the special train would indeed be met by the organizations sponsoring the climb, but at last they were on their way, the young men sitting silently side by side in the car as it jolted and swayed up to plunge into the black of the tunnel. They reached their destination within thirty minutes.

The clatter of climbing gear and the scrape of boots echoed down the artificially lit tunnel as they walked from the Eigerwand Station platform along the slightly down-sloping lateral gallery that gave onto the observation windows. The mood of the group was such that even the reporters gave up asking stupid questions and offered to carry extra coils of rope.

With great economy of communication, the team went to work. The wooden partitions at the end of the gallery were wrenched out with ice axes (while railroad officials reminded Ben that this would have to be paid for) and the first young man stepped out onto the face to plant an anchoring set of pitons. The blast of freezing air they encountered humbled them all. They knew how that cold must be sapping the strength of the men on the face.

Ben would have given anything to lead the group making the rescue, but his experience told him that these young men with all their toes intact and youthful reserves of energy could do the job better than he. Still, he had to fight the desire to make many small corrective suggestions because it seemed to him that they were doing everything just a little bit wrongly.

When the young leader had reconnoitered the face, he crawled back into the gallery. His report was not reassuring. The rock was plastered with a coating of ice half an inch thick—too thin and friable to take an ice piton, but thick enough to cover and hide such viable piton cracks as the rock beneath might have. They would have to peck away at the ice with their axes to bare the rock for each piton. And that would be slow.

But the most disturbing information was that they would not be able to move upward toward the climbers more than ten meters. Above that, the rock face beetled out in an impassable overhang. It looked as though a skillful man could move out as much as a hundred feet to the right or left from the window ledge, but not up.

As the young man gave his report, he slapped his hands against his knees to restore circulation. He had been out on the face for only twenty minutes, but the cold had stiffened and numbed his fingers. With the setting of the sun, the gallery tunnel seemed to grow palpably colder. Low-temperature records would be set that night.

Having established an anchoring base just outside the window, there was nothing to do but wait. The likelihood of the climbers chancing to rope down directly above the window was remote. Even assuming the direct line would go, they had no way to know from above exactly where the window was. Because of the overhang, the first man would be dangling out several yards from the face. They would have to inch over to him, somehow get a line out to him, and pull him in. Once that line was tied down, the retrieval of the others would be easier . . . if they had the strength left to make it down . . . if they had enough rope to pass the overhang . . . if the cold had not stupefied them . . . if their running line did not jam . . . if their anchor point above on the lip of the cliff held.

Every few minutes, one of the young men went out on the face and yodeled up. But there was no answer. Ben paced up and down the gallery, the newsmen sagely pressing against the rock walls to stay out of his way. On one return walk, he cursed and stepped out on the face himself, un-roped, holding one of the anchoring pitons with one hand and leaning out with something of his former insouciant daring. "Come on, Jon!" he shouted up. "Get your ass off that hill!"

No answer.

But something else struck Ben as odd. His voice had carried with abnormal crisp resonance. There was no wind on the Eiger. It was strangely still, and the cold was settling down like a silent, malignant presence. He listened to the eerie silence, broken only occasionally by the artillery crack of a random chunk of rock arcing off from somewhere above and exploding against the base far below.

When he scrambled back in through the gallery window, he slid his back down the tunnel wall and sat crouching among the waiting rescuers, hugging his knees until the shivering stopped, and licking his hand where he had left palm skin on the steel piton.

Someone lit a portable stove, and the inevitable, life-giving tea began to be passed around.

The temperature fell as the daylight at the end of the gallery grew dimmer and bluer.

One of the young men at the mouth of the tunnel yodeled, paused, and yodeled again.

And an answering call came from above!

There was a mumble of excitement in the gallery, then a sudden hush as the young climber yodeled again. And again he received a clear response. A newsman glanced at his watch and scribbled in a notepad, as Ben stepped out on the lip of the window with the three men selected to make contact with the climbers. An exchange of calls was made again. In the windless hush, it was impossible to tell how far from above the calls were coming. The yodeler tried again, and Anderl's voice replied with peculiar clarity. "What is this? A contest?"

A young Austrian in the rescue team grinned and nudged the man next to him. That was Anderl Meyer for you! But Ben detected in the sound of Anderl's voice the last desperate gesture of a proud, spent man. He lifted his hand, and those on the ledge with him were silent. There was a scuffling sound above and to the left. Someone was being lowered over the bulge of rock, far to the left, a hundred and twenty feet from safety. From the clink of snap rings, Ben knew he was coming down in an improvised harness. Then the boots appeared, and Jonathan slipped down slowly, twisting under his line, dangling some ten feet away from the face. Twilight was setting in quickly. While Jonathan continued his slow, twirling descent, the three rescuers began to traverse toward him, chipping away at the treacherous coating of ice, and rapping in pitons each time they uncovered a possible crack. Ben stayed on the ledge by the window, directing the activities of the three. There was no room out there for others who were eager to help.

Ben did not call out encouragement to Jonathan. He knew from the slump of the body in the harness that he was at the very rim of endurance after having broken the way for all three since dawn, and he had no breath to waste on talk. Ben prayed that Jonathan would not succumb to that emotional collapse so common to climbers once the end was almost within grasp.

The three young men could not move quickly. The face was almost vertical with only an iced-over ledge three inches wide for toehold. If they had not been experienced at executing tension traverses against the line, they would not have been able to move at all.

Then Jonathan stopped in mid-descent. He looked up, but could not see over the lip of the overhang.

"What's wrong up there?" Ben called.

"Rope . . . !" Anderl's voice had the gritting of teeth in it. ". . . Jammed!"

"Can you handle it?"

"No! Can Jonathan get on the face and give us a little slack?"

"No!"

There was nothing Jonathan could do to help himself. He turned slowly around on the line, six hundred feet of void below him. What he wanted most of all was to sleep.

Although he was far below them, Ben could hear the voices of Karl and Anderl through the still frigid air. He could not make out the words, but they had the sound of an angry conference.

The three young men continued to move out, now halfway to Jonathan and starting to take chances, knocking in fewer pitons to increase their speed.

"All right!" Anderl's voice called down. "I'll do what I can."

"No!" Karl screamed. "Don't move!"

"Just hold me!"

"I can't!" There was a whimper in the sound. "Anderl, I can't!"

Ben saw the snow come first, shooting over the edge of the overhang, a beautiful golden spray in the last beam of the setting sun. Automatically, he pressed back against the face. In a flash, like one alien frame cut into a movie, he saw the two dark figures rush past him, veiled in a mist of falling snow and ice. One of them struck the lip of the window with an ugly splat. And they were gone.

Snow continued to hiss past; then it stopped.

And it was silent on the face.

The three young men were safe, but frozen in their stances by what they had witnessed.

"Keep moving!" Ben barked, and they collected their emotions and obeyed.

The first shock knocked Jonathan over in his harness, and he hung upside down, swinging violently, his mind swirling in an eddy of semiconsciousness. The thing hit him again, and blood gushed from his nose. He wanted to sleep, and he did not want the thing to hit him again. That was the extent of his demands on life. But for a third time they collided. It was a glancing blow, and their ropes intertwined. Instinctively, Jonathan grasped at it and held it to him. It was Jean-Paul, hanging half out of his bedroll shroud, stiff with death and cold. But Jonathan clung to it.

When Anderl and Karl fell, their weight snapped the line between them and the corpse, and it tumbled over the edge and crashed down on Jonathan. It saved him from falling, counterbalancing his weight on the line that connected them and passed through a snap link and piton high above. They swung side by side in the silent cold.

"Sit up!"

Jonathan heard Ben's voice from a distance, soft and unreal.

"Sit up!"

Jonathan did not mind hanging upside down. He was through. He had had it. *Let me sleep. Why sit up.*

"Pull yourself up, goddamit!"

They won't leave me alone unless I do what they want. What does it matter? He tried to haul himself on Jean-Paul's line, but his fingers would not close. They had no feeling. *What does it matter?*

"Jon! For Christ's sake!"

"Leave me alone," he muttered. "Go away." The valley below was dark, and he did not feel cold any longer. He felt nothing at all. He was going to sleep.

No, that isn't sleep. It's something else. All right, try to sit up. Maybe then they'll leave me alone. Can't breathe. Nose stopped up with blood. Sleep.

Jonathan tried again, but his fingers throbbed, fat and useless. He reached high and wound his arm around the rope. He struggled halfway up, but his grip was slipping. Wildly, he kicked at Jean-Paul's body until he got his legs around it and managed to press himself up until his rope hit him in the forehead.

There. Sitting upright. Now leave me alone. Stupid game. Doesn't matter.

"Try to catch this!"

Jonathan squeezed his eyes shut to break the film from them. There were three men out there. Quite close. Tacked on the wall. *What the hell do they want now? Why don't they leave me alone?*

"Catch this and slip it around you!"

"Go away," he mumbled.

Ben's voice roared from a distance. "Put it around you, goddamit!"

Mustn't piss Ben off. He's mean when he's pissed off. Groggily, Jonathan struggled into the noose of the lasso. *Now that's it. Don't ask any more. Let me sleep. Stop squeezing the goddamned breath out of me!*

Jonathan heard the young men call anxiously back to Ben. "We can't pull him in! Not enough slack!"

Good. Leave me alone, then.

"Jon?" Ben's voice was not angry. He was coaxing some child. "Jon, your axe is still around your wrist."

So what?

"Cut the line above you, Jon."

Ben's gone crazy. He must need sleep.

"Cut the line, ol' buddy. It'll only be a short fall. We've got you."

Go ahead, do it. They'll keep at you until you do. He hacked blindly at the nylon line above him. Again and again with mushy strokes that seldom struck the same place twice. Then a thought slipped into his numb mind, and he stopped.

"What did he say?" Ben called to the rescuers.

"He said that Jean-Paul will fall if he cuts the line."

"Jon? Listen to me. It's all right. Jean-Paul's dead."

Dead? Oh, I remember. He's here and he's dead. Where's Anderl? Where's Karl? They're somewhere else, because they're not dead like Jean-Paul. Is that right? I don't understand it. It doesn't matter anyway. What was I doing? Oh, yes. Cut the fucking rope.

He hacked again and again.

And suddenly it snapped. For an instant the two bodies fell together, then Jean-Paul dropped away alone. Jonathan passed out with the pain of his ribs cracking as the lasso jerked tight. And that was merciful, because he did not feel the impact of his collision with the rock.

THE MALTESE CAT

By Rudyard Kipling

They had good reason to be proud, and better reason to be afraid, all twelve of them; for, though they had fought their way, game by game, up the teams entered for the polo tournament, they were meeting the Archangels that afternoon in the final match; and the Archangels' men were playing with half a dozen ponies apiece. As the game was divided into six quarters of eight minutes each, that meant a fresh pony after every halt. The Skidars' team, even supposing there were no accidents, could only supply one pony for every other change; and two to one is heavy odds. Again, as Shiraz, the gray Syrian, pointed out, they were meeting the pink and pick of the polo ponies of Upper India; ponies that had cost from a thousand rupees each, while they themselves were a cheap lot gathered, often from country carts, by their masters who belonged to a poor but honest native infantry regiment.

"Money means pace and weight," said Shiraz, rubbing his black silk nose dolefully along his neat-fitting boot, "and by the maxims of the game as I know it—"

"Ah, but we aren't playing the maxims," said the Maltese Cat. "We're playing the game, and we've the great advantage of knowing the game. Just think a stride, Shiraz. We've pulled up from bottom to second place in two weeks against all those fellows on the ground here; and that's because we play with our heads as well as with our feet."

"It makes me feel undersized and unhappy all the same," said Kittiwynk, a mouse-colored mare with a red browband and the cleanest pair of legs that ever an aged pony owned. "They've twice our size, these others."

Kittiwynk looked at the gathering and sighed. The hard, dusty Umballa polo ground was lined with thousands of soldiers, black and white, not counting hundreds and hundreds of carriages, and drags, and dogcarts, and ladies with brilliant-colored parasols, and officers in uniform and out of it, and crowds of natives behind them; and orderlies on camels who had halted to watch the game, instead of carrying letters up and down the station, and native horse dealers running about on thin-eared Biluchi mares, looking for a chance to sell a few first-class polo ponies. Then there were the ponies of thirty teams that had entered for the Upper India Free-for-All Cup—nearly every pony of worth and dignity from Mhow to Peshawar, from Allahabad to Multan; prize ponies, Arabs, Syrian, Barb, country-bred, Deccanee, Waziri, and Kabul ponies of every color and shape and temper that you could imagine. Some of them were in mat-roofed stables close to the polo ground, but most were under saddle while their masters, who had been defeated in the earlier games, trotted in and out and told each other exactly how the game should be played.

It was a glorious sight, and the come-and-go of the little quick hoofs, and the incessant salutations of ponies that had met before on other polo grounds or racecourses, were enough to drive a four-footed thing wild.

But the Skidars' team were careful not to know their neighbors, though half the ponies on the ground were anxious to scrape acquaintance with the little fellows that had come from the North, and, so far, had swept the board.

"Let's see," said a soft, golden-colored Arab, who had been playing very badly the day before, to the Maltese Cat, "didn't we meet in Abdul Rahman's stable in Bombay four seasons ago? I won the Paikpattan Cup next season, you may remember."

"Not me," said the Maltese Cat politely. "I was at Malta then, pulling a vegetable cart. I don't race. I play the game."

"O-oh!" said the Arab, cocking his tail and swaggering off.

"Keep yourselves to yourselves," said the Maltese Cat to his companions. "We don't want to rub noses with all those goose-rumped half-breeds of Upper India. When we've won this cup they'll give their shoes to know us."

"We shan't win the cup," said Shiraz. "How do you feel?"

"Stale as last night's feed when a muskrat has run over it," said Polaris, a rather heavy-shouldered gray, and the rest of the team agreed with him.

"The sooner you forget that the better," said the Maltese Cat cheerfully. "They've finished tiffin in the big tent. We shall be wanted now. If your saddles are not comfy, kick. If your bits aren't easy, rear, and let the saises know whether your boots are tight."

Each pony had his sais, his groom, who lived and ate and slept with the pony, and had betted a great deal more than he could afford on the result of the game. There was no chance of anything going wrong, and, to make sure, each sais was shampooing the legs of his pony to the last minute. Behind the saises sat as many of the Skidars' regiment as had to leave to attend that match—about half the native officers, and a hundred or two dark, black-bearded men with the regimental pipers nervously fingering the big be-ribboned bagpipes. The Skidars were what they call a Pioneer regiment; and the bagpipes made the national music of half the men. The native officers held bundles of polo sticks, long cane-handled mallets, and as the grandstand filled after lunch they arranged themselves by ones and twos at different points round the ground, so that if a stick were broken the player would not have far to ride for a new one. An impatient British cavalry band struck up "If you want to know the time, ask a p'leeceman!" and the two umpires in light dust coats danced out on two little excited ponies. The four players of the Archangels' team followed, and the sight of their beautiful mounts made Shiraz groan again.

"Wait till we know," said the Maltese Cat. "Two of 'em are playing in blinkers, and that means they can't see to get out of the way of their own side, or they may shy at the umpires' ponies. They've all got white web reins that are sure to stretch or slip!"

"And," said Kittiwynk, dancing to take the stiffness out of her, "they carry their whips in their hands instead of on their wrists. Hah!"

"True enough. No man can manage his stick and his reins, and his whip that way," said the Maltese Cat. "I've fallen over every square yard of the Malta ground, and I ought to know." He quivered his little flea-bitten withers just to show how satisfied he felt; but his heart was not so light. Ever since he had drifted into India on a troopship, taken, with an old rifle, as part payment for a racing debt, the Maltese Cat had played and preached polo to the Skidars' team on the Skidars' stony polo ground. Now a polo pony is like a poet. If he is born with a love for the game he can be made. The Maltese Cat knew that bamboos grew solely in order that polo balls might be turned from their roots, that grain was given to ponies to keep them in hard condition, and that ponies were shod to prevent them slipping on a turn. But, besides all these things, he knew every trick and device of the finest game of the world, and for two seasons he had been teaching the others all he knew or guessed.

"Remember," he said for the hundredth time as the riders came up, "we must play together, and you must play with your heads. Whatever happens, follow the ball. Who goes out first?"

Kittiwynk, Shiraz, Polaris, and a short high little bay fellow with tremendous hocks and no withers worth speaking of (he was called Corks) were being girthed up, and the soldiers in the background stared with all their eyes.

"I want you men to keep quiet," said Lutyens, the captain of the team, "and especially not to blow your pipes."

"Not if we win, Captain Sahib?" asked a piper.

"If we win, you can do what you please," said Lutyens, with a smile, as he slipped the loop of his stick over his wrist, and wheeled to canter to his place. The Archangels' ponies were a little bit above themselves on account of the many-colored crowd so close to the ground. Their riders were excellent players, but they were a team of crack players instead of a crack team; and that made all the difference in the world. They honestly meant to play together, but it is very hard for four men, each the best of the team he is picked from, to remember that in polo no brilliancy of hitting or riding makes up for playing alone. Their captain shouted his orders to them by name, and it is a curious thing that if you call his name aloud in public after an Englishman you make him hot and fretty. Lutyens said nothing to his men because it had all been said before. He pulled up Shiraz, for he was playing "back," to guard the goal. Powell on Polaris was halfback, and Macnamara and Hughes on Corks and Kittiwynk were forwards. The tough bamboo-root ball was put into the middle of the ground one hundred and fifty yards from the ends, and Hughes crossed sticks, heads up, with the captain of the Archangels, who saw fit to play forward, and that is a place from which you cannot easily control the team. The little click as the cane shafts met was heard all over the ground, and then Hughes made some sort of quick wrist stroke that just dribbled the ball a few yards. Kittiwynk knew that stroke of old, and followed as a cat follows a mouse. While the captain of the Archangels was wrenching his pony round Hughes struck with all his strength, and next instant Kittiwynk was away, Corks following close behind her, their little feet pattering like raindrops on glass.

"Pull out to the left," said Kittiwynk between her teeth, "it's coming our way, Corks!"

The back and halfback of the Archangels were tearing down on her just as she was within reach of the ball. Hughes leaned forward with a loose rein, and cut it away to the left almost under Kittiwynk's feet, and it hopped and skipped off to Corks, who saw that, if he were not quick, it would run beyond the boundaries. That long bouncing drive gave the Archangels time to wheel and send three men across the ground to head off Corks. Kittiwynk stayed where she was, for she knew the game. Corks was on the ball half a fraction of a second before the others came up, and Macnamara, with a back-handed stroke, sent it back across the ground to Hughes, who saw the way clear to the Archangels' goal, and smacked the ball in before any one quite knew what had happened.

"That's luck," said Corks, as they changed ends. "A goal in three minutes for three hits and no riding to speak of."

"Don't know," said Polaris. "We've made 'em angry too soon. Shouldn't wonder if they try to rush us off our feet next time."

"Keep the ball hanging then," said Shiraz. "That wears out every pony that isn't used to it."

Next time there was no easy galloping across the ground. All the Archangels closed up as one man, but there they stayed, for Corks, Kittiwynk, and Polaris were somewhere on the top of the ball, marking time among the rattling sticks, while Shiraz circled about outside, waiting for a chance.

"We can do this all day," said Polaris, ramming his quarters into the side of another pony. "Where do you think you're shoving to?"

"I'll—I'll be driven in an ekka if I know," was the gasping reply, "and I'd give a week's feed to get my blinkers off. I can't see anything."

"The dust is rather bad. Whew! That was one for my off hock. Where's the ball, Corks?"

"Under my tail. At least a man's looking for it there. This is beautiful.

They can't use their sticks, and it's driving 'em wild. Give old blinkers a push and he'll go over!''

"Here, don't touch me! I can't see. I'll—I'll back out, I think," said the pony in blinkers, who knew that if you can't see all round your head you cannot prop yourself against a shock.

Corks was watching the ball where it lay in the dust close to his near fore, with Macnamara's shortened stick tap-tapping it from time to time. Kittiwynk was edging her way out of the scrimmage, whisking her stump of a tail with nervous excitement.

"Ho! They've got it," she snorted. "Let me out!" and she galloped like a rifle bullet just behind a tall lanky pony of the Archangels, whose rider was swinging up his stick for a stroke.

"Not today, thank you," said Hughes, as the blow slid off his raised stick, and Kittiwynk laid her shoulder to the tall pony's quarters, and shoved him aside just as Lutyens on Shiraz sent the ball where it had come from, and the tall pony went skating and slipping away to the left. Kittiwynk, seeing that Polaris had joined Corks in the chase for the ball up the ground, dropped into Polaris's place, and then time was called.

The Skidars' ponies wasted no time in kicking or fuming. They knew each minute's rest meant so much gain, and trotted off to the rails and their saises, who began to scrape and blanket and rub them at once.

"Whew!" said Corks, stiffening up to get all the tickle out of the big vulcanite scraper. "If we were playing pony for pony we'd bend those Archangels double in half an hour. But they'll bring out fresh ones and fresh ones, and fresh ones after that—you see."

"Who cares?" said Polaris. "We've drawn first blood. Is my hock swelling?"

"Looks puffy," said Corks. "You must have had rather a wipe. Don't let it stiffen. You'll be wanted again in half an hour."

"What's the game like?" said the Maltese Cat.

"Ground's like your shoe, except where they've put too much water on it," said Kittiwynk. "Then it's slippery. Don't play in the center. There's a bog there. I don't know how their next four are going to behave, but we kept the ball hanging and made 'em lather for nothing. Who goes out? Two Arabs and a couple of country-breds! That's bad. What a comfort it is to wash your mouth out!"

Kitty was talking with the neck of a leather-covered soda-water bottle between her teeth and trying to look over her withers at the same time. This gave her a very coquettish air.

"What's bad?" said Gray Dawn, giving to the girth and admiring his well-set shoulders.

"You Arabs can't gallop fast enough to keep yourselves warm—that's what Kitty means," said Polaris, limping to show that his hock needed attention. "Are you playing 'back,' Gray Dawn?"

"Looks like it," said Gray Dawn, as Lutyens swung himself up. Powell mounted the Rabbit, a plain bay country-bred much like Corks, but with mulish ears. Macnamara took Faiz Ullah, a handy short-backed little red Arab with a long tail, and Hughes mounted Benami, an old and sullen brown beast, who stood over in front more than a polo pony should.

"Benami looks like business," said Shiraz. "How's your temper, Ben?" The old campaigner hobbled off without answering, and the Maltese Cat looked at the new Archangel ponies prancing about on the ground. They were four beautiful blacks, and they saddled big enough and strong enough to eat the Skidars' team and gallop away with the meal inside them.

"Blinkers again," said the Maltese Cat. "Good enough!"

"They're chargers—cavalry chargers!" said Kittiwynk indignantly. "They'll never see thirteen three again."

"They've all been fairly measured and they've all got their certificates," said the Maltese Cat, "or they wouldn't be here. We must take things as they come along, and keep our eyes on the ball."

The game began, but this time the Skidars were penned to their own end of the ground, and the watching ponies did not approve of that.

"Faiz Ullah is shirking as usual," said Polaris, with a scornful grunt.

"Faiz Ullah is eating whip," said Corks. They could hear the leather-thonged polo quirt lacing the little fellow's well-rounded barrel. Then the Rabbit's shrill neigh came across the ground. "I can't do all the work," he cried.

"Play the game, don't talk," the Maltese Cat whickered; and all the ponies wriggled with excitement, and the soldiers and the grooms gripped the railings and shouted. A black pony with blinkers had singled out old Benami, and was interfering with him in every possible way. They could see Benami shaking his head up and down and flapping his underlip.

"There'll be a fall in a minute," said Polaris. "Benami is getting stuffy."

The game flickered up and down between goal post and goal post, and the black ponies were getting more confident as they felt they had the legs of the others. The ball was hit out of a little scrimmage, and Benami and the Rabbit followed it; Faiz Ullah only too glad to be quiet for an instant.

The blinkered black pony came up like a hawk, with two of his own side behind him, and Benami's eye glittered as he raced. The question was which pony should make way for the other; each rider was perfectly willing to risk a fall in a good cause. The black who had been driven nearly crazy by his blinkers trusted to his weight and his temper; but Benami knew how to apply his weight and how to keep his temper. They met, and there was a cloud of dust. The black was lying on his side with all the breath knocked out of his body. The Rabbit was a hundred yards up the ground with the ball, and Benami was sitting down. He had slid nearly ten yards, but he had had his revenge, and sat cracking his nostrils till the black pony rose.

"That's what you get for interfering. Do you want any more?" said Benami, and he plunged into the game. Nothing was done because Faiz

Ullah would not gallop, though Macnamara beat him whenever he could spare a second. The fall of the black pony had impressed his companions tremendously, and so the Archangels could not profit by Faiz Ullah's bad behavior.

But as the Maltese Cat said, when time was called and the four came back blowing and dripping, Faiz Ullah ought to have been kicked all round Umballa. If he did not behave better next time, the Maltese Cat promised to pull out his Arab tail by the root and eat it.

There was no time to talk, for the third four were ordered out.

The third quarter of a game is generally the hottest, for each side thinks that the others must be pumped; and most of the winning play in a game is made about that time.

Lutyens took over the Maltese Cat with a pat and a hug, for Lutyens valued him more than anything else in the world. Powell had Shikast, a little gray rat with no pedigree and no manners outside polo; Macnamara mounted Bamboo, the largest of the team, and Hughes took Who's Who, alias The Animal. He was supposed to have Australian blood in his veins, but he looked like a clotheshorse, and you could whack him on the legs with an iron crowbar without hurting him.

They went out to meet the very flower of the Archangels' team, and when Who's Who saw their elegantly booted legs and their beautiful satiny skins he grinned a grin through his light, well-worn bridle.

"My word!" said Who's Who. "We must give 'em a little football. Those gentlemen need a rubbing down."

"No biting," said the Maltese Cat warningly, for once or twice in his career Who's Who had been known to forget himself in that way.

"Who said anything about biting? I'm not playing tiddlywinks. I'm playing the game."

The Archangels came down like a wolf on the fold, for they were tired of football and they wanted polo. They got it more and more. Just after the game began, Lutyens hit a ball that was coming towards him rapidly, and it rose in the air, as a ball sometimes will, with the whirr of a frightened partridge. Shikast heard, but could not see it for the minute, though he looked everywhere and up into the air as the Maltese Cat had taught him. When he saw it ahead and overhead he went forward with Powell as fast as he could put foot to ground. It was then that Powell, a quiet and level-headed man as a rule, became inspired and played a stroke that sometimes comes off successfully on a quiet afternoon of long practice. He took his stick in both hands, and standing up in his stirrups, swiped at the ball in the air, Munipore fashion. There was one second of paralyzed astonishment, and then all four sides of the ground went up in a yell of applause and delight as the ball flew true (you could see the amazed Archangels ducking in their saddles to get out of the line of flight, and looking at it with open mouths), and the regimental pipes of the Skidars squealed from the railings as long as the piper had breath.

Shikast heard the stroke; but he heard the head of the stick fly off at the same time. Nine hundred and ninety-nine ponies out of a thousand would have gone tearing on after the ball with a useless player pulling at their heads, but Powell knew him, and he knew Powell; and the instant he felt Powell's right leg shift a trifle on the saddle-flap he headed to the boundary, where a native officer was frantically waving a new stick. Before the shouts had ended Powell was armed again.

Once before in his life the Maltese Cat had heard that very same stroke played off his own back, and had profited by the confusion it made. This time he acted on experience, and leaving Bamboo to guard the goal in case of accidents, came through the others like a flash, head and tail low, Lutyens standing up to ease him—swept on and on before the other side knew what was the matter, and nearly pitched on his head between the Archangels' goal posts as Lutyens tipped the ball in after a straight scurry of a hundred and fifty yards. If there was one thing more than another upon which the Maltese Cat prided himself it was on this quick, streaking kind of run half across the ground. He did not believe in taking balls round the field unless you were clearly overmatched. After this they gave the Archangels five minutes' football, and an expensive fast pony hates football because it rumples his temper.

Who's Who showed himself even better than Polaris in this game. He did not permit any wriggling away, but bored joyfully into the scrimmage as if he had his nose in a feedbox, and were looking for something nice. Little Shikast jumped on the ball the minute it got clear, and every time an Archangel pony followed it he found Shikast standing over it asking what was the matter.

"If we can live through this quarter," said the Maltese Cat, "I shan't care. Don't take it out of yourselves. Let them do the lathering."

So the ponies, as their riders explained afterwards, "shut up." The Archangels kept them tied fast in front of their goal, but it cost the Archangels' ponies all that was left of their tempers; and ponies began to kick, and men began to repeat compliments, and they chopped at the legs of Who's Who, and he set his teeth and stayed where he was, and the dust stood up like a tree over the scrimmage till that hot quarter ended.

They found the ponies very excited and confident when they went to their saises; and the Maltese Cat had to warn them that the worst of the game was coming.

"Now we are all going in for the second time," said he, "and they are trotting out fresh ponies. You'll think you can gallop, but you'll find you can't; and then you'll be sorry."

"But two goals to nothing is a halter-long lead," said Kittiwynk, prancing.

"How long does it take to get a goal?" the Maltese Cat answered. "For pity sake, don't run away with the notion that the game is half-won just because we happen to be in luck now. They'll ride you into the grandstand if they can; you must not give 'em a chance. Follow the ball."

"Football as usual?" said Polaris. "My hock's half as big as a nose bag."

"Don't let them have a look at the ball if you can help it. Now leave me alone. I must get all the rest I can before the last quarter."

He hung down his head and let all his muscles go slack; Shikast, Bamboo, and Who's Who copying his example.

"Better not watch the game," he said. "We aren't playing, and we shall only take it out of ourselves if we grow anxious. Look at the ground and pretend it's flytime."

They did their best, but it was hard advice to follow. The hoofs were drumming and the sticks were rattling all up and down the ground, and yells of applause from the English troops told that the Archangels were pressing the Skidars hard. The native soldiers behind the ponies groaned and grunted, and said things in undertones, and presently they heard a long-drawn shout and a clatter of hurrahs!

"One to the Archangels," said Shikast, without raising his head. "Time's nearly up. Oh, my sire and—dam!"

"Faiz Ullah," said the Maltese Cat, "if you don't play to the last nail in your shoes this time, I'll kick you on the ground before all the other ponies."

"I'll do my best when my times comes," said the little Arab sturdily.

The saises looked at each other gravely as they rubbed their ponies' legs. This was the first time when long purses began to tell, and everybody knew it. Kittiwynk and the others came back with the sweat dripping over their hoofs and their tails telling sad stories.

"They're better than we are," said Shiraz. "I knew how it would be."

"Shut your big head," said the Maltese Cat; "we've one goal to the good yet."

"Yes, but it's two Arabs and two country-breds to play now," said Corks. "Faiz Ullah, remember!" He spoke in a biting voice.

As Lutyens mounted Gray Dawn he looked at his men, and they did not look pretty. They were covered with dust and sweat in streaks. Their yellow boots were almost black, their wrists were red and lumpy, and their eyes seemed two inches deep in their heads, but the expression in the eyes was satisfactory.

"Did you take anything at tiffin?" said Lutyens, and the team shook their heads. They were too dry to talk.

"All right. The Archangels did. They are worse pumped than we are."

"They've got the better ponies," said Powell. "I shan't be sorry when this business is over."

That fifth quarter was a sad one in every way. Faiz Ullah played like a little red demon; and the Rabbit seemed to be everywhere at once, and Benami rode straight at anything and everything that came in his way, while the umpires on their ponies wheeled like gulls outside the shifting game. But the Archangels had the better mounts—they had kept their racers till late in the game—and never allowed the Skidars to play football.

They hit the ball up and down the width of the ground till Benami and the rest were outpaced. Then they went forward, and time and again Lutyens and Gray Dawn were just, and only just, able to send the ball away with a long splitting backhander. Gray Dawn forgot that he was an Arab; and turned from gray to blue as he galloped. Indeed, he forgot too well, for he did not keep his eyes on the ground as an Arab should, but stuck out his nose and scuttled for the dear honor of the game. They had watered the ground once or twice between the quarters, and a careless waterman had emptied the last of his skinful all in one place near the Skidars' goal. It was close to the end of play, and for the tenth time Gray Dawn was bolting after a ball when his near hind foot slipped on the greasy mud and he rolled over and over, pitching Lutyens just clear of the goalpost; and the triumphant Archangels made their goal. Then time was called—two goals all; but Lutyens had to be helped up, and Gray Dawn rose with his near hind leg strained somewhere.

"What's the damage?" said Powell, his arm round Lutyens.

"Collarbone, of course," said Lutyens between his teeth. It was the third time he had broken it in two years, and it hurt him.

Powell and the others whistled. "Game's up," said Hughes.

"Hold on. We've five good minutes yet, and it isn't my right hand," said Lutyens. "We'll stick it out."

"I say," said the captain of the Archangels, trotting up. "Are you hurt, Lutyens? We'll wait if you care to put in a substitute. I wish—I mean—the fact is, you fellows deserve this game if any team does. Wish we could give you a man or some of our ponies—or something."

"You're awfully good, but we'll play to a finish, I think."

The captain of the Archangels stared for a little. "That's not half bad," he said, and went back to his own side, while Lutyens borrowed a scarf from one of his native officers and made a sling of it. Then an Archangel galloped up with a big bath sponge and advised Lutyens to put it under his armpit to ease his shoulder, and between them they tied up his left arm scientifically, and one of the native officers leaped forward with four long glasses that fizzed and bubbled.

The team looked at Lutyens piteously, and he nodded. It was the last quarter, and nothing would matter after that. They drank out the dark golden drink, and wiped their mustaches, and things looked more hopeful.

The Maltese Cat had put his nose into the front of Lutyens' shirt, and was trying to say how sorry he was.

"He knows," said Lutyens, proudly. "The beggar knows. I've played him without a bridle before now—for fun."

"It's no fun now," said Powell. "But we haven't a decent substitute."

"No," said Lutyens. "It's the last quarter, and we've got to make our goal and win. I'll trust the Cat."

"If you fall this time you'll suffer a little," said Macnamara.

"I'll trust the Cat," said Lutyens.

"You hear that?" said the Maltese Cat proudly to the others. "It's worth while playing polo for ten years to have that said of you. Now then, my sons, come along. We'll kick up a little bit, just to show the Archangels this team haven't suffered."

And, sure enough, as they went on to the ground the Maltese Cat, after satisfying himself that Lutyens was home in the saddle, kicked out three or four times, and Lutyens laughed. The reins were caught up anyhow in the tips of his strapped hand, and he never pretended to rely on them. He knew the Cat would answer to the least pressure of the leg, and by way of showing off—for his shoulder hurt him very much—he bent the little fellow in a close figure-of-eight in and out between the goalposts. There was a roar from the native officers and men, who dearly loved a piece of dugabashi (horse-trick work), as they called it, and the pipes very quietly and scornfully droned out the first bars of a common bazaar tune called "Freshly Fresh and Newly New," just as a warning to the other regiments that the Skidars were fit. All the natives laughed.

"And now," said the Cat, as they took their place, "remember that this is the last quarter, and follow the ball!"

"Don't need to be told," said Who's Who.

"Let me go on. All those people on all four sides will begin to crowd in —just as they did at Malta. You'll hear people calling out, and moving forward and being pushed back, and that is going to make the Archangel ponies very unhappy. But if a ball is struck to the boundary, you go after it, and let the people get out of your way. I went over the pole of a four-in-hand once, and picked a game out of the dust by it. Back me up when I run, and follow the ball."

There was a sort of an all-round sound of sympathy and wonder as the last quarter opened, and then there began exactly what the Maltese Cat had foreseen. People crowded in close to the boundaries, and the Archangels' ponies kept looking sideways at the narrowing space. If you know how a man feels to be cramped at tennis—not because he wants to run out of the court, but because he likes to know that he can at a pinch—you will guess how ponies must feel when they are playing in a box of human beings.

"I'll bend some of those men if I can get away," said Who's Who, as he rocketed behind the ball; and Bamboo nodded without speaking. They were playing the last ounce in them, and the Maltese Cat had left the goal undefended to join them. Lutyens gave him every order that he could to bring him back, but this was the first time in his career that the little wise gray had ever played polo on his own responsibility, and he was going to make the most of it.

"What are you doing here?" said Hughes, as the Cat crossed in front of him and rode off an Archangel.

"The Cat's in charge—mind the goal!" shouted Lutyens, and bowing forward hit the ball full, and followed on, forcing the Archangels towards their own goal.

"No football," said the Cat. "Keep the ball by the boundaries and cramp 'em. Play open order and drive 'em to the boundaries."

Across and across the ground in big diagonals flew the ball, and whenever it came to a flying rush and a stroke close to the boundaries the Archangel ponies moved stiffly. They did not care to go headlong at a wall of men and carriages, though if the ground had been open they could have turned on a sixpence.

"Wriggle her up the sides," said the Cat. "Keep her close to the crowd. They hate the carriages. Shikast, keep her up this side."

Shikast with Powell lay left and right behind the uneasy scuffle of an open scrimmage, and every time the ball was hit away Shikast galloped on it at such an angle that Powell was forced to hit it towards the boundary; and when the crowd had been driven away from that side, Lutyens would send the ball over to the other, and Shikast would slide desperately after it till his friends came down to help. It was billiards, and no football, this time—billiards in a corner pocket; and the cues were not well chalked.

"If they get us out in the middle of the ground they'll walk away from us. Dribble her along the sides," cried the Cat.

So they dribbled all along the boundary, where a pony could not come on their right-hand side; and the Archangels were furious, and the umpires had to neglect the game to shout at the people to get back, and several blundering mounted policemen tried to restore order, all close to the scrimmage, and the nerves of the Archangels' ponies stretched and broke like cobwebs.

Five or six times an Archangel hit the ball up into the middle of the ground, and each time the watchful Shikast gave Powell his chance to send it back, and after each return, when the dust had settled, men could see that the Skidars had gained a few yards.

Every now and again there were shouts of " 'Side! Off side!" from the spectators; but the teams were too busy to care, and the umpires had all they could do to keep their maddened ponies clear of the scuffle.

At last Lutyens missed a short easy stroke, and the Skidars had to fly back helter-skelter to protect their own goal, Shikast leading. Powell stopped the ball with a backhander when it was not fifty yards from the goalposts, and Shikast spun round with a wrench that nearly hoisted Powell out of his saddle.

"Now's our last chance," said the Cat, wheeling like a cock-chafer on a pin. "We've got to ride it out. Come along."

Lutyens felt the little chap take a deep breath, and, as it were, crouch under his rider. The ball was hopping towards the right-hand boundary, an Archangel riding for it with both spurs and a whip; but neither spur nor whip would make his pony stretch himself as he neared the crowd. The Maltese Cat glided under his very nose, picking up his hind legs sharp, for there was not a foot to spare between his quarters and the other pony's bit. It was as neat an exhibition as fancy figure-skating. Lutyens hit with all the strength he had left, but the stick slipped a little in his hand, and the ball flew off to the left instead of keeping close to the boundary. Who's Who was far across the ground, thinking hard as he galloped. He repeated, stride for stride, the Cat's maneuvers with another Archangel pony, nipping the ball away from under his bridle, and clearing his opponent by half a fraction of an inch, for Who's Who was clumsy behind. Then he drove away towards the right as the Maltese Cat came up from the left; and Bamboo held a middle course exactly between them. The three were making a sort of Government-broad-arrow-shaped attack; and there was only the Archangels' back to guard the goal; but immediately behind them were three Archangels racing all they knew, and mixed up with them was Powell, sending Shikast along on what he felt was their last hope. It takes a very good man to stand up to the rush of seven crazy ponies in the last quarters of a cup game, when men are riding with their necks for sale, and the ponies are delirious. The Archangels' back missed his stroke, and pulled aside just in time to let the rush go by. Bamboo and Who's Who shortened stride to give the Maltese Cat room, and Lutyens got the goal with a clean, smooth, smacking stroke that was heard all over the field. But there was no stopping the ponies. They poured through the goalposts in one mixed mob, winners and losers together, for the pace had been terrific. The Maltese Cat knew by experience what would happen, and, to save Lutyens, turned to the right with one last effort that strained a back-sinew beyond hope of repair. As he did so he heard the right-hand goalpost crack as a pony cannoned into it—crack, splinter, and fall like a mast. It had been sawed three parts through in case of accidents, but it upset the pony nevertheless, and he blundered into another, who blundered into the left-hand post, and then there was confusion and dust and wood. Bamboo was lying on the ground, seeing stars; an Archangel pony rolled beside him, breathless and angry; Shikast had sat down dog-fashion to avoid falling over the others, and was sliding along on his little bobtail in a cloud of dust; and Powell was sitting on the ground, hammering with his stick and trying to cheer. All the others were shouting at the top of what was left of their voices, and the men who had been split were shouting too. As soon as the people saw no one was hurt, ten thousand native and English shouted and clapped and yelled, and before any one could stop them the pipers of the Skidars broke on to the ground, with all the native officers and men behind them, and marched up and down, playing a wild northern tune called "Zakhme Bagan," and through the insolent blaring of the pipes and the high-pitched native yells you could hear the Archangels' band hammering, "For they are all jolly good fellows," and then reproachfully to the losing team, "Ooh, Kafoozalum! Kafoozalum! Kafoozalum!"

Besides all these things and many more, there was a Commander-in-Chief, and an Inspector-General of Cavalry, and the principal veterinary officer in all India, standing on the top of a regimental coach, yelling like schoolboys; and brigadiers and colonels and commissioners, and hundreds of pretty ladies joined the chorus. But the Maltese Cat stood with his head down, wondering how many legs were left to him; and Lutyens watched the men and ponies pick themselves out of the wreck of the two goalposts, and he patted the Cat very tenderly.

"I say," said the captain of the Archangels, spitting a pebble out of his mouth, "will you take three thousand for that pony—as he stands?"

"No, thank you. I've an idea he's saved my life," said Lutyens, getting off and lying down at full length. Both teams were on the ground too, waving their boots in the air, and coughing and drawing deep breaths, as the saises ran up to take away the ponies, and an officious water-carrier sprinkled the players with dirty water till they sat up.

"My Aunt!" said Powell, rubbing his back and looking at the stumps of the goalposts, "that was a game!"

They played it over again, every stroke of it, that night at the big dinner, when the Free-for-All Cup was filled and passed down the table, and emptied and filled again, and everybody made most eloquent speeches. About two in the morning, when there might have been some singing, a wise little, plain little, gray little head looked in through the open door.

"Hurrah! Bring him in," said the Archangels; and his sais, who was very happy indeed, patted the Maltese Cat on the flank, and he limped into the blaze of light and the glittering uniforms, looking for Lutyens. He was used to messes, and men's bedrooms, and places where ponies are not usually encouraged, and in his youth had jumped on and off a mess table for a bet. So he behaved himself very politely, and ate bread dipped in salt, and was petted all round the table, moving gingerly; and they drank his health, because he had done more to win the Cup than any man or horse on the ground.

That was glory and honor enough for the rest of his days, and the Maltese Cat did not complain much when his veterinary surgeon said that he would be no good for polo any more. When Lutyens married, his wife did not allow him to play, so he was forced to be an umpire; and his pony on these occasions was a flea-bitten gray with a neat polo tail, lame all round, but desperately quick on his feet, and, as everybody knew, Past Pluperfect Prestissimo Player of the Game.

THE YALE-HARVARD BOAT RACE
By Stephen Kiesling

Two weeks into the Ferry we had our next major test, a two-and-a-half-mile race against Navy. Like Dartmouth the previous year, Navy finished well behind us in the Sprints. We knew that we could beat them, but then we should have beaten Dartmouth. We were confident but subdued.

When the bus pulled up to the boathouse at Annapolis, the midshipmen were flying a Yale flag from one of their poles. They greeted us, congratulated us on the Sprints, and escorted us into the boathouse. It was flattering except for their paternalistic concern. Being patronized by oarsmen that we had clobbered only two weeks before was disturbing, especially because they had upset Harvard at a similar race the year before.

The following morning, the coddling continued. During the three-mile paddle to the starting line, they stationed boats to show us the way and gave rather too many people instructions to ensure that we arrived on time. Lulled into a new sense of security, we hardly noticed that the Navy eight was positioned nearly a length ahead of us at the start. The start was supposed to be staggered by one seat because of a slight turn in the course. A seat, not a length. When we pulled closer they politely but firmly told us to get back where we were. The right way, the wrong way and . . . I put the thought out of my mind.

Navy needed more than a length head start; in fact, after a half a mile the race was essentially over. In the first thirty strokes we pulled even and were beginning to pass when Andy warned of a wash from a passing launch. I felt the first rise as the bow hit the wake and then the rapid undulations, but we were prepared and flowed through the bad water without missing a stroke. Navy hit the wake like a deck of cards badly shuffled. Their six man failed to release his oar, transferring the momentum of the shell through the oar into his middle. Had his feet not been tied into the boat, he would have been catapulted into the estuary. Navy resumed rowing almost before the spray had settled, but the race was no longer a contest. They faded away like all the other crews we had raced to lose by eighteen seconds. "A horizon but not quite a time zone," we termed the margin in our new jargon for success. Navy resumed an obviously more strained patronage when we returned to the dock.

We did not get a real test until our second and final four-mile time trial the week after the Navy race. Knowing it would be the last indication of our chances against Harvard, we prepared for the trial as if it were the Race itself. We rested with light practices the day before and adjusted our schedule to row when the tide would be similar to Race Day's. The two lanes of the course had been staked along the river so we would not have to estimate the distance. It was not hard to convince ourselves that the real race had arrived.

Rested and psyched, we charged from the starting line striking a vigorous 42 strokes a minute, settled to 37 and then settled again to a solid 35. A mile into our race the junior varsity joined us for the last three miles. Although they began a little before we arrived at the three-mile mark, we surged past. At the two-mile mark the freshmen also joined the race to ensure that we were pressed until the finish. Again we moved past. In the last five hundred meters we raised the rating for the sprint and finished with the other boats lengths behind. If we rowed like that against Harvard, they would never even see us—or so I believed.

Tony did not say anything immediately after the practice, but called a meeting a few hours later. The sun was bright as we gathered on the porch of the manager's house. The rain that had been with us all week had lifted. All indicators pointed toward success. As we waited for his arrival I imagined the brief advice he would give us. Tony invariably recited the same parables before each race, and I knew most of them thoroughly. He would congratulate us on our performance, tell us to enjoy our day off and close with his favorite story, the story of limits. "There are no limits!" he would conclude at length, and then we would go back to the croquet tournament.

As I watched him come up the steps, I thought for a moment that someone close to him had died. The silver hair, which usually clashed with his youthful frame, made him look old. Clearly he was shaken as he gathered his thoughts. Then slowly, in what became a stunned silence, he explained that while we had rowed a high cadence, the boat was not moving well between strokes. There had not been much "spacing" between the puddles churned up by one stroke and the next. Contrary to what all of us felt, if we rowed as we had that day, we would lose.

A car drove by, the telephone rang, but still no one spoke. I lost myself in contemplation of a new blister and tried to think of a response. Never in my two years with Tony had he ever said anything so directly, believing that we should come to rely on our own judgments. All I knew about rowing was based on being able to trust what felt good. I had faith in my instincts, the faith of an undefeated season, but was it his record or ours? Tony had never beaten Harvard over four miles. For eight years his boats had lost to Harvard at every encounter until we had broken the streak at the Sprints in 1978. Maybe he thought us overconfident, but even if what he said was true, was it right to shake that confidence? We had the strength, the conditioning and the skill to win; that much I knew, but four miles was a long race, a lot of time to face the pain. Relaxation between strokes made the four miles possible, but relaxation was earned by confidence. Harvard's oarsmen could put their faith in Harry Parker knowing that his boats had never lost. They could just do what he told them and expect to win.

For the first time I felt afraid—knowing that fear would kill us. I wanted Tony to know what he had done, yet concealed my own weakness. What would the sophomores feel if they saw the tears forming?

I slunk back to my room to think it over. We had done our best and been told that it was not good enough. Not only was it not good enough, but the criteria for determining what was good had changed. I never checked to see if the spacing was good. I was not sure how to tell. The boat felt good and we had beaten the other two boats: what more could we have done? But if Tony said we were going to lose, then I supposed we were going to lose. No, that was impossible!

For the next few practices, I willed the spacing to improve, but the boat felt the same—and that felt good. After a couple of days Tony declared that the spacing had improved. I imagined that he just wanted us to stop worrying. In any case, I stopped thinking about it. I stopped thinking about much of anything.

The rain returned every day. I contemplated writing letters, but having nothing to say to anyone, I walked into the town of Gales Ferry for a new book. I did not find one, but I saw a few of the Harvard oarsmen. They refused to acknowledge my presence. The townspeople were rooting for us. They did not believe that we would win because so few of them remembered that we ever had won. They root for the underdog. I tried to explain to the postman that we were not the underdogs, that Harvard was expected to lose. He just laughed.

About four days before the Race, Andy Fisher tried to organize a coxswain's race. Traditionally on the day before the races, the coxswains from Yale and Harvard raced in four-oared shells from Gales Ferry to Red Top coxed by the heaviest oarsman from each side; however, because Harvard oarsmen shot water balloons at the Yale coxswains the previous year, Andy refused to race unless the race was switched to finish at Gales Ferry. Switching directions would have been a psychological coup, sixteen losses made any change advantageous, which was why Harvard wanted to maintain tradition. Later, Harvard agreed to the switch if their freshman coach, who had been a coxswain thirteen years before, could compete, but Andy thought it was only fair if both freshman coaches were allowed to compete (Mike Vespoli, our new freshman coach, had rowed in the world champion eight only five years before). I imagined that the Harvard coxswains would row to Gales Ferry while our coxswains rowed to Red Top. The two boatloads of coxswains would not even wave as they passed each other.

Unyielding pride and audacity make good coxswains. Through supreme confidence, coxswains coax oarsmen beyond what their own willpower can accomplish. Craziness, I had thought of their squabble over their race, but that same craziness would help us endure.

By Wednesday the Ferry was drawing to a close. Practices were mild and we were allowed to sleep late in the morning. The veils of exhaustion that had hung over us cleared more each day. Telegrams of encouragement became frequent and the atmosphere more festive. Time to put life in order before the Race.

For those weeks I had lived like a slob—a month spent in my own private locker room with clothes and towels strewn about the floor, kept damp and pungent by the daily rain. I had seldom shaved or even brushed my teeth. My hair, while short, was disheveled. Juxtaposed to the concentration and discipline of practice, disorder had been comforting, a mild rebellion to remind me I was no machine.

I picked the laundry off the floor, found my shaving kit and headed for the washroom. From the porch I looked toward Red Top and down the line of lane markers toward the bridge. The Race seemed for me and for the crew a rite of passage. Winning would establish the maturation of the new era of the Yale crew. Everything had to be in order so that we were free to focus. I considered writing my will and calling in my friends as witnesses.

Ted, our bowman, was completing his scrapbook, four years of newspaper clippings, started at a time when beating Navy was cause for celebration, to 1979, when we swept the championship. The scrapbook, a blue one with *Lux et Veritas* inscribed on the cover, began with an invitation to the freshman reception at President Brewster's house. By the end of the first year it remembered only the races. The graduation announcement that once centered the final page had been moved to make room for the Race program. Ted and the other seniors had graduated two weeks ago in New Haven. They were given a two-day leave to free themselves for the final gesture of their Yale careers. The scrapbook would help keep Ted's stories in line with the facts as we got older.

The final night, when John and I were preparing for sleep, Eric sauntered in and handed John a telegram from the captain of the 1963 crew. "FROM THE LAST CREW TO WIN AND THE FIRST CREW TO LOSE, SIXTEEN YEARS OF ANTICIPATION RIDES WITH YOU . . . GOOD LUCK."

"Thanks a lot," muttered Biglow. I read it and swore. We had been relaxed before reading the note. We needed to forget the burden of those sixteen years, yet it was in part those sixteen years that made the Race so important. As freshmen the three of us had helped break the string of fifteen freshman losses. As sophomores we had won the Sprints for the first time in twenty years, but we tried to forget the past. The last twenty years had nothing to do with the present; time and time again, however, we were told that it did. If we won, we earned that much more glory. If we didn't, nobody really thought it was possible anyway, but the task was clear.

I thought of Tony as he had stood at the head of the banquet table after the previous loss to Harvard. He congratulated us on the season, on how proud he was of us and how much we had accomplished. His voice had been level, encouraging. It was a good race, he explained. We had learned a lot. "Next year . . ." he began calmly, but for an instant the calm broke. Tony drew himself up with a shiver and a newly formed tear. "But we've got to beat Harvard!"

That's his mania, his problem, I thought then. I was tired of being swept along as Tony's paintbrush, in a piece that we had been maneuvered into creating, but was not ours. Trying to do it for Tony or for all those alumni wasn't worth the devastation of defeat.

"Let's do it for Buzz!" The cry rang out for our freshman coach as we passed Harvard. For Buzz we did it freshman year, and for Tony we tried the next, but I realized now that we were not Tony's arms and legs in that race, or any race. Thrown together, with legs, arms, backs, breathing and eventually heartbeats in unison, we were physically and mentally one. Tony would be somewhere behind, silenced by Ivy League rules against coaching during a race and the knowledge that it was out of his hands. The mania, which had come to us as his, was ours.

How fast is Harvard? I wondered. The regular Harvard coxswain had failed to graduate and would not be in the race. Should we win, the alternate cox might become an excuse. I didn't care. Winning no matter what the excuse was preferable to losing. I imagined that Harvard would fall a length behind in the first couple of miles. After that, I didn't know. The previous year, I psyched myself, convinced that we would have to go beyond our capabilities, to row until we dropped and to keep rowing. Now I felt confident. With our best effort we would not be beaten. We had been pampered long enough. No regrets. I drifted into restless dreams.

Gunfire awakened the river. The Race was postponed. No, not postponed. Changed . . . horribly! We marched onto the bridge in rowing shorts and racing shirts, balancing on the guardrail. Every now and then the mist would part, and we could see our opponents, wearing crimson, similarly balanced on the opposite rail. Wind whipped around us, but where we stood was dead calm. Calm enough to load and aim our pistols. One shot each.

The mist was clearing. Occasionally I caught glimpses of the gallery on either bank. The survivors, wearing stained and faded shirts from past years, kept score. The gallery called to the coxswains, who called the shots. The two bowmen fired first, a muffled report and a dull thud. I wondered if Ted saw the smooth hole cut through his forehead before he disappeared, spinning end over end into the mist, but there was no time to worry about Ted. The splash of the bowmen was subsumed under the applause of the galleries. Every time the mist cleared two more shots rang out and two more scores were tallied. Ted, Joe, Matthew, Karl, John. The coxswain called their turns. Each raised his pistol, fired, and disappeared with a clean round hole drilled through his forehead.

How could a team win if no one missed? Only Eric and I were left to face the last of Harvard, and then Eric disappeared, taking with him the seventh of the Harvard eight. No one was going to win at all! Ridiculous! I raised my arm, sighting an inch above the barrel that returned my gaze, and pulled the trigger.

I awakened, struggling in waves of sheets. John was eyeing me curiously from across the room. Nauseated and in no mood to explain, I lurched into the bright sun on the balcony and looked up at our flag. A tailwind. Shit! The oath fell unconsciously. A headwind would have settled the boat, making our size and strength an overwhelming advantage—sealing their fate. The tailwind would favor Harvard. Perhaps the wind would change before dusk, but I doubted it. At least the Rock was still blue. Someone had been up all night protecting it. Already there were ten or twenty yachts at anchor near the finish line. Eric's parents were unpacking themselves from their car. The road must still be open. Eric's parents . . . A bit surprised, I looked down at my underwear and retreated.

All my belongings were packed. Thucydides had moved under the bottle of Kaopectate but was still unread. It would be over in eight hours as if it had never happened. The only loose ends were my racing shirt and shorts hanging above my bed.

All of us had slept fitfully. John looked whiter than usual as he climbed out of bed. "A tailwind," I told him, giving my voice no emphasis.

John shrugged. "Fast race then," and left. I wondered if it was taboo to mention such a disadvantage so soon before the Race. I had tried to keep all judgment out of my voice. Maybe it didn't matter.

After breakfast we paddled three miles down the course and left our boat at the Coast Guard Academy, one mile upstream from the bridge. We would launch that afternoon from the Academy because four miles was too far to row before the Race. The previous year we had left our boat and returned to the Ferry on board an alumnus' cabin cruiser, but the advice we were given during the ride left me so nervous I could barely stand. This time the van arrived to drive us back. The Harvard varsity would also launch from the Academy.

By noon the number of spectators was annoying. Those who visited were relatives, friends or former oarsmen, people who understood and believed in the Race, but each well-wisher meant an extra burden. We might hear them as we neared the finish, but they could not add to the Race itself. The Race would be rowed alone.

Rather than spend the day in worried anticipation, we piled into cars to see the local matinee. It passed the time. We returned to the Ferry in the late afternoon with only an hour left to brood. Most of the spectators had moved across the river or onto boats anchored at the finish. By that point I just felt tired. I remember that Joe walked into the main room, feigning the confidence that none of us felt.

"Gentlemen," he said, mimicking the voice of the starting judge, "my hand is down!"

Dread such as I had never felt before settled upon me. Normally those words brought a shiver of excitement, but now I wanted to leave, to sleep, to be sick.

An hour and a half before the Race, we packed ourselves back into the van and returned to the Coast Guard Academy. Tony had to be in a launch to help officiate at the freshman and junior varsity races so he could not be with us. He had called us together earlier but there had been nothing to say. I thought of Tony's two European championships and his Olympic silver medal. The pair he rowed had been the most successful U.S. pair before or since. Eight times he had watched his crews humiliated in New London. The obsession had grown every year, yet already this race was out of his hands.

The Harvard crew was clustered around a radio, listening to the broadcast of the freshman race, when we arrived. When it became apparent that our freshmen were well ahead I joined them. The mystique about Harvard was ending. Our freshmen had never witnessed the humiliation of a Yale boat losing to Harvard. Perhaps they would never have to. My own freshman year we had gone into the race scared to death. We trailed by a length over the two-mile course until the last few hundred meters when we began to close. We passed Harvard in the final strokes of the race, breaking the fifteen-year freshman losing streak. With our freshmen a length ahead three minutes into the race I felt better about our own chances. The tailwind was still blowing, but by then I too was only thinking of a faster race. If our freshmen could win in a tailwind, then we would have no problem.

Five minutes later the Harvard varsity was cheering. With half a mile to go their freshmen had moved back and were going to pass. I did not listen further. I guess we should have tried to instill a little more fear into our boat. While a freshman victory would have added to our confidence, their loss gave us something to avenge.

Another half hour of stretching and pacing, mostly pacing, and it was time to launch. Harvard on one side of the narrow dock and we on the other, our blades crossed in the middle. We had raced Harvard at the Sprints and passed each other numerous times on the river, but I had no real idea of what they looked like. They did not look that big. They did not look big at all. Maybe there was nothing to worry about. It was their turn to be frightened.

Then came disaster. Karl, our three man, had forgotten to replace a frayed shoelace on his footstretcher. I heard an oath and turned to watch as Karl stared blankly at the broken string in his hand. The remainder was too short, and no one had brought a spare. After a moment's consternation our trainer, who was dockside to help us launch, contributed a lace from his own shoes. One thing always breaks before a big race. Better a shoelace than the oar Eric broke a few days ago. We shoved off, conscious that there was no one to sing the Yale cheer. I was glad. We were alone together.

As we had before our other races, we took a simple warm-up. A few drills, some long three-quarter pressure work, then a few "tens" and starts to get the cadence up. It was a warm-up appropriate for a crew about to row a 2,000-meter race but then so was our strategy. In 1978 we had tried to row down the course at a constant speed, relying on making up at the finish any seats which we allowed Harvard early in the Race. Slow and steady; but we lost by twelve seconds. Seats given up early proved impossible to regain after a couple of miles, so we intended to race now as if it were 2,000 meters. Go out fast, get a lead and hang on. Once in front, we could take control of the Race. If we were ahead after a couple of miles, no one would row through us. I kept thinking about the plan. Attack it! Get ahead in the first mile and commit yourself. So long as we did not fall behind early in the Race everything would be fine. Unlike other large races I was not mumbling "I quit" on every stroke. Neither was I rehearsing what to say to the reporters.

We rowed between the two pillars of the bridge to the starting line, believing that our entire season, indeed Yale rowing for many years, would be judged on the basis of our performance that day. We accepted the challenge. Where before I had been sluggish and stale, I was now powerful and relaxed, the excitement controlled and smooth. Confidently, we backed the stern of our shell into the waiting hands of the stake-boat boy. Hundreds of feet above us, cars whisked by, oblivious to our drama. Up there were the shortcuts, the excuses, the world of infinite possibilities separating man and his potential. We had four miles and the best competition in the nation. We linked hands in a chain down the boat, committing ourselves to each other. I gave a final glance at Harvard, and then looked over my shoulder down the lines of stakes receding into the distance. We were set, the boats were aligned, and both coxswains' hands were down.

"Gentlemen! Both coxswains hands are down!"

"My hand is down!"

"Are you ready? . . . Ready all. . . . Row!"

The blades locking in, backs opening, legs driving. The dull gray water began to boil. Three short strokes to get the boat in motion and twenty high. The cadence increasing with every catch. Remember to breathe and relax up the slide. Breathe and relax. Four miles. Start the rhythm one stroke at a time. Screw that, let's go! The stroke felt higher than usual but solid. Ten strokes gone—only ten more before we settle.

We had left the line at 45 strokes a minute, two strokes higher than in any other race in the season and three strokes over Harvard. Perhaps it was foolish to start so high, but as the commands were called, all the frustration of explaining for an entire year why we lost last time wound its final coil. The command "Row!" unleashed the desire of a year and nothing was going to stop it.

"Oh, you gods!" the Harvard five man had stood up in the shell and chanted to his crew in the shell after winning the San Diego Crew Classic two months before.

"I've got one Harvard god!" screamed Andy.

"I've got two gods! Three gods!"

The crimson blur beside us was dropping back. A seat down after ten strokes, three after fifteen. "Settle in two," yelled Andy. Four seats up.

"Settle!"

With an almost imperceptible hesitation returning up the slide, we dropped the cadence to 38. At the Sprints we had settled to 37. All I knew was that it seemed high but gloriously so. As we had moved to about a length up on Harvard, any doubts I had had about the Race faded. It was worthwhile after all.

I felt a wave of disappointment. The Race, it seemed, would be like any other that season. We would get a length lead early and then gradually pull away. A year's training had gone into these few races and we had won them all in the first few hundred meters. I wanted to win, but I expected more. I expected more until Harvard began pulling back.

In a four-mile race each stroke is at full pressure, but "full pressure" can have different intensities. The strategy for planning special moves during the long race can be critical. At a few hundred meters gone, Harvard took a "power ten" to move back through us. I heard their coxswain calling each stroke and saw their boat surge forward a seat or two, but all this was according to plan. Now it was five hundred meters gone and our turn to make a move. And move we did. We recaptured the distance and kept moving for the little orange ball on the tip of their bow. "I've got their bow deck and I want a bow ball!" screamed Andy, but Harvard held us.

Our cadence had slipped to a more sustainable 35 with Harvard a stroke or so below. The initial burst of adrenaline had been successful, giving us a lead and setting a vigorous pace which I didn't believe Harvard could maintain. I thought of the Sprints a month before. We had been at the thousand-meter mark, halfway home and a length up on Harvard and the rest of the pack. At the thousand Harvard had taken a "twenty." I remembered watching, fascinated, as their stroke cadence came up a beat, and they started to move back. "Relax!" was all Andy yelled, drawing out the syllables in contempt, and Harvard's momentum stopped. I had looked upon Harvard with supreme pity and contempt. That move was all they had, I thought, and it wasn't good enough.

I now looked at Harvard with the same expectation. At some point we would see their last move and we would know it. In the meantime, the Race continued with Harvard taking tens to move, and us countering to regain any distance they made up. Harvard was not getting any closer but neither were they falling back. Our cadence was beginning to feel a bit frenetic. While the timing was good, we were not getting the proper relaxation between strokes. Andy, meanwhile, was not going to let Harvard forget that they were behind. As well as the microphone system which he used to communicate with us. he wore a megaphone for the benefit of the Harvard crew. Whenever we took a seat, Andy called it to Harvard's attention. If a Harvard man swiveled his head to see where we were, Andy exposed him. "The gods are looking!" Being in front, we did not have to turn our heads to see Harvard.

The bridge was not getting much smaller. It still loomed above, mocking our attempts to leave it. With a mile and a quarter gone, the end of a 2,000-meter race, our rating was still too high, and we were beginning to pay for it. Some of the smoothness had definitely left the stroke. I thought that we should drop the rate a beat or two but with Harvard so close I could not be sure. Dropping the cadence properly could maintain the same speed at less cost. Done improperly, the boat would get sluggish. Andy had a marvelous feel for relaxing a stroke at just the right time. He had gotten us two Eastern Championships with the skill, so I resolved to let him worry about it. We had rowed the time trial at a high rating. On the other hand, Harvard had not been on our tail.

At a little more than two miles gone, our plan, so far as it went, had been successful, but I sensed trouble. We were in front as we expected, but Harvard showed no sign of fading. They continued to match us ten for ten; in fact, it seemed that they were taking more on their tens than we recovered with our own. As we passed the Groton submarine dry docks the water became rougher, threatening to throw off our timing. Relax, I kept saying to myself, but to relax took more concentration, more energy, than I had. The Harvard boat which had hugged fairly close to us had drifted well over to the far edge of their lane. With the boats so far apart it was hard to tell who was winning. I was afraid to turn my head in the rough water.

Somewhere in that stretch the boat tipped to starboard and I rolled up the slide and returned without ever setting my blade in the water. The boat balanced again, but during that brief absence of pain the unconscious rhythm had been broken. For a moment it seemed whether the oar was in the water or not made no difference, my legs did the same thing. In panic I rushed up for the next few strokes to prove that I was still there, still pulling. Harvard was clearly moving.

With two and a half miles gone, the boats were dead even. Each catch sent one boat ahead before the other boat took its own catch and moved back. We seesawed back and forth, stroke for stroke, with a mile and a half to go. There were occasional tens but there seemed no difference between moves and the base cadence. The boat hovered in an amorphous fog. My legs had lost all sensation yet my ears rang as if my body was screaming. I could not focus my eyes. Some magic kept my oar and body sychronized with the others, but to my knowledge I was just throwing myself back and forth. Harvard called another ten to move but made no progress. Through the mist that was filling my brain I could hear Andy taunt them, "Not hard enough, Harvard!"

Fury brought me back. Taunting a boat that was moving would make them move faster. Cursing my own prophecy, I heard Harvard's next move and saw them take the lead. I was breathing better and probably pulling harder, but when a boat moves past another after a struggle, triumph will keep it moving. Soon Harvard was a half a length ahead.

Andy was not saying anything so I did my own calculations. With less than a mile to go we were three-quarters of a length down. How much did I have left? At what point could we kick the rating up and sprint ahead? If the rating was called up I knew that I would stay with it; faith and three years of training would see to that. But I also realized that the decision to work harder was no longer mine. I could do more if Andy demanded it of the boat, but I was too exhausted to demand more of myself. I needed Andy to persuade me that I could.

The sound of the crowd from the spectators' yachts focused us as we neared the finish. "Eric, let's go!" I gasped forward, hoping to revive myself with the words. "Please, Andy, call it up." My voice probably had not carried even as far as Eric. I felt old and sluggish—the Race had become slow motion. The ringing in my ears was now the sound of a bell on one of the launches. Harvard was eight seats up but still within range.

Andy called the rating up. Surprisingly, the boat surged forward. Eight seats down, now seven . . . six. So long as the surge continued, we were still in the Race. With twenty strokes to go a blade caught a little water, and the boat rocked to starboard. Nothing special, but we stopped gaining —five or six seats behind and ten strokes from the finish line.

I looked down to pick up my rowing clothes after showering, but my shirt was not there. I searched for several minutes before it occurred to me that the shirt now belonged to Charlie Alterkruse, the Harvard four man. "No one can beat you guys over two thousand meters," he said, as I handed him my shirt. I smiled before I began to cry. We had given all we had. There were no regrets. Next year. The rest of our squad cheered as we returned to the Ferry.

THE NEOPHYTE DIVER

By James Jones

Big Al suddenly swung the wheel hard right, and the little boat made a sharp turn to starboard and headed off in that direction. They were far out on the open bay now. Directly ahead a mile away was the jet airstrip, one of three on the island, almost touching the blacktop road that ran along the water's edge. "It's right off the end of the airstrip, this reef," Bonham said. " 'Bout half a mile out. I got two or three reference points I line up to hit it exact." As violently as he had made the turn, which Grant considered strangely unnecessarily violent, he suddenly cut throttle and Grant grabbed the gunwale to keep from falling forward, as did Ali. For three or four minutes Bonham jockeyed the boat backward and forward, peering down over the side. "There she is," he said. "My special spot."

Grant too looked over the side. Below him in the bluegreen water yellow and brown color-patches swirled and quivered under the water's wash. Just beside these, and as if he were standing shoetips to the edge of a vertical high cliff, he could now and then as the sea flattened catch a glimpse of clear sand far below, dark-green colored through the surface. The sun hot on his back, Grant felt cold at the thought of being immersed in water which was not in a bathtub and whose lack of heat could not be controlled. "Let's get you dressed out," Bonham rumbled from just behind him, and began hauling tanks and gear around as if none of it weighed anything.

As he had before, Grant noticed that Bonham dropped his bad grammar whenever he was giving instructions. Now he kept up a running comment of instruction while the two of them, he and Ali, got the neophyte ready. Flippers first, then the mask spat upon rubbed till it squeaked rinsed and resting on his forehead, rubber wet shirt, weight-belt trimmed to exactly the right weight by Bonham, finally the tank his arms through the shoulder straps crotch strap attached to the weight belt. Grant simply sat, like an electrocutionee he thought, and let himself be handled. The running comment of instruction had to do with clearing his ears and equalizing the pressure in them as he and Bonham went on down, and with what Bonham wanted him to do with his mask, which was to remove it when they reached the bottom of the anchorline, put it back on full of water, and clear it. Grant was to go first, swim forward to the anchorline, descend it ten or twelve feet, and wait for Bonham. Then last, the mask lowered over his eyes and nose, the mouthpiece stuffed into his mouth, and he was falling backward onto the tank on his back while faces and boat wheeled out of sight to be replaced by nothing but bright blue sky, what was he doing here? Then the water closed over him, blinding him.

Still holding the mask to his face with both hands in the approved manner to keep the fall from dislodging it, Grant rolled over quickly but he still could see nothing. He was now lying on the surface. Masses of bubbles formed by the air he had carried under with him rose all around him, blinding him even more effectively than a driving rainstorm would have done up in the air. He waited, vulnerable, what seemed endlessly but was really only seconds. Then, miraculously, everything cleared as the bubbles rose on past him, and he could see. See at least as well as he could on land. Maybe more. Because to his congenital mild myopia everything looked closer. It was supposed to. Snell's Law. (n Sin $a = n'$ Sin a'). Oh, he'd studied all the books—and for years. But this was different. Below him the yellow and brown patches were now clearly delineated fields of yellow and brown coral but in amongst these, invisible from the boat, were smaller patches of almost every color and color combination imaginable. It was breathtaking. And, as far as he could tell, there was nothing dangerous visible.

Tentatively, cautiously, for the first time since he'd gone under, Grant let out a little air and took a tiny breath. By God, it worked! He became aware of the surface swell rolling him and banging the tank against his back. Bending double he dove down to where there was no swell as Bonham had told him, and swam slowly forward along the boat's big shadow above him, toward the slanting anchorline. In the strange silence he could hear odd poppings and cracklings. With each intake of breath the regulator at the back of his neck sang eerily and gonglike, and with each exhale he could hear the flubbering rush of bubbles from it. Everything, all problems, all plans, all worries, 'mistress', her husband, new girl, the new play, sometimes even consciousness of Self itself, seemed to have been swept from his mind by the intensity of the tasting of this new experience, and new world.

At the anchorline, after he managed awkwardly to grab it, he pulled himself down deeper hand over hand until his ears began really to hurt, and then stopped. As Bonham had shown him, he put thumb and forefinger into the hollows in the mask's bottom and pinched his nose shut, and blew. One ear opened up immediately with a loud squeak, but he had to try a second and a third time before he could get the other one completely opened. Then he pulled himself a little deeper, feeling the pressure start to build again, and stopped again. Wrapping his legs around the line, he peered at the diving watch Bonham had sold him and set its outside bezel dial with the zero point over the minute hand. Then he peered at the huge handsome depth gauge beside it which Bonham had also sold him and saw that he was eighteen feet down. On his right arm the enormous Automatic Decompression Meter which Bonham had sold him still read zero; its nitrogen-absorption-measuring needle had not yet even started to move. And so there he hung, having let go with his legs and grabbed the line with a hand, looking around. If Marty Gabel and Herman Levin could only see him now! His nervousness had left him, and he felt a kind of cautious rapture.

To his right and left coral hills forty and fifty feet high stretched away in minor mountain ranges into bluegreen invisibility. Directly in front of him at the foot of the deep end of these rounded ranges, a pure white sea of virgin sand sloped away ever so gently out toward deep water. In between the coral hills he could see down into channels—glaciers; rivers—of sand which debouched onto the vast sand plain. In these channels, varieties of brightly colored fish poked their noses into holes in the coral, or rowed themselves gently along with their pectoral fins like small boats with oars. None of them seemed to be concerned with bothering any of the others, and Grant relaxed even more.

Then, in the corner of his mask which acted like a horse's blinders and cut his field of vision, he caught a flash of silver. Turning his head he saw through the plate of glass a barracuda which appeared to be at least four feet long. It was about twenty feet away. Slowly it swam out of sight beyond his mask and Grant turned again. This process went on until Grant realized the fish was circling him. Regularly, staring at him with its one big eye, it opened and closed its enormous mouth, exposing its dagger teeth, as if flexing its jaws preparatory to taking a bite of Grant. This was its method of breathing of course, he knew, but it didn't look nice just the same. Grant had read that in cases like this you were supposed to swim straight at them as if you intended to take a bite of *them* whereupon they would turn and flee and run away, but he did not feel very much like trying this. Besides, he was not supposed to leave the anchorline. On the other hand he felt he ought not just sit here and let the fish have all the initiative. But before he could make up his mind to do something, and if so then what, another figure swam into his mask's field of vision, further complicating matters till Grant realized what it was.

It was Bonham. Looking like some antennaed stranger from another world, which in a way he was, he swam down on a long slant behind the barracuda, leisurely beating the water with his flippers, his left arm with its hand holding the camera case stretched back at rest along his thigh, his right arm extended out straight before him holding the four-foot speargun. In the green water-air he was gravityless and beautiful, and Grant would have given anything to be like him. As he came on down getting closer, he stopped kicking and, hunching his shoulders in a strange way as if to make himself heavier, coasted down. Just as Grant saw his forearm tightening to squeeze the trigger, the barracuda gave an enormous flirt of its tail and simply disappeared. It didn't go away; it just simply was no longer there, or anywhere visible, with an unbelievable speed if you hadn't seen it. Bonham looked after it, shrugged, and swam on to the line.

There was a great paternalism, protectiveness, about Bonham underwater. He looked Grant over carefully, turning him about and inspecting his gear, then with a violent hand motion downward swam on down the line toward the bottom. Grant followed, his nervousness returning. Twice he had to stop on the line to clear his ears and he suddenly noticed that Bonham apparently did not have to do this at all. On the bottom, like some huge calm great-bellied Buddha, Bonham seated himself crosslegged on the sand, took off his mask, blinked blindly, then put it back on and blew the water out of it by tilting his head to one side and holding the upper side of the mask. Then he motioned for Grant to do the same, as he had, upstairs, warned him that he would.

Grant had done this in the various pools, but down here (his depth gauge Bonham had sold him now read 59 feet) he found it was more scary. It was all that water above you. Kneeling on the sand, he forced himself with the greatest reluctance to reach up and pull off his own mask. When he did, he immediately went blind. The salt water burned his eyes and the insides of his nose. He found himself gasping for breath. Bonham was now only one great blur to him. He made himself breathe deeply several times, and blinked. Then he put the mask back on and cleared it. Not as adept as Bonham, he had to blow several times to get all the water out. But when he looked at Bonham, the big man was nodding happily and holding up his thumb and forefinger in the old circle salute for 'okay'. Then he motioned for Grant to come and went swimming off six or eight feet above the sand. Grant followed, his eyes still smarting. He was ridiculously pleased. At the moment he felt very much the son to Bonham's massive paternalism. This did not irritate him. Instead, it gave him reassurance.

Bonham proceeded to point out the various corals. They were all very beautiful and interesting to look at—in a slimy, repugnant sort of way—but you could only look at coral so long without getting bored. Apparently fully aware of this, Bonham—after pointing out a number of varieties (including two which he warned Grant not to touch by wringing a hand and shaking it as if stung)—chose the exact moment of Grant's increasing restlessness to show him something else. At the end of the coral hillock they had been exploring he swam over to Grant and motioned for him to follow. He led him straight down over the steep side of the hillock to the sand channel bottom (here Grant's depth gauge Bonham had sold him read 63 feet), and there he pointed out two large caves. It was apparently true that Bonham knew this area like Grant knew his backyard. It was also apparent that he was conducting his tour and displaying his treasures one by one with the dramatic sense of a veteran entrepreneur.

To Grant the caves were both exciting and frightening. The one on the left of the sand channel went back in under the coral hill they had just swum over; way back in there some hole running clear to the top of the coral allowed a shaft of sunlight to penetrate all the way to the bottom,

illuminating greenly some strange coral shapes growing on the sand; outside, its entrance was huge, not a real cave mouth at all, but more an
overhang that ran almost the entire length of the side of the hillock. From
under this overhang Grant carefully stayed away, as he looked. By contrast,
Bonham had already swum on in. Turning his head, he motioned Grant to
follow. Biting hard on the two rubber tits of the mouthpiece between his
teeth, tightening his lips over the whole, Grant descended a little and
entered. Scared as he was, it was magnificently beautiful in there. The
ceiling was only fifteen or twenty feet from the sand floor, much lower than
it had looked from outside. Several good-sized tunnels showing sunlight at
their ends led off from it and looked safe for exploring. But Bonham was
already swimming back out, motioning him to follow.

The other cave, across the channel, was really no more than a fissure,
running maybe thirty feet up an almost perpendicular dead-coral cliff,
hardly wide enough to admit a man, and it was to this one now that
Bonham led him.

Gesturing Grant to follow, the big man swam up the fissure to a point
that appeared slightly wider than the rest, snaked himself through, and
disappeared. When Grant followed, he found he had to turn his shoulders
sideways to enter. When he did, his tank banged alarmingly on the rock
behind him. He remembered reading stories of fellows who had cut their
air intake hoses on sharp coral, and who had barely got out alive by luck,
superior experience, and by keeping their heads. Trying to keep his air
intake hose (without being able to see it) somewhere near the center of the
cleft, Grant pulled himself along with his hands on the sucky, unpleasantly
viscid living corals growing here. But when he was in far enough that he
could no longer bend his knees to flutter his feet, the panicky breathless-
ness, the sensation of being unable to breathe, to get enough air, which
panic brings, and which he knew from before, hit him debilitatively. Stopping, he forced himself to breathe deeply but it didn't help. Suddenly his
instinct was to throw off everything and run for the surface blindly, even
though covered by coral rock, get to anywhere where there was air. Instead,
he reached out with his hands and pulled himself further in, trying to keep
his movements slow and liquid, unviolent, though by now he didn't care
whether the coral cut him or not.

Actually, he had only been inches away from freedom. The last pull with
his arms brought him head and shoulders almost to his waist out into the
open. One breast stroke with his arms and he was free, swimming almost
forty feet above the bottom. Bonham, who Grant now realized had been
directly in front of him watching and ready to help, had already rolled over
head down and like an airplane in a full dive was swimming straight down
toward the bottom, his flippers beating leisurely and slow, his arms holding
camera and gun extended backward along his thighs to streamline. For a
moment Grant was seriously angry at him, for taking such a chance with
him on his first dive. Still breathing deeply, though slower and slower now
as his heart and adrenal glands got back to normal, Grant watched in a

kind of witless stupor as Bonham got smaller and smaller and smaller. A few feet above the bottom the big man leveled off over a huge coral toadstool and rolled over face up, and slowly sank to a crosslegged sitting position on it, his head back looking up, for all the world like some great, oneeyed humanoid alien frog from Alpha Centauri or somewhere. Still looking up, he motioned for Grant to come on down. Still staring, still breathing deeply from his fright in the narrow entrance, Grant suddenly realized with a start which brought him back out of his post-panic stupor that he was lying here all stretched out forty feet up in the *air* from this other man, relaxed, his arms out over his head like a man in a bed. Because it really could have been air. *Seemed* like air. The green-tinted water was crystal clear here inside, and Bonham by seating himself on the toadstool had avoided stirring up any sand clouds as they had done outside. For the first time with any real physical appreciation, Grant realized how delicious it was to be totally without gravity like one of the great planing birds; he could go up, he could go down, he could stay right where he was; in the strange spiritual excitement of it, his fear left him completely. Feeling ridiculous again because of his recent panic there, he glanced once at the narrow entrance fissure, then rolled over head down using exactly (though slower) the same body movements he once used to do a full-twisting half gainer, and corkscrewed gently down—relishing the leisurely control— into a vertical dive, his hands and arms straight back along his thighs palms up, his fins beating lazy and slow, as he had seen Bonham do. Only once did he have to clear his ears, and he did it now without pausing. Below him Bonham got larger and larger. Then, duplicating Bonham's maneuver, he rolled over onto his back, exhaled and sank into a sitting position on the giant toadstool beside him, his knees clasped up to his chin. Unable to speak, or even to grin, he gesticulated wildly and waggled his eyebrows to show his enthusiasm. The big man nodded vigorously, then touching him gently, pointed upward, sweeping his arm across the view like a man unveiling a painting. For the first time since he had entered, Grant looked up.

What he saw very nearly took away the breath he had just regained. He was in an immense cavern at least sixty feet high. Apparently the bottom here inside was ten or so feet lower than the sand channel bottom outside. From where he sat at one end the other was almost lost in a hazy near-invisibility. In the dim ceiling a dozen holes allowed clusters of greenish sunrays to strike at varying angles across the interior until they shattered against the sand bottom or rock walls. Each beam wherever it struck against bottom or walls revealed weird outlandish coral sculptures. It was more than breathtaking, it was like having stumbled upon some alien cathedral on some other planet, which some other-world race with their incomprehensible architecture and alien sculpture had ages past built, decorated and dedicated to their unknowable God. Grant was suddenly frightened again, not physically this time, but spiritually. For a moment he forgot he was diving underwater in an aqua-lung. Was that some four-headed

Great Saint whom they worshipped, there on the side wall? Was that seventy-eyed monster, all head and almost no body, resting on the sand floor, the Great Being Himself? And as always, when he found himself alone in an empty church—as he had when a boy, as he had when visiting the great churches and cathedrals of Europe and found one or another of them deserted—Grant felt himself beginning to get an erection in the dim stillness. Was it the privacy? Was it the quiet? Or was it the highceilinged dimness? Or was it maybe the nearness of God? the nearness of Unknowable? Embarrassed, he shifted away sideways, afraid Bonham might notice what was happening inside his tight, scanty bikini, and the feeling began to subside. Anyway he knew one thing for certain. One day while he was here in Ganado Bay he was going to come out here alone—come alone if he had to rent a *row*boat and aqualung from Bonham's competitor—make a dive down here alone, strip off this damned bikini, swim around this cave stark naked with his erection, then sit on this toadstool and masturbate, come like a fury, and watch his milky semen swirl and mingle with the green water which itself swirled about his body with every tiniest movement.

Maybe he'd hire a nondiving native to handle the boat for him. The very secrecy of it, the native up there working the boat and him down here masturbating, made it a tinglingly exciting prospect. But, was this not a too-ambitious project for a neophyte diver just starting out: jerking off underwater? Well, he would find out. The idea of masturbating made him think of his new girl in New York. She, it had turned out, had loved that.

Bonham touched him gently again, on the shoulder, and Grant started guiltily. When he looked over, the other was motioning upward with one hand and beckoning with the other. When Grant asked "Why?" by shrugging up his shoulders and spreading out his hands, Big Al pointed to his watch. Looking at his own Grant saw they had been under 32 minutes, and could hardly believe it. And it reminded him of something else. During his last few breaths it had seemed to Grant that it was getting slightly harder to breathe each time, but the difference was so slight he had thought he was imagining it. Now he tried again and found it was distinctly harder to suck air from the lung. His neophyte's nervousness returned to him suddenly. But neither man had yet pulled his reserve valve!? Grabbing his mouthpiece with one hand and pointing to his tank with the other, Grant made a heaving motion with his chest as if trying to breathe. Bonham nodded. But then he followed the nod by fanning his hands back and forth across each other in a gesture of "Take it easy; don't worry." Gesturing Grant to follow, and without pulling his reserve, he took off from the toadstool with a little leap upward like a bird.

But it was more like a foot-winged Mercury than a bird, Grant thought as he followed. He was no longer nervous. Underwater at least, he now trusted Bonham completely. Forgotten was the momentary anger at Bonham's having taken him through the narrow fissure.

Ahead of him Big Al swam upward on a long diagonal straight across the length of the green cathedral. He did not turn off to the right toward the fissure. Grant assumed, rightly, that there was another entrance—which made him feel good, because he had no liking for the fissure. As he rose on the long diagonal, the air in his tank expanded as the pressure lessened and it became easier to breathe and he understood why Bonham had motioned him not to worry. Only if they had had to descend again into greater pressure, he remembered now from the books, would they have needed their reserve valves. Grant remembered to exhale frequently as he rose to avoid air embolism and when, as he swam, he looked at his Automatic Decompression Meter Bonham had sold him it showed there was no need to worry about decompression. So they were leaving, or—rather—returning.

Ten yards ahead of him Bonham swam into and then out of some of the slanting rays of sunlight which crossed the cave, strangely bright and glowing when he was in one, almost invisible when he was in the darker water in between. Grant could not resist pausing and turning for a look back. He felt a curious sad tranquillity, toward all inevitability, because he had to leave. But when he looked, he found he was already forty-five or fifty feet above the bottom and the toadstool was no longer visible from here. With a second's tingling excitement in his groin he knew now more than ever that, eventually, he would come back here and descend into that invisibility and sitting on that same toadstool looking up, masturbate himself. Play with himself, he added, in the jargon of his parents. Then he swam on.

Ahead of him Bonham had turned the corner into an alcove-cum-tunnel almost at the ceiling of the cavern and was waiting for him. Ahead at the end of it was sunlight, and together in this more than comfortably wide space they swam toward it, then through it and back into the world.

But the dive was still not over. Emotionally, it was, perhaps; but they still had to get back to the boat. Bonham did not even bother to surface and look around but (he really did know this area like his backyard) struck off up and over the coral hillock they had just left the insides of, and which came to within less than ten feet of the surface. Grant could not see boat or anchorline ahead, but Bonham was obviously heading straight for them. Below them as they swam were the tangled, trashy staghorn-coral beds— the brown ones, their hunks of old fishing line caught here and there, rusting beercans in the low spots—which marked the hillock's crest. But now after the cave all that was boring. It was hard to believe they had been inside this hill, and that it was damned near entirely hollow. Grant's sadness at leaving it—out here in the sunlit, brightly coral-studded, open water —was slowly turning into a wild kind of elation. Above him the surface was only a few feet away, and every now and then—as in some silvered but unsolid mirror—he could see himself or Bonham, grossly distorted, reflected back from the underside of it as it moved. His air, without his pulling of the reserve lever but getting harder and harder to draw, lasted just exactly to the side of the boat. At the boat he had a bad moment when, trying to shuck out of his tank straps and pass the lung up to Ali, he went under gulping seawater and almost choked; but then he was over the side and in the boat safe from sharks, barracuda, Portuguese men-o'-war, the bends, air embolism, busted eardrums, and mechanical lung failure. Why the hell had Bonham tried to make it seem so hard? His elation continued to grow.

Behind him Bonham handed up his own lung easily and smoothly, moved his bulk smoothly up the little ladder and over the side and, dripping wet, started the motor. Ali ran forward to haul in the anchor. Before Grant could get himself out of Ali's clinging wet shirt Bonham had sold him, the diver and his helper were headed back to shore full throttle like two men going home from the office, Bonham at the wheel and Ali dismantling the lungs. In the west the sun was still quite a few yards above the big mountain that jutted out into the sea.

TONI SAILER:
GOLD IN THE SNOW

By Maury Allen

Of all the competitive sports, a strong case can be made for skiing as the most emotional, the most exciting, the most satisfying. It may be the most difficult of all sports. Victory, then, is so much sweeter.

In skiing, one's opponent is not the sole consideration. Nature is the true challenger. Cold, ice, and snow must be defeated. The deep hills and the changing flow of a mountainside are the major problems. Only the hearty can survive the challenge of a ski run. Only the brave can fight the curve of the earth, the wind, the cold, the discomfort of skiing. Often only two skis and two poles separate a man from the hazards of winter. In the end, a skier must depend on his own skill, his own nerve, his own courage for survival and success.

In the tiny hamlet of Kitzbühel in Austria's Tyrolean Alps, the winter begins early and lingers long into spring. The first snow falls in October and the last in April. The wind whips across the small streets of the village, piling snowdrifts against the tiny shops and attractive homes. Skiing is not merely a sport in this town. It is a way of life. A blanket of snow covers the town for most of the winter. One learns to get about in snow. It is necessary for work as well as play.

It is not unusual that small children ski almost before they can walk. They ski for pleasure because the sport is so close at hand. They ski because it is a tradition of their village as far back as any of the elders can recall.

On November 17, 1935, a boy was born to the owner of a glass shop in town. His name was Anton Sailer. He was to be a skier because all boys in Kitzbühel are skiers. He was to be a great skier, a champion, because he was willing to work harder than anyone else with whom he skied.

"My parents started me on skis at two years of age," recalled Toni Sailer. "It was typical of all the small boys in my town. It was not typical that I would take to it so quickly and fall in love with skiing so completely."

By the time he was ten, Toni Sailer was an accomplished skier. He could navigate some of the more difficult hills near home. He was fearless on skis and no hill seemed too difficult for him.

"Much of skiing success depends upon losing the fear of falling at an early age," said Sailer. "One must accept that as part of the sport. Every skier falls. Beginners fall and champions fall. It only matters that you get up and try harder next time."

Sailer played soccer in the summertime, was an excellent swimmer, starred on the tennis courts, and loved music.

"As an Austrian, many people expected me to love opera and classical music," he said. "What I really liked most in music was yodeling. I would ski down a hill and yodel to my heart's content."

Toni worked in his father's glass shop after school and during his summer vacation.

"I did it willingly but I was always thinking of the winter and of skiing again. It seemed to be the single thing that interested me at every waking hour," said Sailer.

Toni had two older sisters and through one of them, Rosi, his skiing changed from recreation to his life's passion. Rosi was also an excellent skier and one of her friends was Christian Pravda, already one of the most famous skiers in all Austria.

"I have a brother who is a very good skier," Rosi told Pravda. "Will you take him out and work with him?"

Sailer joined the Kitzbühel Ski Club. There he could ski and practice daily with Pravda and many of the best skiers in all of Austria. By 1953, Sailer was being recognized throughout his country as an excellent prospect for the nation's ski team.

"It is the dream of every skier in my country to ski in the Olympics. This is what we all work for," Sailer said.

Two years before the 1956 Olympics, scheduled to be held in Cortina d'Ampezzo, Italy, Sailer began to train in earnest for a place on the Austrian Olympic team.

"He was a natural from the beginning," said Fred Rosner, the coach of the Austrian team. "It did not take long to recognize Toni as a champion. This was a very special skier."

Sailer trained four hours each day, seven days a week. He would ski down the trails until his legs ached with pain. Then he would ski some more, always perfecting his techniques and working on his form.

In the summer, when there was no snow, he worked hard on preparing his body for the winter season. He exercised regularly each day to build up his arms and his legs.

"A skier must be physically strong," said Rosner. "He must be able to control the skis rather than have the skis control him. He must be the master."

Sailer was careful about his diet, eating only the right foods, making certain that his body was prepared for the grind he was about to face.

"Toni did not eat any strange foods as many skiers do. His only concession was his breakfast drink. He would make a mixture of milk, honey and sugar. Each morning he would sit stirring the combination for five minutes until it all blended into one huge, sticky glob," his coach explained.

Through the winter of 1955 and early in 1956 Sailer practiced his skiing, which wasn't easy. By some strange twist of nature, the snowfall was very light that winter at his Austrian home. He had to travel great distances to find proper snow conditions. Many days passed without any skiing at all because of lack of snow. When he arrived at Cortina with the Austrian ski team, he had been on skis for only 85 hours all winter.

"I fear that it is not quite enough," he said. "I would have liked to have skied 100 hours or more. I am afraid that it will hurt me."

Most of the European skiers had the same problem.

"Toni Sailer will beat us all even if he hasn't skied a day all winter," said one. "He is so good he doesn't need any practice."

By this time Sailer was already considered one of the finest skiers in Europe. He had won most of the Austrian and European skiing championships. He was to make his world reputation at Cortina.

Toni was now twenty years old. He was very handsome, with large blue eyes, blond hair, and a toothpaste-ad smile. He stood 6 feet tall and weighed 174 pounds. He reminded many of the girl skiers of Hollywood movie star Tyrone Power.

"With his muscles, his dimples, and his handsome face," wrote one reporter, "Toni Sailer looks like a Li'l Abner of the Tyrolean Hills."

The local Italian girls, the girl skiers in the competition, and most of the reporters had already picked out Toni Sailer as an Olympic star even before he had skied in a single event.

Sailer was still not sure he could do his best. He had not skied enough in practice because of the lack of snow. The slopes were icy and slippery. Artificial snow had been placed over the runs to help where the hillside was dry. Still it did not seem to be enough to bring out the best in any of the skiers.

The first ski event on the schedule for the 1956 Olympics was the giant slalom. This was run over a course that included 70 gates on the first run and 98 gates on the second run.

In Alpine skiing, the slalom is run in two separate heats. The skiers must weave in and out of the gates, cutting them as closely as possible, without falling, for a final clocking.

As a light snow fell, Toni moved toward the starting line. He wore a white stocking cap, a silk scarf, and a plaid ski jacket. His face was red with cold and his eyes stared ahead at the skier before him.

His Austrian teammate, Anderl Molterer, came down the mountain before him, whirling past the gates, kicking the snow behind him, rushing against the wind, fighting the cold, racing to the finish line. He crossed it as the electric timer stopped at 3:06.3. It was announced as an Olympic record in the giant slalom. Reporters rushed up to Molterer. Photographers aimed their cameras at his face. The Austrian knew the attention would not be his for long.

"I have done nothing," he said. "Toni is not yet come."

Now Toni was coming. Down the course he came, his skis pushing against the snow, his eyes fixed on the next gate, his arms moving smoothly to guide his path. He was gliding on the snow, barely touching it, weaving clearly and softly through the gates, toward the finish line.

The clock ticked off the seconds quickly. Eyes shifted from the small figure of Sailer, high above the finish line, and the huge clock at the bottom. Two minutes, 40 seconds. Two minutes, 45 . . . "Here he comes," someone yelled.

The figure, now larger, moving gracefully to the finish line.

A final snap of the skis, a final turn, a final lunge and Toni Sailer was across the finish line. The time, an Olympic record for the giant slalom, was 3:00.1.

Thousands of spectators rushed to the Austrian skier to embrace and cheer him, to pat his broad back.

"It was the strangest scene," wrote one reporter. "The officials who were supposed to protect Toni from the crowds became part of the crowd. They rushed up to him, pushed paper and pencil at him for his autograph, screamed their affection for him. There were Red Cross nurses at the bottom of the hill on duty in case of any skiing accident and there were tough Italian ambulance drivers ready to lift injured skiers onto stretchers. Suddenly, they left their posts and rushed up to Toni to greet him, shake his hand. It was one of the most exciting shows of affection ever seen at any sports event."

Toni Sailer, shy and gentle, was amazed at the reaction.

"I had won a race everybody thought I would win anyway. I couldn't understand the excitement," he said later.

Sailer had won and he had done it with style and speed. He had earned the gold medal for Austria and he had broken a record. Further, he was a handsome figure and crowds respond to that kind of athlete.

Zeno Colo, an Italian Olympic skier, was asked why the crowd responded so warmly to Toni Sailer.

"He is an artist on skis," he said. "When one watches Toni Sailer ski, one is seeing beauty and poetry."

Even though conditions were less than perfect Toni had put on a marvelous performance. Colo was impressed with Sailer's grace on skis.

"This is a gentle sport," he said. "Toni Sailer is gentle with the snow. He is never rough on the snow or on his skis. He is soft and sweet. He is gentle with them as one would be with a pretty woman."

Colo said that Toni Sailer was the best skier the world had ever seen.

"He has that very special message of the great ones," continued Colo. "The skis talk to the feet, the legs and the body. It is a language unknown to most men and women. It is the whisper Toni Sailer knows best."

Toni Sailer's reactions were less emotional than his great Italian fan's.

"In skiing," he said, "one doesn't really know one's reactions. One must have them. As you come down a hill, there is so little time to think. You do things as you have been trained. It is a reflex. The reflex is there or it is not. Skiing is really a test of subconscious reactions."

Only three skiers in the history of the Olympics had ever won three gold medals. Toni now had his first. There were two events to go, the special slalom and the downhill race. Toni had a record in his first win. No skier had ever won three events and broken records in each. Toni had this chance. It was his Olympian goal.

"There is so little time to enjoy a victory," said Sailer that evening. "One must prepare for the next event. The only time you can fully appreciate what you have done is when the Olympic Games are over. Then in some quiet moment you sit back and think about it. Then it will bring you much joy."

The following afternoon Toni Sailer was preparing for the second major Alpine skiing event, the special slalom.

His major opponent in this event was a tiny Japanese skier named Chiharu Igaya. It was because of Igaya's success in world competition that skiing had become such a popular sport in Japan. Now the Japanese skier aimed to bring glory to his country with a victory in the special slalom.

Igaya was the first down the treacherous slope. The weather had become worse and now the snow and wind blew in the faces of the skiers with biting cold. The small Japanese skier raced down the course. He crossed the finish line in 3:17.3, an excellent time for the difficult run.

At the top, Sailer bent low again, looked down the course and pushed off from the starting gate.

After the giant slalom, he knew the course well and the special slalom presented no problems for him.

"One must always be thinking ahead," said Sailer, "to the next turn, the next ridge, the next curve in the course. While your skis are taking one turn, your mind should be taking the next one."

Down he came again. The crowd moved closer to the finish line. As Sailer passed the end line, the crowd let fly a huge roar. He had defeated the Japanese skier and set an Olympic record of 3:14.7.

"As I received my second medal," said Sailer later, "I could only think of the hours of practice and the cold and the ache in my legs. It all seemed so worthwhile now. I felt a warm glow all over my body."

He had two gold medals and two Olympic records. It had never happened before. Radio and television stations spread the word throughout the world.

An Austrian newspaper headlined a story, "Toni Sailer To Become Movie Star."

Sailer was asked to comment on the report that he had been offered a huge movie contract.

"I am an Olympic skier, an amateur," he said. "The only thing I am interested in right now is the downhill event."

Few events test a man's courage as much as the downhill run. In skiing the straight downhill run is where the accidents occur. The speed generated by the skier is enormous and the danger grows as the skier reaches higher speeds. Even in Cortina, where the greatest in the world had assembled, the downhill run was a major cause for concern.

"It is a terrible course," Sailer told a newsman. "I am afraid not many of us will finish it."

The course was 3,622 meters over rolling mountain terrain. Some of the mountain was actually bare of snow and rock patches hid just under the thin snow.

"The wind is terrible up there," said Sailer, after a practice run. "It will blow many of us off our skis. I don't expect to do very well."

Quickly the word passed among the spectators about the condition of the run. Many skiers among the fans actually feared for the safety of the competitors.

"I would withdraw if I was in the event," said one man. "This is not skiing. This is suicide."

On the morning of the downhill event there was a slight snowfall.

"It helped a little," said Sailer, "but it did nothing about the wind. It was still quite dangerous coming down the hills."

Finally the downhill event was about to begin. One by one the contestants began coming down. One by one they fell. Some were hurt seriously. Others were merely bruised. All complained that conditions were intolerable.

"They ought to give a gold medal to anyone who finishes," said one skier. "It is that kind of a run."

One of the early finishers was Raymond Fellay, a Swiss skier.

"I had a most successful run," he said. "I only fell once."

Now it was Toni's turn. The crowd stared up at the hill waiting for the first view of their favorite.

"I never felt so tense on a run in all my life," said Sailer.

Down he came, faster, faster, faster. He bent his knees deeply and rolled with the curves. He seemed to stay down, under the wind, his back bent low, his legs close to the ground. He picked at the snow with his poles, seeking out the soft spots. He was in complete control of his wonderful body as he came whirling down the course.

Halfway through he almost lost his footing. He stood up quickly, dug his poles deep into the snow, and came out of the turn in control.

Now he was almost at the bottom. The crowd could see him. The clapping started quickly, the sound strangely muffled by the heavy woolen gloves.

His skis charged across the finish line. He had skied the 3,622 yards without a fall. The time was announced as 2:52.2. He had become the fourth man in Olympic history to win three gold medals at the Winter Games and the first to set a record in all three Alpine events, the giant slalom, the special slalom, and the downhill.

"I have never seen such a performance," said Zeno Colo. "No man could do any better. One must always remember that Sailer's performance was under the most uncomfortable of conditions. He sent the messages to his skis and they have answered."

The crowds mobbed him again and small girls rushed up to kiss his cheek. The Austrian smiled at them and patted their heads.

"Thank you," he said. "This is truly the happiest moment of my life."

Three gold medals. Three records. Somebody asked Toni if there were any more at home like him to break records.

"I have a brother, Rudi," he said. "He is eleven and a fine skier. I am afraid he will never be an Olympic champion. He has already lost too much ground. He was three years old, you see, before he put on his first pair of skis."

PELÉ

By Pelé with Robert L. Fish

Göteborg, Sweden—June 1958

The Nya Ulleví Stadium is jammed to capacity, crowded with people come to see the team of the Soviet Union demolish Brazil in this, the third game of their fight in the Jules Rimet Trophy competition for the football championship of the world. Of the sixteen teams in the competition, fourteen have qualified in matches throughout the world the previous year; the other two, West Germany and Sweden, are present as the former champion and the host country, both automatically qualified. Many think Russia might well win the championship, although they concede that Wales is also strong, and one cannot discount West Germany, the champion, nor Sweden, which, although present without having to qualify, is known to always be dangerous.

Newspapermen are here from all over the globe, waiting for the Russian team to appear, anxious to see in person players like Simonian, the agile Armenian center-forward, Iachine, the magnificent goalkeeper, Igor Netto, the left-half and captain, and Salnikov, the highly intelligent inside-left. Radio and television interviewers are anxious for the game to start and then be done with so they can interview the winners, the Russian stars of such noted teams as Moscow Dynamo or Torpedo Moscow or Dynamo Kiev. Other than the Brazilians present, nobody really expects too much from the South American team. True, they had beaten Austria, 3-1, in their first game, but those who saw—and reported—the game knew it had been far from as one-sided as the score seemed to indicate. And the best the Brazilians had been able to do against a weak English team playing without men like Mathews, their great outside-right now retired, or Lofthouse, the squat, powerful center-forward—bringing to the games, in fact, only twenty players although entitled to twenty-two—had been a scoreless tie, and the Brazilians had had to play their hearts out to gain that.

Russia, however, is a different matter. The players on the Big Red team, as it is called, are large and tough, selected from the thousands of subsidized sports clubs throughout the vast land. This is the first time they have entered World Cup competition and they qualified with ease; had they played in all of the previous World Cup matches, they might well have already retired the trophy with three wins. And Brazil has not only never won a championship, but the only time they reached the finals, in 1950— and playing in their own country, on their own field, before their own fans, and against an admittedly weaker team—they had ignominiously lost. And in 1954—well, the less said about the Brazilian effort in 1954 the better! It had not been anything to brag about. So nobody is expecting any miracles from Brazil.

When the teams come trotting out of the tunnel from the dressing rooms, the crowd looks down to see a skinny little black boy in the uniform of Brazil trotting out onto the field, with the others in the same uniform dwarfing him. That skinny little black boy is me—Pelé. Most of the people in the stands have to assume I'm either the team mascot or the son of a friend of the coach; I can't be the son of the coach because the coach is white. Those who had attended the Austria-Brazil and the England-Brazil matches may have remembered me limping onto the field to take my place on the Brazilian bench, screaming my encouragement to the team together with the reserves, as if our few voices could possibly drown out the huge crowds cheering for our opposition.

But this time when the players leave the bench to take their positions on the field, this skinny little black boy—me—also gets up and goes out onto the grass and the people see I am wearing a shirt with a big number 10 on it. I am sure the newspapermen and the radio announcers and the television broadcasters are all consulting their lists to see who the devil No. 10 is; if they are, they will see I am Edson Arantes do Nascimento, seventeen years old. I am sure that some of those in the stands are faintly amused to see a child on the field in a World Cup match, and some are probably outraged that as important an event as a World Cup match should be reduced to parody by having an infant on the field. The more sentimental, however, probably feel pity for a team so reduced in talent as to face the need to bring children along with them. The entire Brazilian team is young as teams go; everyone knows that—but they undoubtedly feel that this is ridiculous!

When the band strikes up the first chords of the Brazilian national anthem, all of us Brazilians feel a strange force within us. I cannot describe it; I doubt if any of us could describe it. If the people in the stands are amazed to see me down there on the field, I am far more amazed. All of us are living in a dream, but none more so than me. I try not to waste time trying to analyze this strange feeling; I know this is no time to be distracted. Instead I try to concentrate on how I will play; but the thought keeps intruding: How is it possible that you are here, in the Brazilian

Selection, in Sweden, about to play for your country in the Jules Rimet matches? It has to be a dream. . . .

The Russian team taking their positions on the field is certainly no dream. A nightmare, possibly, but no dream! Each man is larger than his opposite on our team, and their goalkeeper, Iachine, is a giant. He looks as if all he has to do is spread out his arms and he will cover the entire goal. Getting the ball past this monster, I think with sinking heart, is going to be almost impossible.

To my left as we line up for the game's opening kick is Zagalo; to my right I see Vavá, then Didi, then Garrincha. Garrincha in Portuguese means the cambaxirra, a small bird, and like that small bird Garrincha can dart about the field. We have given him the nickname of Mané; it means fool or half-wit, but less a fool or a half-wit on the field than Mané I have yet to meet. As usual Garrincha even appears slightly bored. I look behind me, more to avoid studying the giants in front than to check our defense. There is Nilton Santos, a tower of strength at mid-field with Zito, the other mid-fielder, grinning at me comfortably. Then, beyond, there is Belini, our captain, Orlando, De Sordi, and behind them all, relaxed and sure, Gilmar, our goalkeeper. Zito claps his hands, winks at me, and calls out loudly:

"Okay, gang! Let's surprise them!"

Vavá looks at him, frowning, but there is a twinkle in his eye:

"What do you mean, surprise them? They expect to get beat! Let's *not* surprise them!"

And then the game has started and I forget the kidding, even forget what I know very well—that the kidding was meant to relax us all, but principally me. I forget the crowds and the stadium and everything. This is just another football game, that beautiful game I love so well, the game I live to play, and nothing else is in my mind. We aren't playing the Russians—we're playing an *opponent,* and winning is all that counts!

The Russians have the ball and they are quite good at handling it, make no mistake—until one of them, oddly enough, does make a mistake and the ball is at the feet of Garrincha. Our little bird takes the ball between his feet and starts down the field in a spectacular dribble that has the crowd on its feet. He evades defenders as if they were not not there. I race over, knowing the Russians will close in on Garrincha in force, but Garrincha is feeling his oats. He dribbles the ball expertly around the nearest man and kicks for the goal with all his force, not even breaking stride to do so. Iachine leaps in the air, extending himself to the fullest, but the ball just clears his fingertips. I have *"Goal!!!"* in my throat when the ball strikes the top crosspiece and bounds back onto the field! I expect Garrincha to swear but he doesn't waste the time. He is a total professional and has judged the ball's trajectory and is prepared to recover it when it returns. Once again he kicks, but this time he is rushed and the ball sails out of bounds.

The game is just beginning but we can already see a great weakness in the Russian defense. The offense is strong, but we are not too worried about that; Nilton Santos and Belini and Orlando and De Sordi and Zito and Gilmar will handle that! Garrincha is inspired; he seems to have been waiting for this game all his life. He goes through the defenders almost at will. The crowd, suddenly aware that the game will not be so easy for the Russians, are screaming at the top of their voices, some of them beginning to root for us. They cheer each dribble we make; each tackle that takes the ball from a bewildered Russian opponent brings increasing yells of appreciation from the fans in the stands. And all we can think of is stuffing the ball past Iachine's gorilla arms into the net!

Didi has the ball and I can read his mind. I dodge between two defenders, prepared for what I know will happen; he kicks the ball toward me as if he had measured the distance with a tape measure. The ball slides past me as I expect and want, and without breaking stride I kick it toward the goal on the dead run. Iachine leaps for it but I know his timing is off; he has not expected the speed of the move. Once again I have the scream of *"Goal!!!"* in my throat—and once again the miserable ball hits the crosspiece and bounds back to the field where Iachine grabs it and hugs it thankfully.

I glare at the goal posts: *"Cagão!"*

Trotting near me, Didi laughs. "Relax, son. It'll go in. Give it time."

My knee is beginning to throb from an injury that had kept me from the first two games and almost from the World Cup games altogether—an injury that is a story in itself that we'll come to in time—but I am in no mood to worry about a mere knee. Didi has the ball again. I get free to let him pass it to me, but a defender is coming over fast to cover me, and Didi, without breaking stride or even indicating his intention by moving his head or his body, passes the ball in a totally different direction to Vavá. Vavá, charging in, has clearly expected the pass, but the Russians have not. Vavá's foot touches the ball lightly to bring it to the proper speed even as he is running, and then in the same motion, he kicks!

Gooooooaaaaaalllll!!!!!! Brazil!!!!!!

We are all over Vavá, screaming, thumping him, pummeling, jumping in the air, waving our fists hysterically. Iachine is stretched out on the ground, looking at us sadly, as if we were bad children who had somehow disappointed a permissive parent.

The game goes on. Now we feel more secure; we feel, in fact, that the game will be easy, and that is always a mistake. As a result we do not score again in that period. I am overanxious. I want to wrap the game up and go back to the hotel where I can hug the memory of it, as a child hugs a favorite toy. My dribbling is good; my evasions, my feints, my tackles, bring shouts of approval from the crowd, now strongly behind us. But I lose two sure goals through not being relaxed enough at the moment of kicking. The others on the Brazilian team are more relaxed but nothing any of us can do results in any more goals and we go back through the tunnel at half time with the score 1-0.

The second half is much the same; the Russians attack strongly, fiercely, but our defense is impregnable. Gilmar has not permitted a goal so far in the tournament, and even getting past Orlando or Nilton Santos or Belini or De Sordi is extremely difficult for the Big Red team, let alone getting a shot at the net with Gilmar guarding it. But the Russian defense has also tightened and—it seems to me—Iachine has grown bigger during half time. There simply does not seem to be any room around him to get into the net. Time is running out, and then I see Didi with the ball again, and from everything he is doing I know he is going to pass the ball to me. He kicks it with that indescribable accuracy of his, as if there were only the two of us on the field, and I stop it momentarily and then start to dribble it in almost the same motion toward the goal. Defenders come in a rush; time is running out for them, as well, and they trail. But we have expected them to do just this, of course, and they have overlooked Vavá, who is totally prepared when, without any indication of purpose, I suddenly pass the ball to him. It slows down as it nears him and Vavá kicks it neatly without losing a step. The defense has attempted to change direction; Iachine swings his large body toward the ball, but even his size cannot compensate for the accuracy of Vavá's kick.

Gooooooaaaaaallllll!!!!!! Brazil!!!!!!

Iachine is sitting up, staring at us with that sad look on his face again. We run for Vavá—he is crying with emotion.

And the game ends: Brazil 2, Russia 0.

That night, after we have celebrated our victory with an incredible meal, and after we have relived the game over and over again, complimenting each other exaggeratedly (our coach, Vicente Feola, lets us do it to get it out of our systems, but we all know that tomorrow he will clamp down relentlessly on such egotism), I go to my room and slowly undress. I climb into bed and lie back, replaying the entire game, move by move, tackle by tackle, dribble by dribble, kick by kick. I realize that I was overanxious. I twinge when I think of the lost opportunities for goals—but I also realize that I hadn't played badly. After all, the World Cup isn't exactly a mere club game against some team from Santo André or Mogí das Cruzes; the Russians aren't exactly pushovers. And we *did* win! Maybe nobody knew who that skinny little black kid, Pelé, was before today, but they do now. I have nothing to be ashamed of. I wonder what they are thinking this moment in Baurú, what my parents are thinking, my brother and sister, my Uncle Jorge and Dona Ambrosina, my grandmother, my friends. I can picture the elation in the streets, and people all talking about Pelé, the little *moleque* who such a short time ago was being punished for kicking a football into the first street light on our street, breaking the bulb, and plunging the neighborhood back into darkness.

I bring my thoughts back to the game. I promise myself that if I am scheduled to play in the next match, I will be calmer, more relaxed—like

Garrincha or Didi or Vavá or Zagalo. I will be more professional, I promise.

I still cannot sleep. My thoughts once more return to Baurú and to all the incredible steps that brought me to this point where I am playing with the Brazilian Selection in the World Cup matches in such a short space of time. It had to be God who did it—but why? Why had He chosen me? What could have been His motive?

I knew it was futile to consider His motives. For whatever reason, though, it had to be a miracle. . . .

Toward the middle of October 1969, the Brazilian press discovered that the number of official goals I had scored since beginning my career with Santos twelve years earlier was approaching the magical number of 1,000. They wrote in their columns that Jimmy MacCrory of the Glasgow Celtics had acquired immortal fame in Great Britain for having scored 500 goals, and they also noted that when he had done so, defenses in general were weaker than they were at the moment. They said that for any player to score 1,000 goals would be to immortalize him, as well as the country that had produced him and his football.

The story was picked up abroad. In the United States the marking of 1,000 goals in soccer was compared to hitting a home run in every game, and that if Babe Ruth had maintained that pace he would have hit more than 2,000 home runs in his years with the Yankees. At that time I had approximately 990 goals in fewer than 900 games, or an average of better than one goal per game, so they felt the comparison was just.

In England it was compared with the records of other great players of the past, and none of them had come close to 1,000 goals. It had always been believed that 1,000 goals was an impossibility, and here was the young Brazilian, Pelé, getting very close. I am sure it was a great story for the press and for the sports fans throughout the world, but personally it made me very nervous. I would have been pleased to have been informed one morning that the day before I had scored the thousandth goal, but to have it ahead of me, and referred to daily in newspapers or on the radio, was unnerving.

Still, as long as we were reasonably far away from the magic number, things continued to go well. On October 15, playing against Portuguesa Desportos—a game Santos won, 6-2—I scored four goals, which were duly enumerated in the media as numbers 990, 991, 992, and 993. The pressure began to build. A week later, playing against Coritiba in the state capital of Paraná, I scored numbers 994 and 995. Now the press came around in force, represented by correspondents from all over the world. Every time I approached the goal area there would be a battery of cameras aimed at me from all sides of the net, and it became quite irritating. In our next game, against Fluminense, our entire team, including myself, went scoreless—but fortunately for us, our opponents did the same. And then, on November 1, I did manage to score number 996 against Flamengo. But after that there was a dearth.

On November 4 Corinthians of São Paulo beat us badly, 4-1, and I scored no goals. The pressure was getting to all of us. Five days later the São Paulo Football Club tied us, 1-1, and our lone goal was not mine. I imagine the newspapers and the radio stations throughout Brazil and the rest of the world must have started to get worried; after all, they had limited budgets and it had begun to look as if they might be paying out travel and per diem expenses to a mob of correspondents for a long time without getting a story in return. In addition, I know the entire Santos team was hoping for the magic number to be reached to permit us to go about our business of playing football without feeling like something on a slide under a microscope.

Then, on November 12, playing against Santa Cruz in Recife, I scored two of our goals in a 4-0 victory, and we were up to number 998. The reporters and television men, the photographers and the radio men, swelled even further at our next game. Number 999 was scored in Paraíba in the northeast, two days later. So when we came to Bahia to play the Esporte Club of Bahia on November 16, I think we probably had every radio in the country tuned into the game.

When I came out onto the field, I felt nervous. I had long wished the thousandth goal was over and done with, but never as much as on this day. I had a sudden cold feeling that I was doomed to go for years and years without scoring another goal, that the elusive Goal Number 1,000 would always be in front of me, taunting me, and preventing me from playing proper football. Nor did the hundreds of cameras that followed every play in which I was involved help in any way. They looked to me like Martian monsters with their single expressionless glass eyes watching me emotionlessly. The Bahian newspapers had bragged that when I made my famous goal that day, the celebration they would throw would shame anything that Rio de Janeiro or São Paulo could possibly have offered. It would demonstrate to the Paulistas and the Cariocas—our word for people from Rio de Janeiro—that Bahian hospitality was the only true hospitality. There was even to be, the newspaper noted, a special thanksgiving mass for the event.

I tried to put my fears aside and play my best, but there is no doubt the constant pressure was having an effect on me and on my game. I never got what I considered a first-class opportunity until just before the game ended, and then I thought I really had it! The ball was passed to me and I dribbled it down the field, avoiding the defense, and then when I was sure I had the goalkeeper beaten on a feint, I kicked as hard as I could without breaking stride. Unfortunately, it struck the crossbar and came bounding back, but before either I or the goalkeeper could get to it, my teammate Jair Bala was there and did what had to be done; he kicked the ball into the net.

The game eventually ended in a tie—1-1—and the thousandth goal still evaded me.

Our next game was against Vasco da Gama in Maracanã Stadium in Rio, and the Cariocas were overjoyed at having the opportunity of seeing the thousandth goal kicked in their home town. I was far from all that happy. In the first place, I was beginning to think the number 1,000 was a jinx and that maybe God never intended that anyone should ever score a thousand goals. And in the second place—confirming my feeling that God was against the idea—that day, November 19, it rained as only it can rain in the tropics when it makes up its mind to rain. The sky seemed to open up and everything wet that had been held up there for a long time came down. One could have cut that rain with a shovel. Still, there were 80,000 spectators who had braved that storm to come and witness the event, and for that number of soaked martyrs one had to do one's best.

Rene, of Vasco da Gama, was guarding me, and Rene was built like Nilton Santos, with legs like tree trunks and a body to give authority to any defense effort he made. On that slippery field, with the rain pelting us in the eyes, and with Rene apparently on every side of me no matter where I turned, I barely touched the ball for the first thirty minutes. Then, at last, I caught him off-balance for a split second, feinted him out of position, and then was off for the goal area, splashing through the rain, before he could recover. I avoided the other defenders who ran to intercept, and kicked with all my force, positive as I watched the ball rise and heard the scream start building up from the spectators that the goal was assured, the jinx licked, the ordeal over! Flash bulbs almost blinded me, but I could still see what I had been hoping I would *not* see—Andrade, the international Argentinian goalkeeper for Vasco, leaped into the air as high as he could and managed to divert the ball over the crossbar with the tips of his outstretched fingers.

I was desperately disappointed, but the play had done one thing for me —it had completely evaporated my nervousness. The thousandth goal, I now realized, was a goal like any other goal; it was simply a matter of putting the ball in the net. The number made no difference. There were no jinx numbers, and God undoubtedly couldn't care less about one football goal. Rene had demonstrated that he could be feinted out of position, and now the thing to do was to calm down, get the goal, and end the nonsense of the magic number once and for all.

I was passed the ball again, once again feinted Rene out of position, and started for the goal area. Once again I dribbled through their defenders and once again I had a good shot and took it. The ball was high and struck the crossbar, but I was prepared to head it in on its return, when Rene, also leaping for the ball, accidentally headed it instead—and the ball bounced into the net for a Santos goal! Making a goal for the opponents always makes a player, as well as his team, feel foolish. I was sure that the mistake would upset Vasco and that opportunities to score would come often that day, despite the weather and the condition of the field. The crowd booed

Rene, but not for scoring a goal for us; it was for preventing me from scoring that magic number 1,000.

There was still plenty of time in the game. Once again I was in mid-field and Clodoaldo of our team made a beautiful pass that split the Vasco defense, and then I had the ball with only the two backs, Rene and Fernando, between me and Andrade, their goalkeeper. And Fernando and Rene were split! I took off as fast as I could, intent upon going between them before they could join forces. Fernando, though, was taking no chances of my getting closer to the goal and scoring; he dove at me, sliding to trip me. The crowd rose with a scream at the referee's whistle: a penalty kick!

A penalty kick certainly wasn't the way I had hoped to make my thousandth goal, but at this point I would have taken it any way I could, just to get the affair over with! I don't know how long I stood over the ball with Andrade watching me intently; I was trying to clear the cobwebs from my mind, trying to forget the importance of this one goal to me, to my game, to my team. I was trying to relax and regain the calmness I had felt only moments before. For one split second I remembered missing that penalty kick in that long-ago infantile game in Santos, but I forced the thought away. Instead, I told myself that just standing there could only increase the chance of missing, and that if I missed, what the hell! I'd get the thousandth goal another time. Then, almost as if my body had gotten tired of waiting while my mind was still discussing the matter, I found I had kicked the ball and was watching it curve nicely past Andrade's outstretched fingers, into the net.

The roar that rose from the crowd was almost enough to hold back the rain; the photographers and reporters mobbed me at once, coming from behind the goal; they were joined almost at once by hundreds upon hundreds that poured from the stands, disregarding the police, and raced across the wet grass to reach for me. My jersey was being torn from my shoulders; I squirmed out of it only to have someone press another jersey on me —this one with the number 1,000 on it. Then I was raised to shoulders and being carried around the field, the tears in my eyes testifying to my emotion. The crowds cheered as we passed them. Then, once I was on my feet again, they demanded that I trot around the field so everyone could admire the new jersey. I jogged slowly past the crowded sections of Maracanã, my heart beating rapidly, pleased the ordeal was over, and happy that I was the man who had done it; the crowd stood and screamed as I went past them.

Then, into the dressing room, and a substitute sent in for me; and I sat there, drained of feeling; then I slowly took off the new jersey with the number 1,000 on it, folded it neatly, and laid it down on the bench beside me to be taken home and treasured forever.

THE WAVES AT WAIKIKI
By Jack London

That is what it is, a royal sport for the natural kings of earth. The grass grows right down to the water at Waikiki Beach, and within fifty feet of the everlasting sea. The trees also grow down to the salty edge of things, and one sits in their shade and looks seaward at a majestic surf thundering in on the beach to one's very feet. Half a mile out, where is the reef, the white-headed combers thrust suddenly skyward out of the placid turquoise-blue and come rolling in to shore. One after another they come, a mile long, with smoking crests, the white battalions of the infinite army of the sea. And one sits and listens to the perpetual roar, and watches the unending procession, and feels tiny and fragile before this tremendous force expressing itself in fury and foam and sound. Indeed, one feels microscopically small, and the thought that one may wrestle with this sea raises in one's imagination a thrill of apprehension, almost of fear. Why, they are a mile long, these bull-mouthed monsters, and they weigh a thousand tons, and they charge in to shore faster than a man can run. What chance? No chance at all, is the verdict of the shrinking ego; and one sits, and looks, and listens, and thinks the grass and the shade are a pretty good place in which to be.

And suddenly, out there where a big smoker lifts skyward, rising like a sea-god from out of the welter of spume and churning white, on the giddy, toppling, overhanging and down-falling, precarious crest appears the dark head of a man. Swiftly he rises through the rushing white. His black shoulders, his chest, his loins, his limbs—all is abruptly projected on one's vision. Where but the moment before was only the wide desolation and invincible roar, is now a man, erect, full-statured, not struggling frantically in that wild movement, not buried and crushed and buffeted by those mighty monsters, but standing above them all, calm and superb, poised on the giddy summit, his feet buried in the churning foam, the salt smoke rising to his knees, and all the rest of him in the free air and flashing sunlight, and he is flying through the air, flying forward, flying fast as the surge on which he stands. He is a Mercury—a brown Mercury. His heels are winged, and in them is the swiftness of the sea. In truth, from out of the sea he has leaped upon the back of the sea, and he is riding the sea that roars and bellows and cannot shake him from its back. But no frantic outreaching and balancing is his. He is impassive, motionless as a statue carved suddenly by some miracle out of the sea's depth from which he rose. And straight on toward shore he flies on his winged heels and the white crest of the breaker. There is a wild burst of foam, a long tumultuous rushing sound as the breaker falls futile and spent on the beach at your feet; and there, at your feet, steps calmly ashore a Kanaka, burnt golden and brown by the tropic sun. Several minutes ago he was a speck a quarter of a mile away. He has "bitted the bull-mouthed breaker" and ridden it in, and the pride in the feat shows in the carriage of his magnificent body as he glances for a moment carelessly at you who sit in the shade of the shore. He is a Kanaka—and more, he is a man, a member of the kingly species that has mastered matter and the brutes and lorded it over creation.

And one sits and thinks of Tristram's last wrestle with the sea on that fatal morning; and one thinks further, to the fact that that Kanaka has done what Tristram never did, and that he knows a joy of the sea that Tristram never knew. And still further one thinks. It is all very well, sitting here in cool shade of the beach, but you are a man, one of the kingly species, and what that Kanaka can do, you can do yourself. Go to. Strip off your clothes that are a nuisance in this mellow clime. Get in and wrestle with the sea; wing your heels with the skill and power that reside in you; bite the sea's breakers, master them, and ride upon their backs as a king should.

And that is how it came about that I tackled surf-riding. And now that I have tackled it, more than ever do I hold it to be a royal sport. But first let me explain the physics of it. A wave is a communicated agitation. The water that composes the body of a wave does not move. If it did, when a stone is thrown into a pond and the ripples spread away in an ever-widening circle, there would appear at the center an ever-increasing hole. No, the water that composes the body of a wave is stationary. Thus, you may watch a particular portion of the ocean's surface and you will see the same water rise and fall a thousand times to the agitation communicated by a thousand successive waves. Now imagine this communicated agitation moving shoreward. As the bottom shoals, the lower portion of the wave strikes land first and is stopped. But water is fluid, and the upper portion has not struck anything, wherefore it keeps on communicating its agitation, keeps on going. And when the top of the wave keeps on going, while the bottom of it lags behind, something is bound to happen. The bottom of the wave drops out from under and the top of the wave falls over, forward, and down, curling and cresting and roaring as it does so. It is the bottom of a wave striking against the top of the land that is the cause of all surfs.

But the transformation from a smooth undulation to a breaker is not abrupt except where the bottom shoals abruptly. Say the bottom shoals gradually for from quarter of a mile to a mile, then an equal distance will be occupied by the transformation. Such a bottom is that off the beach of

Waikiki, and it produces a splendid surf-riding surf. One leaps upon the back of a breaker just as it begins to break, and stays on it as it continues to break all the way in to shore.

And now to the particular physics of surf-riding. Get out on a flat board, six feet long, two feet wide, and roughly oval in shape. Lie down upon it like a small boy on a coaster and paddle with your hands out to deep water, where the waves begin to crest. Lie out there quietly on the board. Sea after sea breaks before, behind, and under and over you, and rushes in to shore, leaving you behind. When a wave crests, it gets steeper. Imagine yourself, on your board, on the face of that steep slope. If it stood still, you would slide down just as a boy slides down a hill on his coaster. "But," you object, "the wave doesn't stand still." Very true, but the water composing the wave stands still, and there you have the secret. If ever you start sliding down the face of that wave, you'll keep on sliding and you'll never reach the bottom. Please don't laugh. The face of that wave may be only six feet, yet you can slide down it a quarter of a mile, or half a mile, and not reach the bottom. For, see, since a wave is only a communicated agitation or impetus, and since the water that composes a wave is changing every instant, new water is rising into the wave as fast as the wave travels. You slide down this new water, and yet remain in your old position on the wave, sliding down the still newer water that is rising and forming the wave. You slide precisely as fast as the wave travels. If it travels fifteen miles an hour, you slide fifteen miles an hour. Between you and shore stretches a quarter of mile of water. As the wave travels, this water obligingly heaps itself into the wave, gravity does the rest, and down you go, sliding the whole length of it. If you still cherish the notion, while sliding, that the water is moving with you, thrust your arms into it and attempt to paddle; you will find that you have to be remarkably quick to get a stroke, for that water is dropping astern just as fast as you are rushing ahead.

And now for another phase of the physics of surf-riding. All rules have their exceptions. It is true that the water in a wave does not travel forward. But there is what may be called the send of the sea. The water in the overtoppling crest does move forward, as you will speedily realize if you are slapped in the face by it, or if you are caught under it and are pounded by one mighty blow down under the surface panting and gasping for a half a minute. The water in the top of a wave rests upon the water in the bottom of the wave. But when the bottom of the wave strikes the land, it stops, while the top goes on. It no longer has the bottom of the wave to hold it up. Where was solid water beneath it, is now air, and for the first time it feels the grip of gravity, and down it falls, at the same time being torn asunder from the lagging bottom of the wave and flung forward. And it is because of this that riding a surfboard is something more than a mere placid sliding down a hill. In truth, one is caught up and hurled shoreward as by some Titan's hand.

I deserted the cool shade, put on a swimming suit, and got hold of a surf-board. It was too small a board. But I didn't know, and nobody told me. I joined some little Kanaka boys in shallow water, where the breakers were well spent and small—a regular kindergarten school. I watched the little Kanaka boys. When a likely-looking breaker came along, they flopped upon their stomachs on their boards, kicked like mad with their feet, and rode the breaker in to the beach. I tried to emulate them. I watched them, tried to do everything that they did, and failed utterly. The breaker swept past, and I was not on it. I tried again and again. I kicked twice as madly as they did, and failed. Half a dozen would be around. We would all leap on our boards in front of a good breaker. Away our feet would churn like the stern-wheels of river steamboats, and away the little rascals would scoot while I remained in disgrace behind.

I tried for a solid hour, and not one wave could I persuade to boost me shoreward. And then arrived a friend, Alexander Hume Ford, a globe trotter by profession, bent ever on the pursuit of sensation. And he had found it at Waikiki. Heading for Australia, he had stopped off for a week to find out if there were any thrills in surf-riding, and he had become wedded to it. He had been at it every day for a month and could not yet see any symptoms of the fascination lessening on him. He spoke with authority.

"Get off that board," he said. "Chuck it away at once. Look at the way you're trying to ride it. If ever the nose of that board hits bottom, you'll be disemboweled. Here, take my board. It's a man's size."

I am always humble when confronted by knowledge. Ford knew. He showed me how properly to mount his board. Then he waited for a good breaker, gave me a shove at the right moment, and started me in. Ah, delicious moment when I felt that breaker grip and fling me! On I dashed, a hundred and fifty feet, and subsided with the breaker on the sand. From that moment I was lost. I waded back to Ford with his board. It was a large one, several inches thick, and weighed all of seventy-five pounds. He gave me advice, much of it. He had had no one to teach him, and all that he had laboriously learned in several weeks he communicated to me in half an hour. I really learned by proxy. And inside of half an hour I was able to start myself and ride in. I did it time after time, and Ford applauded and advised. For instance, he told me to get just so far forward on the board and no farther. But I must have got some farther, for as I came charging in to land, that miserable board poked its nose down to bottom, stopped abruptly, and turned a somersault, at the same time violently severing our relations. I was tossed through the air like a chip and buried ignominiously under the downfalling breaker. And I realized that if it hadn't been for Ford, I'd have been disemboweled. That particular risk is part of the sport, Ford says. Maybe he'll have it happen to him before he leaves Waikiki, and then, I feel confident, his yearning for sensation will be satisfied for a time.

When all is said and done, it is my steadfast belief that homicide is worse than suicide, especially if, in the former case, it is a woman. Ford saved me from being a homicide. "Imagine your legs are a rudder," he said. "Hold them close together, and steer with them." A few minutes later I came charging in on a comber. As I neared the beach, there, in the water, up to her waist, dead in front of me, appeared a woman. How was I to stop that comber on whose back I was? It looked like a dead woman. The board weighed seventy-five pounds, I weighed a hundred and sixty-five. The added weight had a velocity of fifteen miles per hour. The board and I constituted a projectile. I leave it to the physicists to figure out the force of the impact upon that poor, tender woman. And then I remembered my guardian angel, Ford. "Steer with your legs!" rang through my brain. I steered with my legs, I steered sharply, abruptly, with all my legs and with all my might. The board sheered around broadside on the crest. Many things happened simultaneously. The wave gave me a passing buffet, a light tap as the taps of waves go but a tap sufficient to knock me off the board and smash me down through the rushing water to bottom, with which I came in violent collision and upon which I was rolled over and over. I got my head out for a breath of air and then gained my feet. There stood the woman before me. I felt like a hero. I had saved her life. And she laughed at me. It was not hysteria. She had never dreamed of her danger. Anyway, I solaced myself, it was not I but Ford that saved her, and I didn't have to feel like a hero. And besides, that leg-steering was great. In a few minutes more of practice I was able to thread my way in and out past several bathers and to remain on top of my breaker instead of going under it.

"Tomorrow," Ford said, "I am going to take you out into the blue water."

I looked seaward where he pointed, and saw the great smoking combers that made the breakers I had been riding look like ripples. I don't know what I might have said had I not recollected just then that I was one of a kingly species. So all that I did say was, "All right, I'll tackle them tomorrow."

The water that rolls in on Waikiki Beach is just the same as the water that laves the shores of all the Hawaiian Islands; and in ways, especially from the swimmer's standpoint, it is wonderful water. It is cool enough to be comfortable, while it is warm enough to permit a swimmer to stay in all day without experiencing a chill. Under the sun or the stars, at high noon or at midnight, in midwinter or in midsummer, it does not matter when, it is always the same temperature—not too warm, not too cold, just right. It is wonderful water, salt as old ocean itself, pure and crystal-clear. When the nature of the water is considered, it is not so remarkable after all that the Kanakas are one of the most expert of swimming races.

So it was, next morning, when Ford came along, that I plunged into the wonderful water for a swim of indeterminate length. Astride of our surfboards, or, rather, flat down upon them on our stomachs, we paddled out through the kindergarten where the little Kanaka boys were at play. Soon we were out in deep water where the big smokers came roaring in. The mere struggle with them, facing them and paddling seaward over them and through them, was sport enough in itself. One had to have his wits about him, for it was a battle in which mighty blows were struck, on one side, and in which cunning was used on the other side—a struggle between insensate force and intelligence. I soon learned a bit. When a breaker curled over my head, for a swift instant I could see the light of day through its emerald body; then down would go my head, and I would clutch the board with all my strength. Then would come the blow, and to the onlooker on shore I would be blotted out. In reality the board and I have passed through the crest and emerged in the respite of the other side. I should not recommend those smashing blows to an invalid or delicate person. There is weight behind them, and the impact of the driven water is like a sand-blast. Sometimes one passes through half a dozen combers in quick succession, and it is just about that time that he is liable to discover new merits in the stable land and new reasons for being on shore.

Out there in the midst of such a succession of big smoky ones, a third man was added to our party, one Freeth. Shaking the water from my eyes as I emerged from one wave and peered ahead to see what the next one looked like, I saw him tearing in on the back of it, standing upright on his board, carelessly poised, a young god bronzed with sunburn. We went through the wave on the back of which he rode. Ford called to him. He turned an air-spring from his wave, rescued his board from its maw, paddled over to us and joined Ford in showing me things. One thing in particular I learned from Freeth, namely, how to encounter the occasional breaker of exceptional size that rolled in. Such breakers were really ferocious, and it was unsafe to meet them on top of the board. But Freeth showed me, so that whenever I saw one of that caliber rolling down on me, I slid off the rear end of the board and dropped down beneath the surface, my arms over my head and holding the board. Thus, if the wave ripped the board out of my hands and tried to strike me with it (a common trick of such waves), there would be a cushion of water a foot or more in depth, between my head and the blow. When the wave passed, I climbed upon the board and paddled on. Many men have been terribly injured, I learn, by being struck by their boards.

The whole method of surf-riding and surf-fighting, I learned, is one of nonresistance. Dodge the blow that is struck at you. Dive through the wave that is trying to slap you in the face. Sink down, feet first, deep under the surface, and let the big smoker that is trying to smash you go by far overhead. Never be rigid. Relax. Yield yourself to the waters that are ripping and tearing at you. When the undertow catches you and drags you seaward along the bottom, don't struggle against it. If you do, you are liable to be drowned, for it is stronger than you. Yield yourself to that undertow. Swim with it, not against it, and you will find the pressure removed. And, swimming with it, fooling it so that it does not hold you, swim upward at the same time. It will be no trouble at all to reach the surface.

The man who wants to learn surf-riding must be a strong swimmer, and he must be used to going under the water. After that, fair strength and common sense are all that is required. The force of the big comber is rather unexpected. There are mix-ups in which board and rider are torn apart and separated by several hundred feet. The surf-rider must take care of himself. No matter how many riders swim out with him, he cannot depend upon any of them for aid. The fancied security I had in the presence of Ford and Freeth made me forget that it was my first swim out in deep water among the big ones. I recollected, however, and rather suddenly, for a big wave came in, and away went the two men on its back all the way to shore. I could have been drowned a dozen different ways before they got back to me.

One slides down the face of a breaker on his surf-board, but he has to get started to sliding. Board and rider must be moving shoreward at a good rate before the wave overtakes them. When you see the wave coming that you want to ride in, you turn tail to it and paddle shoreward with all your strength, using what is called the windmill stroke. This is a sort of spurt performed immediately in front of the wave. If the board is going fast enough, the wave accelerates it, and the board begins its quarter-of-a-mile slide.

I shall never forget the first big wave I caught out there in the deep water. I saw it coming, turned my back on it and paddled for dear life. Faster and faster my board went, till it seemed my arms would drop off. What was happening behind me I could not tell. One cannot look behind and paddle the windmill stroke. I heard the crest of the wave hissing and churning, and then my board was lifted and flung forward. I scarcely knew what happened the first half-minute. Though I kept my eyes open, I could not see anything, for I was buried in the rushing white of the crest. But I did not mind. I was chiefly conscious of ecstatic bliss at having caught the wave. At the end of the half-minute, however, I began to see things, and to breathe. I saw that three feet of the nose of my board was clear out of water and riding on the air. I shifted my weight forward, and made the nose come down. Then I lay, quite at rest in the midst of the wild movement, and watched the shore and the bathers on the beach grow distinct. I didn't cover quite a quarter of a mile on that wave, because, to prevent the board from diving, I shifted my weight back, but shifted it too far and fell down the rear slope of the wave.

It was my second day at surf-riding, and I was quite proud of myself. I stayed out there four hours, and when it was over, I was resolved that on the morrow I'd come in standing up. But that resolution paved a distant place. On the morrow I was in bed. I was not sick, but I was very unhappy, and I was in bed. When describing the wonderful water of Hawaii I forgot to describe the wonderful sun of Hawaii. It is a tropic sun, and, furthermore, in the first part of June, it is an overhead sun. It is also an insidious, deceitful sun. For the first time in my life I was sunburned unawares. My arms, shoulders, and back had been burned many times in the past and were tough; but not so my legs. And for four hours I had exposed the tender backs of my legs, at right-angles, to that perpendicular Hawaiian sun. It was not until after I got ashore that I discovered the sun had touched me. Sunburn at first is merely warm; after that it grows intense and the blisters come out. Also, the joints, where the skin wrinkles, refuse to bend. That is why I spent the next day in bed. I couldn't walk. And that is why, today, I am writing this in bed. It is easier to than not to. But tomorrow, ah, tomorrow, I shall be out in that wonderful water, and I shall come in standing up, even as Ford and Freeth. And if I fail tomorrow, I shall do it the next day, or the next. Upon one thing I am resolved: the *Snark* shall not sail from Honolulu until I, too, wing my heels with the swiftness of the sea, and become a sunburned, skin-peeling Mercury.

THE SWIMMER

By John Cheever

It was one of those midsummer Sundays when everyone sits around saying, "I *drank* too much last night." You might have heard it whispered by the parishioners leaving church, heard it from the lips of the priest himself, struggling with his cassock in the *vestiarium,* heard it from the golf links and the tennis courts, heard it from the wildlife preserve where the leader of the Audubon group was suffering from a terrible hangover. "I *drank* too much," said Donald Westerhazy. "We all *drank* too much," said Lucinda Merrill. "It must have been the wine," said Helen Westerhazy. "I *drank* too much of that claret."

This was at the edge of the Westerhazys' pool. The pool, fed by an artesian well with a high iron content, was a pale shade of green. It was a fine day. In the west there was a massive stand of cumulus cloud so like a city seen from a distance—from the bow of an approaching ship—that it might have had a name. Lisbon. Hackensack. The sun was hot. Neddy Merrill sat by the green water, one hand in it, one around a glass of gin. He was a slender man—he seemed to have the especial slenderness of youth—and while he was far from young he had slid down his banister that morning and given the bronze backside of Aphrodite on the hall table a smack, as he jogged toward the smell of coffee in his dining room. He might have been compared to a summer's day, particularly the last hours of one, and while he lacked a tennis racket or a sail bag the impression was definitely one of youth, sport, and clement weather. He had been swimming and now he was breathing deeply, stertorously as if he could gulp into his lungs the components of that moment, the heat of the sun, the intenseness of his pleasure. It all seemed to flow into his chest. His own house stood in Bullet Park, eight miles to the south, where his four beautiful daughters would have had their lunch and might be playing tennis. Then it occurred to him that by taking a dogleg to the southwest he could reach his home by water.

His life was not confining and the delight he took in this observation could not be explained by its suggestion of escape. He seemed to see, with a cartographer's eye, that string of swimming pools, that quasi-subterranean stream that curved across the county. He had made a discovery, a contribution to modern geography; he would name the stream Lucinda after his wife. He was not a practical joker nor was he a fool but he was determinedly original and had a vague and modest idea of himself as a legendary figure. The day was beautiful and it seemed to him that a long swim might enlarge and celebrate its beauty.

He took off a sweater that was hung over his shoulders and dove in. He had an inexplicable contempt for men who did not hurl themselves into pools. He swam a choppy crawl, breathing either with every stroke or every fourth stroke and counting somewhere well in the back of his mind the one-two one-two of a flutter kick. It was not a serviceable stroke for long distances but the domestication of swimming had saddled the sport with some customs and in his part of the world a crawl was customary. To be embraced and sustained by the light green water was less a pleasure, it seemed, than the resumption of a natural condition, and he would have liked to swim without trunks, but this was not possible, considering his project. He hoisted himself up on the far curb—he never used the ladder—and started across the lawn. When Lucinda asked where he was going he said he was going to swim home.

The only maps and charts he had to go by were remembered or imaginary but these were clear enough. First there were the Grahams, the Hammers, the Lears, the Howlands, and the Crosscups. He would cross Ditmar Street to the Bunkers and come, after a short portage, to the Levys, the Welchers, and the public pool in Lancaster. Then there were the Hallorans, the Sachses, the Biswangers, Shirley Adams, the Gilmartins, and the Clydes. The day was lovely, and that he lived in a world so generously supplied with water seemed like a clemency, a beneficence. His heart was high and he ran across the grass. Making his way home by an uncommon route gave him the feeling that he was a pilgrim, an explorer, a man with a destiny, and he knew that he would find friends all along the way; friends would line the banks of the Lucinda River.

He went through a hedge that separated the Westerhazys' land from the Grahams', walked under some flowering apple trees, passed the shed that housed their pump and filter, and came out at the Grahams' pool. "Why, Neddy," Mrs. Graham said, "what a marvelous surprise. I've been trying to get you on the phone all morning. Here, let me get you a drink." He saw then, like any explorer, that the hospitable customs and traditions of the natives would have to be handled with diplomacy if he was ever going to reach his destination. He did not want to mystify or seem rude to the Grahams nor did he have the time to linger there. He swam the length of their pool and joined them in the sun and was rescued, a few minutes later, by the arrival of two carloads of friends from Connecticut. During the uproarious reunions he was able to slip away. He went down by the front of the Grahams' house, stepped over a thorny hedge, and crossed a vacant lot to the Hammers'. Mrs. Hammer, looking up from her roses, saw him swim by although she wasn't quite sure who it was. The Lears heard him splashing past the open windows of their living room. The Howlands and the Crosscups were away. After leaving the Howlands' he crossed Ditmar Street and started for the Bunkers', where he could hear, even at that distance, the noise of a party.

The water refracted the sound of voices and laughter and seemed to suspend it in midair. The Bunkers' pool was on a rise and he climbed some stairs to a terrace where twenty-five or thirty men and women were drinking. The only person in the water was Rusty Towers, who floated there on a rubber raft. Oh, how bonny and lush were the banks of the Lucinda River! Prosperous men and women gathered by the sapphire-colored waters while caterer's men in white coats passed them cold gin. Overhead a red de Haviland trainer was circling around and around and around in the sky with something like the glee of a child in a swing. Ned felt a passing affection for the scene, a tenderness for the gathering, as if it was something he might touch. In the distance he heard thunder. As soon as Enid Bunker saw him she began to scream: "Oh, look who's here! What a marvelous surprise! When Lucinda said that you couldn't come I thought I'd *die*." She made her way to him through the crowd, and when they had finished kissing she led him to the bar, a progress that was slowed by the fact that he stopped to kiss eight or ten other women and shake the hands of as many men. A smiling bartender he had seen at a hundred parties gave him a gin and tonic and he stood by the bar for a moment, anxious not to get stuck in any conversation that would delay his voyage. When he seemed about to be surrounded he dove in and swam close to the side to avoid colliding with Rusty's raft. At the far end of the pool he bypassed the Tomlinsons with a broad smile and jogged up the garden path. The gravel cut his feet but this was the only unpleasantness. The party was confined to the pool, and as he went toward the house he heard the brilliant, watery sound of voices fade, heard the noise of a radio from the Bunkers' kitchen, where someone was listening to a ball game. Sunday afternoon. He made his way through the parked cars and down the grassy border of their driveway to Alewives Lane. He did not want to be seen on the road in his bathing trunks but there was no traffic and he made the short distance to the Levys' driveway, marked with a PRIVATE PROPERTY sign and a green tube for *The New York Times*. All the doors and windows of the big house were open but there were no signs of life; not even a dog barked. He went around the side of the house to the pool and saw that the Levys had only recently left. Glasses and bottles and dishes of nuts were on a table at the deep end, where there was a bathhouse or gazebo, hung with Japanese lanterns. After swimming the pool he got himself a glass and poured a drink. It was his fourth or fifth drink and he had swum nearly half the length of the Lucinda River. He felt tired, clean, and pleased at that moment to be alone; pleased with everything.

It would storm. The stand of cumulus cloud—that city—had risen and darkened, and while he sat there he heard the percussiveness of thunder again. The de Haviland trainer was still circling overhead and it seemed to Ned that he could almost hear the pilot laugh with pleasure in the afternoon; but when there was another peal of thunder he took off for home. A train whistle blew and he wondered what time it had gotten to be. Four? Five? He thought of the provincial station at that hour, where a waiter, his tuxedo concealed by a raincoat, a dwarf with some flowers wrapped in newspaper, and a woman who had been crying would be waiting for the local. It was suddenly growing dark; it was that moment when the pinheaded birds seem to organize their song into some acute and knowledgeable recognition of the storm's approach. Then there was a fine noise of rushing water from the crown of an oak at his back, as if a spigot there had been turned. Then the noise of fountains came from the crowns of all the tall trees. Why did he love storms, what was the meaning of his excitement when the door sprang open and the rain wind fled rudely up the stairs, why had the simple task of shutting the windows of an old house seemed fitting and urgent, why did the first watery notes of a storm wind have for him the unmistakable sound of good news, cheer, glad tidings? Then there was an explosion, a smell of cordite, and rain lashed the Japanese lanterns that Mrs. Levy had bought in Kyoto the year before last, or was it the year before that?

He stayed in the Levys' gazebo until the storm had passed. The rain had cooled the air and he shivered. The force of the wind had stripped a maple of its red and yellow leaves and scattered them over the grass and the water. Since it was midsummer the tree must be blighted, and yet he felt a peculiar sadness at this sign of autumn. He braced his shoulders, emptied his glass, and started for the Welchers' pool. This meant crossing the Lindleys' riding ring and he was surprised to find it overgrown with grass and all the jumps dismantled. He wondered if the Lindleys had sold their horses or gone away for the summer and put them out to board. He seemed to remember having heard something about the Lindleys and their horses but the memory was unclear. On he went, barefoot through the wet grass, to the Welchers', where he found their pool was dry.

This breach in his chain of water disappointed him absurdly, and he felt like some explorer who seeks a torrential headwater and finds a dead stream. He was disappointed and mystified. It was common enough to go away for the summer but no one ever drained his pool. The Welchers had definitely gone away. The pool furniture was folded, stacked, and covered with a tarpaulin. The bathhouse was locked. All the windows of the house were shut, and when he went around to the driveway in front he saw a FOR SALE sign nailed to a tree. When had he last heard from the Welchers— when, that is, had he and Lucinda last regretted an invitation to dine with them? It seemed only a week or so ago. Was his memory failing or had he so disciplined it in the repression of unpleasant facts that he had damaged his sense of the truth? Then in the distance he heard the sound of a tennis game. This cheered him, cleared away all his apprehensions and let him regard the overcast sky and the cold air with indifference. This was the day that Neddy Merrill swam across the county. That was the day! He started off then for his most difficult portage.

HAD YOU GONE for a Sunday afternoon ride that day you might have seen him, close to naked, standing on the shoulders of Route 424, waiting for a chance to cross. You might have wondered if he was the victim of foul play, had his car broken down, or was he merely a fool. Standing barefoot in the deposits of the highway—beer cans, rags, and blowout patches— exposed to all kinds of ridicule, he seemed pitiful. He had known when he started that this was a part of his journey—it had been on his maps—but confronted with the lines of traffic, worming through the summery light, he found himself unprepared. He was laughed at, jeered at, a beer can was thrown at him, and he had no dignity or humor to bring to the situation. He could have gone back, back to the Westerhazys', where Lucinda would still be sitting in the sun. He had signed nothing, vowed nothing, pledged nothing, not even to himself. Why, believing as he did, that all human obduracy was susceptible to common sense, was he unable to turn back? Why was he determined to complete his journey even if it meant putting his life in danger? At what point had this prank, this joke, this piece of horseplay become serious? He could not go back, he could not even recall with any clearness the green water at the Westerhazys', the sense of inhaling the day's components, the friendly and relaxed voices saying that they had *drunk* too much. In the space of an hour, more or less, he had covered a distance that made his return impossible.

An old man, tooling down the highway at fifteen miles an hour, let him get to the middle of the road, where there was a grass divider. Here he was exposed to the ridicule of the northbound traffic, but after ten or fifteen minutes he was able to cross. From here he had only a short walk to the Recreation Center at the edge of the village of Lancaster, where there were some handball courts and a public pool.

The effect of the water on voices, the illusion of brilliance and suspense, was the same here as it had been at the Bunkers' but the sounds here were louder, harsher, and more shrill, and as soon as he entered the crowded enclosure he was confronted with regimentation. "ALL SWIMMERS MUST TAKE A SHOWER BEFORE USING THE POOL. ALL SWIMMERS MUST USE THE FOOTBATH. ALL SWIMMERS MUST WEAR THEIR IDENTIFICATION DISKS." He took a shower, washed his feet in a cloudy and bitter solution, and made his way to the edge of the water. It stank of chlorine and looked to him like a sink. A pair of life-guards in a pair of towers blew police whistles at what seemed to be regular intervals and abused the swimmers through a public address system. Neddy remembered the sapphire water at the Bunkers' with longing and thought that he might contaminate himself—damage his own prosperous-ness and charm—by swimming in this murk, but he reminded himself that he was an explorer, a pilgrim, and that this was merely a stagnant bend in the Lucinda River. He dove, scowling with distaste, into the chlorine and had to swim with his head above water to avoid collisions, but even so he was bumped into, splashed, and jostled. When he got to the shallow end both lifeguards were shouting at him: "Hey, you, you without the identification disk, get outa the water." He did, but they had no way of pursuing him and he went through the reek of suntan oil and chlorine out through the hurricane fence and passed the handball courts. By crossing the road he entered the wooded part of the Halloran estate. The woods were not cleared and the footing was treacherous and difficult until he reached the lawn and the clipped beech hedge that encircled their pool.

The Hallorans were friends, an elderly couple of enormous wealth who seemed to bask in the suspicion that they might be Communists. They were zealous reformers but they were not Communists, and yet when they were accused, as they sometimes were, of subversion, it seemed to gratify and excite them. Their beech hedge was yellow and he guessed this had been blighted like the Levys' maple. He called hullo, hullo, to warn the Hallorans of his approach, to palliate his invasion of their privacy. The Hallorans, for reasons that had never been explained to him, did not wear bathing suits. No explanations were in order, really. Their nakedness was a detail in their uncompromising zeal for reform and he stepped politely out of his trunks before he went through the opening in the hedge.

Mrs. Halloran, a stout woman with white hair and a serene face, was reading the *Times*. Mr. Halloran was taking beech leaves out of the water with a scoop. They seemed not surprised or displeased to see him. Their pool was perhaps the oldest in the country, a fieldstone rectangle, fed by a brook. It had no filter or pump and its waters were the opaque gold of the stream.

"I'm swimming across the country," Ned said.

"Why, I didn't know one could," exclaimed Mrs. Halloran.

"Well, I've made it from the Westerhazys'," Ned said. "That must be about four miles."

He left his trunks at the deep end, walked to the shallow end, and swam this stretch. As he was pulling himself out of the water he heard Mrs. Halloran say, "We've been *terribly* sorry to hear about all your misfortunes, Neddy."

"My misfortunes?" Ned asked. "I don't know what you mean."

"Why, we heard that you'd sold the house and that your poor children . . ."

"I don't recall having sold the house," Ned said, "and the girls are at home."

"Yes," Mrs. Halloran sighed. "Yes . . ." Her voice filled the air with an unseasonable melancholy and Ned spoke briskly. "Thank you for the swim."

"Well, have a nice trip," said Mrs. Halloran.

Beyond the hedge he pulled on his trunks and fastened them. They were loose and he wondered if, during the space of an afternoon, he could have lost some weight. He was cold and he was tired and the naked Hallorans and their dark water had depressed him. The swim was too much for his strength but how could he have guessed this, sliding down the banister that morning and sitting in the Westerhazys' sun? His arms were lame. His legs felt rubbery and ached at the joints. The worst of it was the cold in his bones and the feeling that he might never be warm again. Leaves were falling down around him and he smelled wood smoke on the wind. Who would be burning wood at this time of year?

He needed a drink. Whiskey would warm him, pick him up, carry him through the last of his journey, refresh his feeling that it was original and valorous to swim across the county. Channel swimmers took brandy. He needed a stimulant. He crossed the lawn in front of the Hallorans' house and went down a little path to where they had built a house for their only daughter, Helen, and her husband, Eric Sachs. The Sachses' pool was small and he found Helen and her husband there.

"Oh, *Neddy,*" Helen said. "Did you lunch at Mother's?"

"Not *really,*" Ned said. "I *did* stop to see your parents." This seemed to be explanation enough. "I'm terribly sorry to break in on you like this but I've taken a chill and I wonder if you'd give me a drink."

"Why, I'd *love* to," Helen said, "but there hasn't been anything in this house to drink since Eric's operation. That was three years ago."

Was he losing his memory, had his gift for concealing painful facts let him forget that he had sold his house, that his children were in trouble, and that his friend had been ill? His eyes slipped from Eric's face to his abdomen, where he saw three pale, sutured scars, two of them at least a foot long. Gone was his navel, and what, Neddy thought, would the roving hand, bed-checking one's gifts at 3 A.M., make of a belly with no navel, no link to birth, this breach in the succession?

"I'm sure you can get a drink at the Biswangers'," Helen said. "They're having an enormous do. You can hear it from here. Listen!"

She raised her head and from across the road, the lawns, the gardens, the woods, the fields, he heard again the brilliant noise of voices over water. "Well, I'll get wet," he said, still feeling that he had no freedom of choice about his means of travel. He dove into the Sachses' cold water and, gasping, close to drowning, made his way from one end of the pool to the other. "Lucinda and I want *terribly* to see you," he said over his shoulder, his face set toward the Biswangers'. "We're sorry it's been so long and we'll call you *very* soon."

He crossed some fields to the Biswangers' and the sounds of revelry there. They would be honored to give him a drink, they would be happy to give him a drink. The Biswangers invited him and Lucinda for dinner four times a year, six weeks in advance. They were always rebuffed and yet they continued to send out their invitations, unwilling to comprehend the rigid and undemocratic realities of their society. They were the sort of people who discussed the price of things at cocktails, exchanged market tips during dinner, and after dinner told dirty stories to mixed company. They did not belong to Neddy's set—they were not even on Lucinda's Christmas-card list. He went toward their pool with feelings of indifference, charity, and some unease, since it seemed to be getting dark and these were the longest days of the year. The party when he joined it was noisy and large. Grace Biswanger was the kind of hostess who asked the optometrist, the veterinarian, the real-estate dealer, and the dentist. No one was swimming and the twilight, reflected on the water of the pool, had a wintry gleam. There was a bar and he started for this. When Grace Biswanger saw him she came toward him, not affectionately as he had every right to expect, but bellicosely.

"Why, this party has everything," she said loudly, "including a gate crasher."

She could not deal him a social blow—there was no question about this and he did not flinch. "As a gate crasher," he asked politely, "do I rate a drink?"

"Suit yourself," she said. "You don't seem to pay much attention to invitations."

She turned her back on him and joined some guests, and he went to the bar and ordered a whiskey. The bartender served him but he served him rudely. His was a world in which the caterer's men kept the social score, and to be rebuffed by a part-time barkeep meant that he had suffered some loss of social esteem. Or perhaps the man was new and uninformed. Then he heard Grace at his back say: "They went for broke overnight—nothing but income—and he showed up drunk one Sunday and asked us to loan him five thousand dollars. . . ." She was always talking about money. It was worse than eating your peas off a knife. He dove into the pool, swam its length and went away.

The next pool on his list, the last but two, belonged to his old mistress, Shirley Adams. If he had suffered any injuries at the Biswangers' they would be cured here. Love—sexual roughhouse in fact—was the supreme elixir, the pain killer, the brightly colored pill that would put the spring back into his step, the joy of life in his heart. They had had an affair last week, last month, last year. He couldn't remember. It was he who had broken it off, his was the upper hand, and he stepped through the gate of the wall that surrounded her pool with nothing so considered as self-confidence. It seemed in a way to be his pool, as the lover, particularly the illicit lover, enjoys the possessions of his mistress with an authority unknown to holy matrimony. She was there, her hair the color of brass, but her figure, at the edge of the lighted, cerulean water, excited in him no profound memories. It had been, he thought, a lighthearted affair, although she had wept when he broke it off. She seemed confused to see him and he wondered if she was still wounded. Would she, God forbid, weep again?

"What do you want?" she asked.

"I'm swimming across the county."

"Good Christ. Will you ever grow up?"

"What's the matter?"

"If you've come here for money," she said, "I won't give you another cent."

"You could give me a drink."

"I could but I won't. I'm not alone."

"Well, I'm on my way."

He dove in and swam the pool, but when he tried to haul himself up onto the curb he found that the strength in his arms and shoulders had gone, and he paddled to the ladder and climbed out. Looking over his shoulder he saw, in the lighted bathhouse, a young man. Going out onto the dark lawn he smelled chrysanthemums or marigolds—some stubborn autumnal fragrance—on the night air, strong as gas. Looking overhead he saw that the stars had come out, but why should he seem to see Andromeda, Cepheus, and Cassiopeia? What had become of the constellations of midsummer? He began to cry.

It was probably the first time in his adult life that he had ever cried, certainly the first time in his life that he had ever felt so miserable, cold, tired, and bewildered. He could not understand the rudeness of the caterer's barkeep or the rudeness of a mistress who had come to him on her knees and showered his trousers with tears. He had swum too long, he had been immersed too long, and his nose and his throat were sore from the water. What he needed then was a drink, some company, and some clean, dry clothes, and while he could have cut directly across the road to his home he went on to the Gilmartins' pool. Here, for the first time in his life, he did not dive but went down the steps into the icy water and swam a hobbled sidestroke that he might have learned as a youth. He staggered with fatigue on his way to the Clydes' and paddled the length of their pool, stopping again and again with his hand on the curb to rest. He climbed up the ladder and wondered if he had the strength to get home. He had done what he wanted, he had swum the county, but he was so stupefied with exhaustion that his triumph seemed vague. Stooped, holding on to the gateposts for support, he turned up the driveway of his own house.

The place was dark. Was it so late that they had all gone to bed? Had Lucinda stayed at the Westerhazys' for supper? Had the girls joined her there or gone someplace else? Hadn't they agreed, as they usually did on Sunday, to regret all their invitations and stay at home? He tried the garage doors to see what cars were in but the doors were locked and rust came off the handles onto his hands. Going toward the house, he saw that the force of the thunderstorm had knocked one of the rain gutters loose. It hung down over the front door like an umbrella rib, but it could be fixed in the morning. The house was locked, and he thought that the stupid cook or the stupid maid must have locked the place up until he remembered that it had been some time since they had employed a maid or a cook. He shouted, pounded on the door, tried to force it with his shoulder, and then, looking in at the windows, saw that the place was empty.

SWIMMING THE ENGLISH CHANNEL
By Diana Nyad

August 5, 1976. I was wedged into one of British Airway's economy seats, happily accompanied by my two closest friends, who were to act as my trainers, and by an American film crew of seven. We were off to make, assist and record history. I was attempting to become the first woman to complete the double crossing of the English Channel. The swim would be from shore to shore, followed by the permissible ten minutes' rest, and then back again. This was to be one of my toughest moments, and as the date was set for August 15, I had ten days to gather all my assets to a pinpoint focus on the Channel.

It was a night flight; I've always admired people who could sleep sitting up, but I'm not among them, so I dug into the corner of an Adidas bag for Channel swimming literature. *The Channel Swimming Association Handbook* was a bit dry. The list of attempts, successes and records was better; to date only 20 percent of the 1,100 who had attempted the crossing had succeeded. Then I settled down to hundreds of anecdotes of Channel swims, successes as well as failures. Filled with heroism, human drama and fascinating detail, these pages aroused in me once again a tremendous appreciation for this sport, which embraces so much more than the perfecting of specified skills and the mental/physical battle with an opponent. Engrossed by the stories, I also wondered at the fact that, while the English Channel is reputed the world round as the greatest long-distance swimming test, very few people know who has done it or what it involves (except, of course, the enthusiastic and knowledgeable inhabitants of the English coast, who say that had it been dubbed the "French Channel," the interest would have been generated on the other shore).

Who knows the story of Captain Matthew Webb, considered the laughable lunatic of London, who in 1875 set off covered with porpoise oil, with little navigational expertise, slow breast-stroking at one mile per hour, gulping brandy for warmth? Webb was the first to swim across (England to France, 21 hours, 45 minutes), and at the time, his feat was looked upon by those who hadn't actually been witnesses in much the same way as centenarians today view astronauts walking on the moon—pure fiction. (Some weeks later Webb tried to cross the Niagara River four hundred meters above the falls; he is buried at the bottom.) Then there was the man who had been close to losing consciousness an hour from shore, but as he slowly approached the English coast a large wave threw him onto the rocks, at which point he did lose consciousness; as he slipped back into the sea, the next roller tossed him farther than the first, and he thereby completed the swim. And there was barrel-chested Kevin Murphy, who went looking for the first-ever three-way crossing (over, back and over again). One year (1974) he started twelve hours too late: at the fifty-second hour, on his way to the third coast, tremendous winds blew up, forcing him to abandon the effort. Then in July 1976, he began twelve hours too soon, as the light west wind, which switched to an easterly twelve hours after he started, blew diesel fumes straight in his face, inducing many hours of vomiting that reduced him to hopeless exhaustion. And there are scores of stories told of severe jellyfish stings, the famed Channel chop that always seems to come up against you, the icy temperatures, the abrupt changes in weather, different pilots' theories about courses and their almost intuitive interpretation of the tides and wind-force readings.

After a short train ride from London, we checked into the stately White Cliffs Hotel on the harbor front in Dover. One hour later, staring out toward France from my balcony, brimming with fear and excitement, I began to prepare myself.

Swimming has always deserved its reputation as one of the tough sports, the time-consuming sports in which long hours of conditioning can't be avoided. No swimmer arrives at the English Channel or at any other body of water without months and months of strenuous interval training in a pool, monotonous rhythmic hours in open water, and a few long solo crossings under his or her belt. And although I knew the difficulty of conquering the Channel to be highly overrated, despite its public acclaim, my discipline in training for the double crossing hadn't been lax in any way. During the previous five months I had completed three swims of eight, twelve and thirteen hours; and I had put in a hell of a lot of time at the pool, all building toward an intense month of July. Mondays, Wednesdays and Fridays I did ten miles; eight on Tuesdays, and Thursdays; and weekends I would go out for open-water swims in the cold water of the New York area, off Long Island and Fire Island. August meant a welcome tapering, two weeks of light training, loosening up, massages, overresting —and overeating. Except for my weight, I was in perfect physical shape. At 125 pounds, 5 feet 6½ inches, I then had nine days to pump up to what I thought would be an ideal weight of 140. (The very cold Channel temperature—it reads approximately 58 degrees during the summer season—burns up a lot of calories.) No coat of porpoise oil or lanolin can contain body heat and maintain body temperature as well as fatty tissue. Moreover, the caloric output of a marathon swimmer at a decent pace in cold water is from 1,500 to 2,500 calories per hour; and although you feed on liquids rich in glucose while swimming, the calories lost couldn't possibly be reingested fast enough to hold a constant weight. So the prime source of energy becomes the body fat itself.

Gaining weight became one preoccupation. Another was the logistics of the crossing. Through the Channel Swimming Association, the body of officials that organizes, sanctions and records Channel swims, I had prearranged to be piloted by a veteran Channel fisherman named Heath. If most of the stories told could be believed, success was often as dependent on the boat captain as on the swimmer. Evidently, an experienced and interested pilot could guide even the poorest of swimmers across, whereas the best of swimmers could be thwarted in crossing attempts by the inept navigation and bad judgment of an inexperienced one. I was most anxious to meet this Heath.

We took a bus to the next town, wound our way through the cobblestone streets to the wharves and pounded on Heath's door. It opened shortly, a voice with a very strong accent accounced "Auwt beck," and the door was shut again. We traipsed around to the back to find Heath, an almost archetypical old salt, toothless and quiet, with most of his eleven children on the lawn nearby. Introductions went around; my group and his group stepped aside and we held our first meeting, Heath and I, standing arms folded amidst the laundry hanging in his backyard. I trusted him implicitly.

We first discussed the tides. The spring (strong) tides occur every fortnight, three days after the new moon or the full moon. The springs run five to six times faster than a swimmer's speed and are often so strong that breaking in toward shore for landing becomes impossible. Neap (slack) tides also occur every fortnight, three days after the first and last quarters of the moon. Even though the three-to-four-knot strength of the neaps is still faster than average swimming speed for any length of time, a swim, and especially a double crossing, is more easily and safely accomplished during this period. The next neaps were to run from August 17 to 23. The August 15 date I had been given was correct because the tides begin to slacken a couple of days before the neaps actually run.

I was to be second in line with Heath for the mid-August neaps. There would be an all-Arab race on the 15th, weather permitting; he was committed to one of the competitors, and he would then be available to escort me, weather permitting. Weather permitting? Every race I had been to was sent off in any conditions short of a hurricane. Here the wind is measured by the Beaufort scale of wind forces 0 through 17; force 0, up to one mile per hour; force 4, whitecaps are forming; force 7, a gale; and forces 12 to 17, a hurricane. The weather is so unpredictable through the Dover Straits that Coast Guard and shipping forecasts are secured only twelve hours in advance and nobody promises anything. The captain listens for a force 0 to 1, 1 to 2, 2 to 3 or possibly 3 to 4 (if the wind is behind you), and you take off on the next tide, some eleven hours later. Can you imagine showing up at Wimbledon, thoroughly prepared for your moment, only to discover that nobody knows whether you will play the night of the 15th or the afternoon of the 16th; perhaps you will even have to bide your time and hold your peak until the early morning of the 24th, still with no more than twelve hours' notice? If the task of preparation is to peak at a distinct moment, how thorough will the preparation ever be when the moment is so indistinct as to be left in the laps of the Channel weather gods?

The next week's routine was to become one of frustrating but beneficial boredom. Swimming, sleeping and eating. Mostly eating. Sumptuous breakfasts, several light meals during the day, Cadbury chocolate by the pound, dozens of baked potatoes and ears of corn, two or three desserts at dinner. As the Arabs were to compete on the 15th, I thought my starting time would likely be 3:00 A.M. on August 16. I put myself on a descending training schedule: the first few days entailed swimming a few hours and the time spent decreased each day until it was only a matter of thirty to forty-five minutes of relaxed stretching. The sleeping/resting was a system I call overloading. After many months of hard work you reach a point in conditioning that defies fatigue. A tapering period allows for full recovery and sharpening of the edge; and overloading on rest for five or six days before a marathon swim conserves energy and adrenaline until you feel you could explode. Beginning August 12, most of my time was spent quietly, generating the presence of mind to expect the worst and to handle the worst, this time perhaps for a continuous thirty hours. By the 15th I was sky-high and ready, weighing a strong 139 pounds, bursting with confidence and ambition. My head was willing to permit my body any and every abuse.

But the Arab race never set off on the 15th. Or the 16th. Or the 17th. They finally had a chance the morning of the 18th, so I knew my moment would come the following day. Apprehensive about the delay, not having swum for five days, perhaps not as thoroughly peaked as the few days before, I was up again. The film crew was to be on the pilot's boat in the harbor at 9:00 A.M. They would taxi over to Shakespeare Beach, where my trainers would be greasing me. Departure time was set for 10:30, one hour after high water. I downed as many carbohydrates as humanly possible throughout the day—spaghetti, toast and honey, bowls of cereal, baked potatoes. I soaked in a hot bath, tried to relax with a full massage and had ten hours of uneasy sleep. At 7:30 A.M. I was dressing for the preswim meal when the phone rang. Heath—bad weather. Christ, off again. This procedure was to continue in much the same fashion for the following four days. An afternoon forecast at 2:00 would give a tentative go-ahead for the next day, the 6:00 P.M. report would boost my hopes further, but then Heath's call would come through in the morning, canceling day after day, chance after chance. Indefatigable faith began to waver and the physical peak was definitely slipping from its solid groundwork. You can't entirely forgo swimming for ten or twelve—or who knows how many—days before the chance comes; but you can't swim much either, because you may be alerted that you're going off in a few hours and every ounce of reserve will be needed. After passing days and weeks in frustrated waiting, countless swimmers have done a decent training swim in an effort to regain both a mental and physical edge, only to learn the weather has changed and they are scheduled to go that evening at midnight.

August 23 came and went, the last day of the neaps. The film people were anxious, to say the least; this was a hell of an investment and a hell of a risk if no swim was to materialize. I was a nervous wreck, no longer assuring myself how well I would attack the task but wondering if the task would ever offer itself. It did—the next day.

The spring tide beginning to roll, the wind coming at force 2 to 3 from the east, August 24 wouldn't present the glassy mirror of all swimmers' daydreams, but it was an opportunity nonetheless, and we marched determinedly down Shakespeare Beach after the customary ritual of much food and little sleep. With the understandable fear in the back of my mind that the whole thing would be called off at the last minute, I was pensive and took a few minutes for my final meditation. Heath contacted us from the boat on the two-way radio—the swim was on. I was to be greased and waiting for the observer's signal at 1:00 A.M. (An observer is provided by the Channel Swimming Association to officiate a swim, to clock the exact time, and no swim is recognized without one.) I pulled down my suit, and with the aid of an onlooker's flashlight, my two trainers began greasing my torso. It is a singular feeling to stand naked below the towering Shakespeare Cliff in the middle of a cool English night and sense the rubber gloves slapping pounds and pounds of thick grease on your smooth skin. My concoction was 90 percent lanolin, 10 percent paraffin. Some swimmers add silicone fluid as a water repellent; some of the heavier ones have used axle grease; some stick to wool fat, or lanolin by itself; and some go with only Vaseline. If the truth were known, except for the prevention of chafing at the neck, under the arms and between the legs, there isn't a grease made that will serve its intended purpose of keeping in the warmth, keeping out the cold. For me it has become a psychological crutch to know that before a cold-water swim I will start off with six extra pounds of blubber, even though the bulk of it thins and washes off within the first hour.

Heath's boat came within sight at 12:45 A.M.; a rubber inflatable was sent in for the trainers and cameraman; the observer gave the arm signal to begin at 1:03. I stumbled over the rocks at the water's edge, slipped into the cool sea and began stroking. I remembered all the preparations I had made for the thirty-hour swim. I thought of the quick feedings every hour on the hour that would be goals in themselves. I focused on the format of chants and songs I had organized to preoccupy myself during each hour—numbers to count, numbers to reach by the feeding. This hypnotic technique was designed to keep my concentration intact for as long as possible; the isolation and the monotony and the extreme fatigue all seem to eat away at mental control, and when the mental control goes, the will goes and you're through.

From the onset to the first feeding I counted strokes, or each time the left hand entered the water. Eighteen hundred strokes was the goal. The wind coming from the east and my head turning to breathe in almost the same direction meant that I occasionally swallowed water. But during the first hour there were far too many gulps. Stroking, 1,797, 1,798, 1,799, 1,800, 1,801—the trainer's whistle and feeding time. I veered toward the boat, gradually approached the starboard, and reached up for the cup, which was extended to me in a small pan attached to a wooden pole. I would fish into the pan, grab the cup and down the twelve ounces of hot Sustagen (a hot chocolate with tremendous protein, salt, mineral and glucose levels) in less than twenty seconds.

Tossing the cup to the wind, turning again toward France, I began the second hour's counting, the goal being to hit 225 complete "Row, Row, Row Your Boat"'s before the feeding whistle. Only seconds later I vomited heavily, losing the benefit of the first feeding, and as the end of the second hour approached, I was in deep trouble. "Row, row, row . . . life is but a dream," 220, ". . . life is but a dream," 221, the whistle. I took the second cup of chocolate and began vomiting and dry-heaving for twenty minutes, treading water, knowing I couldn't even touch the boat for support. The fifteen people on the boat became alarmed; they tried to communicate with me, tried to suggest ways to combat the nausea. Panic also stirred in my heart—the end was near.

Within minutes I was lying on the deck, wrapped in blankets. Voices at once barraged me with sympathy. Never mind, just bad luck; the Sustagen was too rich to mix with salt water; not such a great day anyway. But I closed my eyes and cried tears for the death of a love that was once the core of my universe. I had swum all over the world with the added pressure of racing world-caliber athletes instead of going it solo. I had held world records across the cold Canadian lakes, from Capri to Naples, down the Argentinian rivers and the Nile. I had held the male and female records for both the north-south crossing of Lake Ontario (18 hours, 20 minutes) and the circling of Manhattan island (7 hours, 57 minutes). Marathon swimming had once offered me the pinnacle of an exhilarating mental/physical/emotional challenge, and now I was faced with the harsh realization that the horizons were no longer wide enough, that the love affair was fading.

My moment of soul-searching had arrived, I suppose, and as our boat slowly puffed back to England and waited two hours to clear immigration, I was enormously depressed. After we docked, we loaded our van and squeezed in; no one spoke as we drove the fifteen minutes back to the hotel. Weary, still swaying and still silent, we dragged ourselves into the foyer, and I solemnly asked if we could all meet for one minute. Everyone pulled up chairs and waited with tired but respectful eyes. I was filled with emotion. Enveloped in greasy blankets, looking from face to face, I spoke slowly and softly. After seven hard years at the top of one of the most difficult sports, I sincerely appreciated the fact that the members of this film company were the first people to believe in what I did, to invest money on the faith that a visual record of what I did would be valuable. (I made more money attempting the English Channel than I did in six years of professional marathon swimming.) They had spent a lot of time and money, my good friends had lent their time and energy, and I was sorry. Almost feeling guilty, I told them that seasickness didn't induce me defeat. I had been seasick a dozen times before, and seasickness doesn't make a champion quit. I said that although physical strength, a fine pilot, efficient trainers, blood sugar replacement and so forth all help you across, only your motivation will actually get you there. If you want to touch the other shore badly enough, barring an impossible situation, you will. If your desire is diluted for any reason, you'll never make it. I said I was like a fighter who was still good, who still made the right moves and who still enjoyed being called the champ, but who just didn't want to take any more punches. The thrill wasn't what it used to be; it had been fading for a couple of years, and if a thrill is no more than a memory, however wonderful, it has no place in the present. I regretted that I had to discover this truth now instead of a month earlier, when I could have analyzed my feelings at home. But I supposed it could have only been discovered swimming again, seeking the thrill again. The group thanked me for sharing my thoughts with them, and we went upstairs.

Dawn broke. I took a bath and swabbed myself with alcohol in another futile attempt to remove the grease. I tried to sleep, but I was anxious, my heart was heavy. I had failed, given up. I had been weak; I hadn't been disciplined enough to make myself do it just because I said I could and would. I felt somehow guilty. Perhaps I had learned a prime lesson for the future—that it was time to move on to something new, but I was still here, there was time to do it right, to leave the old with a grand success instead of a failure.

There were many arguments the next day. Friends said it was a masochistic sport in the first place; wanting to do it again was my intellect speaking, while my words the night before in the foyer came from the heart. Was I really going to do something now that I definitely didn't want to do? I who always bragged that I never, never do anything I don't want to do? Yes, I was. Just this once more and I would go home a winner. And they were with me; the whole crew stayed and believed with me again. The slight change in motivation would make this swim the most difficult of all. It was not the pure desire to win, to finish; it was more the loathing of the self-respect I would lose if I quit.

I asked Heath that night if he would take me again. "Very good swimmer. Of course I will." He had two Indians—a fourteen-year-old girl and a fifty-four-year-old man—in line starting September 1 for the next neaps, so I would have to wait my turn. And before the neaps? That was up to me, he said meaningfully, so I resolved we'd go the first good day, regardless of the tide. The weather came around on August 30. Heath said there would be some wind, force 4 from the northwest, but it would be blowing from behind, so that was all right. But what about swimming back? I was told I should have learned by then not to ask for everything at the Channel.

August 30 was a retake of August 24. Same breakfast, same people doing the same jobs, same fears and nervousness, and once more confidence and desire. The starting time was now 3:30 A.M. and I was again nude on Shakespeare Beach. Other swimmers set off at approximately the same time; from the first stroke I felt fantastically smooth and powerful. Eighteen hundred strokes, first feeding. Two hundred and nineteen "Row, Row, Row Your Boat"'s, second feeding. Thirty-five "Frère Jacques"'s (set of English, French and German), third feeding. I was making splendid headway, I was optimistic and in control, the people on the boat were happy and with me. My only worry was that the seas were beginning to rise; I was thrown about more and more violently and progress was coming to a gradual halt. Two hundred and two "Anything You Can Do, I Can Do Better"'s, and I came in for the fourth feeding. Cramps in the left groin from kicking so hard to catch a breath amidst the waves. I knew that the weather was going to beat me this time. Another fifteen or twenty minutes of trying to straighten my left leg, trying to fight the swells, and that was it. The first time I defeated myself; this time I was had by a greater force than anyone could battle. On the boat I learned that the other swimmers were also out. The wind was now at force 6, all the landlubbers had been violently sick and I saw from a better vantage point that the Channel was a mass of breaking whitecaps. There was no guilt or depression this time. August 30 was without a trace of doubt my mental and physical best. Everyone knew it, and we all talked jovially on the way back to shore. The film crew thought that with a statement from me they could salvage something, although it would not be the film they set out to make. They would head back to New York. My two friends and I decided to go to Paris to throw away the rest of our money.

A hot-water bath and an alcohol bath. No sleep. Drunk with sleeplessness, we zoomed down to Paris, talking of things other than swimming. We stayed in a hundred-dollar-a-night hotel, ate on the Champs Élysées, explored Versailles and happily headed home. We waited at the airport, and through some special nonverbal communication we all knew that I was going back to Dover. We embraced, they flew back to the United States, and I would not be defeated by the English Channel.

Still not having slept for some forty-eight hours except for naps on the train, I went straight to Heath. The Indian girl had tried and failed and the Indian man had hurt his back, so I was first in line again. I asked the observer's daughter to be my trainer, found someone willing to grease me on the shore, and set about regathering new gear, this time at my own expense. Grease, thermoses, Dynamo (a glucose drink that seemed to settle with the salt water better than the rich Sustagen), rubber gloves, towels and blankets, biscuits, ginger ale.

I found a wonderful bed-and-breakfast in Dover, checked into an attic room and tried to catch up on some sleep. It was difficult. I was worried, almost desperate to finally tame this Channel and be done with it. I became more and more nervous each day. Heath didn't call when he said he would, the air and water temperatures were beginning to drop, I wasn't sleeping well and I was losing weight. In five days I read *All the President's Men, Watership Down,* the murder case of *Mary Bell* and Thor Heyerdahl's *Ra Expeditions.*

On September 5, I called the Coast Guard myself and couldn't believe my ears. Force 1 to 2, westerly, for the early evening, probably continuing through the night and not building up again until midday of the 6th. I was frantic. I would not spend one more restless night and take a chance on the weather changing drastically. I called Heath immediately to tell him I wanted to leave on the 10:30 tide that night. It was 2:00, so there was ample time. The first mate, one of his sons, said that was okay, but to be absolutely sure we should wait for the 6:00 P.M. forecast. They would phone me at 6:10 in any case. My hands were shaking, my head was pounding. I felt tremendous pressure, all self-imposed. I was down to 127 pounds, but I was determined to make this swim. I couldn't sleep, so I stared out the attic window at the white cliffs of France, the first time the weather had permitted me to see them. Though twenty-one miles away, they seemed close enough to touch; the water was like a millpond.

I steeled myself, thought that the third time is the lucky one and went downstairs to wait for the word. They were late in calling, as usual, but this time I became furious. How could they be so inconsiderate as to leave me pacing, worrying, wondering with only four hours to prepare? I called the Coast Guard, who reconfirmed the earlier forecast: is was to be beautifully calm all night. At 6:40 I called Heath and aggressively told his son I would be on the beach ready to go at 10:30. He interrupted, "No swim tonight. Bad weather." "You're insane!" I screamed, losing control. "The weather couldn't be better!" He said the old man wasn't going. I hung up and stormed outside.

After cooling down I phoned them back. I argued that this was a business arrangement, that I was paying them to do a job and they were obligated to take me. He said the truth of the matter was that old Heath wasn't feeling so well, and he never liked the night swimming anyway. I could barely think, I was so upset and annoyed. I said again that I was going that night, not the next day, and asked if I would have to get another captain in that case. He said he supposed I would.

There was one skipper with a good reputation available, Burt Reed, who said he would be glad to escort me. He agreed that it was a perfect night, so he would do his best to round his crew up, although it was dangerously short notice. I tried to eat a high-calorie meal about three hours before take-off, but it wouldn't stay down. Reed kept calling to report that he hadn't found his crew yet, but it was still not an impossibility. I felt feverish and ill. Finally at 9:00 he called to say we would have to wait for the morning; he had done his best and that was all he could do.

I fixed my eyes on the delicious flat calm, beginning to feel somewhat fatalistic about the whole thing, and spent one last distressed, sleepless night. Two of the film people, having heard that I was back and trying again, returned to help. It was a welcome diversion; I briefed them and we set off at 11:00 the next morning.

A new boat, new pilot, no experienced trainer; nonetheless, everything was going well. I started on time; the weather was good, although nothing like the night before. During the first hour's counting, I noticed that the water was remarkably colder, and of course my weight loss hadn't helped on that score. First feeding down and I felt fine. Second hour, "Row, Row, Row Your Boat." I began to tremble and just told myself, "It's not so bad, you've been cold before, keep swimming, keep swimming." Third hour, "Frère Jacques." The trembling increased to shaking; I pictured the sun at my solar plexus, a Tibetan meditative technique, trying to feel the warmth move to the limbs. Fourth hour, "Anything You Can Do." As I reached for the fourth feeding my hand was shaking too wildly to grasp the cup, so I skipped it. I found out later that everyone on the boat feared for me at that fourth feeding; they told me my skin had been bluish, and they knew that even willpower couldn't fight the cold. Fifth hour, "I've Been Working on the Railroad." Chilled to the bone, I was quickly losing touch and my concentration was fading. I couldn't count very well and I kept forgetting what I was doing. I thought birds were dive-bombing my cap and goggles; I frantically waved them away. Suddenly, I heard many long pulls on the police whistle accompanied by frenzied shouting; I stopped to look, and surprised and bewildered, I found the boat on my right instead of my left. How did it get over there without my seeing it? Why were they so upset? They were yelling, but I couldn't hear their words. I don't remember much after that. They say I took another feeding and began swimming again, and about forty-five minutes later I started going under. Evidently, they were to me within seconds. I was hauled into the lifeboat, and as they were transferring me to the fishing vessel, I came to and realized what had happened. My body was jerking uncontrollably; they covered me immediately and two of the crew pressed their bodies to me in an offer of the best heat available. One of the mates got some hot bouillon down my throat, and within an hour the trembling began to subside. The captain kneeled beside me and comforted me with a warm hand and large smiling blue eyes. He said I was a good swimmer—I had done ten miles into mid-Channel in a bit more than four hours; I would have reached France in a very short time, indeed; if I put some weight on, I was sure to have a good crack at the record next time; he would be only too pleased to escort me on that occasion; yes, he would.

Unfortunately, the Channel was not a glorious success to be tallied up for the record along with my many other crossings. It was a defeat. Once I weakened mentally, once the weather wouldn't permit success, and ironically, the villain I had originally feared and had set out to vanquish—the cold—was my ultimate downfall. I realized that it is mechanically so easy to walk away from victory swelling with pride and optimism, believing unswervingly in yourself. Walking away from defeat the same way is a true challenge. A champion rekindles enthusiasm, regains confidence, and is willing to set difficult goals for herself again, even after defeat.

Late evening, September 7. British Airways from London to Kennedy. My pulse is racing, my adrenaline is pumping, I am smiling uncontrollably and I can't possibly sit still. Push-ups in the aisle, hyped conversation with anyone and everyone. I feel ecstatically free. The words I am known for quoting to interviewers are flashing through my mind. Life is passing me by. There isn't much time. I have some seventy-five years to live and a third of them are behind me. I feel pressured to do everything, to know everyone, to explore every potential, to press every extreme, high and low. My fervor is renewed.

THE FIRST GOLDEN AGE
By Richard Schickel

It is something like half a century since William Tatem Tilden II was at his peak, something like a quarter century since he died, broke and in disgrace, having served two prison terms—one for committing a homosexual act with a minor, the other for violating a parole that enjoined him from consorting with youngsters. Yet just days after he was released from jail the second time, which happened to be just days before this century turned fifty, an Associated Press poll of sportswriters voted him the greatest athlete in his sport by a margin larger than that achieved by any athlete in any other sport—a judgment from which no knowledgeable tennis authority cares publicly to dissent.

He compiled a wonderful record: seven U.S. singles championships, three Wimbledon singles championships, sixteen wins against just four losses in Davis Cup play, numberless other major titles in singles and in doubles (for which he claimed to have small aptitude). But it was not the number of championships he held that made Tilden the standard against which all other tennis players, including those who in his later years consistently beat him, are judged. It was the moment at which he accomplished his great feats, and the manner he brought to his conquests—and his defeats—which made him, make him, such a singular presence in tennis history.

His moment was that period that used to be known as The Golden Age of Sport—the age of Babe Ruth, Jack Dempsey, Red Grange, Notre Dame's Four Horsemen, and Bobby Jones, with all of whom Tilden stood as an equal. The period may not actually have been suffused with quite the glow nostalgia imparts to memory. None of the major sports was blessed with the depth of talent that has since become commonplace, and it seems likely that the modern athlete is both naturally stronger and the beneficiary of more sophisticated conditioning techniques. (The number of championship tennis matches in past eras that ended with the loser either collapsing or having to be helped from the court after a total expenditure of energy was astonishing.)

Yet the Golden Age was certainly the first in which promoters recognized that sports could be, inevitably would be, a big-money enterprise. It was also the first age in which it was recognized that excellence in a game was not enough, that it had to be combined with a public personality that could be exploited in order to capture the interest of the expanding mass media and their expanding audiences. If tennis had not had Tilden it would have had to invent him or it could not have held its own in the sports pages, in the talk of the nation, might never have developed the beginnings of the broad base of interest on which it currently rests.

Let me put the matter personally. I do not believe that my father, who was the first person to undertake the thankless task of teaching me the game, would have been a player had not the example of Tilden been placed before well-brought-up young men in the Middle West in the 1920s. Nor do I believe that there would have been places for us to play had Tilden not made people outside the country-club belt tennis-conscious. As it was, in the thirties and forties there were courts everywhere. A little farming community, a few miles from our vacation house, had two excellently maintained and rarely used courts to which we could repair for a hit any time we felt like it. Tilden, I firmly believe, was responsible for that fine, tree-shaded stretch of unpopulated asphalt in a place infinitely more interested in the price of corn and tobacco than it was in the USLTA rankings.

I doubt that Tilden ever knew or cared about this aspect of his influence; the evidence is that he was a remarkably shy, self-absorbed, and arrogant man. Yet even for those, like my father, who had never seen him play, he was the ideal incarnation of the tennis player, even the still photographs giving an impression, if not of how the game should be played, then how one should look while playing it. He was tall, slender, and graceful in his immaculate whites, endlessly captured by the camera in attitudes that suggested an effortless flow into position for shots of instruction-manual perfection. The press, the tennis world in general, did not let my father, or the rest of us, in on Tilden's secrets. His sexual proclivities were in that discreet age undiscussed, though there was evidently considerable fear among tennis's rulers that they might become public knowledge and hurt the game. Even such matters as his chain-smoking and his personal slovenliness (off court his clothing was unkempt and without style, and he often avoided the postgame shower because he hated to be seen naked in the locker room) were hushed up, as were the bad habits of other sporting figures who were ridiculously supposed to be setting an example for the nation's youth.

People saw in Tilden what they wanted and needed to see in the game's pre-eminent figure. They knew, for example, that he was a self-made tennis player (he had to be, since as late as 1914 there were only two teaching pros in the entire country), who had not been good enough to make the number-one spot on the tennis team at the small private prep school he attended in his native Philadelphia, or to make the varsity at Penn, which he quit before graduation. Then, however, tragedy struck the Tilden family.

His excessively beloved mother died after a long illness in 1911; four years later his father and his older brother died within months of one another, driving Tilden into a deep depression that lasted for months. An aunt lectured him, telling him he must commit himself to something, anything, lest despondency come to rule his life. There were several things he cared about as much as tennis—music, for example, and bridge and the theater—but it was the sport to which he turned, perhaps because he saw in it a way of exercising some of his taste for the dramatic as well as his need for competitive challenge. Ranked seventieth in the United States, he was put out of the first national championships he entered in the first round. Just two years later, in 1918, he reached the finals, where he lost. He lost again the following year, to "Little Bill" Johnston, largely because "Big Bill's" backhand was no more than a defensive weapon, not an instrument for attack. He passed the winter at the home of a friend who had one of the nation's few indoor tennis courts, working, working, working on his backhand.

In 1920 he went off to Wimbledon and became the first American to win the men's singles title there, defeating the Australian defending champion, Gerald Patterson, with an astonishing bit of gamesmanship. Patterson was known to have a powerful forehand and a feeble backhand, which everyone attacked. In the first set, Tilden disdained it, slamming away at Patterson's forehand, losing the set 6-2. In so doing, however, he was able to study everything the champion could do with his best shot, come to the conclusion that thereafter he—Tilden—could handle it. Patterson thereafter had only weakness—his backhand—to fall back on and Tilden swept the next three sets.

A little later it was time to revenge himself on Johnston. It required five sets to do so, in a match played in the rain and interrupted by a midair plane crash in which two military pilots lost their lives. The accounts of the game insist that it was Tilden's powerful serve which finally broke the game little man, who had to be assisted from the court after the match, but one has the feeling that Tilden was toying with his opponent, blasting him off the court in the first set, deliberately losing the second, staging a dramatic comeback to take the third, then throwing away the fourth when he needed but two points for the match, thus setting up the 6-3, fifth-set crusher. Ever after, Johnston was unable to take a significant match from Tilden.

It all fits. In his memoirs Tilden wrote of the game as he had found it: "They played with an air of elegance—a peculiar courtly grace that seemed to rob the game of its thrills. . . . There was a sort of inhumanity about it." He added: "I believed the game deserved something more vital and fundamental." This was true, as far as it went, but Tilden added more than vitality to the game. What he contributed to it was ferocity. Sometimes, of course, just for the fun of it, or for dramatic effect, he extended a match he should have closed out in straight sets. On one well-known occasion, seeing that he had his opponent hopelessly outclassed, he began offering up the shots this poor soul had shown himself best able to return. Meantime, he began storming at umpire and linesmen until he had worked the crowd into an ugly anti-Tilden mood. At which point he finished the match off briskly and apologized to the official in the chair, H. LeVan Richards: "I'm sorry, Lev. I apologize. But they really deserved a show didn't they?"

More often than not, however, his efforts were directed toward devastating the man across the net, establishing a psychological superiority that would extend beyond the day's match, haunt the fellow down the years in tournament after tournament. Sometimes he would contemptuously pick up, say, four balls, fire the three aces he needed to finish the match, then grandly toss the remaining ball aside as he strode off the court. With Johnston, the next time they met in the U.S. tournament (it was a quarterfinal match) he decided to do without the big serve that everyone had said was the only part of his game that was decidedly superior to "Little Bill's." He beat him trading forehand baseline drives in a game of long rallies. That point settled, Tilden got into a real slugging match with the Californian in the 1922 finals. He let the first two sets get away from him rather easily, much to the delight of the crowd and the assembled officialdom of the USLTA, who by this time had wearied of Tilden's arrogance and his seemingly endless winning streak. He dropped three more games in the third set, then won six consecutive games to turn it— and the match—around. In the locker room afterward, it is said, Johnston was a broken man.

The word now was that Tilden could beat the smaller man only in endurance contests, that he deliberately extended their matches to five sets in order to wear down the frail Johnston. Stung by that criticism, Tilden in the next year's finals came out firing his powerful serve and wiped Johnston out in straight sets. They would meet in one more final, in 1925, and again Tilden would win in a long match, but by that time the truth of the matter must have been clear to the dead-game Johnston: Tilden had deliberately established his superiority in every kind of match, under every sort of condition, and there was simply no way for "Little Bill" to beat his arch-rival.

It should be emphasized, in the age of Jimmy Connors, that ferocity did not imply viciousness. There were many players who detested Tilden, principally for his inability to tolerate debate over his pronouncements about how the game should be played, for the way he dominated any room he entered, but it was never said that he was anything but a perfect sportsman on court. "Peach!" he would cry when delighted by an opponent's excellent winner, and he was famous for giving up the next point when he felt a linesman's error had done the man across the net out of a point. In 1922, when both Tilden and Johnston had won the U.S. title twice and were playing for permanent possession of the cup that was supposed to be the only tangible reward for winning. Johnston wearily told his nemesis after the match, "If I can't have the cup myself, I would prefer you of all men to have it." It may indeed be that Tilden won his second Wimbledon because he was such a fine—or at least self-consciously showy—sportsman. His opponent was B. I. C. Norton of South Africa, who found himself serving for match point. Tilden returned deep, thought it was out, and came chugging up to the net to congratulate Norton. The shot, however, was in. Norton thought Tilden was charging to volley and flubbed his return. Tilden went on to win the last set 7-5.

Such is the stuff from which legends are woven. Some, indeed, say that Norton was so impressed by Tilden that he threw the match, unwilling to take the Wimbledon title from a man who was known to be sick, who had spent the week prior to defending his title in a nursing home. Be that as it may, even legends age and Tilden, who had come to greatness rather late (he was twenty-seven before winning a major title), would in the last half of "his" decade prove vulnerable to that remarkable group of Frenchmen known as the Musketeers—Jean Borotra, Henri Cochet and René Lacoste, and their quietly efficient fourth, Jacques "Toto" Brugnon, who played expert doubles. It took all of them to end Tilden's domination of the game, and only one of them, Cochet, appears to have established a definitive psychological edge on the American, although that too is open to debate.

Borotra, "the Bounding Basque" of the sportswriters' leads, was the most colorful of the group. He generally wore a cocky beret and generally came to the net after serving—the first major player to do so. A stylist of flash and dash, he had learned the game while vacationing in England as a child, catching on to its intricacies after perhaps a day of instruction, helped by the fact that he had played pelota, the handball game native to his region. Cochet was a cheerful, lazy-seeming sometime ballboy, weak of serve and backhand, but possessed of an uncanny ability to take shots on the rise—the best way of turning an opponent's power back on him—and particularly demoralizing, for some reason, to Tilden. Lacoste was the son of a wealthy industrialist, had a frail constitution, and was forced to virtually retire from the game when he was only twenty-five. Until then he was famous for keeping a book on other players, noting strengths, weaknesses, and their propensities for certain shots in certain situations.

They began competing at Wimbledon in 1922, the year the old challenge-round system—in which the defending champion was not forced to defend his title until the final (or "challenge") round—was abandoned, and G. L. Patterson regained the title he had lost to Tilden. The Frenchmen did a little better the next year, when the All England Club abandoned its old grounds in the Worple Road and moved to its present site in Church Street, though "Little Bill" Johnston gained his only Wimbledon title that year, with Tilden absent. It was not until the following year's "fortnight" —1924—that Borotra, who often commuted from his job in Paris to Wimbledon by plane, began a great French winning streak—six straight Wimbledon championships—by taking the title from Lacoste in the first all-French final round.

The following year they met again in the finals and this time the results were reversed. It was obvious that the French were coming on. In 1925 and '26 they reached the Davis Cup challenge round and were set down by the Tilden-Johnston duo 5-0 and 4-1, Lacoste administering Tilden's first defeat in cup competition at the second meeting. Cochet, volleying with deadly effectiveness, also managed to put Tilden out of Forest Hills in the quarterfinals in 1926, and it was clear that the following summer would bring to a crisis the question of American leadership in international tennis.

Things began well enough for Tilden. He defeated Cochet in the French semifinals and lost to Lacoste in the finals in a five-set, three-hour match in which it appeared that Tilden had actually won when he seemed to have aced Lacoste on match point at 9-8 in the final set. The serve was called out, however. Lacoste steadied and went on to win the deciding set 11-9.

Tilden met Cochet again in the semifinals at Wimbledon and was blowing the young Frenchman off the court, leading 6-2, 6-4, and 5-1 in the third set when, suddenly, "Big Bill" lost seventeen points in a row and the set 7-5. He promptly lost the next two sets 6-4, 6-3. The umpire, an eighteen-year Wimbledon veteran, called the turnabout "the most astonishing event that has happened in my time at Wimbledon," especially since many who saw the match believed that the first two-and-a-half sets may have been the finest tennis Tilden ever played.

There were a dozen theories as to what had gone wrong. Tilden declared that Cochet, with his back against the wall, had simply risen to heights Tilden could not match. Others said Tilden tanked the match so that Cochet would be chosen for Davis Cup play where Tilden could then gain dramatic revenge. Others say the entrance of King Alfonso of Spain into the royal box just as Tilden was on the verge of victory distracted him—or perhaps encouraged him to extend the match an extra set in order to treat His Majesty to some first-class tennis. Others say Tilden was simply too tired to go five sets against his younger opponent, though the day was a cool one and Tilden went on to win plenty of long matches in the years to come. Given his love of drama and his supreme confidence, it seems likely that Tilden did let up just a little—lost his edge and never regained it, even as you and I do when we permit self-satisfaction to outrun common sense on days when for a time we seem miraculously able to do no wrong. Whatever happened, Cochet gained not only an important win (he went on to defeat Borotra in the final), but a career-long hoodoo on Tilden, who only rarely took him in important matches thereafter.

Now events began to conspire to produce what was perhaps the most dramatic of all Davis Cup competitions. Combining with Frank T. Hunter, Tilden won the doubles championships over the Cochet-Brugnon team at both Wimbledon and Forest Hills, while losing to Lacoste in the singles at the latter tournament. In those days, even for an egotist like Tilden, playing for your country for the cup was considered a higher honor than merely playing for yourself at Wimbledon or Forest Hills. Indeed, the nationalistic overtones of these matches had much to do with exciting tennis interest among nonplayers. They reveled in the fantasy that a country's honor was somehow at stake in the exclusive stadiums where these mysterious people played their mysterious game.

The opening-round pairings pitted Lacoste against Johnston, Tilden against Cochet, with their opponents reversed in the second singles round. In the first match Johnston was pathetic, Lacoste taking him in short, straight sets. Tilden, however, temporarily exorcised the Cochet jinx in four hard sets, giving the United States hope if it could win the doubles. Here USLTA officialdom, despite the desperate situation, decided to teach the arrogant and unpopular Tilden a lesson. They informed him, on the morning of the match, that a player named Dick Williams would be substituted for Frank Hunter as Tilden's partner, despite the fact that that year Tilden-Hunter had proved themselves the world's premier doubles team. Tilden told the men in the blue blazers that he would play with Hunter, one of his few close friends among his fellow competitors—they called themselves "the Smarties"—or he would not play at all. He was informed that he must follow instructions, which was the wrong approach to "Big Bill" Tilden. "Gentlemen," he is said to have said, "I will be playing bridge, and when you have decided to name Mr. Hunter as my partner, come and inform me." With that, he settled back for a day at his second-favorite game.

Periodically through the day, USLTA officials and their emissaries pleaded with Tilden. They were finally told to stop interrupting the bridge game. The audience was in its seats before officialdom conceded their match to the champion and informed Tilden that he could play with Hunter after all. "Fine. I'll dress as soon as we finish this rubber," he told them in his most imperious manner, rather like Sir Francis Drake finishing his game of bowls before taking on the Spanish Armada.

The French Armada, however, did not have everything staked on a single battle. It would be sufficient, after Tilden's hard-fought win over Cochet, simply to extend him as far as they could, wearing him down for Lacoste, who was to play him in the singles next day. It required five sets for Tilden and Hunter to defeat Borotra and Brugnon, and when it was over, Tilden said later, he was "absolutely through . . . I was nervous. My reserves were used up in the bickering."

His only hope the next day against Lacoste was to try for a quick, straight-set victory and he came out firing the big serve. Lacoste, with his book and his brilliant tennis brain, resolved simply to keep everything in play, to run Tilden into the ground. The strategy worked: "The monotonous regularity with which that unsmiling, drab, almost dull man returned the best I could hit . . . often filled me with a wild desire to throw my racket at him," Tilden wrote in his autobiography many years later. He was able to take only one set from the Frenchman, twelve years his junior. It was true, as many witnesses to Tilden's career have testified, that even in defeat he carried himself like a victor, much to everyone's annoyance. This time, however, the crowd at the Germantown Cricket Club took him at his own assessment and when he left the court, they rose in wild ovation—for the first and only time nonplussing Tilden in public. He was used to the galleries' being against him, often worked them around to that mood in order to fire himself up. He did not know what to do with this outburst of affection and raised his arms over his head like a boxer.

Now it was up to the aging and frail Johnston to try to keep the cup in the United States, where it had resided for six years. No one could see how this consistent loser to Tilden could possibly pull out a victory over Cochet, Tilden's most consistent nemesis, yet at the end of two sets they were even. The third set and the early games of the fourth set went easily to Cochet. Johnston, making his last major appearance, rallied, pulling up from 2-5 to 4-5 and holding a 30-0 lead in the game that would even the set and very likely even the match. It was a gallant bid, but Johnston was either overanxious or put off by the uproar of the crowd. He finally lost his service, the set, and the match at 6-4, as Tilden sat in the stands next to Lacoste, who was bundled in two sweaters and an overcoat against a nervous chill which even the warm weather and his recent exertions could not penetrate. "God bless you, Little Bill," a woman called out as Johnston's last stand was finally crushed and there was another ovation, this time one washed with tears.

But if the Johnston story in essence ended that day in Philadelphia, the Tilden legend was burnished by defeat. On his return to France Lacoste declared, "Tilden could not be beaten by one player; he was beaten by a team," and the French, who had by this time built a brand new arena, the Stade Roland Garros, mainly to provide a proper setting for the Musketeers, could hardly wait to see them have a go at Tilden on soft red clay.

The USLTA rulers, however, decided that the aging Tilden, supported by Hunter in the doubles and with the undistinguished F. J. Hennessey in the number two singles spot had, in 1928, no real chance of returning the Davis Cup to its native shores. The time was ripe, they fondly believed, for another assault on Tilden. All through the glory years he had listed his occupation as "newspaperman" and, indeed, before becoming a champion he had written on both sports and the theater for the Philadelphia *Ledger*. Ever since, he had filed for sundry syndicates whenever he was engaged in a major championship and he was not the only alleged amateur who picked up some spare change by so doing. The LTA did not much care for the practice, but until now it had chosen to look the other way. This year, however, in a spasm of purity, it decided to suspend Tilden for six months because of the articles he had written from Wimbledon. He was not required for the Inter-Zone finals against Italy, but the French, with tickets to the challenge round at Roland Garros sold out, were beside themselves when it appeared that Tilden would not be permitted to play there. He thoroughly enjoyed his role as international martyr to hypocritical amateurism and must have enjoyed a particular thrill of satisfaction when the

American ambassador in Paris, Myron T. Herrick, acting under pressure from President Coolidge himself, intervened in the affair and worked out a compromise that postponed the suspension until Forest Hills. His excellency made the announcement of the deal at a lunch just before the challenge round was to begin. Tilden rushed out to practice and was, according to reports, so hysterical that he could hit nothing. And he had to face Lacoste—now four consecutive times a victor over him—in the first round. Worse, he would be facing him on clay, extraordinarily suitable to the Frenchman's game and before a home crowd.

Lacoste won the first set easily, 6-1. Then, suddenly, Tilden abandoned his customary big game and started chopping the ball back at Lacoste with a maddening variety of spins and cuts, utterly bewildering the Frenchman and taking the match in five sets. In the locker room afterward, Lacoste spoke to the press: "Two years ago I knew at last how to beat him. Now, on my own court, he beats me. I never knew how the ball would come off the racket, he concealed it so. I had to wait to see how much it was spinning, and sometimes it didn't spin at all. Is he not the greatest player of them all?"

It was the only match Tilden and the Americans won and, indeed, it was 1933 before France gave up the Davis Cup—to a team from Great Britain headed by Fred Perry and H. W. "Bunny" Austin. In the intervening years Tilden was, until he turned pro in 1931, always in the American side and, with Lacoste retired, generally able to defeat Borotra, but never Cochet. Nevertheless, he was by no means washed up. In 1929, when Cochet did not defend his Forest Hills title, Tilden won it for the last time, defeating his pal Hunter in the finals.

Then at Wimbledon in 1930 Wilmer Allison, a fine young American player, defeated Cochet in the quarterfinals, and Tilden, now thirty-seven, took Borotra in the semifinals and downed Allison in the anticlimactic finals. It was a magnificent accomplishment for a player of his age, and he provided an interesting response to René Lacoste, who in *Lacoste on Tennis,* two years before, had stated that it would be interesting to compare the style of the 1920 Wimbledon winner with that of the 1930 winner, implying that the intervening decade would have worked considerable change on the style of the champion. Maybe it did. Certainly the 1930 champion was slower, less vigorous, somewhat cannier in his methods of attack. But the name was the same—Tilden, William Tatem Tilden II.

And he had one more contribution to make to the game. As early as 1926 he had been approached by the legendary C. C. "Cash and Carry" Pyle, the sports promoter, with a $50,000 offer to turn pro, money that neither the hard-hitting and very promising Vinnie Richards nor the great Suzanne Lenglen had been able to resist. "Mr. Tilden, I think you're a damned fool," Pyle had said when Tilden finally turned him down, and Tilden replied, "Mr. Pyle, I think you are probably right." Now, however, he had his last chance to turn his gift to profit and he signed with MGM to make some movies. He was madly stage-struck, having even appeared as Dracula in a New York production. His movie career never amounted to much—he was a very bad actor off the tennis court—but he did launch a profitable pro tour pitted against the Czech champion, Karel Kozeluh, and Richards, both of whom he was able more or less regularly to defeat.

A couple of years later Cochet and Ellsworth Vines, a hard hitter whom many had expected to reach Tildenesque heights, joined the tour. Now Tilden found he could handle Cochet and he generally fought Vines, eighteen years his junior, on even terms, as a little later he would the great Fred Perry, his successor as the dominant figure in world amateur tennis. In fact, Tilden later toured with the much younger Don Budge and with Bobby Riggs, playing solid tennis when he was in his fifties. There was even a fabled occasion, during World War II, when Gardner Mulloy arranged some exhibition matches for the benefit of the Navy and asked Tilden to play a warm-up match before Mulloy took on Ted Schroeder, the Forest Hills champion. Tilden said he would play only if given a shot at Schroeder. Mulloy at first demurred, unwilling to be a party to the old gentleman's humiliation, but finally succumbed. Tilden snappily defeated Schroeder 6-2, 6-2. He was capable of that almost until the day he died— short bursts of absolutely superlative tennis against anyone.

More important, however, his presence in professional ranks gave that struggling game a respectability it might otherwise not have had in the thirties and forties. Because he had made the jump, others could follow and by so doing they kept a steady pressure on the amateur game to reform, to open itself to professionalism. In the thirties and forties I can remember men of my father's age wondering why in the world, if open golf tournaments were so successful, open tennis tournaments could not be equally so; why the best players in the world were somehow prevented from competing in the world's best tournaments. It may be that Tilden's final victory over the clubmen, the shamans of shamateurism who had sniped away at him all during the years when he was their meal ticket, the star who sold admissions at their box offices, came during the years when his example served to lure their new attractions away from them prematurely, when wandering the world he and his various troupes brought exemplary, world-class tennis to places which otherwise would never have had the chance to see it, extending interest in the game beyond the boundaries of the country-club lawns.

True to form, they turned their back on him when he entered upon his time of troubles in the late forties. He appeared at Forest Hills after serving his jail terms and was snubbed unmercifully. Some literally turned their backs on him when he approached. His name was purged from the alumni files at Penn, his pictures taken down from the walls at his home club, the Germantown Cricket Club. You can find his picture—an old wire-service snap—mixed indiscriminately among those of the other champions (none of whom are legends in quite the Tilden manner) in the men's locker room at Forest Hills. But that's it. There is today no other monument of any sort, anywhere in the small official world of tennis, to the man who made the great world conscious of the game—its beauty, its glory. For a sport that sets such store by tradition it is a very odd omission. Or is it, perhaps, all too characteristic of it?

ARTHUR ASHE VS. CLARK GRAEBNER
AT FOREST HILLS

By John McPhee

There are two identical, adjacent rooms under the grandstands at Forest Hills—long, panelled, wedge-shaped, narrow, each containing a table, a chair, a shower stall, towels, hot tea, Coca-Cola, Gatorade. Graebner throws off his clothes and hurries into a shower, still wearing his glasses. Ashe, on the other side of the wall, sits down and slowly prepares to change his shirt. Graebner rubs soap on his glasses and rinses them. He is thinking, among other things, "One lucky shot here or there makes all the difference in the world."

"The fourth set is for all the ice cream," Ashe is telling himself. His father is with him. Dr. Johnson comes into the room and reminds Arthur to concentrate, and to be sure, when he returns to the court, to win the first point.

To Ashe and to Graebner this tournament and this match are high and important moments—but passing moments, nonetheless—on the way to Australia. All year, they have played together to get the United States into position for the first time in four years to challenge the Australians, and the concentration of these efforts has resulted in part in a general elevation of each player's game. Ashe, Graebner, Pasarell, Lutz, Smith, Osborne—the United States Davis Cup Team has been a self-improving institution, and had Ashe and Graebner not been on the team it is possible that neither would have come this far at Forest Hills or reached the semifinals at Wimbledon, as both did. In three months' time, they will go to Australia. Ashe and Graebner will play the singles matches, and the team will come home with the Davis Cup. Meanwhile, under the grandstands at Forest Hills, their captain, Donald Dell, has the problem of telling each how to beat the other.

Dell, who is thirty, is an attorney in the District of Columbia. He has sandy hair and he looks like half the older brothers in the world. He was a friend of Senator Robert Kennedy, he worked for a time as a special assistant to Sargent Shriver in the Office of Economic Opportunity, and there is about him a veneer of nice politics, of wheeling and dealing at the compound level. Beneath this veneer is a man of luck, wit, decision, and outspoken fairness, and as man and politician Dell has made a team out of a half-dozen blatantly individual tennis players. The level of his own game could be described as first-rate once removed, so his words have where-withal. Pasarell is with him. They visit Graebner first. Graebner is putting on fresh clothes.

"Hey, Clark, how you feeling?"

"I just can't beat this guy. I can't beat him. He *always* beats me. I can't play the guy. It's not that I'm psyched out by him, but I'm playing great and he hits three all-time winners in a row. I can't beat him."

"Then take a shower and let's go back to the clubhouse and have a nice beer and default the fourth set. Then you can go home."

"I didn't mean that."

"Don't think like that. Go out there and work your tail off. Don't wake up tomorrow morning regretting that you didn't give a hundred per cent. Win the fourth set and Arthur's morale will go down. You'll have to work your *ass* off. He's playing well now. But you get one break in the fourth set and you're back in the match. Go out there and guts it out. Scramble. When he aces, don't worry. When he hits a wood volley, don't worry about it. Don't worry what people in Cleveland are thinking, watching the tube."

"I'm playing better than Wimbledon."

"Just play Arthur."

"I've been reading him unbelievably well. But when he starts closing his eyes, nobody knows where the ball will go."

Pasarell asks Graebner, "Is there anything I can get you? Anything you need?"

"I need your game for the next hour, Charlie."

Dell says, "Clark, I'm going to see Arthur now. Is there anything you want me to tell him?"

"Yeah. Tell him to turn pro."

Three minutes remain of the interval. Arthur has dried himself off with a towel and changed his shirt, but has made no further effort to cool himself after the infernal heat outside. He doesn't believe in mid-match showers. "They cool you too much, draw too much heat off and sap your energy, even if they *are* refreshing. Back on the court, you've got to use a lot of energy just to get your body working full blast again."

Dell and Pasarell come into the room.

"I'm not serving well," Ashe says.

"Spin it in. And move in faster to the net," Dell tells him.

"I'm not returning well."

"Bend over. Move your feet. Keep your ball on the racquet longer. You're wasting too many shots. You're flailing too many returns. Move your damn feet on the returns. You're gambling too much for winners when it isn't necessary. Play percentage tennis. Hit a three-quarter spin serve and get into the net. He'll chip. Get in there and cover the chip.

Arthur, this is the biggest tournament of your life. This is a big chance.
The finals are tomorrow. You've got a chance to win the whole thing.''
    Ashe looks up at Pasarell to see what he might have to say. Pasarell says,
"You were asleep in the first set. Wake up.''

By the umpire's chair, Graebner unfolds a fresh dental towel, puts it in his
pocket, rubs sawdust all over his racquet handle, returns to the court, and
slams back Ashe's first two serves of the fourth set. Love-thirty. It is an
inaccurately auspicious beginning, for Ashe now begins to hit shots as if
God Himself had given them a written guarantee. He plays full, free wind-
milling tennis. He hits untouchable forty-five-degree volleys. He hits over-
heads that skid through no man's land and ricochet off the stadium wall.
His backhands win everywhere—crosscourt, down the line—and one of
them, a return of a second serve, is almost an exact repetition of the
extraordinary shot that finished the third set. "When you're confident, you
can do anything," Ashe tells himself. Both he and Graebner are, for the
most part, hitting the ball even harder than they have been previously, and
the average number of shots per point, which rose slightly in the second
and third sets, is down again, to 2.5. Graebner is not in any sense out of the
match. His serve seems stronger. His volleys are decisive. Ashe sends a
big, flat serve down the middle, and Graebner, standing on the center mark,
hits the ball off his forehand so hard that Ashe cannot get near it—an all
but impossible shot from that position, requiring phenomenal power. Ashe
serves again to Graebner's forehand. Graebner drives another hard return,
and runs for the net. Ashe is now playing almost consistently on the level
he stepped up to in the last three shots of the third set. Moving fast, he
intercepts, and sends a light and graceful putaway past Graebner, down the
line.
    There are very few places in the world where Ashe feels at ease or at
home. One, of course, is Gum Spring, Virginia, where the milieu he moves
in is entirely black. His defenses are alert everywhere else he goes, with
only four exceptions—Australia, the islands of the South Pacific, Sweden,
and Spain. ''A Negro draws stares in Australia, but you can pretty much
tell they're not malicious. They only mean 'What the hell is *he* doing
here?' I don't look like an aborigine. When I first played in Spain, I could
tell by the way the Spanish tennis players acted that I had nothing to worry
about. The Spaniards would just as soon hustle my sister, if I had one.
They don't care. It's a great feeling to get away from all this crap in the
United States. Mentally and spiritually, it's like taking a vacation. It's like
going from New York to the black world of Richmond and Gum Spring.
Your guard goes down. Everywhere else I go, my sensors are out. Everywhere. It's a waste of energy, but maybe I can do two things at one time—
think about something else and have my sensors out, too.''
    In 1960, Arthur was sent to St. Louis for his senior year of high school,

and it is generally assumed that this arrangement was made (by Dr. Johnson) because Arthur was not allowed to compete with white tennis players in Richmond. This was true but not relevant. By that time, there was no tennis player of any color in or near Richmond who could play points with him. Tennis is a game of levels, and it is practically impossible for a player who is on one level to play successfully with a player on any other. Arthur needed high-level competition the year around, and St. Louis was full of McKinleys and Buchholzes and indoor courts. There were a few problems. One young St. Louis tennis player took Arthur to a private tennis club one day that spring, and as Arthur was beginning to hit, a voice called out to him, "Hey, you! Get off there. We don't allow colored in this club." Arthur left. He was graduated from Sumner High School with the highest grades in his class. On the summer tennis circuit, he went to every length to attract no attention, to cause no difficulty. Moving in and out of expensive white atmospheres, he used the manners that his father and Dr. Johnson had taught him, and he noticed that the manners of the white players, and much of their general behavior, tended to suggest a lower standard. "When an experience is new, you're not sure of yourself mentally, but basic politeness got me through." Meanwhile, he would look down at his plate and find two steaks there. He knew what was happening. A message had come from the kitchen, on the Afro-American telegraph.

While he was at U.C.L.A., the level of his game became so high that he was made an honorary member of the Beverly Hills Tennis Club, where he played with people like Hank Greenberg and Charlton Heston. Of Heston he says, "He's not that coördinated. He plays tennis like he drives a chariot." Of Greenberg he says, "He's a tennis buff. He covers the court well. He's a big guy. A big, big guy. Jesus!" On a street in the Bronx, Ashe once played tennis with John Lindsay ("Good forehand"), and in the Washington ghetto he played with Bobby Kennedy ("Another good forehand"). In tennis, the nearest black was light-years below him now, and he became, in his own words, "a sociological phenomenon." He has been kept extremely busy on the U-Rent-a-Negro circuit. He has been invited to the White House four times. Only two years ago, he was very hesitant about walking into the dining room of the West Side Tennis Club, in Forest Hills. Sometimes when his phone rings in his rooms at West Point, he picks it up and an anonymous voice says to him, for instance, "You have your nerve running your black ass around the country playing tennis while my son is fighting in Vietnam."

Ashe leads two games to one in the fourth set. He moves in on Graebner's second serve and tries one more backhand crosscourt megablast. Out. By inches. Fifteen-love.

Graebner's next serve is wide to Ashe's backhand. Ashe drives the ball down the line to Graebner's forehand, following to the net. Ashe admits to himself, "In effect, I'm saying to him, 'O.K., Clark, I can beat you on your forehand.' I'm being a little arrogant." Graebner catches the ball at the limit of his reach and sends back an unforceful volley. Ashe wipes the point away with his backhand. Fifteen-all.

Graebner's big serve goes down the middle. Ashe leaps for it and blocks it back. Graebner hits a low, underspun crosscourt backhand. Ashe runs to it and answers with a backhand even more acutely angled. Graebner has to dive for it, but he gets it, hitting a slow deep volley. Ashe, on the backhand again, drives the ball—much too fast to be contested—down the line. "Get in there!" he shouts, and the ball gets in there. Fifteen-thirty. Graebner thinks, "If I had his backhand and he had my forehand, we'd be invincible."

Ashe's forehand is something to see as it is. Graebner rocks, goes up, and—to Ashe's forehand—smashes the ball. Ashe slams it back through the service box and out the side of the court. "Most players hit a shot like that once in a lifetime," says Donald Dell. Fifteen-forty.

Ashe now has two chances to break Graebner. He looses a heavy backhand return, but Graebner stops it and hits it to the baseline. Ashe lobs. At the service line, Graebner moves in under the overhead and brings down the paper cutter. The shot goes within four feet of Ashe but is too powerful to be as much as touched. Thirty-forty.

Break point No. 2. Graebner rocks, and lifts the ball. Crunch. Unmanageable. Right down the middle. Deuce.

Graebner serves. Fault. Again. Double fault. Advantage Ashe.

Graebner faults once more, then hits a wide slice to Ashe's backhand. Ashe moves to it and explodes another all-time winner down the line. Game to Ashe. Games are three–one, fourth set. Graebner is broken.

Because Ashe is black, many people expect him to be something more than a tennis player—in fact, demand that he be a leader in a general way. The more he wins, the more people look to him for words and acts beyond the court. The black press has criticized him for not doing enough for the cause. He has repeatedly been asked to march and picket, and he has refused. Militant blacks have urged him to resign from the Davis Cup Team. Inevitably, they have called him an Uncle Tom. Once, in Milwaukee, he was asked to march with Stokely Carmichael but said no, and on the same day he visited a number of Milwaukee playgrounds, showing black children and white children how to play tennis. The demands of others have never moved him to do anything out of character. He will say what he thinks, though, if someone asks him. "Intrinsically, I disapprove of what black militants do. Human nature being what it is, I can understand why they have such a strong following. If you had nothing going for you and you were just a black kid in a ghetto, you'd have historical momentum behind you and it would be chic to be a black militant—easy to do, very fashionable. You'd have your picture and name in the paper because you'd be screaming your head off. They sound like fire-and-brimstone preachers in Holy Roller churches. But you must listen to them. You can't completely ignore them. Their appeal is to the here and now. If I were a penniless junkie, I'd go for it, too. I'd have nothing to lose, nowhere to go but up.

But you can't change people overnight. If you took a demographic survey of blacks, you'd find, I think, that the farther up the socio-economic scale you got, the fewer people would be behind Stokely. I'm not a marcher. I'm not a sign carrier. I'm a tennis player. If you are a leader in any field, and black, you are a hero to all blacks, and you are expected to be a leader in other fields. It's beautiful. People in Richmond look upon me as a leader whether I like it or not. That's the beautiful part of it. The other side of the coin is that they expect the same of some light-heavyweight boxer that they do of me. But he doesn't have my brain. *He* tries to get into politics, and we lose some leverage.

"Guerrilla warfare is going to start. Businesses will burn. There will be more riots. More nationally known political figures may be killed. But eventually more middle-class blacks will become involved in human rights. Extreme militants will lose their power and influence. So I am cautiously optimistic. I define the cause as the most good for the most people in the least amount of time, and that has absolutely nothing to do, specifically, with color. Anything I can do to help the cause is good. Nobody listens to a loser. If I put myself in a position where I can't compete, I am merely a martyr. We don't need any more martyrs right now. One must separate the emotional from the practical. Don't bite off more than you can chew. A little bit is better than nothing, no matter how you may feel. Progress and improvement do not come in big hunks, they come in little pieces, and the sooner people accept this the better off they'll be. I wouldn't tell my son to content himself that things will come gradually. You've got to push. You've got to act as though you expect it to come tomorrow. But when you know it's not going to come, don't give up. We're outnumbered ten to one. We'll advance by quiet negotiation and slow infiltration—and by objective, well-planned education, not an education in which you're brainwashed. Education reflects a culture's values. If that culture is warped, you get a warped education, with white Janes and Dicks in the schoolbooks and white pale-faced guys who made history. There are so many insidious ways you can get brainwashed to think white equals good—white Howdy-Doody, white Captain Kangaroo. I didn't feel like a crusader once. I do now. I've always been fair with all people. I always wanted to be a solid citizen. I went to college. I graduated. I have put in time in the armed services. I treat all people equally—rich, poor, black, white. I am fairly generous. Nobody can find fault with that. But in the spirit of the times—in some people's eyes—I'm an Uncle Tom. The phrase is empty."

"His racquet is his bag," Ronald Charity's wife, Ruth, says. "Arthur has to fight in his own way." Arthur's sensors are still extremely active. He boils within when he hears a white man call him "boy" or "son." He says, "Do I look like your son?" He also can't stand blacks who tell him not to trust whites, and he says he feels sorry for Negroes who become upset when they see a Negro woman with a white man. At U.C.L.A., he was fond of a white girl, and he saw her with some frequency until her mother saw *him* on TV. He laughs out loud when he tells the story. "It's funny now," he says. "It stung then." He uses "black" and "Negro" interchangeably. In hotels, somewhat inconsistently, he often asks, "Where's the boy for the bags?" He thinks there is a certain inherent motor superiority in black athletes. "At an early age, we seem to be a little looser, a little more athletic than white kids. You go through Harlem and you'll see kids less than five feet tall with pretty good jump shots and hook shots. White kids that age don't have those shots." He is suspicious of Greek standards in art. He wonders where all the other races were when Polyclitus was shaping his canon. He urges white American friends to refresh their perspectives by living in Asia, he pays his annual dues to the National Association for the Advancement of Colored People, and he is not at all troubled by men like Alabama's George Wallace. "Wallace is beautiful. He's doing his own thing. He's actually got a little bit of soul. What I worry about is people who say one thing and do another. Wallace is in his bag, and he enjoys it." Ashe's particular hero is Jackie Robinson— "because of what he went through, the self-control, the perseverance." Asked if he has any white heroes, he says, "Yes, I have. John F. Kennedy, Robert Kennedy, Benjamin Franklin, and Pancho Gonzales."

Tilting forward, looking up, Ashe whips his racquet over the ball and aces Graebner with a sharp-angled serve. "I stood as far over as I possibly could and still he aced me," Graebner mumbles. Ashe misses his next first serve, then follows an American twist recklessly to the net. Graebner chips. Ashe hits the world's most unorthodox volley, on the dead run, drawing his racquet back all the way and smashing the ball out of the air, out of sight, with a full round-house swing. "He just pulls his racquet back and slaps," Clark's father comments, but there is only mild disparagement in the remark, for he adds, "That's what Laver does." (Before the year is out, Laver and Ashe will be ranked first and second in the world.) Ashe hits another wide serve—unmanageable. Donald Dell says, "Arthur is knocking the hell out of the ball." Graebner thinks, "He's smashing every God-damned first serve, and they're all going in." Ashe leads four games to one, fourth set. His game is so big now that it is beyond containment. There is something about it that suggests a very large aircraft beginning its descent for Kennedy. In Graebner remain sporadic aces.

Twenty-six hours hence, beside the Marquee, Dell, Pasarell, and Graebner will meet spontaneously, from separate parts of the stadium, and go to press-section seats, close to one end of the court. Their teammate will be in the fifth set of the finals, against the Dutch player Tom Okker, and they will help draw him through it—"Move your feet, Arthur." . . . "Bend your knees." . . . "Spin it." . . . "Chip the returns, Arthur." . . . "Get your first serve in." Graebner, Pasarell, and Dell will shout these things in moments when the crowd is clapping, because coaching from the grandstand is not strictly approved. When Ashe breaks through Okker's serve, in the fifth game, he will look up at the Davis Cup group and close his fist, and when the match is over he will turn, point up to them with the handle of his racquet, and bow to them, giving them something of his moment as the winner of the first United States Open Championship. "Subdued disbelief," in his words, is what he will feel, but he will speak with nonchalant clarity into microphones and he will put an arm around his weeping father. When he returns to the United States Military Academy, he will have dinner with the cadet corps, and all the cadets will stand up and cheer for him for three and a half minutes while he pushes his glasses into place and affectionately looks them over.

Meanwhile, he aces Graebner for the last time. Graebner looks at the ball as it goes by, watches it hit the stadium wall, shakes his head, then looks again at the empty air beside him where the ball was and thinks, "I can't believe he can hit it that hard. I didn't even *see* the ball. Arthur is just playing too well. He's forcing me into errors." Games are five—two, fourth set.

Graebner serves to Ashe's forehand. Ashe drives the ball up the middle. Graebner hits hard for Ashe's backhand corner, and misses. Love-fifteen.

Ashe chips a return into the net. Fifteen-all.

Ashe blocks another return into Graebner's forehand service court, and Graebner, rushing in, tries a drop half volley, the extraordinarily difficult shot that has almost been Ashe's signature in this match—that Ashe has scored with time after time. Graebner fails to make it good. He whips himself. "An unbelievable shot for me to try—difficult in the first place, and under this pressure ridiculous. Stupid." Fifteen-thirty.

Graebner now sends his farewell ace past Ashe. Crunch. Right down the middle. Thirty-all.

Graebner rocks, swings, hits. Fault. He lifts the ball again. Double fault. Thirty-forty.

"Match point," Ashe tells himself. "Now I'll definitely play it safe." But Graebner hits the big serve into the net, then hits his second serve to Ashe's backhand. The ball and the match are spinning into perfect range. Ashe's racquet is back. The temptation is just too great, and caution fades. He hits for it all. Game, set, match to Lieutenant Ashe. When the stroke is finished, he is standing on his toes, his arms flung open, wide, and high.

THE FRONT RUNNER
By Patricia Nell Warren

It was just a few minutes before the 5,000 final began.

Those minutes, plus the thirteen-odd minutes that the race would last, and another day, and we could all go home.

The twelve runners were jogging up and down the track, keeping warm and loose until the moment the officials told them to go to the line. In the infield, the high-jump finals were going on. The marathon was out being run on its 26.2-mile course through Montreal, and would finish up here later. Right after the 5,000 the 1,500 final would be run—the race that Vince should have been in, and wasn't.

The murmur of the stadium spilled down onto the track. Nobody was watching the high jumpers. They were all watching the two slender runners jogging around, Billy and Armas Sepponan. I knew that the eye of the TV cameras would be fixed on them. Via satellite, their image would be flashed to millions of viewers in dozens of countries. It was safe to say that the entire civilized world was looking at Billy at that moment.

He was unaware, inward, alert, as he jogged along the straight, then wheeled gently and came back. His number 928 was pinned to his breast. Dellinger passed him jogging the other way, but they didn't look at each other.

Vince was by me, wearing his sleeveless jerkin. Next to him was Mike Stella, who had bombed out in the 5,000 heats.

Vince looked at me. "Harlan, right now he's not even thinking about you." He smiled a little.

"I hope not," I said.

The crowd's murmur grew. The officials were motioning the runners to the line. They stood there in a ragged little row, loose, doing their final psychs, hands on hips, looking around a little. Then their line straightened, crisp, military, each man bent and toeing the mark.

We scarcely heard the starter's pistol as the crowd yelled them off.

I sat there keeping track of Billy's laps. This time around, I was a bit more relaxed. Possibly, as I looked back on it, it was the months of fatigue setting in. Even if he loses, I was thinking, he'll still have the gold from the 10,000. Very likely he'll get a silver or a bronze here. It won't be a great tragedy, really. He will have made his point.

With his usual cheerful willingness to be the guinea pig, Billy had put his body up front. He was clipping along at a near-world record pace. He wasn't running away this time, just teasing them on at that punishing tempo. The field went with him, Sepponan running in next-to-last place. They were nicely bunched. Billy pulled them through the first 3,000 meters, averaging 62 seconds a lap.

At 3,000 Billy shook up the field by accelerating sharply. They started stringing out behind him. The next lap he gave them a 58.1. Doggedly, Bob Dellinger had moved into the No. 2 slot, and Sepponan was forced to start moving up.

"Here we go," said Vince. "The show's on."

In the next lap, Billy raised the ante to 57.3. With the runners well into the last half of the race, the crowd noise was swelling. So intense was their concentration that you didn't feel the usual "dead space" that the crowd sometimes feels in these long-distance races on the track.

The field, a little shaken by his display of confidence, was really stringing out now, and Sepponan moving up on the outside. Billy led by thirty yards. Dellinger struggled gamely to stay ahead of Armas, then let go, and Armas was in the clear.

The crowd had surged to its feet and the yell had risen to its Olympic shriek—that massed yell of humanity that you hear only at the Games, high-pitched, deafening as the keening of a hurricane wind.

They went into the next-to-last lap. Now it was Billy and Armas's race, with the rest trailing and shattered. Armas was kicking, rapidly closing the gap between himself and Billy. Vince had his hand clenched on my arm so tightly that it might have hurt had I been more aware.

Through my glasses, I watched that distant pale figure, stretched out in full flight, with his long hanging slow stride. His sweaty face was as calm as if he were swinging along a trail in the woods. Mike was yelling hoarsely and jumping half out of his seat. Betsy was shrieking on the other side of me.

They came streaking down the straight and into the final lap. The bell clanged. Their long legs were devouring the track. Armas was now fifteen yards behind Billy. Billy had forced him to start his kick early, but still . . . I started wondering. It was possible that we had gambled wrong, and that Billy should have tried a runaway after all. He possibly was going to kill himself with this last blazing lap, and fade near the finish, letting Armas gun him down.

Billy turned his head quickly and saw Armas hauling him down. Incredibly he accelerated again. Everyone around us seemed to be going berserk. Vince and Mike weren't yelling any more, just sitting and staring.

"This last lap," said Vince, "is going to be murder. They're *sprinting*."

"Yeah," I said numbly, "it looks like it's going to be under 50 seconds. The last mile is going to be under 4."

I thought distractedly of the rare occasions when a last lap like this was run. Juha Vaatainen in the Helsinki Games 10,000 meter in 1971. Marty Liquori and Jim Ryun in the Martin Luther King Games.

The two of them swept into the first turn of the last lap. In the infield, the high jumpers had knocked off because they couldn't concentrate. For a few moments, all I could see through my glasses were the two men's sweat-soaked backs. Armas' hair flopped wetly, and ahead, Billy's curls lifted moistly.

Then, as they rounded the turn, their profiles came into view. They were both hurting now, and both blocking that hurt. Armas' face was twisted into a grimace. Billy's face was still smooth, but the pain was in his eyes, in his open mouth with the teeth showing slightly, in the slight rhythmic jerk of his head.

They stormed into the backstraight, Armas now five yards behind.

I felt that deep prickling rise of my hackles, as always on the few occasions when Billy really awed me. Actually, they both awed me. We were watching some elemental force of nature, a storm at sea, a volcano erupting, an earthquake.

So much history, so many lives, went into each of their strides. From centuries of genes and family affairs to the last red corpuscle crammed in at high altitude. In Billy's case, I knew the factors more intimately: the clash about his training, the hills on the Prescott trails, the kiss in the movie theater, my efforts to shield his peace of mind, right down to the tender loving and the massage last night. Even the people who'd hassled him had helped forge his stubbornness. It was all being put together now.

As his great strides gulped up the backstraight, I could see him again on the Prescott track that first morning, reeling out those beautiful 60-second quarters. I could hear him saying, "I'm thinking of the Olympics," and myself saying, "That's a big order."

As they went into the last turn, I stood dead silent, with chills running up and down me. They were both splendid as the sun, terrible as an army with banners. There was no doubt in the mind of anybody in that stadium that this was going to be one of the great runs, and a record at the end of it that would stand for a long time.

As they had peeled out of the last turn, Armas had pulled up to Billy's shoulder. They both looked sick now, both deeply in oxygen debt, both dizzy and calling on the last bit of glycogen. They were both running like animals.

Armas hung at Billy's shoulder for about ten strides. And then, almost in mid-stride, he cracked. Billy had broken him. With whatever his final fatal edge was, gay desperation or maybe just Vitamin E pills, he had broken the iron Finn.

Still in control, though dying himself, Billy pulled away. He was a yard ahead, then two yards, as Armas came apart at the seams.

I felt my muscles go limp with relief. Vince grabbed my arm and shook me with silent joyous delirium.

The two were halfway down the straight to the finish line, with those two yards between them and Armas staggering, when it happened.

Later on, in the videotape, I would see it in slow motion. Billy seemed to falter a little, and his head snapped a little to the left. Then his legs gave way under him, just as if somebody had flicked the switch powering his legs to ''off.'' Still burning forward, yet falling at the same time, he slumped slowly, fully to the track.

As he hit the red tartan, the jolt snapped through his body. He slid a little on his left side, his right leg sliding forward as if to take one last stride. His head struck heavily against the low board rim on the inside of the track.

Actually, it happened so fast that the crowd didn't burst its lungs with a huge scream until it was over.

On the videotape, you could see Armas, dazed, glancing down at Billy as he passed him. ''I thought it was luck,'' Armas would say later. Then he gathered himself and ran heavily on, easing the pace sharply because he didn't have to worry about anybody catching him. When he hit the tape, he was staggering.

Back up the straight, Billy lay sprawled by the board, in lane 1. He didn't move. The other runners were skirting him, looking at him, running on.

I was horrified, not even thinking of the lost medal. What could have happened? All kinds of crazy possibilities ran through my mind. At the least, a terrible muscle pull. A concussion as his head hit the board. A massive leg cramp. A heart attack.

Beyond the finish line, Armas was on his hands and knees, looking more like a spent decathlete. Officials were running toward Billy. I also saw the U.S. team doctor and distance coach Taplinger running toward him. The stadium was a sea of babbling and comment. Many people were applauding Armas' victory, but just as many were standing, their eyes fixed on Billy.

He did not move.

I was already scrambling down to the track, pushing and shoving blindly. Vince and Mike were behind me.

We were on the track. Several officials tried to stop us. I shouldered one out of the way. Vince punched one. Three of them caught Mike and held him.

Vince and I ran up the track.

A number of people were already bending around Billy. Tay Parker was kneeling by his head, and motioning them back. ''Give him air,'' he said. ''Get away.''

Billy lay on his left side, with his left arm flung forward on the track, the gold ring glinting on it. His face was turned down and his hair fell forward, hiding it. He had fallen with such force that his glasses had been jolted off. They lay just ahead of him, shattered. The only motion in him was the sweat trickling earthward on his limbs. It seemed incredible that this body, which seconds ago had been moving as fast as a distance-running man is capable, could be so still.

"He may have hit his head on the board there," Tay Parker was saying.

Then we saw a little pool of blood spreading from under his hair. It was the darkish blood of a runner deep in oxygen debt. I told myself that I didn't see it.

"Christ," said Parker. "He couldn't have hit himself *that* hard."

The officials, bug-eyed, were crowding around. Parker motioned them away again. Vince was kneeling by Billy's feet.

Gently Parker turned Billy over. Then we saw what his hair had hid. The whole left temple and part of his forehead was gone. In their place was a pink and white bleeding crater. Bits of bone, blood and brain had exploded down his face and into his hair. Pieces of bone, with hair attached, came away in Parker's hands.

I told myself that I did not see this.

Parker was shaking his head, dazed. He was feeling in Billy's hair on the other side of his head.

"I can't believe this," he said. "It's a bullet wound."

"A bullet wound?" I repeated stupidly.

"I was a medic in Nam, I've seen plenty of them," said Parker. "Look, here's where it went in." He showed us the small, dark red hole, parting Billy's hair so that the sunlight hit it.

I was kneeling there clutching Billy's warm, limp hand as he lay there with his head on Parker's knees. It was beginning to occur to me that that hand would never squeeze mine again.

I looked dumbly up at all their faces. They were all silent, stunned, not reacting yet. Gus Lindquist had just come up and shouldered through the group, and was getting his first look at Billy's bloody head. Our eyes met. At that minute, I think, Lindquist began to understand the tragedy that he had participated in.

It was Vince who cried the unutterable cry for me. He bent down over Billy's feet, his head almost touching them, and he gave a sound like an animal being crushed to death in a press. He stayed there like that, holding Billy's spiked feet, and sobbing in that suffocated way, as if there were no air in his lungs.

Slowly I let Billy's hand go. I picked up his broken glasses and my fingers closed around them so hard that the glass cracked. On the track where he had lain, there was a wet imprint of sweat from his limbs. It was already drying. I looked at his eyes. They were half-open, gazing softly, so clear, so empty now. The left eye had a film of blood over it.

Some of the runners had come jogging back up the track to see what the trouble was. Armas, somewhat recovered now, was with them. He bent beside me, looked at Billy, muttered something in Finnish, and put one hand over his eyes. His shoulders started to shake. Someone pulled him to his feet and led him away.

Someone put his arms across my shoulders. I looked blankly up, into Mike Stella's face. He was dead white, and the tears had run clear down to his jaws. Tay Parker was kneeling there with Billy's head on his knees, crying. More and more people were coming across the infield. A photographer shouldered his way through the group and flashed a picture. Then another one.

It began to occur to me that it was strange—all these tears, but none in my own eyes. I was clenching the broken glasses so hard that my hand was cut.

Suddenly the voice of the announcer cut through everything.

"Ladies and gentlemen, Billy Sive is badly hurt . . . the information reaching us from the track is garbled . . . a correction, we regret to announce . . ." The announcer's voice was breaking. "We regret . . . Billy Sive is dead . . ."

A wave of gasps and screams went through that huge place. Even in my benumbed state I felt it.

". . . Dead . . . apparently shot from the stands . . ."

Screams of panic at the thought of a gunman loose in the crowd.

". . . Ladies and gentlemen, please, no panic . . . the police have arrested the gunman as . . . trying to leave the stadium . . ."

The voice was cutting through my head.

"Billy Sive is dead . . ." The announcer himself breaking up, trying to control his voice.

The high jumpers and officials beginning to run across the infield, abandoning their event.

Somebody was prying my hand open, taking away from me the broken glasses, mopping my hand with a handkerchief. I was helping Tay to carry Billy. He was so warm and limp, and his shattered head rolled against my breast. They had killed him, right there on the track where we'd thought he was safest.

". . . Dead . . . shocking . . . tragic . . . keep calm . . . the athletes are . . ."

In the first-aid room, Tay was picking the glass out of my hand and taking a few stitches. Billy was on a stretcher, covered with a sheet. Someone was jabbing a sedative shot into Vince's shoulder to quiet him down.

My eyes were dry. They were almost unblinking.

The times were still up there on the huge scoreboard.

ARMAS SEPPONAN FINLAND 13:04.5
FRANCOIS GEFFROY FRANCE 13:10.1
JOHN FELTS AUSTRALIA 13:10.9
VITALIY KOSTENKO USSR 13:11.4
BOB DELLINGER USA 13:11.6

It was not until later that I was able to reflect on the irony. Only death could force my front-runner to give away a world record, like the one he gave to Armas.

It was not until later that I was able to reflect on it as history. At Munich and Mexico City they had slaughtered the innocents out of sight, behind the scenes. Here they had slaughtered the innocent in full sight of the crowd, at the peak of his life.

THE LONELINESS OF THE LONG-DISTANCE RUNNER

By Alan Sillitoe

The pop-eyed potbellied governor said to a pop-eyed potbellied Member of Parliament who sat next to his pop-eyed potbellied whore of a wife that I was his only hope for getting the Borstal Blue Ribbon Prize Cup For Long Distance Cross Country Running (All England), which I was, and it set me laughing to myself inside, and I didn't say a word to any potbellied pop-eyed bastard that might give them real hope, though I knew the governor anyway took my quietness to mean he'd got that cup already stuck on the bookshelf in his office among the few other mildewed trophies.

"He might take up running in a sort of professional way when he gets out," and it wasn't until he'd said this and I'd heard it with my own flaptabs that I realized it might be possible to do such a thing, run for money, trot for wages on piece work at a bob a puff rising bit by bit to a guinea a gasp and retiring through old age at thirty-two because of lace-curtain lungs, a football heart, and legs like varicose beanstalks. But I'd have a wife and car and get my grinning long-distance clock in the papers and have a smashing secretary to answer piles of letters sent by tarts who'd mob me when they saw who I was as I pushed my way into Woolworth's for a packet of razor blades and a cup of tea. It was something to think about all right, and sure enough the governor knew he'd got me when he said, turning to me as if I would at any rate have to be consulted about it all: "How does this matter strike you, then, Smith, my lad?"

A line of potbellied pop-eyes gleamed at me and a row of goldfish mouths opened and wiggled gold teeth at me, so I gave them the answer they wanted because I'd hold my trump card until later. "It'd suit me fine, sir," I said.

"Good lad. Good show. Right spirit. Splendid."

"Well," the governor said, "get that cup for us today and I'll do all I can for you. I'll get you trained so that you whack every man in the Free World." And I had a picture in my brain of me running and beating everybody in the world, leaving them all behind until only I was trot-trotting across a big wide moor alone, doing a marvellous speed as I ripped

between boulders and reed-clumps, when suddenly: CRACK! CRACK!—
bullets that can go faster than any man running, coming from a copper's
rifle planted in a tree, winged me and split my gizzard in spite of my
perfect running, and down I fell.

The potbellies expected me to say something else. "Thank you, sir," I
said.

Told to go, I trotted down the pavilion steps, out on to the field because
the big cross-country was about to begin and the two entries from
Gunthorpe had fixed themselves early at the starting line and were ready to
move off like white kangaroos. The sports ground looked a treat: with big
tea-tents all round and flags flying and seats for families—empty because
no mam or dad had known what opening day meant—and boys still running heats for the hundred yards, and lords and ladies walking from stall to
stall, and the Borstal Boys Brass Band in blue uniforms; and up on the
stands the brown jackets of Hucknall as well as our own grey blazers, and
then the Gunthorpe lot with shirt sleeves rolled. The blue sky was full of
sunshine and it couldn't have been a better day, and all of the big show was
like something out of Invahoe that we'd seen on the pictures a few days
before.

"Come on, Smith," Roach the sports master called to me, "we don't
want you to be late for the big race, eh? Although I dare say you'd catch
them up if you were." The othrs cat-called and grunted at this, but I took
no notice and placed myself between Gunthorpe and one of the Aylesham
trusties, dropped on my knees and plucked a few grass blades to suck on
the way round. So the big racc it was, for them, watching from the grandstand under a fluttering Union Jack, a race for the governor, that he had
been waiting for, and I hoped he and all the rest of his pop-eyed gang were
busy placing big bets on me, hundred to one to win, all the money they had
in their pockets, all the wages they were going to get for the next five years,
and the more they placed the happier I'd be. Because here was a dead cert
going to die on the big name they'd built for him, going to go down dying
with laughter whether it choked him or not. My knees felt the cool soil
pressing into them, and out of my eye's corner I saw Roach lift his hand.
The Gunthorpe boy twitched before the signal was given; somebody
cheered too soon; Medway bent forward; then the gun went, and I was
away.

We went once around the field and then along a half-mile drive of elms,
being cheered all the way, and I seemed to feel I was in the lead as we went
out by the gate and into the lane, though I wasn't interested enough to find
out. The five-mile course was marked by splashes of whitewash gleaming
on gateposts and trunks and stiles and stones, and a boy with a waterbottle
and bandage-box stood every half-mile waiting for those that dropped out
or fainted. Over the first stile, without trying, I was still nearly in the lead
but one; and if any of you want tips about running, never be in a hurry, and
never let any of the other runners know you are in a hurry even if you are.
You can always overtake on long-distance running without letting the oth-

ers smell the hurry in you; and when you've used your craft like this to
reach the two or three up front then you can do a big dash later that puts
everybody else's hurry in the shade because you've not had to make haste
up till then. I ran to a steady jog-trot rhythm, and soon it was so smooth
that I forgot I was running, and I was hardly able to know that my legs were
lifting and falling and my arms going in and out, and my lungs didn't seem
to be working at all, and my heart stopped that wicked thumping I always
get at the beginning of a run. Because you see I never race at all; I just run,
and somehow I know that if I forget I'm racing and only jog-trot along
until I don't know I'm running I always win the race. For when my eyes
recognize that I'm getting near the end of the course—by seeing a stile or
cottage corner—I put on a spurt, and such a fast big spurt it is because I
feel that up till then I haven't been running and that I've used up no energy
at all. And I've been able to do this because I've been thinking; and I
wonder if I'm the only one in the running business with this system of
forgetting that I'm running because I'm too busy thinking; and I wonder if
any of the other lads are on to the same lark, though I know for a fact that
they aren't. Off like the wind along the cobbled footpath and rutted lane,
smoother than the flat grass track on the field and better for thinking
because it's not too smooth, and I was in my element that afternoon
knowing that nobody could beat me at running but intending to beat myself
before the day was over. For when the governor talked to me of being
honest when I first came in he didn't know what the word meant or he
wouldn't have had me here in this race, trotting along in shimmy and
shorts and sunshine. He'd have had me where I'd have had him if I'd been
in his place: in a quarry breaking rocks until he broke his back. At least old
Hitler-face the plain-clothes dick was honester than the governor, because
he at any rate had had it in for me and I for him, and when my case was
coming up in court a copper knocked at our front door at four o'clock in
the morning and got my mother out of bed when she was paralytic tired,
reminding her she had to be in court at dead on half past nine. It was the
finest bit of spite I've ever heard of, but I would call it honest, the same as
my mam's words were honest when she really told that copper what she
thought of him and called him all the dirty names she'd ever heard of,
which took her half an hour and woke the terrace up.

I trotted on along the edge of a field bordered by the sunken lane,
smelling green grass and honeysuckle, and I felt as though I came from a
long line of whippets trained to run on two legs, only I couldn't see a toy
rabbit in front and there wasn't a collier's cosh behind to make me keep up
the pace. I passed the Gunthorpe runner whose shimmy was already black
with sweat and I could just see the corner of the fenced-up copse in front
where the only man I had to pass to win the race was going all out to gain
the half-way mark. Then he turned into a tongue of trees and bushes where
I couldn't see him anymore, and I couldn't see anybody, and I knew what
the loneliness of the long-distance runner running across country felt like,
realizing that as far as I was concerned this feeling was the only honesty

and realness there was in the world and I knowing it would be no different ever, no matter what I felt at odd times, and no matter what anybody else tried to tell me. The runner behind me must have been a long way off because it was so quiet, and there was even less noise and movement than there had been at five o'clock of a frosty winter morning. It was hard to understand, and all I knew was that you had to run, run, run, without knowing why you were running, but on you went through fields you didn't understand and into woods that made you afraid, over hills without knowing you'd been up and down, and shooting across streams that would have cut the heart out of you had you fallen into them. And the winning post was no end to it, even though crowds might be cheering you in, because on you had to go before you got your breath back, and the only time you stopped really was when you tripped over a tree trunk and broke your neck or fell into a disused well and stayed dead in the darkness forever. So I thought: they aren't going to get me on this racing lark, this running and trying to win, this jog-trotting for a bit of blue ribbon, because it's not the way to go on at all, though they swear blind that it is. You should think about nobody and go your own way, not on a course marked out for you by people holding mugs of water and bottles of iodine in case you fall and cut yourself so that they can pick you up—even if you want to stay where you are—and get you moving again.

On I went, out of the wood, passing the man leading without knowing I was going to do so. Flip-flap, flip-flap, jog-trot, jog-trot, crunchslap-crunchslap, across the middle of a broad field again, rhythmically running in my greyhound effortless fashion, knowing I had won the race though it wasn't half over, won it if I wanted it, could go on for ten or fifteen or twenty miles if I had to and drop dead at the finish of it, which would be the same, in the end, as living an honest life like the governor wanted me to. It amounted to: win the race and be honest, and on trot-trotting I went, having the time of my life, loving my progress because it did me good and set me thinking which by now I liked to do, but not caring at all when I remembered that I had to win this race as well as run it. One of the two, I had to win the race or run it, and I knew I could do both because my legs had carried me well in front —now coming to the short cut down the bramble bank and over the sunken road—and would carry me further because they seemed made of electric cable and easily alive to keep on slapping at those ruts and roots, but I'm not going to win because the only way I'd see I came in first would be if winning meant that I was going to escape the coppers after doing the biggest bank job of my life, but winning means the exact opposite, no matter how they try to kill or kid me, means running right into their white-gloved wall-barred hands and grinning mugs and staying there for the rest of my natural long life of stone-breaking anyway, but stone-breaking in the way I want to do it and not in the way they tell me.

Another honest thought that comes is that I could swing left at the next hedge of the field, and under its cover beat my slow retreat away from the sports ground winning post. I could do three or six or a dozen miles across the turf like this and cut a few main roads behind me so's they'd never know which one I'd taken; and maybe on the last one when it got dark I could thumb a lorry-lift and get a free ride north with somebody who might not give me away. But no, I said I wasn't daft didn't I? I won't pull out with only six months left, and besides there's nothing I want to dodge and run away from; I only want a bit of my own back on the In-laws and Potbellies by letting them sit up there on their big posh seats and watch me lose this race, though as sure as God made me I know that when I do lose I'll get the dirtiest crap and kitchen jobs in the months to go before my time is up. I won't be worth a threpp'ny-bit to anybody here, which will be all the thanks I get for being honest in the only way I know. For when the governor told me to be honest it was meant to be in his way not mine, and if I kept on being honest in the way he wanted and won my race for him he'd see I got the cushiest six months still left to run; but in my own way, well, it's not allowed, and if I find a way of doing it such as I've got now then I'll get what-for in every mean trick he can set his mind to. And if you look at it in my way, who can blame him? For this is war—and ain't I said so?—and when I hit him in the only place he knows he'll be sure to get his own back on me for not collaring that cup when his heart's been set for ages on seeing himself standing up at the end of the afternoon to clap me on the back as I take the cup from Lord Earwig or some such chinless wonder with a name like that. And so I'll hit him where it hurts a lot, and he'll do all he can to get his own back, tit for tat, though I'll enjoy it most because I'm hitting first, and because I planned it longer. I don't know why I think these thoughts are better than any I've ever had, but I do, and I don't care why. I suppose it took me a long time to get going on all this because I've had no time and peace in all my bandit life, and now my thoughts are coming pat and the only trouble is I often can't stop, even when my brain feels as if it's got cramp, frostbite and creeping paralysis all rolled into one and I have to give it a rest by slap-dashing down through the brambles of the sunken lane. And all this is another upper-cut I'm getting in first at people like the governor, to show how—if I can—his races are never won even though some bloke always comes unknowingly in first, how in the end the governor is going to be doomed while blokes like me will take the pickings of his roasted bones and dance like maniacs around his Borstal's ruins. And so this story's like the race and once again I won't bring off a winner to suit the governor; no, I'm being honest like he told me to, without him knowing what he means, though I don't suppose he'll ever come in with a story of his own, even if he reads this one of mine and knows who I'm talking about.

I've just come up out of the sunken lane, kneed and elbowed, thumped and bramble-scratched, and the race is two-thirds over, and a voice is going like a wireless in my mind saying that when you've had enough of feeling good like the first man on earth of a frosty morning, and you've known how it is to be taken bad like the last man on earth on a summer's afternoon, then you get at last to being like the only man on earth and don't give a bogger about either good or bad, but just trot on with your slippers slapping the good dry soil that at least would never do you a bad turn. Now the words are like coming from a crystal-set that's broken down, and something's happening inside the shell-case of my guts that bothers me and I don't know why or what to blame it on, a grinding near my ticker as though a bag of rusty screws is loose inside me and I shake them up every time I trot forward. Now and again I break my rhythm to feel my left shoulder blade by swinging a right hand across my chest as if to rub the knife away that has somehow got stuck there. But I know it's nothing to bother about, that more likely it's caused by too much thinking that now and again I take for worry. For sometimes I'm the greatest worrier in the world I think (as you twigged I'll bet from me having got this story out) which is funny anyway because my mam don't know the meaning of the word so I don't take after her; though dad had a hard time of worry all his life up to when he filled his bedroom with hot blood and kicked the bucket that morning when nobody was in the house. I'll never forget it, straight I won't, because I was the one that found him and I often wished I hadn't. Back from a session on the fruit-machines at the fish-and-chip shop, jingling my three-lemon loot to a nail-dead house, as soon as I got in I knew something was wrong, stood leaning my head against the cold mirror above the mantelpiece trying not to open my eyes and see my stone-cold clock—because I knew I'd gone as white as a piece of chalk since coming in as if I'd been got at by a Dracula-vampire and even my penny-pocket winnings kept quiet on purpose.

Gunthorpe nearly caught me up. Birds were singing from the briar hedge, and a couple of thrushies flew like lightning into some thorny bushes. Corn had grown high in the next field and would be cut down soon with scythes and mowers; but I never wanted to notice much while running in case it put me off my stroke, so by the haystack I decided to leave it all behind and put on such a spurt, in spite of nails in my guts, that before long I'd left both Gunthorpe and the birds a good way off; I wasn't far now from going into that last mile and a half like a knife through margarine, but the quietness I suddenly trotted into between two pickets was like opening my eyes underwater and looking at the pebbles on a stream bottom, reminding me again of going back that morning to the house in which my old man had croaked, which is funny because I hadn't thought about it at all since it happened and even then I didn't brood much on it. I wonder why? I suppose that since I started to think on these long-distance runs I'm liable to have anything crop up and pester at my tripes and innards, and now that I see my bloody dad behind each grass-blade in my barmy runner-brain I'm not so sure I like to think and that it's such a good thing after all. I choke my phlegm and keep on running anyway and curse the Borstal-builders and their athletics—flappity-flap, slop-slop, crunch-slap-crunch-slap-crunchslap—who've maybe got their own back on me from the bright beginning by sliding magic-lantern slides into my head that never stood a chance before. Only if I take whatever comes like this in my runner's stride can I keep on keeping on like my old self and beat them back; and now I've thought on this far I know I'll win, in the crunchslap end. So anyway after a bit I went upstairs one step at a time not thinking anything about how I should find dad and what I'd do when I did. But now I'm making up for it by going over the rotten life mam led him ever since I can remember, knocking-on with different men even when he was alive and fit and she not caring whether he knew it or not, and most of the time he wasn't so blind as she thought and cursed and roared and threatened to punch her tab, and I had to stand up to stop him even though I knew she deserved it. What a life for all of us. Well, I'm not grumbling, because if I did I might just as well win this bleeding race, which I'm not going to do, though if I don't lose speed I'll win it before I know where I am, and then where would I be?

Now I can hear the sportsground noise and music as I head back for the flags and the lead-in drive, the fresh new feel of underfoot gravel going against the iron muscles of my legs. I'm nowhere near puffed despite that bag of nails that rattles as much as ever, and I can still give a big last leap like gale-force wind if I want to, but everything is under control and I know now that there ain't another long-distance cross-country running runner in England to touch my speed and style. Our doddering bastard of a governor, our half-dead gangrened gaffer is hollow like an empty petrol drum, and he wants me and my running life to give him glory, to put in him blood and throbbing veins he never had, wants his potbellied pals to be his witnesses as I gasp and stagger up to his winning post so's he can say: "My Borstal gets that cup, you see. I win my bet, because it pays to be honest and try to gain the prizes I offer to my lads, and they know it, have known it all along. They'll always be honest now, because I made them so." And his pals will think: "He trains his lads to live right, after all; he deserves a medal but we'll get him made a Sir"—and at this very moment as the birds come back to whistling I can tell myself I'll never care a sod what any of the chinless spineless In-laws think or say. They've seen me and they're cheering now and loudspeakers set around the field like elephant's ears are spreading out the big news that I'm well in the lead, and can't do anything else but stay there. But I'm still thinking of the Out-law death my dad died, telling the doctors to scat from the house when they wanted him to finish up in hospital (like a bleeding guinea-pig, he raved at them). He got up in bed to throw them out and even followed them down the stairs in his shirt though he was no more than skin and stick. They tried to tell him he'd want some drugs but he didn't fall for it, and only took the pain-killer that mam and I got from a herb-seller in the next street. It's not till now that I know what guts he had, and when I went into the room that morning he was lying on his stomach with the clothes thrown back, looking like a skinned rabbit, his grey head resting just on the edge of the bed, and on the floor must have been all the blood he'd had in his body, right from his toe-nails up, for nearly all of the lino and carpet was covered in it, thin and pink.

And down the drive I went, carrying a heart blocked up like Boulder Dam across my arteries, the nail-bag clamped down tighter and tighter as though in a woodwork vice, yet with my feet like birdwings and arms like talons ready to fly across the field except that I didn't want to give anybody that much of a show, or win the race by accident. I smell the hot dry day now as I run towards the end, passing a mountain-heap of grass emptied from cans hooked on to the fronts of lawn-mowers pushed by my pals; I rip a piece of tree-bark with my fingers and stuff it in my mouth, chewing wood and dust and maybe maggots as I run until I'm nearly sick, yet swallowing what I can of it just the same because a little birdie whistled to me that I've got to go on living for at least a bloody sight longer yet but that for six months I'm not going to smell that grass or taste that dusty bark or trot this lovely path. I hate to have to say this but something bloody-well made me cry, and crying is a thing I haven't bloody-well done since I was a kid of two or three. Because I'm slowing down now for Gunthorpe to catch me up, and I'm doing it in a place just where the drive turns in to the sportsfield— where they can see what I'm doing, especially the governor and his gang from the grandstand, and I'm going so slow I'm almost marking time. Those on the nearest seats haven't caught on yet to what's happening and are still cheering like mad ready for when I make that mark, and I keep on wondering when the bleeding hell Gunthorpe behind me is going to nip by on to the field because I can't hold this up all day, and I think Oh Christ it's just my rotten luck that Gunthorpe's dropped out and that I'll be here for half an hour before the next bloke comes up, but even so, I say, I won't budge, I won't go for that last hundred yards if I have to sit down cross-legged on the grass and have the governor and his chinless wonders pick me up and carry me there, which is against their rules so you can bet they'd never do it because they're not clever enough to break the rules—like I would be in their place—even though they are their own. No, I'll show him what honesty means if it's the last thing I do, though I'm sure he'll never understand because if he and all them like him did it'd mean they'd be on my side which is impossible. By God I'll stick this out like my dad stuck out his pain and kicked them doctors down the stairs: if he had guts for that then I've got guts for this and here I stay waiting for Gunthorpe or Aylesham to bash that turf and go right slap-up against that bit of clothes-line stretched across the winning post. As for me, the only time I'll hit that clothes-line will be when I'm dead and a comfortable coffin's been got ready on the other side. Until then I'm a long-distance runner, crossing country all on my own no matter how bad it feels.

The Essex boys were shouting themselves blue in the face telling me to get a move on, waving their arms, standing up and making as if to run at that rope themselves because they were only a few yards to the side of it. You cranky lot, I thought, stuck at that winning post, and yet I knew they didn't mean what they were shouting, were really on my side and always would be, not able to keep their maulers to themselves, in and out of cop-shops and clink. And there they were now having the time of their lives letting themselves go in cheering me which made the governor think they were heart and soul on his side when he wouldn't have thought any such thing if he'd had a grain of sense. And I could hear the lords and ladies now from the grandstand, and could see them standing up to wave me in: "Run!" they were shouting in their posh voices. "Run!" But I was deaf, daft and blind, and stood where I was, still tasting the bark in my mouth and still blubbing like a baby, blubbing now out of gladness that I'd got them beat at last.

Because I heard a roar and saw the Gunthorpe gang throwing their coats up in the air and I felt the pat-pat of feet on the drive behind me getting closer and closer and suddenly a smell of sweat and a pair of lungs on their last gasp passed me by and went swinging on towards that rope, all shagged out and rocking from side to side, grunting like a Zulu that didn't know any better, like the ghost of me at ninety when I'm heading for that fat upholstered coffin. I could have cheered him myself: "Go on, go on, get cracking. Knot yourself up on that piece of tape." But he was already there, and so I went on, trot-trotting after him until I got to the rope, and collapsed, with a murderous sounding roar going up through my ears while I was still on the wrong side of it.

It's about time to stop; though don't think I'm not still running, because I am, one way or another. The governor at Borstal proved me right; he didn't respect my honesty at all; not that I expected him to, or tried to explain it to him, but if he's supposed to be educated then he should have more or less twigged it. He got his own back right enough, or thought he did, because he had me carting dustbins about every morning from the big full-working kitchen to the garden-bottoms where I had to empty them; and in the afternoon I spread out slops over spuds and carrots growing in the allotments. In the evenings I scrubbed floors, miles and miles of them. But it wasn't a bad life for six months, which was another thing he could never understand and would have made it grimmer if he could, and it was worth it when I look back on it, considering all the thinking I did, and the fact that the boys caught on to me losing the race on purpose and never had enough good words to say about me, or curses to throw out (to themselves) at the governor.

The work didn't break me; if anything it made me stronger in many ways, and the governor knew, when I left, that his spite had got him nowhere. For since leaving Borstal they tried to get me in the army, but I didn't pass the medical and I'll tell you why. No sooner was I out, after that final run and six-months hard, that I went down with pleurisy, which means as far as I'm concerned that I lost the governor's race all right, and won my own twice over, because I know for certain that if I hadn't raced my race I wouldn't have got this pleurisy, which keeps me out of khaki but doesn't stop me doing the sort of work my itchy fingers want to do.

I'm out now and the heat's switched on again, but the rats haven't got me for the last big thing I pulled. I counted six hundred and twenty-eight pounds and am still living off it because I did the job all on my own, and after it I had the peace to write all this, and it'll be money enough to keep me going until I finish my plans for doing an even bigger snatch, something up my sleeve I wouldn't tell to a living soul. I worked out my systems and hiding-places while pushing scrubbing-brushes around them Borstal floors, planned my outward life of innocence and honest work, yet at the same time grew perfect in the razor-edges of my craft for what I knew I had to do once free; and what I'll do again if netted by the poaching coppers.

In the meantime (as they say in one or two books I've read since, useless though because all of them ended on a winning post and didn't teach me a thing) I'm going to give this story to a pal of mine and tell him that if I do get captured again by the coppers he can try and get it put into a book or something, because I'd like to see the governor's face when he reads it, if he does, which I don't suppose he will; even if he did read it though I don't think he'd know what it was all about. And if I don't get caught the bloke I give this story to will never give me away; he's lived in our terrace for as long as I can remember, and he's my pal. That I do know.

BEYOND THE DIVIDE

By Colin Fletcher

The little Forest Service ranger station nestled among trees, a hundred yards from the end of the road. Late afternoon shadows had reached out around it, softening the heat. I parked outside and went in.

The ranger was young, redheaded, new to the job, still eager. "Wish I was coming with you," he said as he filled out my fire permit. "Haven't had a chance to get over into the main valley yet, but they say it's a beautiful place."

"So I hear."

"Be doing some fishing?"

"Maybe. I'll take a rod along, anyway. Little five-piecer. Fits into my pack."

"How far d'you aim to go?"

"Oh, over the divide and down into the valley, for sure—but . . . well, it really doesn't matter much. Guess I'll go as far as the spirit moves me. Right now, I just feel I want to get the hell out."

"I know what you mean," said the ranger. He handed over the permit. "Yes, I'd have to say you look as if you could do with a spell out there."

We chatted some more and arranged that because I was going alone he would special-watchdog for me. I would stay overnight in the nearby campground, then get an early start next morning. If I didn't check out with the ranger by nightfall seven days later, he would know I was in trouble and would institute a search.

An hour later I was standing at the tailgate of my station wagon making a final check of the gear in my pack when a man came out of the Winnebago that was the only other vehicle in the campground. He walked over and stood looking at my outspread gear.

"You don't take a little TV set, or even a radio?"

"No."

"What d'you do then, out there for a whole week?"

"Oh, there's always plenty to do. Never seems to be enough time."

"But what do you *do?* Just hike like crazy?"

"Well, some trips I do a lot of walking, sure. Every day, morning and afternoon. But sometimes I just . . . do a lot of sitting around."

The man shook his head. He stood there for a few minutes, watching, then turned on his heel, walked back to his fortress and went inside and shut the door. I was left wondering why I had once again failed to come up with a coherent let alone satisfactory answer to a recurring question.

Next morning I began the long, steep climb toward the crest that lay between roadhead and the valley.

The night at roadhead had partway acclimatized me to the elevation, but I found myself struggling. Hour after hour I labored upward under a heavy load and hot summer sun, following a trail that wound through trees and then across open granite. But even as I labored, one sector of my mind remained content: a day's hard sweating, it said to the rest of me, would help slough off the human world; would begin to work me into the week.

All day, though, I kept meeting echoes.

In the course of the morning I passed no less than seven people, in parties of two and three, coming down the trail. Mostly we exchanged only monosyllables, but one markedly comely damsel wore shorts bearing the printed message: "Dangerous curves ahead!" The shorts fitted her perfectly. At noon I lunched beside a rockbound lake, and had barely finished eating when a dozen college-age kids, paired males and females, erupted onto the far shore, a hundred yards away. They promptly stripped off and dived into the lake, then stood around in shallow water, talking and flirting. Fifteen minutes passed before one of the girls noticed me and the show ended.

In late afternoon, thunderclouds assembled, coalesced. The air cooled. By the time I camped at sunset beside a smaller and starker lake, innocent of skinny-dippers, the clouds were dispersing and shafts of sunlight struck vivid on granite cliffs. A double rainbow arched over castellated peaks. The silence of high places reigned. As I set up camp beside the gnarled and curlicue trunk of a juniper tree, it seemed as if I had finally left the human world behind; but next morning, as I labored on up the last steep stretch below the crest, I found I still needed to sweat something out.

The view from the 10,000-foot pass, though magnificent, was not quite what I had expected. All I could see, clearly, was a long, sloping land of rocky spurs and side canyons. The valley itself lay hidden, several miles away, almost a vertical mile below. I could make out the line of its axis but little else.

I rested briefly at the pass, relishing the vista and nibbling goodies. Then I began the long descent. Soon, I struck away from the trail and started to detour around a string of lakes. I think I broke away from the trail to celebrate having crossed the divide, thereby cutting off the outer world and finally freeing myself; but I had barely reached the first lake and was following a faint game trail and a train of thought that I had been trying to board for a long time when a young couple with a small black dog materialized from a stand of trees. They seemed a pleasant enough pair. But they somehow succeeded in achieving an effect that takes some doing when you have only two human bodies and a dog at your command: they crowded around me.

"Isn't it wonderful up here, away from everybody?" gushed the man.

"So peaceful," said his mate. "Why, only yesterday we were still on the main trail, over on the other side of that ridge, and we met fourteen people inside of two hours. *Fourteen!*"

I held my peace.

"Yes, that was just too much of a crowd for us," said the man. "So we struck away from the trail."

"And now it's wonderful, being out here on our own. We're camped beside the lake, you know. You're the first person we've seen all day."

I began to ease on down the game trail. My companions took up escort positions.

"Yes, it's so much better over here," the man said to the back of my head. "I mean, that's what you come up into the mountains for, isn't it? Getting away from people."

His mate, who had stationed herself in front of me, with the dog, halted and pointed off to the right. "Our camp's just down there. Wouldn't you like to come and have a cup o' coffee with us?"

I declined, tried to edge forward.

"But it's just beautiful down there. So quiet."

I managed to step around her and get moving again. I set a stiff pace.

They kept up gamely, close behind, still chattering in tandem. I suppose I grunted a response from time to time. the dog remained mercifully silent.

We must have progressed like that for a couple of hundred yards. It began to feel like a scene from a bad movie. At last I stopped and turned and fixed the man with what I hoped was only a semi-steely gaze. "Look, I really have to agree with you that the reason we come up into the mountains is to get away from people. I certainly do. And at the moment I simply want to be alone."

Both of them looked disappointed, almost shocked. I rather think the dog's tail went between its legs. Just for a moment, I regretted having been so blunt. "Sorry," I said. "I hope you'll understand."

But they gave no obvious sign that they did, and there was nothing left for me to do except turn and walk on down the game trail.

As I walked, I kept telling myself it was ridiculous to let the incident disturb me. They were no doubt perfectly nice people, just a little rattled by the unaccustomed condition of being alone. Rattled and unaware of it. Unaware, that is, of the gulf that yawns between loneliness and solitude— those two internal states that both arise from the physical condition of being alone, yet stand poles apart. The fact remained, though, that the train of thought that had been steaming up just before I met them had long since left the station, and in its place surged an unruly mob. For at least half an hour I kept striding fiercely on—around the string of lakes, then over a low ridge and back onto the man-made trail.

The lonely young couple turned out to be the last of the echoes, though, and before long the walking and the mountains began to work their therapy.

The trail lipped over into the head of a long side canyon and began to wind down it, following the line of a tiny creek, threading a tortuous route among huge granite boulders that littered the canyon's floor. Many of the boulders lay at odd angles, like a giant's forgotten playthings. Some of their flanks had been glaciated smooth as glass, others roughed and greened by lichen.

The creek gained stature, began to support more greenery, even small meadows. When I took my hourly rest in one of the meadows I watched a surprisingly trusting gopher come clear out of his hole, scythe down a plant that must have been all of three feet distant, return to his hole with the harvest stored in puffed cheeks, then close the hole from inside— apparently by bunting up with his rear end some soil he had just excavated, head down, a few inches below the entrance. Long before afternoon eased over into evening I had begun to merge with the country.

I was far down the side canyon, with the peaks standing well behind me and the day dying, when the trail for the first time cut away from the creek and began to angle up the flank of a rocky spur. I halted and stood looking down the canyon's deep glaciated U; stood there deliberating.

The topo map offered conflicting evidence about my options. It showed that the trail would curve around the crest of the spur before dropping down into the main valley; and this apparent rejection of the side canyon as a route made me suspect that at some stage it became impassable. When I checked the part of the map that represented what was clearly the crucial stretch—the point at which the side canyon fell steeply away into the main valley—tightly packed contours seemed at first to confirm my suspicions. But the more closely I examined the contours, the more hopeful I became that there might be a way through. Other things came into it, too. With the sun now only a glowing memory behind jagged peaks, I would soon have to camp, and from where I stood the lower part of the side canyon— tumbling creek and attendant strip of green cradled between steep granite walls—looked very inviting. Neither map nor eye showed a man-made trail. That in itself promised well. And a quarter of a mile ahead I could see a little meadow with a rocky outcrop on one flank, and trees protecting it. The creek bent around the outcrop's buttresses like a moat around a castle.

I did not stand there on the trail for very long, debating. I suppose there was never much doubt, really; and before long I hitched the pack a notch higher on my hips, stepped off the trail and began to walk down toward the meadow.

I think it was in that moment, as I broke free from the man-made trail, with almost two days of walking tucked safely under my hip belt and five more stretching out ahead, that I finally moved from one world into another.

I walked at first through open brush, following my instincts, then a game trail. As I walked I kept glancing ahead. The meadow had slipped from view, but the moated-castle outcrop still jutted up like a beacon. For the second straight afternoon, dark thunderclouds had failed to reach a climax, and now, as they dispersed northward, they reflected the last of the sun's glow onto the castle's granite walls. I found myself smiling. It is not every day that you walk toward a place you have never been before and feel that you are coming home.

The open brush gave way to scattered conifers, then aspen groves. The game trail cut confidently through them. From time to time I could still glimpse the castle outcrop, up ahead.

I walked on, taking my time, savoring the taper of the day.

By the time I reached the edge of the meadow the light was seeping away, but the castle outcrop, even with its reflected illumination gone, still invited. On its lower flanks I found, sure enough, a perfect campsite: a small, level, grass-carpeted ledge, just far enough from the creek to avoid any danger of my polluting it but close enough for easy water supply and for music.

The view from my little ledge embraced meadow, canyon, sawtooth peaks. Everything except a lingering glow behind the peaks had subsided now to a study in subdued greens and grays. The scene cried out, in its quiet way, to be contemplated; but after the long day's walking there were other, more insistent demands.

I slipped the aluminum-framed pack off my back and stood it upright near one end of the green-carpeted ledge and propped it there with my bamboo staff jammed at an angle against a convenient rock wall. I opened the pack, took out the black plastic groundsheet and spread it on the grass in front of the pack. Next, because the air had suddenly chilled, I put on my down jacket and an Orlon balaclava. Then I rolled out the foam pad on the groundsheet, spread the sleeping bag on the pad, and unpacked and deposited the kitchen—food bag, pots and pans, stove—on the right side of the groundsheet, near its head.

Next, I took a white plastic tarpaulin out of the pack and stood with it in my hand, pondering. The afternoon thunderclouds had vanished now, off to the north, and it seemed unlikely they would return during the night. Besides, the view from the ledge, still softening toward night, was not one you could in decency block out with plastic. I set the tarp down beside the groundsheet, on the opposite side from the kitchen, where it would be ready for pulling over the bag if my weather forecasting turned out to have been lousy, and also for use as a dew-defying shroud for any other gear, including boots, that would find a night-place on that side of the bed. Then I took all three quart-size plastic water canteens out of the pack and walked down to the creek.

I was filling the last canteen when I heard, somewhere downstream, a splash that might have been a big trout or an otter or a muskrat or possibly a beaver—or could even, I suppose, have been dismissed as imagination had it not, almost at once, come again. I peered into the shadows. Nothing

—except the deep U of the canyon framing a moonlit blueness that I knew was the space above the valley.

I walked back to camp and put the canteens down beside the ground-sheet—one in the kitchen, two on the opposite side—and unzippered the sleeping bag halfway and sat down on it. I leaned back against the pack and took off first one boot and then the other, removed my socks and slid both legs into the sleeping bag. I rezippered the bag far enough for it to snug tight against the down jacket so that bag and jacket together formed an uninterrupted shell around my body. Then I paused, relishing the cozy assurance of warmth.

The moon, hanging above my left shoulder, was vanquishing the rearguard daylight. The meadow, and the lines of the canyon, had begun to regain definition. A different, moon-blued definition. High above, the outline of the peaks was fading. I sat looking at it all for a moment; then I reached back and took the flashlight from a side pocket of the pack and slipped its attached loop of nylon cord around my neck.

All at once I felt tired, uninterested in cooking. I knew, though, that the one thing guaranteed to re-motivate me was a shot of fast-acting calories. So I reached back into another side pocket of the pack, took out a plastic bag of candies, unwrapped two, slipped them into my mouth and began to set up the kitchen. Within minutes I had the stove unpacked and standing ready, one pot half full of water, and a foil package of "chili con carne" lying beside it, top torn open. Two more minutes and I had the stove roaring and the pot standing on it, and I could lean back once more against the soft, half-empty pack bag.

The stars were out now. The peaks had become little more than a broad and jagged saw of blackness, blacker than the sky only because it was devoid of stars. A night breeze already flowed down the canyon, cool on my face. I pulled the jacket hood over my head. The roar of the stove built an igloo of sound around me.

The pot on the stove muttered. I switched on the flashlight and saw, sure enough, steam rising from around the pot lid. With bandanna-wrapped fingers I removed the lid, poured the chili mix into the water, stirred, turned the stove to low, slipped an asbestos-lined wire gauze—the kind you used at school with Bunsen burners—between it and the pot, and sat back again while dinner simmered.

The stove only whispered now. Far up the canyon, a coyote yowled. Then, behind the stove's whisper, there was only silence, filling the canyon, cold and solid. I sat watching moonlight rout the last of the day. Soon, it filled the canyon, blue and solid, in tandem with the silence.

I checked my watch. Ten minutes. I lifted the lid from the pot and ladled a first serving of chili into the metal cup. In the flashlight beam it steamed, brown and appetizing. It tasted almost elegant, and I sat there and ate it, spoonful by spoonful, looking out over sleeping bag and meadow and cold blue canyon but no longer seeing very much. By the time I had finished the fourth and last cupful of chili and had scraped most of the goo from the pot and poured a little water into it to aid final cleaning in the morning, I was barely awake enough to eat my ordained piece of meal-ending chocolate. I think I was still eating it—oblivious, now, of the view—when I fell asleep. When I came half-awake again I was still sitting up, leaning against the pack, and my watch reported that two hours had passed. I slid down into the sleeping bag, pulled it loosely around me, and once more slept.

In the morning, before breakfast, two fawns stood beside the creek, ears alert, bodies silhouetted in the first sunlight against lush green grass. And after breakfast, as I sat considering how soon to move on, a coyote emerged from the trees on the far side of the meadow and trotted out into the open, legs tripping doglike and dainty among the tussocks. It quartered twice across the middle of the meadow, then began to move, nose to ground, into the breeze that had just begun to ease gently up the canyon. I reached out, very slowly, lifted my binoculars from the boot in which they had spent the night, and focused on the hunting coyote. Almost at once, it pounced, like a kitten on a ball of wool, on some unseen target. Clearly, the coyote had missed its prey. For it stood there looking down—no doubt into a gopher hole—its body as eloquent of frustration as a golfer's after a missed two-foot putt. But a few minutes later I watched it, after another pounce, fling back its head, readjust a small, dark, struggling shape held in its teeth, chomp a couple of times, swallow, then resume its breakfasteering. Twice more in the next five minutes it pounced and missed. Just after the second miss it moved out of sight behind a rock wall of my little ledge that angled down, six feet beyond the kitchen. I slid out of bed and very slowly, on hands and knees, eased toward the wall. I reached it, peered over. Off to my right, a chipmunk chirped alarm. Out in the meadow, the coyote swung its head toward me, froze for a moment—and then was racing away across the open grass—legs no longer dainty but frantic, digging turf. Within seconds the streaking brown body had vanished into dark trees.

Half an hour later I struck camp and walked on down toward the space, hanging blue at the canyon's mouth, that I knew was the valley.

Almost at once, the country mutated. The canyon began to slope more steeply, the creek to tumble more boisterously. The meadows grew smaller and less frequent, the conifer stands between them, taller and more stately. The granite boulders studding the canyon floor crowded closer.

Above all, though, there were the flowers. A quartet of crimson columbines—five trumpets per player—extemporized in sun-filled silence to a captive bracken audience. Beside a rotting juniper log, a saprophytic snow plant spiked up through dead leaves, scarlet buds bunched tight around its core like a string of small, rather tattered pomegranates. I walked on down among the tumbled boulders. In a natural granite courtyard beside the creek, nodding tiger lilies curved up and gracefully over, each flower with its yellow, brown-spotted petals peeling back on themselves into delicate yet startling orbs; each orb with its ring of six flattened-miniature-taco stamens dangling like wind chimes. Against a lush mossy backdrop, a galaxy of shooting stars—chocolate-brown cones, yellow tail bands, pale pink plumes—hung suspended in plunging stationary orbit.

I had just passed the shooting stars when I stepped onto a granite ledge and found myself looking out over the valley.

A lot depends, of course, on the mood you are in when you first see a place. But I am sure that even without the flowers' Elysian prelude I would have halted in surprise on that open granite ledge. The valley was deeper and more dramatic than I had expected. It was, to an extent the topo map had somehow not prepared me for, a canyon rather than a valley—almost in the same way that Yosemite is a canyon, though it too is always called "Valley." But the plunging granite side walls did no more than frame the picture. Tall, elegant conifers clothed the valley in a dense green mat. Shadows cast by the trees' spired summits gave the mat depth and texture. Wedges of deeper shadow, from spurs on the valley's rim, drew sharper, communal contrasts. And down the center of the valley, furrowing its mat, meandered a river that was a chain of white rapids, mottled brown shallows and blue-green pools.

Yet the elements of the scene were not its core. Even in that first moment there was something else about the valley—the morning light, perhaps, or my flower-decked mood—that invited; that left me slightly breathless. I had been afraid, I think, that the weeks of anticipating the trip might have created an expectancy barrier. Standing on that granite ledge, I knew I need not have worried.

I stayed on the ledge only long enough to savor through binoculars the close-woven richness of green-tree mat and beckoning river; but while I stood there a military jet cut down the valley's cleavage, so low that it kept vanishing below my line of sight. The jet tore the quiet air, bouncing crass thunder off the plunging rock walls. By rights, I should have cursed its pilot—for breaking sensible flying regulations, for disturbing my peace. Yet, just as had happened once before, years earlier, in a similar situation, I found myself instead admiring his competence and thrust and lawlessness; found myself acknowledging the vivid way he represented us restless, driving humans. I stood listening until the plane's last echoes died away, then brought my mind back to practical matters.

Below the ledge, a jumble of rocks slanted steeply away. It was far from clear whether I would be able to find a route down. I scrambled off one end of the ledge and began the descent.

At first I had to thread my way through a chaos of huge granite boulders. But between them plunged precipitous, loose gravel slopes, and I slipped and slid down these runways, scaled route-blocking boulders big as cottages, then returned to gravel. Ten minutes, and the worst seemed over. Trees began, in among the boulders: junipers with their warm, twist-pattern trunks; firs with soft, green-tipped pagoda branches; then huge, stately ponderosa pines. It was hot now, even in the shade, and the air grew heavy with the sweet toffee smell of pine sap.

At last the gravel runways began to flatten out and the trees to grow closer together, so that you could call the place a forest. Soon I was walking on almost level ground across a cushioning carpet of pine needles, and the pines rose huge and silent and there was almost no undergrowth, just the towering trees. It was big, dignified country. Before long I could hear the river.

I found a flawless campsite a hundred feet from the river, near a side creek that was just a healthy trickle, really, but had a natural log dam that broadened it out into a miniature pool, two feet across, with a walkway down into it and a triangular stone exquisitely placed in a moss-bank setting. I rolled out my groundsheet and pad under a big ponderosa pine. A squirrel rasped up a neighboring tree, then peered at me around one side of it and complained. When I had set up camp and brewed a pot of tea I found myself just sitting there, leaning against my pack, suddenly content, after all the hard walking, to do nothing.

And that was almost all I did for the rest of the day: just sat and looked around. In the due course of time, though, I began—as nearly always happens when you stay for a while in one place—to notice details that at first had melded into the backdrop. Mind you, I saw nothing that could be called even remotely exciting. I watched cobwebs drift by on silent journeys that were invisible, too, except in slanting beams of sunlight. I watched the labored flights of clapper-rattle grasshoppers that clappered on the way down and not, as you would expect, when taking off and gaining height. I watched a litle brown bundle of a bird land on a twig, seven feet away, and sit there, body pulsating, beady eye casing me, until I reached for the camera; and as it departed I resolved for the hundredth time in ten years to get myself a bird book and at least learn to identify the most common species. I watched an ant carry a small catkin head, six times bulkier than itself, for a vast distance over an obstacle course of pine needles and then across the cleared space that was my kitchen; carry it, presumably, toward some goal—yet pass on the way, every few inches, catkins that to me looked identical to the one that formed its prodigious burden. I watched the obvious frustration of a mosquito that settled on my shirt sleeve; smelling warm flesh below, it kept boring down with its slender proboscis but never managed to drill quite deep enough to strike blood. Once, I watched a bat, looking rather lost in bright sunlight, stutter an erratic course downriver. And all the time, sitting there at my ease, I half-heard the tinkle of the little side creek and, as the afternoon wore on, the brush of wind across treetops.

Once, in midafternoon, I got up and walked to the riverbank and sat on a tree that beavers had felled. The tree's tip lay out in the main current and its whole trunk pulsated. I sat there, feeling the river's ceaseless life, gazing without real thought at a patch of willows that grew on an island— or rather, on what would earlier in the year be an island but was now surrounded by an open expanse of dry pebbles that you would be able to walk over, even at dusk, without fear of treading on a concealed rattle- snake. I got up and strolled out onto the smooth, water-rounded pebbles.

On one of them lay the mottled brown husk of a helgramite, split neatly down its center. The split was so clean, so eloquent, that I could almost see the new, transformed insect emerging, unfurling its wings, then flying up and away into the new, surprising element of air. I walked out onto the tip of the willow patch. Upstream, below a rapid, there was a long, gentle run —not quite a pool but not a shallow either—in which the water had just the right movement and just the right depth of color. At that hour, with the sun beating down, there was no sign of fish. Somehow, anyway, it was not yet time to fish. I walked back to camp and brewed more tea.

By the time I had finished drinking it the afternoon clouds were building their black threat, and I stretched my white plastic tarpaulin out between the trunk of the big pine tree and a pair of nearby saplings. I rigged the tarp high, so that although it would protect me from a thunderstorm there was still plenty of space under its eaves for me to look out at the forest. With the sun cut off and a grayness lying heavy, nothing much seemed to be happening there. But a spider undertook a long diagonal trip across the tarp and I lay watching its progress. All I could see through the white plastic, except for a blurred suggestion of the body, was the circular pattern of its outspread legs at the points they touched the tarp. Watching the moving pattern, it occurred to me that this was what an insect-eating fish, such as a trout, must see when a fly or spider came floating down the river, out in the broad expanse of mirrorlike reflecting surface that would fill all its view except for a small window above its head. Within that window the trout's angle of sight was wide enough for light to be refracted through the water instead of reflected, and through the window the trout could look out into the nonwatery world and sometimes detect, near the window's edge, bulky two-legged animals waving thin poles to and fro; animals that the trout knew, from instinct or experience, were not to be trusted in any damned way. When the current carried an insect downstream into the circular window, the trout could see the whole insect instead of just the pattern of leg-prints previously visible on the water's mirror surface; and the fish could therefore make a final decision about whether it should rise in the water and engulf the morsel. Lying under my white plastic tarp, I watched the spider complete its journey, vanish. It was a long time, I realized, since I had thought like a trout, the way I used to as a kid—and as a man ostensibly much older than a kid. It was a long time since I had fished, even. Sudden sunlight transformed the white plastic into a glaring expanse. I stuck my head outside. The thunderclouds had slid away, frustrated, and the sun was reclaiming the day. I took down my tarp and went back to watching the forest.

I suppose I did not really spend all that first day watching the forest. I do not think I opened the paperback I had brought, and I cannot remember anything else I did—nothing I can put a finger on, I mean—so I'm tempted to say that I sat there under my pine tree, thinking. But "thinking" is the wrong word, really. What you do at such times, I find, is not proper thinking. Even what we normally call "thinking" is not an easy process to pin down. Perhaps Robert Musil came close when he wrote, "It is not the case that we reflect on things. Rather, things think themselves out within us." Sitting under a tree when you are pleasantly tired and giving yourself up to the forest is certainly a very passive business. Still, thoughts trip by. And at some point that afternoon, as I sat there contentedly under my big ponderosa pine, doing what would to anyone else have looked like nothing —and would probably have looked like it to me, had I considered the matter—I for some reason found myself remembering the Winnebago man in the campground, three days earlier, and the way I had once again failed to come up with a satisfactory answer to his central question; and all at once there popped up into my mind, apparently unbidden, a memory that had lain unpopped for more than thirty years.

Back when I was ten or eleven there was a boy at my school in England who lived on a farm and who, when asked what he had done on a free day or weekend or long vacation, always produced the same answer. His response became so predictable that we little embryo terrorists would on every possible occasion ask him, "John, what did you do this weekend?" —or whatever the period had been. Then we would wait in delicious expectation. And John always produced. Without fail, he would give his slow smile and say, "Oh, just mucked about." Sitting there under my pine tree, I found myself understanding, thirty years late, the rightness and richness of his response.

The hours passed and I sat and mucked statically about. First, I think, I began to itemize the wealth of detail. A pale blur on a rotting tree trunk focused into the orange remnants of a pine cone, half dismantled and left lying there in the dining room of the squirrel that had chided me when I arrived but was now accepting enough, or at least resigned enough, to sit out on a branch and just watch me before flouncing off on a safari to quieter parts. When I looked out across the hidden river I found myself not just seeing tangled forest canopy but zeroing in for some reason on a particularly tall ponderosa pine; found myself appreciating the way its ruler-straight trunk thrust up orange against the pale gray of the valley's granite wall, and the way big green cones bent its branches in delicate downcurves, like a loaded Christmas tree's; found myself delighted by the way sunlight kept bouncing off the cones' resin so that the tree sometimes glistened as if dusted with Christmas frosting. Back closer to my couch, around the boles of mature pines, dried-out cones lay thick, as if big, rough, circular tarpaulins had been spread there. Closer still, the ants still scurried, busier than beavers. Offstage, the ceaseless river whispered. And always there were the trees, in all their slow chapters: slender saplings; thrusting mid-lifers; towering, triumphant giants; snags, gaunt and stark as skeletons; then rotting, moss-shrouded windfall. I sat on, idly watching, details often fading back into the whole, so that I was aware only of a glorious richness, prodigality, wantonness.

The day faded toward extinction. But I did not light a fire. I like to watch night fall, then become a part of the shadowed darkness, and a fire, for all its cheer, cuts you off. Soon, bats were flitting silent against pale sky. Then the moon rose. My eyes and mind wandered among blue shadows, then up to and along the great waves of gray that were the valley's limits.

In the morning, at first eye-open, there was a deer standing barely twenty paces away, so camouflaged by a fir sapling that I could see only the black-tipped white tail and, through slowly raised binoculars, a single big eye, unblinking but somehow full of fearfulness. For a long moment we examined each other. Then there was only the sapling.

Before breakfast, I went fishing.

Out in the "civilized" world, the human population can be divided, with no more than routine oversimplification, into three groups: those who regard all fishing as a cruel and near-criminal aberration (and who commonly climb to their elevated opinions from a firm base of ignorance); those who "sport-fish" merely to catch fish (and who may indeed treat fish with cruel and near-criminal disregard); and those who understand that the catching of fish is largely a means to an end and that the essence of fishing is a close-to-innocent pleasure that can border on, even lap over into, sheer artistry. These graduates are often—though by no means exclusively—people who fly-fish for trout.

It was barely seven o'clock when I walked eagerly down to the river. The sun had not yet cleared the valley's rim, and along the riverbank the air was cold, going on bloody cold. But because I knew I would have to wade a little in order to fish the run above the willow-patch island I wore shorts, and leather moccasins on bare feet. I had my heavy down jacket on, though, with its hood pulled tight. I walked across the isthmus of water-rounded pebbles that joined the island to the bank, looked for and failed to find the split-open helgramite husk, came to the foot of the run, hesitated, took off the moccasins, stuffed them into the fishing satchel slung around my neck, hesitated again, then waded out into the river.

The water felt bitterly cold. My feet slipped and slithered on smooth, slime-coated pebbles. I waded carefully out until the willow patch was far enough behind my right shoulder to give me room to cast. The water barely reached my knees but my feet were already almost numb. From its little holding ring just above the rod's cork handle, I unhooked the artificial fly —a dainty confection of fur and feather, with the feather wound spirally around the hook so that its fibers stood out like the legs of a real fly or spider. Then I began false-casting: flexing the rod to and fro so that the stiff, heavy line extended forward, then backward. With my left hand I kept stripping more and more line off the reel so that its airborne part, reaching out in a constantly mobile curl, grew steadily longer. At first I kept turning my head to watch the line flow backward on its smooth and beautiful path. I watched mainly to make sure that at its full extension, when it hung for an instant, green and almost straight against the shadows of the far bank, the fly at the end of the gut leader did not snag the willow patch. But I also watched because it was a long time since I had fished, and watching the line helps you regain your timing—a delicate response to the rhythm of the cast that is transmitted to your fingers down the slender and supple rod. When the line was long enough, I let one forward cast follow through to completion. The line curled out upstream, over the edge of the run. At its full extent, the pale fly hung poised for an instant, a foot above the water. Then it landed, delicate as thistledown, and began floating with the current, back toward me. With my left hand I kept pulling in line, so that if a fish rose and engulfed the fly there would be little or no slack line between us and I could tighten before he sensed that there was something wrong. Like the casting and many other things, this keeping in touch with the fly by constant retrieving of the line was something I still did almost automatically, the way I had done it as a kid during those long, glorious days when such arts were the only things that mattered. Were sometimes the only things that existed.

The first three or four casts, no fish rose. Then one splashed untidily at the fly. Automatically, I tightened. I knew at once that it was a small fish, but because of my long abstinence there was still a mild thrill when the fish fought against the pressure and the rod came alive in my hand. I reeled in and held the little rainbow trout, barely six inches long, on the surface of the water, close beside my left knee. It lay there on its side, momentarily exhausted. It was so young that there were still vertical black parr marks at intervals along the gleaming, rainbow-hued flanks. I tucked the rod into my right armpit, reached down with my left hand, grasped the fish gently but firmly, still in the water, and with my right forefinger and thumb pressed back and down on the hook so that the barb disengaged and I could slip the fly free. I opened the palm of my hand partway so that the fish, though no longer captive, was held upright in normal swimming position. For a long moment it stayed there, unmoving. Then with a flick of its tail it darted forward, streaked out into the run and vanished. Because it had not been exposed to air or to a dry, slime-removing hand, it would suffer no harm. In bright sunlight, when I could see everything that happened, I had once watched a small trout that I had just caught and released, in just this way, rise almost immediately to the same fly floated down over the same place.

A little farther up the run, the tip of a dark nose broke the surface and annexed an invisible insect. I eased forward a couple of steps—and discovered that my feet were now so numb that it was all I could do to keep my balance. The fish rose a second time. I reforgot my feet and recast upstream. The fly landed dead on target, four or five feet above the place the fish had risen, and began to float down with the current. As I retrieved line with my left hand I found myself imagining the trout, poised in its feeding place, watching the mirrorlike surface that stretched away upstream; watching a circular, outspread pattern that was the imprint of the hackle tips at the points they touched the water; watching the pattern move swiftly down toward the window above its head, where it would be able to see the whole body of the expected fly or spider. Up in my reality, above the surface, I watched intently as the pale and barely visible blur of feather hackle swept on downstream. I kept imagining that it had moved into the trout's window and that the fish was at that moment making its decision to eat or not to eat. For long, ticking seconds, the fly kept floating down with the current; and then, when I felt sure it had passed beyond the trout's window, the dark nose broke the surface again and the pale blur that was my fly had vanished. I flicked my wrist back, felt the fish, solid. Then line was cutting out across the run at an angle and then the fish was cartwheeling through the air, a bar of glorious, glistening silver; and then the pressure of the rod was too much for it and it was coming back toward me, still struggling but already halfway defeated. Within a minute I had it lying quietly at the surface, close beside my knee. It was ten or eleven inches long: perfect eating size. I tucked the rod under my arm again, reached down and grasped the fish firmly in my left hand, lifted it clear of the water, put my right thumb in its mouth, ball upward, laid my right forefinger along the top of the head, and jerked the thumb smartly backward. I felt the neck break. The fish, already dead, quivered, then lay still. For a long moment I let it lie there in my open palm while I admired the glistening spotted scales and still-shimmering rainbow tints. Then I took a plastic bag out of the satchel slung around my neck, slid the fish into the bag, slipped the bag into the satchel.

In the next twenty minutes I caught two more pan-size rainbows. And then, at the very head of the run, on the same pale dry fly, I hooked a bigger fish that careened almost to the far side of the river before I brought it back and eventually landed it by stumbling to the bank and coaxing the now exhausted and almost immobile fish into water so shallow that it could no longer swim freely and I could grasp it with reasonable safety and quickly break its neck. It was only then that I realized I could barely feel my feet. I also realized for the first time that the sun had cleared the far rim of the valley. I took stock. Four fish were plenty for the morning, for food as well as fun. I sat down on the smooth, dry pebbles, rubbed my benumbed feet halfway dry and slid them into the moccasins. And all at once, there on the open pebbles, it was warm. I took off the down jacket, began cleaning the trout. By the time I came to the last one I had taken off my shirt and the sun was beating hot on my bare shoulders.

Afterward, when I looked back at the week as a whole, it almost seemed as if nothing much happened after I caught those first trout: the rest of the week gave an impression of tapering off in anticlimax. At the time, though, it did not feel like that at all. Very much the reverse. Yet while the fishing on that fourth morning was in no sense a climax it turned out, I guess, to be the last "new" thing I did all week. Perhaps that is the point: afterward, I did nothing different from what I had already done. Just more of the same. Let there be no doubt, though—for three more days the valley continued to hold me content in the palm of its cupped hand.

After a trout breakfast on that fourth morning, I toyed with the idea of striking camp and exploring upriver. But after giving the matter some thought—that is, by letting the possibility swirl around my head for a while and then pulling it out and remeasuring it—I decided that the week was not going to evolve into one of my hard-walking treks. The first two and a half days had taken care of all that. So I did not strike camp for another twenty-four hours.

Some of that time I sat and read, or simply went on looking around at the forest. Two or three times, I took local strolls. On one of them I met a rattlesnake, but he lay out in the middle of an open patch of pine needles and was therefore almost as visible and unthreatening as he would have been on smooth pebbles. He rattled at me, anyway, when I was still a dozen paces away, so I did not even suffer the kind of scare you get from almost treading on one. During that same stroll I talked briefly to a couple of people camped half a mile downstream, under a rocky overhang. They were pleasant folks, out on their first weeklong trip, and reveling in the experience. Later, a packtrain passed close to my camp, heading upriver on the main trail, and I exchanged a few words with the man on the last of the seven or eight horses. He was relaxed and amiable, up there under his big hat. Yes, he said, the valley was just the same for several miles downstream. Just as beautiful.

That evening I fished again—for dinner and next morning's breakfast. I also fished for other things, of course. And although I had within half an hour caught four trout big enough to complement two meals, I went on fishing—under a new rubric: If I caught more fish I would release them.

As it turned out, I went on fishing far too long—just the way I always did as a kid, and as a young man too—and eventually, although my timing had now improved, I snagged the fly in a branch that I had not seen in the fading light. I could not reach the branch (even though I wore boots this time, and did not wade, because I was exploring some distance upstream), and I had to break the leader. To tie on a new fly I had to hold the hook's tiny eye up against the palest sector of sky, and even then I could barely see either it or the end of the fine gut leader. As I fought the familiar reluctance of the gut to be threaded through the eye I was vaguely conscious of the dark tips of conifers, high against the sky, just as I had often been with other trees, other skies, in many other places—almost, it seemed, in other lives. Then the fly was safely knotted on at last and I was casting up into the gloaming, into a calm pool, and guessing, most of the time, just where my fly might be floating. On one cast I saw the ripples of a widening circle, up on the flat surface of the pool, roughly where the fly could have been, and almost instinctively I raised the rod. Just for a moment there was a weight on the line—a more solid weight, it seemed to me, than any other of the day's fish had generated. Then the weight had gone and the line was slack and I was left trying to decide if the fish had really been so much bigger than all the rest or whether I should attribute the impression to a vivid imagination. Somehow, by now, it did not matter very much, and I went on casting up into the paleness that was the pool. Soon it was too dark even for that, even for me, and I fumbled the flashlight out of my satchel and turned and walked home to camp.

Next morning, after an early breakfast, I stowed everything into my pack and walked downstream along the main trail. It was good to feel the weight of the pack on my hips again, and the smooth surface of the bamboo staff in my right hand; good to feel the rhythmic stride I fell into, almost without thinking. The sun beat down on my bare shoulders. It was not yet hot, though—only warm and comforting.

The valley floor kept opening up into broad, lush meadows. Each of these meadows, too, cried out in its own way to be contemplated, but I kept walking. Now, somehow suddenly, I had only two days left.

That day, I walked barely five miles. At the far end of the biggest and lushest meadow, I paused. The map showed that half a mile ahead the trail struck away from the valley floor; and there was another thing, too. I could see that less than a mile downstream the steep granite walls began to flatten out. Beyond that point, the valley would be a different place. So I cut away from the trail, toward the river, and found a good campsite on the meadow's edge, a hundred feet short of the river, in an aspen grove.

Most of that day I just sat in camp with the meadow spread golden-green before me and aspens whispering at my elbow and the pale blue sky overhead slowly filling with clouds. Up in another world, jets kept painting white contrails across that sky. Fortunately, contrails rarely seem to intrude on my solitude. They are too remote, too unreal. Some people, I know, feel differently—though an honest fellow backpacker once admitted, "Well, maybe I just mean that they wreck my photography."

In late afternoon I went fishing again. I caught nothing big enough to eat —perhaps because the fish, too, were disturbed by the way the day's clouds, spreading down the valley from invisible peaks, had a new, determined look. Soon, little flurries of spinning wind began to push across the meadow, printing whirligig patterns in the tall grass, then erasing them. The clouds built thicker, blacker. The gloom deepened. At last, a few drops of rain fell, cold and heavy. When the storm exploded I was safely back under my little white tarp, which I had tied to neighboring aspen trunks. I sat listening with pleasure to the way the tarp prattled under the lashing rain and heaved in response to the swaying aspens. By nightfall the thunderstorm had blown itself out, and I took the tarp down and dined by freshly laundered starlight.

Next morning, with the whole world washed clean and shining, I went for a walk along the river, watched trout rising, then came back to my aspen trees. I sat there, leaning against my pack, for half an hour. But by then I knew I could procrastinate no longer. Around noon, I struck camp. Twenty minutes later I began climbing the steep side trail that slanted toward the divide.

I did not say goodbye to the valley. In midafternoon I became aware, too late, that I had crossed a shallow rise that cut me off from it. From its floor, anyway. All I could see was the upper part of the now familiar granite wall.

Somehow it did not matter too much. I knew, now, that I would be coming back.

That night I camped in high country again, among granite slabs and boulders, beside a dead juniper tree with its curlicue bark bleached palest orange. By midafternoon next day I was climbing toward the pass that would take me back, over the divide, into the little valley in which the ranger station stood.

The pass was lower than the one I had crossed on the second day, and softer. As I approached it, a deer wandered over the skyline, skirted a snowbank, then sauntered down through a sloping bed of blue lupines that was bigger than the statutory football field. I reached the crest. The air buzzed with bees beelining to and from the lupines. All around, sun-lit space rested on a maze of peaks that sawtoothed away into immense, hazy distances. Below, the ranger-station valley lay green and inviting. The whole scene fitted together. Everything fitted together now. There was none of the gaping meaninglessness that had hung so heavy on me, seven days earlier.

I started down the slope, into the little valley. Another hour, and I could see the ranger station tucked in among its trees. Just before five o'clock I climbed up the steps onto the wooden veranda, slipped the pack off my back and went in through the screen door.

The young redheaded ranger looked up from his desk, glanced at his watch, smiled. "I was beginning to wonder," he said. "Had a good time?"

"Great."

"Do some fishing?"

"Sure."

"Any luck?"

"Oh, all I needed—and more."

"Good," said the ranger. He got up and moved toward the counter. "What else did you get to do?"

"Well, you know how it is, I walked and fished and . . ." I hesitated. "Oh, I just mucked about."

The ranger nodded. "I know what you mean," he said. He reached the counter, shook my hand, ran his eye over me. "Well, one thing's for sure. Whatever you did out there, it's done you a whole lot of good."

MY AMERICAN TOUR: CASEY BERGER, THE TEXAS CHAMP

By Sir Atholl Oakeley

A few days later Garsh came round to tell me that I was to appear at the 71st Armoury, one of the largest American stadiums after Madison Square Garden.

'Who against?' I asked.

'The Texas Champ. Oh boy, am I worried. It's a real tough assignment. Maybe we made a mistake letting Curley see you the other day. You sure look good now. I figure they're having second thoughts and taking no chances.'

So at last my great day arrived. Alfred drove Bill and me to the stadium. Pojello was already there looking more like a professor than ever. With his usual smile he said, 'Atol, I tink you give big Champion prescription. You believe what I say. Karl knows best. You take things steady. No rush. This man, big man. Very strong man. You no let him get grip or you finish upside down. You wait right time. Take great opportunity soon you see it. No try pin. Just grab foot. You try submission. I tell you. I know you listen. You win! You very big drawing card. Everyone come to see you. You will say, "Thank you, Mr. Pojello. You tell truth." You like very much Mr. Pojello.'

The main fight was for the world heavyweight championship between Ray Steele, a leading contender, and Jim Londos, Champion of Greece and reigning world champion. The stadium had been sold out for days.

Unlike the British journalists, American pressmen know how to write up wrestling, and wrestling here I found was very big business. A few weeks previously ninety thousand people had paid to see Gus Sonnenberg. Crowds of sixty thousand and more were commonplace. Wrestling had then completely eclipsed boxing, whose chief heavyweight and former wrestling champion, the Italian Primo Carnera, had failed to draw the paying customers on any great scale. This was due to his size, power and weight, which dwarfed his opponents. Boxing attendances were right down. The public do not pay to see a vast great man beating a small man.

They like to see small men beat big men. So it has always been since the days of Goliath.

Primo Carnera, a giant 6 ft 7 in wrestler weighing nineteen stone, had invaded the sacred rights of the glove game and had, in his prime, easily demolished the lot, without knowing much about the art. He punched so hard that in training they made him wear 24 oz gloves. With ordinary boxing gloves he killed Schaaf. After this he lost his nerve. Primo was invincible as a glove fighter, as the world and America found out. But once he had killed a man Primo told me that he could no longer hit hard in case he killed anyone else. Thereafter, he said, he always pulled his punches. In due course he sank back into that oblivion which he enjoyed until Paul Journee (for Jeff Dickson) found him wrestling all comers, fifteen a night, in France. But more about Carnera later.

Meantime I found myself in a large dressing room completely surrounded by huge men, muscled like gorillas, and about as big. Some were seven feet in height. The smallest, other than Londos the champion, measured at least six foot. I saw no one there except Londos who was anywhere near my size. The smallest of the giants was nineteen stone. Even the champion was of a much heavier build than I was.

Jack Pfeiffer, Curley's manager, came into the dressing room and told the preliminaries to get a move on. He came over to me and asked:

'Well, Cap, how you feel?'

I looked at Pfeiffer, who was around five foot eight and a hundred and twenty pounds. 'Pleased to find someone smaller than myself,' I replied: 'Okay, Jack, and could I be told which of these giants is Mr. Berger?' He said: 'You'll find out. You're not on till after the main bout anyway. See you later.'

When he returned to the dressing room Pfeiffer said: 'Now listen to me, Cap, we all admire you for coming all this way from little old England to do battle with our big boys. We have decided to give you a break. You're up against Casey Berger, Texas Champ. It's a thirty-minute match. We know how you paid your round-trip over and we've billed you real good.'

(He certainly had; 'Captain Atholl Oakeley, Scion of Kings', was my billing!)

'We don't aim to make you lose face at home so we're going to do you proud. Casey will give you a five-minute exhibition. After that we'll put up a card. Then you gotta do your best. This gives you five minutes' sure good chance to show yourself to the American public. After five minutes Casey aims to beat you right away because he is a great champion and he has his reputation to consider. You can go home and tell your folks you stayed five minutes against our champion.'

Good old Jack Pfeiffer! I was deeply touched. Here was I in a foreign country, bombastically challenging men much bigger than I was. An Englishman at that, and the English, despite statements to the contrary, are usually much too stuck up to be really popular in the States. Here was a little American manager saying they did not wish to hurt me but, in their own way, try to enhance my reputation.

Irslinger, who had spent hours advising me in England as to what I might expect in America, had not prepared me for such generosity.

'Atol,' he had said, 'your heavyweights do not get enough experience in England to take on Americans in their own country. Your country produces great champions only in the lighter weights. Even if an English heavyweight *was* able to win over an American champ in America, or even looked like doing so, the ref would disqualify him.

'I figure, over in the States where there are 20,000 heavies, no English heavyweight is able to beat even their fourth raters. But maybe you can succeed. You have lots of experience against the best Europeans. You train a long time. You also got what it takes to make a champ—courage and speed.'

Perhaps Henri believed that I might have a chance in America because of my size and style. He had impressed upon me that their heavyweight wrestling champions at that time were men of great size and strength who, compared with me, would be slow and ponderous. Their strength made it imperative that at all costs I should avoid being caught in any grip from which I would be unable to escape.

Henri said that, being accustomed to fighting men of their own size, these giant champions from nations all over the world would think nothing of me. If I ever let them get a grip they would crush me.

This kind of talk, from so experienced a fighter as Henri Irslinger (remember he had won the open 'London Tournament' of 1908), had made me all the more determined to win.

But now I felt a small, rather insignificant little Englishman surrounded by giants in a foreign country. I did not even know which of these men was Casey Berger, my first opponent.

But I was not kept long in suspense. A good-looking Hercules came over and drawled, 'Hiya. I'm Berger. Casey Berger. Glad to know you, Cap.' He smiled, then ambled away with the measured gate of a Southerner. This then was Casey Berger. He looked all that Karl had said he was.

I continued thinking:

'This is a strong and determined man. I must not be fooled by that smile. Casey is not going to take any chances against a little fifteen-stoner. My only chance of winning will be speed and a ferocious attack—as rough as possible, *à l'Irslinger,* and right from the start. I must show him I am no pushover.'

I remembered how I had blacked the eye of world champion Svediquist in the final of the championships in Brussels three years previously. The American press regarded all Englishmen as (outwardly) over-polite and (inwardly) perfidious. Casey would not expect rough tactics. More likely, as I later heard, he expected me to follow the usual pattern. Namely retiring with a cut eye or flinging myself horizontal, holding my steel protector-cap and screaming 'foul' at the top of my voice.

It may well have been that the Texas champion took me too lightly. In view of performances by other British heavyweights, who had ventured into the lion's den of the American ring, one could hardly blame him.

I awoke from my day dreams with a bang.

'You're on now, Cap. Get goin',' called out Jack Pfeiffer. As I passed him, wearing my black and white silk dressing gown, skin-tight black tights trimmed with chocolate and gold (my regimental Athletic Team colours), he said:

'Say, you look all right. I hope they hoovered the mat for you, Cap.'

Then he saw my knee-pads:

'What you aim to do—play cricket?'

As I walked up the aisle I heard people saying:

'This is the English aristocrat. My, but he looks a smart little fellow.'

'Surely they're not putting that little guy on with Berger. He'll get killed.'

'Heard he came over from England just to challenge us.' 'Yes, I hoid all that befoire. Last Big British Palooka ended up on his back yelling foul.'

Someone else replied: 'That little fellow won't get a chance to yell foul.'

Then suddenly an English voice called out:

'Come on, England. We're all rooting for you to show these Yanks where they get off. Rule, Britannia, old boy, and don't bloody well forget it!'

That effort clinched it! I would beat this Texan or never again enter a wrestling ring! I climbed up the steps, vaulted the ropes and went over to my corner.

My appearance was greeted with one big howl of laughter. I bowed sedately and was greeted, if possible, by even louder laughter. There were shouts of, 'This game ought to suit British heavyweights. Why don't you lie down like the rest of your champions? You look more natural horizontal!'

'You English send your Prince of Wales to South America. *You,* son of a bitch, they send to us.'

'How long before *your* eye opens up, Cap?'

Casey followed me in at a slow pace, and stepped nonchalantly over the top rope. He bowed slightly to the crowd and ignored me.

He got a terrific reception. Texans are very popular in the States, as well they might be. Casey Berger was a great drawing card, and rightly thought much of by the American sporting public.

'Hey, Casey', I heard someone call, 'why you put on against welter-weights? What happened to all the heavies?'

The referee followed Casey. I at once recognised Gunboat Smith—one of the most famous of all boxers. One who knew ring fighters, of both fight games, from A to Z. A professional who had forgotten more than all the ex-amateur heavyweights of later generations ever knew.

The announcer, Mr. Humphries (who wore a hat), said, 'Ladies and gentlemen. It gives me pleasure to present Captain Atholl Oakeley, Champion of England, who has come to our shores to make good his challenge to beat our champions. Give the Captain a hand.'

There was some polite clapping.

'And in this corner Casey Berger whom you all know.'

Uproar again for their idol.

'Hiya, Casey. Do your stuff, boy,' I heard someone shout.

Casey's face remained a mask.

We went to our corners and took off our dressing gowns—or 'robes' as the Americans call them.

I walked to the centre of the ring and held out my hand. Casey brushed it aside and got booed.

Without more ado I stepped in, grabbed a headlock and buttocked him. All his nineteen stone went crashing to the mat. The Texan pulled loose and stood up. He walked crabwise across the ring and stood in a corner.

Someone called out, 'Two minutes.'

Casey came out of the corner bulling in the initial headhold then using brute force to bring me to my knees. Changing to a half nelson he levered me onto my shoulders and held me. I raised one shoulder clear, thus 'stopping' a fall with the bent leg check as taught us at the Ashdown. Casey seemed puzzled at this. 'Four minutes,' called the timekeeper.

One minute to go. I stayed, held as in a vice. This man was not only heavy; he was much stronger than anyone I had met before. I would have to keep clear. I thought, 'If I let this big chap get a firm hold on me I'm done for.'

Casey slacked the half nelson. I rolled on my stomach, knelt up, shot my legs forward into a sitting position, turned to my left and stood up.

'Five minutes.'

I suddenly saw, mat level, Casey's chief second hold a card towards me. On it was written:

'You're on your own Cap.'

Casey glanced casually towards his corner and like a flash I was on him. All the best Irslinger tactics! Three hard forearms, left, right, left, I put into his face, then, double wrist-locking him, I brought him to the mat before he realised what was going on. Neck scissors (he broke it) followed by a straight scissors and face bar. His nose bled.

'First blood to me,' I thought. 'So far so good.'

I hauled his head back and heard his neck creak.

Casey, by this time, was acting like an infuriated bull. He broke the scissors, throwing me off and storming to his feet.

We had a furious fist fight in a corner. Our four seconds and the referee intervened to separate us.

'Son of a bitch,' growled Berger to the ref. 'What the hell is this, a wrestling match or a god damned prize fight?'

'Cap,' says the ref, 'I don't go for rough tactics. Quit all that bare knuckle stuff or out you go. Now fight on.'

Casey, really roused, threw me with a 'supplice'. I grabbed the bottom rope and hauled myself out of the ring. I fell on the floor with a bang. Re-entering the ring I ran into an American flying mare and got shot out of the ring the other side. This time I knocked over an elderly man wearing glasses. Again I got back into the ring. ('Nine minutes,' called the time-keeper.)

'Cap's greasy,' said Casey to the ref.

Gunboat Smith called for a towel and dried me.

'What you got on? Looks like grease to me.'

'Sure slippery,' says the Texan. 'I can't hold him. Get him dried.'

The referee dried me again with some force.

'Okay now. Fight on!'

The next five minutes was a real tear-up. Casey grabbed every hold in the book but so slippery was I that he failed to hold me. The more he tried and failed the more furious he became. I felt his strength was so great that only counter-moves, and slips, executed with great speed, could save me.

I nearly got caught with a chancery and bar; then by a figure four scissors, then in a short arm scissors, and finally a Further Nelson. I managed to escape from all these—the last one by 'spinning'.

Casey, now really angry at sarcastic shouts from the crowd who were beginning to get excited and vociferous, went back into the initial head hold and bulled me into a corner, where he forced a crotch hold and body-slammed me very hard indeed.

Somewhat winded by the force of the impact I managed to slip free and so under the ropes.

Minute after minute this went on with Casey furiously trying to hold me, while time and again I slipped free.

By the time the twenty-fourth minute was called the whole arena was in a pandemonium. The noise was ear-splitting, one gigantic deafening roar nearly breaking my ear drums. Hundreds of people were jumping up and down in their seats, all bawling at Casey who replied by again picking me up and slamming me, then throwing himself onto me in a desperate effort to get the fall. With one shoulder down I screwed my hips round and slipped out of his clutches.

Then it was that I saw the card which sent me hopping mad:

'Okay Casey go for a draw.'

As I say, this card so infuriated me that all the hereditary instincts of my prize-fighting grandfather came welling up inside me. I knew then it was a case of 'do or die', and that everything rested on one fast and bold move.

Having returned once again from my usual escape-exit under the ropes I saw this giant of a man standing, legs apart, his great hands on his hips, waiting for me.

'This,' I remember thinking, 'Is Kyburz all over again.' I knew what I was going to get. In a flashback I saw myself once more in hospital just as I was after that terrible body slam at the Salle Wagram in Paris, when referee Davis saw World Champion Kyburz raise the dust sky high as, from high overhead, he crashed me to the canvas, into oblivion and hospital.

With all my waning strength and speed, I catapulted myself between and through the Texan's legs. Berger must have wondered where I had gone to!

Then like a swimmer at the turn, as quick as lightning, I twisted round, locking one of his ankles with my left arm, one with my right. I hauled in my shoulders against his huge calves, I felt like a maniac. Would Casey fall? For a moment he stood. Then, like a falling tree, this colossal Texan Champion shivered, and crashed full length to the canvas . . . !

I whipped up both legs, stepped over them and barred his mouth, savagely digging in my knuckles and straining his head back. Still this steelman did not tap. I pulled my bare knuckles up under his nose which was already streaming blood.

I leant forward till I felt his knee joint creak. Casey, most gallant of all men, only groaned but still did not submit. A minute ticked by.

I released the face lock and concentrated on the leg lock. The noise in the stadium was absolutely deafening. The sound seemed as if all the devils in hell had been let loose. Still Casey would not submit. It became fantastic, unreal, like a dream. The din grew even worse.

Blood and sweat poured from Casey's face, now deathly white. I remembered Irslinger's final advice.

'If they won't submit, frighten them.'

But how could one frighten this Texan? Nothing ever frightens these Texans.

Casey just wasn't the type to be frightened. As a man he was superb, his courage was magnificent. He was caught and he knew it, but he would never surrender. What a man!

Desperately I turned my back on the ref and deliberately twisted one foot, with a circular movement, against the ankle joint: one of the sinister moves taught me by Irslinger. Determined to remember the lesson of Phil Scott and others I knew I had to win this fight.

Casey, furious and now in dire agony, pointed to his foot. The referee bawled 'Stop that, Cap.' But his voice sounded miles away. It all seemed utterly unreal, I felt as if in a dream.

The twenty-fifth minute came up.

I forced my knuckles under Berger's arm-pits and I thrust them through, grinding them down so taking double arm locks.

With both legs trapped in step-over toe holds and both arms drawn right up his back with double arm locks into barred hammer locks the Texan could not move one single inch in any direction.

In another 35 seconds, as I increased to full pressure, he tapped. I heard someone yell, 'My God he's beaten him!'

It took the seconds, his and mine, helped by the referee, at least another two minutes to unravel us, so interlocked were our legs. I think I must have fainted.

The next thing I remember was someone lifting me, like a corpse, clear over the ropes. People grabbed me. Some man had me on his shoulder and was carrying me out. All around a sea of faces, a surging milling crowd, buffeted us. I remember thinking, 'If this was a hostile crowd I would certainly be lynched.'

But they were not hostile. Their champion had fallen but, like our British crowds, they were grand sportsmen. David had slain Goliath. That is what fight crowds all over the world go mad to see and have done since time immemorial.

Men were shouting 'Well done, little guy—guess you got what it takes', and 'The King will sure be proud of you'.

But the King was not proud of me. He never knew, because the British press suppressed all reference to the fight.

TRANSATLANTIC RACE

By Carleton Mitchell

F riday, *July 18. 2:45* A.M.: During the night wind and sea moderated, and we are back to a comfortable but satisfying 8 to 8.5 on the Kenyon. The wind also shifted slightly. It is now about south-southwest at 12 to 15 knots. We reel off the miles. As Bunny Rigg might say if he were aboard: "Those Plymouth girls have us by a nylon towrope!"

I write this in the cockpit by flashlight. Beside my notebook lies the chronometer-watch we use on deck, and the navigator's notebook. I wait to take time when Frank can shoot the stars. He stands by the mizzen rigging, watching, occasionally squinting through the sextant to see if the horizon is yet well enough defined for a sight.

To the north more than to the east there is the first paling of the sky. While we slept the overcast cleared away, but scattered clouds lie ahead, in the east, and another mass is clustered to the southward. Directly above the sky is clear and the stars are brilliant. Nearer the horizon they are less distinct, as though a thin haze might be forming.

The ritual of morning stars is one of the most beautiful moments of the day: the navigator standing ready, at first a barely discernible silhouette as he identifies his prey by altitude and azimuth. Then an almost imperceptible glow begins to dissolve the weld of sea and sky, and gradually the line of the horizon becomes distinct. The day grows lighter, and the dimmer stars fade. The sky goes from black to gray and slowly assumes delicate shadings of yellow and pink. Patches of foam from breaking crests appear pale gray against the darker gray of the sea, as though the water is loath to give up the stored blackness of the night.

"Stand by!" suddenly calls the navigator. "Stand by!" you repeat, mumbling seconds as the hand of the watch scurries around the dial . . . "Mark!" There is urgency in the command, the sense of communication of a precise instant in the eternity of time . . . You record hour, minute, and second, and the altitude, and the musical names assigned the stars by the ancients: Vega, Kochab, Altair, Capella, Jupiter, Dubhe, Aldebaran . . . Somehow it is a wonderful way to begin a day, a combining of old mysteries and modern precision. And you always feel grateful that again you are fixed on the earth's surface in relation to all other objects: to the islands, to the continents, to the reefs. Somehow you feel less alone.

9:25 A.M.: Around the horizon is a collection of clouds that prior to this passage would have had me standing at the weather rail. Now I sit in the companionway and watch them with a somewhat jaundiced and dispassionate eye. Since Bermuda too many have cried "wolf" for us to get excited by anything not equipped with neon lights, cowcatcher, and siren. Also large red crosses painted on sides and bottom.

North Atlantic clouds come in assorted sizes, shapes, and colors, and the showcase is usually full. At the moment I have only to raise my head to see tufted silver ones ahead, ragged gray ones to starboard, funereal black ones astern, and an odd bank of purplish-blue ones to port. Meanwhile nothing special happens. The track of the barograph remains comparatively level, the breeze blows at about the same velocity from the south-southwest, and we scoot along under the same combination of sails. After a while you seem to get used to living with any sort of threat on a companionably relaxed basis—even a volcano or the atom bomb.

Going along so comfortably, our only worry is chafe. It is really amazing how quickly any two surfaces in intermittent contact can show signs of wear. The problem usually greatest when carrying a spinnaker with the wind well forward, the working of the after guy against the main shrouds, we have solved by use of a wire guy and large rollers—exactly like spools for thread, but about 5 inches in diameter—bound to the shrouds. Elsewhere we are festooned with lengths of split hose, wrappings of canvas, and just plain tape. Miles and miles of each, it seems. Every adjustment of the sheets means endless shifting of bits and pieces of chafing gear. But the funniest chafe of all is along the luff of the mizzen staysail, where a procession of overfed types from cockpit to galley to cockpit has worn away the cloth where they squeeze past. Either we have to go on shorter rations or sew leather along the luff at tummy height! Add a new chapter to hazards of the sea.

11:35 A.M.: After a half hour at the helm I am willing to admit we are overcanvased. My arms feel as though I have been trying to lift an elevator to the top of the Empire State Building with a hand crank. The breeze is back into the twenties and the sea is causing us to sheer. Yet we are going so well and there are so many minor variations of force and direction even within this consistent breeze I hate to change to a genoa. If it would blow 5 miles harder, or the breeze would go another point ahead, there would be no question. But each time I get ready to suggest the shift, the wind moderates a hair, or swings a little farther aft. So as a compromise have dropped the mizzen to ease the helm. It has helped: we still show over 9 knots and Bobby reports the wheel better.

This is glorious going. The sun is breaking through the current overhead assortment of clouds, small flannelly jobs with a warp and woof crosshatch of blue sky between, and it is almost warm. Occasionally a little crest slaps aboard forward, a tiny spatter of sparkling drops, just enough to keep the foredeck wet; and occasionally a sea races under the quarter wave to curl over the counter and run forward along the lee waterway. The spinnaker sheet fore guy is rigid enough to use as a chinning bar, you can jump up and down on the sheet, and we run down the miles for England. As Jack said a moment ago: "We don't even have a Bermuda Race-and-a-half left to go." I cautioned him against such comparisons later for fear of hurting the feelings of sensitive types, but it is true: the remaining distance seems like nothing. If this wind holds.

A trio of whales is off to leeward pacing us. They seem to be puffing mightily in an effort to keep up, but are not quite making it on a boat-for-boat basis. However, as they appear to be strictly Class B whales in over-all length I suppose we have to give them time. Which reminds me: where is *Samuel Pepys,* and what the hell is she doing?

7:40 P.M.: At 5:00 this afternoon, while I slept peacefully, *Caribbee* ran out from under a cover of clouds into brilliant sunshine. When Dick called me at 6:00 the after stateroom was brighter than it had been for days. For a few moments I lay in my bunk and looked across the cabin and through the porthole over the opposite bunk. I could tell we had been freed by the position of the main boom, and because we were standing up straighter while the water went past just as fast. As *Caribbee* rolled I would see only white rushing foam, a few feet beyond the port; then she would lift, and I would see the green-gray North Atlantic seas; and she would roll still farther and I would be looking up at a blue ellipse of cloudless sky. There would be a moment's pause as she poised on a crest, then she would shoot ahead, rolling, and the whole cycle would begin again.

The sunshine held during the cockpit cocktail session, adding a second reason for the gathering being the most noisy and cheerful in days. Gone with the calm are the long faces and quiet voices; when water bubbles under the counter, our spirits bubble in time. Now we bubble 9 knots' worth—a lot of bubbling. Both for *Caribbee* and for us.

But as our watch was finishing dinner before taking over, Dick came below and said: "There's a black cloud bank coming up from astern. I can't tell what it means but you'd better bring oilies." And when I stuck my head through the companionway slide, there it was: from horizon to horizon it stretched, flat on top, dark and ominous, extending down to the water as a solid curtain. It lacked the neon lights and the red crosses, but everything else seemed to be present.

I stood by the weather backstay and watched. It gained fast. All afternoon there had been a pronounced swell from the northwest, persistent and heavy enough to buck the waves kicked up by our present southwest breeze, and this looked as though it might be the force behind those outriders. This is it, I kept thinking; this has to be it, the northwest gale so long overdue. A boat can't cross the ocean and not take a beating somewhere; we can't go on talking about the Great Atlantic Calm of '52 and making derisive noises without Father Neptune doing something about it.

. . . Now we're going to get it, we puny mortals who have been wanting wind!

Wispy clouds raced overhead, low enough to rip their bellies on the mainmast, with the denser mass close behind—and we saw we had been fooled by the low sun: the clouds were not heavy and ominous at all, but only our traveling companion of the last 2 days, the flannel sky, temporarily left behind and hurrying to catch up. Now, as I write this, its leading edge is well ahead, although I can still see a narrow band of blue at the horizon, and we are all happy: the cloud, *Caribbee,* and us, because under the flannel cloud is just the wind we want: not too little, not too much, so we continue at 9 knots as peacefully as babes riding a carriage in the park.

10:35 P.M.: I am finally convinced the true southwesterly of the middle latitudes has come in. On going over the log, I find it was at 8:10 Wednesday night I noted: "Breeze hauling. On spinnaker." Now it has been aloft for 50-odd hours. There have been only minor variations in the strength and direction of the wind during that period, and we have run down a degree of longitude every five hours or less. Up here at latitude 51 degrees, a degree of longitude is only 37.9 nautical miles in length. We have thus taken a great leap forward on the track chart.

So at last we have the winds we expected to ride all the way across, those "prevailing westerlies" of the pilot charts. Having had a little leisure during this watch, I studied the log and found some interesting things. Beginning at noon of Friday, July 4, we sailed 635 miles, the distance of the course from Newport to Bermuda, in 72 hours 53 minutes. That figure represents an average speed over the bottom of 8.72 knots. The Cruising Club of America yearbook lists the Bermuda Race record for the present course as 75 hours 32 minutes, set by *Bolero* in 1950. So far good enough. But then beginning at 8:00 A.M., July 8, it took us 196 hours to sail the next 635 miles, a heartbreaking average of 3.24 knots. And in the 1946 Bermuda Race, the slowest since the war, the *last* boat in the fleet whose time was recorded made it to the finish line in 178 hours! Thus in two successive stretches across the Atlantic, *Caribbee* exceeded two records for another similar stretch: the fastest and the slowest. Now, if the wind holds, we will probably better our earlier pace.

So it has been a period of mad weather, when nature sharply reminds man his attempts to catalog her are futile. We had fresh breezes where the books said we might expect the light variables of the horse latitudes, and light variables from the east when we arrived in the charted area of the prevailing westerlies. Meanwhile the radio brings reports of record heat waves around the rim of the Atlantic, both in North America and in Europe.

Also in my study of the log I was reminded of something else: how terrible was the period of aimless slatting and fruitless beating which reached its nadir on the morning of the sixteenth. Sails up, sails down, tacking endlessly on headers, getting nowhere, until Frank looked up from the chart in disgust and said: "We're going back and forth on the same damned line. It's just getting blacker and blacker from the pencil marks.'' Only the arrival of the first stages of this breeze in the morning kept us from a run that might have averaged less than a knot for 24 miles—1 mile per hour for working continuously, changing sails, calling them, tacking endlessly. Believe me: I have learned record passages are the pleasant ones!

As the winds have fluctuated, so have our moods. I know these notes reveal me as a person of ''ups-ies'' and ''downs-ies.'' It is a characteristic for which I do not apologize; it appears even in the writings of the most outwardly stoic of the old adventurers. But this afternoon Bobby passed along a remark by Dick which shed some light on the curious rise or fall in the spirits of sailors on long passages as the speed goes up or down: you always think of the passage as continuing at the rate you are moving at the moment. It seems to be a universal failing. If you're enjoying a fair breeze and making 8 knots, you calculate how long it will take to cover the remaining miles at 8 knots, completely forgetting that wind is the most fickle and undependable of commodities. You rub your hands and say gleefully, ''We'll be in next Tuesday.'' Everyone is elated. But then the breeze dies, or goes ahead, and the speed drops. You're making 2 knots. Immediately there is a new calculation and faces grow long. Someone growls, ''Hell, we won't get there before Christmas.'' You feel cheated and vow you'll never let your hopes soar again. And you don't, until the next fair slant.

Saturday, July 19. 6:45 A.M.: The midnight log entry opens with the notation: ''This day commences with pleasant westerly. Carrying spinnaker, balloon forestaysail, main, mizzen staysail, and mizzen.'' Yet for me this past 4-hour watch, now almost ended, has been one of the most tense and wearing ones of the passage. While dressing, after being routed out of my snug bunk at 2:45, I could tell things were rugged on deck. From my difficulty in maintaining balance against the lurch and roll I knew steering would be hard, and that the wind had freshened and the sea built. There was a roaring of water along the lee deck, a feeling of burying that indicated we might be on the verge of carrying too much sail.

Deck wasn't cheering: there was a slight glimmer of light in the east, but the whole sky was leaden and gray. A fine misting rain fell, and visibility was bad. The wind had backed still farther into the south, so we were carrying the spinnaker pole as far forward as it would go, right against the headstay. The sail was constantly on edge, even so. Even in the poor light I could see it curl.

I confess my inclination was to shift to a genoa while both watches were together. But then I thought perhaps things looked worse than they really were, as is always the case when first coming into a nasty night from a deep sleep, and did not want to give way to that first-awake letdown, the old predawn loss of courage, when the tides in men are at their lowest ebb. And we would be comfortable again if only the wind would veer a couple of points to the west. Dick settled my doubts by telling me the wind had freed in the last half hour and showed signs of continuing around.

So we set ourselves at our stations and the port watch disappeared down the companionway sack-wards faster than any gophers ever popped into holes. I watched them with envy. But not for long, as there was plenty to keep us busy. Steering was particularly hard. The northwest swell still rolled in under the wind waves of our sou'wester, the same as yesterday, but both much bigger: the result was a nasty bucking sea, occasionally combining to make *Caribbee* take a violent sheer. With each sheer the spinnaker would curl deeply, and the man forward would call frantically: "Go down! Go down!" Sometimes the rudder would take effect; at other times the spinnaker would break and refill with a resounding crash. But we carried on, reluctant to do anything which might slow us, although we did strike the mizzen and mizzen staysail to ease steering.

And then we got it. We were asking for it, and we got it. I was at the wheel when suddenly there was a *ping!* from aloft, a sound like a breaking ukulele string magnified a few hundred times. The whole boat gave a jump, as though Father Neptune had given us a good swift boot in the stern. The spinnaker sagged, but then held and filled again.

At the moment of the ping I began bearing away as fast as I could grind the wheel, and as soon as we came off before the wind yelled: "What the hell happened?" For a moment no one knew, despite a cluster forward looking up the mast. Then Frank spotted the trouble: one spinnaker halyard had let go, cause for the moment unknown, and the sail had been caught by the other one. I have noted that for this race we installed twin halyards, so one backs up the other. Fortunately, it turns out.

It was a very minor accident compared to what might have happened, so we took the hint and switched to a genoa. Immediately there was an amazing change in conditions—in apparent conditions, that is. What a moment before had been a wild dawn—the break occurred at 4:50—became merely unpleasant: a fresh southerly wind thick with fine rain setting up a bobble of a sea, neither particularly vicious. Good seamanship and good sense dictated a switch. But ocean racing? We have dropped a knot on the Kenyon, and wait impatiently for more light so a man can go aloft to find what happened, and make repairs.

8:50 A.M.: After breakfast both watches assembled on deck. It was still blowing well over twenty, and the wind had moved even more to the south, putting it forward of the beam. The conflicting seas seemed more pronounced than ever, so it was almost impossible to walk along the deck without holding onto the liferail or some other stable object. Yet we rigged the bosun's chair and tied Frank in securely and up he went: up some 75 feet into the cold raw wind, the chill spitting rain. Around us the sea and the sky were gray and lonely. No gallery to applaud, no one to know or care except the knot of oilskinned shipmates hauling on the halyard; just one more unseen vignette of the countless thousands that have occurred on the empty ocean.

From amidships I watched him trace wild arcs as *Caribbee* plunged along at better than 8 knots: he would work awhile, hold on awhile as a particularly bad combination of seas made the motion worse, and lean to leeward for a while. It took me a little time to figure that the latter gesture was for the better downwind distribution of his breakfast pancakes. But finally he signaled to come down, and was lowered away, and we found what had happened: the strain on the halyard aloft had pulled out a splice in the strap that held the block. The ends of the wire looked like steel spaghetti. Frank had transferred the block to a spare strap at the masthead, and we were back in business. But it is not altogether pleasant to contemplate what might have happened if the second halyard had not been in place, and held: a huge nylon bag suddenly collapsing under our bows, fast to the ship by 150 feet of wire halyard, a wire foreguy, and two heavy linen sheets.

As amazed as I was at the news that a splice had pulled, I was even more amazed by Frank's color when he reached the deck. On starting up, he had blended with his shipmates; on coming down he was exactly the color of pea soup—a rich green. He drank a cup of hot tea, to which I added a good slug of rum, and now sleeps. Just before dropping off he assured Henry that he was indeed the finest of cooks: the pancakes tasted as good coming up as they had going down.

10:00 A.M.: Now I have finally gotten to my bunk I am not sleepy, although while sitting on deck in the rain I could hardly wait, and a silly paraphrase from *Alice in Wonderland* kept running through my head in tuneless and monotonous repetition: "Sack of the evening, beautiful sack." As for the first time everything below is wet and clammy, perhaps I am staying awake to savor a little longer the sheer animal satisfaction of being dry and warm. Oilskins and sweaters hang throughout the cabin in odd places. Damp socks are jammed behind light bulbs and in the front of the bookcase. There isn't much difference in temperature between cockpit and main cabin, and unless the rain stops and we get some drying weather we will have to dig deep into our stock of spare gear.

Fuel is the only miscalculation we made in our advance planning. We could carry only a small supply of briquettes for the main cabin fireplace, to heat and dry the living quarters in case of necessity, but have a fair amount left despite keeping a fire going a couple of days on the Grand Banks. I will have Henry stoke up the grate before lunch. Our real shortage is in alcohol for the cooking stove. Neither Henry nor I took into consideration that on a long passage there would be more baking and midnight snacking. Or perhaps I should be more honest and say we didn't realize as a crew that we would be capable of eating 24 hours a day, less only time for sleep and a few deck chores. We began the voyage by each watch putting on a kettle of water about a half hour before calling the other, at night; after dressing, you could struggle to the galley for a mug-up of coffee, tea, soup, or cocoa. This noble practice degenerated into a kettle bubbling almost constantly, especially during the waking hours of those supermen, the port watch. So a couple of days ago, to the great sorrow of all hands, I had to decree rationing: stove on at night only at the three o'clock change in watches, a cold lunch, and no more baking. Really rugged! Shades of Thomas James and the other old searchers for the Northwest Passage! No more hot cornbread, no more apple pie! Survival does indeed become a matter of chance, and from now on *Caribbee* will be sailed with the desperation of men willing to risk all in a desperate gamble —no Plymouth, no pie. . . . But seriously, if I were ever again making a long passage in the higher latitudes I would allow double the usual consumption of cooking fuel for shorter trips in warmer climes, and add a little bit more as a reserve.

Otherwise we are in fine shape. Our planning for food was on the basis of a 3-week passage, with another 2 weeks of emergency food in reserve— real "iron rations," Coast Guard-approved survival food for use in lifeboats, the daily supply per man having less bulk than a package of cigarettes. What a comedown that would be! But Henry assures me we are in no danger of descending to such levels. While our consumption has been as great as is humanly possible there is still an ample reserve. One reason for this was the food already on the boat when the Trans-Atlantic stores came aboard in Bermuda: our planning had been done on a "bare boat" basis, so the 21-day supply was entirely in addition to canned goods left over from the Bermuda Race, and the "just in case" extras hidden deep in lockers and bilge.

I marvel at how well we have eaten. Italian spaghetti and meat balls; German sauerkraut and wieners; Chinese chop suey and chow mein; New England codfish balls and mashed potatoes; New Orleans crawfish bisque and shimp jambalaya; Boston baked beans; Mexican chili and tamales; Scotch kippers and Dutch ham and Alaskan salmon—our menu is cosmopolitan and varied. There seems to be nothing which cannot be found in canned form, even bread. On previous passages bread has been a real problem, for there are times when even the hardiest cook cannot bake in a small boat's oven; now bread comes in neat tins, and after weeks at sea tastes almost as good as the spanking-fresh product of the corner bakery. Rye, white, or whole wheat, take your choice. And I do not believe it is only our seagoing appetites that make everything so palatable: canned food when prepared with care and imagination can compare favorably with fresh, especially when enough thought goes into planning menus so there is no feeling of repetition. *Henri du Caribbee* has done well on all counts. One hazard I did not anticipate on this passage was having to turn sideways to get up the companionway.

Dick just came down to get the balloon jib. As he stood talking, water collected in a puddle at his feet. It still rains, and the wind remains too far forward to carry a spinnaker. Hence the ballooner, in hopes of coaxing the speed back to 9 knots.

Seeing Dick cold and dripping made me feel even more snug, and suddenly sleepy. Lights out. Let her howl for somebody else—for the next 2 hours, anyway.

4:45 P.M.: We continue to be gluttons for punishment and work, but it is a form of gluttony that eats up the miles.

On deck at 1:00 to the same leaden sky and splitting rain, but found the wind trending slightly more toward the west. So all hands kept close watch on the masthead fly. By 2:00 the apparent breeze was a bit forward of the beam, by 2:30 it had come abeam, and by 2:45 the spinnaker was set and drawing. As it is now. And the wind has continued on around until we log it as a true southwester. Again the Kenyon has climbed to 9. The sea followed the wind aft, and steering is not too bad, although occasionally a big one will rise above the level of the taffrail to shoulder the stern high, bury the bow, and cause *Caribbee* to slice across the sea ahead. But this wind lacks the weight to make the process vicious.

Two hundred seven miles today, 212 yesterday. We're in the groove, really rolling. Now have less than one Bermuda Race left to go—about a Miami-Nassau plus a St. Pete-Havana. With continuing luck we could make the finish in another 3 days. "Continuing luck" of course means continuing wind and no major catastrophes to gear; by the law of averages we should get the first, and I'm not too concerned about the second.

Thinking back, I believe we have consistently gotten the maximum speed possible in the conditions we encountered. There were times when we went mighty slow—when we didn't go at all—but we can have the satisfaction of knowing we did everything possible with what we had. It is customary for a skipper to pay tribute to his crew, but in this case I feel every page of these notes tells a story that could not be summed up by any amount of flowery compliments. I can only add I do not believe there was ever a keener or more efficient crew, which let down less or remained as cheerful under trying conditions. And nothing could be more difficult than the old nightmare sensation of running like hell but staying in the same place, while in your imagination the goblins pursue like Olympic hurdlers.

7:15 P.M.: It is strange but I feel in the last few days we all have a different attitude about this race. At first there was constant speculation about the other boats, their qualities and potentials, and how they would be sailed. In a sense, for the first few days we were sailing hard because we were racing the others, a purely competitive sensation. But now I believe our concentration is solely on *Caribbee*. It has become a fetish to keep her moving as fast as possible; it has also become our greatest pleasure. She seems to us so wonderful, this supposedly inanimate object, we can do nothing else. She has carried us almost across an ocean, kept us safe and comfortable, responded to our every demand, forgiven our excesses. In return, we have learned her whims and desires, and are willing slaves to both.

It would not be accurate if I said we do not frequently speculate on the other boats—sometimes pessimistically, feeling they might have skirted the calm while we lay helpless; sometimes optimistically, thinking the light weather must have been widespread enough to trap them, too. But now such speculation is more objective and fatalistic. The race is less important than the personal fact that we have made this passage, have shared this experience. If some super-radar could suddenly show us the others either fantastically ahead or behind, so our efforts from here to the finish would make no difference to the outcome of the race, I am sure we would sail exactly the same way as we do now—as hard and well as we can.

This passage has clarified my perspective, as well as taught me more of the sea than I could have learned in another lifetime of coastal cruising. And I know, even as I calculate the miles to the finish, I would somehow be happier if it was 6000 instead of 600 miles. I know I shall be excited and delighted when we sail into Plymouth—yet sad. Even now I can re-member vividly the moment almost exactly 20 years ago when the battered old ketch *Temptress* crawled into Ft. Pierce inlet ahead of an unseasonal tropical storm, 17 days out of the Chesapeake, the three of us aboard exhausted from being buffeted by a succession of gales off Cape Hatteras. It was my first passage on the open ocean. I had been frightened, I can say honestly: the deep roar of wind in the rigging, the heavy slam of seas rolling out of the night, the sheer insensitiveness and pitilessness of the ocean, not willing to quit when man had enough and begged for mercy. . . . Yet when we gained calm water beyond the roaring hell of the inlet, breaking heavily from the first swells of the advancing hurricane, I was sad. I knew something had ended that could never be had again, not in exactly the same way. And after a time even the fear and the exhaustion were part of the perfection of the memory.

As the most important memories of this crossing will remain not as a race but as a passage.

Acknowledgments

Grateful acknowledgments are listed here for permissions to reprint copyrighted works included in this anthology:

"Attending the 64th Olympic Games: 520 B.C." from *The Praise Singer* by Mary Renault. Copyright © The Estate of Mary Renault 1978. Reproduced with permission of Curtis Brown Ltd., London on behalf of the Estate of Mary Renault.

"The Thousand-Mile Auto Race (Mille Miglia 1955)" from *My Greatest Race* by Stirling Moss. Copyright © 1974. By permission of the author.

"The Redheaded Outfield" from *On the Diamond* by Zane Grey. Copyright © 1920 by Zane Grey. Renewed 1948 by Lina Elise Grey. Reprinted by permission of Zane Grey, Inc.

"The Magnificent Moment: The Called-Shot Home Run" from *Babe— The Legend Come to Life* by Robert W. Creamer. Copyright © 1974 by Robert W. Creamer. Reprinted by permission of Simon & Schuster, Inc. Reprinted by permission of Sterling Lord Literistic, Inc.

"Mystic Baseball: A New Age Look" from *Heaven on Earth* by Michael D'Antonio. Copyright © 1992 by Michael D'Antonio. By permission of the author.

"Winning and Losing" from *Killer Instinct* by Bob Cousy with John Devaney. Copyright © 1975 by Robert Cousy and John Devaney. Reprinted by permission of Random House, Inc.

"Three Cushions" from *McGoorty: A Billiard Hustler's Life* by Dan McGoorty as told to Robert Byrne. Copyright © 1972, 1984 by Robert Byrne. Published by arrangement with Carol Publishing Group.

"Moonlight Cruising" from *Cruising Is Fun* by Brandt Aymar. Copyright © 1941 by Greenberg, Publishers, Inc. By permission of the author.

"Bomaye" from *The Greatest: My Own Story* by Muhammad Ali with Richard Durham. Copyright © 1975 by Muhammad Ali, Herbert Muhammad, Richard Durham. By permission of the author.

"The Patterson–Liston Fight" from *The Presidential Papers* by Norman Mailer. Copyright © 1963 by Norman Mailer. Reprinted by permission of the author and the author's agents, Scott Meredith Literary Agency, Inc., 845 Third Avenue, New York, New York, 10022.